Micah

Illuminations

C. L. Seow, General Editor

Scott C. Jones, Brennan W. Breed,
  and Susanne Gillmayr-Bucher,
  Hebrew Bible/Old Testament

Judith H. Newman, *Deuterocanonicals/Apocrypha*

Loren Stuckenbruck, *New Testament*

Micah

Introduction and Commentary

Carolyn J. Sharp

William B. Eerdmans Publishing Company
Grand Rapids, Michigan

Wm. B. Eerdmans Publishing Co.
2006 44th Street SE, Grand Rapids, MI 49508
www.eerdmans.com

© 2025 Carolyn J. Sharp
All rights reserved
Published 2025
Printed in the United States of America

30 30 29 28 27 26 25   1 2 3 4 5 6 7

ISBN 978-0-8028-6832-9

Library of Congress Cataloging-in-Publication Data

A catalog record for this book is available from the Library of Congress.

Contents

List of Illustrations	ix
To the Reader	xi
Preface	xiii
List of Abbreviations	xvi

INTRODUCTION — 1

1. **Historical Contexts, Compositional Growth, and Textual Versions** — 3
   - 1.1 Composition and Redaction of Micah — 11
   - 1.2 Micah within the Book of the Twelve — 19
   - 1.3 The Masoretic Text of Micah — 22
   - 1.4 The Septuagint Translation of Micah — 22
   - 1.5 Fragments of Micah Texts from the Judean Desert — 23

2. **Literary Dimensions of Micah** — 24
   - 2.1 Structure and Themes of Micah — 26
   - 2.2 The Persona of the Prophet — 29
   - 2.3 Poetic Artistry in Micah — 31

3. **Prophecy, Politics, and Theology** — 42
   - 3.1 Political and Economic Dimensions of Prophecy in Ancient Judah — 42
   - 3.2 Theological Traditions in Micah — 45
   - 3.3 Feminist Amplifying of Micah — 46
     - 3.3.1 Micah as KILLJOY — 52
     - 3.3.2 Micah and FUGITIVITY — 53
   - 3.4 Micah and Ecological Justice — 57

v

Contents

4. Overview of the History of Consequences	60
4.1 Micah in Jewish Traditions	60
4.1.1 *Midrashic Interpretations*	63
4.1.2 *Modern Jewish Interpretations*	78
4.2 Micah in Christian Traditions	83
4.2.1 *Early Christian Interpretations*	86
4.2.2 *Medieval Christian Interpretations*	95
4.2.3 *Early Modern to Contemporary Christian Interpretations*	100
4.2.4 *Micah in Christian Liturgies*	119
4.2.5 *Micah in Social Justice Movements*	120
Bibliography	124
COMMENTARY	131
Micah 1	133
Interpretation	135
Superscription (1:1)	136
Divine Wrath Descends from on High (1:2-7)	136
The Prophet Laments (1:8-9)	138
Cartography of Destruction (1:10-16)	138
Retrospect	143
Micah 1 and Ecological Justice	145
Commentary	146
Bibliography	175
Micah 2	179
Interpretation	181
Woe to Those Who Practice Injustice (2:1-5)	181
The Insolence of Oppressors (2:6-11)	183
Exile as Divinely Ordained Punishment (2:12-13)	185
Retrospect	189
Micah 2 and Ecological Justice	191
Commentary	193
Bibliography	214
Micah 3	217
Interpretation	219
Indictment of Judean Leaders (3:1-4)	219

Contents

False Prophets Shamed, but Micah Empowered (3:5-8)	221
The Razing of Jerusalem Foreseen (3:9-12)	223
Retrospect	228
Micah 3 and Ecological Justice	230
Commentary	232
Bibliography	248

Micah 4 — 251
   Interpretation — 253
     Zion as Pinnacle of Godly Peace (4:1-4) — 255
     Communal Identity (4:5) — 256
     Zion's Restoration and Renewed Dominion (4:6-8) — 257
     *Catastrophe, Then Rescue by Y*HWH *(4:9-13b)* — 257
     *Zion Pledges the Spoils to Y*HWH *(4:13c)* — 259
     Israel under Threat (4:14 [Eng. 5:1]) — 259
   Retrospect — 265
   Micah 4 and Ecological Justice — 267
   Commentary — 269
   Bibliography — 289

Micah 5 — 291
   Interpretation — 293
     Rise of a Godly Ruler (5:1-4a [Eng. 2-5a]) — 293
     *Israel's Defeat of Assyria and Ritual Shout to Y*HWH
       as Divine Warrior (5:4b-8 [Eng. 5b-9]) — 295
     War Song of Divine Vengeance (5:9-14 [Eng. 10-15]) — 296
   Retrospect — 300
   Micah 5 and Ecological Justice — 303
   Commentary — 305
   Bibliography — 324

Micah 6 — 325
   Interpretation — 327
     *Juridical Defense of Y*HWH*'s Fidelity (6:1-5)* — 329
     Dialogue on Covenantal Obligations (6:6-8) — 330
     Indictment of the Corrupt City (6:9-16) — 331
   Retrospect — 337
   Micah 6 and Ecological Justice — 340
   Commentary — 342
   Bibliography — 364

Contents

Micah 7	367
Interpretation	370
Daughter Zion Laments (7:1-4a)	374
A Gibe at False Prophets (7:4b)	375
Micah as Faithful Sentinel (7:5-7)	376
Daughter Zion Speaks (7:8-10)	376
Micah Consoles Daughter Zion (7:11-13)	377
Micah Intercedes and Yhwh Responds (7:14-15)	378
Micah's Doxology of Hope (7:16-20)	378
Retrospect	383
Micah 7 and Ecological Justice	385
Commentary	388
Bibliography	408
General Bibliography	409
Subject Index	425
Author Index	436
Scripture Index	443
Ancient Sources Index	462

Illustrations

Fig. 1 The prophet Micah. Byzantine mosaic in the Cathedral of San Marco, Venice. 2
Fig. 2 Shephelat Judea: Nahal Hevron, 1954. 4
Fig. 3 *St. Jerome Writing*, ca. 1606, by Caravaggio (Michelangelo Merisi da Caravaggio, 1571–1610). 89
Fig. 4 John Calvin. Engraving by Georg Osterwald. 100
Fig. 5 *Jonathan Edwards (Princeton Portrait)*, 1860, by Henry Augustus Loop (1831–1895). 105
Fig. 6 Judah after the fall of the Northern Kingdom of Israel. 132
Fig. 7 Initial V: An Angel before Micah, ca. 1270. Illuminated manuscript by unknown artist, likely in Lille, France. 137
Fig. 8 The Golden Gate in the eastern wall of the Temple Mount. Built in the sixth or seventh century CE, likely the oldest gate in Jerusalem. 163
Fig. 9 The fall of Lachish: King Sennacherib reviews Judean prisoners. Detail from wall relief in the throne room of Sennacherib's Southwest Palace at Nineveh. 170
Fig. 10 The prophet Micah, ca. 1099–1100, carved by Wiligelmo de Modena (fl. ca. 1099–1120). 183
Fig. 11 Jonah, Micah, and Isaiah. Stained glass, thirteenth century. In the Basilika St. Kunibert in Cologne, Germany. 204
Fig. 12 *Mystic Wheel (The Vision of Ezekiel)*, 1451–1452, by Fra Angelico (Guido di Pietro, ca. 1395–1455). 222
Fig. 13 Micah, Victorian-era stained glass. St. Edmundsbury Cathedral in Bury St. Edmunds, Suffolk, England. 242
Fig. 14 Tympanum of Micah beating a sword into a plowshare, ca. 1220–1270. Basilique Cathédrale Notre-Dame d'Amiens. 256

Illustrations

Fig. 15	*Let Us Beat Swords into Ploughshares*, by Evgeniy Vuchetich (1908–1974). Bronze sculpture.	276
Fig. 16	Schwerter zu Pflugscharen patch. Textile badge affixed by East German peace activists to clothing and bags.	277
Fig. 17	Virgin Annunciate and the prophet Micah, 1432. Detail from the Ghent Altarpiece by Jan van Eyck (1390–1441) with Hubert van Eyck (1370–1426).	294
Fig. 18	Micah with laboring Jerusalem in Tree of Jesse, ca. 1331. Marble façade of the cathedral in Orvieto, Italy.	308
Fig. 19	Assyrian palace wall relief from Kalhu (Nimrud) during the reign of Tiglath-Pileser III, ca. 730–727 BCE, showing an Assyrian attack on an enemy town.	311
Fig. 20	*Michäas*, by Karl Mayer (1810–1876).	331
Fig. 21	*Micah Exhorting the Israelites to Repentance*, 1866, by Gustave Doré (1832–1883).	351
Fig. 22	*Prophetarum Laudabilis Numerus*, 1447, by Fra Angelico (ca. 1395–1455).	403
Fig. 23	*Micah, Elijah, Gideon*, 1497. Russian Orthodox icon by unknown artist.	407

To the Reader

ILLUMINATIONS is an innovative resource for all who are interested in engaging the Bible in depth. The author of each volume employs the full range of biblical scholarship to illumine the text from a wide variety of perspectives, including the engagement and impact of the text through the centuries.

The volumes are designed to be accessible and enjoyable. To that end, discussion of each portion of the text begins with the author's INTERPRETATION, written in fluid style and with minimal use of foreign languages, technical jargon, reporting of alternative proposals, and citations of secondary literature. Most readers may find it sufficient to read this portion and turn to the following material only for reference.

The COMMENTARY that follows the INTERPRETATION provides a thorough accounting of the text in its original language and an engagement of other scholars. The discussions here support the author's interpretation and serve as a reference work on the individual words and phrases of the text.

Modern interpreters have increasingly come to recognize that it is insufficient merely to reconstruct what a biblical text might have meant in its original context or to consider what it might mean in the present. Rather, the Bible is always encountered as it has come to mean. It is a collection of texts with a long history, and every aspect of that history is a part of their meaning. Like a Chinese landscape painting, the value of the work resides not merely in the work of the original "artist," but also in the ongoing conversation that the "painting" has engendered over time. Part of the aim of this series is to alert the reader to the history of conversation surrounding biblical texts and to invite the reader to join that conversation.

Those who explore this history have variously named their enterprise "history of interpretation," "history of effects," "history of influence," or

To the Reader

"history of reception." Though often used interchangeably, these labels in fact emphasize different aspects of the evidence scholars evince, including all manner of encounter with the biblical tradition. They include exegesis in commentaries, theological expositions, and homilies, but also the interpretive moves entailed in the introduction of vowel letters and the punctuation to the Hebrew text, translations and paraphrases, and artistic renderings. They also involve works in various genres and media inspired by or reacting to the biblical tradition, appropriations of it in liturgy, explicit and implicit justifications for actions, polemics, conduct arising from encounters with it, and unwitting results—including nefarious consequences—of its use. In recognition of the reality that these texts produced results both witting and unwitting, both actively received and passively endured, this series uses the rubric "history of consequences," meaning "consequences" in the sense of all that comes after the Bible, as well as "consequences" in the sense of the direct or indirect results of interpretation and reception.

C. L. SEOW, *General Editor*

SCOTT C. JONES, BRENNAN W. BREED, AND SUSANNE GILLMAYR-BUCHER, *Hebrew Bible/Old Testament*

JUDITH H. NEWMAN, *Deuterocanonicals/Apocrypha*

LOREN STUCKENBRUCK, *New Testament*

Preface

My gratitude is offered to Choon-Leong Seow for his invitation to contribute to this series and for the inspiring example of his Job 1–21 commentary. Andrew Knapp at Eerdmans has been unfailingly responsive and supportive throughout this project; I am deeply grateful to him. Thanks are due as well to my editor, Brennan Breed, who made several important suggestions related to reception history.

The labors of many wise scholars of Micah have assisted my progress in this work. I have learned much from the foundational commentary of Francis Andersen and David Noel Freedman, the judicious work of Rainer Kessler, the astute feminist analysis of Julia O'Brien, and the erudite 2019 volume by Riemer Roukema on Christian reception of Micah in antiquity. For work on the textual traditions of Micah, I have been guided by the expertise of Dominique Barthélemy, Anthony Gelston, and Edward Glenny. I wish to record my appreciation for the work of Ehud Ben Zvi, who has been steadfast in his efforts to shift scholarly debate about the Latter Prophets from a historicist mindset to a more nuanced understanding of the prophetic books as sophisticated constructions of scribal memory centuries later than the historical settings of those ancient works. Two edited collections have proved invaluable, and I offer my gratitude to the editors and contributors: *The Book of the Twelve: Composition, Reception, and Interpretation* (2020), edited by Lena-Sofia Tiemeyer and Jakob Wöhrle, and *The Oxford Handbook of the Minor Prophets* (2021), edited by Julia O'Brien. I am grateful for the highly intelligent work of Chip Dobbs-Allsopp regarding lineation and other features of Biblical Hebrew poetry. I offer robust thanks to Marquis Bey for their inspiring work on Black trans feminism.

I offer my warm appreciation to the Henry L. Slack Dean of Yale Divinity School, Gregory E. Sterling, for his unflagging kindness and generous support of my research. Thanks are due to Kenneth Minkema, who was helpful

Preface

in guiding me into Jonathan Edwards' citations of Micah. The Yale Divinity School library staff is a treasure; I offer special thanks to Suzanne Estelle-Holmer and Soli Johnson, who assisted me at several junctures during this research. I thank Daryl Denelle and Meredith Barges for helping me avoid ableist valences in my translation of *hlk* in Micah 6:8.

The steady encouragement of cherished friends in biblical studies, homiletics, feminist writing, ecological activism, and pastoral ministry has been essential for my stamina in researching and writing this book, the third in a spate of three commentaries I've written. Joyful thanks go to Christl Maier, Roy Heller, Jaime Clark-Soles, Julie Claassens, Louis Stulman, Jeanette Stokes, Mary Moschella, Rebecca Wall, Beverly Mitchell, Marion Thullbery, Márcia Rego, Rachael Wooten, Marcy Lytle, Dale Wood Peterson, Lisabeth Huck, Donyelle McCray, Melanie Ross, Jennifer Herdt, Brandon Nappi, Julie Kelsey, Tom Long, and Leah Schade. The sustaining witness of several congregations has kept me energized for this work: I wish to thank St. Thomas's Episcopal Church in New Haven, Connecticut; St. John's Episcopal Church in Essex, Connecticut; the Marquand Chapel community at Yale Divinity School; and The Chapel of the Cross in Chapel Hill, North Carolina.

In North America, land acknowledgments keep us mindful of indigenous peoples whose ancestors were harassed, forcibly displaced, tortured, and killed in militarized colonization processes instigated by settlers of European heritage. The persistent economic, social, and political challenges with which Native groups contend today are due in no small part to that history of injustice and cultural trauma, and to the failure of governmental agencies, educational institutions, and ecclesial judicatories to make meaningful reparations. Yale University acknowledges that indigenous peoples and nations, including Mohegan, Mashantucket Pequot, Eastern Pequot, Schaghticoke, Golden Hill Paugussett, Niantic, and the Quinnipiac and other Algonquian-speaking peoples, have stewarded through generations the lands and waterways of what is now Connecticut. My office, the Yale libraries that support my research, the classrooms in which I teach, and my home study are located on unceded land of Quinnipiac and Niantic peoples. I honor their historical and continuing presence in the terrain, literal and figurative, in which I have worked to amplify Micah's call for justice.

Words cannot express the depth of my gratitude to my family for their love and good humor during the intense time I was working on this commentary. I rely daily on the cheery support, hilarious wit, and unreserved warmth of our offspring, Cedar and Jake. When I began my career in biblical studies, the children were preschoolers. Now grown, they are pursuing fascinating careers, Cedar in comparative literature and queer studies, and Jake in geopolitical consultation with a focus on China. It has been a joy to watch their growth in wisdom and skill in their chosen life paths, and I have been inspired by them as I have turned toward new possibilities within my own academic vocation. My spouse, Leo Lensing, has been my rock. Constant in love and a model of intellectual stamina and verve, Leo has continued to accomplish much in German studies and film studies while tending skillfully to hearth and home. I owe him more than I could possibly say. Other family members, too, have been vital to my well-being during this project: I offer special affirmation to my twin sister, Libby Tilghman, her husband, Bill Tilghman, my brother, Jim Sharp, and our stepmother, Sandra Sharp.

This volume is dedicated to the memory of my stepfather, David H. McAlpin (1928–2022), a Presbyterian pastor, philanthropist, and longtime leader and supporter of the Greater Trenton Habitat for Humanity in New Jersey. Through his compassionate presence and unstinting support of good causes, Mac exemplified Micah's vision of believers who do justice, cherish fidelity, and proceed humbly with their God.

CJS
Feast of the Nativity of John the Baptist
June 2024

Abbreviations

1 Apol.	Justin Martyr, *First Apology*. Pages 163-87 in *The Apostolic Fathers with Justin Martyr and Irenaeus*. ANF 1. Grand Rapids: Eerdmans, 1996.
1QpMic	*pesher* commentary on Mic 1:5-6 found in Cave 1 at Qumran
4Q168	fragments of Mic 4:8-12 found in Cave 4 at Qumran
8HevXIIgr	fragments of a Greek scroll of the Minor Prophets found at Nahal Hever
ÄAT	Ägypten und Altes Testament
AB	Anchor (Yale) Bible
ABRL	Anchor (Yale) Bible Reference Library
ABS	Archaeology and Biblical Studies
abs.	absolute
ACCS	Ancient Christian Commentary on Scripture. Vol. 14: *The Twelve Prophets*. Edited by A. Ferreiro. Downers Grove, IL: InterVarsity Press, 2003.
AcT	*Acta Theologica*
ACT	Ancient Christian Texts
AIL	Ancient Israel and Its Literature
AJSR	*Association for Jewish Studies Review*
ANEATP	*The Ancient Near East: An Anthology of Texts and Pictures*. Edited by J. B. Pritchard. Princeton: Princeton University Press, 2011.
ANEM	Ancient Near East Monographs/Monografías sobre el Antiguo Cercano Oriente
ANF	Ante-Nicene Fathers. Edited by Alexander Roberts and James Donaldson. 10 vols. Edinburgh: T&T Clark, 1885-1887.
Ant.	Flavius Josephus, *Jewish Antiquities*
AOTC	Abingdon Old Testament Commentary
ArBib	The Aramaic Bible

ATD	Das Alte Testament Deutsch
AThR	*Anglican Theological Review*
b.	Babylonian Talmud tractate
B. Bat.	Baba Batra
BASOR	*Bulletin of the American Schools of Oriental Research*
BCE	Before the Common Era
BCOTPB	Baker Commentary on the Old Testament: Prophetic Books
BDAG	Danker, F. W., W. Bauer, W. F. Arndt, and F. W. Gingrich. *Greek-English Lexicon of the New Testament and Other Early Christian Literature*. 3rd ed. Chicago: University of Chicago Press, 2000.
BETL	Bibliotheca Ephemeridum Theologicarum Lovaniensium
BHQ	*Biblia Hebraica Quinta*. Edited by A. Schenker et al. Stuttgart: Deutsche Bibelgesellschaft, 2004– . Fascicle 13, *The Twelve Minor Prophets*, prepared by A. Gelston, 2010.
BHS	*Biblia Hebraica Stuttgartensia*. Edited by K. Elliger and W. Rudolph. Stuttgart: Deutsche Bibelgesellschaft, 1983.
Bib	*Biblica*
BibInt	*Biblical Interpretation*
BibInt	Biblical Interpretation Series
BibS(N)	Biblische Studien (Neukirchen)
BigS	*Die Bibel in gerechter Sprache*. Gütersloh: Gütersloher Verlagshaus, 2006.
BN	*Biblische Notizen*
BRLJ	Brill Reference Library of Judaism
BTS	Biblical Tools and Studies
BTTS	Bonaventure Texts in Translation Series
BZAW	Beihefte zur Zeitschrift für die alttestamentliche Wissenschaft
Cat.	Cyril of Jerusalem, *Catecheses 13–18: Mystagogical Lectures*. Vol. 2 of *The Works of Saint Cyril of Jerusalem*. Translated by L. P. McCauley and A. A. Stephenson. FC 64. Washington, DC: Catholic University of America Press, 1970.
CBC	Cambridge Bible Commentary
CBQ	*Catholic Biblical Quarterly*
CC	Continental Commentaries
CE	Common Era
CGL	*The Cambridge Greek Lexicon*. Edited by J. Diggle, B. L. Fraser, P. James, O. B. Simkin, A. A. Thompson, and S. J. Westripp. 2 vols. Cambridge: Cambridge University Press, 2021.

Abbreviations

CHANE	Culture and History of the Ancient Near East
City of God	Augustine, *The City of God, Books XVII–XXII*. Translated by G. G. Walsh and D. J. Honan. FC 24. Washington, DC: Catholic University of America Press, 1954.
Comm.^{CA}	Cyril of Alexandria, *Commentary on the Twelve Prophets*. Vol. 2. Translated by R. C. Hill. FC 116. Washington, DC: Catholic University of America Press, 2008.
Comm. Mich.	Jerome, *Commentariorum in Michaeum libri II*. Pages 40–113 in vol. 1 of *Commentaries on the Twelve Prophets*. Edited by T. P. Scheck. Micah translated by A. Cazares. 2 vols. ACT. Downers Grove, IL: IVP Academic, 2016.
Comm.™	Theodore of Mopsuestia, *Commentary on the Twelve Prophets*. Translated by R. C. Hill. FC 108. Washington, DC: Catholic University of America Press, 2004.
cpl	common plural
cs	common singular
CS	Cistercian Studies
CTAT	*Ézéchiel, Daniel et les 12 Prophètes*. Vol. 3 of *Critique textuelle de l'Ancien Testament*. Edited by D. Barthélemy. 5 vols. OBO 50.3. Fribourg: Éditions Universitaires; Göttingen: Vandenhoeck & Ruprecht, 1982–2015.
CurBR	*Currents in Biblical Research*
CurTM	*Currents in Theology and Mission*
CWS	Classics of Western Spirituality
Deut. Rab.	*Midrash Rabbah, 7: Deuteronomy, Lamentations*. 3rd ed. Translated by J. Rabbinowitz. London: Soncino, 1983.
Dial.	Justin Martyr, *Dialogue with Trypho*. Pages 194–270 in *The Apostolic Fathers with Justin Martyr and Irenaeus*. ANF 1. Grand Rapids: Eerdmans, 1996.
DJD	Discoveries in the Judaean Desert
EBR	*Encyclopedia of the Bible and Its Reception*. Edited by C. M. Furey et al. Berlin: De Gruyter, 2009–.
ECC	Eerdmans Critical Commentary
Eccl. Rab.	*Midrash Rabbah, 8: Ruth, Ecclesiastes*. 3rd ed. Translated by A. Cohen. London: Soncino, 1983.
ECL	Early Christianity and Its Literature
EJL	Early Judaism and Its Literature
En.	Enoch
EncJud	*Encyclopaedia Judaica*. Edited by F. Skolnik and M. Berenbaum. 2nd ed. 22 vols. Detroit: Macmillan Reference USA, 2007.

Abbreviations

Eng.	English
Esth. Rab.	*Midrash Rabbah, 9: Esther*. 3rd ed. Translated by M. Simon. London: Soncino, 1983.
ESV	English Standard Version (2011)
Exod. Rab.	*Midrash Rabbah, 3: Exodus*. 3rd ed. Translated by S. M. Lehrman. London: Soncino, 1983.
FAT	Forschungen zum Alten Testament
FB	Forschung zur Bibel
FC	Fathers of the Church
FCB	Feminist Companion to the Bible
FCMC	Fathers of the Church: Medieval Continuations
FOTL	Forms of the Old Testament Literature
fp	feminine plural
FRLANT	Forschungen zur Religion und Literatur des Alten und Neuen Testaments
fs	feminine singular
Gen. Rab.	*Midrash Rabbah, 1: Genesis*. 3rd ed. 2 vols. Translated by H. Freedman. London: Soncino, 1983.
GKC	*Gesenius' Hebrew Grammar*. Edited by E. Kautzsch. Translated by A. E. Cowley. 2nd ed. Oxford: Clarendon, 1910.
Gos. Thom.	Gospel of Thomas
Haer.	Irenaeus of Lyons, *Against Heresies*. Pages 315–567 in *The Apostolic Fathers with Justin Martyr and Irenaeus*. ANF 1. Grand Rapids: Eerdmans, 1996.
HALOT	*The Hebrew and Aramaic Lexicon of the Old Testament*. L. Koehler, W. Baumgartner, and J. J. Stamm. Translated and edited under the supervision of M. E. Richardson. 5 vols. Leiden: Brill, 1994–2000.
HBM	Hebrew Bible Monographs
HBV	The Hebrew Bible and Its Versions
HCOT	Historical Commentary on the Old Testament
Heb.	Hebrew
Herm. Vis.	Shepherd of Hermas, Vision(s)
hiph.	hiphil
hithp.	hithpael
Hom. Gen.	Origen, *Homilies on Genesis and Exodus*. Translated by R. E. Heine. FC 71. Washington, DC: Catholic University of America Press, 1981.
Hom. Lev.	Origen, *Homilies on Leviticus: 1–16*. Translated by G. W. Bark-

	ley. FC 83. Washington, DC: Catholic University of America Press, 1990.
Hom. Lk.	Origen, *Homilies on Luke*. Translated by J. T. Lienhard. FC 94. Washington, DC: Catholic University of America Press, 1996.
Hom. Jer.	Origen, *Homilies on Jeremiah and 1 Kings 28*. Translated by J. C. Smith. FC 97. Washington, DC: Catholic University of America Press, 1998.
Hom. Josh.	Origen, *Homilies on Joshua*. Translated by B. J. Bruce. FC 105. Washington, DC: Catholic University of America Press, 2002.
Hom. Matt.	St. Chrysostom, *Homilies on the Gospel of Saint Matthew*. Translated by G. Prevost; revised with notes by M. B. Riddle. NPNF[1] 10. Peabody, MA: Hendrickson, 1995. Homily 29: 195–98. Homily 68: 414–20.
Hom. Ps.	Basil of Caesarea, homilies on the Psalms in *Exegetic Homilies*. Translated by A. C. Way. FC 46. Washington, DC: Catholic University of America Press, 1963.
HThKAT	Herders Theologischer Kommentar zum Alten Testament
HTR	*Harvard Theological Review*
HvTSt	*HTS Teologiese Studies/Theological Studies*
IBHS	*An Introduction to Biblical Hebrew Syntax*. B. K. Waltke and M. P. O'Connor. Winona Lake, IN: Eisenbrauns, 1990.
ICC	International Critical Commentary
IECOT	International Exegetical Commentary on the Old Testament
IJH	*International Journal of Homiletics*
IJPT	*International Journal of Public Theology*
impf.	imperfect or nonperfective form
impv.	imperative
inf.	infinitive
Int	*Interpretation*
IPBES	Intergovernmental Science-Policy Platform on Biodiversity and Ecosystem Services
	2019: The Global Assessment Report: Summary for Policymakers.
	2020: Status and Trends—Nature.
IPCC	Intergovernmental Panel on Climate Change
	2022: Climate Change 2022—Impacts, Adaptation and Vulnerability: Summary for Policymakers: Working Group II Contribution to the Sixth Assessment Report. https://www.ipcc.ch/report/ar6/wg2/.

Abbreviations

	2023: Climate Change Synthesis Report of the IPCC Sixth Assessment Report (AR6). https://www.ipcc.ch/report/sixth-assessment-report-cycle/.
ISBL	Indiana Studies in Biblical Literature
Jac.	Ambrose of Milan, *Jacob and the Happy Life*. Pages 119–84 in *Seven Exegetical Works*. Translated by M. P. McHugh. FC 65. Washington, DC: Catholic University of America Press, 1972.
JANER	*Journal of Ancient Near Eastern Religions*
JETS	*Journal of the Evangelical Theological Society*
JNES	*Journal of Near Eastern Studies*
Joüon	Joüon, Paul. *A Grammar of Biblical Hebrew*. Translated and revised by T. Muraoka. 2 vols. Rome: Pontifical Biblical Institute, 1991.
JPsTh	*Journal of Psychology and Theology*
JSLHR	*Journal of Speech, Language, and Hearing Research*
JSOT	*Journal for the Study of the Old Testament*
JSOTSup	Journal for the Study of the Old Testament Supplement Series
JSS	*Journal of Semitic Studies*
JTI	*Journal of Theological Interpretation*
Jub.	Jubilees
KAT	Kommentar zum Alten Testament
LAI	Library of Ancient Israel
Lam. Rab.	*Midrash Rabbah, 7: Deuteronomy, Lamentations*. 3rd ed. Translated by A. Cohen. London: Soncino, 1983.
LCC	Library of Christian Classics
Lev. Rab.	*Midrash Rabbah, 4: Leviticus*. 3rd ed. Chapters 1–19 translated by J. Israelstam; chapters 20–37 translated by J. J. Slotki. London: Soncino, 1983.
LHBOTS	Library of Hebrew Bible/Old Testament Studies
LNTS	Library of New Testament Studies
LXX	Septuagint
Mak.	Makkot
Mart. Pol.	Martyrdom of Polycarp
Micah^{LXX}	Septuagint text of Micah
Micah^{MT}	Masoretic text of Micah
mp	masculine plural
ms	masculine singular
MSV	Vatican Manuscript Codex 30 of Genesis Rabbah, containing midrashic commentary on Gen 46–48

xxi

Abbreviations

MT	Masoretic Text
NAC	New American Commentary
NCBC	New Collegeville Bible Commentary
NEAEHL	*The New Encyclopedia of Archaeological Excavations in the Holy Land.* Edited by E. Stern. Vols. 1–4: Jerusalem: Israel Exploration Society; Carta, 1993. Vol. 5: Jerusalem: Israel Exploration Society, 2008.
NETS	New English Translation of the Septuagint and the Other Greek Translations Traditionally Included under That Title. Edited by A. Pietersma and B. G. Wright. Michaias translated by G. E. Howard. Oxford: Oxford University Press, 2007.
NICOT	New International Commentary on the Old Testament
NJPS	*Tanakh: The Holy Scriptures: The New JPS Translation according to the Traditional Hebrew Text*
Noet.	Hippolytus. Pages 223–31 in *Against the Heresy of One Noetus.* In *Ante-Nicene Fathers: Hippolytus, Cyprian, Caius, Novatian.* ANF 5. Grand Rapids: Eerdmans, 1996.
NPNF[1]	Nicene and Post-Nicene Fathers, Series 1
NPNF[2]	Nicene and Post-Nicene Fathers, Series 2
NRSV	New Revised Standard Version (1989)
NSKAT	Neuer Stuttgarter Kommentar, Altes Testament
Num. Rab.	*Midrash Rabbah, 5: Numbers.* 3rd ed. 2 vols. Translated by J. J. Slotki. London: Soncino, 1983.
OBO	Orbis Biblicus et Orientalis
OBT	Overtures to Biblical Theology
OEANE	*The Oxford Encyclopedia of Archaeology in the Near East.* Edited by E. M. Meyers. 5 vols. New York: Oxford, 1997. Current online version, 2011.
OHAL	*The Oxford Handbook of the Archaeology of the Levant c. 8000–332 BCE.* Edited by M. L. Steiner and A. E. Killebrew. Oxford: Oxford University Press, 2014.
OHMP	*The Oxford Handbook of the Minor Prophets.* Edited by J. M. O'Brien. Oxford: Oxford University Press, 2021.
OHP	*The Oxford Handbook of the Prophets.* Edited by C. J. Sharp. Oxford: Oxford University Press, 2016.
OSJCB	Osnabrücker Studien zur Jüdischen und Christlichen Bibel
OTL	Old Testament Library
OTS	Old Testament Studies
OtSt	Oudtestamentische Studiën

pers. com.	personal communication
pf.	perfect or perfective form
PG	Patrologia Graeca [= Patrologiae Cursus Completus: Series Graeca]. Edited by J.-P. Migne. 161 vols. Paris, 1857–1886.
PIBA	*Proceedings of the Irish Biblical Association*
r.	reign
R.	Rabbi or Rav
Rab.	Rabbah
RB	*Revue biblique*
RBS	Resources for Biblical Study
RCL	Revised Common Lectionary (1994)
ResQ	*Restoration Quarterly*
RRBS	Recent Research in Biblical Studies
Ruth Rab.	*Midrash Rabbah, 8: Ruth.* 3rd ed. Translated by J. I. Rabinowitz. London: Soncino, 1983.
RVR	Reina-Valera Revision (1995)
Šabb.	Šabbat
SBLDS	Society of Biblical Literature Dissertation Series
SBLStBL	Society of Biblical Literature Studies in Biblical Literature
SBR	Studies of the Bible and Its Reception
SBS	Stuttgarter Bibelstudien
SEÅ	*Svensk exegetisk årsbok*
SemeiaSt	Semeia Studies
Sent. I	Peter Lombard, *Sentences, Book 1: The Mystery of the Trinity*. Translated by G. Silano. Mediaeval Sources in Translation 42. Toronto: Pontifical Institute of Mediaeval Studies, 2007.
SHANE	Studies in the History of the Ancient Near East
SHBC	Smyth & Helwys Bible Commentary
SJT	*Scottish Journal of Theology*
Song Rab.	*Midrash Rabbah, 9: Esther, Song of Songs.* 3rd ed. Translated by M. Simon. London: Soncino, 1983.
Strom.	Clement of Alexandria, *Stromateis*
SVTG	Septuaginta: Vetus Testamentum Graecum
SWBA	Social World of Biblical Antiquity Second Series
SymS	Symposium Series
Tg. Mic	Micah in *The Targum of the Minor Prophets*. ArBib 14. Translated and annotated by K. J. Cathcart and R. P. Gordon. Wilmington, DE: Glazier, 1989.
THBC	Two Horizons Biblical Commentary

Abbreviations

TJ	*Trinity Journal*
Tract. Ev. Jo.	Augustine, *Tractates on the Gospel of John: 28–54*. Translated by J. W. Rettig. FC 88. Washington, DC: Catholic University of America Press, 1993.
TSAJ	Texte und Studien zum antiken Judentum/Texts and Studies in Ancient Judaism
Vitae Proph.	Vitae Prophetarum
vrss.	versions
VT	*Vetus Testamentum*
VTSup	Supplements to Vetus Testamentum
WAWSup	Writings from the Ancient World Supplement Series
WJE	*The Works of Jonathan Edwards*. 26 vols. New Haven: Yale University Press, 1977–2009. Online archive: http:/edwards.yale.edu.
WJE 4	Edwards, J. 1972. *The Great Awakening*. Edited by C. C. Groen. WJE 4. New Haven: Yale University Press, 1972.
WJE 5	Edwards, J. *Apocalyptic Writings*. Edited by S. J. Stein. WJE 5. New Haven: Yale University Press, 1973.
WJE 8	Edwards, J. *Ethical Writings*. Edited by P. Ramsey. WJE 8. New Haven: Yale University Press, 1989.
WJE 9	Edwards, J. *A History of the Work of Redemption*. Edited by J. F. Wilson. WJE 9. New Haven: Yale University Press, 1989.
WJE 11	Edwards, J. *Typological Writings*. "Images of Divine Things" and "Types." Edited by W. E. Anderson. "Types of the Messiah." Edited by M. I. Lowance Jr. with D. H. Watters. WJE 11. New Haven: Yale University Press, 1993.
WJE 13	Edwards, J. *The "Miscellanies," Entry Nos. a-z, aa-zz, 1–500*. Edited by T. A. Schafer. WJE 13. New Haven: Yale University Press, 1994.
WJE 14	Edwards, J. *Sermons and Discourses, 1723–1729*. Edited by K. P. Minkema. WJE 14. New Haven: Yale University Press, 1997.
WJE 15	Edwards, J. *Notes on Scripture*. Edited by S. J. Stein. WJE 15. New Haven: Yale University Press, 1998.
WJE 17	Edwards, J. *Sermons and Discourses 1730–1733*. Edited by M. Valeri. WJE 17. New Haven: Yale University Press, 1999.
WJE 19	Edwards, J. *Sermons and Discourses: 1734–1738*. Edited by M. X. Lesser. WJE 19. New Haven: Yale University Press, 2001.
WJE 20	Edwards, J. *The "Miscellanies," Entry Nos. 833–1152*. Edited by A. P. Pauw. WJE 20. New Haven: Yale University Press, 2002.

Abbreviations

WJE 21	Edwards, J. *Writings on the Trinity, Grace, and Faith*. Edited by S. H. Lee. WJE 21. New Haven: Yale University Press, 2003.
WJE 22	Edwards, J. *Sermons and Discourses, 1739–1742*. Edited by H. S. Stout and N. O. Hatch, with K. P. Farley. WJE 22. New Haven: Yale University Press, 2003.
WJE 23	Edwards, J. *The "Miscellanies," Entry Nos. 1153–1360*. Edited by D. A. Sweeney. WJE 23. New Haven: Yale University Press, 2004.
WJE 24	Edwards, J. *The "Blank Bible."* Edited by S. J. Stein. 2 vols. WJE 24. New Haven: Yale University Press, 2006.
WJE 25	Edwards, J. *Sermons and Discourses: 1743–1758*. Edited by W. H. Kimnach. WJE 25. New Haven: Yale University Press, 2006.
WO	*Die Welt des Orients*
ZAW	*Zeitschrift für die alttestamentliche Wissenschaft*
ZUR	*Zürcher Bibel*, 2nd ed.

Introduction

Fig. 1. The prophet Micah. Byzantine mosaic in the Cathedral of San Marco, Venice.

The oracles and traditions attributed to the prophet Micah are riveting expressions of political dissent and theological activism grounded, per the superscription and remembered traces of a first-person speaker, in the lived experience and wisdom of an eighth-century Judean. Micah hailed from Moresheth, a village scholars identify with contemporary Tell ej-Judeideh in the Shephelah, the rolling Judean foothills to the west of Jerusalem that serve as a fertile transitional region between more prominent inland hills and the coastal plain. While the Micah traditions give us nothing of Micah's biography, it seems likely from the oracles attributed to him that Micah's perspective would not have been that of an urban powerbroker. The prophet's name, *mîkāh*, may be a hypocoristic representation of a rhetorical question, "Who is like Yah?," which finds an analogue theologically in the rhetorical question of Mic 7:18: *mî-'ēl kāmôkā*, "Who is a God like you?"

1. HISTORICAL CONTEXTS, COMPOSITIONAL GROWTH, AND TEXTUAL VERSIONS

The poetry of Micah is artful, drawing hearers and readers into powerfully dramatized moments of historical, theological, and ethical significance for the Judean community across a span of historical contexts. Some passages are difficult to understand fully, though Henri Cazelles and David Sperling might overstate the challenges when they say the text of Micah "swarms with philological difficulties" and characterize 1:10–16; 2:6–11; and 7:11–12 as "unintelligible" (2007, 163). The book of Micah moves fluidly between two historical perspectives. One lens is focused on the Neo-Assyrian period, a time of dread when the fall of Samaria alarmed neighboring regions and, to astute observers of the time, might have seemed to presage the imminent

Introduction

Fig. 2. Shephelat Judea: Nahal Hevron, 1954.

doom of Jerusalem. Within that context, some have proposed that the Syro-Ephraimite war of 734-732 is relevant here, in which a regional coalition sought to coerce Judah into joining their rebellion against the Assyrian ruler Tiglath-Pileser III (r. 745-727; note that regnal dates in this commentary include the accession year). This protracted conflict may be visible in the background of some passages in Mic 4-5 (so, e.g., de Moor 2015, 192). The relevant biblical texts on the Syro-Ephraimite war include 2 Kgs 15-17; Isa 7-10; 1 Chr 5:6; and 2 Chr 28:20. Of the outcomes of Tiglath-pileser's aggressively expansionist military campaigns across the Levant, Josette Elayi writes,

> He used the policy of massive deportation in order to prevent possible future rebellions. The largest groups of deportees were mainly taken

from Damascus, Israel, and Samsi's people [in Arabia]. The recorded number of deportees in his inscriptions is 16,620. . . . The province of Damascus was created, including Transjordan, from Gilead to Abel-Shittim. The kingdom of Israel was turned into a smaller district called Bît-Humria in the Assyrian inscriptions: it was limited to Samaria and its vicinity west of the Jordan and south of Jezreel. The kings of both Israel and Judah became Assyrian vassals. . . . Tiglath-pileser left behind him not only ruined cities but also monuments in recollection of his power and sovereignty. (2022, 152)

In the Micah traditions, a second lens is trained on the Neo-Babylonian period. Babylon is expressly named in 4:10 as a site of diaspora for Judean captives; other Micah texts, too, have indisputably been shaped in light of concerns later than the Neo-Assyrian period, including passages that envision and lament the desolation of Daughter Zion and passages that offer luminous hope for Israel's and Judah's restoration. As Francesco Arena observes, "the book of Micah (its core included) has been vastly edited to address the future of Jerusalem after the Babylonian invasion and the exile, which represents the background against which the redactors intended it to be read" (2020, 157). Both of these Levantine historical contexts are situated within the Iron Age. The chronological subdivisions are debated among archaeologists, because changes in material culture and the dating of destruction layers are assessed in divergent ways depending on methodologies, weighting of evidence, and other critical judgments used (see Sharon 2014, 58–63). This commentary uses the dates provided by the Levantine Ceramics Project: Iron Age I is taken as 1200–1000, Iron Age IIA as 1000–900, IIB as 900–700, and Iron Age IIC as 700–587. I do depart from the Levantine Ceramics Project date of 586 for the destruction of Jerusalem since, with Rainer Albertz, Christl Maier, and others, I am persuaded that Neo-Babylonian troops launched the siege of Jerusalem in January 588 and the city fell in July 587.

Critical differences were manifest in the geopolitics of the region and the lived experiences of Israelites and Judeans. Assyrian dominance, from 912 BCE onward, came to an end with the destruction of Nineveh in 612. The opening of the scroll of Micah's oracles holds Samaria and Jerusalem together: "Who constitutes the transgression of Jacob? Is it not Samaria? And who constitutes the high places of Judah? Is it not Jerusalem?" (1:5b). Micah 1:1–7 reflects knowledge of the fall of Samaria, the capital of the Northern Kingdom of Israel, in 722 to the Assyrians (Elayi 2017, 46). Assyrian military

Introduction

strength was formidable. Though historical records of military forces were regularly inflated by royal scribes in antiquity, according to Christopher Hays and Peter Machinist, the Assyrian Empire apparently did maintain "tens of thousands in their standing armies," and the impressive "scale of the Assyrian military is also suggested by the incredible 160,000 kilograms (352,740 pounds) of iron found in a single room at Sargon II's palace at Khorsabad" (2016, 58).

Shalmaneser V (r. 727–722) had launched a three-year siege of Samaria. After his death, Samaria was finally captured by Sargon II (r. 722–705), of whom Elayi offers, "Sargon was not a charismatic leader, like Alexander the Great, for example. He seems to have been just as terrifying to his own troops as he was to his enemies," and adds, "he often made displays of barbaric treatment and slaughter of his enemies and their families" (2017, 19–20). Sargon boasted in an inscription about his conquest of Samaria: "I led away as prisoners 27,290 inhabitants of it (and) [equipped] from among [them] . . . 50 chariots for my royal corps. . . . [The town I] re[built] better than (it was) before and [settled] therein people from countries which [I] myself [had con]quered" (*ANEATP*, 266). After the fall of Samaria and Assyria's forcible deportation of captives, it is highly likely that many Israelite survivors "fled southward as refugees and were incorporated into Judean society" (Hays with Machinist 2016, 48; so also Elayi 2017, 52). The dramatic oracles of Mic 1 attest to the dread experienced by Judean villages as the Assyrian military threat advanced toward Jerusalem. Whether the oracles had been composed by the historical Micah after he saw traumatized Israelite refugees flood into the region or their vivid imagery was imagined as a powerful cultural memory by a later scribe cannot be known with certainty. In any event, Elayi observes, "Sargon's reign had an immense impact on Palestine. . . . The kingdom of Israel was suppressed and its inhabitants scattered through deportations, most of the Philistine cities were reduced to subjugation, and the kingdom of Judah was subdued as an Assyrian vassal state" (2017, 61).

The fall of Samaria could be construed from a later scribal perspective as a warning to Jerusalem about the threat of the Neo-Babylonian Empire. This is clear from 2 Kgs 17:1–20, where the sins of the Northern Kingdom of Israel are detailed, Israel's defeat by the Neo-Assyrian Empire is framed as Yhwh's retribution for Israel's refusal to reform its sinful ways, and a link to Judah is made explicitly in 17:19–20, "Judah also did not keep the commandments of the Lord their God but walked in the customs that Israel had introduced," and a more expansive use of the designation "Israel" encompasses divine punishment of both Israel and Judah: "the Lord rejected all the descendants

Historical Contexts, Compositional Growth, and Textual Versions

of Israel; [Yhwh] punished them and gave them into the hand of plunderers, until [Yhwh] had banished them from [Yhwh's] presence."*

Some 130 years later, the Babylonian military juggernaut would leave Jerusalem with its monumental structures burned or reduced to rubble and the region around Jerusalem devastated. Yet the Neo-Babylonian Empire would meet its own end when Babylon was conquered by the troops of Cyrus of Persia. The final form of the book of Micah seems to have all of this in view; many contemporary scholars would agree with Johannes de Moor that Mic 1–7 "is the product of several centuries of editorial shaping" (2015, 191). Of the numerous dramatic effects created by this bifocal perspective, I would highlight two. First, the reign of the coming "One of Peace" (5:1–4a [Eng. 2–5a]) can be seen to embrace all of Israel's and Judah's history: consolation and flourishing will be the portion for all, including the descendants of those terrorized and displaced in the Northern Kingdom long ago and those more recently (from the perspective of postexilic prophetic scribes) who were traumatized by the fall of Jerusalem. A second effect of the expansive scope of this scroll: the lamenting of Micah himself (1:8–9) and Daughter Zion (7:1–4a), and Zion's and the community's affirmations of enduring resilience vis-à-vis their enemies (4:13c; 5:4b–8 [Eng. 5b–9]; 7:8–13), resonate as positions of strength not just for a particular historical moment, but for all time. This people will stand strong against any adversary that has ever risen or will rise against the covenant people.

Two passages in Mic 1–3 envisage the defeat of Judah and destruction of Jerusalem: 2:12–13 (this being a devastating ironic image of exile very like Amos 6:4–7, not an awkwardly placed oracle of divine protection; see the commentary) and 3:12 ("Zion will be plowed as a field"). These passages may constitute advance prophetic warning that Jerusalem, too, will fall as Samaria did if Judean leaders do not correct their ethical and religious failings. But it is also possible that these are traces left by scribes who preserved and shaped the book of Micah in the time of the Babylonian exile after the fall of Jerusalem to Nebuchadrezzar II over a century later, or in the postexilic period, that is, after Cyrus of Persia defeated Babylon in 539 BCE and issued an edict in 538 that Judeans in Babylonia were free to return home. An explicit reference to the Neo-Babylonian era in 4:10 ("you will go to Babylon") makes clear that some of the Micah traditions were brought to their final literary form during or later than the Neo-Babylonian hegemony over Judah, for this

---

* Translations of biblical passages from books other than Micah are from the NRSV unless otherwise noted.

Introduction

verse seems to demonstrate awareness of Nebuchadrezzar's deportations of Judean captives to Babylonia in 597 and 587 BCE (see Jer 52:15, 28-30).

There is a strong turn back to the focus on Assyria in Mic 5:5b-6, which expresses deep anxiety about an impending Assyrian invasion of Judah. These lines likely constitute a poetic reflection on that historical moment from a vantage point at some distance from the relevant events. This passage seems to know of the fall of Samaria and the campaign of Sennacherib (r. 705-681) against Jerusalem in 701, crafting a perspective framed as being offered just prior to the Assyrian invasion either for dramatic effect or to underline the accuracy of Micah's prophetic vision ("when he invades our land"). That military campaign is reflected in a lengthy royal inscription on an artifact known as the Prism of Sennacherib. The Assyrian ruler boasts of a number of victories: having subdued Hatti, with "Luli, king of Sidon, whom the terror-inspiring glamor of my lordship had overwhelmed," so he "fled far overseas and perished"; having subjugated "the kings of Amurru" and compelling them to pay heavy tribute, these vassals including Sidon, Ashdod, Moab, and Edom; having routed others, including Ekron and its Egyptian and Ethiopian allies, providing gruesome details about having killed the Ekron "officials and patricians" who had rebelled and having "hung their bodies on poles surrounding the city," the public display of tortured and mutilated corpses functioning as a spectacle designed to intimidate onlookers and weaken potential political resistance in the future (*ANEATP*, 269-70; Elayi 2018, 68). The section most relevant to Judah and Jerusalem reads:

> As to Hezekiah the Jew, he did not submit to my yoke; I laid siege to 46 of his strong cities, walled forts and to the countless small villages in their vicinity, and conquered them by means of well-stamped (earth-)ramps, and battering rams brought (thus) near (to the walls) (combined with) the attack by foot soldiers. . . . I drove out (of them) 200,150 people, young and old, male and female, horses, mules, donkeys, camels, big and small cattle beyond counting, and considered (them) booty. Himself [viz., Hezekiah] I made a prisoner in Jerusalem, his royal residence, like a bird in a cage. (*ANEATP*, 270-71)

Micah 5 imagines Assyria as a potent threat and, though likely composed later, artistically reflects a Judean perspective as voiced prior to the defeat of the Assyrians by Babylonia. Given what had happened to the Northern Kingdom of Israel, Judeans' terror at the prospect of forced deportation must have been intense and would have resonated long afterward in Israel's formative literary traditions. Jonathan Valk observes, "Mass deportation is an outgrowth of the longstanding ancient Near Eastern practice of counting human beings as part of the spoils of war, to be subjugated and employed according to the designs of their captors," and the Neo-Assyrian Empire was notorious for this practice: "The Assyrian kings of the first millennium B.C.E. boast repeatedly in their inscriptions that they uprooted entire peoples from their homes and resettled them elsewhere," and "these were not idle boasts," for according to one scholarly estimate, well over four million people were forced into exile by the Assyrians over a span of three centuries (2020, 77). It was tactically advantageous and economically beneficial for the Assyrian Empire to secure the unpaid labor of prisoners of war and subjugated noncombatants alike. These "vast slave raids" constituted "a fundamentally punitive mechanism designed . . . to pacify areas of resistance and deter unrest" (78). This intimidation strategy is manifestly evident in Assyrian inscriptions and wall sculpture: "figurative representations of deportees in Assyrian reliefs portray men, women, and children being marched out of ruined landscapes while others are butchered and tortured around them" (92). Forcible depopulation could cause lasting harm to the infrastructure of affected regions, imperiling life in those areas long after the Assyrian army had left: "Assyrian campaigns and deportations in the Levant left enduring demographic scars. . . . In the southern Levant, many regions were left desolate. The Lower Galilee and the hill country of Ephraim were left almost entirely deserted" (89). The advance of Assyrian troops would have terrorized vulnerable population groups throughout the Levant for many generations, and we see that anxiety in Mic 5. Valk comments (80) that "deportation in the Levant was most intensively practiced in the period from Tiglath-pileser III to Sennacherib (745–681 B.C.E.)," precisely the time in which Judah's scribes situate the prophesying of Micah of Moresheth.

Viewed through the dual lenses of the Neo-Assyrian and Neo-Babylonian eras, the oracles of Mic 6 should be heard as an impassioned warning to Judah that could apply in every historical context the implied audience could imagine, from the reign of Omri on through the Persian period. The prophet works artfully with a venerable tradition refracted in many Hebrew Bible texts from different eras: Israel's miraculous redemption by Yhwh in days of old. In the foreground is Israel's exodus from Egyptian enslavement under the leadership of Moses, Aaron, and Miriam, with threats successfully overcome during the journey represented in the figures of the Moabite ruler Balak and the seer Balaam. Narrative markers frame a cultural geography involving formative events narrated in the Pentateuch through Joshua and

Introduction

stretching "from Shittim to Gilgal" (6:4-5). Judah need only strive to obey the will of Yhwh as laid out in the community's own history. Ehud Ben Zvi observes, "This divine will includes a requirement from the audience to behave in accordance with some of Yhwh's attributes (cf. Lev 19:2), while at the same time maintaining a constant awareness of the unbridgeable gap between humanity and Yhwh" (2000, 153).

The historical context is not recoverable for the collection of poems in Mic 7, though its artful interweaving of allusions to other Hebrew Bible traditions suggests a likely time of composition in the Persian period. The speaker in 7:1-4, 8-10 is Daughter Zion, not the prophet (see the commentary). Micah responds to Zion in 7:5-7 and 7:11-13, then turns to Yhwh in 7:14-20, offering prophetic intercession for his people and exhorting Yhwh to display divine saving power as in days of old. Relevant to Mic 7, and other Micah materials as well, is the speculation of some scholars that "prophetic drama" or "liturgy" is an appropriate formal designation for materials in the Latter Prophets that seem to be intentional about staging dialogue among several voices. Klaus Baltzer has argued this for Deutero-Isaiah (see Sharp 2003 for my critique). Joyce Rilett Wood (2000) and Helmut Utzschneider (1999, 2005) have pressed the case for Micah in some detail, the latter arguing for Micah as a dramatic text in two acts, 1:2-5:14 and 6:1-7:20 (2005, 11-21). Ben Zvi raises the cogent objection that there is no persuasive evidence for such a thing as a "prophetic liturgy," thus the *Sitz im Buch*, rather than some putative "unmentioned oral performance," should guide its interpretation (2000, 180). Nevertheless, the point continues to be pressed by scholars who assert that dialogical voicing within this polished literature requires that we imagine a *Sitz im Leben* within an actual worship liturgy. But even allowing that there are dramaturgical and hymnic resonances in some of Micah's lines, the suggestion of prophetic performance as staged falls short of being fully convincing. The present writer finds most persuasive the nuanced position articulated by Walter Dietrich concerning Nahum: "The text could have been consciously formed in such a way that the readers or those listening to the reading could imagine a drama having taken place. . . . The point of view would be shifted from one angle to another, [and] changing scenes would demand the audience's attention" (2016, 22). Vivid imagery, shifting perspectives, and intense dialogical engagement between speakers, this last facilitated through rhetorical questions and the quoting of ventriloquized adversaries, are characteristic of every chapter of Micah, albeit in a more muted way in Mic 5:1-5 (Eng. 2-8). Riveting indeed is the drama of Micah's public proclamation, unfolding against the backdrop of his community's

Historical Contexts, Compositional Growth, and Textual Versions

terror and the sneering disregard of Judean powerbrokers. The postexilic prophetic scribes who amplified the preaching of Micah of Moresheth show something of that same dramatic sensibility themselves.

1.1 Composition and Redaction of Micah

There are numerous proposals for reconstruction of the compositional and editorial processes that yielded the book of Micah in its final form in the Masoretic tradition (Micah^{MT}). Two understandings of the compositional and redactional growth of Micah have drawn interpreters' attention in critical scholarship. One theory suggests, in broad strokes, that some oracles delivered by the historical Micah of Moresheth in the eighth century BCE were amplified by editing that is sometimes, though not always, characterized as Deuteronomistic. That is, the book of Micah is seen to have been expanded by small-scale interpolations and larger blocks of material written by scribes working in continuity with the diction and traditions deemed central to Deuteronomy and the Deuteronomistic History. The scribes responsible for later redaction of Micah worked after Jerusalem had fallen to the Neo-Babylonian Empire in 587 BCE—thus the final form of Micah^{MT} arrived at its present complex shape, aptly characterized by James Nogalski as "a composite unity" (2017c, 181), in the exilic era or, more likely, the postexilic period. Scholars working within this framework have made lively proposals and counterproposals about which Micah texts were composed earlier and which seem to have been generated in later historical times. Scribal textual traditions were fluid, and some scribes would have been highly skilled at blending their own later work with earlier discourse, smoothing literary transitions and adopting lexical and ideological features of earlier texts, even purposefully archaizing as the literary context might require. Within the theoretical framework of redaction criticism generally, many scholars hold the view that Micah was shaped editorially first in a smaller collection that included Hosea, Amos, and Zephaniah, known as the Book of the Four. For more on that, see §1.2 below.

A second theoretical framework, brought to comprehensive expression by Ben Zvi, suggests that the prophetic books—and other Hebrew Bible texts as well—should be interpreted as the products of scribal social memory in the Persian period. Though traditions were certainly known before that time, confirmable facts regarding the evolution of significantly earlier written texts over several stages cannot be recovered. This yields Micah as

Introduction

an erudite compositional performance from centuries later than the events ostensibly reflected in the poetry—not a core of eighth-century material later redacted and amplified by Deuteronomistic or other tradents (Ben Zvi 1999a). Julia O'Brien follows Ben Zvi on this, situating the composition of Micah between 539 and 400 BCE (2015, xlix). Where Ben Zvi musters arguments focused on the social functions of literary representation and cultural memory, O'Brien takes a more historical tack in her reasoning, seeking to illuminate material conditions of Judeans' lives in Persian-period Yehud. She argues for an early fifth-century provenance for Micah, in part from the absence of "urgency" about rebuilding the Jerusalem temple (presumably because it had already been rebuilt, thus after 516–515 BCE) and "before the [re]building of the city walls, generally dated to 445 BCE" (xlix-l).

In redaction-critical scholarship, certain literary features of composite texts are taken as markers of scribal editing. Such features have included: unexpected or awkward shifts of implicit addressee or topical emphasis; diction that seems to sit uneasily in its literary context and is found more fully integrated into the discourse of other biblical sources; the presence of brief prose snippets in a literary environment otherwise dominated by poetic expression; and semantic gestures that seem to interrupt, correct, or redirect the ideational flow of thought in a passage. In scholarly debates about composition and redaction, many scholars offer minutely detailed proposals for redactional activity, engaging in lively dispute about local textual issues and the conclusions that may or may not viably be drawn from the same. A highly intelligent discussion of compositional and redaction-critical debates in Micah research can be found in Jan Wagenaar (2001, 6–45). Key points about historical context and ideological *Tendenzen* are often tacitly stipulated within such discussions. For example, regularly found in scholarship of the nineteenth and twentieth centuries was the idea that earlier traditions in the Latter Prophets—assumed to go back to oral performances of the historical prophet—focused on oracles of divine judgment and scenarios of defeat and trauma in military conflict; traditions proclaiming joyous celebration of YHWH's power and restoration of Israel and Judah were thought to be later and often redactional in character. There are excellent grounds on which to argue this case as regards many passages in Isaiah, Jeremiah, and elsewhere, but the reasoning does not stand in every case, especially where a prophet or prophetic tradition is working skillfully with ironic reversals. In another arena of scholarly debate are those scholars interested in the literary and theological effects of various dimensions of the final form of the text. Reading the final form of the text—even with diachronic considerations in mind—is for this group of scholars an intellec-

Historical Contexts, Compositional Growth, and Textual Versions

tually meaningful and fascinating endeavor. That would not change even if some effects of literary juxtaposition, amplification of themes, redirection of motifs, introduction of new diction, and the like could be known to be coincidental byproducts of scribal processes that did not have as authorial or editorial goals the communication of those effects.

Relevant for Micah is another rich nexus of scholarly debates that involve theorizing thematic links and redaction within subgroups of the Minor Prophets and across the Book of the Twelve as a whole (Redditt and Schart 2003; Ben Zvi and Nogalski 2009; Boda, Floyd, and Toffelmire 2015; Di Pede and Scaiola 2016; Wenzel 2018). Diachronic approaches to multiple layers in biblical texts or groups of texts and synchronic approaches to effects of the final form of those texts can never be performed in isolation. It is an observable fact of academic culture that some redaction critics have little patience for sophisticated literary readings that do not take textual layers and reconstructed historical contexts into account; synchronic readings are studiously ignored in redaction-critical commentaries, and only rarely does one see a redaction critic engaging the implicit or explicit challenge that a well-analyzed and eloquently described larger trajectory might pose for piecemeal analysis of (reconstructed) layers and interpolations. For their part, literary and theological scholars who analyze thematic or final-form dimensions of the textual signifying in Micah may balk at the high level of speculation built into redaction-critical arguments, find assertions about scribal microinterventions at the level of words or half-clauses to be inherently implausible, and be bemused by the proliferation of schemata and the levels of textual complexity at which some redaction critics arrive, especially when they confidently assign a different scribal hand to each discernible textual feature. On the proliferation of redaction-critical proposals, the objection of Rex Mason (2004, 16) may be taken as cautionary: "Remarkable variations in conclusions remind us that there is inevitably a large element of subjectivity in [redaction-critical] approaches to the text." Ben Zvi observes, "the necessarily sequential construction of (hypothetical) texts building on each other quickly increases the likelihood that the entire reconstruction will be more likely wrong than correct," and continues, "I am *not* denying that redactional processes took place in prophetic literature," but "the level of uncertainty associated with all these matters is far higher" than that attending "historical reading-oriented approaches" focused on what we do know from the Persian period onward (Ben Zvi and Nogalski 2009, 62–63).

For readers who are not engrossed by these scholarly dialogues and disputes, they might remember only that Micah[MT] assuredly moved through several stages of literary growth and editing, showing that the Micah tradi-

Introduction

tions were of absorbing importance to Judean scribes for generations (this is confirmed by the quotation of Micah in Jer 26:18-19), and that the final form of Micah[MT] is a richly complex work of literary art. Prophets and scribes surely worked together, their efforts mutually reinforcing and perhaps sometimes contestatory, along a fluid spectrum of creative formulation, public proclamation, and preservation for future generations. Prophets' delivery of original prophetic discourse—whether orally in public performances or in originally written form, as is indisputably the case with much of Ezekiel— should not be conceived in terms that are fully or rigidly separate from the work of scribes, especially given the dramatically narrativized and fascinating relationship between the prophet Jeremiah and his scribe Baruch. Prophets may have been literate themselves or may have worked closely with scribal groups. Redactors were not unimaginative technical functionaries; they too had passionate convictions and keen vision regarding the workings of Yhwh in the history of their communities and in their present moment. In these pages, I use the terms "prophetic scribe" and "prophetic scribal memory" regularly, to honor the contributions of later redactors as visionary and artistic in their own right and to keep us mindful that the prophetic sensibility of Micah of Moresheth was not necessarily the only prophetic temperament involved in the production of the book that bears his name.

Below, I review several theories from the past fifty years about the growth and shaping of the Micah traditions. These theories are presented not in exhaustive detail but in a focalized way, *in nuce* and with emphasis on the arguments I find most important (see also Sharp 2011). I commend to the reader two investigations of the coherence of the final form of Micah: the work of Mignon Jacobs on conceptual coherence (2001; see 16-44 for her review of the scholarly literature) and the volume by Kenneth Cuffey on literary coherence (2015; see 6-72 for his literature review). My goal in this commentary is to point readers toward potential significances of various passages and subsections of Micah and to ponder, then, how we might understand the literary effects of the book as a whole. I decline to follow the older practice of sketching a comprehensive filiation schema of the well-known European and North American male scholars from the nineteenth century onward who have proposed a possible reading for a particular Micah word, clause, strophe, larger literary unit, or redactional stratum. While their work is highly intelligent and can certainly be consulted with profit, this citation strategy belongs to an era in which historicist speculation was heavily privileged in biblical studies, emendation of the biblical text was undertaken with gusto whether or not ancient versions supported the constructed alternatives, an atomistic approach was regnant regarding genres and formulaic gestures spied within small units of text, redaction-critical theories relied on an astonishing degree of speculation and tautological reasoning, and sophisticated literary analysis was seldom foregrounded. Women scholars and scholars of color are seldom cited in these sorts of reproductions of scholarly lineages, even in works produced well after doctoral programs in biblical studies had begun admitting those constituencies and the number of publications by women and scholars of color increased. The reader eager to experience traditional academic discourses of filiation might consult William McKane (1998) or Francis Andersen and David Noel Freedman (2000). To illustrate the point: on Mic 2:1, McKane notes the contributions of Wellhausen, H. Schmidt, Smith, Weiser, van der Woude, Duhm, Ehrlich, Wolff, Robinson, Rudolph, Hillers, Willis, Kimḥi, and Rashi. On the same verse, Andersen and Freedman cite the positions of Fohrer, Bardtke, Avishur, Melamed, Gerstenberger, Clifford, Williams, Janzen, Clements, Hillers, Mowinckel, Westermann, Wildberger, Wellhausen, Willis, Budde, Duhm, Halévy, Robinson, Sellin, Bruno, Ehrlich, Margolis, Wade, Fishbane, Beck, Hetzron, Kogut, Watson, Cross, Delcor, and Graham.

James Luther Mays (1976) argues well for a more literary approach over against redaction-critical atomizing of the text: "When the book is studied carefully with an interest not in what makes it come apart, but in what holds it together, then a variety of integrating features begin to appear," including "catchwords and repeated motifs." He sees in Micah two structural blocks, 1:2-5:15 and 6:1-7:20 (2-3). The first part has "been shaped to serve as a prophetic proclamation of Yhwh's reign over the nations," while the second block of material "is concerned directly and intimately with the relationship between Yhwh and Israel" (8-9). He acknowledges some "revision of . . . language at a few places, and brief expansions inserted" in Mic 1-5 and addition of Mic 6-7 during the Neo-Babylonian period, but insists that "chs. 6-7 were given their final shape by the same concerns which shaped chs. 1-5" (24-33).

Hans Walter Wolff (1990; orig. pub. 1982) argues for three "sketches"— dramatic scenes of prophetic proclamation—that go back to the historical Micah. The first comprises 1:6, 7b-13a, 14-16; the second is found in 2:1-4, 6-11; and the third is 3:1-12 (12-13, 26). Added to this material over time were "Deuteronomistic commentaries," "interpolations and changes," and shaping for liturgical use (26). In Mic 4-7, Wolff says, "we find hardly a text whose language is comparable to Micah's": chapters 4-5 "contain not one sentence of accusation or proclamation of judgment against Judah or Jerusalem," and

Introduction

were likely added no earlier than the dedication of the second Jerusalem temple in 515 (13, 26). In 6:2-7:7, while the "language ... is somewhat more reminiscent of Micah's," the justice theme is "not treated the same" as in earlier chapters (13-14). Micah 7:8-20 is redactional: hymnic language—"three psalms"—with some editorial glosses, in an overarching effect liturgically designed to lift up the voice of the worshipping community (24-25, 27).

Delbert Hillers (1984) notes the longevity of the thesis, going back to Bernhard Stade in 1881 or even earlier, that only the doom oracles of Mic 1-3 could have been uttered or thought by the historical Micah, bracketing 2:12-13, which many consider (wrongly, in my view) to be an oracle of promise. Hillers takes the redactional schema defended by Wolff as representative, and says, "if convincing, such an interpretive approach would go far to resolve a central dilemma in Micah: the presence of widely disparate, almost clashing elements" (Hillers 1984, 3). But for Hillers, "redaction-criticism of Micah fails to carry a satisfying degree of conviction" and is "hypothetical at too many points to be interesting" (3). Hillers cannot subscribe to the high degree of scribal intentionality and "constant growth" demanded by redaction-critical models, which fail to account satisfactorily for "accidental or deliberate omission of materials in the process of transmission"—that is, "loss"—and "underestimates the place that chance, the irrational, the unpredictable, may have in the forming of a text" (4). On the theme of restoration being necessarily later than the time of Micah per redaction-critical logics, Hillers offers a cogent objection: across cultures, protest movements can and do emerge in many eras; political, social, or religious "revitalization is a recurring phenomenon in human history and the history of given societies" (8). For one of several examples that spur him to balk at redactional analyses, Hillers says of 1:1, "attempts to fit the superscription into a detailed account of the growth of the collection do not rise above the level of guesses. It is significant that the painstaking studies of [Theodor] Lescow and Jörg Jeremias reach opposite conclusions as to what is new and old here" (15; see Lescow 1972; Jeremias 1971).

McKane (1998) affirms the contributions of Wolff, while hesitating as regards the "deliberate redactional techniques" for which Wolff argues regarding the presence of Mic 4-5 in the book. While more focused on erudite atomistic analysis verse by verse and word by word, McKane does press for "the mention of foreign nations at the beginning of chapter 1 ... and at the end of chapter 5 ... to be taken more seriously as the opening and closing brackets of a redaction, a calculated attempt to define the scope, the beginning and end, of a piece of literature" (19).

Historical Contexts, Compositional Growth, and Textual Versions

Andersen and Freedman (2000) find it likely that the eighth-century prophets, Amos, Hosea, Isaiah, and Micah, "were edited in conjunction or succession by the early seventh century to constitute a kind of proto-corpus of prophetic writings" (105), speculating that there is virtually no biographical or other historical-contextual information in these books due to "the availability of the needed background material in the form of the Primary History" comprising Genesis–Kings (106). They perceive Micah as structured in a Book of Doom (chs. 1-3), a Book of Visions (chs. 4-5), and a Book of Contention and Conciliation (chs. 6-7), finding it significant that the imperative "Hear!" (šimʻû) is the first word in Mic 1–3 and the first word in Mic 6–7, occurring three times in each of those blocks of material (137).

Jacobs (2001) makes a number of needed interventions in the standard logics of structural and redactional analysis, among them that "the repetition of a given formula within a text is not itself indicative of the significance of that formula to the macro-structure" a scholar may have discerned (65), that markers of genre "do not by themselves signal the relationship of the units they introduce" (85), and that a shift of tone does not necessarily indicate composition by a different hand or a theological position of a different historical era—as, for example, the shift between Mic 3 and Mic 4, which she sees as a subsection of a coherent larger unit, Mic 1–5 (71). The complex conceptual themes she identifies include justice, judgment, and hope, a concept engaged "throughout the book of Micah" (216), *pace* numerous interpreters.

Nogalski (2011) finds that the literary "complexity of Micah suggests that the material traced specifically to an early prophetic messenger appears only in early portions of Micah 1–3" and was edited later toward closer semantic linkages with Hosea and Amos (511–12). Micah is best characterized, per Nogalski, as "a composite unity" made up of discrete units that "were originally independent of one another"—a standard assumption that, I would gently object, in many instances cannot be proved—and that these units have been made more coherent through "deliberate arrangement" in the final form of the book (516). Nogalski's observations about the contributions of Micah within the Book of the Twelve are illuminating: "As the last eighth-century writing in the Book of the Twelve, Micah foreshadows the major themes of the next three writings," not least by "[laying] the groundwork for the Assyrian threat . . . which is the subject of Nahum" and by describing "the situation of Judah . . . in Micah 6:1–7:7" in ways that foreshadow "the status of Judah in Habakkuk 1:2–4" and motifs in Zephaniah (518–19). Nogalski concludes: "as the midpoint of the Book of the Twelve,

Introduction

Micah 4-5 plays a significant role by rehearsing many of the themes of the Twelve," including future restoration for Judah and the complicated place of the nations (520).

Focusing mainly on literary resonances with Neo-Assyrian texts, Bob Becking (2013) argues for the following structure: Mic 1, "an original, but distorted prophecy" that has been transmitted in some disorder; Mic 2-5, "a prophetic futurology based on a variety of reworked sayings from the Micah tradition"; and Mic 6-7, "a Josianic treatise based on pseudepigraphy" (2013, 112).

Cuffey (2015) rightly notes that coherence can be perceived on multiple levels and to varying degrees in ways influenced by cultural norms, social location, and other factors unique to the reader, but especially through "internal links, structure, perspective, and theme" (112-20). Recurring terms may in fact be conveying differing semantic senses, and their recurrence could have come about through a mixture of intentional usage, chance, and later amplification of an earlier source, leaving their structural significance unclear (126-29). Cuffey finds insufficient the arguments for a "three-fold alternation of doom and hope" in a perceived macrostructure of Mic 1-3, 4-5, and 6-7 or 1-2, 3-5, and 6-7, whether on historical or literary grounds (135-40, 153-61); against the first structure there, he cogently observes that the "vivid contrast" between 3:12 and 4:1 may show not disjunctive perspectives but a complex, intentionally crafted response to the fall of Jerusalem (139). He argues for a fourfold structure of doom and hope in Mic 1-2; 3:1-4:8; 4:9-5:15; and 6-7, highlighting the significance of the notion of "remnant" in 2:12-13; 4:6-7; 5:6-7; and 7:18 as key to organization of the book around the "kerygmatic point" that Yhwh is a "God who punishes, yet restores" (217, 230, 276-82). I do dissent from the common misreading of 2:12-13 as an oracle of hope; in my view, those verses constitute an ironic performance of judgment along the lines of what Micah's adversaries wish to hear (see the commentary). Cuffey's richly detailed study should be consulted by every scholar interested in the literary features of Micah.

The above review is offered not as a comprehensive survey but as an invitation to the reader to observe shifts of tone, diction, imagery, and themes as Micah^{MT} unfolds, to ponder the diverse kinds of interplay between social and political contexts and creative expression, and to read Micah with close attention to effects of the voicing created by prophetic scribes to dramatize the speakers in the book: Yhwh, Micah of Moresheth, Micah's opponents, Judah's enemies, and Daughter Zion. I am persuaded that the book of Micah in its final form was shaped as a written composition that draws skillfully on cultural memories of the fall of Samaria (722) and the Neo-Assyrian

Historical Contexts, Compositional Growth, and Textual Versions

advance through the Levant in the time of Sennacherib (701) as meaningful for the postexilic context in which these prophetic scribes were working.

1.2 Micah within the Book of the Twelve

The sequences of books in the Book of the Twelve are various in the MT, Vaticanus manuscripts of the LXX, and the Babylonian Talmud, demonstrating the fluidity of these biblical traditions in the centuries in which they were formed and preserved. Differences in order may point to differing implicit criteria by which smaller collections within the Twelve were envisioned by different scribal groups. Here are the orders represented in the MT and the LXX; for details on the sequences in specific ancient manuscripts, see Jennifer Dines (2012).

MT	LXX
Hosea	Hosea
Joel	Amos
Amos	Micah
Obadiah	Joel
Jonah	Obadiah
Micah	Jonah
Nahum	Nahum
Habakkuk	Habakkuk
Zephaniah	Zephaniah
Haggai	Haggai
Zechariah	Zechariah
Malachi	Malachi

Keywords, shared motifs, diachronic considerations (such as a rough trajectory from earlier to later), and other factors may have been at play in the arrangement of the MT sequence. For an example relevant to Micah: the end of Micah (7:18-20) draws on Exod 34:6-7, and the opening of Nahum (Nah 1:2-3) does as well. It may be that the LXX translators moved Jonah—a third book that draws on Exod 34:6-7, in Jon 4:2—to a position contiguous with Nahum to link those books' judgment against Nineveh (Alfaro 2021, 89). In the Babylonian Talmud tractate B. Bat. 14b-15a, the rabbis discuss the order of the Latter Prophets and the Writings in chronological terms:

Introduction

along with Isaiah, the prophets who prophesied earliest in history were Hosea, Amos, and Micah.

Thematic links across the Book of the Twelve may be taken as evidence for shared ideation important to Israelite and Judean prophetic discourse, and, in some cases, that scribes shaped this literature toward literary congruence. Explicit reference to the day of Yhwh (*yôm yhwh*) is deployed in sophisticated ways in Joel, Amos, Obadiah, Zephaniah, and Malachi (see Joel 1:15; 2:1, 11; 3:4; 4:14; Amos 5:18, 20; Obad 15; Zeph 1:7, 14; Mal 3:23). Roy Garton (2012) points to the centrality of the theme of Israel's wilderness traditions in the Twelve, as seen in Hos 2, 9, 11, 12, 13; Amos 2, 3, 5, 9; Mic 6, 7; Hag 2; and Mal 3. Further, scholars have mustered detailed redactional and literary arguments that scribes framed the preexilic prophesying of Micah within a subgroup of books within the Twelve that took shape in the exilic period: Hosea, Amos, Micah, and Zephaniah, dubbed the Book of the Four by Nogalski (1993; see Albertz 2003, 204-16). Scholars who have made defining contributions to the theory of a circulating Book of the Four include Nogalski, Aaron Schart, Nicholas Werse, and Jacob Wöhrle (2008, 2012, 2020). Literary linkages are evident that weave the end of one book with the beginning of the next, though objections can always be raised that one or another catchword link could be coincidental. Jill Middlemas sums up shared themes within the Four as follows: "The prophets are described as bearers of the divine message that, once rejected, leads to divine judgment including the loss of land. Common to all is the prominent theme that judgment is purifying and leads to a future-oriented salvation" (2016, 46). Among Werse's incisive observations (2019) are these: "Micah contains strikingly few references to idolatry, fueling the suspicion that the two primary occurrences of the theme emerge from the later editing of the text" (184); as many have noticed, "Mic 4-5 functions as a literary echo chamber for other prophetic texts and themes" (188-89); further along those lines, interpreters should take seriously the major differences between Mic 6 and Mic 1-3, including that in Mic 6 the prophet accuses not just leaders but the whole people, "introduces a sudden string of allusions to the exodus and wilderness traditions" not featured earlier in the book, and makes "reference to northern kings" in a way that is anomalous for the book (201); and that in his view, "the five strongest cases for editorial activity assuming a Book of the Four literary horizon in Micah consist of Mic 1:1, 5b-7 (and v. 9); 2:3, 12-13; 6:9-16" (213). Wöhrle (2020) summarizes arguments for Deuteronomistic redactional supplementation of the four prophetic books in diction that displays affinities to material in 2 Kgs 17-18, insisting, "The large number of cross-references

Historical Contexts, Compositional Growth, and Textual Versions

between the so-called dtr.[Deuteronomistic] additions to the books of Hosea, Amos, Micah, and Zephaniah and the books of Kings cannot be a coincidence," but rather proves that "the same hand brought . . . the dtr. additions into these books" (27-29). The interpolations Wöhrle identifies in Micah are 1:1, 5b-7, 9, 12b; 5:9-13; and 6:2-4a, 9aα, 10-15 (23). Interpreters not already persuaded of the methodological assumptions undergirding much redaction criticism might balk, but all readers should be interested—even if simply from a final-form literary perspective—in Wöhrle's claim that the relevant added materials expand or critique perspectives in Kings, in that for these four prophets, "not only cultic, but also social and political issues, especially from the part of the upper classes, caused Yhwh to intervene" in judgment against the Northern and Southern Kingdoms (31-33).

Thematic links may, of course, gesture toward the power of a shared intellectual heritage more generally, rather than targeted use of earlier texts or scribal editorial interventions. A theme vividly explored in the Book of the Four, but not often noticed, involves a nexus of metaphors concerning devouring and famine. Metaphors of greedy consumption, deprivation, and feasting are deployed brilliantly in each of these four prophetic books to portray the greed and covenantal disobedience of Israelites or Judeans, the punishment that will come through the agency of a furious Yhwh, and the agricultural abundance awaiting the covenant people in the eschatological future governed by Yhwh's sovereignty. Per Hosea, Yhwh will kill the disobedient covenant people with thirst (Hos 2:3); "wild animals" and "the new moon" will devour them (2:12; 5:7); a futility curse will be in effect that keeps the people from being satiated (4:7-10); the people devour their rulers (7:7); and more (see Sharp 2010). In Amos, fire will devour the strongholds of enemy nations and Judah (Amos 1:7, 10, 12, 14; 2:2, 5); Yhwh created food shortages (4:6), withheld rain so villagers were at risk from thirst (4:7-8), appointed blight and locusts to devour the harvest (4:9; 7:1-2), and will send fire to devour Bethel, the ocean, and the land (5:6; 7:4). In Micah, corrupt leaders are portrayed as cannibalizing their people (3:1-3); a divinely appointed futility curse will keep the people from satiety (6:14); and Daughter Zion can find no produce to eat (7:1). Finally, Zephaniah portrays a gruesome feast of Yhwh at which the guests will be consecrated and—this is implicit—consumed (Zeph 1:7); Jerusalem's corrupt officials and judges are like lions roaring after prey and ravening wolves "that leave nothing until the morning" (3:3). This thematic interest in devouring and deprivation (viz., thirst and famine) is explored artfully in particular ways grounded in the prophesying of Hosea, Amos, Micah, and Zephaniah. These motifs

Introduction

are organic to the literary genius and unique idioms of each prophet; they cannot be demonstrated to have arisen through literary dependence, and are certainly not the product of redaction.

Proponents of the historical existence of a Book of the Four should address the objection that the ordering of the twelve Minor Prophets has separated the four in two different ways in the MT and the LXX. It is not sufficient, logically speaking, to argue for the principles of ordering that do seem to underlie the MT and LXX orders. If an earlier scroll had so closely associated Hosea, Amos, Micah, and Zephaniah, and those books had been known as a collection, such that their linkages were perceived, redactionally reinforced, and explored interpretively by ancient scribes, then to have dismembered the grouping would not have been something scribal tradents would have undertaken lightly.

1.3 The Masoretic Text of Micah

The MT of Micah is relatively unproblematic. I have assessed differences between Karl Elliger's *BHS* Micah and the 2010 *BHQ* Micah prepared by Anthony Gelston; these are few and concern only lineation, not changes to the Hebrew text. I have found *BHQ* an improvement in every instance of variation (for one of several examples: in setting 2:3 as prose), and follow it here.

1.4 The Septuagint Translation of Micah

This commentary engages the LXX text of Micah as established in the critical edition of Joseph Ziegler (2016). While there are a number of minor local divergences between the Greek and Hebrew text traditions, there is nothing on the scale of, say, the larger divergences seen in the book of Jeremiah. The text of Micah^{LXX} is relatively close to that of Micah^{MT} except in those instances where the LXX translators were evidently baffled by the Hebrew. Philippe Guillaume has argued that while some Dead Sea scrolls contain fragments of several texts within the Book of the Twelve, we should be cautious about taking this as evidence that all twelve books of the Minor Prophets were known to comprise a single scroll before the LXX translation was completed in Alexandria. Though it is likely that all the books of the Twelve were "translated by a single person," nevertheless it is significant that "a good century after Ben Sira's mention of the XII, we still have no physical evidence of a scroll upon which all the Minor Prophets were copied together" (2007, 10-11). Even though "the number of Minor Prophets copied

Historical Contexts, Compositional Growth, and Textual Versions

on individual scrolls increases as time goes by and scrolls holding multiple books appear in Palestine in Greek as early as their Hebrew counterparts," there is no collection of all twelve books "earlier than the first century BCE," and thus material evidence is lacking for support of "claims that the XII formed a collection before their translation in Greek" (12).

Dominique Barthélemy notes of the Ziegler LXX edition, along with editions of previous editors, that Ziegler has been "overly influenced by the divisions" in the MT, which "sometimes leads him to propose unsatisfactory syntactic groupings" (2012, 412). Barthélemy offers an important observation about the structure of Micah as signaled in major manuscript traditions of Micah^{LXX}:

> Vaticanus and Barberini both divide Micah into seven pericopes: Per. 2 begins with 1:10, per. 3 with 3:5, per. 4 with 4:1, per. 5 with 6:1, per. 6 with 6:9b, and per. 7 with 7:7. Their agreement is all the more striking since these two manuscripts belong to two distinctly different textual traditions. Vaticanus is the paradigm of the Alexandrian text, while Barberini is clearly Antiochene—confirmed by the fact that most of its text serves as lemmas for a commentary of Theodoret. (2012, 422)

When we consider the major sections of Micah^{LXX} per the Vaticanus manuscript tradition as translated by Edward Glenny (2015, 18–37), this yields the following structure:

1:1–1:9
1:10–3:4
3:5–3:12
4:1–5:15
6:1–6:9b
6:9c–7:6
7:7–7:20

Noteworthy specific departures from Micah^{MT} in the Greek text tradition will be referenced in the commentary ad loc.

1.5 Fragments of Micah Texts from the Judean Desert

A dozen manuscripts of the Minor Prophets have been discovered in the Judean desert. Some of these, such as 4Q76 (4QXII^a), do not contain Micah. Scroll 4Q82 (4QXII^g) is extremely fragmentary, showing phrases from Mic 1:7, 12–15;

Introduction

2:3-4; 3:12; 4:1-2; 5:6-7; and 7:2-3, 20 (Ego et al. 2004). A Hebrew scroll of the Twelve was discovered in Wadi Murabba'at in "heavily damaged" condition (de Moor 2020, 1) in 1955. This text, known as Mur 12, is dated by some to 75-100 CE (Jinbachian 2012, 137) and by others to about 135 CE. It contains fragments of every book of the Twelve except Hosea and Malachi, including all of Micah except 6:8-10 (Fuller 2020, 276). Scroll 1Q14 (1QpMic) is a fragment of a pesher commentary on 1:2-9 and 6:14-16. Scroll 4Q168 (4QpMic) may be a fragment of pesher on 4:8-12 or the actual Micah passage (Simkovich 2021, 234).

Fragments of an ancient Greek manuscript of the Book of the Twelve, designated 8Ḥev 1 (8ḤevXIIgr), were found in 1953 and 1961 in Cave 8 on the southern bank of Naḥal Ḥever, a wadi running through the Judean desert between Ein Gedi and Masada to the Dead Sea. Of the ten caves at Naḥal Ḥever, Cave 8 is noteworthy for the 1955 discovery of more than forty skeletons from antiquity, apparently the remains of Jewish resistance fighters and others who had fled the besieged fort at Masada during the Bar Kokhba revolt (132-135 CE). This discovery of human remains prompted archaeologist Yoḥanan Aharoni to dub the site the "Cave of Horror." The manuscript of the Twelve is dated to the first century BCE (Jinbachian 2012, 137; Tov 2022, 78; for reconstructed Micah lines from 1:1-6:4 and annotations on the reconstructions, see Tov 1990, 32-43, 85-89). Its grammatical and syntactical features proved important for the thesis of Barthélemy regarding a so-called *kaige* revision of books of the Septuagint toward congruity with the Hebrew text that became the MT, or, in a small number of cases, possibly the original translation into Greek, rather than a revision of an existing Old Greek text (Aitken 2015, 21-24). In the assessment of Russell Fuller, "4QXII^b, 4QXII^c, 4QXII^e, and 4QXII^g from cave 4 at Qumran ... are reasonably likely to have originally held complete collections of the Twelve," and "this is even more likely for the later manuscripts, 8ḤevXIIgr and MurXII" (2020, 275).

For parallel transcriptions of Micah^{MT}, Micah^{LXX}, and the Micah fragments in 8Ḥev 1 (8ḤevXIIgr), 4Q76 (4QXII^g), 1Q14 (1QpMic), 4Q 168 (4QpMic), and Mur 12, see the volume in *Biblia Qumranica* edited by Beate Ego, Armin Lange, Hermann Lichtenberger, and Kristin De Troyer (Ego et al. 2004).

2. LITERARY DIMENSIONS OF MICAH

The book of Micah offers incontrovertible signs of artistic design that signal attentive crafting for aural reception, literary shaping within and across

Literary Dimensions of Micah

oracles, and brilliant intentionality about numerous subtle linkages of theology, ethics, and performative speech across the entire collection. These rhetorical choices and literary linkages are perceptible from micro levels of local sound-play and clausal echoes to macrostructural links and themes. Ben Zvi argues concerning 1:2-16, and the book of Micah more generally, that the "actual, historical, rhetorical situation" of this material, "at least in its present form," should be understood as "not that of a living prophet orally addressing the people, but of a community of readers (re-)reading and meditating upon a written text" constructed by literati who serve as "brokers of divine knowledge" for the postexilic Judean community (1998, 118-19).

In my view, the fascinating combination of artistically crafted language and structural elegance, on the one hand, and several textual sites of considerable strangeness and obscurity, on the other, suggest the composition and shaping of Micah traditions over time: first in an earlier setting in which dramatic public performance may have obtained, and later in contexts in which scribes polished and amplified this authoritative material as written. Those processes could have overlapped and reinforced each other during the lifetime of Micah of Moresheth, and were assuredly carried on by scribal tradents long after Micah's time; but beyond that, interpreters simply cannot know the details. I am not persuaded that the book of Micah as an original composition—in the main or in its entirety—should be dated to the postexilic era or the Persian period in Yehud. Nor am I persuaded by arguments that the *ipsissima vox* of the historical prophet Micah can be discerned with confidence in "earlier" oracles of doom but not in "later" material of promise. Every chapter of Micah is constructed around a powerfully articulated sense of dread—this is true even of Mic 4, Mic 5, Mic 6, and Mic 7. In Mic 1-3, the material that confronts the implied audience first in any sequential performance or reading of the oracles of Micah, the terrifying figure of the prophet himself is the focal point of an implicit and chastened hope. (Mic 2:12-13 is not an oracle of hope; it should be read on analogy with Ps 125:5 and Amos 4:3; 6:7. See commentary to Mic 2.) The hope to which the audience can cling in Mic 1-3 is the prophet himself: this lamenting, howling performer of the purposes of Yhwh (1:8), this scorned preacher of unwelcome but desperately needed truth (2:6-7), this spiritual leader filled with the power of the spirit of Yhwh to testify unceasingly to the need for justice and communal reform (3:8). In Mic 4-7, the material conditions of dread remain, something that is emphasized too little among scholars who are hearing the new notes of promise as dominant in those oracles. The implied audience has been educated via the material earlier in the Micah

Introduction

collection to look to Micah as authoritative spiritual leader. This audience is offered, now, visions of a different reality—one in which the community of believers chooses to live in deep accord with the purposes of Yhwh. But Assyria and Babylonia continue to threaten, and unthinkable violation and forced displacement loom (4:9-11); divine retribution against all sinners, even those in Judah, will continue (5:9-14 [Eng. 10-15]; 6:9-16; 7:4b, 9, 13); and militarized conflict will continue to ravage both Judah and the nations (4:12-14 [Eng. 5:1]; 5:4b-14 [Eng. 5b-15]; 7:10, 16-17). Shot through all of this material, from Mic 1 to Mic 7, is an extraordinarily effective and subversive artistry that makes a terrifying dread audible as a counter to false hope—and makes hope audible within conditions of terrifying dread.

The overarching organization of the oracles in Mic 1-7 can be understood within a literary framework showing that "resistance to misuses of power in Micah 1-3 yields to reconfigurations of theology and ethics in community (chs. 4-6) and a renewed focus on God as the agent of transformation" in Mic 7 (Tisdale and Sharp 2016, 649). Within that sweeping trajectory, many brilliant moves are made within and across oracles and oracle groups.

2.1 Structure and Themes of Micah

An abundance of proposals about the structure of Micah have been advanced in the scholarly literature, each offering a degree of coherence and plausibility. In my view, the final form of the book of Micah unfolds in artfully crafted poetic oracles arranged in a diptych, each panel of which explores vivid images and motifs from the perspective of Yhwh and from two other perspectives: that of the prophet, and that of a quoted adversary, whether a malfeasant constituency within the covenant people or an enemy from beyond the boundaries of Judean identity. The first panel of the diptych comprises 1:2-3:12, material entirely concerned with terrifying judgment leveled by a wrathful Yhwh against Samaria and Judah for their egregious sins (2:12-13 is not an exception; it is an oracle of impending catastrophe fully congruent with what precedes it, not an oracle of hope). The second panel comprises 4:1-7:20, material that anticipates the dawning of Zion's restoration and renewed dominion, even as the challenges in the present circumstances of the community are acknowledged and continue to be forcefully addressed by Yhwh. My proposal is by no means redaction-critical in nature; I hope this is obvious. I tend to be underwhelmed by redaction-critical logics as deployed across large swaths of text, finding redactional arguments from even the most erudite of scholars to be rife with speculation and tautologies. Broad themes (such as sin, restoration, the day of Yhwh, and so on) can seldom be counted as reliable guides to a specific scribal intention that can also be proved, on substantive different grounds, to have originated from an ancillary or interpolative position over against an earlier base text.

Within my proposed diptych framework, I attend to three features of the book of Micah: (1) the insistent featuring of Jerusalem, including the voicing of Daughter Zion to a degree greater than some interpreters have perceived; (2) reversals yielding desolation and exile, a rhetorical strategy of world-unmaking that is constitutive of the way in which Micah exercises prophetic authority; and (3) reported discourse as a tool for the strategic shaping of the implied audience's communal understanding. First: Reading Micah, we see Jerusalem as the formidable yet vulnerable seat of Judean political life, Jerusalem as future site of universal torah learning and peacemaking, and Jerusalem personified as the threatened, lamenting, and resolutely faithful Daughter Zion. The corruption and promise of this magnificent city lie at the very heart of Micah's prophetic witness.

Second: In every chapter of Micah, a dramatic reversal of a unique sort is effected through the prophet's discursive praxis. Micah's poetic images and words may be theorized as drawing on the tacit assumptions of his implied audience and, subtly and powerfully, reversing something vital about how they can be construed to have thought about Yhwh and their community. In Amos, the opening rhetoric of entrapment and a sustained ironizing of exodus traditions are foundational to how the book of Amos functions for its many audiences (Sharp 2009, 151–69). Similarly in Micah, a prophetic praxis of insistent reversal is of significant import for how the Micah material functions. The praxis is meaningful regardless of whether an interpreter reconstructs a historical prophet standing behind the artful design or sees this instead as generated by scribal practices of composition and redaction at work in several historical contexts.

Third: A crucial structural organizing feature of these oracles is the reported or imagined discourse of antagonists. The two panels in the larger diptych are linked by a "hinge" of reported discourse in 4:2, quoting nations—implicitly, Judeans among them—who honor Yhwh and seek to study the ways of torah. In the first panel of this diptych, here are the words of antagonists whose distorted theopolitical understandings Micah seeks to refute:

Introduction

"We are utterly ruined! He exchanges the portion of my people. How he removes what belongs to me! To an apostate he apportions our fields." (2:4)

"Do not preach! They must not preach such things! Disgrace will not overtake [us]." (2:6)

"Is not Yhwh in our midst? Calamity will not come upon us!" (3:11)

The prophet responds brilliantly to each of the three adversarial quotations. First, "what belongs to" the people is no longer relevant, since Judean oppressors themselves have become the equivalent of an enemy, driving their own people from the portions they had claimed and ruining the land (2:8–10). Second, because the prophet's interlocutors wish to hear a positive oracle rather than doom, Micah performs a faux oracle of hope with razor-sharp irony, barely veiling the truth that the people and their leader will be incarcerated in a transit center and forcibly deported (2:12–13). Third, calamity will inevitably come: Jerusalem will be plowed into rubble (3:12).

Micah 4:1–5 constitutes a structural hinge linking images of the inescapable and devastating judgment explored in Mic 1–3 with images of Yhwh's deliverance and Zion's return to preeminence in Mic 4–7. Central to this passage is reported discourse in 4:2 that holds together the first panel, which details Yhwh's judgment on Jerusalem, and the second panel, which celebrates the reestablishment of Zion's dominion:

"Come, let us go up to the mountain of Yhwh,
 to the house of the God of Jacob,
so [Yhwh] may give us instruction in [Yhwh's] ways
 and we may walk in [Yhwh's] paths!" (4:2)

The second panel of Micah's diptych, then, uses further reported discourse of antagonists to catalyze the decisive response of those allied with Yhwh: first Daughter Zion, returned to her preeminent position of dominion over those who wish her harm, then Micah, then Daughter Zion again:

"Let her be defiled, and let our gaze rove over Zion!" (4:11)

"With what should I come before Yhwh,
 bow down before God on High?

> Should I come before [Yhwh] with burnt offerings,
>   with year-old calves?
> Will Yhwh be pleased with thousands of rams,
>   with myriad torrents of oil?" (6:6-7)

"Where is Yhwh your God?" (7:10)

These discursive attacks are answered decisively. The prophetic scribe responds in language that anticipates Zion's rising to thresh her enemies (4:13), lays out clearly the expectations of Yhwh for the faithful community (6:8), and claims the power of ancient tradition to show that Yhwh was with Israel not only in days of old, but also now and for all time (7:14-20).

2.2 The Persona of the Prophet

There is no account of Micah's prophetic commissioning or biography-style representations of aspects of the life of the prophet. The absence of these two features is noteworthy, given that several books of the Latter Prophets contain detailed material on the social and political contexts of prophetic functioning, including the prophet's encounters with others, the performance of sign-acts, and the narration of vision reports (see Isa 36-37; much in Jeremiah and Ezekiel; Hos 1-3; the vision reports in Amos 7-9; Jonah 1-4; Hag 1-2; Zech 1-8). There are several literary gestures in the book of Micah that do effectively work to limn the persona of the prophet—that is, that characterize Micah in his public mode of prophetic functioning, along with qualities that matter for his performance of the role of prophet. He is identified as a Moreshethite; he is characterized as one to whom the word of Yhwh came during the reigns of three Judean rulers and as a prophet who speaks reliable messages concerning both Samaria and Jerusalem (1:1). First-person speech dramatizes his role as one who publicly laments the ruin of Samaria and the looming threat to Jerusalem (1:8-9), who claims his right to speak words of judgment (3:1), and who is energized for his prophetic vocation by "the power of the spirit of Yhwh" (3:8). Antagonism toward prophetic utterances of doom ("Do not preach.... They must not preach such things," 2:6, with plural verb forms) subtly signals that Micah is experiencing opposition, though this is not sketched in such detail as, for example, the fierce disputes dramatized in the laments of Jeremiah and Deutero-Jeremianic prose narratives concerning the prophet's opponents within his community.

Introduction

I read Mic 7:7, "But as for me, for Yhwh I will keep watch," as portraying Micah as faithful sentinel over the house of Judah, and 7:14-15a is uttered by Micah in the venerable prophetic role of intercessor.

Micah may have prophesied over decades (1:1), but we cannot know the age at which he began his work of public proclamation. We cannot know whether he was a priest or Levite (*pace* Cook 1999, 228-31); we cannot know whether he worked the fields as a farmer or was employed in some other way. Interpreters' suppositions about the persona of the prophet are guided in every instance by their assumptions about the oracles written under his name in the Book of the Twelve. Wolff describes Micah as possessed of "fearless self-assurance," motivated by "love for those who experience bodily suffering," and so deeply in solidarity with his community that when an enemy strikes against the gate of Jerusalem, "Micah is experiencing that deathblow in his own body" (1978, 5-6, 8). Richard Phillips offers that Micah's name, "Who is like the Lord?," suggests that the prophet from Moresheth "identified with his name" and that "at the heart of his faith was joy for the saving grace of God" (2010, 136). Whatever the historical reality may have been, biblical traditions show Micah as connected to the land and his local community, as outraged by injustice, and as daring to challenge the powerbrokers of his day on behalf of those who suffer. Micah is represented, in the words of Ellen Davis, as an agrarian prophet and practical theologian (2019, 232).

We may imagine several possibilities for how Micah of Moresheth came to be constructed as the representational figure we have in the book that bears his name. Hailing from a small village, Micah may have begun speaking as a young iconoclast frustrated at the ways in which his community was alternately exploited and ignored by those in power locally and their confederates in the Jerusalem political hierarchy. Alternatively, he may have prophesied as a midlife householder appalled at the way in which he saw elite officials manipulate and coerce those like him—and perhaps his own family—into giving up their patrimonial lands. Over the years, Micah may have been, or become, a village elder who could no longer bear to remain silent as he watched grave economic and social injustices undermining the stability of families and causing despair in those around him. We cannot know. What we do know is that the book of Micah presents this prophet as a fiery, uncompromising idealist empowered by the spirit of Yhwh to declare the sinfulness of what he has seen locally and in Jerusalem. We also know that scribes of later generations saw Micah as an authoritative and compelling prophetic figure (see Jer 26:18) whose visionary utterances could have included, or did include, words of consolation and healing for a community that had been terrified by the Assyrians and ravaged by the Babylonians.

Sigmund Mowinckel (1884-1965) offers an interesting assessment of the temperament of prophets whose words and experiences are on offer in Isaiah, Jeremiah, Ezekiel, and the Twelve. Mowinckel's bias against experiential knowing through visions and ecstatic experience is clear as he frames the writing prophets over against intermediaries portrayed in the Deuteronomistic History as customarily falling into ecstatic trances:

> This ecstatic element in its primitive and exaggerated forms is very much toned down in the reforming prophets.... Their utterances are given in a finished artistic form; to the solemn words of judgment they generally add a clear, reasoned, moral and religious exposition; and their words do not come to them as a wild, stammering glossolalia—as involuntary, conscious words accompanied by unconscious reflex actions—but as moral and religious apprehensions of inexorable facts, apprehensions that "rise up" in them from the depths of the subconscious to attain lucidity, merging into their moral and religious personality. (2002, 86-87)

Gerhard von Rad argues that the writing prophets saw themselves as mandated to assay or test their people's faithfulness, a role that "demanded sustained vigilance in passing judgment upon [people] and circumstances." This prophetic role was inhabited by those "of extreme intellectual versatility, whose judgment was incorruptible, who possessed a profound knowledge of human nature, and who, above all, were very familiar with the religious traditions." The one "appointed to hear the word of God ... surrenders much ... freedom," but they also "enjoy an entirely new kind of freedom" as they are "drawn into ever [closer] converse with God," being "privy to divine purposes and ... given the authority to enter into a unique kind of converse" with those in their community (2001, 74-76). Joseph Blenkinsopp sees in the literary construction of Hosea, Micah, Isaiah, and Amos as prophets an identity belonging "to the very small minority of the population that was literate and educated," involved in a "tradition of dissident intellectualism and social criticism" that was not common for intermediaries in other cultures in antiquity (1995, 154).

2.3 Poetic Artistry in Micah

Poetic oracles constitute the overwhelming majority of the extant traditions in Micah. Biblical Hebrew poetic expression is often highly figurative and

Introduction

elliptical; it can be characterized by a rich density of sound-play that sometimes incorporates mimetic aspects. Biblical poetry is often found in elegantly structured word pairs, clauses, lines, strophes, and larger blocks, the structuring itself not only contributing to the artfulness of expression but signaling potential meaning through combinatory relationships perceptible at many levels (Berlin 2008). The poetic artistry of Micah's oracles is dramatic and captivating, not least because of what Robert Alter calls the "archetypifying force of vocative poetry in the Prophets" (2011, 183). The theological and ethical messages—plural, particular, and powerful—of discrete strophes and larger units of poetry within Micah are performed and made more persuasive, not only for the implied or explicitly addressed immediate audience in the text but also for readers across the centuries, by means of the literary artfulness through which they are conveyed. What Carol Dempsey notes of Mic 2–3 is true of Micah as a whole and of biblical prophetic discourse more generally: "the various forms and literary techniques have an effect on the moral imagination and memory of the intended and unintended readers of the text" and thereby convey "an ethical message that is biting, intense, provocative and unforgettable" (1999, 118). Dempsey rightly observes also the high level of skill presumed of audiences by the prophetic scribes who shaped the Micah traditions: "the intended audience of the book of Micah was comprised of highly gifted readers . . . able to recognize literary, sophisticated techniques, to understand the allusions, ironic twists, insinuations within rhetorical questions and the . . . subtle relations created by precise word choice" (127–28).

There are four prosaic exceptions to Micah's intense focalizing through the medium of poetic expression: the prose superscription in 1:1; the prose oracle in 2:3; the prose pronouncement in 2:5; and the prose comment in 4:5. The provenance of these more prosaic lines cannot be known, but they have the character of later scribal insertions intended to amplify the poetic expression in a particular direction or to guide the implied audience in understanding the more elliptical oracles of the prophet.

Poetic strophes in Mic 1–7 are built, in the vast majority of cases, on bicola: series of couplets characterized by a poetic parallelism that communicates a perceptibly close and meaningful semantic relation to one another. James Kugel has made an essential contribution to the theorizing of Biblical Hebrew poetry in his exploration of heightening, to be understood as many kinds of intensification across pairs or trios of clauses and lines. The poetic operation of heightening was made memorable for generations of scholars and students via Kugel's offering of a simple descriptor for its implied semantic effect: "A, and what's more, B" (1998, 54). As Kugel describes it,

Literary Dimensions of Micah

with considerable nuance and allowing that poetry and prose exist on a fluid spectrum of semantic performances (59–95), Biblical Hebrew poetry can be recognized by its participation in "a complex of heightening effects used in combinations and intensities that vary widely" and by "consistently binary sentences, an obvious regard for terseness, and a high degree of semantic parallelism" (94). Adele Berlin offers an expansive review of the kinds of morphological, phonological, grammatical, lexical, and semantic parallelism operative in Biblical Hebrew poetry; her work emphasizes the interplay of equivalence and difference along multiple axes of combination (2008). In his artisanal readings of biblical poetic texts, Alter demonstrates the ways in which parallelistic poetic expression creates lively dramatic worlds. "Lines of biblical poetry are informed by an often fierce or mesmerizing energy of assertion that sweeps from one part of the line to its parallel member and, frequently, from the line to a whole sequence within the poem. . . . There is subtlety as well as insistence in these seeming repetitions," Alter avers, and the reader experiences poetry's subtle gestures and tonal changes as narrative: "utterances develop and change, miniature stories unfold" (2011, xi). Movement—from word to word, clause to clause, line to line, strophe to strophe—suggests progressive development, a kind of deepening or complexifying, the emerging of a richer nexus of possibilities. The differences expressed within partial or seeming equivalence in Biblical Hebrew poetry create semantic sense: "the elegance of the formal structure" of parallelistic verse "is also a subtle instrument for the development of meaning," Alter says—or more precisely, parallelistic structure generates "a delicate dialectic interplay of meanings" (2011, 17–18). The ways in which a biblical author alters expected parallelistic relations can draw the attention of the audience as well. Andersen and Freedman observe that "much of the interest of Micah's poetry is created by his use of pairs" that differ from the "stock pairs generally preferred by Hebrew poets" (2000, 261). They cite an example in 2:1: in the expressions translated here as "those who devise wickedness" (ḥōšǎbê-ʾāwen) and "those who work out evil" (pōʿălê-rāʿ), "Micah has switched the nouns" from the standard pairings found commonly in the Hebrew Bible, and his formulations are found only here.

F. W. Dobbs-Allsopp attends to the line as vitally important for the signifying power of Biblical Hebrew poetry, which is "dominantly distichic" (2015, 88) and generally organized into couplets or triplets, less often into quatrains, and rarely but notably in isolated single lines. Dobbs-Allsopp notes, "Grouping or chunking" through the semantic linking of lines "is the central mechanism by which the specific patterns or shapes of energy—those runs

Introduction

of recurrence riven by difference and variation," are themselves shaped through the broader "rhythmic hierarchies" that secure the audience's interest and communicate meaning in Biblical Hebrew poetry (111–12). In the poetic establishment of rhythmic equivalences, differences, and elaborations, the "experience of continuance is crucial," for "rhythm creates anticipation" (108), one of the features of prophetic poetry that would have made it so compelling to hearers and interpreters in antiquity and through the centuries.

Dobbs-Allsopp argues that the interplay of various schemata of syllabic stress and lineation creates "beats or pulses," something that "effectively pushes poetry ever forward in its pulsating ebb and flow and in the process creates coherence and a basic ground against which other more complex rhythmic clusters or contours may play" (123). As regards the "basic ground" of lineation in Micah, the poetic discourse of this prophetic book pours forth bicola in the speech of Yhwh, the prophet, and Daughter Zion. These are artful indeed. We may notice, then, a variety of "more complex rhythmic structures" in Micah as well. Dobbs-Allsopp remarks a tricolon in 1:7, where the punishment of Samaria is detailed. It may be that "the change in grouping strategy [helps] to signal the oracle's impending conclusion" (140); perhaps more important, the three images of pulverizing, igniting, and devastation of Samaria's idols communicate the comprehensiveness and inescapability of divine retribution. A striking density of tricola can be seen in Mic 2, in the ventriloquized speech of opponents in 2:6, 11 and in the ironic oracle of "hope"—actually doom—in 2:12–13. It is unquestionably the case that the regular flow of bicola is disrupted in those three textual sites. In each instance, the metrical anomaly causes a hitch in the linguistic flow for the hearer or reader, requiring that they pay closer attention to what is being said—which in each case is deceptive: manipulative on the part of Micah's opponents and false prophets (2:6, 11) and saturated with irony in Micah's own response, mimicking deception with a profoundly serious aim (2:12–13). Tricola in 3:2–3 make more protracted the moment in which the implied audience must witness, as it were, the flaying of the people by elite oppressors. This semantic disruption may serve to disorient the audience, intensifying and prolonging their sense of horror. Other noteworthy tricola pile up references to malfeasant agents as the cause of the destruction of Jerusalem (3:11, 12); amplify the identifiers for the throngs of those whom Yhwh will gather from diaspora (4:6); heighten the impact of Yhwh's powerful rhetorical questions challenging Judah (6:3); draw out poignantly the waiting of Daughter Zion for Yhwh (7:7); and extend the imagery of Zion's subjugated enemies crawling in dread toward Yhwh (7:17).

Literary Dimensions of Micah

Tod Linafelt emphasizes the constitutive importance of lineation as shaped through the medium of discursive utterance: "Biblical Hebrew poetry exhibits a rhythmic patterning and syntactical compression that results in genuine *line structure*" that is "always represented as *direct discourse*; that is, as the words of a speaking subject, even if the speaker is anonymous" (2021, 688 [emphasis original]). Linafelt goes on, "Biblical poetry is much more *verbally inventive* . . . than biblical prose narrative," clarifying further, "if biblical prose narrative generally avoids both descriptive and figurative language, biblical verse fairly revels in" such language (689 [emphasis original]). Over against the formal constraints of prose signifying, Linafelt celebrates as unique to poetic expression an "endless interpretability" generated by the elliptical nature and "verbal inventiveness" of poetry (699).

Following is a brief illustrative review of poetic features in Micah, organized alphabetically by the key concept under discussion.

Alliteration, the repetition of consonantal sounds in close proximity, and especially those in initial positions of words, can delight the ear and subtly reinforce or deepen the audience's understanding of meaningful semantic connection between or among the relevant terms. Perhaps the most famous arena of wordplay in Micah, involving both alliteration and assonance, is 1:10–15, in which names of towns and villages under threat from the Neo-Assyrian military advance toward Jerusalem are amplified sonically by warnings that repeat consonant and vocalic sounds from the names of the relevant sites. For more on these, see commentary to 1:10–16.

In 2:4, several alliterative and assonant sequences tumble over one another in a cascade of artfully designed sonic effects. In "they will lament with bitter wailing," repetition of the voiceless fricative *heh* mimics the gasping that can accompany paroxysms of sobbing. If we include the word *māšāl* from a few words earlier, no fewer than five sibilants (four with the letter *shin*) hiss through the line. Other consonants, too, are repeated, including bilabial *mem* and fricative *khet*, yielding a spellbinding example of tightly constructed ancient Hebrew poetic art. Another good example of alliteration presents itself in 4:14 (Eng. 5:1) in language about striking the "judge" with the "rod," *baššēbeṭ . . . šōpēṭ*.

Allusion is the deployment of recognizable elements of language from other sources, often an "established literary tradition" (Cuddon 2014, 25), to generate a depth of background or to bring into the foreground a particular thread, or threads, within a rich tapestry of potential meanings. Micah's oracles brim with allusions. Among the most powerful are allusions to Israel's

35

Introduction

wilderness wandering in 6:4-5 and to the patriarchal narratives and exodus traditions in 7:15, 18-20.

Apostrophe, the direct address of an absent person, a thing, or an idea "as if present and capable of understanding" (Cuddon 2014, 49), is regularly deployed in the poetry of Micah. The prophet apostrophizes corrupt Judean leadership throughout the book; whether Judean officials were actually present for any of his invective, in the late eighth century or as read aloud in a later time, cannot be known. Micah also addresses all peoples, the earth itself, mountains, and the earth's foundations (1:2; 6:2); entire villages and their inhabitants (1:10-16); personified Jerusalem (4:8-14 [Eng. 5:1]; 7:11-13); personified Bethlehem (5:1 [Eng. 2]); unspecified adversaries that likely included both Judah and other nations (5:9-14 [Eng. 10-15]); the entire people of Judah (6:3-5, 8, 9 ["O tribe"]); and false prophets (7:4b).

Assonance, the repetition of the same or similar vowel sounds, is pervasive in Biblical Hebrew prose and poetry, due to foundational semantic features of the language, including the prevalence of certain sounds in plural and dual noun endings in the absolute state (*-îm, -ôt,* and *-ayim*) and in the various construct states. But the importance of vocalic sound-play for Biblical Hebrew poetry, and for the oracles of Micah, goes beyond that. For two examples: Andersen and Freedman observe that in the oracle against Samaria in 1:5-7, "the assonance in *šĕmāmâ* makes an inclusion with *Samaria* in v 6aA," an artful move that focalizes the destruction of Samaria sonically (2000, 182); in 1:8, as the prophet discusses how he laments, a soundscape of keening is created by the repetition of long-*e* sounds.

Concatenation, the linking of multiple elements in a chain of expressions, serves to build aural and semantic intensity and deepens meaning, or makes its significance more expansive, as elements are added. Concatenation may be discerned in 1:10-16 as the prophet calls out name after name of villages threatened by the advance of enemy invaders through the region of the Judean Shephelah and nearby: Gath, Beth-leaphrah, Shaphir, Zaanan, Beth-ezel, Maroth, Jerusalem, Lachish, Moresheth-Gath, Achzib, Mareshah, and Adullam sketch out a landscape of terror. In retrospective reflection, or upon a new hearing or rereading of Mic 1, the seasoned interpreter may begin, consciously or unconsciously, to add "Jerusalem," the last word in the preceding verse (1:15), as the first city in the concatenation, its presence underscored, then, as "Jerusalem" and its linked word "gate" (*šaʿar*) from 1:9 recur in the middle of the list at 1:12.

Another example of concatenation unfolds in the dramatic war song of divine vengeance in 5:9-14 (Eng. 10-15). In these highly structured poetic lines using repeated deployment of the verbal clause "I will cut down" (*hikrattî*) as anchor along with several other verbs, Yhwh's fury is directed at a long chain of targets identified with the enemy: horses, chariots, cities, fortifications, sorceries, soothsayers, idolatrous images, sacred pillars, sacred poles, and cities (again). Brief but lyrical concatenation may be seen in the poetic description in 7:12 of the diaspora sites from which Israelites and Judeans will return to Zion: "from Assyria and the cities of Egypt, and from Egypt to the River" (that is, the Euphrates), "from sea to sea and mountain to mountain."

Heightening of one or another dimension of meaning is a constitutive feature of Biblical Hebrew poetry. Heightening involves the perceptible semantic linkage of two or more elements—sounds, parts of words, whole words, clauses, lines, strophes, or larger units—in a way that generates intensification and creates the effect of meaning. Heightening is rhetorically powerful and inherently interesting. It can be captivating for an audience to move from a more familiar term to a more exotic or rare formulation, to be swept from a simple verb to a more complex, more robust, or more volatile verb, and so on. Examples of heightening in Micah are too numerous to discuss in a comprehensive way. Here are illustrative examples from several chapters of Micah.

In 1:4b, heightening can be seen in the move from the slow but inexorable melting of wax in the vicinity of a fire to the forceful flooding of rushing waters down a slope. In 1:6, not only will the dressed stones of Samaria's monumental structures tumble down into the valley, but their very foundations will be laid bare, an example of heightening that drives home the completeness of the destruction. In 2:4, not only will ruined elites have their possessions removed, but their "fields"—a more specific term that brings into focus the grave threat to their economic security—have been distributed to "an apostate," which makes the expropriation all the more appalling. In this example, syntactical complexity increases: the first clause consists of three simple words of one syllable, two syllables, and one syllable respectively: *'êk yāmîš lî*, while the second clause has three three-syllable words: *ləšôbēb śādênû yəḥallēq*. In 2:9, not only will women be driven from their homes, but—all the more poignant—even their young children will be dispossessed. In 3:2–3, a gruesome heightening is perceptible in the predatory actions of oppressors moving from the outside of the victims' body (flaying) to the deeper tissue (devouring the flesh) and finally the innermost part (breaking the bones).

In 6:4, in the first clause Yhwh speaks of "bringing up" Israel from "the land of Egypt" generally; this is heightened in the second clause, in which

Introduction

the divine action is remembered with a more dramatic verb, "redeemed," and a more precise and dramatic context, "from the house of slavery." In 6:6-7, grammatical and semantic heightening are in evidence in at least four dimensions of the language. The ventriloquized worshipper muses about bringing "burnt offerings," this noun being a single word in Hebrew, and then "year-old calves," with heightening in the more complex three-word noun phrase. The pair of nouns in 6:6b (burnt offerings/year-old calves) is dramatically intensified as the worshipper waxes hyperbolic in 6:7a, imagining "thousands of rams" and "myriad torrents of oil" being brought to the altar of Yhwh. Finally, the most precious offering of all is imagined in 6:7b: the worshipper's own firstborn child, the offspring of their body. Within that last pair, the audience relishes another small-scale instance of heightening, from the single Hebrew word "my firstborn" to a two-word clause, "the fruit of my body."

Hyperbole, exaggeration for effect, is a venerable tool of artistic, political, and social discourse. Among its potential effects in communication are these: rendering untrustworthy an overwrought or unnuanced voice; amplifying what is seen to be at stake in a particular perspective; and engendering passionate or inflammatory responses in the implied audience. Abraham Heschel has noted the hyperbolic nature of prophetic representations (see below). Micah has regular recourse to hyperbolic language as he characterizes sinful, corrupt, and cruel behaviors. Among numerous examples, the most graphic is in 3:2-3, where the leaders of the Judean administration are characterized in vivid detail as cannibalistic, rendering repellent the economic dealings by which they enrich themselves at the expense of those less powerful. O'Brien observes that "hyperbole may be in the eyes of the beholder," such that some interpreters may read a passage as entirely straightforward in its signifying, rather than crafted hyperbolically for effect (2016, 249). The same may be said for the perception of ambiguity, irony, and many other effects of aurally performed or written artfulness: reception of the constitutive features of literature, music, art, and all creative productions is invariably conditioned, culturally and socially, by what is thinkable or expected on the part of the interpreters.

Imagery is important in poetry, not only for the vividness and drama of poetic expression as a means of persuasion, but for imaginative worldbuilding in the communities of reception gathered around the text. Relevant throughout Mic 1-7 is Alter's observation about the contrastive use of imagery in oracles in the Latter Prophets:

The monitory poems of the prophets are dominated by images of wasteland, uprooting and burning, darkness, enslavement and humiliation, stripping of garments, divorce and sexual abandoning, earthquake and storm. The poems of consolation are dominated by images of flourishing vineyards and fields, planting and building, shining light, liberation and regal dignity, splendid garb, marital reconciliation and sexual union, firm foundations and calm. (2011, 196)

Irony suffuses the prophetic discourse in Micah. Verbal irony works with the complex interplay of the said and the unsaid. As I have suggested elsewhere, interpretation of a given ironic text "will be more persuasive to the degree that it can account for multiple axes along which the unreliable 'said' may be seen to signal incongruity" and to the extent that it "takes seriously the particulars of the 'said' in its construction of the 'unsaid'" (Sharp 2009, 33; for literature on the theorizing of irony, 10–35). Ironic communication works "to persuade us of something that is subtler, more complex, or more profound than the apparent meaning" of that which has been ostensibly said, ushering the implied audience "into an experience of alterity that moves [them] toward new insight by problematizing false understandings" (24).

Lineation is an important structural feature of Biblical Hebrew poetry. James Longenbach says, "Poetry is the sound of language organized in lines," and the feature of lineation contributes to the experience of meaning-making, for poetic expression "does not simply describe a movement of thought; it embodies and complicates that movement through the relationship of syntax and line" (2008, xi, 13). Especially in a formally structured, parallelistically patterned mode of poetic expression, as we have in Biblical Hebrew poetry such as the oracles of Micah, lineation is a powerful element within the patterning. Longenbach observes, "the drama of lineation lies in the simultaneous making and breaking of our expectation for pattern" (70).

Metaphor as a richly layered form of expression is important in Micah's oracles. Metaphors establish multiple avenues of potential meaning through the juxtaposing of disparate frames of reference. As Mason Lancaster observes, "Metaphors are systematic mappings between conceptual domains . . . not merely the comparisons of two isolated entities, but whole *sets* of corresponding elements between two domains of experience" (2021a, 244 [emphasis original]). Active reader involvement is necessary to produce

Introduction

meaning that makes intelligent sense of the vehicle of the metaphor while gesturing toward a nuanced other sense in light of the (perceived) tenor of the metaphor. Metaphorical discourse seeks to enlighten and persuade through subtle uses of analogy, ellipsis or gapping, and the complex interplay between equivalence and difference in ways that produce experiences of congruence, unexpected shifts of focus, and discord for the implied audience. Exploring dimensions of selected theories of metaphor from Aristotle to Benjamin Harshav, Juan Cruz has noted the relation of metaphor to ideology and its important structuring role in the discursive practices of the book of Micah (2016, esp. 17-46, 64-65, 232-37). The rich diversity of metaphors in the poetry of Micah illumines for the implied audience central features of theology and social ethics.

Onomatopoeia uses sound to evoke aurally and enact sonically that which is being described. Onomatopoeia is effective whether a word or phrase is actually spoken aloud or is simply audiated (heard in one's imagination) as one is reading. Rich onomatopoeic interplay between the sound of a word or clause and the meaning being signified can delight the audience and, moreover, can serve subtly not only to enrich the imagery offered for the audience's consideration but to undergird the point being made. In 1:4, the sound of the verb *bqʿ*, with its medial velar and final voiced guttural, aurally evokes the "splitting apart" of the valleys. In 1:7, the verb *ktt* evokes the pulverizing or crushing into fragments of Samaria's idols; this verb is used in 4:3 as well for metalworkers beating swords into plowshares, evoking not crushing but hammering sounds. In 1:8 and 7:1, the verb *yll* and the interjection *ʾaləlay* powerfully enact sonic representation of a lamenting prophet and a wailing Daughter Zion. In 2:4, mockers will taunt devastated Judeans; their imitation of gasping sobs is represented by a sequence with repeated nasal *n* and voiceless fricative *h* in rapid succession. Some interpreters suggest that in 2:6, *nṭp* as a verb for preaching is meant derisively to evoke the annoying sound of dripping water or the spray of saliva (Dempster 2017, 88; cf. *nṭp* for utterances in Job 29:22; Prov 5:3; Song 4:11). In 2:12, the verb *hmh*, used in the Hebrew Bible for a rich range of sounds from cheeping and barking to groaning and roaring (*HALOT* 1:250), evokes the tumult of sheep in a pen and—the tenor of the simile—prisoners of war being prepared for deportation.

Repetition is a powerful way to underline a point and, if the repeated language or imagery is vivid, to create an increasingly intense experience of understanding or affective response in the implied audience. In 5:4b-5 (Eng. 5b-6), the image of Assyria's invasion of Judah is painted dramatically in two repeated lines, *kî-yābô' bə'arṣēnû wəkî yidrōk*, "when he invades our land and treads within" with divergent objects of the transitive verb: "our fortresses" (v. 4b [Eng. 5b]) and "our territory" (v. 5b [Eng. 6b]). The repetition of these lines gives the impression that the advance of the Assyrian troops is inexorable. The variation of the direct object at the ends of the two lines constitutes a marked difference within the equivalence established by strong poetic parallelism. Reading the relationship of the two direct objects as significant, one sees the Assyrian assault not only on fortified cities but more broadly on the entire territory of Judah, the threat affecting all regions within its borders. Further, the audience may be spurred to hear the sound of tramping boots through the poet's repetition of the two-syllable *yidrōk* ("tread"). In Yhwh's war song of divine vengeance in 5:9-14, "I will cut down" (*hikrattî*) is utilized four times, suggesting the repeated slashing of a blade. In 7:11-12, a deictic exclamation is repeated with subtle variations to draw the audience's attention to a long-distant time of restoration: "A day!" (*yôm*, 7:11a), "That very day!" (*yôm hahû'*, 7:11b), and "That day!" (*yôm hû'*, 7:12).

Rhetorical questions are persuasive means of inviting, or even subtly coercing, the assent of the implied audience to a position or perspective favored by the speaker. In Biblical Hebrew, a question may be marked with an animate pronoun ("Who?"), an inanimate pronoun ("What?"), a locative particle ("Where?"), a temporal particle ("When?"), or a proclitic interrogative particle (*hă-, ha-,* or *he-*) attached to the first word of the question (*IBHS* §18.1c; *HALOT* 1:236). A good number of questions in Biblical Hebrew—rhetorical and otherwise—are left unmarked and "must be recognized from context" (*IBHS* §18.2f). Especially as regards rhetorical questions, unmarked instances may be mistaken for statements or even emphatic pronouncements rather than questions. Among the Latter Prophets, Amos deploys rhetorical questions with something akin to genius (see Amos 3:3, 4, 5, 6, 8; 5:20, 25; 6:2, 3, 12, 13; 7:2, 5; 8:8; 9:7). Micah, too, uses the form with deft sophistication. Rhetorical questions occur in Micah at 1:5; 2:7; 3:1, 11; 4:9; 6:3, 6, 7, 9, 10, 11; 7:10, 18. There are often elements of irony involved, sometimes in a dynamic in which the assent of the implied audience serves to entrap or convict them of misunderstanding, malfeasance, or worse.

Space constraints preclude further detailing here of the breathtaking artfulness of Micah's oracles. Chiasmus, ellipsis, synecdoche, and many more poetic features enliven the lines, strophes, and larger blocks of material, capturing the attention of the implied audience and enhancing the elegance and persuasiveness of the prophet's communication.

Introduction

3. PROPHECY, POLITICS, AND THEOLOGY

In every Hebrew Bible text, narrative and poetic claims about the deity and construals of divine actions and purposes—in a word, theology—are inextricably intertwined with the social and political values of the visionaries, word-artists, tradents, and redactors who created, shaped, and preserved the material. Intermediation between the divine and the human always involves valences of power and social authority, whether it is performed live in a public space, represented or described, or interpreted in other ways.

3.1 Political and Economic Dimensions of Prophecy in Ancient Judah

Theological discourses, poetry, and narratives that perform or represent prophecy in the Hebrew Bible are inevitably political in nature. Religious hierarchies involving access to the divine unfailingly stake claims about authenticity and authority within social and political structures embedded in, or adjacent to, religious spaces and sources of power.

Tactically key to the organization of avenues of influence and means of social power in any society are national and regional policies and practices that enhance the wealth of the powerful, virtually always at the expense of those of lower status and wealth—enslaved persons, agricultural laborers, the working poor in urban centers—whose labor and its fruits are commodified and controlled by political elites. Many oracles of Micah focus on the plight of those who are doubly injured: first, by the military incursions and forced displacements perpetrated by enemy troops, with the catastrophic blows that militarized conflict deals to the stability, physical health, emotional well-being, and economic survival of families; and second, by exploitative economic practices within Judean society itself, especially as fostered under the extractive policies of the monarchical system and the injustices perpetrated by elite officials vested in that system. To understand the tenor of Micah's prophesying, it is essential to illumine dimensions of poverty that have diminished human lives and challenged communities both in ancient Judah and in other contexts across the centuries. Toward this end, I employ a bifocal lens: I draw on biblical scholarship that analyzes poverty in Israel and Judah in antiquity, and I turn to poverty studies more broadly for analytical observations pertinent to the contexts of contemporary readers who encounter Micah's polemics against economic exploitation from their own positions as interpreters in the ongoing reception history of Micah.

CL Wren Radford writes, "Engaging with lived experiences of marginalisation has become a vital practice for academics and activists seeking to address unjust social and political relations" (2022, 1). Of course, every context is unique in which greed, dispossession, and neglect have ravaged the lives of individuals, families, and communities. Even for members of a marginalized constituency living in the same location at a particular time, what each person or family experiences is particular to them and cannot be smoothed into a dominant narrative that captures adequately what they may have suffered. For those who struggle with homelessness or forced migration, food insecurity, lack of access to medical care, being defrauded financially, surviving militarized conflict or incarceration, or another vector of diminishment, every experience of suffering is unique, constituted by particular constellations of injury, risk, and resistance, specific vectors of harm and potential aid, and countless unreproducible elements having to do with intersectional oppressions, privilege and disprivilege, trauma and healing, cultural factors, and indefinable qualities of personhood in relationship. Every experience of despair and resilience is unique. Nevertheless, it is intellectually important and ethically generative to consider the experiences of those living in poverty or precarity across social formations and historical times, listening for dissonances and resonances. The reader of Micah who does not reflect on lived experiences—ancient and contemporary—is not hearing these ancient oracles with the deep attention that Micah and later prophetic scribes are asking of their implied audiences.

Roland Boer has studied extractive economies in ancient Israel, Judah, and surrounding regions, theorizing the modes and means of resource allocation, exploitation, and resilience deployed across various forms of social organization, from subsistence-level herding and agriculture in households, larger kinship groups, and village collectives in the Bronze Age to estate-centered patron-client relations, local urban-rural hierarchies of exchange, and international trade in later centuries. At the bottom of social and political hierarchies, laborers worked extremely hard, and control of the fruits of their labors was not theirs; "economic and gender exploitation" was rife (Boer 2015, 109), as it has been in countless economies across the millennia, including in the production processes that drive late capitalism in the present day. In the ancient Near Eastern estates that supplied urban centers, ruling elites who were vested in temple and palace hierarchies wielded significant and often unchecked power over agricultural workers—whether permanent or temporary, including slaves and tenant farmers—who had become laborers "by various means, whether as captives from war (typically boys and girls), as deportees, or as refugees from

Introduction

the sanctions of customary law, from catastrophic drought or flood, from the need to pay off debts, and so on" (119). The lack of recourse available to oppressed householders and other nonelite Judeans is on vivid display in Mic 2:1–2 and 7:3.

Marvin Chaney has analyzed the political and economic transition in ancient Israel from a loose network of agricultural land holdings farmed for the subsistence of kinship groups and villages to a centralized monarchical regime that appropriated agricultural yields for the needs of the royal house and for regional and international trade, with the financial gains of trade going not to the farmers but into the royal coffers. Drawing on archaeological evidence, economic historiography, and sociological insights, Chaney offers this portrayal of the life of farmers under the Israelite and Judean monarchies:

> Many of the agricultural "surpluses" once retained by freeholding peasants in the hill country were extracted by a variety of taxes and rents to fill state coffers and fund an increasingly consumptive lifestyle among the upper classes. Rain agriculture in Palestine was subject to the vicissitudes of periodic drought, blight, and pestilence. . . . Once the monarchic state and its ruling elite began to extract "surpluses" to pay for luxury and strategic items . . . the peasants' margin grew [even] slimmer. . . . Usurious interest rates ensured frequent foreclosures; debt instruments thus served to transfer land from peasant freehold to large estates, reducing previously free and independent farmers to landless day-laborers or debt-slaves. (2017, 76)

Chaney and others have described the interrelated factors and processes of this transition as agricultural intensification. This process included: increasing specialization of agricultural products for purposes of export; the narrowing of a prior and beneficial multiuse approach to land use for agriculture and herding that had spread and thus mitigated risk; the enforcement of debt contracts that regularly forced foreclosure on farmers' holdings; and other indicators of social stratification, not only in urban centers but in large towns and smaller villages caught up in the larger economic system (Chaney 2017, 125–34, 205–9; for his cogent rebuttal of several interlocutors, see 137–46). Gale Yee has identified a variety of "overlapping levels" of marginalization of the peasant class in ancient Israel and Judah. These included: exploitative taxation that "drained off peasant surpluses" and forced some workers into debt slavery; the disenfranchisement of women "with respect to descent, inheritance, marriage residence, and other social customs"; "ethnocentric laws and ideologies that diminished the stranger and immigrant"; and social stratification that included "rituals of honor, entitlement, and privilege that the elite enjoyed in contrast to the ... insults to dignity, forced deference, humiliations, and physical beatings that the exploited often endured," as well as ongoing "fear of reprisals" for resistance (2007, 12, 18).

Jason Silverman (2021) provides an excellent overview of economic issues in the southern Levant related to subsistence production, land tenure and debt, involuntary labor, systems of exchange, and more. Regarding the polemics in Mic 3:9-12 against Judean elites, he offers these thought-provoking words: "'Bribe,' 'price,' and 'silver' appear in parallel as illicit recompenses for legal decisions, priestly teachings, and oracles, respectively. Does this ... imply that leaders ought to perform all these activities gratis, that they charged too much for their services, or ... that the product was tailored inappropriately to the audience?" (332). Silverman observes, "the prophets address justice on a moral basis rather than on the level of economic structures," and "their vision of proper treatment of the poor is echoed in royal and proverbial texts" in many cultures throughout the ancient Near East (333), showing that the biblical prophets stand in a venerable tradition of advocacy for those living in poverty or experiencing disenfranchisement by social elites.

3.2 Theological Traditions in Micah

A central question for scholarship on Micah is the extent to which Deuteronomistic ideology may be demonstrated to have influenced these oracles. Claims for Deuteronomism are grounded on two chief ways of reasoning. First, scholars point to shared lexical items occurring in Micah and in Deuteronomy or the Deuteronomistic History, and sometimes—though the incidence of tautology increases in such arguments—in other biblical texts that have themselves been seen as showing Deuteronomistic influence, such as the prose in Jeremiah. Arguments on the basis of shared language should show that such language is characteristic of Deuteronomy or the Deuteronomistic History (rather than incidental), seems to be unusual or not characteristic of the Micah or other biblical text otherwise, and does not occur so broadly in the Hebrew Bible as to make determination of provenance impossible. Traditional arguments for Deuteronomistic influence

Introduction

regularly fail to persuade, especially on the second and third counts just mentioned, and it is the decision of this commentary that in the absence of persuasive evidence to the contrary, the readings presented here will not rely on speculation about Deuteronomistic influence. For example, some scholars point to Micah's use of the lexical term *pāsîl*, "image, idol" (Mic 1:7; 5:12) as being congruent with polemics against idolatry found in Deuteronomy and the Deuteronomistic corpus (see forms of *pāsîl* at Deut 7:5, 25; 12:3; 2 Kgs 17:41), and with the general tenor of the account of Josiah's reform in 2 Kgs 23, though that particular lexical item does not occur there. One might object, however, that *pāsîl* occurs also in Hos 11:2, in poetic material that explores metaphors of childhood, disobedience, and parental nurture that are characteristic of Hosea; thus the grounds are tenuous on which to argue that Mic 1:7 and 5:12 were influenced by Deuteronomism rather than, say, by Micah traditionists' knowledge of Hosea's oracles. Many other such examples could be cited.

3.3 Feminist Amplifying of Micah

In its marvelously variegated purposes and effects, feminist interpretation may be understood as performing several modes of engagement of power relations expressed or intimated through texts and traditions, as well as the power relations performed by communities that historically have understood themselves to be addressed by those texts and traditions. Feminist interpretation is foundationally intersectional, probing and analyzing the countless ways in which explicit norms and subterranean biases shape issues related to gender, sexuality, racialization, bodied capability, access to economic resources, and more. Among feminist interpretive possibilities are: retrieving the presence and agency of women and gender-nonconforming persons throughout history, plausibly imagining and reconstructing the same wherever texts have erased or muted the voices and actions of nonmale persons; plying deconstructive theories and initiatives that unravel distorted views of the subject framed by biblical discourse; engaging in constructive visioning and strategic work to foster ideational and material change; and promoting discursive practices that honor liminality, becoming, and contestation. Feminist interpretation strives to make visible, resist, and dismantle structures and processes of gender-based oppression and violence, engaging—in all possible ways—the intersectional consequences of such structures and processes, and the spiral of harms they generate. Feminist work centrally involves building pedagogical, political, and social systems and pathways for the envisioning and enactment of justice. This work is powerfully resonant with the prophetic vision offered in the book of Micah, a vision that continues to generate responses as the history of consequences of this biblical text unfolds. As Jewish feminist theologian Judith Plaskow writes, "Feminists can affirm our debt to and continuity with prophetic insistence on connecting faith and justice, even while we extend the prophets' social and religious critique beyond anything they themselves envisioned" (1990, 217). The "beyond" articulated by Plaskow includes postmodernist ways of reading and counterreading gender in Micah. On this, I find valuable the work of Erin Runions (2001), who offers incisive insights about Micah's formation of the implied audience and the weaknesses of some gendered interpretations of Micah. Reading Runions, interpreters will be empowered: to counter tacit understandings of Zion as "a damsel in distress, punished and rescued by a male ruler" (210); to engage the profound ambiguities and liminality on offer in Micah passages; to decline the "passive acceptance of an identity of a nation led into domination over other nations" (211); to consider how the wounded remnant might be being trained to emulate or mimic the colonizing power that has harmed them (215-17); and, for those readers vested with social or economic power, to wrestle with how to position themselves authentically with regard to justice when they might find themselves "between the conqueror and the crushed," rather than clearly one or the other (232).

It is axiomatic in feminist work to identify the social locations that have shaped one's perceptions and values. Keenly aware that this move is still made seldom in biblical commentaries, I here note dimensions of my identity as commentator that shape how I construe relevant issues in Micah along historical, translational, hermeneutical, literary, and theological trajectories. I write as a scholar trained in critical thinking at Wesleyan University, Yale Divinity School, and the Yale Graduate School of Arts and Sciences. I write as a lifelong resident of the United States, of English and Scottish heritage, claiming a postcolonial resistant posture over against the British imperial condescension toward Americans that I have encountered not infrequently in the academy. I write as one who has benefited from and interrogated white privilege, educational privilege, and cishetero privilege, while also withstanding and rejecting the regular erasure and diminishment of women's contributions in the fields in which I have gained expertise. I write as one who strives to be an emancipatory educator in the classroom, in presentations for nonscholarly groups, and in my writing.

Introduction

I am persuaded that praxes within many classrooms and in academia more broadly are still biased against women, gender-nonconforming persons, nonwhite persons, persons without substantial economic resources, and persons without a significant family history in higher education. Biases, often unwitting, affect professors' evaluation of student work, faculty hiring and promotion processes, research citation practices, and protocols for attendance and networking at expensive national and international conferences as a condition of visibility in the guild. I write as one shaped by Christian theological claims, especially as regards sacramental theology and liturgy, Christology, and practices of progressive Protestant dissent. I write as a preacher and as an Episcopal priest.

Considerations of justice and injustice articulated in the book of Micah are of vital interest for feminist interpreters of sacred texts. Women are present in Micah's discourse, both as historical persons in the prophet's community whose fate engages Micah's attention, and as figured in Daughter Zion and the female-gendered enemy of 7:8-10. Judean women and gender-nonconforming persons were present in the history of Judah, in the community in which Micah of Moresheth lived, and in the communities of the later scribes who redacted the book of Micah. Further, as Jimmy Hoke comments, "Queer wo/men were there." Hoke rightly observes that "androcentric, heteronormative scholarship denies the existence of wo/men and queerness, only admitting their existence if their presence is explicitly mentioned" (2021, 28). The role of a commentator includes analyzing vestigial traces or silences regarding what may have been suppressed, what may have been relegated to the background of a text's concerns, and what may constitute ideological distortion of the lived experience out of which a biblical text was generated and the political and social conditions of contexts salient in the history of its reception.

Micah stands among the earliest prophets whose visionary exhortations to justice have been canonized in the Hebrew Bible. With Micah in the cohort of eighth-century prophets who use discursive practices of words and embodied performances (sign-acts) to intervene in systems of oppression and violence are Amos and Isaiah of Jerusalem. Standing with them, too, are later scribal redactors who honed and expanded the earliest forms of prophetic oracles into the layered and complex textual witnesses that are authoritative for communities across cultures from the rabbinic era and early Christianity on into the present.

Three passages on themes of justice and violence have proved particularly resonant through centuries of reception history.

> Let justice roll down like waters,
>> and righteousness like an ever-flowing stream. (Amos 5:24)
>
> They will beat their swords into plowshares
> and their spears into pruning hooks.
> Nation will not lift up sword against nation,
> and they will no longer study war. (Mic 4:3 // Isa 2:4)
>
> [Yhwh] has told you, O mortal!
>> What is good?
>> What does Yhwh require of you?
> Nothing other than to do justice, to cherish fidelity,
>> and to proceed humbly with your God. (Mic 6:8)

Thus justice work and peacemaking have venerable pedigrees within the biblical prophetic corpus and in the centuries of reception history that have followed. Feminist visions of justice and communal transformation seek to address the intersectional oppressions of persons, communities, and other living beings, interrogating and speaking truth about every dimension in which harms injure bodies and quash spirits. In oppressive systems, sustained violence—militarized, economic, cultural, educational—relies on ongoing imbalances of power at every level from global to communal to personal, terrorizing and silencing those who dissent and perpetrating more subterranean but equally insidious obstruction to resources that individuals, families, groups, and communities need to survive and flourish. Feminist scholars create and deploy critical interrogative and constructive discourses and practices of justice-making to secure the well-being of women and girls, children generally, nonbinary and gender-nonconforming persons, all people in circumstances of oppression or precarity, and—per the vital witness of ecofeminism—other living beings as well.

As feminist activists have long underlined, cultural constructions and lived experiences of gender are inextricably intertwined with issues of power, both in generative vectors of power used for renewal, resistance, and revitalization, and harmful vectors of disempowerment, distortion, and death-dealing. I have written elsewhere that my feminist work has been characterized by three commitments:

1. *to honor all subjects*, attending to those whose experiences and truths are erased, silenced, or distorted in patriarchal and other violent rhet-

Introduction

oric, whether rhetoric of the biblical texts or of later commentary on those texts;

2. *to interrogate relations of power* . . . within biblical texts and also those performed via assumptions underlying methods of interpretation, the pressures of reception history, and scholarly norms for what counts as viable analysis;

3. *to reform community*, especially by opening spaces for new visions and the fierce contestation of harms perpetrated over the centuries by those gathered around these sacred texts. (Sharp 2022a, 49 [emphasis original]; further on feminist hermeneutics, queer readings, and feminist translation praxis, 50–72)

I pursue these goals as fully as I can in the pages of this commentary.

Special mention must be made of O'Brien's excellent volume on Micah in the feminist Wisdom Commentary series published by Liturgical Press. Among the cogent positions she articulates, I would highlight three important points that should texture the discussion of all interpreters of Micah. First, observing that "the voice of the privileged ally"—in the persona of Micah of Moresheth—"is not the same as the voice of the oppressed," O'Brien is careful to "insist on the distinction between the voice of the scribe and the interests of the average person in ancient Yehud," for entanglement in the hierarchy of imperial privileges enjoyed by the scribal literati will assuredly have "shaped the author's imagination" in these oracles (2015, liii). Second, noting that access to food resources has been limited for many women living in impoverished communities across cultures, O'Brien avers that "gendered aspects of hunger and poverty" are largely overlooked in Micah, who gives his attention to "leaders and elites," allowing them to "monopolize the stage," whereas "in Micah women are generic objects of pity rather than individuals in pain" (lv). Third, while Micah sharply critiques Judean leaders for moral corruption and failing in their duties, he does not critique the centralized hierarchy as such in which he is embedded. O'Brien poses the trenchant question, "Would a world in which all people stream to Jerusalem have benefitted those who did not share power in Jerusalem—women and men living in small villages?" (lxii).

The prophetic interventions that come to voice in the Micah traditions have rippled through Western literary and social history. The force of these rearticulations may be theorized as a significant dimension of the history of consequences of this prophetic book, even in instances in which a Micah passage is not mentioned directly and Micah's language is not quoted.

In this commentary, I seek to gesture toward the rich panoply of ways in which contemporary feminist and queer scholars might interrogate and explore Micah's rhetoric and call for justice beyond feminist retrieval of the reconstructed or imagined intentions of the biblical authors and later redactors, whose minds can never be known.

Bonnie Honig has astutely observed "the breadth and depth of patriarchy's grasp, its imbrication in everything we love as well as in the structures and powers we resist" (2021, 13). Honig theorizes three modes of refusal as performed in Euripides's *Bacchae* and engaged in contemporary critical theory and the arts. Micah, too, is an iconic performer of refusal. Micah declines the idolatries—literal and metaphorical—that distort his community's identity and dishonor their God (1:5-7; cf. 5:11-13). Micah rejects the heartless exploitation perceived to be characteristic of Judean elites' dealings with agrarian householders (2:1-2, 8-9; 3:2-3, 10-11) and interrogates the culture of violence enacted by the greedy and the malevolent (7:2-3, 13, 16-17). Micah attends explicitly to the harms done to women and children (1:16; 2:2, 9) as a sign of Judah's desolation. And Micah lifts up the ancestor Miriam (6:4) as one of three paradigmatic leaders commissioned by Yhwh to lead Israel out of enslavement, tacitly declining the erasure of Miriam that we perceive otherwise, beyond the few mentions of her in Pentateuchal narratives and genealogies. Thus the book of Micah may be claimed as a valuable resource for feminist hermeneuts seeking biblical traditions in which to ground a politics of refusal. As a feminist translator, I note here one instance of my own refusal: I decline to inscribe theological androcentrism in this twenty-first-century translation. Wherever masculine singular pronouns are used and the referent is unambiguously the deity, I supply "[Yhwh]" or "[Yhwh's]" instead. That ancient Israelite and Judean scribes understood Yhwh as a masculine deity is clear in Micah and numerous other biblical texts, though the full significance of that masculine theological language, even historically, could be robustly debated. I trust the reader will not be confused by my decision not to reproduce theological androcentrism in my own voice.

For my feminist amplification of Micah's tropes and traditions, I draw extensively on two interdisciplinary works of signal importance for critical reflection on issues of gender, identity, and power: Sara Ahmed's *Living a Feminist Life* (2017) and Marquis Bey's *Black Trans Feminism* (2022). Insights from these volumes are offered in the Retrospect section of each chapter as catalysts for readers' sustained explorations, interrogations, and amplifications of Micah texts in their own cultural, social, and educational contexts.

Introduction

The book of Micah is a valuable companion text for the emancipatory work of feminist, womanist, trans, and queer ethics, theology, and historiography constructed via the retrospective critical gaze.

3.3.1 Micah as Killjoy

In her perspicuous *Living a Feminist Life*, Ahmed continues the work of theorizing the notion of the feminist KILLJOY that she explored in her 2014 book, *Willful Subjects*. There, Ahmed constructed willfulness as intentional and strategic resistance to structures and processes of harm and erasure: "Willfulness could be thought of as political art, a practical craft that is acquired through involvement in political struggle. . . . Feminist, queer, and antiracist histories can be thought of as histories of those who are willing to be willful" (2014, 133–34). What Ahmed predicates of willful subjects may be applied readily to many of the Latter Prophets, especially Hosea, Amos, Micah, Jeremiah, and Ezekiel: "willfulness as audacity, willfulness as standing against, willfulness as creativity" (134). In Judean antiquity, Micah was willing to be willful. Micah—the prophet as constructed in the literary composition—was creative and audacious in his standing against the idolatry and exploitation that he saw in the behavior of the powerful of his society. The book of Micah may be considered what Ahmed calls a "willfulness archive" (134).

Standing in the reception history of the book of Micah myself, I submit that the figure of the willful feminist KILLJOY is generative for amplifying prophetic resistance of all kinds—centrally including, but not limited to, resistance to gender-based oppression and the many forms of harm entangled with that. The feminist KILLJOY dares to name the sordid and tragic truth of systemic patriarchal violence: its robust androcentric distortions, its barely veiled misogynistic norms and ideologies, and its countless specific violations of the bodies and spirits of all under its sway. The feminist KILLJOY disrupts patriarchal cultural complacency, making audible and visible the forms of erasure, silencing, and subjugation that patriarchy uses to quash dissent. The feminist KILLJOY leads the revision of inadequate norms and fosters the envisioning of new possibilities for the community's future. Micah, too, dares to disrupt the explicit and implicit cultural narratives that ground acts of unholiness and injustice in idolatrous and distorted ideation. The prophet rails against the literally idolatrous worship of gods other than YHWH (1:7; 5:12), the false claiming of divine authority for words YHWH has not spoken (3:5–7), and the purveying of faux prophecies out of mercenary motivation (3:11; 7:4). Moreover, Micah fulminates against the metaphorically idolatrous reifications of economic and social power that dishonor Yhwh and the vulnerable constituents within Judean society whom the covenant community should be protecting and assisting. Because Micah attends to the disastrous consequences of Judean sin for women and children in his community, and because he claims the leadership of Miriam as paradigmatic for the fulfilment of Yhwh's purposes (6:4, the only reference to Miriam's important communal role outside of the Pentateuch, when we bracket two genealogical references in 1 Chr 4:17; 6:3), we can stand in the reception history of this passionate prophetic book and claim Micah as a protofeminist KILLJOY. Within the Retrospect section of each Micah chapter, I craft a linkage between Micah's prophetic resistance of harms in ancient Judah and Ahmed's notion of the KILLJOY who resists contemporary patriarchal violence.

3.3.2 Micah and FUGITIVITY

According to the superscription in Mic 1:1, the chief historical context in which the Micah traditions are to be understood is the period from the late eighth to the early seventh centuries BCE. During the era of Neo-Assyrian hegemony, many thousands of people from Israel, Judah, and other regions were taken prisoner, enslaved, and forcibly removed to Assyria or another location. Eckhart Frahm writes,

> Attempted escape from the harsh conditions under which slaves lived was a regular occurrence across the Assyrian Empire, all the more so as cases of manumission seem to have been rare.... A handbook on legal practices known from Middle Assyrian and Neo-Assyrian copies instructs the owners of undependable slaves to engrave on their faces the phrase ḫalaq ṣabat, "He is a runaway—seize him!" Before this is taken as another sign of a specifically Assyrian—or Mesopotamian—penchant for inhumanity, it must be stressed that later civilizations had very similar procedures in place. In ancient Greece, the foreheads of runaway slaves were marked with the words *kátekhé me pheúgo*, "Seize me, I am a fugitive," while the Romans forced slaves to wear metal rings around their necks that were inscribed with the Latin phrase *fugi tene me*, which means the same. Later, in the American South, fugitive slaves, if they were caught, had the letter R (for "runaway") branded on their cheeks. (2023, 315)

Introduction

It is transparently clear that the state of fugitivity and the mindsets and actions of fugitives, in their diverse historical contexts and varied cultural figurations, are of profound relevance for understanding the book of Micah and its reverberations through the history of interpretation, from antiquity to the present moment of reading.

In their richly theorized book, *Black Trans Feminism*, Bey works historically and textually to foster the abolition of forms of subjugation that define, regulate, and harm countless persons and communities through racialized, gendered, and sexualized ideologies of normativity. Such ideologies fund systemic and interpersonal violence, punitive and carceral responses to difference, and continual quotidian diminishment of those who resist or seek to live otherwise. Bey theorizes and engages a modality through which blackness, transness, and acts of resistance have been understood in works of critical theory: FUGITIVITY, grounded in part through a critical emancipatory reading of the history and lived experience of Black African persons fleeing enslavement by white and European captors in the United States and elsewhere. Tavia Nyong'o explains, "From early maroon societies in the eighteenth century to underground revolutionaries in the late twentieth and twenty-first centuries, the fugitive is an enduring figure in Black history and culture. The fugitive might even be the foundational figure of black resistance" (2019, 92). Paula von Gleich observes of FUGITIVITY, understood as a vital concept in North American Black feminist theory and Black American literature, that the notion works to reconfigure the Afro-pessimist position that within the antiblackness structures of United States society, Black persons are construed as "socially dead"; explorations of FUGITIVITY can serve to "testify to the fact of their refusing, enduring, resisting, and thinking beyond that status toward future possibilities of unconfined freedom" (2022, 5, 23). FUGITIVITY "points to the historical legacy of physical, mental, and cultural practices of individual and communal forms of refusal of, survival despite, resistance against, and flight from anti-black violence by Black diasporic communities for centuries" (52). The notion is of paramount importance for every contemporary reader of Micah who has been enculturated in explicit and implicit tenets of white supremacy or antiblackness—whether in the United States or elsewhere, and whether such hateful distortions have been encountered in the public square or in private, in the Eurocentrism of Western academic biblical studies and theological discourse or in the history of interpretation of Micah.

Bey celebrates FUGITIVITY as "an escapeful slitheriness that power's hands cannot contain" (16). For Bey, the embodied locus of emancipatory resistance that is boldest and most promising in theoretical and material terms is Black trans feminism. They observe, "Gender is one of the chief forms through which coercive, compulsory violence and captivity are carried out," and further, "sex and gender assignment can be read as . . . a primordial violence seeking to quell the mutiny of black anoriginal lawlessness or unruly transitivity" (2022, 25). Bey's work on blackness, queerness, and un/gendered FUGITIVITY is "in primary service of the eradication of violence, of which normative impositions are prime culprits" (55). Relevant here is critical work on the self as a "plural event" and anoriginality as a way of talking about ontology produced not in a static originary essence but in irreducible difference in relation (Benjamin 2017). Such difference is continually expressed and performed, not fixed or vulnerable to being commodified. Nyong'o suggests one may define FUGITIVITY "paradoxically, as constant transformation without escape" (2019, 197), and that definition is cogent. But untrammeled and untamable transformation, even within implacably oppressive social structures or material conditions of diminishment, may constitute a kind of escape after all. Bey lauds the radical abolition performed by guiding figures who resist, who express their subjectivities in ways that are purposefully illegible to—not understandable, not intelligible, not capturable by—the violent logics of antiblackness, gender policing, and cishetero distortions. One such figure of resistance, Alexis Pauline Gumbs, writes poetry that enacts "a refusal of racialized and gendered normativities, which incites the possibility of other worlds and epistemologies" (2022, 119). Bey stands with Gumbs in "moving toward an escape from patriarchy and white supremacist taxonomizing and the attending modes of supposed life that these regimes entail" (145). When "gender and sexual normativity are destabilized," Bey writes, the resulting "crisis" offers "an opportunity to enact new forms of assemblages, coalitions, collectivities, affinities, and life" (60). Bey offers a prophetic call to "an alternative and otherwise mode of living, grounded in a radically nonexclusionary sociality that escapes captive and captivating logics of subjectivity," instead promoting an abolitional freedom through "byzantine, rhizomatic relational affinities" (69).

Claiming my own position in the reception history of Micah, I submit that the witness of the poet Micah of Moresheth, too, incites flight from dehumanizing violence, envisioning the possibility of other worlds and new collectivities energized by life-giving mutuality. Micah exhorts his audience to embrace an alternative epistemology that reframes what communal ethics and the holy require. Micah can assist us in dismantling the carceral

Introduction

ideologies that keep believers and others complicit in, trapped within, and hunted by death-dealing hierarchies of violence, these justified over and over again in antiblack, misogynist, and queer-hating public and religious discourse via forms of authorization that, I suggest, are not only toxic but idolatrous. Within the Retrospect section of each Micah chapter, I reflect on connections between Bey's notion of FUGITIVITY and three levels of FUGITIVITY discernible in the book of Micah. The Judeans known or remembered in the time of the Micah traditions—writ broadly as the late eighth century to the sixth century BCE—were FUGITIVES. They were Judeans without Judah, thousands deported to captivity in Babylonia (Jer 52:27-30), others having fled to Moab, Ammon, Edom, Egypt (see, e.g., Jer 44), or elsewhere. They were denizens of Jerusalem whose city had been breached and had been made a smoking heap of rubble (Mic 3:12; Jer 39:8; 52:13). They were YHWH-believers without YHWH, a deity who had not saved them from Neo-Assyrian and Neo-Babylonian invasions, whose theophanic arrival signals the divine intent to beat and kill them (1:3-7; 2:3; 6:13), and who will hide the divine face when the community cries out in terror for YHWH's assistance (3:4-7). Judeans are FUGITIVES from violence: from the horror of enemy troops surging through the region and encamping at the gate of Jerusalem (1:9, 12), and from monstrous exploitation, corruption, and bloodshed within their own community (2:1-2; 3:1-4, 9-11; 6:11-12; 7:2-4).

FUGITIVITY matters in Micah. First and foremost, this prophet pays attention to, and laments on behalf of, his FUGITIVE compatriots who have been terrorized and yearn for freedom from imperial violence (1:10-16; 2:8-9). Second, the rhetoric of Micah makes audible a wounded Daughter Zion (1:9; 3:12), a Zion who suffers and is afraid (4:9-11; 7:1-4) but who nevertheless persists in her defiance (7:8-10), a FUGITIVE Zion who has discursively escaped the obliteration willed for her by her enemies and who will be restored—which is to say, a Zion who has survived. Third, the book of Micah, read in the complex polyphony of its final form, creates and holds a liminal space of FUGITIVITY within which Judah can experience its past, present, and future in YHWH (4:1-4, 6-7; 5:3 [Eng. 4]; 6:8; 7:14-15, 18-20) as a daring though as yet undecidable escape from the violent social and theological logics of exploitation, retribution, and annihilation.

It is urgent that feminist and other emancipatory modes of biblical interpretation be fostered through holistic radical pedagogy in undergraduate, master's-level, and doctoral classrooms, as well as in less formal educational settings. Feminist theorizing of social contexts and texts of antiquity, interrogation of the history of consequences of particular interpretations of biblical texts, and exploration of persuasive readings enlivened by sophisticated understandings of dynamics of gender, race, and power: all these are vital for the flourishing of the bodies and spirits of our students and for the communities in which they offer leadership, collaborative work, and creative vision for the common good. Because commentaries cannot be assigned in their entirety as reading for students, I have constructed pedagogical tools for the commentaries I have written, this Micah volume being the third. For my Joshua commentary (2019b), I have a resource with my "For the Preacher" sidebars, designed to assist those who grapple with theological and ethical issues of that biblical book while still claiming it as sacred Scripture. For my Jer 26–52 commentary (2022a), I have a resource with subversive feminist "hauntings" of Jeremiah texts, designed to invite readers to claim lament, utopian vision, and queer resistance and alliance-building as vital dimensions of prophetic witness. For this Micah commentary, I have created a resource with my KILLJOY and FUGITIVITY comments inspired by Ahmed and Bey, and a resource with this commentary's ecojustice subsections. Any reader who would find these resources helpful should email me (carolyn.sharp@yale.edu); I will gladly share them.

3.4 MICAH AND ECOLOGICAL JUSTICE

The living biospheres and creatures of Earth are under grave threat. Humans, land mammals, reptiles, marine creatures, birds, insects, trees, shrubs, grasses, mosses: all living things are confronting unnaturally rapid and injurious changes to the environments that sustain their life. The ecological networks of relation that create biodiversity for a flourishing planet are failing, and doom approaches. In our present moment, the creation of every new work of art and performance takes place in the crucible of catastrophic climate change. The ecological emergency is the context for every novel and poetry chapbook and biblical commentary, every painting and sculpture and film, every sermon and song created anew for the love of God, the pursuit of truth, or the transformation of community. This is true whether or not the writer, artist, or performer directly addresses the climate crisis in their work. We may take as paradigmatic a powerful comment from the reformer John Calvin:

> When we behold the entire order of nature, we see nothing, high or low, that is not resplendent with God's glory. Yet at the same time, nothing

Introduction

has escaped corruption.... Its corruption is the fruit of our sins. Our own pollution has infected the sky and the earth; and, although God created everything good, there remains nothing which has not been corrupted or cursed. And why is that? Because of us. In the same way that the rising morning fog obscures the air, we have polluted the earth, air, and sky. That is the point that Micah is making here. (2003, 104–5; for more on Calvin, see the Overview of the History of Consequences)

The above is Calvin's response to the prophet's scathing rhetorical question in 2:7 about the ruination of the people: "Are these [Yhwh's] deeds?" Calvin is speaking in theological and ethical terms, of course, as he holds sinners accountable for the punishing consequences they are experiencing from the hand of God. Yet one staggering dimension of human sin, the despoiling of the living community of Earth in countless ways, may be glimpsed in those words from a towering theologian of the preindustrial age. What Laurie Braaten says of Hos 4:1–10 is relevant to the agrarian ethos of Micah as well: "Ecological devastation is a moral issue, grounded primarily in lack of proper religious instruction. A failure to understand the God who created and cares for Earth results in human behavior that destroys creation.... Not living in faithful relationship with God and others is a violation of the moral order with cosmic consequences" (2022, 155).

Every reader in the present day is reading Micah in the context of global ecosystem collapse. There are no exceptions, whether the reader chooses to consider the climate emergency or not. Reception of the book of Micah in these days requires honest assessment of the profound ecological harms caused or exacerbated by the misguided practices of sinful human beings: by industrialization and continual warfare across the globe, by failure adequately to regulate corporate extractions of natural resources, by relentless exploitation and exhaustion of fertile lands in service of agribusiness greed, and by ignorance and heartlessness concerning the sufferings of nonhuman creatures whose habitats are being rendered unlivable by timber clear-cutting, the unchecked sprawl of urbanization and other forms of development, the dumping of toxic waste, and rising sea levels. In his prophetic discourse, Micah calls out the arrogance, greed, and exploitative practices of leaders in ancient Judah and urges that his community protect the vulnerable by doing justice (6:8). Those of us who appreciate the book of Micah as a valuable cultural artifact or who gather around Micah as Scripture must learn wisdom from Micah's thunderous oracles of judgment and magnificent oracles of promise. In this season of ecological catastrophe, wisdom requires naming the harms we have perpetrated against the living community of Earth and against our brothers, sisters, and siblings living in poverty or ecological precarity.

The focus of Micah is on the exploitation of those in his community who experience impaired access to economic resources and political power. The Intergovernmental Panel on Climate Change has repeatedly confirmed the irrefutable point, demonstrated in climate science for decades, that global warming and biodiversity loss exacerbate existing "inequity and poverty," yielding "disproportionate exposure and impacts for most vulnerable groups" (IPCC 2022 §C.3.1), and further, "vulnerable communities who have historically contributed the least to current climate change are disproportionately affected" (IPCC 2023 §A.2). Those who understand our communities to include not just humans but all living creatures will find Micah's prophetic outrage relevant as regards the callous disregard for trees and plants, animals, birds, marine life, and insects as well. As the Intergovernmental Science-Policy Platform on Biodiversity and Ecosystem Services has shown, "The global rate of species extinction is already at least tens to hundreds of times higher than the average rate over the past 10 million years, and is accelerating," and further, "the numbers of threatened species that will go extinct if the drivers that threaten them continue, and the numbers of 'dead species walking' that will die out even without any further habitat deterioration or loss, dwarf the numbers of species already driven extinct by human actions" (IPBES 2020 §2.2.5.2.4a). Readers of Micah should consider the prospect of disastrous ecological decline confronting the western coastal plain of Israel, a bioregion that may have been less than twenty-five miles from the prophet's home, if he lived in Moresheth-Gath: "Mediterranean forests, woodlands, fynbos and scrub . . . harbour an extremely high diversity of species originating from almost all known biogeographic realms of the world. . . . The Mediterranean biome has the second lowest level of land protection among terrestrial biomes . . . and is projected to experience the largest future proportional loss of biodiversity" (IPBES 2020 §2.2.7.4). Wisdom requires that every reader of Micah consider how this ancient prophetic text can illumine the urgency of ecological repentance, reform, and transformative action on behalf of the vulnerable, not only humans but everything that lives in our broader biotic communities.

In the Retrospect section of each chapter of this commentary, I will offer a reflection on Micah's relevance for ecological justice. These reflections claim their rightful place in the history of consequences of Micah's prophetic witness as the Anthropocene era careens toward its end. I honor Micah of Moresheth as a wise guide for contemporary articulation of truths about the scope of human sin in our era of global warming, weather-related disasters, mass

Introduction

extinctions of creatures, and untold human suffering in communities of economically and politically marginalized persons and creaturely suffering in biomes undergoing drastic changes in livability. Though the consequences of our rapacious misuse of lands and waterways cannot be undone, clear-eyed acknowledgement of our injurious sins and renewal of Earth-honoring lifeways remain vitally important. Repentance is still the right path.

Micah 1 signals that the Holy One will be known in a terrifying avalanche of judgment. Communities barely surviving in economic precarity and climate-related threat are already experiencing the devastation to which Micah points. Will we root out the sins that are in the process of creating a postapocalyptic landscape before our very eyes? Reflecting on desert terrain in the southwestern United States, Terry Tempest Williams offers this:

> The paradox found in the peace and restlessness of these desert lands, where rockslides, flash floods, and drought are commonplace, allows us to embrace the hardscrabble truths of change. In the process of being broken open, worn down, and reshaped, an uncommon tranquility can follow. Our undoing is also our becoming. (2020, xi)

If biotic life is to thrive on this planet, it is indisputable that the unbridled human commodification of living beings and their habitats must be broken open and reshaped by an ethos of mutuality. The ringing exhortation of Mic 6:8 can guide us to do ecological justice, to cherish fidelity to the living biospheres and creaturely networks of Earth, and to proceed humbly in our daily living and ethical choices with the Creator of all that is.

4. OVERVIEW OF THE HISTORY OF CONSEQUENCES

The book of Micah is only 105 verses long, but its importance over the centuries, especially for grounding Jewish and Christian ethical considerations and messianic hopes, has been enormous.

4.1 MICAH IN JEWISH TRADITIONS

Micah of Moresheth is mentioned by name in Jer 26, a postexilic text describing a dramatic scene in which Jeremiah is about to be executed on the grounds of sedition for having exhorted "all the cities of Judah that come to worship in the house of the Lord" to repent of their sinful ways and return to torah observance, else Yhwh will destroy the temple and make Jerusalem "a curse for all the nations of the earth" (26:2-6). In Jeremiah's defense, the example of Micah is cited as a powerful prophetic precedent: Micah spoke an oracle of judgment against Jerusalem (Mic 3:12 is quoted) that, far from constituting sedition, caused Hezekiah to repent and saved the city from the siege warfare being waged by the Assyrian army under the command of Sennacherib in 701. This incident is neither recorded nor hinted at in the book of Micah, which contains no prose narratives.

John Smith notes that Micah does not address his oracles directly to Hezekiah or any other king: "Micah seems to have denounced the nobles and councillors of the king rather than the king himself" (26). Sennacherib's assault on Judah, Hezekiah's donning of sackcloth and dispatching of intermediaries to consult the prophet Isaiah, and Hezekiah's plea to Yhwh during the crisis are recounted in exquisite detail in Isa 36-37 (// 2 Kgs 18:13-19:37), but there is no Isaianic oracle in that narrative that Jerusalem will be destroyed; rather, Isaiah assures the delegation from Hezekiah that all will be well and relays an oracle of judgment against Assyria, after which an avenging angel of Yhwh strikes down 185,000 Assyrian soldiers. The reference to Micah of Moresheth in Jer 26, while not congruent with the traditions in Isaiah and 2 Kings just discussed, nevertheless conveys something of Micah's authority and renown as a prophet and the weight that the oracle in Mic 3:12 carried in postexilic tradition.

The Book of the Twelve is mentioned as early as the work of Jesus ben Sira, a second-century BCE book known as Sirach or Ecclesiasticus. In a lyrical review of heroic ancestors in Israelite and Judean history (Sir 44:1-50:29), Ben Sira writes, "May the bones of the Twelve Prophets send forth new life from where they lie, for they comforted the people of Jacob and delivered them with confident hope" (49:10). Though this reference to the Twelve is elliptical (see Ueberschaer 2020, 353-54), it is taken by many scholars as a signal that the books of the Minor Prophets were already being considered together as a single united work. In 1 Maccabees, dated to the late second century or early first century BCE, are unmistakable echoes of the visions of peace articulated in Mic 4:4 and Zech 8:4. Lauding the high priesthood and governorship of Simon Maccabeus, the author of 1 Maccabees writes, "The land had rest all the days of Simon. He sought the good of his nation. . . . They tilled their land in peace; the ground gave its increase, and the trees of the plains their fruit. Old men sat in the streets; they all talked together of good things. . . . All the people sat under their own vines

Introduction

and fig trees, and there was none to make them afraid" (1 Macc 14:4, 8-9, 12; Ueberschaer 2020, 374-77).

Micah is treated briefly in the Vitae Prophetarum, a work composed at the beginning of the Common Era that provides biographical sketches of twenty-three prophets, including the twelve Minor Prophets. His Ephraimite tribal identity is noted, because the ancient scribe has conflated him with Micaiah ben Imlah, a prophet in 1 Kgs 22 who prophesies during the reign of Ahab of Israel, more than a century earlier than the time of Micah of Moresheth. Anna Maria Schwemer argues that the conflation was not from ignorance but purposeful, amplifying the prophetic persona of Micah/Micaiah because of two correspondences: the striking on the cheek in 1 Kgs 22:24 and Mic 4:14 (Eng. 5:1), and "Hear, you peoples, all of you!" in 1 Kgs 22:28b and the similar prophetic apostrophe in Mic 1:2 (Schwemer 2020, 420). The Vitae Prophetarum account of the death of Micah/Micaiah fits with the timeline of Micaiah, though Micaiah's death is not narrated in the Hebrew Bible. Ahab's son Jehoram throws the prophet off a cliff "because he rebuked him for the impieties of his fathers," and the prophet's body is buried in Moresheth, in a grave near "the cemetery of the Enakim" (420-21). Schwemer observes that Sirach and the Vitae Prophetarum "have in common an interest in the graves of the prophets and in the hope of eschatological resurrection" (2020, 437).

In the mishnaic and talmudic tractate Makkot, a number of biblical texts are expounded in the teaching of R. Simlai as distillations of the 613 torah commandments (*miṣwôt*), 365 prohibitions and 248 positive directives, parsed as 611 *miṣwôt* received by Moses on Sinai plus the first two commandments of the Decalogue spoken directly from the mouth of God (b. Mak. 23b-24a). Several prophetic figures guide believers into deeper understanding of the 613 *miṣwôt* in a series of increasingly concentrated foci, moving from eleven to six to three to two to one (b. Mak. 24a). In Ps 15, David describes eleven attributes that will help ensure the believer's admittance to the world to come. Isaiah 33:15 elucidates six character attributes of the righteous. Micah 6:8 establishes the 613 *miṣwôt* upon three attributes: doing justice, performing acts of *ḥesed*, and walking humbly with God. Isaiah 56:1 is cited as grounding torah obedience in two mandates ("maintain justice and do what is right"). Next comes Amos 5:4, in which Yhwh commands one thing: "Seek me and live." Last in this catena of distillations of the essence of torah obedience is Hab 2:4 with one mandate: "the righteous live by their faith."

In the Babylonian Talmud tractate Sukkah 49b, R. Elazar explains the third mandate of Mic 6:8, to proceed humbly with God, as follows: "This is referring to taking the indigent dead out for burial and accompanying a poor bride to her wedding canopy, both of which must be performed without fanfare." An elaboration follows from the Gemara: funerals and weddings normally are public affairs, thus "to proceed humbly" means to conduct such business privately, just as making charitable donations and studying torah are activities best done in private.

Clay Alan Ham notes that the talmudic tractate b. Soṭah 49b "alludes to Mic. 7.6 in its explanation of the increase in evil and degradation during the war with Vespasian," citing Micah also on the motif of intrahousehold conflict or betrayal in Jub. 23:16–19 and 1 En. 56:7 (2019, 48).

The targum to the Minor Prophets, a subdivision of Targum Jonathan, is a paraphrastic Aramaic rendering of the Book of the Twelve leavened with numerous intratextual amplifications. According to Kevin Cathcart, the targum to the Minor Prophets likely originated in literary form in Palestine in the period after 70 CE, seems to have been redacted in Babylonia, and was being cited as "an already established tradition of interpretation" no later than the fourth century (Tg. Mic, 1, 12–18). Because the readings are so closely tied to the Hebrew text of Micah, I treat illustrative examples of targumic commentary in the commentary section of each chapter of Micah, rather than seeking to summarize them here.

4.1.1 Midrashic Interpretations

In the Midrash Rabbah are several dozen references to Micah passages embedded in rabbinic reflections on other focal biblical texts. These compendia of rabbinic reflections on the books of the Torah and the Five Scrolls achieved their final forms over centuries of composition and redaction. Per David Gottlieb, the earliest, Genesis Rabbah, was shaped in the late fourth to early fifth century CE. He gives dates of the others as follows. Exodus Rabbah "appears to combine a 10th-century text in chs. 1–14 with earlier midrashim in chs. 15–52"; Leviticus Rabbah, late fifth to early sixth century; Numbers Rabbah "attained its final form in southern France sometime after the 11th century"; Deuteronomy Rabbah "occurs in different versions, dating variously to the 4th and 8th century"; Song of Songs Rabbah, late sixth to early seventh century; Ruth Rabbah, about 500 CE; Lamentations Rabbah, late fifth to early sixth century; Qohelet Rabbah, eighth century; finally, Esther Rabbah is "a composite text" from the fifth and eleventh centuries (2021, 42–43). Rabbinic midrashic work with Micah articulates and accomplishes many things in the larger project of seeking to illuminate the

Introduction

ways of God with the covenant people and their antagonists, remembering a sacred past and exploring its possibilities so as to live faithfully in their present moment and, further, imagine consolations and joys to come in the eschatological future. Gottlieb suggests the exegetical and homiletical dimensions of midrashic interpretation "link the reader of these works to the ancestral and covenantal narratives through which Jewish peoplehood is established and renewed" (2021, 44). Womanist interpreter Wilda Gafney observes,

> Traditional midrash is . . . mystical, imaginative, revelatory, and, above all, religious. Midrash interprets not only the text before the reader, but also the text behind and beyond the text and the text between the lines of the text. In rabbinic thinking, each letter and the spaces between the letters are available for interpretive work. Midrash is rarely comprehensive and occasionally contradictory, raising as many questions as it answers. (2017, 4–5)

Tamar Kadari offers, "The midrashic enterprise encompasses a surprising range of forms: delicately close readings alongside wildly imaginative renderings; legends that ascend the most sublime heights of religious thought, alongside comic descriptions; and more," exemplifying a "polysemic multiplicity" that many scholars of rabbinic literature have deemed meaningful for communities of Jewish hermeneutical praxis (2022, xix, xxiii; Fraade 2007).

We enter into the stream of midrashic observations that utilize Micah via a focal text in the book of Ecclesiastes. Qohelet's lament that all things are wearisome is applied to "words of heresy," offered with reference to the regret of R. Eliezer for having commended an argument presented by a *min* (heretic) who had cited Mic **1:7**. For failing to ignore or repudiate the heretic, Eliezer had been arrested as a heretic himself (*Eccl. Rab.* 1.8.3 to Eccl 1:8; 26–28). Of the threat in Mic **1:15** about YHWH unleashing punishment upon Adullam, rabbinic commentary suggests that this was in response to the sin of the patriarch Judah, who had settled near Hirah the Adullamite and later sinned against Tamar, daughter of a nearby family (*Gen. Rab.* 85.1 to Gen 38:1; 2:787).

Rabbi Abba b. Kahana applies the image in Mic **2:1** of evildoers plotting by night upon their beds to the ten tribes of the Northern Kingdom of Israel during the divided monarchy (see 1 Kgs 12:1–20), prompting mention of the grievous sin of Judah and Benjamin by R. Berekiah and the abhor-

Overview of the History of Consequences

rent practices of (gentile) dwellers in coastal cities by R. Huna. The three malfeasant constituencies are observed to have been more sinful than antediluvian humanity and the citizenry of Sodom (*Gen. Rab.* 28.5 to Gen 6:7; 1:226–27). Rabbi Berekiah makes a similar claim in the name of R. Eleazar: the ten tribes were more sinful than the generation of the flood because the latter sinned all day long (a literal understanding of the closing adverbial clause in Gen 6:5), whereas the ten tribes sinned both at night and in the morning, per Mic **2:1** (*Song Rab.* 1.4.3 to Song 1:4; 44). The bitter wailing forecast in Mic **2:4** is framed as a response to the despised Persian ruler Ahasuerus carousing while Jerusalem's temple lay in ruins (*Esth. Rab.* 1.10 to Esth 1:2; 25–26). Illustrating that the words of the teachers of Jewish oral tradition are more beloved—that is, observed with more care—than the "words of the Torah and the prophets," Rabbi Ḥanina son of R. Adda offers in the name of R. Tanḥum b. Aḥa that Micah had been rudely forbidden to preach, per Mic **2:6**; Maurice Simon says the implication is "that prophecy can be interrupted, but not so the teaching of the Sages" (*Song Rab.* 1.2 to Song 1:2; 32).

Rabbi Judah b. Ila'i uses Mic **2:8** to amplify the divine words to Moses on Sinai about the people having been "quick to turn aside from the way that I commanded them" when they fashioned the golden calf (Exod 32:1–8). In the Micah verse, the rabbi takes "my people" (*'ammî*) as the subject of *yəqômēm*, saying that the people's fervent declaration of obedience to Yhwh (Exod 24:7, "All that the Lord has spoken we will do") had "since yesterday" (*'ethmûl*) turned to an idolatrous asseveration about the golden calf (*Exod. Rab.* 42.7 to Exod 32:8; 489). In an exposition of harms that befell Israel for its failure to heed the covenant with Yhwh, the forced migration depicted in Mic **2:9** is adduced: having neither hearkened to the commandments nor performed them faithfully, "the ten tribes," all but Judah and Benjamin, were carried into diaspora by the Assyrians, and displaced captives from other conquered nations were settled in their place (2 Kgs 17:1–24). The casting out of women and children described in Mic **2:9** is explicated as follows: married women were sexually violated by other Israelite men, such that their husbands divorced them; per Deut 23:3 (Eng. 2), the children produced by rape were to be excluded from the worshipping assembly, thus the glory of God was taken away from them. The command to depart, then, in Mic **2:10** is tied in this same midrashic discussion to the Israelites' having engaged in adultery: "For other sins," God says to Israel, divine forbearance had been on offer, "but seeing that you have stretched forth your hand to commit adultery" and thus to "defile the inheritance" of Jacob, the ten tribes'

Introduction

"doom was sealed" and they were banished from the land (*Num. Rab.* 9.7 to Num 5:12; 1:243-46).

In Mic **2:13**, the image of the "one who breaks out/breaks through" (*happōrēṣ*) and goes before the people is important for rabbinic interpreters, who refer to this verse at least a dozen times in midrashic commentary, more often than any other verse in Micah. In one instance, the image is woven into a sequence of references in which divine promises should be understood to be fulfilled in a threefold sense: "in the wilderness," "in the Land," and "in the Messianic future." That is, each biblical reference is considered to be meaningful first in a sense appropriate to the wilderness wandering of Israel under Moses's leadership; then in a sense appropriate to Israel's and Judah's communal life in Canaan territories allotted to Israel, per Deuteronomistic historiography, once Joshua and the Israelite army had annihilated or dispossessed the Canaanite indigenous inhabitants; and finally in a sense appropriate to the eschatological future of Israel. Rabbi Ḥiyya offers that as a divine reward offered to Abraham for having "stood by" the angelic beings as they refreshed themselves at the oaks of Mamre (Gen 18:8), Yhwh accompanied Israel through the wilderness (in the pillar of cloud by day and fire by night, per Exod 13:21), has stood in "the congregation of God" (*baʿădat-ʾēl*, Ps 82:1) during Israel's time in the land, and will go before the covenant people in the messianic future (alluding to Mic 2:13; *Gen. Rab.* 48.10 to Gen 18:8; 1:411-12). Yhwh's leadership as *happōrēṣ* features also in a midrashic reference to the dividing of the Red Sea as the Israelites fled their Egyptian captors (*Gen. Rab.* 69.5 to Gen 28:14; 2:632-33).

This image of Yhwh as *happōrēṣ* in Mic **2:13** is used by R. Levi in an exquisite catena of reflections on Israel's betrothal to Yhwh, organized by linkages drawn between the Song of Moses at the Red Sea and Song of Songs 4 (*Exod. Rab.* 23.5 to Exod 15:1; 283). The betrothal of Israel and God is explored further in a dialogue between R. Ḥanina and R. Simon: Israel gave God thirteen gifts in the offering detailed in Exod 25:3-7; God reciprocated with thirteen gifts as described in Ezek 16:10-13; other paired correspondences include the golden diadem fashioned for the head of Aaron (Exod 39:30) and the divine Shekinah at Israel's head, per Mic **2:13** (*Song Rab.* 4.12.2 to Song 4:13; 220-22).

Of Jacob's growth in economic resources through strategic animal husbandry while in the service of Laban, R. Simeon b. Abba plays twice on the verb *prṣ* in his comment that "an opening . . . was broken through . . . for [Jacob] of the nature of the World to Come" (*Gen. Rab.* 73.11 to Gen 30:43 and *Gen. Rab.* 96 [MSV] to Gen 47:29; 2:675, 923; also *Eccl. Rab.* 9.11.1 to Eccl 9:11; 244).

When Tamar gives birth to twins Perez and Zerah, her observation that the firstborn has made a breach for himself is interpreted in midrashic commentary as Tamar prophesying that the Messiah—*happōrēṣ*—will come from the lineage of Perez (*Gen. Rab.* 85.14 to Gen 38:29; 2:799). Micah **2:13** comes up in a reflection about the "tears of the oppressed" (Eccl 4:1), a metonym taken by Daniel the Tailor to represent illegitimate children unfairly excluded from the worshipping assembly per torah mandate (Deut 23:3). That these "exiles" are seen by God as golden and will be comforted in the world to come is prophesied in the vision of Zech 4:2, where the bowl (*gullâ*) atop a golden lampstand suggests either that the Shekinah—the divine presence—accompanied the oppressed into diaspora or that the divine Redeemer as *happōrēṣ* will bring them out (*Lev. Rab.* 32.8 to Lev 24:10; 416-17; also *Eccl. Rab.* 4.1 to Eccl 4:1; 111-12). In a rich discussion of the deployment of tribal encampments during the wilderness wandering, rabbinic expositors point to Mic **2:13** for Judah's preeminence as the tribe from which the king—implicitly, David and the Davidic monarchy—had arisen (*Num. Rab.* 2.10 to Num 2:3; 1:36).

Reflecting on Daughter Zion's suffering, rabbinic commentators craft a sequence in which Israel's and Judah's sins correspond to the kind of distress suffered in their divinely ordained punishment and, later, the sort of consolation Israel experiences. "They sinned with 'head,' were punished with it and comforted with it," the midrash says, in the first example of metonymic body parts (ear, eye, nose, mouth, tongue, heart, hand, foot) standing for sin, punishment, and consolation. The midrash observes that Israel had sinned in the wilderness by asking for a "head"—a new leader (Num 14:4)—so Israel's "head" was punished (quoting Isa 1:5, "the whole head is sick"). Micah **2:13** is then deployed for its image, interpreted as consolation, that the people will be comforted by being led out of diaspora with Yhwh at their head (*Lam. Rab.* 1.57 to Lam 1:22; 146-47).

Midrashic commentary on sinners unconcerned about divinely appointed punishment begins with Amos 6:1—"Alas for those who are at ease in Zion!"—and reviews other incautious sinners who lacked apprehension about looming catastrophe. In their ranks are found Judah and Benjamin, the ten other tribes, idolaters, and the corrupt Judean officials, priests, and prophets ventriloquized in Mic **3:11** (*Num. Rab.* 10.3 to Num 6:2; 1:350).

The portrayal in Mic **3:12** of Zion being "plowed as a field" is adduced by R. Joshua of Siknin to illumine the cause of the disagreement between Cain and Abel. The rabbi offers that the brothers were arguing over on whose land the temple should be built: the fatal dispute arising "when they were in the field" (Gen 4:8) signifies, when refracted through Mic **3:12** with its

Introduction

simile of a field, that they were, in fact, in the Jerusalem temple (*Gen. Rab.* 22.7 to Gen 4:8; 1:187). "Field" as signifying the temple is revisited via rabbinic interpretation of the poetic utterance of Isaac when, visually impaired and relying on scent, he recognizes "Esau" (Jacob in disguise) and says, "The smell of my son is like the smell of a field that the Lord has blessed." There, Mic **3:12** is adduced in the midrashic explanation, "the Holy One ... showed him [Isaac] the Temple built, destroyed, and rebuilt": the Micah verse speaks to the temple's destruction, and the divine blessing in Isaac's speech "hints at it being rebuilt and perfected in the Messianic future" (*Gen. Rab.* 65.23 to Gen 27:27; 2:600).

The plowed "field," Zion, is cited as seat of the sovereignty of the Holy One in a rabbinic comment on Eccl 5:9 (*Lev. Rab.* 22.2 to Lev 17:3; 278; also *Eccl. Rab.* 5.8f.3 to Eccl 5:9; 139). A halakic mandate to put outside the camp those deemed ritually impure due to a skin condition, discharge, or contact with a corpse is read in a moral register, taken to concern the exile of Israelites who have committed the transgression of idolatry, sexual immorality, bloodshed, or "neglect of the septennial rest of the land" (see Exod 23:10–11; Lev 25:2–12). In this discussion, the razing of Zion per Mic **3:12** is adduced as divine retribution for those transgressions (*Num. Rab.* 7.10 to Num 5:2; 1:198). Midrashic reflection on the "oracle concerning the valley of vision" in Isa 22 offers as context for the divine call to weeping in 22:12 the "destruction of the first and second Temples," citing Mic **3:12** (*Lam. Rab.* Proem 24; 39–40).

Among midrashim on the inauguration of the Passover festival is a citation of Mic **4:5** concerning the nations following other gods. The Micah verse, linked with Isa 2:5–21, spurs a reflection on the eschatological future: "In the Time to Come when all the idolaters will bring their idols to save them ... God will dissolve the idols, and they shall behold and be ashamed of them and cast them away and go and hide themselves in caves and among the rocks" (*Exod. Rab.* 15.15 to Exod 12:1; 179).

In a reflection on the second set of stone tablets Moses hews for inscription of the Ten Commandments, the oracle in Mic **4:6** promising restoration of Israel—identified by Yhwh as "those whom I had harmed"—is cited in a midrashic dramatization of Israel pleading for divine mercy. The covenant people protests that though they do sin, none other than their Creator had placed the "evil inclination" within humankind. God acknowledges this originary act of divine affliction as the harm mentioned in Mic **4:6** and promises to remove humans' propensity for sin "in the Time to Come" (*Exod. Rab.* 46.4 to Exod 34:1; 532). In Byzantine-era midrashic traditions known as the Tanḥuma-Yelammedenu literature, the point that God created the

Overview of the History of Consequences

"evil inclination" (*yetzer hara*) in humankind is used by R. Hama bar Hanina to defend Israel from divine judgment: he links humanity's "evil inclination" to Israel's disobedience that had been punished per Mic **4:6**, reading the verse as an expression of Yhwh's regret for having afflicted the people (Weiss 2022, 262-65). In a later reflection on that teaching by an anonymous Tanḥuma-Yelammedenu sage, Jer 18 is deployed in a dialogue in which Israel avers that it is the potter's responsibility when a flawed vessel is fashioned; Yhwh's response in Mic 4:6 is interpreted as the divine intention to remove the "evil inclination" from humankind (Weiss, 265-67).

A teaching of R. 'Azariah in the name of R. Judah b. Simeon frames the identity of the "judge of Israel" being struck per Mic **4:14** with reference to the commissioning of the prophets Isaiah, Amos, Micah himself, the seventy elders who receive the spirit of prophecy in Num 11:24-25, and Elisha (*Lev. Rab.* 10.2 to Lev 8:1-4; 122). Another midrash links the tears on the cheeks of Daughter Zion with Jerusalem's lamenting "on account of her judges," citing the judge being struck on the cheek per Mic **4:14**; this is presumably an example of the Babylonians' violence against judicial leaders in Jerusalem, a line of thinking made clearer in a subsequent example of Babylonian invaders binding Judean men (*Lam. Rab.* 1.25 to Lam 1:2; 95-96).

Micah **5:2** (Eng. 3) is adduced in reflection on the delay in Israel's deliverance from, as one sage puts it, "the exile in which we are at present living and in which we are defiled with iniquities." The circumstance is deemed analogous to four things: a grain harvest, since premature reaping yields useless produce; a grape harvest, since early grapes make for sour wine and poor vinegar; to spices gathered when they are not yet dry, because their aroma will be compromised; and to a woman in childbirth, who must labor at the appropriate time if the child is to live. On that last simile, Mic **5:2** (Eng. 3) is brought in to support the point (*Song Rab.* 8.14.1 to Song 8:14; 324-27).

The image in Lam 1:13 of Yhwh having spread a net to entangle Zion's feet spurs a midrashic reverie on circumstances in which one might look for "the feet of the Messiah": R. Abba b. Kahana says when Judah has "benches filled with Babylonians," that is, captive Babylonian troops; R. Simeon b. Yoḥai suggests when "a Persian horse [is] tethered in Eretz Israel," envisioning Persia's defeat of the Neo-Babylonian Empire and quoting Mic **5:4** (Eng. 5) to demonstrate, "this shall be peace" (*Lam. Rab.* 1.41 to Lam 1:13; 121-22). In that teaching and another midrash, we see "Assyria" in Mic **5:4** interpreted as a reference to Persia; Maurice Simon observes that "Assyria" is "a name frequently given by the Rabbis to the Persians" (*Esth. Rab.* 1.18 to Esth 1:3; 31n7). A spirited rabbinic discussion of Ps 60:9-10 (Eng. 7-8) has

Introduction

one stream of tradition taking the seven named regions there as pointing to the "three kings and four commoners" who "have no share in the World to Come": the rulers Jeroboam, Ahab, and Manasseh, plus Balaam son of Beor, Doeg the Edomite, David's disloyal adviser Ahithophel, and Elisha's duplicitous servant Gehazi. Another line of thinking argues for seven or eight saviors based on Mic **5:4** (Eng. 5), though that position is declined in favor of four saviors per other prooftexts (*Num. Rab.* 14.1 to Num 7:48; 2:556–58). Elsewhere in the midrash, the seven shepherds of Mic **5:4** are identified as Adam, Seth, Methuselah, David, Abraham, Jacob, and Moses; the eight princes are "Jesse, Saul, Samuel, Amos, Zephaniah, Hezekiah," or in other sources Zedekiah, "Elijah, and the Messiah" (*Song Rab.* 8.9.3 to Song 8:9; 317; cf. Stavsky 2009, 39).

The rabbis attributed to divine inspiration via King Solomon an elaboration of benefits for Israel that correspond to fulfillment of the blessing Isaac had spoken over Jacob. Where Isaac had said, "May God give you of the dew of heaven" (Gen 27:28), Mic **5:6**, with its imagery of the "remnant of Jacob" being "like dew from Yhwh," is deployed as confirmation of that detail of the blessing (*Gen. Rab.* 75.8 to Gen 32:3; 2:693). This image of dew also comes up in a captivating midrashic sequence about how God can cause deadly or beneficial things to rain down from heaven: fire and brimstone upon the people of Sodom (Gen 19:24); dew upon the remnant of Jacob (Mic **5:6**); manna for the Israelites wandering in the wilderness (Exod 16:4; Ps 78:24–25); plagues upon the Egyptians (Exod 7–12); huge stones upon Amorite troops (Josh 10:11); celestial opposition in battle against Sisera and other Canaanite adversaries (Judg 5:20); and actual rain for agricultural abundance and other blessings for God's people (Deut 28:12; *Exod. Rab.* 25.1 to Exod 16:4; 301). In midrashic commentary on Leviticus, there is a lively rabbinic debate concerning the deeper significance of *wayyəhî* and *wəhāyâ* verbal forms in texts throughout the Hebrew Bible. Simeon b. R. Abba musters the Mic **5:6** promise that the remnant of Jacob will be (*wəhāyâ*) like dew from Yhwh in a list of five citations that, he argues, indicate occasions for unparalleled rejoicing (*Lev. Rab.* 11.7 to Lev 9:1; 149; also *Esth. Rab.* Proem 11; 16). The image in Mic **5:7** of Israel as a lion is focalized in a rabbinic comment about the Jews slaughtering the Persians in the story of Esther: Israel was "mighty like a lion attacking a flock of sheep and smiting without let or hindrance, there being none to deliver" (*Esth. Rab.* 10.11 to Esth 9:2; 120). In a Tanḥuma Buber teaching on the theme of God having offered the torah to the nations, Mic **5:14** is mustered in an explication of ways in which the nations have not been obedient (Ottenheijm 2022, 277, 284): they have neither heeded the torah nor upheld the seven Noahide laws by which all humanity is bound, those comprising prohibitions on idolatry, cursing God, murder, eating flesh from a still-living creature, sexual immorality, and stealing, plus the constructive obligation to establish courts of justice.

On Joseph's brothers derisively dismissing Joseph's prophetic dream about having dominion over them, the divine lawsuit introduced in Mic **6:1** is cited to show that the prophets rebuke malfeasant persons who seek to thwart God's purposes (*Gen. Rab.* 84.10 to Gen 37:5–6; 2:776). Micah **6:2** features in at least eight midrashim. One teaching imagines an anxious query from the Israelites just before they seek to escape Egyptian enslavement. The people ask where God is, and Moses calms them with Song 2:8, "Look, he comes, leaping upon the mountains." Rabbi Judah explains that while God would not redeem that sinful generation of Israelites on their own merits, divine mercy would nevertheless be forthcoming for the sake of the ancestors, figured as "mountains" in Mic **6:2** (*Exod. Rab.* 15.4 to Exod 12:1; 163). These mountains recur as symbol of the patriarchs in a midrashic analogy about a royal builder frustrated by suboptimal conditions. Similarly, God was unable to found the world due to the pressure of primordial waters—representing human wickedness—until "the patriarchs came and showed themselves righteous," whereupon the deity could say, "On these I will establish my world," the patriarch "mountains" understood, then, as the pillars of the earth belonging to Yhwh, per 1 Sam 2:8 (*Exod. Rab.* 15.7 to Exod 12:2; 168). Further on the mountains as signifying the patriarchs, Mic **6:2** is adduced in a rumination on the splendor of God's sovereignty. While "no evil can touch the throne of God," Israel and Judah did sin and their rulers declined in power; through those centuries, the patriarchs (the "mountains" in Ps 72:3 read via Mic **6:2**) offered prayers of intercession, until the blinding of Zedekiah and the destruction of the temple by the Neo-Babylonian Empire, after which Yhwh began praying for the covenant people (per Num 6:26; *Exod. Rab.* 15.26 to Exod 12:2; 197–98). The intercessory benefits of the patriarchs as "mountains" per Mic **6:2** are imagined in a beautiful midrash on Moses being called to meet God atop Mount Sinai: Moses "went up in a cloud and descended in a cloud," and "the merits of the fathers ascended and descended with him" (*Exod. Rab.* 28.2 to Exod 19:3; 332).

The covenant lawsuit in Mic **6:2–3** is cited in midrashic commentary as one of three occasions on which Yhwh has sought "a settlement of accounts" with Israel. In each instance, tied to the verb *ykḥ* in Isa 1:18 and the noun *rîb* in Mic **6:2** and Hos 12:3, adversarial nations gleefully anticipate Israel's punishment; the nations are disappointed when Yhwh does not

Introduction

"exterminate [Israel] from the world" but instead turns divine rebuke into favor (*Lev. Rab.* 27.6 to Lev 22:27; 349–51; also *Num. Rab.* 10.1 to Num 6:2; 1:333; *Song Rab.* 5.16.2 to Song 5:16; 251–52). Of Yhwh's rhetorical question in Mic **6:3**, "How have I wearied you?," and the deity having dispatched Moses, Aaron, and Miriam per **6:4**, R. Berekiah offers that far from those three leaders having depleted the Israelites' food and water or troubling them in some other way, in fact Israel received manna for the sake of Moses (Exod 16:1–18), the well of fresh water for the sake of Miriam, and clouds of glory for the sake of Aaron (*Num. Rab.* 1.2 to Num 1:1; 1:4–5; also *Num. Rab.*13.20 to Num 7:45; 2:553). As regards Miriam and Aaron, the death of the ancestor followed immediately by notice of a misfortune serves to ground the rabbinic logic that the merits of the ancestor, while living, had secured the benefit. A miraculously mobile well of inexhaustible fresh water is linked to Miriam because notice of her death in Num 20:1 is followed in 20:2 by the mention of a lack of water for the Israelites, and shortly thereafter, the reader encounters the enigmatic Song of the Well in Num 21:17–18. (Further on Miriam's well in Jewish traditions, see Baskin 2021.) Similarly, the cloud of the divine presence is first noticed when Aaron is speaking to the Israelites (Exod 16:10), and immediately after Aaron's death, Israel is attacked by Canaanites, suggesting that the protective cloud was no longer present (Num 20:28–21:1). Further on divine forbearance per Mic **6:3**, R. Isaac underlines the solicitude of the Holy One in that God allowed the Israelites to fulfill their obligation to recite the Shema (Deut 6:7) conveniently while they were sitting, walking, lying down, or rising (*Lev. Rab.* 27.6 to Lev 22:27; 350–51). Another midrash illustrates the Holy One's generosity by underscoring that God could have required Israel to bring "burnt-offerings from the beasts that are in the mountains" rather than the domesticated livestock that were ready to hand (*Num. Rab.* 20.5 to Num 22:5; 2:790).

The reference in Mic **6:4** to Yhwh having sent Moses, Aaron, and Miriam to guide the people is interpreted through Ps 43:3, where the psalmist asks that God send out God's "light and truth" to lead the believer. "This"—the paired noun sequence—"refers to Moses and Aaron," per the midrash, but Moses balked at leading the people (Exod 3:11), so God was compelled to descend and guide them (*Exod. Rab.* 15.14 to Exod 12:2; 177). Rabbi Simeon b. Yoḥai teaches that the name of Yhwh is magnified in the world whenever the deity "executes justice on the wicked," and that in Mic **6:5**, understanding the righteous acts of Yhwh means recognizing divine retributive justice (*Lev. Rab.* 24.1 to Lev 19:2; 304). As regards the mention of Balaam in Mic **6:5**: R. Abba b. Kahana offers, with searing derision, that the Mesopotamian seer

Overview of the History of Consequences

was "one of three persons whom the Holy One . . . examined and found to be a vessel full of urine": Cain because he lied to the Sovereign of the Universe when questioned on the whereabouts of Abel (Gen 4:9); Hezekiah because he boasted to Isaiah, "a prophet of the Omnipresent," about having shown his treasury to Babylonian envoys (Isa 39:1-7 // 2 Kgs 20:12-18); and Balaam because he answered the Sovereign of the Universe without due respect (*Num. Rab.* 20.6 to Num 22:2; 2:791-92). The image in Lam 1:10 of enemies stretching out their hands over the precious things in Jerusalem's treasuries yields an imagined moment when Ammonites and Moabites "ran to plunder" not silver and gold but "the Torah for the purpose of expunging" the ban on their membership in the assembly of Yhwh (Deut 23:4). In this context, the Moabite ruler Balak in Mic **6:5** comes into view: the rabbis consider ways in which Abraham's care for Lot had been repaid with harm by Lot's descendants, and one of those was the scheming of Balak to have Balaam curse Israel (*Lam. Rab.* 1.38 to Lam 1:10; 115).

Rabbi Joshua of Siknin hears the rhetorical question of Mic **6:6**, "Should I give my firstborn for my transgression?," as referring to Abraham's near-sacrifice of Isaac (*Gen Rab.* 55:5 to Gen 22:1; 1:485). To proceed humbly with God per Mic **6:8** is linked, in a midrash translating the adverbial infinitive *haṣnēaʿ* as "modestly," to God speaking with Moses in the tent of meeting rather than in a more public setting (*Num. Rab.* 1.3 to Num 1:1; 1:7). In a mapping of ten journeys made by the divine Shekinah as envisioned by Ezekiel, Mic **6:9** is cited: Yhwh calling to the city is framed within a trajectory of the Shekinah proceeding from the temple's east gate to the court to the roof, thence to the altar to the wall of the city (this is per Mic 6:9), and onward to the Mount of Olives, where, according to R. Jonathan, the Shekinah waited in vain for three and a half years for Israel to repent (*Lam. Rab.* Proem 25; 50-51). The polemic in Mic **6:11** against deceit in economic dealings appears in a midrashic reflection on the woes that inevitably follow when "the words of the Torah [are] despised" by the "common people," by sages "versed in the Torah," by judges, and, per R. Berekiah teaching in the name of R. Abba, by an entire generation given to unrighteousness (*Ruth Rab.* 1.2 to Ruth 1:1; 16-18).

A blighted vineyard is in view in a midrashic dialogue that considers enemy nations and Israel's sinfulness as metaphorized in Isaiah's Song of the Vineyard (Isa 5:1-10). Rabbi Judan cites Mic **7:1**, "there is no cluster of grapes to eat," to demonstrate that Israel's sin has blighted its heritage. Rabbi Berekiah adds that the agents of destruction are "the four kingdoms," likely to be understood via Dan 7:1-27. Maurice Simon's annotation offers that

Introduction

for rabbinic commentators, the empires are Babylon, Persia, Greece, and Rome; contemporary scholars might read the Daniel passage as pointing to Babylonia, Media, Persia, and Greece. That Israel's "vineyard" has not yet borne fruit is due to the lack of any righteous person, as per Mic 7:2, except Noah, Daniel, and Job (cf. Ezek 14:14, 20; *Song Rab.* 2.15.2 to Song 2:15; 137-38, and 137n7).

The lament in Mic 7:2 that no pious or righteous person remains is quoted in a richly layered exposition of debate in the heavens about God's "harsh decree" barring Moses from the land of Canaan. Moses's persuasiveness as intercessor is emphasized: "His prayer was like a sword which tears and cuts its way through everything, and spares nothing," so when Moses objects to his exclusion from Canaan and begins to pray that the decree be reversed, an anxious God commands the angels, "Descend quickly; bolt all the gates of every heaven, because the voice of prayer threatens to force its way to heaven" (*Deut. Rab.* 11.10 to Deut 31:14; 180-82). This midrash goes on to portray the incomparable holiness and brilliance of Moses through reflection on his miraculous attributes, as told by Moses himself: he could converse on the day he was born; he prophesied at three months of age; as leader of Israel he not only performed the miracles narrated in Exodus, Numbers, and Deuteronomy, but also "ascended heaven . . . and engaged in battle with the angels, and received the law of fire, and sojourned under [God's] Throne of fire, and took shelter under the pillar of fire, and spoke with God face to face." Confronted by the wicked angel Sammael, Moses beats him with the staff engraved "with the Ineffable Name," removes his glory, and blinds him. As God and three angels descend to take Moses's soul to heaven, the soul begs to remain in Moses's pure body; as Moses finally dies, the lament of Mic 7:2 is quoted with none other than the heavens weeping as this godly man perishes (*Deut. Rab.* 11.10 to Deut 31:14; 181-87).

A spirited discussion of identities of potential foes per Mic 7:6, "the enemies of a man are those of his own household," reviews candidates as disparate as a disloyal wife who has her husband executed by a political official, a venomous snake, "the Tempter" active throughout a believer's life, and "insects, vermin, and flies" that take up residence in the home (*Gen. Rab.* 54.1 to Gen 21:22; 1:475-76). Midrashic commentary cites the discord portrayed in Mic 7:6 as a sign of the intractable conflict and pervasive oppression that will be characteristic of the unrighteous age just before the Messiah appears. "The wise men of the generation will die and the rest will waste away with grief and sorrow and much trouble will come upon the community and cruel decrees will be promulgated," the rabbis teach, and, from R. Nehorai citing the Micah verse, "the young will insult their elders." Rabbi Nehemiah adds, "there will be great poverty and scarcity ... the whole of the government will be converted to *minuth* ['heresy'] and there will be no reproof," and per R. Jannai, generation after generation will be "cursing and blaspheming" (*Song Rab.* 2.13.4 to Song 2:10; 127). Joel Marcus notes similar passages in Jewish apocalyptic literature (2009, 887-88).

A midrashic retrospect lays out moments of abjection in Israel's history, each later overturned by a marvelous reversal of status: the Israelites' enslavement in Egypt, where they had to "work with bricks and mortar and they were repulsive and contemptible in the eyes of the Egyptians" (Exod 1:13-14; 8:26); Joseph's imprisonment in Egypt (Gen 39:20-41:14); David's flight from Saul (1 Sam 19-24); and Mordecai's humbling himself in sackcloth and ashes (Esth 4:1). After this historical review, a citation of Mic **7:8** identifies the "Community of Israel" as the speaker, addressing its defiant "whenever I have fallen, I rise" to "the other nations" generally (*Song Rab.* 6.12.1 to Song 6:12; 273-74). In a midrash narrating conflict in the heavens between Sammael, "the chief of all the accusing angels," and the mighty archangel Michael, the latter quotes Mic **7:8**, saying he had "fallen" because of the death of Moses, yet he "'shall arise,' on account of the leadership displayed by Joshua when he shall have defeated the thirty-one kings" (cf. Josh 12; *Deut. Rab.* 11.10 to Deut 31:14; 183).

On YHWH being light to the faithful believer, midrashic exposition connects the cardinal directions for encampment of the tribes of Israel in the wilderness with four corresponding archangels: Michael with Reuben on the south, Gabriel with Judah on the east, Uriel with Dan on the north, and Raphael with Ephraim on the west. Symbolic meanings of these connections are explored; Mic **7:8**, "YHWH has been my light," is cited to demonstrate, as does the meaning of the angelic name "Uriel," that God has been light to the tribe of Dan and to all Israel (*Num. Rab.* 2.10 to Num 2:3; 1:39). Micah **7:8** is deployed in a beautiful midrashic simile comparing "the greatness of Israel" to the gradual increase of dawning light and the gradual increase in stature of Mordecai in the book of Esther (*Esth. Rab.* 10.14 to Esth 8:15; 123). Rabbi Ḥiyya and R. Simeon b. Ḥalafta are said to be walking together when they observe the dawn breaking, and R. Ḥiyya comments, "Even so shall the deliverance of Israel break forth," citing Mic **7:8**. He continues, "first it comes on little by little, then it begins to sparkle, then it gathers strength, and then it spreads over the sky"; further, just as there are heavenly luminaries to rule the day and the night (Gen 1:16-18), "so Israel shall have a place both in this world and in the next" (*Song Rab.* 6.10.1 to Song 6:10; 268).

Introduction

The allusion in Mic 7:15 to "the days when [Israel] came out of the land of Egypt" anchors reflection on a catena of divine acts of redemption, all seen as rooted in the month in which Passover was established as a divinely appointed "season of rejoicing." In this same month, the midrash offers, Isaac was born; Isaac was bound by Abraham (and—left unspoken but transparently clear—was released when the deity provided a ram instead to reconfigure sacrifice; Gen 22:1-14); Jacob received Isaac's blessings (Gen 27:28-29); in redeeming Israel from enslavement in Egypt, God brought Israel from death to life and "from a yoke of iron to the yoke of the Torah"; and in time to come, God will wreak vengeance upon Israel's enemies (citing Jer 50:34 and Isa 43:4; *Exod. Rab.* 15.11 to Exod 12:2; 173-74). Micah's oracle prophesying Judean dominion over the nations in Mic 7:16 is rooted in Jacob's deathbed blessing over Judah about the nations offering tribute and obedience to him (*Gen. Rab.* 99.8 to Gen 49:10; 2:982).

God's characteristic pardoning of Israel's iniquity per Mic 7:18 is couched as divine instruction to Moses when the people complain at Rephidim about the lack of water (Exod 17:1-7). God telling Moses to pass on before the people is heard as an adjuration to Moses to forgive their antagonistic words, explicated further by R. Meir as a command that Moses seek to resemble God in repaying good for evil (*Exod. Rab.* 26.2 to Exod 17:8; 317-18). Within a collection of halakic regulations in Exod 21-23, verses about God's angel guiding Israel (23:20-21) underscore that the angel will not be forgiving of rebellion; this is contrasted with God as pardoning iniquity per Mic 7:18, highlighting God's mercy and signaling that angels must never be worshipped as if they were God (*Exod. Rab.* 32.4 to Exod 23:21; 408). A midrash on the power of prayer has Cain quoting Mic 7:18 to God in a plea for mercy after having murdered Abel and being sentenced to a life of wandering; God relents regarding the fugitivity curse, allowing Cain to settle in the land of Nod (Gen 4:14-16; *Deut. Rab.* 8.1 to Deut 30:11; 147-48). The celebration of God's forgiving nature in Mic 7:18 is mustered among texts affirming divine goodness to those who wait for God, taken as signaling divine favor to all who are pure of heart and honor the paths of torah (*Lam. Rab.* 3.9 to Lam 3:25; 202-3).

The incomparable divine compassion in which Israel trusts per Mic 7:19 is illustrated through a series of contrasts between self-serving human actions and merciful divine actions. Human creditors demand payment, while God suppresses Israel's debt; a human pupil carries the lantern for the teacher, while God goes before Israel as a pillar of cloud by day and (left tacit) a pillar of fire by night; servants wash, clothe, carry, and guard their masters during sleep, while God is the one who washes and clothes Israel (citing Ezek 16:9-10), bears Israel on eagles' wings (Exod 19:4), and guards Israel during sleep (Ps 121:4; *Exod. Rab.* 25.6 to Exod 16:4; 306). God's "fidelity to Abraham" remembered in Mic 7:20 is linked to God having preserved Abram's life during famine when the patriarch journeyed to Egypt (*Gen. Rab.* 40.1 to Gen 12:10; 1:326) and to God's compassionate action in response to Rachel's plea for children (*Gen. Rab.* 73.2 to Gen 30:22; 2:668). Per R. Abin teaching in the name of R. Berekiah the Elder, that same divine fidelity was also demonstrated by God having communicated with Abraham "by way of both word and vision," a signal honor for the patriarch (*Lev. Rab.* 1.4 to Lev 1:1; 7).

The melodious polyphony of midrashic tradition has continued from the early centuries of the Common Era through medieval times and into the present day. Plaskow finds in the play and possibility of midrashic interpretation a radical methodological hope for the continuing reformation of worshipping and learning communities within Judaism toward full inclusion and equity for believers of every gender. As she sees it, "Midrash expands and burrows, invents the forgotten and prods the memory, takes from history and asks for more. It gives us the inner life history cannot follow, building links between the stories of our foremothers and our own joy and pain," and "[transforming] them into living memory" (1990, 59). The creativity of midrashic writing is life-giving for those who see as urgent the need to rewrite and amplify biblical traditions. As with any system of theory, lived experience, and prescriptive praxis shaped under cisheteropatriarchal cultural constraints, this rich and meaningful heritage can also diminish the community, and particular constituents within it, through hierarchical norms and exclusionary practices. Midrashic polyphony continues, enlivening and irrepressible, as feminist communities—Jewish and otherwise—continue to engage in lively debate about readings and counterreadings of these sacred texts. Midrash offers a precedent for engaging in such debate with as much intellectual acumen, spiritual passion, and creativity as each feminist believer can muster. Gafney insists, "Midrashic exegesis is not limited to rabbis or the authoritative classic literature of rabbinic Judaism. It continues whenever and wherever people study and teach the Scriptures" (2017, 5). Plaskow grounds the generative freedom of midrash in covenantal hermeneutics: "In the realm of Jewish religious expression, invention is permitted and even encouraged. Midrash is not a violation of historical canons but an enactment of commitment to the fruitfulness and relevance of biblical texts" (1990, 56). Such "remembering

Introduction

and inventing together," as Plaskow puts it, has been and continues to be a transformative means of "reshaping Jewish memory" (56) in light of the One who created the intellect and the heart of every believer for the faithful study of Scripture.

Rabbinic interpreters in the medieval period offered a rich tapestry of commentaries on many aspects of verses in Micah. Among prolific commentators on Micah were Rashi (Shlomo Yitzhaqi, 1040-1105), Joseph Kara (ca. 1065-ca. 1135), Abraham Ibn Ezra (ca. 1092-ca. 1167), and David Kimhi (1160-1235). Space constraints preclude my offering illustrative examples here or striving to summarize dominant trajectories of interpretation, something that would be a herculean task. The reader may consult the work of Naomi Grunhaus (Macchi et al. 2020, 1104-7) for a brief overview of medieval exegetical works on Micah, including three "Rabbanite commentaries written in Arabic/Judeo-Arabic" (1105); for a historical survey of medieval Jewish philological interpretation, see Eran Viezel (2017). Where possible, I have incorporated key insights from medieval rabbinic interpreters into the commentary sections of my Micah chapters.

4.1.2 Modern Jewish Interpretations

In the modern era, two Jewish interpreters of the biblical prophets have been particularly influential for scholars and spiritual seekers: Martin Buber and Abraham Heschel. The Austrian and Israeli philosopher Martin Buber (1878-1965) wrote extensively in Jewish mysticism and the philosophy of religion, among other intellectual arenas, attracting global attention with his book *Ich und Du* (1923); he famously translated the Hebrew Bible into German with Franz Rosenzweig. In *The Prophetic Faith*, first published in Hebrew in 1942 and in English in 1949, Buber describes Micah as one who "takes to himself the teaching of Isaiah, of which we find many traces in his sayings," while being "more radical and inexorable in manner" than Isaiah. Buber says Micah goes "further than his master" in three things: "the criticism of [the] social order" as regards injustice, "the crystallization of the divine demand" in Mic 6, and "the completeness of the punishment" of Judeans for their corruption and violence (2016, 193-94).

The Polish-American rabbi and scholar Abraham Heschel (1907-1972) wrote lyrically about the Latter Prophets. His book *The Prophets*, first published in 1962, was offered as a project in Jewish theology and ethics meant to correct the distortions and limitations of dogmatic theological readings and psychological analysis of these ancient figures (2001, xxi-xxii). Heschel's magnificent opening description of the intense sensitivities and hyperbolic language of the prophets is worthy of attention by every interpreter of the writing prophets. In Heschel's characterization of the prophets, one may hear incipient resonances with liberation theology across religious traditions, and also with the notion of the feminist KILLJOY as prophetic witness:

> Instead of dealing with the timeless issues of being and becoming, of matter and form, of definitions and demonstrations, [the reader finds] orations about widows and orphans, about the corruption of judges and affairs of the market place. Instead of showing us a way through the elegant mansions of the mind, the prophets take us to the slums. The world is a proud place, full of beauty, but the prophets are scandalized, and rave as if the whole world were a slum. . . . To us a single act of injustice—cheating in business, exploitation of the poor—is slight; to the prophets, a disaster. To us injustice is injurious to the welfare of the people; to the prophets it is a deathblow to existence: to us, an episode; to them, a catastrophe, a threat to the world. Their breathless impatience with injustice may strike us as hysteria. We ourselves witness continually acts of injustice, manifestations of hypocrisy, falsehood, outrage, misery, but we rarely grow indignant or overly excited. To the prophets even a minor injustice assumes cosmic proportions. (2001, 3-4)

While idolatry is featured in two passages of Micah (1:5-7; 5:11-13 [Eng. 12-14]), Heschel rightly observes that Micah's response is muted to "the sin of idolatry, to the people who bow down to the work of their own hands, to the sorcerers and soothsayers," for in Micah's view, "the fatal sin is the sin of moral corruption" (2001, 125). For Micah, YHWH is a God of social and political justice: "The prophets proclaimed that the heart of God is on the side of the weaker. God's special concern is not for the mighty and successful, but for the lowly and the downtrodden, for the stranger and the poor, for the widow and the orphan. The heart of God goes out to the humble, to the vanquished, to those not cared for" (213).

From Marc Saperstein's magisterial work on Jewish preaching during times of militarized conflict in the nineteenth and twentieth centuries, we may consider two representative sermons relevant for Micah. A sermon entitled "God Protects Our Fatherland" was preached by Rabbi David Woolf Marks (1811-1909) to the West London Synagogue of British Jews on 7 Octo-

Introduction

ber 1857, against the backdrop of the Crimean War and with a focus on the fierce conflict that raged between British colonial forces and indigenous resistance fighters in India (Saperstein 2008, 121–41). British citizens were appalled by reports of "atrocities committed by the Indian rebels: torture and rape, mutilation of men, women, and children, massacres of Europeans and plundering of their property" (128). The reports, while based on documented violence, were exaggerated for political effect, and as might be expected, the British public was not as well informed about the atrocities committed by British troops (128–29). Many British preachers denounced the violence of the Indian "insurgents" and called for public support of the British armed response, emphasizing—with no irony—the "ingratitude demonstrated by the rebels towards a benevolent, humane, and enlightened British rule" (129). Among the voices lifted in outcry, Londoners heard influential Baptist preacher Charles Spurgeon (1834–1892), who explicitly put aside his pacifism in this instance, urging that his hearers lament and prepare for "spiritual battle" (Sharp 2021, 621). Marks takes as his focal text Ps 3:9, "With the Lord is help," and brings his hearers immediately into a dramatic confrontation with the gruesome consequences unleashed by "the wildest passions of savage nature" in India (132). While he does not quote Mic 3:12 on the destruction of Jerusalem, his description of the horrors of war brings that text to mind in his catena of military crises facing "the Hebrew people" in "what part soever of the Bible we turn," including—he does explicitly name—Sennacherib's siege of Jerusalem in the time of Hezekiah (135). In this vivid passage, Marks quotes the towering Unitarian minister and antiwar activist William Ellery Channing (1780–1842):

> Wheresoever [war] rages, industry ceases. . . . It impoverishes whole communities, reduces to ashes the homesteads of thousands, "moistens the soil with human gore, makes mothers widows and children orphans, and it rarely opens for the conqueror a path that does not lie over putrefying heaps of mortality, over pillaged cities, ravaged fields and smoking ruins." (133)

Having considered the devastations of war, Marks nevertheless makes a turn, urging support for the British suppression of the Indian insurrection. He asks his hearers not only to pray but to "make ourselves useful according to our several capacities, and to employ all the means at our command . . . to re-establish the authority of the Law," until "the Messiah's advent, when all existing political relations will be adapted to the glorious events consequent upon the coming of the regenerator of the human race" (135, 138). The discerning reader can hear in this approach the preacher's holding of liminal space between Mic 3:12 and 4:1-3. The atrocities and horrific destruction of war have been suffered throughout Jewish history, the preacher reminds his congregation, from the time when Moses and the Israelites stood at the Red Sea through the many armed conflicts during David's monarchy to Sennacherib's invasion of Judah to the threat of "utter extermination ... of the Jewish exiles in the dominions of Persia" as narrated in the book of Esther (133-35). Until the Messiah comes, "to be stern in the day of battle and to be moderate and merciful in the hour of victory is a maxim that every pulpit ought to inculcate," Marks preaches; the importance of mercy notwithstanding, the British citizen should not for a moment "indulge in maudlin sentimentality" toward the criminal acts of the enemy (139). Rather, Marks urges that believers make it possible for all to perceive "God's blessing ... in the readiness with which" British citizens respond to the Crown's "summons 'To arms'" (140-41).

A sermon entitled "A Time for War, and a Time for Peace" was preached by Rabbi J. Leonard Levy (1865-1917) to the Reform congregation Rodef Shalom in Pittsburgh, Pennsylvania, on 8 April 1917, two days after the United States Congress had voted to declare war on Germany, thus catapulting the United States into World War I (Saperstein 2008, 324-45). As Saperstein describes the context, Levy had served as a military chaplain and as vice president of the International Peace Union. His preaching from 1914 onward was initially grounded in pacifism but moved toward acknowledgement of the inevitability of armed conflict. In the early days of the war, Levy had affirmed his high esteem for German art, culture, and medical science, and he had vigorously insisted that war was not God's will (325-28). But in his sermon on Eccl 3:8 just days after the United States had entered the war, he preached to his American congregants about "national obligation and responsibility," asking that all "place at the disposal of our nation ... their life, their sacred liberties, [and] their possessions" so as to ensure victory (330). He urges that believers "not blame God for this war" (332), but underlines that it is imperative for those seeking God's righteousness to "defend the principles of justice" (334). The preacher emphasizes that he still believes in peace (336)—indeed, peace and war are linked: "in times of war we should organize for peace, an enduring peace, a durable peace, an international peace.... The lurid flames of war will be quenched. The red rivers of gore will evaporate. The curtain of fire will be extinguished" (342). Citing the first Passover, when "Israel was liberated in the name of the Author of Liberty"

Introduction

(344), Levy reaches the apex of his powerful sermonic performance. "The emancipation of a handful of slaves on the banks of the Nile was a sign and token of the ultimate emancipation of the human race," he thunders, pointing to an age yet to dawn, when "'every man shall sit under his own vine and under his own fig-tree, and there shall be none to make him afraid.'" The vision of Mic 4:4 is to be cherished, yes, but it is "an ideal," and the current circumstances require something other than pacifism: "The time for peace will come.... The time for war is here" (345).

Yakov Nagen, senior rabbi at the Otniel Yeshiva in Israel and director of Ohr Torah Stone's Beit Midrash for Judaism and Humanity and Blickle Institute for Interfaith Dialogue, writes of the luminous material in Isa 2:2-4 and Mic 4:1-3, "An inextricable part of the prophetic vision for civilization's progress is building connections among all nations.... Torah does not go forth by itself from Zion, nor the word of God from Jerusalem. The Jewish people play a crucial role in spreading Torah," and further, "spreading God's Torah to all of humanity, through the people of Israel, is more than a prophetic vision; it is a deep part of the destiny of the people of Israel from its beginning" (2022, 29, 34). Nagen cites rabbinic comments in b. Soṭah 32a and 36a on Deut 27:8, in which Moses and the elders of Israel command the people regarding building an altar of unhewn stones on Mount Ebal, "You shall write on the stones all the words of this law very clearly": the sages took "very clearly" to mean "the Torah was written in 70 languages, so that all the nations could partake and understand" (34). He also lauds the renowned rabbi Jonathan Sacks (1948-2020) for "his ability to teach and share the Torah on the world stage in a way that gave humanity insights and tools for dealing with the profound contemporary problems with which many nations are concerned" (43).

Micah texts are featured in a number of contemporary Hebrew songs. For example, the motif of the torah proceeding from Zion (Mic 4:1) is the focal theme of settings of *Ki MiTzion teitzei Torah*, per Ora Weinbach (pers. comm.) often sung on the celebratory holiday of Simchat Torah, which concludes the week-long observance of Sukkot. Micah 4:4 provides a central motif of *Vine and Fig Tree*, also known as *Lo Yisa Goy*, composed by Shalom Altman in 1948; this song reflects the Isaiah version of the parallel texts Isa 2:4 // Mic 4:3. Other songs drawing on Micah include *Maoz Tzur*, a Hanukkah song that closes with a prayer that God raise up "the seven shepherds" (Mic 5:4b [Eng. 5b], with thanks to Ora Weinbach for the reference); *Yishmaeni Elohai* ("My God Will Hear Me," 7:7), composed by Christene Jackman in 2009; and *Mi Chamocha* ("Who Is Like You?," 7:18), composed by Todd Herzog in 2009.

4.2 Micah in Christian Traditions

Highly visible in Christian reception history has been the theological move to confirm Jesus as anointed Redeemer or Christ via the mention in Mic 5 of Bethlehem as the birthplace of the Messiah. The exhortations in Mic 6:8 have dominated reception of this prophetic book in social ethics and theologically grounded political activism.

The Gospel of Matthew quotes Mic 5:1 (Eng. 2), underlining that Bethlehem is the birthplace of Jesus of Nazareth (Matt 2:1), in a catena of prooftexts from the Hebrew Scriptures intended to show that Jesus is the long-awaited Messiah (2:6). Walter Wilson remarks that Matthew's quotation "differs significantly from both the MT and the LXX," with Matthew changing "Ephrathah" to "the land of Judah," negating the adjective "insignificant" (*oudamōs elachistē*, "by no means least"), omitting "in Israel" in the Micah phrase "ruler in Israel," and shaping the point about shepherding in Mic 5:3 (Eng. 4) via the language of 2 Sam 5:2b (2022, 1:55-56). C. A. Ham and others have interpreted the force of Matthew's intentional reversal of the point about Bethlehem's insignificance as demonstrating that "since Jesus the Messiah has been born there, glory has come to Bethlehem, that is, it is now 'no longer least'" (2019, 43). Luke places Jesus's birth in Bethlehem as well (Luke 2:4-16), without quoting Mic 5; the Gospel of John makes a similar move in a dramatized discourse about the origins of the Messiah (John 7:42).

Ham notes the prevalence of this move in the early church, citing among its proponents Justin Martyr (ca. 100-ca. 165), Irenaeus (ca. 130-ca. 203), and Tertullian (ca. 155-ca. 220). He cites as illustrative the argument of Eusebius (ca. 260-ca. 339) that "only two famous men have been born in Bethlehem, David and Jesus, and . . . since David lived and died long before, the prophecy in Micah must refer to Jesus" (Ham 2019, 43). Not all contemporary scholars are persuaded that the locale of Jesus's birth was in fact Bethlehem (Marcus 2009, 848), but the accuracy of the claim was not in dispute for premodern readers.

Matthew offers the quotation of Mic 5 not in the narrator's voice but as something confirmed by "all the chief priests and scribes of the people" (Matt 2:4). This voicing on the part of the First Evangelist is noteworthy. Ham observes that the Matthean quotation, "placed on the lips of the chief priests and scribes," evokes a text that "contrasts a weakened ruler of Israel (Mic. 4.9, 14) with a new ruler for Israel . . . who will revive the ancient dynasty of David" (Ham 2019, 42). The contrast may be heard in its Matthean context as ironizing Judean leadership, including religious leadership, at

Introduction

the time of Jesus's birth. According to Ulrich Luz, the quotation takes on "an anti-Jewish sharpness: although the scribes of the people of God recognize that they are talking about the hoped-for messianic shepherd of God's people Israel, instead of acting on that knowledge they become Herod's accomplices" (2007, 113). Dorothy Jean Weaver, too, notes the vector of critique in which this Matthean quotation participates: "identifying Jesus as the one who will 'shepherd . . . Israel,' even as these same people are later depicted by Jesus himself (9:36; 15:24) as 'the lost sheep of the house of Israel,'" shows that the people are "apparently 'unshepherded' by their designated religious leaders" (Weaver 2017, 69 [emphasis removed]).

John 7:42 offers a refraction of the Mic 5 tradition that the Messiah will be born in Bethlehem. A dispute arises among some in Jerusalem during the Sukkot festival about whether Jesus, who has been performing healings in Galilee (John 7:1), could be the one prophesied by Micah. "Surely the Messiah does not come from Galilee, does he?" argue those who, on the basis of Mic 5, are unpersuaded about the origin of Jesus. Maarten Menken sees the dispute as another instance of the "Johannine misunderstandings" crafted in the Fourth Gospel, in which "spiritual realities" are wrongly interpreted by Jesus's opponents (2019, 93; similarly Thompson 2015, 177, and many scholars).

The Gospels of Matthew and Luke may be alluding to Mic 6:15, "You will sow but not reap" (*sy spereis kai ou mē amēsēs*), in Jesus's parable of the talents. Wilson hears the characterization of the harsh master as one who reaps where he did not sow (Matt 25:24 // Luke 19:21) as a potential "inversion" of that Micah verse (2022, 2:316). Wilson also hears a resonance between the vignette of a hungry Jesus finding no figs on a fig tree (Matt 21:18-19 // Mark 11:12-13) and the lament in Mic 7:1 (2022, 2:193).

Matthew and Luke quote Mic 7:6 on family discord marking the new era that Jesus has inaugurated through his ministry (Matt 10:35-36 // Luke 12:53). A tradition of intrafamily betrayal, adduced as one aspect of the coming persecution of Christians and represented in all three Synoptic Gospels (Matt 10:21-22 // Mark 13:12-13 // Luke 21:16-17), is pertinent, though it cannot be demonstrated to reflect literary dependence solely on Mic 7:6 as such. This material may be articulating a more general knowledge of the theme of pervasive conflict in kinship groups in apocalyptic times; Marcus explains that a number of Second Temple and later "apocalyptic texts portray alienation from family members as one of the end-time woes to be endured until God shortens the time and saves [God's] people" (Marcus 2000, 280). But Mic 7:6 is assuredly one source for the early Christian view

Overview of the History of Consequences

that "the proclamation of the gospel inevitably encounters persecution, manifest primarily in hostility of governing authorities . . . and polarized responses among family," the motif of strife and betrayal within households also being audible in Gos. Thom. logion 16 and Mart. Pol. 6 (Ham 2019, 48), as well as in the gnostic text Pistis Sophia Book 3.113 (Roukema 2019, 35). Huub van de Sandt argues that the Q material (the hypothetical written sayings source underlying shared material in Matthew and Luke that is not found in Mark) has to do with "the threat of apocalyptic judgment," and the addition of a crucial temporal phrase in Luke 12:52, "from now on" (*apo tou nyn*), "shifts the conflict from the eschaton to the present," suggesting it is an "immediate effect of Jesus's ministry" (2019, 60).

In Matt 10, after material about persecutions to come, Jesus says, "But the one who endures to the end will be saved" (Matt 10:22b // Mark 13:13b; cf. Luke 21:19b, "By your endurance you will gain your souls"). Wilson muses that this "may have been inspired by Mic 7:7" (2022, 1:358).

In the early centuries of the Christian church, many theologians wrote commentaries on the Twelve Prophets. Favored loci for christological readings included the eschatological vision that opens Mic 4 as pointing to the coming reign of Christ and the prophecies of the coming messianic ruler in Mic 5:1–4a (Eng. 2–5a). For example, in book 18, chapter 30 of *The City of God*, which Augustine of Hippo (354–430) began in 413 and finished in 426, the theologian reads Mic 4:1–2 symbolically to argue that Mount Zion is Christ; he begins, "The prophet Micah, representing Christ under the figure of a great mountain," and goes on to quote 4:1–3a. Of 5:1 (Eng. 2), Augustine relays the broad Christian consensus that here Micah "foretold even the place in which Christ was to be born" (*City of God*, 126). Christian interpreters explicated many other passages in Micah as well with reference to Jesus of Nazareth as the Christ.

It is ethically urgent to acknowledge that from the first century of the Common Era onward, some Christian interpretations of Hebrew Scripture texts, including passages from Micah and other books of the Latter Prophets, have been marred by the repellent ideologies of supersessionism, anti-Judaism, and anti-Semitism (Levine 2022). Scholarly works in reception history of the prophets that are instructive on the history of Christian anti-Jewish theology, ecclesiology, and ethics include: John Sawyer's *The Fifth Gospel: Isaiah in the History of Christianity* (1996), Yvonne Sherwood's *A Biblical Text and Its Afterlives: The Survival of Jonah in Western Culture* (2000), and an article by Charles Meeks on Hos 1–3 (2020). While some analyses of New Testament texts authored by Jewish Christians have been unnuanced

Introduction

in their framing of the pertinent issues, the pervasiveness of Christian supersessionism, anti-Judaism, and anti-Semitism is undeniable and deplorable. Such noxious positions, which do grievous harm up to the present day, must be unflinchingly examined and incisively dismantled as we strive to understand what writers in antiquity, the medieval period, and the modern period were doing when they grounded Christian claims in the authority of the Hebrew Scriptures.

4.2.1 Early Christian Interpretations

Origen of Alexandria (ca. 185-ca. 253), the erudite textual scholar and philosophical theologian, focuses in his exegetical writings and sermons on Christian allegorical and symbolic meanings to be drawn from the Hebrew Scriptures. Riemer Roukema notes that Origen wrote the first commentary on the Twelve "probably in 245-246, but except for two fragments it is lost to us" (2019, 11). In a homily taking its starting point from Lev 12:2 on postpartum impurity, Origen underscores Christ's identity as spiritual physician (Matt 9:12; Mark 2:17; Luke 5:31) and observes that though the incarnate Lord was born in an impoverished place, Bethlehem, he was rich per his divine nature, as 2 Cor 8:9 and Phil 2:6-8 suggest (*Hom. Lev.* 8.4.3 [160]). In his homilies on Joshua, Origen frames the many battles against Canaanite indigenous groups narrated in Joshua as spiritual battles within the heart of the believer against the cosmic powers and spiritual forces of evil (Eph 6:12) that "await us after baptism," the walls of Jericho signifying "the proud walls of sin" that must be destroyed before believers can, as per Mic 4:4, rest under their own vine, "which is Christ Jesus" (*Hom. Josh.* 5.2 [61]; 15.7 [150]; 16.4 [155]). Joshua is to be understood as a type of Jesus Christ, as Origen and many early church theologians suggested. Thus when Joshua is said to have conquered all the territory of Canaanite groups, Origen can aver that though the geopolitical territory of Canaan never knew peace in its fullness, "in my Lord Jesus Christ" there is true peace for the believer, since "your land has ceased from wars if you still 'carry around the death of Jesus Christ in your body'" (*Hom. Josh.* 15.7 [150]; cf. 2 Cor 4:10).

Preaching on Jeremiah's cry of woe in Jer 15:10, Origen suggests "Jeremiah" is better understood as Christ, proved from the speaker claiming to be "judged and disputed" across "the whole earth" in that verse. Origen proposes, then, that the Savior who lamented over Jerusalem (Matt 23:37-39 // Luke 13:34-35) is also the lamenting speaker in Mic 7:1-2: the Incarnate Lord descended to earth but could find no righteous person (*Hom. Jer.* 14.5-14.6

[141-142]). Of the speaker who has sought in vain to find grapes to harvest (Mic 7:1), Origen objects that the referent could not be Jeremiah: "Does the Prophet have a farm? . . . It is proper to no one to *gather* both all from the harvest and what has been planted except to the Lord and Savior Jesus Christ." Origen argues that Christ's lament is actually about the fruitlessness of "the churches," and he exhorts his hearers to search within themselves: "Will the Son of God discover something in [each of us] to pick or harvest? . . . Even if we have still a little in ourselves, two or three kernels, our sins are many against us. . . . Who among us has *clusters* of virtue?" (Hom. Jer. 15.3 [160]).

Roukema writes that Eusebius "referred to a large number of texts from Micah in his apologetic work *The Proof of the Gospel* (*Demonstratio euangelica*) from ca. 318," mustering these as prooftexts about the advent of Jesus as the Messiah, and that when the interpretations of Eusebius and Jerome coincide, the two authors "likely . . . borrowed them from Origen" (2019, 13).

Athanasius of Alexandria (ca. 296-373), the influential theologian known especially for his refutation of Arianism, notes in his *On the Incarnation* concerning Micah's prophecy about beating swords into plowshares (Mic 4:3 // Isa 2:4), "Who is He . . . that has united in peace [people] that hated one another, save the beloved Son of the Father . . . Jesus Christ?" Athanasius adds that Christ's teaching can turn "barbarians who have an innate savagery" to agriculture, so that "instead of arming their hands with weapons they raise them in prayer" (NPNF² 4:64). Athanasius mentions the joyous call to go up to Zion (Mic 4:2 // Isa 2:3) in his Easter letter for 334 as he calls his hearers to virtue and spiritual diligence (letter 6.11; NPNF² 4:522). In his letter to Epictetus, bishop of Corinth, defending orthodox Nicene Christology, Athanasius draws a sharp contrast between authoritative teaching and heretical propositions about Christ and the Trinity. Having read what had been sent by Epictetus, Athanasius quotes Micah's language of the law going forth from Zion and the word of Yhwh from Jerusalem (Mic 4:2 // Isa 2:3) as he dismisses the authority of heretical doctrine, thundering, "But whence came forth this? What lower region has vomited the statement that the Body born of Mary is coessential with the Godhead of the Word? Or . . . that what hung upon the tree was not the body, but the very creative Essence and Wisdom? Or . . . that to pronounce the Lord's Body to be of Mary is to hold a Tetrad instead of a Triad in the Godhead?" (letter 59.2; NPNF² 4:570-71).

Ambrose of Milan (339-397) muses on the biblical ancestor Jacob as a model of holiness, drawing on Isaac's blessing of Jacob (Gen 27:27) to suggest that

Introduction

Jacob was fragrant with virtue as a field is fragrant. He links Jacob to Christ's atoning death for the sake of the world, and musters here Micah's image of peaceful refreshment under the grapevine and fig tree (Mic 4:4): "In this field the grape is found that was pressed and poured out blood and washed the world clean. In this field is the tree, and beneath it the saints will find rest and be renewed by a good and spiritual grace" (*Jac.* 2.1.3; FC 65:148). Roukema describes Ambrose's exposition of the significance of Bethlehem, literally "house of bread," in 5:1 (Eng. 2): Ephrathah connotes "'the house of the one who sees wrath,'" alluding to Herod's slaughter of the infants and toddlers in and around Bethlehem (Matt 2:16); "although Christ was born in the house of wrath, it became a house of bread because it received the Bread that came down from heaven, i.e. Christ (John 6:33, 41, 51), so that 'in the place of cruelty, there is now piety'" (2019, 133).

The venerable biblical scholar **Jerome** (ca. 347-420) wrote commentaries on Nahum, Micah, Zephaniah, Haggai, and Habakkuk in the space of a single year in 392 or thereabouts, per Thomas Scheck, before proceeding to write commentaries on each of the other books of the Twelve, Isaiah, Jeremiah, and Ezekiel (*Comm. Mich.*, xxiii). In his Micah commentary, Jerome first amplifies the plain sense of the Hebrew text, always providing the LXX and engaging it, as well as critiquing its infelicities, in his discussion; he cites the Greek translation of Symmachus on occasion also. Then Jerome proceeds to his chief interpretive interest: arguing in diverse ways, via allegorical, tropological, and anagogical hermeneutical moves, that Micah's oracles of promise point to God's redemptive work in Christ, while the oracles of doom serve as proleptic condemnations of Hellenistic philosophers and (Christian) heretics. For example, of the image in 1:9 of divinely sent retribution reaching the gate of Jerusalem, Jerome notes of his dualistic opponents, "Both the Marcionites and the Manicheans use this scripture to show that the God of the law is the creator of evil things" (*Comm. Mich.*, 49; Roukema 2019, 32). Of the "house of derision" in 1:10 LXX—monumental architecture built by the kings of Israel, according to the plain sense of the text—he argues that on an anagogical reading, the builders are "the princes of the heretics" and "the leaders of perverse dogmas; for theirs, indeed, are the empty houses that were built in vain" (*Comm. Mich.*, 50). His hermeneutical openness extends to the reader, whom he empowers to decline any perspective that is unpersuasive. Using another commentator's reading of John 1:3 as illustration, Jerome says if readers find a trajectory of interpretation "excessively forced . . . and explained in a way that is contrary to the

Fig. 3. *St. Jerome Writing*, ca. 1606, by Caravaggio (Michelangelo Merisi da Caravaggio, 1571–1610). Oil on canvas.

simplicity of the Scriptures, more by the artifice of eloquent speech than by the true interpretation," such readers should "follow the exposition [they themselves have] discovered" (59).

Jerome's respect for the Hebrew Scriptures does not prevent him from articulating a Christian supersessionist position, as when he brings Rom 11 into his discussion of the dual images of the righteous and the enemy of God in Mic 2:6–8, though he does urge Christians to "be careful not to mock those who fall," since "all would require God's mercy" (55–56). He perpetuates the canard, all too common in Christian interpretation since the composing of the Gospels of Matthew and John, that "the Jews" played a central role in the execution of Jesus, when he observes of the shorn, lamenting mother in 1:16, the "grace, by which [Judaism] once flourished before God, has completely departed. For where is the prophet? Where the teacher of the law? . . . Jerusalem has been shaven bald . . . and her children, who cried out against the Lord: 'Crucify, crucify him,' were led into captivity" (51, 52; cf. Matt 27:22–23; Mark 15:13; Luke 23:21; John 19:6). Illustrating his interest in multiple levels of meaning, Jerome expounds various senses that readers might discern in the reference in Mic 2:1 to God's retribution against those who devise wick-

Introduction

edness (53-54). First, Israel experiences divinely ordained exile at the hands of the Neo-Assyrian and Neo-Babylonian Empires; second, the Jews were subjugated by the Romans "because they worked evil things against the Lord Jesus"; and on a third level of theological significance, "the whole discourse is directed to the human soul, which fell from paradise into the captivity of this world" (53). Those things from which sinners cannot lift their necks (2:3) can be understood as vices, as "one demon casts a cord of fornication, another of avarice, another of murder; this one holds the strings of perjury"; such captives will be freed only when Christ comes again (54).

At the beginning of his second volume on Micah, Jerome offers a fascinating glimpse into ancient polemics about authorship and literary influence, sharing his frustration with Paula of Rome (347-404) and her daughter Eustochium (ca. 368-ca. 419), Christian ascetics and close companions of Jerome. Paula studied Scripture with Jerome and served as patron of his translation work; she and Eustochium established several monasteries and lodging for pilgrims and other travelers in Bethlehem. Jerome complains to his sainted friends,

> The prefaces of our books silence the curses of the envious who assert publicly that I write nonsense, sterile and barren of speech. . . . I beseech you, O Paula and Eustochium, to close your ears to barking like this. . . . For what they say, that I compile from the books of Origen and that it is not becoming for the writings of ancients to be plagiarized . . . which they think is a vehement curse, I regard . . . as a very great praise. For I wish to imitate one who, I do not doubt, pleases you and all experienced people. (*Comm. Mich.*, 74-75)

Jerome goes on to list worthies of Roman literary antiquity who drew heavily on antecedents in Greek literature, and cites the way in which Hilary of Poitiers borrowed from Origen (75-76).

Theodore of Mopsuestia (ca. 350-428) avers in his commentary on the Twelve Prophets that Micah received divine revelations relevant not only to the eighth century BCE but to the Neo-Babylonian period (*Comm.*™, 206, 209, 219-22, 229, 232). His annotations are judiciously paraphrastic of the Micah[LXX] text or explicative of historical or literal dimensions of each passage. Theodore understands Micah's oracles of doom as designed to catalyze repentance broadly, both in the Jewish believers of Micah's era and in subsequent generations: "By mention of the impending retribution he wanted you to desist from evildoing; but you were not willing to heed. . . . God's words . . . were meant for your improvement. Since you did not respond, however, they were obliged to manifest their inherent truth to you in your failure to repent" (214).

As a leading figure in the Antiochene school of exegesis, Theodore generally refrains from christological or other allegorizing readings, sometimes explicitly rejecting typological approaches. For example, he dismisses the suggestion that Mic 4:2, about "the word of Lord" proceeding from Jerusalem, should be read in light of Jesus's dialogue with the Samaritan woman at the well in John 4:7-26 (220). He cannot entirely eschew the strong view of his time that mention of the ruler in 5:1 (Eng., LXX 2) must be linked to Christ, but he is more cautious than many about how he acknowledges this. The literal referent is Zerubbabel, he insists, even if this prophecy also does foretell Christ; he studiously avoids reference to Mary the mother of Jesus when discussing the prophecy in the following verse of a pregnant woman giving birth (226-28). Theodore does not wield razor-sharp political or ecclesiological applications concerning his own time, in the manner of Jerome or John Calvin. But he can be caustic about fanciful hermeneutics, for example, finding proponents of "highly imaginative" explications of the Hebrew idiom "seven plus eight" in 5:4 (Eng., LXX 5) to have "come up with old wives' tales so as to appear to have something to say" (230-31). Robert Hill observes of Theodore's lengthy discussion on this point, "Theodore's prolixity intends to disabuse the pervasive Christian tendency to read as a prophecy of Christ's Resurrection any mention of seven and eight in the OT" (232). Other biblical prophetic books constitute influential intertexts for Theodore, even if he seldom cites them by name (though see an explicit reference to Amos, 242). He is drawing on Ezek 38-39 when mentioning Gog several times as he comments on Micah (e.g., 224, 226-27, 229); in his treatment of Mic 6:2, he may have Amos 8:3; Jer 7:32-8:2; or Ezek 37:1-2 in mind when he offers this paraphrase of the divine voice about Jerusalem: "Later, it held . . . many corpses all of a sudden lying in its midst of those who shortly before had high opinions of themselves" (235). Theodore has noticed the shift from divine punishment in Mic 1-3 to (mainly) oracles of hope in Mic 4-7, and finds it spiritually salutary: the prophet's "disclosure of pleasant things after the experience of harsh things" serves a dual function for the hearers, "bringing them to their senses by the mention of baleful things and encouraging them by the brighter to hold fast to hope in God" (219).

Cyril of Alexandria (ca. 375-444) offers commentary on the Twelve with a capacious hermeneutic that allows for the potential polyphony of Scripture and tradition. He takes seriously the historical contexts of Micah oracles

Introduction

and teaches about geographical and political particulars, sometimes with an observation such as, "there is . . . a definite need to discern the difference in periods of time" when considering shifts of theme or the mention of Babylon when Assyria had been in view earlier (*Comm.*^{CA}, 231). But Cyril also urges readers to "go beyond a material impression and rise to a more subtle understanding"—moral or theological, and often christological—in their pondering of the prophet's words (185). God coming forth from the divine place and treading upon high places (1:3) signals the incarnation and Christ's subjugation of "the spiritual forces of wickedness" (186). Of the geological disruptions described in the theophany imagery of 1:4, Cyril finds the convulsing "mountains" to refer to "those who outranked others" who will "be shifted from their positions of privilege," while the melting "valleys" signify "the lowly and abject . . . the masses, being very obdurate and reluctant to respond to the divine oracles" (185). Yet the moral lesson, to love God wholeheartedly and "shake off one's lethargy in good works, to do no harm in any way to one's neighbors," applies to all (188). In another example, he interprets the vision of peace offered in 4:3-4 historically, with apparent reference to the *Pax Romana*, as the cessation of local hostilities under the hegemony of the Roman Empire; but he also offers, "If . . . you chose to interpret the passage spiritually, you would understand . . . that it was with Christ dispensing peace to us out of his characteristic clemency" that believers learned to cultivate "the fruits of righteousness" (225-26).

Cyril recognizes that biblical texts can be "marked by artistry and irony" (190), and accordingly, he often suggests several ways of understanding a passage, offering figurative readings side by side with instruction focused on the material history of ancient Judah. For example, the malfeasant leaders to be cast out per Micah^{LXX} 2:9 may be understood as those in the prophet's time "capable of helping their subjects with instruction and lawgiving, the guides and elders, the shepherds and presidents" who had harmed their constituents, but their characterization could "be applied also to the Jews at the time of the Incarnation, who followed the views of the scribes and Pharisees" (206-7). Of Micah's prophecy of a ruler from Bethlehem in 5:1 (Eng., LXX 2), Cyril articulates the consensus view of early Christian interpreters: "With great clarity he refers to the restoration that has occurred in Christ" (233). But the context could be understood also in other ways, as concerning Israel or humankind more generally. "Israel was ruled in the beginning by God" but "preferred human government instead, and asked for Saul as king," a grievous sin, so "to bring Israel back to their original state . . . serving under God as king," Micah prophesied the advent of Christ

(233). Cyril allows, "It would not be at variance with the purpose, however, ... to give the passage a general interpretation," according to which "we people on earth had rejected God's royal rule" and submitted ourselves to the "yoke" of "an arrogant apostate—namely, Satan," such that all humanity stands in need of redemption through Christ (233-34).

Cyril, with many others of his time, expounds supersessionist readings. In one of many examples, he makes much of the people's lament in 2:4 that their fields have been distributed by the enemy: "At the time of the Incarnation," the Jews suffered this dispossession because "by their frenzy against Christ they forfeited their inheritance." Cyril elaborates, with reference to Rom 9-11; Matt 3:8-9 // Luke 3:8; and Eph 2:19, that the gentiles "sprang up in [Israel's] place, and to them Christ allotted the splendid and desirable inheritance of the heavenly goods" (202). Of the "everlasting mountains" (*oresin aiōniois*) addressees of Mic[LXX] 2:9 are adjured to approach, Cyril allows that the figure might allude to actual mountains of "the land of the Persians and Armenians," such as Mount Ararat, to which sinful Judean elites will be deported, but he offers a figurative reading as well: these majestic peaks might be the Gospel writers, "the heralds and ministers of the New Covenant telling of the mystery of Christ, who were celebrated, conspicuous, and resplendent with the achievements of virtue," and to whose Gospels Jewish believers should draw near, so as to find rest in "the teachings of Christ" (207).

Other early Christian readings of Micah will be adumbrated here just fleetingly, with a focus on interpreters not yet mentioned. Comprehensiveness in this regard would be impossible; I draw on Roukema's erudite and meticulously detailed survey for these final gestures toward the richness of early Christian interpretation. **Hesychius** (died ca. 450) suggests that "the mountains were shaken under the Lord [Mic 1:4] on the day of the cross, by which he means Christ's crucifixion" (Roukema 2019, 51). Regarding the Micah[LXX] wording in the first clause of 1:15, "the heirs" (over against Micah[MT] "the dispossessor"), **Theodoret of Cyrrhus** remarks a singular reading, "the heir," in Aquila and suggests, via the parable in Matt 21:33-41 about violent tenants of a vineyard who kill the owner's son, that the heir is Christ, who "'freed not only Lachis but also the whole world from the bondage to useless idols'" (Roukema 2019, 67). Of Mic 2:10, "this cannot be the resting place," **Gregory of Nazianzus** (329-390) muses that his own episcopal ministry "should not be orientated to the earthly things that do not give rest, but [to] the heavenly things" (Roukema 2019, 79). Expounding on the cannibalism imagery in 3:2-3, Hesychius proffers allegorical meanings for the body parts

Introduction

as believers' capacities under assault by false teachers: the skin signifies "'the divine commandments by which the virtues, as it were the flesh ... protect themselves'"; the bones represent "'the powers of the soul'"; and those faculties are "cut in pieces" (3:3) by the divisive and erroneous traditions of false teachers (Roukema 2019, 92). **Didymus of Alexandria** (ca. 313–ca. 398) reads 3:8, Micah's asseveration that his witness is energized by the spirit of Yhwh, as "a testimony to the divinity of the Holy Spirit and [the Spirit's] close collaboration with God the Father and the Son" (Roukema 2019, 98).

Regarding the torah that will go forth from Zion, a **Pseudo-Cyprian** work entitled *On the Two Mountains Sinai and Zion*, possibly a sermon and likely to be dated to the third century, draws a contrast between "Sinai, from which the law of Moses went forth," and Zion, from which a "new law" will proceed that signifies "the holy cross of Christ" (Roukema 2019, 107), perhaps an oblique allusion to the supersessionist theologizing of Sinai and Zion in Heb 12:18-24. On the accoutrements of warfare and idolatry to be demolished by Yhwh in Mic 5:9-13 (Eng. 10-14), allegorizing readings are offered by some interpreters, including Ambrose of Milan and Hesychius. Ambrose "says that the soul's chariots will be suppressed," elaborating that those are "'the irrational impulses and movements of its body,'" while Hesychius reads the doomed horses and chariots as "'the voluptuous thoughts' and 'the bestial inclinations' respectively" (Roukema 2019, 154, 157). Roukema (163) notes that in his Homily 68, **John Chrysostom** (ca. 347-407) hears resonances of the divine pathos in 6:3-5—misattributing the material to Isaiah—as expressed by Jesus to the Jewish antagonists who have rejected him (Matt 21:42-45, quoting Ps 118:22-23; *Hom. Matt.*, 198). In his Homily 29, Chrysostom musters Yhwh's rhetorical questions in Mic 6:3 and the query, "Saul, Saul, why do you persecute me?," put by the risen Christ to Saul of Tarsus (Acts 9:4) as examples of divine meekness that teach the Christian believer to "use gentleness to eradicate the disease" of sin in another "by bestowing attention and tender care" (*Hom. Matt.*, 416). In a sermon delivered in 399 in Constantinople, Chrysostom deploys Mic 6:3 in a polemic against "Christians who, on Good Friday, preferred the horse races and the theatre to the worship services" (242). Roukema describes a homily that may have been given by a student of Chrysostom, **Proclus of Constantinople** (d. 446), in which layers of typological significance are unfolded regarding the mention of Moses, Aaron, and Miriam in 6:4:

> The homilist briefly mentions three of Jesus' healings, of two men and one woman, and his resurrection of three deceased persons, again of

two men and one woman. Then he refers to the parallel of the three leaders . . . Moses, Aaron, and Miriam, whom he considers representatives . . . of the law, the prophets, and the Church respectively. He elaborates only on the Church, which, like Miriam, praises God for being set free from the spiritual . . . Pharaoh, the devil. (Roukema 2019, 166)

In addition to Origen, as noted above, interpreters hearing the lamenting voice in 7:1-3 as Christ include Ambrose of Milan and Didymus of Alexandria (Roukema 2019, 183-85). Ambrose understands 7:8, "Do not rejoice over me, O my enemy," and what follows to be "testimony attributed to the soul that, in spite of its previous conversion, stumbled and fell back," but has repented and looks once more for God; "the soul then addresses its true enemy, the flesh," which taunts the soul with "Where is your God?" (cf. 7:10) during times of affliction, "when the soul suffers temptations [such as] bodily pain or the loss of children," but the soul "should not listen to her" (Roukema 2019, 198-99). In the exposition of Cyril of Alexandria regarding the bucolic imagery in 7:7, the speaker is "either God the Father who speaks to the Son, or the prophet who addresses Emmanuel (i.e., Christ). . . . Cyril explains that Christ's people, tribe, sheep, and inheritance have not been justified by works of the law, but rather by faith," and goes on, "Christ does not shepherd them with an iron rod, as Ps 2:9 says, but with gentleness. . . . So while he crushes with an iron rod those who do not believe in him, he pastures the believers among lilies and leads them to good grazing," Cyril taking the "rich pasture as a reference to the inspired Scripture whose hidden meaning is clarified by the Spirit" (207). Hesychius argues that the disciplining rod of Mic 7:14 should be understood as "'the cross, for it has become a rod to those who are disobedient,'" while the peaceable grazing in Bashan and Gilead signifies "'the new and old covenant, when they begin to be shepherded by the cross'" (Roukema 2019, 210). The image of God hurling sins into the sea in 7:19 has been taken as a reference to Christian baptism at least as early as the fourth century, that reading being cited by Basil of Caesarea (ca. 329-379), Ambrose, Jerome, Theodoret of Cyrrhus, and Hesychius (Roukema 2019, 212-15).

4.2.2 Medieval Christian Interpretations

In the medieval period, the monk, reformer, and cardinal **Peter Damian** (1007-1072) mentions Micah once in his extensive correspondence. In letter 1, written in 1040 or 1041 to a nobleman named Honestus, Damian draws

Introduction

on Hebrew Scripture texts for a variety of arguments designed to refute Jewish interlocutors who "deny the Trinity"; who do not believe God "begot the Word" incarnate as Jesus of Nazareth; who do not agree that David (i.e., the psalmist), Daniel, Isaiah, Jeremiah, Habakkuk, and other prophets prophesied Christ's suffering, death, resurrection, and eschatological dominion; and who generally deny that Jesus is the Messiah (1989, 37-83). Employing instances of direct address to an imagined Jewish hearer, and characterizing his own hermeneutical efforts as having summoned "a cloud of witnesses" (72), Damian suggests that his hope for the Jewish interlocutor is nothing less than to "attract you to faith in Christ" (79). In this endeavor, Damian quotes Mic 4:1-3 in full, as Augustine and others before him had done, as evidence of that prophet's "witnessing to Christ." He observes drily, "to strengthen the position I have taken, I do not hesitate to write once again what the Holy Spirit wished to repeat through the mouths of two prophets," then citing the parallel passage in Isa 2 (1989, 45). Simple quotation and citation suffice to make the point, per Damian as for Augustine, though Damian adds a word of explanation at the end of the letter: "I did not try to employ the flowers of rhetorical eloquence nor the sharp arguments of the dialecticians. . . . I did not wish to burden you with wordy and extended proofs. Wherefore, in placing before you almost bare texts from Scripture, I have sent you, as it were, a bundle of arrows for your quiver" (83). For many theologians in the early church through the medieval period, the power of catenas of biblical texts should not be underestimated.

The physician and writer **Peter Alfonsi** (d. 1116), a Spanish Jew originally named Moses Sephardi who converted to Christianity and was baptized in 1106, mentions Micah in his *The Dialogue against the Jews*, a work styled as polemical by many, though as Ritva Palmén and Heikki Koskinen note, the "tone is congenial, occasionally even friendly" (2016, 381). Such disputations had been known since the second-century *Dialogue with Trypho* of Justin Martyr. Per Daniel Lasker (1996, 162-63), in the twelfth century, theological dialogues framed between Christian and Jewish disputants were written by Gilbert Crispin (1055-1117), Odo of Tournai (ca. 1060-1113), William of Champeaux (1070-1121), Peter Abelard (1079-1142), and Peter the Venerable (ca. 1092-1156). Alfonsi's work musters points in defense of Christian theology not only from biblical interpretation but from scientific empiricism and natural philosophy as well (Palmén and Koskinen 2016, 381-84). Micah 5:1 (Eng. 2) is mustered in the eighth of twelve dialogues Alfonsi constructs between "Moses" and "Peter." As Katharina Heyden comments, this work "is staged as an encounter between Alfonsi's former Jewish" identity "and his new Christian one," intended as "a reappraisal of Alfonsi's own conversion and a self-justification given face-to-face with his former religious self," such that "in the end, Moses will convert" (Heyden 2022, 6–7). The particular nub of their debate here concerns the divine and human natures unified in the person of Christ, a notion that "Moses" finds unpersuasive. In a catena of prooftexts from Isa 9, 11, 25, 40, and 41, as well as Zech 12 and Pss 8 and 44, "Peter" adduces Mic 5:1. He explains that the coming forth of one to be a ruler in Israel "is said with respect to the body"—that is, the humanity of the incarnate Christ—while his going forth as "'from the beginning, from the days of eternity' implies the everlasting nature of divinity" (Alfonsi 2006, 191). Other points of argument follow, with "Peter" concluding that Yhwh's promise of an eternally established Davidic throne in 1 Chr 17:11-12 points not to Solomon but to Christ. This mode of argumentation is characteristic of other sections of the work as well; Alfonsi's "goal is to show that the whole Old Testament testifies to Christ" (Heyden 2022, 7).

Dominican theologian **Albert the Great** (ca. 1200–1280) cites Micah in his treatise *On Resurrection*, written likely in the period from 1233–1242 and redacted up to 1248 (2020, 9). The work is structured in four tractates presenting *quaestiones* on issues fiercely disputed by scholastic theologians of the thirteenth century regarding the resurrection of Christ and of the body generally. In his second tractate, the seventh question concerns scriptural proofs written prior to Christ's resurrection. Albert quotes Mic 2:12 in the Vulgate—misattributing the quotation to Amos—as one such proof that points to Christ's ascension: "Christ 'ascended opening the way before them'" (*ascendit enim pandens iter ante eos*; 2020, 96). Further on the ascension, in the ninth question of this tractate Albert quotes the same line, this time with proper attribution to Micah. He argues first that Christ ascended, according to the divine nature, not to a physical place but to "the Trinity's heaven" as expressed through metalepsis in Eph 4:10, since "the Trinity is not enclosed in any created or corporeal place" (150). He argues that Christ was not "lifted up" in a passive way, as in the doctrine of the Assumption of Mary or through being carried by angels, but actively ascended by his own power; Albert quotes Mic 2:13 at this juncture presumably for its active verb, "he ascended" (153).

The Dominican philosophical theologian **Thomas Aquinas** (ca. 1225–1274) mentions Micah several times in his twenty occasional academic sermons, most of which Mark-Robin Hoogland says Thomas preached to Dominican and Franciscan friars in Paris (Aquinas 2010, 8). In sermon 1, "Veniet Desideratus," preached on the first Sunday of Advent (year unknown), Thomas

Introduction

describes ways in which the world needed and desired Christ's incarnation so as to experience hitherto unknown grades of perfection, union, generation, justice, mercy, and glory (2010, 23-33). Micah 7:17, on the approach of the nations to Yhwh, is quoted to show that humanity, suffering the "incurable wound" of original sin and afflicted by the same as if "oppressed by an unbearable tyrant," longed for "a pleasing dominion" instead, something also demonstrated, according to Thomas, by the utterance, "I will expect God my Savior," in 7:7. That the awaited and beloved savior is Jesus Christ can be known, per Thomas as with innumerable Christian interpreters, from the prophecy about Bethlehem in 5:1 (Eng. 2, refracted through Matt 2:6; 31-32). Sermon 8, "Puer Jesus," delivered on the first Sunday after Epiphany, likely between 1268 and 1272, focuses on Jesus having "advanced in age and wisdom and in grace with God and the people" (Luke 2:52; 87-107). Addressing dimensions of biological and spiritual growth, Thomas elaborates on inner peace as a sign of the latter, warning via a quotation of Mic 7:6 that believers must guard against discord with family and "friends of the flesh" if they are to progress in grace (98).

Sermon 13, "Homo Quidam Fecit Cenam Magnam," was preached on the second Sunday after the Feast of the Holy Trinity, likely between 1268 and 1272 (171-94). Taking as his point of departure Jesus's parable of the wedding banquet in Luke 14, Thomas explores the theme of spiritual refreshment on offer through God's "magnificent provision" of the living bread that came down from heaven, that is, Christ (John 6:51). This "sacramental refreshment" helps believers not to fear, delights and satisfies them, and is life-giving for all who are called to the feast. Pondering those in the parable who decline to attend, Thomas highlights their ignorance, lack of rectitude, and lack of faith, quoting Mic 7:2, "the saint has disappeared from the earth, and a righteous [person] is not found among the people," on the second of those flaws (191). Finally, in sermon 16, "Inveni David," delivered on the Feast of St. Nicholas, December 6 (year unknown), Thomas expounds dimensions of God having found and anointed David (Ps 82:21 [Eng. 20]) and—for this liturgical occasion—St. Nicholas, both characterized as devout, powerful, and virtuous (233-41). Arguing that Nicholas was possessed of "a matured virtue that is rare in young men," Thomas quotes Mic 7:1 on "early-ripening figs" as a metaphor for "boys who preserve their sanctity in their boyhood" and are willing to bear "the yoke of the Lord" in their youth (235).

Dominican theologian **Henry Suso** (Heinrich Seuse, ca. 1300-1366) alludes to Micah texts several times in his *Wisdom's Watch upon the Hours*, an influential work of medieval mystical theology (Suso 2019). Suso opens book 1 with a quotation of Wis 8:2 about the lifelong yearning for wisdom, framing a narrative about Christian discipleship through the trope of a youthful believer ardently seeking divine wisdom, resisting the temptation toward Epicureanism, and struggling through moments of incomprehension and unfulfilled longing (1.1). A dialogue unfolds between the disciple and Wisdom, who is Christ, as evidenced by lines such as, "I went out with the eleven and made my way to the Mount of Olives, where . . . it would scarcely be believable . . . with what anguishes, what powerful and terrible terrors of death my delicate nature, horrified at the approach of my death, was then possessed" (1.3.1). Through this dialogue, the believer is given to consider the nature of sin and the decline of virtue in the church, the "incomprehensible boundlessness" of Christ's love (1.3.20), the fearsome torments of hell and joys of heaven, and the spiritual benefits of meditating on the "precious treasure" of Christ's passion (1.14.1). Suso's first quotation of Micah comes when the anguished soul, lamenting the sins that had driven away Christ her spouse, is comforted by "Eternal Wisdom, Son of the heavenly Father, the messenger of mercy, the prince of clemency, the lawgiver of lovingkindness," who stands "ready to pity and conceal 'your sins, and cast them into the bottom of the sea'" (Mic 7:19; 1.4.11). Suso deploys a second quotation of Micah in a dramatic vision experienced by the disciple, who sees a pilgrim with a staff standing with troubled countenance near the ruins of an ancient city. Wisdom (Christ) explains, "I am that pilgrim," clarifying that the ruined city is "the Christian religion, once fervent and devout" but now fallen into decay through the corruption, venality, and other vices of its denizens (1.5.1–2); the pilgrim's staff "signifies the death that I endured on the cross, which I offer to the faithful as a sign of love, so that they may . . . turn to me with their whole hearts" (1.5.11). Here Wisdom quotes Mic 7:6, about antagonism within households, in a catena of references to the deplorably injurious ways in which believers treat one another (1.5.6). Suso's third reference to Micah occurs in the response of radiant Wisdom to a query from the enraptured disciple, "Tell us your name and your lineage." She quotes Mic 5:2 on her mysterious origin as being "from the beginning, from the days of eternity," in a cascade of lyrical references drawn from Sir 24, Prov 8, and other texts (1.6.6). Book 2 of *Wisdom's Watch upon the Hours* proceeds to address the importance of sinners' fearing the Lord, preparing with equanimity for death, cultivating purity of heart and detachment from the things of this world, receiving the Eucharist in devout humility, and living in continual praise of God and divine Wisdom.

Introduction

4.2.3 Early Modern to Contemporary Christian Interpretations

John Calvin (1509–1564) delivered twenty-eight sermons on Micah at the Cathédrale Saint-Pierre in Geneva between November 12, 1550, and January 10, 1551. He preached, apparently without notes, Monday through Saturday in alternate weeks; each sermon lasted roughly an hour (Calvin 2003, viii; Parsons 2006, 2). As preacher, Calvin understood himself to be inhabiting a role similar to that of the prophets of the Hebrew Scriptures (Gordon 2009, 293): assailing idolatry and ethical malfeasance, calling his people to repent of their sins, urging his hearers to return to a deeper and more committed faith in God. Calvin honors the biblical text as offering enduring and unassailable truth not only historically, in the time of the prophet, but also throughout the centuries and in his own contemporary circumstances in Geneva. Michael Parsons observes that Calvin repeatedly "underlines the Word's authority, its force and power, its effectiveness and the inexcusability and sheer folly of rejecting it" (2006, 8). Exegetically compelling expository preaching was vital for hearers, in Calvin's view (Scales 2018, 18).

Fig. 4. John Calvin. Engraving by Georg Osterwald. Bibliothèque publique et universitaire de Neuchâtel.

In many of his Micah sermons, Calvin levels fierce critique at magistrates and other officials in Geneva, Roman Catholic authorities, Anabaptists, and the influential group known as the Libertines (2003, vii). He views cities generally as sites of unbridled corruption (22) and sees an urgent need for reform at every level of society: "In our time ... the world is so perverted that one need hardly travel to a city to find cunning and evil, for the rural folk are equally corrupt. But . . . such evil originates in cities, and . . . malice has spread everywhere" (29). While polemicizing frequently against the sins of the Geneva elite and merchants, Calvin is merciless regarding the laxity and immorality of believers of every social class: "The common [person] is equally arrogant. Admittedly, the rich and the mighty are intoxicated with their grandeur. . . . They are guiltier of greater excess and extortion. But, at the same time, we observe how corrupt the lowly [person] is. [That one] too possesses an evil conscience and is guilty of a host of condemnable practices" (23).

In his proclamation, Calvin's language regularly veers into the hyperbolic, as, for example, when he avers that ecclesial leaders are "debauched," "impious," and "totally devoted to evil" (2003, 381). Characteristic of his view of the Roman Catholic Church is this polemic: "As soon as one vice is corrected, the papists preserve as many others as possible. . . . Rome is an abyss of iniquity. The Devil reigns in every part of it. . . . His diseases and stench infect the entire world" (34). In a similar way, though usually with less vitriol than that aimed at Roman Catholicism, Calvin attacks "the Jews" in ways that are inflammatory and offensive. Though, tragically, Calvin's rhetoric is in line with distorted thinking within Christian traditions going back to the first century, there is no excuse for Calvin's persistent anti-Judaism. He does hold Christians responsible for sin as well: "Not for a moment can we discharge ourselves from the ranks of those whose greater condemnation is addressed here. And since our world is no better now than it was in his time, our Lord willed that his sentence of condemnation, proclaimed first against the Jews, should remain in effect until the end of time" (4). Reflecting on Calvin's commentary on Romans, Bruce Gordon offers a measured assessment of Calvin's understanding of Judaism that can be helpful for our consideration of Micah:

> There is nothing evil in the Law itself, but it reveals the extent of evil, as no person is able to meet its standard of perfection. Calvin . . . spoke of [Paul] the Apostle's love for his people and his concern for their salvation. . . . Moses was a preacher of the Gospel. . . . However, because Christ remained behind a veil, not evident to the Israelites, Moses had to teach a form of works righteousness. . . . [Calvin] was clear that the Jews should be honoured on account of the station granted them by God. . . . Christians should not denigrate the Jews, but neither should the Jews themselves be flattered into thinking that all is well without accepting Christ. (2009, 116–17)

Introduction

Calvin sees Micah's oracles of doom as designed rhetorically for reform of the sinner, a point he makes over and over from the pulpit: "God has to address us harshly, manifesting [divine] ire and displeasure at us, before we can appreciate [God's] grace and love. . . . We have to experience God's wrath, until it wounds the depth of our hearts, before we can truly appreciate God's love and infinite bounty" (2003, 7). Or again, "Whenever misfortune and trouble overtake us, we are experiencing God's hand by means of which [God] corrects us whenever we fall short. And in doing so, God makes us look to [God] again," for "if we want to be true Christians, it is essential to be reformed by God's spirit" (98–99). The position is an orthodox one affirmed by many interpreters through the ages. For example, Cyril of Alexandria avers of the imagery of devastation in the war song of divine vengeance that closes Mic 5, "even by calling sinners to account, God works for their benefit" (*Comm.*^{CA}, 244). So too in every sermon, Calvin articulates the idea that God inflicts harm upon humanity for purposes of instruction and spiritual formation. In Calvin's theology, God performs

> vengeance against those who disdain to be guided by God's grace. . . . Believers are also afflicted. And sometimes our Lord treats [God's] children more harshly than [the Lord] does strangers. For when [God] sees that we are about to follow our evil affections, [God] sends us afflictions in order to divert us from them. At the same time, [God] converts all of our miseries into good, in order that they might serve toward our salvation. (61)

Calvin underlines the point over and over again in his preaching, insisting, "God actively executes [divine] judgments in this world, not just at the end of time" (88), for "God's purpose is to purge us from sin" (252).

Gordon asks, "How effective were Calvin's sermons?" Calvin spoke openly of feeling dejected at his preaching's apparent lack of efficacy in turning Genevans from hypocrisy, greed, and ingratitude toward God. "In fact," Gordon offers, "his appeal was quite magnetic, and his sermons drew large congregations, such that by the middle of the 1550s he was preaching at the morning and afternoon services in Saint-Pierre to accommodate the numbers. Calvin was the star" (2009, 294). Becoming "desperately concerned that he should not become the object of a personality cult," Calvin devised a rota for sharing homiletical duties with other ministers in Geneva and "would attend the sermons of other ministers—doubtless a daunting prospect for them" (295). Preaching and biblical scholarship were central to Calvin's Christian vocation to the end of his life. In his final decline in 1563–1564, though his health deteriorated precipitously, "he was carried to church in a chair, and still preached" (332).

Congregationalist theologian and renowned preacher **Jonathan Edwards** (1703–1758) preached in Northampton, Massachusetts, and elsewhere, offering sermons designed to kindle or reawaken Christian piety in his hearers. Edwards's preaching ministry lasted almost forty years, and according to Kenneth Minkema, over twelve hundred of Edwards's sermon manuscripts are extant (2021, 387). In the 1730s and 1740s, he was a leading light in the first wave of New England Protestant revivalism known as the Great Awakening. C. C. Goen observes that the ground had been tilled through a series of "reformations"—including "five 'harvests' during [Solomon] Stoddard's sixty-year pastorate" in the Northampton church where Edwards succeeded him, and "while George Whitefield, by virtue of his flamboyant itinerancy and its consequent influence on evangelistic method, may be called the 'founder' of American revivalism, it was Jonathan Edwards who began the historical documentation and theological defense which have sustained it as an ongoing tradition" (WJE 4:1, 5). M. X. Lesser describes the period 1734–1738 as the zenith of Edwards's homiletical art, a time in which his sermons, structured in the "triadic Puritan form" of textual exposition, theological doctrine, and application, married "technical mastery with great optimism concerning what could be accomplished through pastoral preaching" (WJE 19:xi, 6).

Edwards studied the Bible continually, and his sermons are saturated with Scripture references. Stephen Stein relays that Edwards wrote down a "private resolution in the closing months of 1722 while serving as a supply minister in New York City: *Resolved*, To study the Scriptures so steadily, constantly and frequently" that he might be assured of growth in wisdom (WJE 15:1). Edwards took copious notes on biblical texts in preparation for developing sermons; these included everything from lists of references, word studies, simple expository description, and stubs of themes to sustained exegetical and theological reflections. Douglas Sweeney observes that Edwards maintained various "sets of private notebooks" in which he would "rough out his theological reflections," utilizing "these intellectual workbooks to extend and clarify his ideas about an exceptionally wide range of issues and themes" (WJE 23:1). According to Stein, his *Miscellaneous Observations on the Holy Scriptures*, called the "Blank Bible" by Edwards, "contains more than 5,500 notes and entries by Edwards relating to biblical texts" (WJE 24:1). Edwards's annotation material "ranges widely across textual, linguistic, syn-

Introduction

tactical, historical, theological, polemical, devotional, and personal issues," and he maintained this resource at least from "the middle to late months of 1730" to 1749 (*WJE* 24:23, 91). After 1730, Stein says, "Edwards tended to write longer entries in the 'Notes on Scripture' and shorter entries in the 'Blank Bible'" (*WJE* 24:92). Relevant to Micah is the observation of Stein that in the "Blank Bible" were some nine hundred entries on texts in the Latter Prophets. In Stein's estimation, "No section of the Bible is more consonant with Edwards's self-conception and his sense of responsibility as a Christian minister than the prophetic books of the Old Testament" (*WJE* 24:41). The following illustrations of Edwards's hermeneutical and theological work with Micah proceed in the order of Micah chapter and verse, rather than in chronological order, though where a particular verse is focal for several sermons, chronology structures the presentation here. In Edwards's work, we see him regularly returning to the same or similar ways of thinking about a particular passage across the years. His exegetical and theological work with Scripture was of utmost importance to him as a preacher. Eloquence, clarity, and zeal were required to lead the people of God:

> We that are ministers not only have need of some true experience of the saving influence of the Spirit of God upon our heart, but we need a double portion of the Spirit of God . . . we had need to be as full of light as a glass is, that is held out in the sun; and with respect to love and zeal, we had need at this day to be like the angels, that are a flame of fire [Ps. 104:4]. (*WJE* 4:507)

The "Miscellanies" notebook entry #863, written between May and October 1741 (*WJE* 20:38), elaborates on the theme, "Conflagration. Misery of the Damned." In these pages, Edwards jots some musings on the fiery horror that the earth will become for sinners in the last judgment. Taking 2 Pet 3:12 as his point of departure, Edwards speculates that "'tis very probable that the fire of the conflagration will be such as to dissolve the rocks, and melt the mountains and the ground, and turn all into a kind of liquid fire." Fumes and other "volatile parts" will remain mixed rather than being carried off by the then-nonexistent atmosphere, so that mountains will literally melt. Here, Mic 1:3–4 is cited within a list of biblical prooftexts. The waters of the earth will boil, and "the whole world will probably be converted into a great lake and liquid globe of fire, a vast, shoreless ocean of fire." Volcanoes help us to imagine what hell will be like: "it will be a sea of fire that will always be in a tempest," continuing "in an exceeding perturbation" in which "all

Fig. 5. *Jonathan Edwards (Princeton Portrait)*, 1860, by Henry Augustus Loop (1831–1895). Oil on canvas. In the Princeton University Art Museum, Princeton, New Jersey.

shall be agitated by the wrath of God." The condemned will tumble about in ceaseless "rage and fury and hideous confusion and uproar . . . having no rest, day nor night, with vast waves and billows of fire continually rolling over their heads, bigger than the highest mountains." Finally, "the whole visible world shall be destroyed with one great and general destruction" (*WJE* 20:92–94).

Introduction

In the numbered entries of *Images of Divine Things*, Edwards strives to show, per Wallace Anderson, that "all 'outward' and created things are specifically designated by God to 'represent spiritual things,'" Anderson here quoting "Miscellanies" no. 362 (*WJE* 11:7). In Anderson's estimation, Edwards made "an important innovation in Christian typology and philosophy," successfully avoiding the excesses of medieval allegory while nevertheless "linking the natural and the supernatural in a compelling and dynamic unity in God" (*WJE* 11:33). For an example relevant to Micah: in entry no. 204, written between 1753 and 1754, Edwards says of owls, "These are birds of the night, that shun daylight and live in darkness," and further, of "those creatures that are in Scripture called dragons, as referred to in Mic. 1:8, 'I will make a wailing like dragons, and mourning as the owls,'" Edwards explains, "the wailing of those dragons and owls represents the misery and wailing of devils, who are often called dragons, and of other spirits that dwell in eternal darkness" (*WJE* 11:127).

"Sin and Wickedness Bring Calamity and Misery on a People" is a sermon Edwards preached in Northampton in December 1729 and twice more, once in April 1753 to hearers that included Native Americans at Stockbridge (*WJE* 14:485-486). Minkema identifies these hearers as Mahican and Mohawk Indians; almost two hundred of Edwards's sermons to them are extant (2021, 400). In what Minkema describes as "the classic jeremiadic mode," Edwards deploys Mic 3:1-2 in a polemic against corrupt civil officials and magistrates. Emphasizing that there is already "a great deal of wickedness in the heart of every" person, Edwards thunders that many are "scandalously ignorant" of God, "grossly superstitious," and living "openly vicious lives," and their rulers "countenance vice and wickedness" and "rule unjustly," thus demonstrating the "general corruption" of society (*WJE* 14:488-91). He makes a similar point in a thematic note (#174) for a sermon on 3:11, within a batch of sermons dated fall 1730-spring 1731: "A pretense of trusting Christ is a vain pretense, as long as [people] live wicked lives" (*WJE* 17:450).

With innumerable Christian preachers over two millennia, Edwards sees the vision of the nations joyfully streaming to Zion and the dawning of universal peace per Mic 4 as pointing to the coming reign of Christ. In "True Saints, When Absent from the Body, are Present with the Lord," a sermon preached on 12 October 1747, Edwards crafts a sequence about the meek inheriting the earth and the coming peace that will reign, asserting, "Is. 2:4, Mic. 4:3, Is. 11:6-9, and many other parallel places" show us that "the saints in heaven will be as much with Christ in reigning over the nations, and in the glory of his dominion at that time, as they will be with him in the honor of judging the world at the last day" (*WJE* 25:240 [emphasis added]). In a 1748 treatise entitled *An Humble Attempt*, published when evangelical fervor was on the wane, Stephen Stein says Edwards "called for united prayer" among congregations local and farther afield, articulating "his conception of prophecy in the life of the church" (*WJE* 5:36). Quoting Zech 8:20-22 on nations coming to worship Yhwh of Hosts in Jerusalem, then adducing Isa 60:2-4, Mic 4:1-3, and "Is. 2 at the beginning" on the same motif, Edwards offers: "There has been nothing yet brought to pass, in any measure to answer these prophecies," so the fulfillment still lay in the future (*WJE* 5:312–313). He urges that "this future glorious advancement of the church of God should be brought on . . . by great multitudes in different towns and countries taking up a *joint resolution*, and coming into an express and visible *agreement*, that they will, by united and extraordinary *prayer*, seek to God that [God] would . . . grant the tokens and fruits of [God's] gracious presence" (314 [emphasis original]; cf. 336). Edwards advocated for this universal day of prayer and fasting, a similar plan for a dedicated day of prayer having taken place in Edinburgh beginning in 1743 and continuing in subsequent years, but his efforts met with only limited success (*WJE* 5:39).

Edwards's *A History of the Work of Redemption* comprises thirty sermons that he preached to his church in Northampton between March and August in 1739, having written the sermons in twelve small booklets "designed to be held in the palm of his hand" (*WJE* 9:5). In the twenty-seventh sermon in this series, Edwards's eagerness for divine retribution against malefactors and his yearning for universal peace are intertwined. With Isa 51:8 as his focal text for the series (Minkema 2021, 388), he expounds a number of other passages from the Latter Prophets, including Isa 2:4; 11:6–9; and Jer 33:9. "Satan's heathenish kingdom" will be "overthrown" and "the kingdom of Christ" will be "set up on the ruins of it everywhere, throughout the whole habitable globe," Edwards preaches, while "terrible judgments and fearful destruction" will "be executed on God's enemies," including "blasphemers, deists, and obstinate heretics," as well as "the cruel persecutors that belong to the church of Rome" (471, 473, 475). He goes on to rhapsodize, "The church on earth and the church in heaven shall both gloriously rejoice and praise God as with one heart" (477), citing Mic 4:4 as he envisions a time in which "holiness of heart and life shall abundantly prevail," life will be marked by unparalleled prosperity and blessing, and believers will "receive all manner of tokens of God's presence, and acceptance, and favor" (481, 485).

"Types of the Messiah," which is the same as "Miscellanies" no. 1069, is "a long treatise on the subject of biblical typology, composed between 1744

Introduction

and 1749," during Edwards's ministry in Northampton, according to Mason Lowance Jr. (*WJE* 11:157). Micah **4:13**, "Arise and thresh, O daughter of Zion," is mustered in Edwards's discussion of "Israel's victory over the Canaanites under Deborah," which he sees as pointing typologically toward "the church's victory over her enemies in the Messiah's times" (*WJE* 11:247). The language in Mic 4 about the dominion of Daughter Zion is taken up again by Edwards in "God's People Tried by a Battle Lost," a sermon preached on 28 August 1755. Edwards makes a thunderous claim, "'Tis promised that the enemies of God's church shall never prevail. . . . The church's Redeemer is mighty, that the church shall finally prevail against all his enemies in the most complete and glorious manner often foretold," supporting his point by several prooftexts, including Mic **4:11-13** (*WJE* 25:693–694).

With many Christian interpreters before and after him, Edwards reads **5:1** (Eng. 2) as a prooftext for the claim that the Second Person of the Trinity, the preexistent Logos, existed before the dawn of time: "the Son of God, as a distinct person, was from eternity" (*WJE* 23:91). He makes this point against Isaac Watts's position that the human soul of Jesus was preexistent in the "Miscellanies" entry no. 1174, to be dated sometime before March 1751 (*WJE* 23:35, 89–92). Edwards rearticulates the point in entry no. 1349, written before 1757, and entry no. 1358, written in 1757 or 1758 (*WJE* 23:36, 417, 636).

Edwards provides a lengthy word study related to Mic **5:2** (Heb. 1) in entry no. 501a in his series of exegetical notebooks entitled, "Notes on Scripture" (*WJE* 15:594–98). This entry, written sometime later than 1757, focuses on the Hebrew verb *yṣ'*, to "come forth" or "go forth" or "proceed." Edwards underlines that this Micah passage has "great doctrines taught in it" that might be revealed through close study of the word. Reviewing occurrences of the verb across the Hebrew Scriptures, Edwards highlights the semantic contexts in which it signifies the "flowing forth" of water, the rising of the sun, "the springing or sprouting of plants," the utterance of a word or sounding of a voice, and "proceeding by generation, both as from the father and the mother." He cites Balaam's prophecy in Num 24:17 of a star rising out of Jacob (though the verb *yṣ'* is not used there) to figure the birth of Christ as the rising of a luminary, then avers that the semantic sense of generation—being born—is most likely intended in Mic 5:2 (Heb. 1). His conclusion is that the "goings forth . . . of everlasting" in this Micah verse concern "Christ, with respect to his proceeding from the Father . . . represented as the Father's glory and brightness . . . as brightness from a luminary, and as the Father's 'word.'"

Sermon fragments from Edwards have been catalogued: extant are many hundreds of single sentences, these being either focal verses from Scripture or embryonic ideas on possible sermon themes. Sermon fragment #753, dated August 1744, is tied to Mic **5:7-8**, where the prophet unfolds vivid imagery of the remnant of Jacob being like a ravening lion that will trample and eviscerate enemy nations. Edwards contemplated a potential sermonic theme for this passage that is nothing short of fascinating: "The same means of grace are attended with a quite diverse and contrary influence and consequence on different persons" (*WJE* 25:722).

In "The Sacrifice of Christ Acceptable," a sermon preached in Northampton in late October 1729, Edwards explores the obedience of Christ to the will of the Father. Citing Ps 50:7-10 to discount burnt offerings as having any propitiatory efficacy, Edwards underlines that the sacrifices made by ancient Israel were holy simply because God had commanded Israel to make them. Relying on the supersessionist framework of the Epistle to the Hebrews, Edwards offers that the "sweet savor" of Noah's offering and later Israelite sacrifices delighted God only because they evoked the substance—Christ—that was adumbrated in the shadow of Israelite ritual. The sacrificial system of Israelite antiquity had profound didactic purposes regarding humans' sinfulness and our need for atonement, as mediated by the obedience of Christ in offering himself to death for the sake of "the justice of God." Edwards alludes to Mic **6:7** as he argues that "we are God's, and all that we have is [God's], so that [if] we should offer, as the Prophet says, the fruit of our bodies for the sin of our souls," we would be offering what already belongs to God (*WJE* 14:444-51). The sermon ends in a paean to the excellence of Christ's sacrifice (456-57).

In "Mercy and Not Sacrifice," a sermon preached in Northampton in January 1740, Edwards crafts an impressive catena of biblical texts to demonstrate that God esteems actions of "moral duty" in mercy toward others more highly than "the external act of worship." Featured in Edwards's brilliant argument are Luke 3:10-11, the Sermon on the Mount, ten New Testament epistles, Isa 1:12-17; Amos 5:21-24; Mic **6:7-8**; Isa 58:5-7; Zech 7:2-10; Jer 7:2-3; Matt 15:3-9; Isa 58:1-4; Jer 6:13; Jas 2:18; and more, urging his hearers to show their love of God in Christ through "deeds of righteousness, faithfulness, mercy and love towards your neighbor" (*WJE* 22:114-35). In *Some Thoughts concerning the Revival*, part 5: "Shewing Positively What Ought to Be Done to Promote This Work," published in full in 1743, Edwards complains that Communion, that "holy and sweet ordinance," was not being observed as often as was desirable. From there, he argues that love of neighbor eclipses love of God in worship; he cites Isa 1:12-18; Amos 5:21-24; Mic **6:7-8**; Isa 58:5-7; and other passages to prove Christians should take "a proportionable care

Introduction

to abound in moral duties, such as acts of righteousness, truth, meekness, forgiveness and love towards our neighbor," which are more important to God "than all the externals of . . . worship" (*WJE* 4:522).

In a notebook of twenty pages begun in February 1729, Edwards expounds at length on "Signs of Godliness" as manifested through faith and Christian praxis (*WJE* 21:469–510). Spiritual fruitfulness requires that believers do good works, "cleaving to God" and "persevering through all trials and difficulties," keeping God's commands, "mortifying our sensual and fleshly lusts," "denying ourselves and selling all for Christ," moderating their speech, and "believing the difficult, the spiritual and abasing doctrines of Christianity." Edwards avers that believers should be continually "hungering and thirsting after spiritual good," demonstrating "a meek and forgiving spirit," giving themselves to deeds of love and charity, while "really believing and being heartily convinced that Jesus Christ is the Son of God and the Savior of the World." Trusting in God, fearing God, repenting of sin, and standing before God in humility are characteristics of true Christian godliness. On that last quality, being humble, Mic 6:8 is among the biblical texts mustered for Edwards's definition of humility: "a broken and contrite heart, a being poor in spirit, sensibleness of our own vileness and unworthiness, self-abasement before God, disclaiming all worthiness and glory, mourning for sin" (*WJE* 21:502).

In "The Duty of Charity to the Poor," a sermon preached in January 1733, Edwards cites Mic **6:8**, saying of the prophet's exhortation to love mercy that it is "one of the three great things that are the sum of all religion," and elaborates, "I know of scarce any particular duty that is so much insisted upon, so pressed and urged upon us, both in the Old Testament and New, as this duty of charity to the poor" (*WJE* 17:369, 375). In "Continuing God's Presence," a sermon preached in July 1735, Edwards moves from Ezek 39:28–29, with its motifs of God pouring out the divine Spirit upon Israel and never again hiding the divine face, to the beneficial "tokens of God's presence": people repent and are joyful, preaching bears good fruit, peace is experienced in the community, and believers are brought "to an high pitch of blessedness." Next, Edwards musters biblical texts to affirm God's continuing presence and mercy (Luke 11:11–13; Deut 4:34; 1 Sam 12:22; 1 Kgs 6:13; Ezek 34:24–25; Isa 62:4), underscoring the need for sinners to plead for God's mighty succor (Ps 138:8; Deut 3:24). Edwards argues that believers' steadfast commitment to showing love of neighbor is vital if God is not to withdraw from them. He cites 1 John 4:21 and Mic **6:8** to show that love of God and love of neighbor are inextricably linked, then explores specific applications, commending prayer and spiritual self-examination—believers should "be very watchful of the inward frame of their hearts"—and urging that believers avoid missteps such as developing a "careless spirit" or indulging in irritation at being admonished by others (WJE 19:392–417).

In a sermon preached on 9 December 1742, "On occasion of burning of John Lyman's house and children, which was on Wed. night, Dec. 8, 1742," Edwards chooses as his focal text Mic **6:9**, on God crying out to the city in rebuke, as he addresses a conflagration in which two of Lyman's children had died (WJE 22:551). Instructing the children of his congregation about divine wrath, Edwards is said to have "walked them over to view the charred remains of the structure" as an object lesson (Minkema 2011, 163).

Entry no. 68 in *Images of Divine Things*, "probably written during the winter [or] spring of 1737-1738" (WJE 11:42), concerns wheat, wine, and oil as types of spiritual food. On this, Edwards deploys Micah: "Oil, that great type of the grace of the Holy Spirit, is procured by treading and pressing the olives (Mic. **6:15**). But this Holy Spirit is the sum of all the benefits of Christ, procured for us by his sufferings" (WJE 11:73 [emphasis added]).

In a "Blank Bible" annotation to **7:16**, on the ears of the nations being deafened as they approach Yhwh in dread, Edwards offers this: "'Tis a figurative expression representing as though their senses should be perfectly overcome and stupefied by the greatness of the things they should see and hear, as the sight is dazzled, and [people] are struck blind by a sudden and great light and glory, and their ears deafened with a sudden, great, and astonishing sound" (WJE 24:802). In the "Miscellanies" entry no. 461, in two paragraphs entitled "The End of the Creation," with "end" used in the sense of ultimate purpose, Edwards muses on the character of God. He avers that God "delights in goodness for its own sake . . . acts justly because 'tis agreeable to [God's] nature," and "speaks the truth, because [God] delights in truth for its own sake" (WJE 13:502–3). Micah **7:18** is the first biblical text Edwards musters (along with Ezek 18:23, 32 and Lam 3:33) for this enormously important point about God delighting in mercy—a point that is visible elsewhere in Edwards's writings, perhaps to the surprise of those who associate with Edwards the uncompromising Puritan theology of his most famous sermon, preached in Enfield, Connecticut, in July 1741 and likely repreached more than once thereafter (Minkema 2021, 398): "Sinners in the Hands of an Angry God."

A comprehensive survey of Christian preaching on Micah from the eighteenth century to the present day is not possible in these pages. Several

Introduction

illustrative sermons will have to suffice here as gestures toward the homiletical possibilities preachers have glimpsed. In "An Oration on the Beauties of Liberty; Or, the Essential Rights of the Americans," a Thanksgiving Day sermon delivered on 3 December 1772 by Baptist minister John Allen in the Second Baptist Church in Boston, Massachusetts, and subsequently published widely, the preacher responds to American anticolonial fighters' action of burning a British schooner, *HMS Gaspée*, on June 10 of that year and British fulminations about extradition of the perpetrators. Allen describes the love of liberty as foundational to the character of Americans, lifts up the prophet as sentinel to suggest that "the watchmen of America" will guard their people "from every invasion of power and destruction," and uses the polemic in Mic 7:3 to shame the British monarchy as a corrupt and "arbitrary despotic power" greedily desirous that "British streets may be paved with American gold."

In "A Threshing Sermon," preached in 1851 in Detroit, Michigan, the African Methodist Episcopal (AME) Zion evangelist Julia Foote focuses on the imperative to Daughter Zion in 4:13 to "arise and thresh." She avers that not only "preachers of the word" but "all God's people" are to heed this call to "destroy the works of the devil" (quoting 1 John 3:8) and thus carry out the "gracious designs" of the risen Christ. She invites her hearers to imagine the "gospel flail" as a means by which "the devil is threshed out of sinners," identifying this instrument further as the "sword of the Spirit" (Eph 6:17). Foote adjures those who wield the gospel flail to do so "in a kind and loving spirit." The consequences of such threshing are to be welcomed by the "penitent soul" as "potent and salutary." In what may be an oblique reference to Rom 6:1–11, Foote links such spiritual discipline to being crucified with Christ so that sin may be "put to death" and Christ "may live and reign" in the believer "without a rival" (Collier-Thomas 1998, 60–65).

In "Antipathy to Woman Preachers," a sermon preached by AME Zion pastor Florence Spearing Randolph around 1930 to her congregation at Wallace Chapel in Summit, New Jersey, Randolph links the prophetic promise of restoration of Daughter Zion in Isa 62:11, along with refractions of Zech 9:9 in Matt 21:5 and John 12:15, with exhortations to "fear not" delivered to Hagar, Isaac, Jacob, the Israelites at the Red Sea, and Moses before the battle with Og of Bashan (Gen 21:17; 26:24; 46:3; Exod 14:13; Num 21:34). Mentioning Jeremiah, Ezekiel, and Daniel as additional sources of admonitions not to fear, Randolph moves to the New Testament, underlining that "after the resurrection the first words spoken to the first preachers of the gospel

Overview of the History of Consequences

are the words 'Fear not ye'" (Mark 16:6). In a move of homiletical imagination, she turns in direct address to the women at the tomb: "Preach the first gospel sermon, take the message to those who are to be the teachers of the whole human race"—that is, the disciples—for "you have been faithful, you persevered for the truth and hence you are honored by God and are first commissioned." Addressing the fact that there "still is great antipathy to women preachers," she insists that God has called women to preach, closing with a catena of prooftexts: Gal 3:28 on there being neither "male nor female" in Christ, Mic 6:4 on "Miriam the prophetess [being] reckoned among the deliverers of Israel," and the judge Deborah, a "wife and mother" whose "capacious soul embraced more than her own family," reaching "thousands on the outside." In an abrupt closing that surely would have had powerful resonances for Black listeners in the Jim Crow era, Randolph suggests a comparison between Deborah and Moses: Deborah was "a great liberator" whose "people were oppressed and enslaved" (Collier-Thomas 1998, 105-6, 126-27). Lynchings of African Americans by white racist mobs were still an appallingly common occurrence in the United States at this time. While precise numbers will never be known and it is reasonable to expect that lynching events have been significantly underreported, it is generally accepted that from 1882 to 1968, well over 4,000 lynchings took place across the United States, often in public spectacles attended by white racist mobs of hundreds or thousands (Equal Justice Initiative 2017). As of November 2020, the Tuskegee University Archives collection on lynchings put the estimated total number of victims at 4,734. As context for Randolph's sermon, I note that the Tuskegee University Archives report 301 documented lynchings of African Americans between 1920 and 1930. In 1930, when Randolph likely preached this sermon, two African American men, J. Thomas Shipp and Abraham S. Smith, were lynched in Indiana and at least eighteen others were lynched across the United States (Johnson 2020). The Ku Klux Klan was active in New Jersey from 1921 through the late 1920s (Chalmers 1987, 243-53), and the racist organization was officially disbanded in that state only in 1944. We can well imagine that in 1930, Randolph's sermonic theme about not being afraid, her enlisting of women preachers as liberators in the spiritual lineage of Miriam and Deborah, and her closing words about oppression and enslavement would have been deeply stirring to her listeners.

Nan Stewart, born in 1850 to parents enslaved on the Hunt plantation in Charleston, West Virginia, explains in a 1937 oral-history interview (Stewart 1941, 86-91) how she came to understand freedom in light of Mic 4:4:

Introduction

> Culured preachahs use to cum to plantashun an' dey would read de Bible to us. I 'member one special passage preachahs read an' I neber understood it 'til I cross de riber at Buffinton Island. It wuz, "But they shall sit every man under his own vine and under his fig tree; and none shall make them afraid; for the mouth of the Lord of Hosts hath spoken it." Micah 4:4. Den I knows it is de fulfillment ob dat promis; "I would soon be undah my own vine an' fig tree" and hab no feah of bein' sold down de riber to a mean Marse. I recalls der wuz Thorton Powell, Ben Sales and Charley Releford among de preachahs. (89)

Stewart mentions Buffington Island, an island in the Ohio River near Ravenswood, West Virginia. Thought to have been a station on the Underground Railroad, the island was the site of a Civil War battle on 19 July 1863 won by Union troops.

In "Good without God," a sermon on **6:6-8** preached in England between July 1937 and 1939, the Methodist minister William Sangster (1900-1960) deplores the growing separation he perceives between morality and committed religious praxis. He ventriloquizes secularists who insist ethical action is possible apart from "sermons and sacraments, prayers and parsons, churches and chants, hymns and amens" (1971, 346). Sangster cheerfully concedes that the Israelites may not have been skilled warriors ("the Philistines proved that") or adept farmers ("their inability to squeeze from the soil as much as the Canaanites explains the seductiveness of the Baalim"), but lauds their "great spiritual insight . . . that the holy God required a holy people" (346). While "mere ceremonies" are indeed meaningless to God, and believers cannot accomplish the "devotion of clean hearts and ordered lives" on our own, "grace was thrown like a bridge across the abyss" through the mediation of Jesus Christ (346-47). Strategically choosing not to mention death-dealing atrocities committed under the banner of Christianity over the centuries, Sangster boldly declares, "Almost everyone alive to-day owes an incalculable debt to Christianity, whether they embrace the faith themselves or not," averring that if more people had heeded "the ethic of Christ" concerning love and care for others, "Europe to-day would not be a continent in arms," the emancipation of women would not have been delayed, and slavery would have been rightly adjudged "incompatible with His teaching" (347-48). Suppressing "the religion of Christ," as the Nazis are doing when they "kill or imprison her pastors," leads to appalling outcomes: "Freedom dies. . . . Truth yields place to propaganda. Oppression and bad faith become too common to excite surprise," and worst of all, "Jews are persecuted in the country which gave birth to Heinrich Heine, Jacob Mendelssohn, and Albert Einstein" (350).

Alluding to the cannibalism imagery in Mic **3:2-3**, United Methodist pastor Charles Aaron affirms that contemporary preachers on Micah must dare to confront appalling injustices in their own times: they "have an obligation to shine the spotlight on inhuman working conditions, commercialization of children's sexuality, the persistence of slavery in some countries, and other ways in which God's children are 'chewed up and spit out' by those callous enough to get rich at the expense of others" (2005, 95). In "A Vision in Stained Glass," a sermon on Mic **4:1-5** preached at Waterloo Theological Seminary in Ontario, Canada, sometime between 2001 and 2004, David Schnasa Jacobsen invites listeners to consider that in every time of disaster or threat, "God is doing the work of peace" by "gathering broken folks like us into a new people," for "God will give us peace by piecing together our brokenness." Weaving eucharistic imagery into the theological claim, Jacobsen says, "Micah's vision was hopeful precisely because it met a nation where it was most broken. . . . We who are bound together by gracious symbols of a broken body and blood poured out should know. It's just how God operates" (Aaron 2005, 109-10). In "Check!," a sermon preached on the first day of classes at Perkins School of Theology in August 2000, Alyce McKenzie suggests that Mic **6:8** constitutes a divine "syllabus" on "walking attentively with God": the Lord "requires that the condition of the helpless and the poor, the struggling and the lonely, make a claim on our passion, our conduct, and our attention" (Aaron 2005, 142).

In "A Resurrection Option," a sermon on Mic **4:1-5** delivered on 4 May 2003 at Grace and Holy Trinity Cathedral in Kansas City, Missouri, the United Church of Christ preacher Walter Brueggemann lifts up Micah's eschatological vision as a promise that "things will not stay as they are" for those who must eke out an existence "under the grinding reality of one empire after another," for "God will not stop until the world has been healed and brought to its senses" (2011, 259). The "key mark of God's future is disarmament": believers should align themselves with peacemaking rather than the world's "mantras of aggressive patriotism," repenting of "our consumer appetites that are endless in need and desire" and choosing to live modestly—"one vine and one fig tree, not great vineyards or groves of fig trees"—so that there is enough for all (260-62).

In "The People's Court (Micah 7:18-20)," a sermon preached on 18 October 2015 at the Beech Street Christian Church in Ashland, Kentucky, Rob O'Lynn highlights Judean leaders' "open disregard" for justice, presses the

Introduction

point that the people too were complicit in injustice, and elaborates on the divine mandate, via **6:8**, that believers "[order] our entire lives around God's word." Mustering texts from Genesis, Exodus, Joshua, the Psalms, Isaiah, Jeremiah, 1 John, and Ephesians in a rich tapestry of biblical promises, O'Lynn focalizes the incomparability of a compassionate God via Mic **7:18–20** for his hearers: the coming Messiah (**5:2–4**) will restore and shepherd the faithful, and God stands ready to forgive and bless.

For a 2016 sermon by Episcopal priest Wilda Gafney that amplifies Micah's call to act for justice (**6:8**) on behalf of those harmed by oppressions based on race, gender, sexuality, economic class, and more, see the History of Consequences textbox for Mic 6. For a 2020 sermon by Protestant minister and activist William J. Barber II that uses Mic **2** to shed light on economic injustice in the United States, see the History of Consequences textbox for Mic 2.

In "This or That?," a sermon delivered on 11 July 2021 in the Duke University Chapel in Durham, North Carolina, Episcopalian preacher Ellen Davis emphasizes Micah's identity as "a farmer from the hinterland" to point up the radical nature of Micah's claim that God's Spirit has fallen on him. Davis draws a sharp contrast between Micah and the "highly elite profession of prophecy" otherwise across the ancient Near East. Prophets tended to be "dignitaries, public intellectuals . . . well-paid advisors to kings," but unlike these court prophets, "Micah the farmer" would have been seen as "a plain-spoken clod walking around the capital city barefoot and half-naked, like someone in mourning" (**1:8**), "an embodied declaration that something was wrong—cosmically wrong." The names of the *shalom* prophets have since disappeared in the mists of time, Davis observes, but Micah's words have echoed powerfully down through the centuries, because Micah spoke "the truth of God." In "the daily news from the eighth century," Micah watched the terrifying approach of the Neo-Assyrian Empire and Judean officials' expropriations of lands, crops, and bodies—warriors, laborers—to fuel Judah's own military defenses. Davis shows us a Judean landscape crowded with war refugees, debt slaves, and displaced and hungry families, then links this to the "massive global homelessness" of our own time, with countless "war refugees, economic refugees, [and] environmental refugees" struggling to survive. The perpetrators of injustice today are "multinational corporations, often in collaboration with governments and elite private investors," who "dominate food production and distribution in this country and around the globe" in an industrialized agricultural juggernaut that continues to disenfranchise innumerable farmers and has become "the chief driver of environmental degradation" across the planet. Micah interweaves "outrage"

Overview of the History of Consequences

and "a wildly hopeful vision" throughout his prophesying. Positioned at "the exact middle" of the Book of the Twelve is his articulation of two possible futures: a Jerusalem in ruins (3:12) and a Jerusalem exalted as a beacon of peace and land care for all (4:1-4). Davis urges her hearers to understand this liminal moment as a time of decision for the faithful today, when "all life hangs in the balance. Which will it be?" Do we choose "violence and hunger" or "God's dream for the world"—swords or plowshares?

Lutheran minister Leah Schade preached a sermon series on Micah in Lexington, Kentucky in 2022. Her first sermon, "The Volcanic Warning—and Promise—of Micah 1:1-7, 2:12-13," was delivered to Hunter Presbyterian Church on 12 June 2022. In it, Schade observes the "volcanic landslide of consequences" that weaken a community marked by violence and injustice. Taking the Ten Commandments as foundational, Schade calls believers to an alternative ethic of ecological justice for people, the land, and all living creatures. Schade preached her second sermon, "Casting a New Vision for Appalachia: A Meditation on Micah Chapters 3, 4, and 5," on 4 October 2022 in a worship service celebrating the Feast of St. Francis of Assisi and marking the end of the Season of Creation, led by Lexington Theological Seminary and the Laudato Si' Commission of the Roman Catholic Diocese of Lexington, Kentucky. Telling the story of a toxic sludge spill in 2000 that devastated aquatic life and property for thirty miles along Kentucky's Tug Fork River, Schade echoes Mic 2-3 on the importance of bearing witness to "the ravages of predatory industries" and calls her hearers to engage in micro acts of "protection, trust, care, and love" for Appalachia. Schade's final sermon in the series, "Justice, Kindness, and Walking Humbly with God's Creation," was delivered on 9 October 2022 to Central Christian Church in Lexington, Kentucky. Using the courtroom trope of Mic 6, Schade takes the role of advocate for our "Earth that is sick with pollution, fossil-fueled greenhouse gases, and plastics that choke waterways as well as our own bloodstream." Referencing 6:1-2, she poses the rhetorical question, "Who is in the jury box? The Earth. All of God's creation. The mountains and hills, the rivers and streams, the elephants and chickadees. The very planet itself" will judge human callousness and greed. To invite spiritual and emotional connection to living creatures, Schade evokes the sacred beauty of the Blanton Forest in Kentucky: its "stream with darting minnows," its "boulders robed in lichen," its "rhododendrons [kneeling] in prayer," and the "drenching baptism" of a sudden rainstorm. Schade closes with a call to the congregation to trust the "marvelous things" (7:15) God has in store for those who "do justice, love kindness, and walk humbly" in care for God's creation.

Introduction

Australian Anglican priest Andrew McGowan preached a sermon entitled "What Does the Lord Require? The Economy of Grace and the Sacrifice of Tyre Nichols," at St. Paul's Episcopal Church in Cleveland Heights, Ohio, on 29 January 2023. Noting the economic dimensions of sacrifice in antiquity, McGowan traces the exploitative logic underlying a pervasive culture of brutality against Black men in the United States, lifting up the death of twenty-nine-year-old Tyre Nichols in Memphis on 10 January due to injuries sustained in a savage police beating: "Tyre was not simply the victim of horrifying violence by a few, but a sacrifice offered by an economic and political system to the false gods of privilege and accumulation." McGowan urges his hearers to align themselves instead with the economy of divine grace operative in the Eucharist, which is a transformative gift offered to all in "the infinite love of God."

Across the centuries, artists have represented Micah texts in inked engravings, carved wood, oil paintings, tempera on wood, frescoes, sculpted marble façades of cathedrals, bronze sculptures, stained glass, music, and other media. Central themes in the history of reception include: the prophet depicted excoriating the Israelites for their sins; the nations beating their swords into plowshares (4:3); Micah prophesying the coming of the Messiah (5:1-4a [Eng. 2-5a]); and Micah's exhortation to believers to do justice, to cherish fidelity or "love mercy," and to proceed or "walk" humbly with God (6:8).

In Christian cantatas, anthems, and hymnody, motifs from Micah feature prominently. Johann Sebastian Bach set Mic 6:8 in his Cantata BWV 45, "Es ist dir gesagt, Mensch, was gut ist," composed in Leipzig for the eighth Sunday after the Feast of the Trinity and performed for the first time on 11 August 1726. Prolific Swedish composer Johan Helmich Roman (1694-1758) composed a motet on 7:18-19, "Vem är en sådana Gud som Du är" (HRV 856). The line from Mic 2:10, "this cannot be the resting place," is reflected in the hymn, "This Is Not My Place of Resting," composed by Horatius Bonar (1808-1889), and likely influenced the lyrics of "My God, I Thank Thee Who Hast Made," a hymn composed in 1858 by Adelaide A. Procter. The vision of cessation of hostilities among nations in Mic 4:1-4 may have shaped "O Day of Peace That Dimly Shines," composed by Carl P. Daw in 1982, while Isaiah's peaceable kingdom (Isa 11:6-9) is most audible in that hymn's lyrics; the line "May swords of hate fall from our hands" reflects Mic 4:3. Micah's irenic vision is featured in "Christ Is the World's True Light," composed in 1931 by George Wallace Briggs, which reframes the prophets' focus on Mount Zion as global union in Christ, enthroned as Prince of Peace ("In Christ all races meet, their ancient feuds forgotten ... all shall forsake their fear, to ploughshare beat the sword, to pruning-hook the spear"); this vision of peace can be heard also in "The Day Is Coming—God Has Promised," composed by Calvin Seerveld in 1985. Bethlehem as the site of the Savior's birth (Mic 5:1 [Eng. 2]), refracted through the innerbiblical quotation in Matt 2:1-6, can be heard in many Christian compositions celebrating Christ's incarnation, including these: the fourteenth-century "Puer natus in Bethlehem"; "Once in Royal David's City," composed by Cecil Frances Alexander in 1848; "O Little Town of Bethlehem," composed by Phillips Brooks in 1868; the anthem "Bethlehem Down," composed by Peter Warlock (Philip Arnold Heseltine) in 1927; and "Little Bethlehem of Judah," composed by Calvin Seerveld in 1986. The exhortations of Mic 6:8 are reflected in many anthems and hymns, including: "Humbly, My God, with Thee I Walk," composed by James Montgomery (1771-1854); "Humble Thyself to Walk with God," composed by Johnson Oatman (1856-1922); "What Does the Lord Require," composed by Albert F. Bayly in 1949; "Listen, O You Mountains (Humbly Walk with God)," composed by K. Lee Scott in 2000; and "With What Shall I Come?," composed by Rosephanye Powell in 2015 and scored for SATB and violin. Traci West describes the public singing of 6:8 in "national protests by the United Methodist Church's Reconciling Movement Network" by those advocating for full inclusion of lesbian, gay, bisexual, and trans believers in the life of the church. West observes, "The Micah text was used as a musical ritual" that "ritualized a liberationist Christian ethics of dissent," articulating "a public accusation of hypocrisy against the majority of delegates who walked into the hall to vote to retain the discriminatory rules maintaining the [supposed] innate superiority of heterosexuals" in the United Methodist tradition (West 2016, 604). Micah 7:19 is audible in the line "Our sins shall sink beneath the sea," in the hymn "In Vain We Lavish out Our Lives," composed by Isaac Watts (1674-1748).

4.2.4 Micah in Christian Liturgies

Passages from Micah are known to have been read in ancient liturgies. Roukema writes that extant are Armenian and Georgian translations of a now-lost Greek lectionary from Jerusalem, the original possibly dating to the fourth century. According to him (2019, 232-33), these resources indicate the following schedule of readings: Mic 4:1-7 for the second Wednesday in Lent (Armenian); 5:1-6 (Eng. 2-7) for Christmas Eve (Georgian) or the eve of the Feast of the Epiphany (Armenian), the latter to be read "on the Site of the Shepherds near Bethlehem"; 6:1-9b for the third Tuesday in Lent (Geor-

Introduction

gian); on the Feast of the Twelve Prophets, 7:7-9 was to be read according to the Armenian lectionary, while for that holy day, the Georgian lectionary assigns 4:1-5, 6-13; 6:1-9b; and 7:7-20, that last passage also scheduled for the sixth Monday in Lent. Roukema observes that a group of medieval liturgical manuscripts prescribe "that the Minor Prophets be read in the nocturnal offices in November," a practice that may go back to earlier than the eighth century (2019, 234). Centuries later, the "*Missale Romanum* of Milan, from 1474," schedules the reading of Mic 7:14, 16, 18, 20 "for Ember Saturday in the third week of September" (235). Micah 6:1-8, or just 6:3-4a, have been featured in Good Friday liturgies from Jerusalem at least as early as the fourth century, from the seventh century onward in Spain, and elsewhere; for details, see the fascinating discussion of Roukema (2019, 235-44).

In contemporary times, the Revised Common Lectionary (1994), a table of biblical lessons designated for worship services in mainline Protestant traditions in the United States and Canada, deploys only three passages from Micah in its three-year liturgical cycle. Micah 3:5-12 is read on Proper 26 in Year A, Mic 5:2-5a (Eng.) is read on the fourth Sunday of Advent in Year C, and Mic 6:1-8 is read on the fourth Sunday of Epiphany in Year C. Thus worshippers attending only on Sundays in traditions that follow the RCL hear not a single line from Micah in Year B, and encounter no passage in any liturgical year drawn from Micah 1, 2, 4, or 7. The Roman Catholic lectionary used in many countries, the *Ordo Lectionum Missae* (1981), along with the Roman Catholic *Lectionary for Mass: For Use in the Dioceses of the United States of America*, volume 1 for Sunday masses (1998), show only a single Micah reading: 5:1-4a is listed for the fourth Sunday of Advent in Year C. In volumes 2-4 (2002), which list many more readings designated for weekday masses, five Micah passages are deployed: 2:1-5; 5:1-4a; 6:1-4, 6-8; 7:7-9; and 7:14-15, 18-20. Roman Catholic liturgical reading of 7:14-20 on Ember Days may date back to the seventh century (Sumani 2016). In the Greek Orthodox lectionary, Mic 5:2-5 is read in the First Hour on the Eve of the Nativity of Christ, and 4:6-7 + 5:2-4 is read during Vespers in that evening.

4.2.5 Micah in Social Justice Movements

Numerous faith-based and social justice organizations have grounded their vision, mission, or programmatic initiatives in passages from Micah, overwhelmingly with reference to two passages: 4:3 on beating swords into plowshares, and the first of the three imperatives in the final clause of 6:8, "do justice." Many peace movements and nonprofit organizations have chosen the name "Swords to Plowshares." One such organization, founded in 1974 in San Francisco, provides policy advocacy and direct services addressing poverty, housing precarity, posttraumatic stress disorder and other mental illnesses, unemployment, insufficient disability compensation, and other challenges experienced by United States veterans. In the former East Germany, peace initiatives led by Christian pastors and youth groups as early as 1980 catalyzed support for nonviolence and an end to the proliferation of nuclear weapons using bookmarks and textile patches emblazoned with the motto, "Schwerter zu Pflugscharen" (image on p. 277); activists displaying the insignia were at risk of punitive consequences by DDR authorities. Swords to Plowshares Northeast, established in 2017 in New Haven, Connecticut, by founders from the United Church of Christ, Episcopal, and Jewish traditions, works with local law enforcement to acquire handguns and rifles through gun buyback programs, then has incarcerated persons and volunteer blacksmiths melt down the weapons for garden tools and works of art. In May 2023, the Class of 2023 of Berkeley Divinity School at Yale gifted the school with a processional cross around which are entwined stunning wrought-iron lilies crafted by blacksmith Peter Catchpole of Iron Ore Art in Milford, Connecticut. Graduating student Paul J. Keene said in his remarks, "We asked Peter to procure weapons, to break them, to shatter them, and to reforge them into this cross as a testament to God's transformative power to turn the weapons of death into the tools of life."

An official statement crafted in March 1992 by Canadian Christian leaders draws on Mic 4:4—translated as "and no one shall make them afraid"— to elucidate causes of violence against women, including "imbalance of power . . . a distorted view of sexuality and the objectification of the female body," and a cultural failure to educate people "on resolving problems nonviolently," and to press for changes in theological-school and church curricula, development of "pastoral and liturgical resources to help acknowledge and deal with violence in human communities," and advocacy in public policy to secure "economic justice for women," shelters and other housing for survivors of abuse, and "programs for rehabilitating abusers" (Gervais et al. 1992, 27–28). The statement was signed by the Canadian Conference of Catholic Bishops, the Anglican Church of Canada, the United Church of Canada, the Evangelical Lutheran Church in Canada, the Evangelical Fellowship of Canada, the Presbyterian Church in Canada, the Salvation Army for the territory of Canada and Bermuda, the Mennonite Central Committee of Canada, the Council of Christian Reformed Churches in Canada, the Women's Inter-Church Council of Canada, and the Church Council on Justice and

Introduction

Corrections, a breadth of jurisdictions that surely makes this one of the furthest-reaching promotions in Christian history of ethical application of a Micah passage other than 4:3 (swords into plowshares) or 6:8.

Saint Louis University in St. Louis, Missouri, offers a Micah Program, founded in 1996, described as "focusing on pillars of academics, service, leadership, and interfaith community," with membership open to all students, with or without religious commitments, who wish to live together in community and work for social justice. Nine congregations collaborating in Micah Ecumenical Ministries in Fredericksburg, Virginia, have been working since 2005 to alleviate homelessness. In 2011, Fuller Theological Seminary began seven pilot Micah Groups as part of a cohort-based preaching initiative for the spiritual formation of developing preachers committed to justice; the seminary reports there are now almost 150 Micah Groups worldwide. Facing the problem of homelessness in St. Paul, Minnesota, the Metropolitan Interfaith Council on Affordable Housing (MICAH) advocates for policy and justice initiatives designed to secure a living wage, access to education, good healthcare, and affordable housing for all. A network of thirty-nine congregations in Wisconsin called Milwaukee Inner-City Congregations Allied for Hope (MICAH) organizes events for local residents on criminal justice and prison reform, health-care equity, employment and economic development, and more.

Micah Global, a Christian network headquartered in England, partners with other groups on advocacy and public education related to alleviating world hunger, extreme poverty, and the refugee crisis; provides fellowships for personnel in hospitals and nongovernmental organizations in developing countries; and offers support for innovative technologies and tools addressing neglected tropical diseases. In 2004, the World Evangelical Alliance and associated Christian relief and development agencies launched the Micah Challenge, a global network of not-for-profit groups, communities, and individuals that now has justice initiatives underway in more than forty countries. Groups participating in the Micah Challenge had worked on the eight Millennium Development Goals promoted by the United Nations through 2015, and since that year have addressed the seventeen United Nations Supportable Development Goals, which include: ending poverty and gender oppression; ensuring worldwide access to education and clean energy; building resilient and innovative infrastructure in human settlements; and taking urgent measures to combat climate change and its deleterious consequences in terrestrial and marine environments.

Chicago's Samuel DeWitt Proctor Conference sponsors a Micah Institute that offers education for Christian leaders and congregations wishing to

Overview of the History of Consequences

explore the interrelationship of practices of faith and the use of financial resources. Youth pastor Amy Jacober uses the notion of ḥesed in Mic 6:8 to ground her call for youth ministries to work toward expansive inclusion of teens with disabilities as essential for the abundant life to which God calls us (2019). Finally, untold numbers of scholars and others who hold Jewish or Christian faith commitments have found ways to articulate the importance of Micah's theology and ethics for contemporary communities facing political corruption, economic exploitation, or injurious social policies that harm the most vulnerable members of society.

This commentary now takes its place in the stream of reception history of the book of Micah. In popular discourse in contemporary United States culture and in the perspectives of scholars in theological education whose expertise is not in biblical studies, I have seen a tenacious reductionism concerning what biblical prophecy connotes. A number of educated people seem to equate prophecy with a harsh and simplistic call for social justice. In some quarters, there seems to be little awareness of the brilliantly nuanced means by which the books of the Latter Prophets perform their art toward a multitude of richly variegated rhetorical purposes for their communities, understood, of course, as plural for prophetic books redacted over generations. I have urged that activists, artists, preachers, and writers reflect on the biblical heritage of the Latter Prophets in terms of a fuller range of possibilities for contemporary responses (Sharp 2019a, 225–27). With Isaiah, Hosea, and others in the biblical prophetic corpus, and with prophets from antiquity whose teachings and oracles are lost to us, Micah offers compelling wisdom and fresh visioning for believers and communities that yearn to do justice, cherish fidelity, and proceed humbly with the God whom they worship. Here is the spectrum of creative possibilities I invite readers to explore in the Retrospect section of each Micah chapter:

→ resilience → resistance → reformation → rejoicing

As I understand these practices, they represent not a linear progression but a spiral of concurrent possibilities that fluidly influence, complexify, and displace one another in their articulations in community, shifting as contextual factors change and new voices emerge.

As each reader's appreciation of Micah will be shaped by their own beliefs and values, so my own suggestions in each Retrospect section have been formed not only through my training as a biblical scholar and practi-

Introduction

cal theologian, but through my lived values as a peace-loving, ecologically minded feminist Christian opposed to every kind of violence. For decades, I have claimed pacifism and reject as indefensible the horrific harms perpetrated by planned military violence against combatants and noncombatants alike. Those harms include: mass deaths with untold repercussions for multigenerational bereavement and communal despair; bodily maiming; rampant sexual violence, both in conflict zones and within the ranks of military organizations; emotional trauma and moral injury of a magnitude that is virtually immeasurable; the obliteration of countless homes, infrastructures essential to community life, and irreplaceable cultural artifacts; and the desecration of holy spaces and other venues where survivors of war might have found consolation. For decades, I have claimed feminism as a life-giving nexus of insights and practices designed to honor the agency and integrity of girls and women, gender-nonconforming persons, boys and men, and other living beings. For communities committed to justice, constant vigilance and fierce resistance are needed in response to countless expressions of gender-based oppression and violence, distorted cisheteropatriarchal ideology, and the intersectionally linked hierarchies of domination and exploitation based on white supremacy or other racialized systems of harm, suppression of indigenous groups, and the profound violence of economic subjugation. Words fail me to describe the depth, complexity, and blazing urgency of the feminist struggle.

In oracle after beautifully crafted oracle, through diverse and artful rhetorical means, Micah teaches his community to remain resilient through national and regional traumas; he urges them to engage in active resistance of the depredations of the elite and the violence of invading armies; he exhorts them to reform their understanding of Yhwh's requirements for ethical life and faithful theological praxis; and he invites them to rejoice in the divine deliverance they had known in days of old and can envision for the future restoration of Zion. As contemporary readers and communities gather around the book of Micah, we too can find in its pages extraordinary resources for resilience, resistance, reformation, and rejoicing.

BIBLIOGRAPHY

Aaron, C. L., Jr. 2005. *Preaching Hosea, Amos, and Micah*. Preaching Classic Texts. St. Louis: Chalice.

Aitken, J. K. 2015. "The Origins of ΚΑΙ ΓΕ." Pages 21–40 in *Biblical Greek in*

Context: Essays in Honour of John A. L. Lee. Edited by J. K. Aitken and T. V. Evans. BTS 22. Leuven: Peeters.

Albert the Great. 2020. *On Resurrection.* Translated by I. M. Resnick and F. T. Harkins. FCMC 20. Washington, DC: Catholic University of America Press.

Albertz, R. 2003. *Israel in Exile: The History and Literature of the Sixth Century B.C.E.* Translated by D. Green. SBLStBL 3. Atlanta: Society of Biblical Literature.

Alfaro, J. 2021. "The Old Greek of Jonah and Its Revisions." *BN* 190:87-99.

Alfonsi, P. 2006. *Dialogue against the Jews.* Translated by I. M. Resnick. FCMC 8. Washington, DC: Catholic University of America Press.

Allen, J. 1772. "An Oration upon the Beauties of Liberty; Or, the Essential Rights of the Americans." National Humanities Center, America in Class. https://americainclass.org/sources/makingrevolution/crisis/text6/allenorationbeauties.pdf.

Aquinas, T. 2010. *The Academic Sermons.* Translated by M.-R. Hoogland. FCMC 11. Washington, DC: Catholic University of America Press.

Baskin, J. R. 2021. "Miriam's Well." *EBR* 19:329-30. doi:10.1515/ebr.miriamswell.

Ben Zvi, E., and J. D. Nogalski. 2009. *Two Sides of a Coin: Juxtaposing Views on Interpreting the Book of the Twelve.* Analecta Gorgiana 201. Piscataway, NJ: Gorgias.

Benjamin, A. 2017. "Recovering Anoriginal Relationality." *Research in Phenomenology* 47:250-61. doi:10.1163/15691640-12341370.

Berlin, A. 2008. *The Dynamics of Biblical Parallelism.* 2nd ed. Biblical Resource Series. Grand Rapids: Eerdmans.

Brueggemann, W. 2011. "A Resurrection Option." Pages 259-62 in *The Collected Sermons of Walter Brueggemann.* Vol. 1. Louisville: Westminster John Knox.

Buber, M. 1923. *Ich und Du.* Leipzig: Insel.

Chalmers, D. M. 1987. *Hooded Americanism: The History of the Ku Klux Klan.* 3rd ed. Durham, NC: Duke University Press.

Collier-Thomas, B. 1998. *Daughters of Thunder: Black Women Preachers and Their Sermons, 1850-1979.* San Francisco: Jossey-Bass.

Damian, P. 1989. *Letters 1-30.* Translated by O. J. Blum. FCMC 1. Washington, DC: Catholic University of America Press.

Dietrich, W. 2016. *Nahum, Habakkuk, Zephaniah.* Translated by P. Altmann. IECOT. Stuttgart: Kohlhammer.

Dines, J. 2012. "Verbal and Thematic Links between the Books of the Twelve in Greek and Their Relevance to the Differing Manuscript Sequences."

Introduction

Pages 355–70 in *Perspectives on the Formation of the Book of the Twelve: Methodological Foundations—Redactional Processes—Historical Insights.* Edited by R. Albertz, J. D. Nogalski, and J. Wöhrle. BZAW 433. Berlin: De Gruyter. doi:10.1515/9783110283761.355.

Ego, B., A. Lange, H. Lichtenberger, and K. De Troyer. 2004. "Micah, Based on Transcriptions of R. E. Fuller, A. Lange, J. T. Milik, and E. Tov." Pages 89–111 in *Biblia Qumranica*. Vol. 3B: *Minor Prophets*. Leiden: Brill.

Equal Justice Initiative. 2017. "Lynching in America: Confronting the Legacy of Racial Terror." 3rd ed. https://lynchinginamerica.eji.org/report/.

Eshel, H., and H. M Cotton. 2021. "Ḥever, Naḥal." Pages 357–59 in vol. 1 of *Encyclopedia of the Dead Sea Scrolls*. Edited by L. H. Schiffman and J. C. VanderKam. 2 vols. Oxford: Oxford University Press.

Fraade, S. D. 2007. "Rabbinic Polysemy and Pluralism Revisited: Between Praxis and Thematization." *AJSR* 31:1–40. doi:10.1017/S0364009907000219.

Fuller, R. 2020. "The Book of the Twelve at Qumran." Pages 271–85 in *The Book of the Twelve: Composition, Reception, and Interpretation*. Edited by L.-S. Tiemeyer and J. Wöhrle. VTSup 184. Leiden: Brill. doi:10.1163/9789004424326_019.

Gafney, W. C. 2017. *Womanist Midrash: A Reintroduction to the Women of the Torah and the Throne*. Louisville: Westminster John Knox.

Garton, R. E. 2012. "Rattling the Bones of the Twelve: Wilderness Reflections in the Formation of the Book of the Twelve." Pages 237–51 in *Perspectives on the Formation of the Book of the Twelve: Methodological Foundations—Redactional Processes—Historical Insights*. Edited by R. Albertz, J. D. Nogalski, and J. Wöhrle. BZAW 433. Berlin: De Gruyter. doi:10.1515/9783110283761.237.

Gervais, M., et al. 1992 (June). "And No One Shall Make Them Afraid (Micah 4:4): The Church Leaders' Submission to the Canadian Panel on Violence Against Women." *Ecumenism* 106:27–29.

Gordon, B. 2009. *Calvin*. New Haven: Yale University Press.

Gottlieb, D. N. 2021. "Midrash Rabbah (MidRab): I. Rabbinic Judaism." *EBR* 19:42–44.

Guillaume, P. 2007. "A Reconsideration of Manuscripts Classified as Scrolls of the Twelve Minor Prophets (XII)." *JHS* 7, article 16. doi:10.5508/jhs.2007.v7.a16.

Ham, C. A. 2019. "The Minor Prophets in Matthew's Gospel." Pages 39–56 in *The Minor Prophets in the New Testament*. Edited by M. J. J. Menken and S. Moyise. LNTS 377. London: T&T Clark.

Heyden, K. 2022. "Dialogue as a Means of Religious Co-Production: Historical Perspectives." *Religions* 13:150. doi:10.3390/rel13020150.

Hoke, J. 2021. *Feminism, Queerness, Affect, and Romans*. ECL 30. Atlanta: SBL Press.

Honig, B. 2021. *A Feminist Theory of Refusal*. Cambridge: Harvard University Press.

Jacober, A. E. 2019. "*Hesed*: How Youth Ministry with Teens with Disabilities Helps Restore an Abundant Community." *Journal of Youth Ministry* 17:34–57.

Jeremias, J. 1971. "Die Deutung der Gerichtsworte Michas in der Exilzeit." *ZAW* 83:330–54.

Johnson, C. W. 2020. "Lynching Information." Tuskegee University Archives Repository. http://archive.tuskegee.edu/repository/digital-collection/lynching-information/.

Kadari, T. 2022. "The Enchanted World of Midrash and Its Unexpected Return in Recent Generations." Pages xiii–xxxii in *Dirshuni: Contemporary Women's Midrash*. Edited by T. Biala. HBI Series on Jewish Women. Waltham, MA: Brandeis University Press. doi:10.2307/j.ctv2cmr99d.3.

Lasker, D. J. 1996. "Jewish-Christian Polemics at the Turning Point: Jewish Evidence from the Twelfth Century." *HTR* 89:161–73. doi:10.1017/S0017816000031965.

Lescow, T. 1972. "Redaktionsgeschichtliche Analyse von Micha 1–5." *ZAW* 84:61–64.

Longenbach, J. 2008. *The Art of the Poetic Line*. Minneapolis: Graywolf.

Macchi, J.-D., M. Albl, R. Fuller, B. D. Walfish, N. Grunhaus, J. Rosenbaum, R. Roukema, S. R. Burge, O. Z. Soltes, and N. H. Petersen. 2020. "Micah (Book and Person)." *EBR* 18:1096–1116. doi:10.1515/ebr.micahbookandperson.

Menken, M. J. J. 2019. "The Minor Prophets in John's Gospel." Pages 79–96 in *The Minor Prophets in the New Testament*. Edited by M. J. J. Menken and S. Moyise. LNTS 377. London: T&T Clark.

Minkema, K. P. 2011. "Informing of the Child's Understanding, Influencing His Heart, and Directing Its Practice: Jonathan Edwards on Education." *AcT* 31.2:159–89. doi:10.4314/actat.v31i2.8.

———. 2021. "Writing and Preaching Sermons." Pages 387–403 in *The Oxford Handbook of Jonathan Edwards*. Edited by D. A. Sweeney and J. Stievermann. Oxford: Oxford University Press. doi:10.1093/oxfordhb/9780198754060.013.29.

Nagen, Y. 2022. "Sharing Torah with the World: The Jewish People's Responsibility to Non-Jews." Translated by R. G. Schultz. *Tradition* 54.3:29–50.

Nogalski, J. D. 1993. *Literary Precursors to the Book of the Twelve.* BZAW 217. Berlin: De Gruyter.

Ottenheijm, E. 2022. "*Meshalim* on Election and Power: Two Examples in Tanhuma Buber." Pages 270–89 in *Studies in the Tanhuma-Yelammedenu Literature.* Edited by R. Nikolsky and A. Atzmon. BRLJ 70. Leiden: Brill. doi:10.1163/9789004469198_014.

Palmén, R., and K. J. Koskinen. 2016. "Mediated Recognition and the Quest for a Common Rational Field of Discussion in Three Early Medieval Dialogues." *Open Theology* 2:374–90. doi:10.1515/opth-2016-0031.

Parsons, M. 2006. *Calvin's Preaching on the Prophet Micah: The 1550–1551 Sermons in Geneva.* Lewiston, NY: Mellen.

Sandt, H. van de. 2019. "The Minor Prophets in Luke–Acts." Pages 57–77 in *The Minor Prophets in the New Testament.* Edited by M. J. J. Menken and S. Moyise. LNTS 377. London: T&T Clark.

Sangster, W. E. 1971. "Good without God." Pages 345–50 in vol. 11 of *20 Centuries of Great Preaching: An Encyclopedia of Preaching.* Edited by C. E. Fant Jr. and W. M. Pinson. 13 vols. Waco, TX: Word.

Saperstein, M. 2008. *Jewish Preaching in Times of War, 1800–2001.* Oxford: Littman Library of Jewish Civilization.

Scales, A. T. 2018. "Justice and Equity: John Calvin's 1550 Sermon on Micah 2:1." *IJH* 3:16–29. doi:10.21827/ijh.2018.39449.

Sharp, C. J. 2003. Review of *Deutero-Isaiah,* by Klaus Baltzer. *SJT* 56:103–6.

———. 2010. "Hewn by the Prophet: An Analysis of Violence and Sexual Transgression in Hosea with Reference to the Homiletical Aesthetic of Jeremiah Wright." Pages 50–71 in *Aesthetics of Violence in the Prophets.* Edited by C. Franke and J. M. O'Brien. LHBOTS 517. London: T&T Clark.

Silverman, J. M. 2021. "Historical Economics and the Minor Prophets." *OHMP,* 323–40. doi:10.1093/oxfordhb/9780190673208.013.23.

Simkovich, M. Z. 2021. "The Minor Prophets in Early Judaism." *OHMP,* 229–42. doi:10.1093/oxfordhb/9780190673208.013.38.

Stewart, N. 1941. Oral history interview with Sarah Probst, reporter, and Audrey Meighen, author-editor. Pages 86–91 in *Slave Narratives: A Folk History of Slave Narratives in the United States from Interviews with Former Slaves: Typewritten Records Prepared by the Federal Writers' Project, 1936–1938.* Vol. 12: *Ohio Narratives.* Washington, DC: Federal Writers' Project of the Works Progress Administration for the State of Ohio.

Sumani, W. 2016. "Easter Vigil as the 'Mother of All Vigils': The Significance of Structural Parallels between the Easter Vigil and the Vigils of Pentecost and the Tempora in the Roman Rite." *Ecclesia orans* 33:7–48.

Suso, H. 2019. *Wisdom's Watch upon the Hours*. Translated by E. Colledge. FCMC 4. Washington, DC: Catholic University of America Press.

Thompson, M. M. 2015. *John: A Commentary*. NTL. Louisville: Westminster John Knox.

Tov, E., with the collaboration of R. A. Kraft and a contribution by P. J. Parsons. 1990. *The Greek Minor Prophets Scroll from Naḥal Ḥever (8ḤevXIIgr)*. Seiyâl Collection 1. DJD 8. Oxford: Oxford University Press.

Ueberschaer, F. 2020. "The Book of the Twelve in Early Jewish Literature." Pages 352–84 in *The Book of the Twelve: Composition, Reception, and Interpretation*. Edited by L.-S. Tiemeyer and J. Wöhrle. VTSup 184. Leiden: Brill. doi:10.1163/9789004424326_023.

Viezel, E. 2017. "The Rise and Fall of Jewish Philological Exegesis on the Bible in the Middle Ages: Causes and Effects." *Review of Rabbinic Judaism* 20:48–88. doi:10.1163/15700704-12341319.

Weiss, D. 2022. "Dramatic Dialogues in the Tanhuma-Yelammedenu Midrashim." Pages 249–69 in *Studies in the Tanhuma-Yelammedenu Literature*. Edited by R. Nikolsky and A. Atzmon. BRLJ 70. Leiden: Brill. doi:10.1163/9789004469198_013.

Werse, N. R. 2019. *Reconsidering the Book of the Four: The Shaping of Hosea, Amos, Micah, and Zephaniah as an Early Prophetic Collection*. BZAW 517. Berlin: De Gruyter.

Wöhrle, J. 2008. "'No Future for the Proud Exultant Ones': The Exilic Book of the Four Prophets (Hos., Am., Mic., Zeph.) as a Concept Opposed to the Deuteronomistic History." *VT* 58:608–27. doi:10.1163/156853308X344532.

———. 2012. "So Many Cross-References! Methodological Reflections on the Problem of Intertextual Relationships and Their Significance for Redaction Critical Analysis." Pages 3–20 in *Perspectives on the Formation of the Book of the Twelve: Methodological Foundations, Redactional Processes, Historical Insights*. Edited by R. Albert, J. D. Nogalski, and J. Wöhrle. BZAW 433. Berlin: De Gruyter. doi:10.1515/9783110283761.3.

———. 2020. "The Book of the Four." Pages 15–37 in *The Book of the Twelve: Composition, Reception, and Interpretation*. Edited by L.-S. Tiemeyer and J. Wöhrle. VTSup 184. Leiden: Brill. doi:10.1163/9789004424326_003.

Commentary

Fig. 6. Judah after the fall of the Northern Kingdom of Israel.

MICAH 1

Superscription

1:1

¹The word of Yhwh that came to Micah the Moreshethite in the days of Jotham, Ahaz, [and] Hezekiah—kings of Judah—which he saw concerning Samaria and Jerusalem.

Divine Wrath Descends from on High

1:2–7

>²Pay attention, all you peoples!
>>Give heed, O earth and all that fills it!
>
>And may the Lord God serve as a witness against you {*mp*},
>>the Lord from [Yhwh's]* holy temple.
>
>³For ^(mark this:) Yhwh is coming forth from [Yhwh's] place
>>and will come down and tread upon the high places of the earth.
>
>⁴The mountains will melt under [Yhwh],
>>and the valleys will split apart,
>
>like wax yielding to the fire,
>>like waters flooding down a slope.

---

* As a feminist translator, I decline to inscribe theological androcentrism in this translation by using masculine pronouns for the deity. Where needed for clarity, I supply "Yhwh" or "Yhwh's" in brackets. The emphatic particle *hinnēh* is translated as "mark this" in superscript at 1:3 and 2:3 to note the presence of the particle without giving it undue weight.

Micah 1

⁵All this is for the transgression of Jacob
    and for the sins of the house of Israel.
Who constitutes the transgression of Jacob?
    Is it not Samaria?
And who constitutes the high places of Judah?
    Is it not Jerusalem?
⁶So I will make Samaria a heap of rubble in the field,
    a place for planting vineyards.
I will pour her stones into the valley,
    and her foundations I will lay bare.
⁷All her images will be pulverized,
    and all her wages will be set ablaze,
        and all her idols I will make a desolation;
for as from the wage of a prostitute she has gathered [them],
    thus as the wage of a prostitute they will return.

The Prophet Laments

1:8–9

⁸Concerning this I will lament and howl;
    I will go about barefoot and stripped.
I will make lamentation like the jackals,
    and mourning like the ostriches:
⁹"Indeed, she has been fatally weakened by her wounds!
    For it {*fs*} has come as far as Judah.
He has struck as far as the gate of my people,
    as far as Jerusalem."

Cartography of Destruction

1:10–16

¹⁰In Gath, do not announce {*mp*} it;
    do not weep bitterly {*fs*}!
In Beth-leaphrah,
    roll yourself {*fs*} in the dust!
¹¹Pass by {*fs*} for your {*mp*} own sake,
    O inhabitant of Shaphir: nakedness, shame!

The inhabitant of Zaanan has not gone forth.
The lamentation of Beth-ezel:
    he has robbed you of its place to take a stand.
¹²Though the inhabitant of Maroth longs for good,
    surely calamity has come down from Yhwh
        to the gate of Jerusalem.

¹³Harness {*ms*} the horses to the chariot,
    O inhabitant of Lachish:
this [was] the beginning of sin for Daughter Zion,
    for in you {*fs*} have been found the transgressions of Israel.
¹⁴Therefore you will give parting gifts
    to Moresheth-gath;
the houses of Achzib have become deception
    for the kings of Israel.
¹⁵Again I will bring the dispossessor against you,
    O inhabitant of Mareshah.
As far as Adullam will come the Glory of Israel.

¹⁶Make yourself bald and cut off your hair {*fs*}
    because of your treasured children!
Make your baldness as extensive as that of the vulture,
    for they have gone into exile from you.

INTERPRETATION

Micah 1 propels us into the public theological witness of the prophet Micah during the reigns of three kings of Judah: Jotham, Ahaz, and Hezekiah. The prophetic witness opens with a dramatic portrayal of Yhwh descending from heaven to wreak judgment on Israel and Judah (1:5) for their sins. The poetry expresses in vivid terms an earthquake of divine retribution that will crush mountains and open massive rifts in valleys. All that lies beneath the feet of Yhwh melts and crumbles and pours downhill, is deconstructed and falls into rubble, is pulverized into fragments and set ablaze. The shock waves of Yhwh's fury will spread inexorably through the landscape, dismantling built structures in Samaria, the capital of the Northern Kingdom of Israel, and reaching to the gates of Jerusalem. The effects of this divine reckoning will leave inhabitants of surrounding villages stunned and in

Micah 1

mourning (1:10-15); Israelite and Judean children alike will be forced into exile (1:16). All of Judah suffers. Families in tiny villages—places that aren't even on the map, literally and figuratively—must hide in terror from enemy troops ravaging the land. In the time of Micah, the threat is clothed in Assyrian garb, and later, destruction will march into Judah under the insignia of the Neo-Babylonian Empire. Neither imperial power will hesitate to slaughter Judeans and force prisoners of war into diaspora. These conflicts would leave the land decimated, with surviving Judeans traumatized and at risk of the famine that can come in the wake of militarized destruction.

Superscription (1:1)

The historical context explicitly claimed in the superscription places the witness of the prophet in a volatile time in the Judean community. Reflected artfully in Mic 1 and material throughout the book of Micah is knowledge of devastating military incursions launched by the Neo-Assyrian Empire against the Levant. First was an assault against the Northern Kingdom under the leadership of Shalmaneser V, king from 727 to 722 BCE. Upon his death, his successor, Sargon II, captured Samaria immediately; Sargon II would sit on the Assyrian throne from 722 to 705 BCE. Later came an assault against Judah and Jerusalem led by the son of Sargon II, Sennacherib (r. 705-681). Sennacherib besieged Jerusalem in 701. His annals report that he was victorious, while the perspective of biblical texts is that Yhwh intervened to strike down the Assyrian troops (2 Kgs 18-19 and the parallel text in Isa 36-37; see also 2 Chr 32:1-23). But the focus of Mic 1 is not on the mighty victory of Yhwh over the enemies of Samaria and Jerusalem. Rather, the prophet causes his audience to linger in that liminal moment when devastation loomed for numerous smaller cities and villages in Judah.

Divine Wrath Descends from on High (1:2-7)

Micah 1-3 is framed by an *inclusio* with vivid images of devastation. The poetry of 1:6 dramatizes Samaria, the capital of the Northern Kingdom, being toppled into a heap of rubble in the open field and becoming unbuilt—reduced to a bare hill for planting terraced vineyards. The downward motion signaled by several verbs depicts an inexorable cascade effect: The implied audience witnesses an unstoppable avalanche of judgment that wrecks ev-

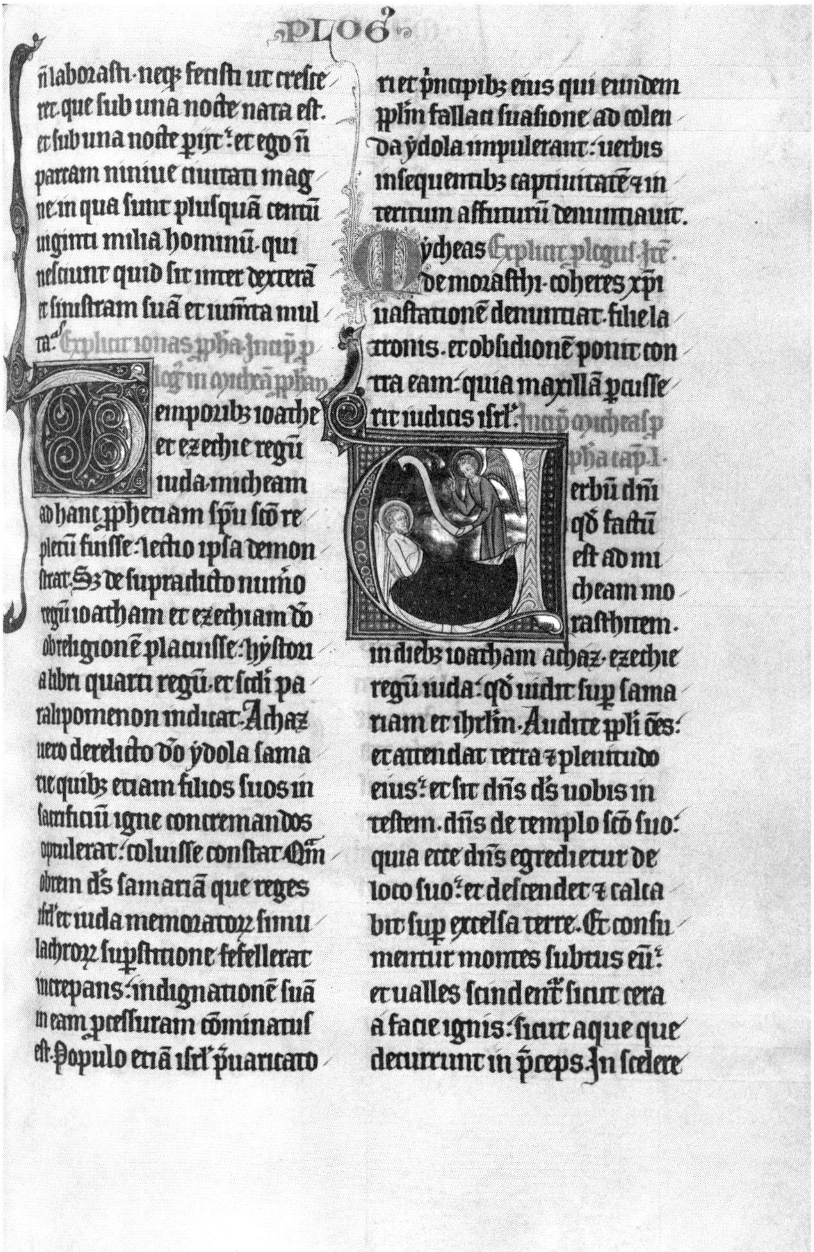

Divine Wrath Descends from on High 1:2–7

Fig. 7. Initial V: An Angel before Micah, ca. 1270. Illuminated manuscript by unknown artist, likely in Lille, France. Tempera, black ink, and gold leaf.

erything in its path. The lesson offered by the prophet may be reflecting on the ruins of the palace of Omri, king of Israel (r. 884–873) in Samaria. The Omride lineage was powerful: Omri was on the throne twelve years, then Ahab ruled for twenty-two years, Ahaziah for two years, Jehoram for twelve years, and then Athaliah, a queen mother in the Omride dynasty, reigned for six years (841–835). The dynasty as a whole seems to have lasted over fifty years. Yet it, too, fell to rubble. This cautionary word from Micah would have been effective for his own generation and for subsequent circles of hearers gathered around his oracles: No matter how strong an empire may be, no matter how invincible an economic system of exploitation and commodification might seem, no matter how intractable greed and bias against those living in poverty, Micah counsels that Yhwh will dismantle and leave in ruins the structures that cause social and cultural devastation. The imagery of destruction, with monumental buildings being brought low, will be reiterated and intensified in 3:12: Zion will be plowed like a field, Jerusalem will become heaps of rubble, and the Temple Mount will be like high places of the forest.

The Prophet Laments (1:8–9)

Micah gives his audience to imagine him wailing and lamenting the harm moving inexorably toward Jerusalem. This is a dramatic, even shocking performance rhetorically, whether the naked, howling prophet was perceived in actual performance or the image of Micah was only imagined as Mic 1 was read aloud. Jerusalem—the holy city of Zion, political center of Judah and the earthly locale held most sacred as the place of Yhwh's enthronement— is situated at the heart of this calamity. In the more expansive view of terrain from north to south, the destruction of Samaria (1:6–7) has spurred the prophet to cry out in lamentation, and the sound of his wailing carries across terrain and time alike: Micah turns toward Jerusalem (1:9), his lamentation and mourning audible, as it were, from the Assyrians' destruction of Samaria in 722 to the threat Assyria presses against Jerusalem in 701.

Cartography of Destruction (1:10–16)

Three eighth-century prophets in the Book of the Twelve, Hosea, Amos, and Micah, use place-names to dramatic effect in their prophetic oracles.

Cartography of Destruction 1:10–16

Hosea uses a welter of names—Jezreel, Gilgal, Beth-aven, Mizpah, Shittim, Gibeah, and many more—to construct a cartography of sin, a tradition-history map of sites in Israel's history where the covenant people had transgressed and offended Yhwh (Sharp 2010). Amos uses place-names in a rhetoric of entrapment, launching oracles in Amos 1–2 against a list of enemies—Damascus, the Philistines, Edom, the Ammonites—and then, in a move that would have scandalized his audience, Amos names Judah and Israel at the end of that list, targeted for destruction along with the enemies of Yhwh's people. For his part, Micah uses language beautifully designed for aural processing: wordplay with place-names both captivates and shocks the implied audience.

Micah's direct address to residents of the various threatened towns seems to be enacting how news would spread by word of mouth as the Assyrian invaders stormed through each locale. The poetic artfulness of the sound-play initially delights the ear; then the audience's delight turns to horror as they decipher what the prophet is suggesting about the fate of each place. An analogous effect in this author's context would be created if Micah appeared on the town green in New Haven, Connecticut, and thundered, "'New Haven'? More like 'New Craven,' you will be so terrified when divine retribution comes!" Towns and villages in the region surrounding Jerusalem panic and lament as they witness and experience the havoc wreaked by the enemy juggernaut. The razor-sharp prophetic critique of 1:10–12 is aimed sarcastically at some municipalities' failure to understand the full implications of what has been unfolding. No war alarm need be raised in Gath, Zaanan has not mustered for battle, and Maroth still hopes to avoid disaster, the prophet observes acidly. Those who understand Micah's irony know the truth, as would those rereading this text in later generations: Yhwh is deploying an enemy to punish sinful Judah, and escape will be impossible. In 1:10–16, the prophet appeals to the implied audience as if they were inhabitants of the doomed towns. This rhetorical choice is dramatic and effective: even two millennia later, the chill of dread can run down the spine of a reader who encounters the imperatives to lament and hide as doom approaches.

Jerusalem is positioned at the center of Micah's poem in 1:10–16, anchoring a chiastic structure in which Jerusalem (1:12) and Zion (1:13) are enveloped by the villages and towns that surround the capital city. It is powerfully effective for the prophet to situate the preeminent city of Judah in this list comprising names of small and unimportant towns, Gath and Lachish aside. The prophet's poetry gives us to imagine Jerusalem being surrounded as the

Micah 1

siege net tightens. Jerusalem is surrounded literally by decimated villages in the geographical region of Judah—covered by the dust of Beth-leaphrah (1:10), clothed by the shame of Shaphir (1:11), tasting the bitterness of Maroth (1:12)—and surrounded aurally in this poetry, too, by the sounds of chaos, panic, and terror.

Concluding Mic 1 is a stark image of desolation: Mother Zion is adjured to tear out her hair as she mourns for her children forced into captivity. Exile was a predictable and devastating consequence of military defeat a number of times in the history of ancient Israel and Judah, including in Micah's day. In 722 the Northern Kingdom of Samaria fell to the Neo-Assyrians, Shalmaneser V launching the siege and, upon his death, Sargon II then capturing the city. Many inhabitants of Samaria were forcibly deported to other countries according to 2 Kgs 17 and the boasting of Sargon II himself: an inscription in his voice says he exiled over 27,000 people from Samaria, in what Eckart Frahm calls "the most famous mass deportation ever carried out in Neo-Assyrian times" (2023, 148). As Mic 1 closes, the implied audience is left in stunned silence, bereft, perhaps imagining their own children being put in chains and led into exile, the flowering strength of a culture crushed, the hope of future generations all but extinguished.

History of Consequences

For illustrative comments on Mic 1 in rabbinic midrash, see the introduction under §4.1.1 Midrashic Interpretations.

Clement of Alexandria (150–ca. 215) cites Micah's apostrophe of the earth in 1:2 in his *Stromateis*, suggesting "earth" is a signifier for sinners—those who are "senseless and disobedient," who have chosen "ignorance and hardness of heart," and who "cleave to the things of sense" rather than contemplating heavenly things (*Strom.* 4.26; ANF 2:440).

Origen of Alexandria (ca. 185–ca. 253) reads God's descent from heaven as signaling pastoral attentiveness: God "is said to descend when [God] deigns to have concern for human frailty" (*Hom. Gen.*, 108). Preaching on Gen 18:21, Origen quotes 1:3 on God's descent as showing concern for humanity. He moves to John 3:13 and Phil 2:7: the incarnation of Christ demonstrates God's mercy "not only to care for us, but also to bear the things that are ours" (108). In his homiletical treatment of the embalming of Israel (i.e., Jacob; Gen 50:2-3), Origen also presses Mic 1:5 into the service of his supersessionist understanding of the truth of God in Christ as over against torah obedience. Of the "impiety" of Jacob and the sin of Israel, Origen reads with the plain sense that the transgression was idolatry, then elaborates that the sin of Jeroboam's golden calves (1 Kgs 12:28-30) "blinded and closed the eyes of Israel," and that "just as the true Joseph, our Lord and Savior, put his physical hand on the eyes of the blind man and restored his sight" (Mark 8:22-25; John 9:1-7), "so also he put his spiritual hands on the eyes of the Law, which had been blinded by the corporeal understanding of the Scribes and Pharisees, and he restored sight to them" (*Hom. Gen.*, 213).

Pachomius (ca. 290-346), an Egyptian monk credited with founding the Christian communal monastic tradition, tells a story about an angelic theophany experienced by his disciple Theodorus of Tabennese while Theodorus was reading Micah. Theodorus is perplexed by the image in 1:4 of waters coursing down. The angel offers, "Is it not obvious that it is the water of the river [of life] coming down from Paradise?" (Pachomius 1980, 215).

Jerome (ca. 347-420) reads Micah's call to all peoples (1:2) as applying to the church, while the next vocative phrase, to the earth and all that fills it, "applies to the heretics," who, per 1:7, "fabricate idols with their own skilled hand and with their imaginative mind"; the transgression of Jacob, viz., Samaria (1:5), "is the assemblies of the heretics" (*Comm. Mich.*, 42-43, 45). His other primary target being the philosophers, Jerome suggests the mountains being shaken (1:4) signals the crushing of "the teachings of the philosophers [and] the eminent kingdoms" by the incarnation of Christ (43). His reading of "barefoot and stripped" (1:8), which contemporary scholars take to refer to Micah enacting public lamentation, is fascinating: when heretics learn the truth of Christ, "they will put aside from their feet whatever they had that was liable to cause death . . . and they will cast away all the clothing of their fornication . . . so that they can put on the garment of Christ" (45). This interpretation likely shows the influence of texts such as Gal 3:27 ("As many of you as were baptized into Christ have clothed yourselves with Christ"); Eph 4:22-24 ("put away your former way of life, corrupt and deluded . . . clothe yourselves with the new self, created according to the likeness of God in true righteousness and holiness"); and Col 3:9-10 ("you have stripped off the old self with its practices and have clothed yourselves with the new self, which is being renewed in knowledge according to the image of its creator"; cf. Rom 13:14). The image of removing the footwear of heresy may constitute an oblique nod to Eph 6:15, which exhorts Christians, "as shoes for your feet put on whatever will make you ready to proclaim the gospel of peace."

John Calvin (1509-1564) comments on the mention of Hezekiah in the superscription, taking it as relevant to the bleak spiritual landscape of Micah's time and his own. In a sermon on 12 November 1550, Calvin avers, despite the prophets God had sent, no one "repented or became reformed . . . until the time of Hezekiah. And to show how steeped in malignity the entire world was, we are given a saintly king whose only wish was to guide the world back to God. But what happened? . . . He was unsuccessful in his efforts to convert the people, or to save them from further iniquities, though he employed all his power to eliminate their idolatrous practices and superstitions. For, until God intervenes, that is how entrenched the Devil is in human hearts" (2003, 3). Calvin takes literally the prophet's apostrophe of all peoples and the earth in 1:2: "Micah speaks as he does, desiring that every living creature hear him, and that his voice be heard by every nation of peoples, to the ends of the earth" (13).

In a sermon on 14 November 1550, Calvin deploys Micah's polemic against idolatry (1:7) as a weapon against Roman Catholic spiritual practices: "The papists . . . think they are genuinely pleasing God by going on their pilgrimages, muttering before their idols, and abstaining from meat on certain days. . . . They establish masses in honor of different saints, attend matins, and observe certain feast days. . . . Would you not agree that they transform God into something carnal like themselves?" (37). Commenting on "the wage of a prostitute," Calvin offers, "One cannot enter a single church of the papacy without being more defiled than if one had entered a bordello" (44).

Jesuit priest, poet, and peace activist Daniel Berrigan (1921-2016) offers of the town names in 1:10-15, "Think of American cities and the claim implicit in their names, to 'newness': New York, New Canaan, New London, New Brunswick, Newton, Newburgh, New Haven, and so forth. . . . How speedily the claims are canceled, the boast proven empty . . . in these 'new' settings! We venture on the streets of any 'new town' in the land. Crimes abound, socialized indifference and numbing, homelessness, evictions, political chicanery and greed, racism. . . . The crimes are old as those denounced by Micah" (1995, 216).

RETROSPECT

Micah's articulation of Yhwh's rage at idolatry in 1:7 and his dramatized embodiment of terror in 1:8 anticipate a key element of Sara Ahmed's notion of the feminist KILLJOY: fractured volatility. Ahmed writes that the feminist KILLJOY "flies off the handle" in the "suddenness of anger": she "not only causes her own breakage, she breaks the thread of a connection. Feminism as self-breakage: history enacted as judgment. Or feminism as a tear in the social fabric; history enacted as loss" (2017, 171). As Ahmed notes, it can be exhausting to deal with the feminist prophetic voice, for its utterances seem to generate crisis, even when the prophetic words are merely responding to an existing crisis that has been ignored or framed as unimportant—something against which Micah rages (2:6, 11). As prophets and martyrs throughout history have known, the personal cost of bearing witness can be devastating. We can imagine Micah the howling, lamenting prophet (1:8) agreeing with Ahmed that "the costs of struggling against injustice can be personal" and acute, even overwhelming (172). But Micah's prophetic mission requires bold, embodied risk-taking for the sake of the purposes of Yhwh, though the world adjudges the prophet as unbalanced (see Hos 9:7). "To be willing to killjoy," Ahmed writes, "is to transform a judgment into a project . . . a politics of transformation, a politics that intends to cause the end of a system" (255) and that ends the scheming and obliviousness that had allowed the system to continue to operate. Regarding women's studies and feminist activism, Ahmed could have been interpreting Mic 1:2–6 when she thunders, "the point is to transform the very ground on which we build. We want to shatter the foundations" (176). As regards intervening in the predatory economic hierarchies that Micah decries and against which contemporary prophets fulminate, Julio Boltvinik and Susan Archer Mann would agree: "The seismic transformations in social life over the last half century require equally seismic transformations in social thought and political praxis if we are to understand and respond adequately to the crises of global rural poverty" (2016, 16–17).

Marquis Bey finds transformative the power of radical resistance to political structures and social discourses that violate the integrity of Black, trans, and queer persons. Such resistance is prophetic, involving political dissent and social activism, rejection of distorted ideologies, and envisioning new ways of living in relationships of mutuality rather than dominance. What Bey says of Black trans feminism can be predicated of the rhetoric of dismantling in Mic 1:2–7: it "ends the world in order to claim the world,

Micah 1

a world emerging in the rubble of this world, anew" (2022, 32). Solidarity, vital for this work, can be fostered through public lamentation of harms suffered by those on the underside of the power structures dominant in the present world. Micah laments the impending devastation of Jerusalem (1:8-9), and he makes audible the stunned silence and wailing of those in unwalled villages and fortified cities as enemy troops rampage through the Judean countryside (1:10-11). Such public witness to the ravages of militarized predation can spur survivors, and audiences in future generations, to strive for an "unsubjugated life" (61) for themselves and their communities. With racialized oppression in mind, Bey asserts that "a substantive solidarity rests not in how one has been treated—which almost exclusively gets tied to historical terror and trauma . . . —but with how one approaches world-changing, politicality, and thus radical politics to beget a more habitable world" (48). The dramatic poetry in Mic 1–3 moves the implied audience to solidarity with terrorized Judean FUGITIVES hiding in the ruins of their villages (1:11), driven from their homes (2:9-10, 12-13), and mauled by Judean political elites (3:2-3). Solidarity with the wounded and dispossessed, then, catalyzes the (postexilic) community to yearn for the kind of covenantal obedience that will secure their flourishing in a peaceful and habitable world (4:1-4; 6:1-8).

As elucidated in the introduction, here is the spectrum of possibilities I have traced for contemporary responses to Micah's prophetic witness: → resilience → resistance → reformation → rejoicing. Micah 1 builds *resilience* in its audiences over the centuries by depicting the solidarity of the prophet—and by extension, the prophetic tradition more broadly—with those who are suffering: the prophet sees the atrocities and terror of those who are powerless and laments the situation publicly (1:8), showing that he understands the gravity of the community's fear and vulnerability. Micah 1 catalyzes *resistance* to the bland assurances of unscrupulous political elites that calamity will not come, drawing the audience's gaze to the ruinous fate of Samaria (1:6-7) as unmistakable historical evidence that no society is impregnable. Micah 1 calls for *reformation* of practices of idolatry, whether meant literally as the worship of things that are not God (1:7), or figuratively as misguided reliance on economic and military strength and the deceptive imperial discourses (1:14) that keep those chimeras at the center of communal hope. Finally, Mic 1 holds space for *rejoicing* in the cosmic power of Yhwh, who does see the noxious harms perpetrated by oppressors across the globe, something to be celebrated by those who find themselves exploited, injured, disregarded, or abandoned by social structures and political regimes. Micah 1 assures those who are powerless that YHWH will descend in invincible holiness and righteousness (1:2–4) to hold malefactors accountable.

MICAH 1 AND ECOLOGICAL JUSTICE

Micah 1:2 calls the living community of earth to bear witness to the righteous indignation of YHWH. All of creation—the "earth and all that fills it"—is to observe as YHWH descends in wrath to testify against Israel and Judah. The prophet teaches his Judean audience that they worship a God whose appearing (theophany) and punitive anger have profound consequences for the ecology of mountains, valleys, fields, and vineyards, and for the soundness of built structures in villages and cities. The political, religious, and cultural dimensions of life in human communities are under dire threat when the sins of leaders and people offend YHWH.

In the opening poetic lines, the effects of YHWH's wrath are imagined. First, the earth's surface will convulse, with mountains imagined as melting under the footfall of the Holy One and valleys splitting apart. This cataclysmic response is framed in terms of the most powerful topographical event the ancients would have known: the earthquake, which triggers landslides and creates sudden fissures and gaping chasms in the ground. Second, urban structures—the center of human community—will collapse into rubble, the foundations of monumental buildings and the implied foundations of human cultural institutions laid bare (1:6) by the deity. The capital city Samaria, hub of political power, commerce and trade, and religious life, will be returned to its predeveloped state, "a place for planting vineyards" (1:6), natural terrain no longer defiled by the predations and idolatries of sinful human beings.

Contemporary activists have paid attention to the ecological injuries resulting from corporations' and political leaders' exploitation of natural terrain, with untold havoc wreaked by the engines of industrialization, extractive economies, and war. "Human-induced climate change, including more frequent and extreme events, has caused widespread adverse impacts and related losses and damages to nature and people," the IPCC warns, and "near-term warming and increased frequency, severity and duration of extreme events will place many terrestrial, freshwater, coastal and marine ecosystems at high or very high risks of biodiversity loss" (IPCC 2022 §§B1.1; B.3.1). Grievous harms have been done to human families and countless other living creatures across the globe by the unbridled greed for profit from natural resources. Extractive policies have been pursued since ancient times. Roland Boer speaks of "the many faces of plunder," including violent plunder enacted by invading armies and "polite" forms of plunder—internal and external—driven by elite powerholders via "tribute, taxation, and exchange," all means of extraction that have in common "the underlying purpose [of] acquisition through some form of extortion" (2015, 6-7). Governments and other groups too many to list have perpetrated brutal colonization of inhabited territories, displacement of wild creatures and destruction or repurposing of habitats, enslavement of persons and commodification of their bodies and labor, and agricultural overworking and depletion of fields and vineyards.

Micah envisages the disastrous effects of human sin as Judah's vulnerability to the military violence of Neo-Assyrian troops, whose invasion of Judah is construed as divine punishment for Judean leaders' lack of fidelity to the covenant with Yhwh. Evoking public performance, Micah offers lamentation barefoot, stripped, and howling, taking cues from wild creatures of the desert (1:8) and observing bitterly that his bereft community will have to do the same (1:16). Jackals hunt and scavenge at the edges of human culture, and their wailing cries at dusk and dawn can sound eerie to the human listener. Ostriches, the largest birds in the world, are powerful creatures. In addition to trilling and chirping, ostriches can hiss and growl, and males can create a booming sound as a warning cry. Vultures are intimidating carrion-eating birds that live on the edges of built spaces. The baldness of the vulture cited in Micah's imperative evokes a human ritual gesture of lament—tearing out the hair—as signaling a graphic tableau of death and decomposition. Human sin has catastrophic effects on cultures and civilizations, including irremediable damage to wild creatures; the IPCC notes that in the mid-range future, "very high extinction risk for endemic species in biodiversity hotspots is projected to at least double from 2% between 1.5°C and 2°C global warming levels and to increase at least tenfold if warming rises . . . to 3°C" (IPCC 2022 §B.4.1). In Micah's theology of retribution, human sin will make us kin to the wild animals roaming desert terrain. A bitter irony of the present age is that human choices are making that terrain more inhospitable than Micah could have imagined.

COMMENTARY

Micah 1 opens with a superscription directing the implied audience to understand what follows to have been revealed to Micah of Moresheth by none other than Yhwh. Abraham Heschel muses, "The prophets tell us little of how the divine word came to them or how they knew it to be the word of the very God. . . . What stands out as essential, unique, and decisive is *the prophet's participation*, his affecting and witnessing the thinking of the Lord" (2001, 555 [emphasis original]). Ruling this out as some kind of "personal experience" of the prophet, mere "inner illumination," Heschel underscores the magnitude of the claim of the superscription and the demands of relaying what has been witnessed in terms that are national and even cosmic in scope: "It takes great inner power to address a nation; it takes divine strength to address heaven and earth" (556).

1:1 Micah. The name "Micah" (*mîkâ*) may suggest a short form of a rhetorical question, "Who is like Yah?" (or "Yahu"). That rhetorical question is more visible in the name of the prophet with whom Micah has sometimes been confused in reception history: Micaiah (1 Kgs 22:1–28). Here in the scroll of Micah, the opening appellation of the prophet will find resonance in the rhetorical question to Yhwh that comes near the close of the book: "Who is a God like you?" (*mî-ʾēl kāmôkā*, 7:18).

in the days of Jotham, Ahaz, [and] Hezekiah. The reigns of three Judean rulers anchor the prophetic witness of Micah in geographical and chronological terms. Jotham son of Uzziah is said in 2 Kgs 15:33 to have reigned sixteen years: from 759 to 743 BCE per Thomas Römer (2010, 556), 756–741 per James Nogalski (2011, 511), or 742–735 per William McKane (1998, 25); Rainer Kessler affirms that 759 or 756 was Jotham's accession year (2000a, 74). Ahaz succeeded Jotham, with regnal dates for which the chronological sources are in dispute: 743 to 727 or 735 to 715 (Römer 2010, 556), but 742–725 per Nogalski (2011, 511). Hezekiah reigned from 727 to 698 or 715 to 687 (Römer 2010, 560; McKane chooses the latter range), but 725–696 per Nogalski (2011, 511); Kessler says Hezekiah died either in 700 or 697 (2000a, 75). Francis Andersen and David Noel Freedman observe that the Micah superscription "places Micah's work as beginning later than that of the other three eighth-century prophets, although not necessarily continuing later than that of Isaiah, whose activity went on at least to the end of the century" (2000, 112).

Because Micah could have begun prophesying early or late in the reign of Jotham and could have ceased delivering oracles early or late in the reign of Hezekiah, the superscription allows us to say with precision only that Micah prophesied for anywhere from perhaps a dozen years to over sixty years; Francesco Arena suggests "from 20 to 53 years of prophetic activity"

Micah 1

(2020, 160). Manuel Jinbachian observes, "it is unclear whether he prophesied during the reigns of the first two kings, since he is completely silent on the Syro-Ephraimite war, the appeal of Ahaz to the Assyrians for help, and the deportation of the Naphtalites to Assyria, as recorded in 2 Kgs 15:29" (2012, 138). A short range may be more imaginable for the extant material, but there is no way to ascertain the length of intervals between Micah's oracles or when the first and last were delivered. He may have spoken—or been remembered as having spoken—many oracles that were not preserved. In any case, Micah would have known of the Neo-Assyrian Empire's siege of Samaria begun under Shalmaneser V and Samaria's fall in 722 to Sargon II; he may also have known of Sennacherib's unsuccessful siege of Jerusalem in 701. For those who, with Ehud Ben Zvi, prefer to consider "Micah" as a remembered figure constructed by scribes in Persian Yehud, the historical question becomes instead the hermeneutical issue of how and why "Micah" is being constructed—from a vantage point centuries later—as an eighth-century prophetic figure who would have experienced those events (see Ben Zvi 1998; 2000, 9-11). Burkard Zapff (2022, 31-32) takes seriously the regnal names in the superscription as guiding Micah's audience toward linkages with the prophesying of Hosea, Amos, and Isaiah of Jerusalem.

Samaria and Jerusalem. Samaria is mentioned in Micah only in 1:1, 5, 6. The close pairing of the capitals of Israel and Judah here signals the way in which the fates of those northern and southern geopolitical entities were seen as closely intertwined, something discernible in northern and southern prophetic traditions alike in the Latter Prophets. Within the Book of the Twelve, Hosea pays intense negative attention to the northern region of Ephraim and Samaria: "the corruption of Ephraim" is paired with "the wicked deeds of Samaria" (Hos 7:1); inhabitants of Samaria offered worship at a shrine in Bethel, perceived as idolatrous by Hosea and styled metonymically as Samaria's "calf" perhaps because of an image or statue of a calf there (1 Kgs 12:25-30), and the "calf" will be broken and carried away to Assyria (Hos 8:5-6; 10:5-6); the king of Samaria "shall perish like a chip on the face of the waters" (10:7); and Samaria will face mutilation and death on the battlefield as a consequence of its sins (14:1 [Eng. 13:16]). Amos depicts Samaria as a place of "great tumults," "oppressions," "violence and robbery" (Amos 3:9-12), callous indifference to the vulnerable (4:1), and the misplaced complacency of elites (6:1, paired with Zion). Samaria will be destroyed (8:14); survivors of Samaria's fall will be considered as a "remnant" only in the sense that dismembered body parts might be considered remnants (3:12). Obadiah 19 prophesies that Ephraim and Samaria will be subjugated mili-

Commentary

tarily and controlled by "those of the Negeb" when a restored Judah expands its territory after the Neo-Babylonian Empire has been defeated. Elsewhere in the Latter Prophets, Isaiah addresses Samaria in a focalized way in chapters 7–10, critiquing the arrogance of the Syro-Ephraimite coalition, and otherwise only in Isa 36:19 as an example of a locale that had fallen before the Neo-Assyrian military juggernaut. The place-name occurs in Jeremiah just three times: in Jer 23:13 we find an indictment of the prophets in Samaria for having prophesied by Baal; in 31:5 is a lyrical image of viticultural restoration of the mountains of Samaria; and in 41:5, "Samaria" occurs as an ancillary reference within a gruesome story of the slaughter of eighty pilgrims by Ishmael son of Nethaniah and his men. In Ezek 16 and 23, Samaria is personified in florid hypersexualized terms as the sister of Jerusalem and an object lesson in the consequences of shameless (geopolitical) infidelity, her example then eclipsed by the "abominations" and "whorings" committed by Jerusalem (Ezek 16:51; 23:11); apart from these elaborate indictments, Samaria is mentioned not at all in Ezekiel. The subjugation of Samaria by the Neo-Assyrian Empire (see 2 Kgs 17), an event that would have generated fascination and horror across the Levant, is refracted in Judean scribal circles as instructive for Judah. The reader of Mic 1 should consider Julia O'Brien's feminist caveat (2015, 9) regarding the intersectional ways in which gender and class affect the marginalization of different constituencies in societies: "Although the opening oracle of Micah casts whole cities as transgressing," we might be "suspicious of Micah's totalizing language," given that "not all persons shared equally" in economic resources and political power, and thus in the accountability for the divinely wrought calamity the prophet envisions as looming for those cities.

1:2 *Pay attention . . . give heed!* Edgar Conrad notes that Isaiah, Joel, and Micah "all begin with a command to hear immediately following the superscription" (Isa 1:2; Joel 1:2; Mic 1:2) and "all three include a vision of desolation of the land" while also envisioning a restored temple of Yhwh (2003, 206). The mp impv. *šimʿû*, "Pay attention!" or "Hear!" or "Listen!," occurs in Micah at 1:2; 3:1, 9; 6:1, 2, 9; it is addressed to "all peoples," the "heads of Jacob and rulers of the house of Israel," "mountains and everlasting foundations of the earth," and an unspecified paradigmatic "tribe." Thus Micah regularly offers a call to attention with the character of warning, and the command has sometimes been taken as a marker of a larger structural pattern (Mason 2004, 15). Within the Book of the Twelve, the impv. *šimʿû* is a central feature of prophetic discursive praxis, being found in the following passages with

Micah 1

the indicated addressees, human and inanimate: Hos 4:1 (people of Israel); 5:1 (priests); Joel 1:2 (elders); Amos 3:1, 13 (people of Israel); 4:1 ("cows of Bashan who are on Mount Samaria"); 5:1 (house of Israel); 8:4 ("you who trample on the needy"); and the six times in Micah referenced above.

The fs impv. *haqšîbî* occurs only in Isa 10:30 and Mic 1:2 in the Hebrew Bible. It is notable that in the larger literary contexts of both passages, Mic 1:10–16 and Isa 10:27b–32 present cartographies of locales terrorized by the advance of Neo-Assyrian troops and use the chilling rhetorical strategy of direct address to some of the doomed towns. In Mic 1, mention of the Assyrian threat advancing on "the gate of Jerusalem" (1:9) is amplified further by the mapping of the terror through Gath, Beth-leaphrah, Shaphir, Zaanan, Beth-ezel, Maroth paired with another mention of "the gate of Jerusalem," then Lachish, Moresheth-gath, Achzib, Mareshah, and Adullam. In Isa 10, the rhetorical trajectory is the reverse: the mapped terrain of doom includes Rimmon, Aiath, Migron, Michmash, Geba, Ramah, Gibeah, Gallim, Laishah, Anathoth, Madmenah, Gebim, and Nob, with the threat ending at "the hill of Jerusalem."

In the Latter Prophets, the imperative can drive forward a rhetorical move that suggests Yhwh is putting Israel or Judah on trial, metaphorically speaking, for breaking the stipulations of covenantal fidelity to Yhwh as sovereign. The controversy or disputation trope, in Biblical Hebrew the *rîb*, was regularly called the "covenant lawsuit" by twentieth-century biblical scholars; that term is avoided by some interpreters today as implying with unwarranted precision either a formal juridical process in ancient Israel or Judah—this to have generated the metaphorical usage in prophetic discourse—or too pointed a forensic sense, whether taken in literal or figurative terms. The notion of *rîb* has been perceived in many Hebrew Bible texts containing that noun or the related verb, including Hos 4:1–5 and Mic 6:1–8. The disputation has also been discerned in texts that do not supply any overt semantic expression of the trope but seem to imagine a trial procedure with witnesses and testimony. The disputation trope is best understood as a complex signal within ancient Israelite rhetoric that invites a sense of shame and heightening anxiety in the implied audience addressed as a malefactor being held to account by the deity. As Walter Brueggemann puts it, "the lawsuit form asserts the abrasion and alienation that are at work between [Yhwh] and Israel, which arise from Israel's recalcitrant way of life and issue in vexation and suffering for recalcitrant Israel at the hands of [Yhwh]," and moreover, the prophets "are remarkably skillful in driving from the horizon any other explanation for the trouble or well-being of Israel" (1997, 636).

Commentary

all you peoples . . . O earth. McKane notes that while some rabbinic and other interpreters have translated these nouns as referring only to Israelite peoples and the "land" of Israel, the interpretive position that these nouns "refer to all the people of the earth is irresistible" (1998, 27). The linkage of *ʾereṣ* (or *tēbēl*) and *məlōʾāh* (or a similar form) is not unknown in biblical texts discussing the land of Israel—see, for example, Lev 19:29; Ezek 19:7; 30:12. But it is more common in an expansive pairing, often explicit, of heavens and earth, as in Deut 33:16; Pss 50:12; 89:12; Isa 34:1; and that is the rhetorical move being made here in Mic 1:2. Andersen and Freedman comment, "'Earth' (vv. 2, 3) retains its mythic connotations and the 'mountains and valleys' likewise belong more in primal creation stories than in contemporary geography" (2000, 137).

the Lord God. The divine appellation "the Lord God" (*ʾădōnāy yhwh*, with the Tetragrammaton pointed by the Masoretes as *ʾĕlōhîm*) occurs in Micah only here. In the Twelve, it occurs also at Obad 1, Zeph 1:7, and, strikingly, twenty times in Amos. Micah[LXX] has only *kyrios* here; Anthony Gelston observes, "G often omits one of the divine names in this formation" (*BHQ*, 95).

serve as a witness against you. The targeted group ("against you," *bākem*) is left unspecified for the first three verses of the indictment (1:2-4), as the prophet allows a terrifying ambiguity to grow regarding the antecedent for the pronoun: perhaps all the peoples of the earth and all earth's creatures (1:2) are being called to pay attention as their own destruction unfolds. The referential ambiguity will be resolved in 1:5: Israel and Judah are those being indicted. The gaze of all the peoples and the living creatures that fill the earth will turn, as it were, and be trained on Samaria and Jerusalem. Ben Zvi highlights another ambiguity, this one tied to possible valences of the preposition: Yhwh could be "among you" or "against you" (1998, 105-7). While the melting mountains and splitting valleys would be alarming signals of theophany, the purpose of Yhwh's descent becomes chillingly clear only as 1:5 unfolds: Yhwh is descending in fearsome wrath for the purpose of punishing transgression.

Characteristically redirecting its audience from too anthropomorphic an understanding of Yhwh and Yhwh's actions, the targum to 1:2 makes an insertion: it is the word of Yhwh, "the *Memra of* the Lord," that will bear witness against the people.

from [Yhwh's] holy temple. In view here is not the actual Jerusalem temple but the heavenly place of divine enthronement from which Yhwh comes forth to tread upon the earth. Isaiah offers an unforgettable descrip-

Micah 1

tion: "I saw the Lord sitting on a throne, high and lofty, and the hem of [Yhwh's] robe filled the temple. Seraphs were in attendance above [Yhwh]; each had six wings: with two they covered their faces, and with two they covered their feet, and with two they flew. And one called to another and said, 'Holy, holy, holy is the Lord of hosts; the whole earth is full of [Yhwh's] glory.' The pivots on the thresholds shook at the voices of those who called, and the house filled with smoke" (Isa 6:1-3; cf. the elaborate temple vision in Ezek 40:1-47:12).

1:3 Yhwh is coming forth ... will come down and tread. In evidence here is the influential ancient Near Eastern tradition of the divine warrior, whose appearance is said to be signaled by convulsive responses in the weather and topography of the natural world: storm clouds, thunder, lightning, rain, hail, whirlwind, the earth quaking, rocks splitting, floods, and oceanic upheavals. In Hebrew Bible poetic traditions, such natural signs are said to accompany Yhwh's march before the Israelites through the wilderness and divine leadership in battle on behalf of the people (see, among many passages, Exod 19:16-20; Judg 5:4-5; Pss 18:8-16 [Eng. 7-15]; 68:7-8; 77:16-20; Isa 42:13; Hab 3:3-15). Commentators such as Kessler (2016, 216) have noted the similarity of Mic 1:3b and Amos 4:13. In Amos, the clause belongs to the first of three doxologies in which the power of Yhwh to destroy becomes increasingly clear (cf. Amos 5:8-9; 9:5-6). In Tg. Mic 1:3, several additions secure distance from potentially anthropomorphizing (mis)understandings: Yhwh "*is appearing from the place of the house of his Shekinah,*" that latter term signifying the divine presence among the people in a unique and non-anthropomorphizing way. The rabbinic interpreter known as the Malbim (Meir Leibush ben Yehiel Michel Wisser, 1809-1879) draws a parallel between Yhwh's direct action in 1:3 and in the final plague, the slaughter of the Egyptian firstborn, as noted in Exod 11:1 and 12:29: "Here too, God ... will exact the punishment due and will not rely on Divine agents" (Stavsky 2009, 4).

high places. The polyvalent term *bāmôt* here has two potential primary meanings (*HALOT* 1:136-37): elevated topographical features such as hills, knolls, and mountain ridges; or outdoor shrines or other worship installations, sometimes built in elevated places. In the second sense, *bāmôt* are portrayed in many Hebrew Bible texts as illegitimate either due to the deity worshipped or the religious praxis conducted there or, in the case of Yhwh worship, due to the location not being a centrally authorized site. Hebrew *bāmôt* occurs in Micah only in 1:3, 5 and 3:12, forging a strong link between the rhetoric of judgment here and the prophet's oracle against Jerusalem there and suggesting an increasingly intense focus, from the "high places of the earth" (1:3) to the "high places of Judah" (1:5) to the Temple Mount being destroyed and left as "high places of the forest."

of the earth. That the whole earth is in view initially is suggested not only by the call to many "peoples" (1:2) but also from the implied contrast between Yhwh's place above and that which lies below (1:3). Micah's skillful linkage of the instances of *bāmôt* in 1:3 and 5 creates the impression that the powerful tread of Yhwh will crush not only the tallest mountains but also, the audience realizes as the prophetic language becomes increasingly focalized, the illegitimate shrines of Judah. That impression is made vivid in the unambiguous oracle in 3:12 about the coming destruction of Zion: the rubble imagined by the audience in 1:6 of Samaria becomes the rubble of beloved Jerusalem, and the "mountain of the House"—that is, the temple—becomes nothing more than *bāmôt* of the forest. The bifocal gaze of the horrified implied audience moves, then, from an expansive view of the entire earth to a finer-grained focus on the vulnerable places of their own land. I find cogent the reading of Ben Zvi that the term 'ereṣ "seems to play a Janus role, looking both forward and backwards" in 1:2-7, "associating vv. 3-4 with v. 2 on the one hand, and with vv. 5-7 on the other" (1998, 108).

1:4 *mountains will melt . . . valleys will split apart.* The earth is riven by seismic responses to the proximity of Yhwh. Dominic Irudayaraj argues that the allusion to topographical high and low places constitutes a merism "[signaling] that God's coming up and down has a cataclysmic impact on the entire world" (2021, 707).

like wax yielding to the fire. Translating the prepositional phrase *mippənê* in the third clause of 1:4 as "yielding to" expresses the subtle resonances of antagonistic confrontation evoked by no fewer than three words in this verse. First, the mountains "melting" (*mss*, niphal) recalls the metaphorical melting of enemies' hearts in terror (Deut 1:28; 20:8; Josh 2:11; 5:1; 7:5; 2 Sam 17:10; Isa 8:6; 13:7; 19:1; Ezek 21:12; Nah 2:11). Next, the verb for the valleys "splitting apart" (*bqʿ*, hithp.) is used in contexts of armed conflict for breaching military defenses, hacking enemies with blade weapons, and dashing enemies to pieces (see 2 Sam 23:16; 2 Kgs 2:24; 8:12; 15:16; 25:4; 1 Chr 11:18; 2 Chr 21:17; 25:12; 32:1; Hos 13:8; 14:1; Amos 1:13; Jer 52:7; Ezek 26:10; 30:16). Finally, *mppny* can mean "from before" in the sense of facing or being routed by an adversary (e.g., Judg 6:2, 6; 9:21; Ps 61:4; Isa 17:9; Lam 2:3; 5:9), just as *lpny* can signal an adversarial stance or presentation for armed conflict. Psalm 68:2 (Heb. 3) offers that the wicked will perish before God "as

Micah 1

wax melts before the fire." As Yhwh descends, then, the semantic freight of the imagery signals both incomparable holiness and inescapable menace.

like waters flooding down a slope. This image suggests the inexorable force of divine judgment cascading down an incline, unstoppable and washing away everything in its path. Abraham ibn Ezra (ca. 1092–ca. 1167) offers that the denizens of the Northern Kingdom "will be split apart and scattered among the gentile nations like a waterfall whose water sprays in all directions as it hits the ground" (Stavsky 2009, 5). James Luther Mays perceives a dimension of warning here: "all the earth, mountain and plain, gives way and begins to disintegrate before the force of [Yhwh's] appearance ... the most permanent topography of the world cannot maintain itself when [Yhwh] appears. How much less [people] who oppose [Yhwh]!" (1976, 43).

1:5 Who constitutes the transgression of Jacob? The prophet could have chosen the inanimate interrogative, *mah*, if the two cities in this verse, Samaria and Jerusalem, had been in view as antecedents in a more literal way. The point of these rhetorical questions and answers is not that Samaria itself constitutes the transgression of Jacob and Jerusalem is tantamount to *bāmôt* in Judah. Rather, it is unspoken yet powerfully audible in the animate interrogative "Who?" that the leaders of those cities have led their people astray. Bruce Waltke and Michael O'Connor assert that "English idiom requires" the use of the interrogative "What?" for cases of *mî* in which "a thing is closely associated with the person or is pregnant with the idea of a person, or where persons are understood and implied" (*IBHS* §18.2d). That is not so; more semantically daring choices are certainly available to one translating into English. A flattening translation of the interrogative into "What?" mutes the vital importance of the implied personal agency in the formulation in 1:5. Andersen and Freedman keep the interrogative as it is written, followed by a dash rather than smoothing the awkward syntax (2000, 172-73). Compare Isa 3:8, "Jerusalem has stumbled, and Judah has fallen," which is clarified further in 3:12, "O my people, your leaders mislead you." In contemporary diatribes about incompetent national leadership in the United States, one hears, "Washington is broken," meaning, of course, not the municipality but those charged with governance there. Invective against leaders is well in keeping with the prophet's scathing indictment of the powerful in 2:1-2 and political leaders in 3:1-4. In Tg. Mic 1:5, expansions indicate the locations are being interpreted with a steadfast literalism: "*Where did the people of the house of Jacob transgress? Was it not in Samaria? Where did the people of the house of Judah commit sin? Was it not in Jerusalem?*"

Jacob. This is a political term using the name of the eponymous ancestor in the patriarchal narratives of Genesis as a marker of belonging. Occurring twice in this verse and nine other times in Micah, "Jacob" is a significant identifier across all the major sections of the book (2:7, 12; 3:1, 8, 9; 4:2; 5:6, 7; 7:20). Here, in parallel with Samaria, it stands for the Northern Kingdom (Nogalski 2011, 525). In other Micah usages, it is equally clear that the term represents the entire covenant people. Andersen and Freedman observe, "In our study of the political terminology of this book we found no reason to restrict either of the names 'Jacob' and 'Israel' to only one of the two kingdoms" (2000, 388).

Israel . . . Judah. The rhetorical move from Israel to Judah in 1:5 is the first signal of a complex geopolitics connecting the Northern and Southern Kingdoms in the theology of Micah. Some argue that the inclusion of Judah in 1:5b is secondary, given that the focal target of Yhwh's wrath is Samaria alone in 1:6-7 (McKane 1998, 31-32). To be sure, there are texts in the Hebrew Bible in which the northern region of Samaria is at the center of the scribes' attention and comments about Judah seem to exhibit a patently secondary character, suggesting later interpolation during the compositional growth of the text. Well-known examples include certain lines or clauses in Hos 5:5; 6:11; 8:14; and 2 Kgs 17:19. In some biblical texts, the disastrous fate of the Northern Kingdom—falling to the Neo-Assyrian Empire in 722—serves as a cautionary example to Judah. But more than that, Micah is linking the fates of Samaria and Jerusalem. Nogalski says, "Samaria's role in Micah plays a purely editorial function whose purpose is to link the pronouncements of Amos and Hosea against Samaria with Micah's warning to Jerusalem" (2017a, 203). "Purely editorial" may underestimate how integral Samaria is to the witness of Micah. On the other side, the judgment of Andersen and Freedman that "the whole book is about both cities" (127) may be a bit overstated. But the destinies of the two cities are assuredly seen together through a single prophetic lens.

1:6 *I will make Samaria a heap of rubble.* Yhwh roars the divine plan to raze Samaria, the capital of the Northern Kingdom of Israel, as punishment for its transgression. Identified today with Sebastia, a village lying northwest of Nablus, ancient Samaria was destroyed in 722 BCE, after the Assyrians had besieged the city for three years. There is dramatic foreshadowing here of the coming destruction of Jerusalem, a linkage secured by the shared language of each capital city being made into a "field" (*śādeh*) in 1:6 and 3:12. The means of divine retribution, left unspoken here, would have been

Micah 1

understood by Micah or a later prophetic scribe as warfare generally and siege in particular. Samaria was on a "high hill (430 m above sea level), towering over its surroundings," per Nahman Avigad (1993, 1300). Omer Sergi and Yuval Gadot underline that the visibility of such royal palaces, signaling both control and "conspicuous consumption" of local resources, "serves as an active symbol, conveying the iconography of political power spatially" (2017, 104). Israel Finkelstein notes, "the monumental palace was constructed in a building effort that included the shaping of the summit of the rocky hill"—Sergi and Gadot elaborate that "the highest part of the rocky summit was leveled off and separated from its surroundings by an artificial, ca. 4 m. high rock-cut scarp" (2017, 105)—and further, while "in its early days the palace was apparently surrounded by agricultural installations . . . the construction of a monumental royal compound with casemate fortification, elevated on large-scale fills, came in a somewhat later phase of the Omride dynasty" (Finkelstein 2011, 234). The royal quarters were on the acropolis (upper city), which had two fortification walls. The outer wall "was 1.6 m thick and built of fine ashlar masonry laid in carefully fitted headers and stretchers," while "the inner wall, the city's earliest wall, was attributed . . . to Omri" and was "not particularly strong," which explains why the outer wall was later built—it was "much stronger" (Avigad 1993, 1302). Avigad offers, "The Israelite masonry at Samaria is renowned for its outstanding quality," adding these details: "the upper, visible courses were smoothly dressed. All the ashlars were set dry—that is, without mortar—and with outstanding precision" (1303). The breaching and destruction of the walls and buildings of Samaria would surely have shocked Israelites and Judeans who knew the area. Micah's description of Yhwh's resolve to obliterate the city is rhetorically effective in dramatizing the scene. Sergi and Gadot: "As the Omride dynasty collapsed and the Nimshides came to power"—see 2 Kgs 10 for the coup led by Jehu son of Nimshi—"the changes in socio-political conditions made their mark on the landscape. Samaria and Megiddo were completely reshaped and rebuilt, effectively erasing or hiding the former architectural symbols of Omride hegemony" (110). The poetic diatribe in Mic 1:2-7 suggests a similar erasure of Samarian power in a later generation, something expressly linked to the pejorative cultural memory of Omri and Ahab in 6:16.

Hans Walter Wolff assumes that the fall of Samaria marks the last moment when Micah could have composed 1:6-16: "722 is the terminus ad quem for the entire text in 1:6-16 originally from Micah," with "734 as the terminus a quo, the year when the troops of Tiglath-Pileser III, in his first campaign against Palestine, stormed over Gaza in Philistia and on toward the south . . . bringing terror to the inhabitants of . . . the southwestern Shephelah" (1990, 4). While such historicist reasoning is still seen in redaction-critical schemata in some contemporary scholarship, it is important to recognize that sophisticated prophetic texts need not be conceived as having been generated in the historical context narrated, or assumed, in these poetic oracles (or in the prose of other prophetic books); this material could have been shaped later. Andersen and Freedman suggest something of the craftsmanship of 1:2-7 when they call attention to "the intricate word patterns that link the whole together into a tapestry of ideas" (2000, 135).

1:7 *her images will be pulverized*. The verb here for pulverizing, *yukkattû*, suggests complete and utter destruction. This particular form is used only elsewhere in the Hebrew Bible at Job 4:20, where it describes the fragility of mortals before the invincible righteousness of their Creator, and Jer 46:5, where it describes the destruction of Egyptian warriors by the Babylonian ruler Nebuchadrezzar. The 2 Kgs 23 narrative of the religious reforms of Hezekiah—named, of course, in the superscription of Mic 1:1—describes that king's removal and burning of cultic vessels that had been "made for Baal, for Asherah, and for the host of heaven"; his destruction of an image of Asherah, sculptures of horses and chariots dedicated to the sun, illicit altars including one at Bethel, and sacred pillars; and his defiling of Topheth and other cultic sites used for worship of Molech, Astarte, Chemosh, and Milcom.

all her wages. The metaphorization of Israel and Judah as adulterous wives and sex workers is explored in feverish detail in the Latter Prophets, particularly in Hosea and Ezekiel; Isaiah and Jeremiah also participate in that prophetic scribal tradition, albeit to a lesser degree and with diction that is less intimate than that of Hosea and less vulgar than that of Ezekiel. Micah shows knowledge of this tradition only at 1:7, where, immediately following parallelistic pairing of Samaria and Jerusalem (1:5), not Judah but Samaria is likened to a sex worker. To my ear, the silence of Micah around Judah's metaphorical adultery or sexual shame is thunderous. Micah here declines the inflammatory tradition so virulently on display in Hosea and Ezekiel: blaming Israel/Judah in sexualized terms for the geopolitical threats and military catastrophes that put the social body of Yhwh's people at profound risk. Concerning 1:7, Gerlinde Baumann surmises that "probably this is meant to set up Samaria as a counter-figure to 'daughter-Zion,' who plays an important role from Mic 1:13 onward" (2003, 208). Andersen

Micah 1

and Freedman remark (2000, 181), "The noun *earnings* fits *burn* by a kind of transference because the verb 'burn' is associated with the penalty for prostitution, especially in a priestly family (Gen 38:24; Lev 21:9)." Underscoring the centrality of the metaphor of prostitution in Hosea, Kessler remarks, "It is nearly impossible to understand Micah 1:7 without having read Hosea first.... Micah 1:2-7 relies on the text of Hosea" (2016, 217, 220).

as the wage of a prostitute they will return. Micah's word of judgment here is elliptical for two reasons. First, the prepositional sequence *min . . . wəʿad* is difficult, and second, Micah is working with metaphorical vehicle and tenor in ways that blur the boundaries between those dimensions of signifying. He may be suggesting that wealth gained from illicit political or trade connections with other nations will be treated by an enraged Yhwh as earnings from sex work might be treated: as shameful and worthy of destruction. The pulverizing of engraved images and idols, objects forbidden in Deut 4:15-30 and destroyed in Josiah's reform (2 Kgs 23:4-20), may be in view in this material as well. Illicit gain, gathered as sex workers might gather their fees, will now go back to the customers—as it were—in the shattered condition that Yhwh requires for the covenant people's treatment of idols. Waltke reads more literally, confident that "the conquering Assyrian army . . . would use the precious metals of gold and silver that formerly overlaid Samaria's rich idols . . . to pay the Assyrian cult prostitutes, providing revenue for their cultic centers" (2007, 55). His assumption about the historical existence of sex workers in cultic roles in Assyria is not shared by many today (see DeGrado 2018). The idols have been obliterated, metaphorically speaking, in the preceding line. The sex-work imagery here is not common for Micah; resonances are audible with the more florid diction of Hosea (e.g., McKeating 1971, 158). The targum to 1:7 clarifies the MT locution "they will return" with a highly specific fuller predicate: *"they shall be handed over to the temple of those worshipping idols."*

1:8 I will lament and howl. The first-person subject is unambiguous in Micah[MT]. Most interpreters, including the present author, see the prophet as the agent of the action. Considering Julia Kristeva's reading of abjection in Leviticus (1984, 93-109), noting that "my people" is spoken by Yhwh many dozens of times more often in the Hebrew Bible than by any human speaker, and adducing Jer 48:30-33, a passage in which the speaker could be argued to be either Yhwh or the prophet, Timothy Beal (1994) has argued that in Mic 1:8-9, Yhwh is the lamenting subject: "In both of these intensely passionate prophetic discourses, we find Yhwh making radical shifts between devastating wrath on the one hand and wild dirge-like lament on the other" as the deity moves "through the cities, among the piles of unclean corpses" that divine wrath has created (182–83). A similar case has been pressed for the identity of the lamenting voice in Jer 8:22–9:3 (Heb. 9:2) as being that of Yhwh. I agree with Beal generally about the irrepressible intertextuality of biblical texts and the productive ways in which slippages and tensions are produced between and among speakers and addressees in Biblical Hebrew poetry, both within the porous "borders" of a single passage and in textual landscapes writ larger. Beal observes, "No interpretation can settle the meaning of a text absolutely. There are always ruptures, or traces, which, when given sustained attention, can open to new readerly possibilities" (185). Indeed—but here in Mic 1:8–9, to my sustained gaze, the demarcations between divine and human speaker seem clear, not least because the image of the deity going barefoot and stripped is, though metaphorical, highly counterintuitive. If anything, the use of "my people" could be considered a polemical move by the howling prophet, a challenge flung at the deity whose destructive power has laid waste to Samaria and now threatens Jerusalem.

O'Brien underscores the importance of lament for the book of Micah: "Significantly, Jerusalem's fate in Micah is not simply *depicted* but extensively *lamented*, a task associated in the ancient Near East primarily with women" (2015, 17 [emphasis original]), though she is less taken with the gender slippage here than are interpreters who find the male prophet lamenting to be a noteworthy moment of gender-queering. What Anathea Portier-Young observes regarding the use of first-person commissioning accounts in Isaiah, Jeremiah, and Ezekiel is relevant here as well: "First-person narration . . . heightens audience identification, immersion, and affective engagement, opening pathways for audiences to participate in the embodiment of encounter, revelation, call, and mission" (2024, 78), or, in the case of Micah, invites the audience to participate in lamenting. This will form hearers and readers through affective connection to the prophet's horror and wracking grief, rather than to the faux confidence and denial purveyed by Micah's opponents. In Micah[LXX] 1:8, third-person singular verbs yield either Samaria—the closest expressed antecedent—or Jerusalem as the implied lamenting subject, something recognized by interpreters in antiquity, such as Cyril of Alexandria (*Comm.*[CA], 190). In Tg. Mic 1:8 are verbs in the third-person plural: those lamenting, wailing, and going about stripped *"in chains"* are the people of Israel and Judah (so Cathcart and Gordon 1989, 113n20), and possibly also survivors of the obliterated Samaria.

Micah 1

In the MT, an important interpretive issue has to do with the tone of 1:8, which prepares the implied audience to hear a cascade of images of fatal injury, humiliation, shame, and loss (1:9-16). Is the prophet modeling public lament in this way, howling like a wild animal, in earnest, or is this a "elegiac taunt," as Ze'ev Weisman suggests (1998, 21)? Is this faux lament of the sort that many have correctly identified in more than one passage in Amos (e.g., Amos 6:1-7), or is Micah portraying authentic anguish at the fate of Jerusalem and the villages of Judah? The options should not be kept separate in too strict a fashion, for the biblical prophetic traditions are artful at mixing expressions of grief and condemnation in the same utterance, as is evident in Jer 8:21-9:10 (Eng. 9:11). Weisman argues that the puns on village names in Mic 1:10-15 communicate "derision" and "a trace of malicious pleasure" at the retribution coming to these sites (1998, 22). But Micah's polemic is directed entirely at Judean elites, here (cf. "the houses of Achzib" and the "kings of Israel," 1:14) and throughout the book. His invective is aimed neither at his traumatized people as a whole nor at the women and children of dispossessed Judean families. If this howling prophet has crafted poetic linkages between the names of towns and the terrible fate of their inhabitants, that may be better understood as an artful way of showing the inescapability of approaching doom than as glee at the decimation of entire population centers.

barefoot and stripped. On "barefoot," I take the *ketiv* (*šēlāl*) seriously because of the importance of sound-play here. Jörg Jeremias (2007, 129) suggests the morphology of the *ketiv* has been influenced by the two preceding words with *tsere yod* vowels; so too Gelston (*BHQ*, 96), who notes, as also per the Masorah Magna for Micah, that the spelling in the *qere* (*šôlāl*) can be seen at Job 12:17, 19. Rather than attributing the *ketiv* of this adjective to scribal error, I suggest the prophet has purposefully created a soundscape of wailing sounds with repeated long-*e* vowels. That *šēlāl* would evoke *šôlāl* for an ancient audience—whether hearing the line performed or audiating it during reading—seems obvious and would constitute an artistic and strategic choice on the part of Micah. In ancient Israel and Judah, purposefully walking unshod—when one had the means otherwise to don footwear—can signal a disruption of mundane life due to loss, violation, or other trauma (2 Sam 15:30; Isa 20:1-4). Prophetic sign-acts involving stripping off clothing or footwear include Jer 13:1-11, where Jeremiah dons and then takes off and buries a loincloth, abandoning it for a long time so that its deteriorated condition can represent visually the ruination of Judah, and Ezek 24:15-24, where YHWH warns Ezekiel that his spouse will die suddenly, but he may not mourn her with the expected signs of grief, including having no sandals on his feet. Heschel remarks, "To walk about without the outer garment was . . . a sign of mourning. . . . Similarly, to walk about without sandals was a sign of great poverty or of deep mourning. . . . Removing the shoes as a sign of mourning is observed to this day by traditional Jews" (2001, 511).

Jackals . . . ostriches. Jackals (*tannîm*) and ostriches (*bənôt yaʿănâ*) are paired also in Job 30:29; Isa 34:13; 43:20. In the Hebrew Bible, the jackal serves as an iconic figure for wilderness or wasteland, ruination, and the desolation of abandoned or destroyed cities. Jackals roam landscapes inhospitable to human flourishing; see, for example, Ps 44:20 (Eng. 19; likely not a reference to mythopoetic dragons or sea monsters, though there is philological overlap in the semantic ranges of those homonyms in Biblical Hebrew poetry); Isa 13:22; 35:7; Jer 9:10 (Eng. 11); 10:22; 49:33; 51:37; and Mal 1:3. The cry of the jackal is unsettling; the sound has been described by a bioacoustics researcher as a "needling" sort of "shriek, or a wail, as if someone had set a banshee free in the forest" (Lloyd 2021, 36). Ostriches are figured as cruel in Lam 4:33.

1:9 *"Indeed, she has been fatally weakened . . ."* These two verses are the content of Micah's bitter lamentation. The opening fs adjective refers to the unexpressed subject, Daughter Samaria, who has been wounded to the point that no cure is possible. It is not the wounds (plural, standing in number discord with the adjective) that are incurable: it is personified Samaria who will not recover and about whose fate Micah wails. The fate of Samaria unmistakably throws into sharp relief the threat looming for Daughter Zion. In Jer 30:12–15 is similar language concerning Zion's incurable woundedness and suffering as the result of Yhwh's punishment via an enemy (there, the Neo-Babylonian army) wielded as divine weapon. Amy Kalmanofsky argues that imagery of Israel, Judah, or Zion as a beaten, infected, or gravely wounded body is intended to shock the implied audience, to evoke horror and sympathy, and to spur the rejection of behaviors that, per prophetic indictments, have led to the violation of the body of the covenant people. She observes, "Diseased and dying bodies . . . are rhetorically powerful because they register Israel's sinful state and God's displeasure. . . . Prophets use images of shocking bodies in order to initiate reform. . . . They want their audience to view decaying, dismembered, diseased, beaten, and female bodies, and to be changed" (2016, 557).

it has come as far as Judah. The unexpressed fs subject of *bāʾâ* should be left ambiguous, precisely as the prophetic poetry has it, which heightens

Micah 1

the dread experienced by the implied audience. The implied subject is the violent force causing the region's wounds: the fs noun *milḥāmâ*, "battle, war," is likely alluded to here, envisioned as progressing inexorably to the very gates of Jerusalem. This noun is important in Micah. In 2:8, *milḥāmâ* will be named outright—tellingly, in a phrase that emphasizes the risk to those who are (naïvely) trusting and recoil from *milḥāmâ*, but who are now experiencing the trauma of militarized dispossession at the direction of YHWH. Two powerful reversals await the reader who continues through the oracles of Micah. In 3:5, the false prophets disingenuously proclaim peace as the state of things, but wage *milḥāmâ* (metaphorically speaking) against those who do not compensate them for their mercenary activity. In the irenic vision of 4:3, warfare—*milḥāmâ*—will be a thing of the past as YHWH arbitrates among nations and soldiers lay down their weapons, refashioning them into implements of agriculture for the benefit of the community.

He has struck . . . as far as Jerusalem. That the attacking 3ms subject remains unidentified here only intensifies the sense of looming menace: behind the human assailant figured here (the Assyrian ruler or his army commander), we glimpse the outline of a punitive and rageful YHWH deploying Assyrian troops as a weapon, as in Isa 10:5-6, where YHWH roars, "Ah, Assyria, the rod of my anger—the club in their hands is my fury! Against a godless nation I send him, and against the people of my wrath I command him, to take spoil and seize plunder, and to tread them down like the mire of the streets." Considering the relationship of the metaphors of Mic 1:8-9 to the dramatic imagery of 1:10-16, Juan Cruz offers this nuanced analysis: "As the plague of Samaria's wounds spreads to Jerusalem, so does the lament begin to encompass the towns surrounding the latter city. Mourning spreads from an individual in v. 8 to several groups of female figures in the verses that follow," and the implied audience might imagine themselves swept into a soundscape of terror and grief: "the mourning from different locations creates a reverberating sound that echoes around the surrounding towns of Judah, lending the poem an additional emotive and auditory impact" (2016, 109).

the gate of my people. In ancient Judah, gates of fortified cities "had wooden double doors, which were metal-plated to withstand fire" and "secured by a locking bar of bronze or iron . . . held in place by sockets in the doorposts" (King 1988, 75). The breaking of bars is a trope for destruction of a city's defenses (Jer 51:30; Lam 2:9; Amos 1:5; Nah 3:13). Here is the first occurrence of the term *'ammî*, "my people," in Micah. It inaugurates a sequence that unfolds throughout the book: Micah will use this term eight

Commentary

Fig. 8. The Golden Gate in the eastern wall of the Temple Mount. Built in the sixth or seventh century CE, it is likely the oldest gate in Jerusalem.

more times to express intense fear, sadness, or indignation from a position of solidarity with his people, whether speaking in his own voice, ventriloquizing lamenting denizens of Judah, or speaking for Yhwh (see 2:4, 8, 9; 3:3, 5; 6:3, 5, 16). In the verses that follow, Andersen and Freedman observe, the tone is one of "panic" and "hysteria" (201).

1:10 *Gath.* The mention of Gath launches a sequence of twelve town names that map a cultural terrain marked by desolation, chaos, and fear. Matthew Suriano notes that there is movement southward in 1:10–12 from Gath toward Lachish in 1:13, and movement northward in 1:13–15, from Lachish toward Adullam (2010, 438). Andersen and Freedman observe that these locations "don't correspond to any military campaign that can be realistically constructed, except in a vague and general way" (214), though they suggest that the geopolitical context fits the reign of the beleaguered Ahaz, under threat "by Edom (2 Kgs 16:6), by the Philistines who raided the cities of the Shephelah (2 Chr 28:17–18)," and by adversaries during the Syro-Ephraimite war (235, 244; Shaw 1987). Many others, including Nadav Na'aman (1995, 527), find that Sennacherib's invasion of the Levant seems to fit better the mood of overwhelming alarm. I agree, underscoring that this need not mean

163

the oracles were composed shortly after 701, but simply that the cultural memory brought to expression so vividly in these verses—even if from a much later generation—would evoke those circumstances. Yair Hoffman offers a nuanced proposal that expands the chronological possibilities to three: 738–734 for the original lament, later edited with reference to the Assyrian assault on Ashdod in 712 and Sennacherib's advance on Jerusalem in 701 (2008, 95–97). As is true of 1:2-7, so also Micah's ironic and artful warnings in 1:10-16 to vulnerable villages (Beth-leaphrah, Shaphir, Zaanan, Beth-ezel, Maroth, Moresheth-gath, Achzib, Mareshah, Adullam) and larger fortified towns (Gath, Lachish) could have been composed as the product of prophetic scribal memory of a later generation. Beginning with a well-known city—some argue that Gath would have been a relatively impressive "territorial kingdom" by the late Bronze Age (Panitz-Cohen 2014, 545)—would secure the implied audience's attention in a way that opening with an obscure backwater would not. Hoffman writes, "The settlement list anchors the lament in a distinct geographical area, as if leading the listener/reader on a guided tour of explicit populated sites, seemingly providing... an intimate eyewitness view of the disaster" (2008, 90).

Some find it unlikely that this Gath would have been the well-known Philistine city-state, given that "all the other places that can be identified lie in the vicinity of Micah's hometown" (208), but Andersen and Freedman observe, with others, that the conquest of Gath by Neo-Assyrian troops in 711 BCE means that city would have shared the experience of militarized trauma into which the lesser-known and unknown locales in this material have been swept (208). I find imaginative but implausible their related speculation that from 1:5-13 is sketched "the trail of the spread of the cult of the goddess from Samaria to Jerusalem via Lachish" (230).

Gath, which came to be inhabited by the Philistines during the waves of migrations of mixed groups from the Aegean Sea region and elsewhere in the early Iron Age, is identified by most scholars with Tell eṣ-Ṣafi, situated approximately halfway between Jerusalem and Ashkelon (for a detailed overview of the site with photos, see Maeir 2012, 1–66). Archaeological evidence suggests that Gath and another Philistine city, Ekron, saw considerable expansion of built structures between Iron I and Iron IIA, a measure of economic prosperity and regional influence. Gath thrived through the mid- to late ninth century BCE. Despite its massive fortifications, which included a city wall some ten feet thick, Gath was destroyed in the final decades of the ninth century, sometime between about 830 and 800 BCE, an event some scholars correlate with the notice in 2 Kgs 12:17 that the Aramean

Commentary

ruler Hazael conquered Gath (so Maeir 2012, 26). Archaeologists digging at Gath have found "impressive amounts of Early Bronze Age pottery" and a "unique, well-preserved ivory cylinder seal . . . with an extraordinary, naturalistic depiction of a standing lion" (Maier 2012, 12–13), as well as many finds from later periods. Archaeologists have uncovered large siege works, including a deep siege trench "surrounding the city on three sides" (Ehrlich 2016, 374–75), and evidence of a breach—a noticeable gap—in the fortified city wall. Gath is mentioned at the beginning of David's lamentation over Saul and Jonathan in the Song of the Bow (2 Sam 1:20). If the relevant clause of Mic 1:10 is an intended allusion to that tradition, quite possible given the shared language with *bəgat ʾal-taggîdû* (McKane 1998, 40; Andersen and Freedman 2000, 240), the prophet may be enacting a complex proleptic reference to the death of Judah's leader or the destruction of Judean royal lineage more decisively.

Andersen and Freedman aver that "the long inventory of place-names" and wordplay in this section "point to planned, sustained literary work" (204). Defending that point in light of the numerous interpretive challenges within the text of 1:10–16, they offer two possibilities for understanding the genesis of these lines: "Either they are an accurate transcript of a spontaneous outburst," the prophet offering word and image associations "in broken sobs," or these verses constitute an "artistic composition such as would be made by a dramatist, capturing the feelings of desolation and grief that must be felt by any participant in events so catastrophic" (206).

Beth-leaphrah. This locale is mentioned only here in the Hebrew Bible; scholarly proposals have identified it with Khirbet et-Ṭayyibeh, Ṭayyibet el-ʿIsm, or Tell el-ʿAreini/Tel Erani (Suriano, 440–46). The wordplay here is clear: the second half of the place-name, *ʿaprâ*, sounds like the dust, *ʿāpār*, in which the inhabitants will roll in grief. Naʾaman revocalizes *lə* to *lōʾ*, arguing that the epithet "House-of-No-Dust" shows more clearly the ironic reversal in Micah's wordplay (1995, 519). Micah[LXX] 1:10 is different from Micah[MT] in several particulars. The MT of 1:10, "Do not weep bitterly! In Beth-leaphrah, roll yourself in the dust," is in the Greek translation something like, "You {*pl*} in Akim, do not rebuild from a house a mockery; strew dirt on your mockery." "In Akim" indicates the LXX scribe has read a prepositional *b* plus place-name for the Hebrew infinitive absolute *bākô* (McKane 1998, 40; *BHQ*, 96). Amitai Baruchi-Unna arranges the relevant MT consonantal sequence as *bbyt[ʾ]l ʿprh*, presuming an *aleph* has been omitted due to scribal error in "Bethel." The emendation yields three place-names and this translation: "In Gath tell it not. Do not weep in Bethel at all. Ophrah,

165

Micah 1

roll yourself in dust" (2008, 630). A striking number of biblical passages do associate Bethel with weeping (Gen 35:8; Judg 2:1^LXX; 20:26; 21:2; Hos 12:5). With appreciation for the ingenuity of Baruchi-Unna's proposed emendation, I stop short of adopting it here because that reading is attested by no textual version (so also Suriano 2010, 435).

roll yourself. Reading not the first-singular pf. of the *ketiv* but, rather, a fs impv. with the *qere* for the sense and for congruence with fs addressees throughout this section. The personification of these threatened villages and towns as feminine, congruent with the personification of Jerusalem throughout the book of Micah as Daughter Zion, is semantically powerful. The *hithp.* of *plš* occurs also in contexts of public lamentation at Jer 6:26; 25:34; Ezek 27:30.

1:11 *Pass by for your own sake, O inhabitant.* Wordplay again: the "inhabitant," *yôšebet*, will experience shame, *bōšet*. Here, the reader encounters a fs impv., then a 2mp pronoun, then an apostrophized fs noun representing the denizens of Shaphir. In 1:11, 12, 13, and 15, "inhabitant" is a fs addressee, standing for the collective inhabitants of these locales. The move to represent all inhabitants of a place with the feminine singular is a regular occurrence in the Latter Prophets.

Shaphir. This place-name is not known; it is mentioned only here in the Hebrew Bible.

nakedness, shame! The inhabitant of Zaanan has not gone forth. Zaanan is not known to contemporary scholars. The syntax of the first clause is somewhat unusual, with two nouns linked by *maqqep* (*ʿeryâ -bōšet*) and no preposition present to signal an adverbial complement; the *atnach* may encourage us to read the "nakedness, shame" compound term with what precedes. The targum elaborates graphically on the sense: "Shaphir, *with genitals uncovered,* naked and ashamed." Micah^LXX may betray the confusion of the Greek translator, who interprets ʿryh as "her cities" (*tas poleis autēs*), with the implication—the meaning is not entirely clear—that Zaanan remained behind its protective fortifications: the inhabitants "have not gone out to mourn its adjoining house" (McKane 1998, 41). Edward Glenny renders the entire verse as, "Though inhabiting well her cities, the one inhabiting Sennaar did not come out. Mourn for the house next to her; she shall receive a painful blow from you" (2015, 21). The "nakedness, shame" (*ʿeryâ-bōšet*) linked in the MT clause are not to be imagined as mundane consequences of unclothed hasty flight from the invaders or the generic loss of status experienced by those routed in battle. The NJPS translates the line as an unmarked

Commentary

rhetorical question: "Did not the inhabitants of Zaanan have to go forth in nakedness and shame?" But this is better interpreted as a verbless shout of horror functioning as a warning to the inhabitants of Shaphir.

The next line amplifies the warning. "Zaanan" sounds like the verb for "going forth," *yāṣəʾâ*, often used in Biblical Hebrew for an army advancing to meet the enemy. Since Zaanan does not go forth, that suggests those inhabitants are cowering in fear, remaining in hiding—something that would have been considered shameful—rather than choosing to engage the enemy or assist injured Judeans. Peggy Day argues that the nakedness referenced here results from victorious foes "stripping captives of war" and is a metonymic signal of rape (2008, 69). Violation of female, male, and gender-nonconforming captives has been perpetrated as a form of torture, as a public display of the victor's power, and as a means of traumatizing and breaking the will of entire communities. Sexual violence has, tragically, been common both as a spontaneous, unplanned crime and as a planned military strategy in conflict zones across the globe from antiquity to the present day.

Beth-ezel. This place-name occurs nowhere else in the Hebrew Bible, and the location is not known. Naʾaman revocalizes once again to yield an appellation, "House-of-No-Shade," which he sees as an ironic taunt about the Assyrian king's inability to provide protection, combined in the second clause with an understanding of *ʿemdâ* as "tax" demanded by the Assyrian overlord (1995, 520-21; see below for *ʿemdâ*), but this is strained in the context of an invasion unleashing chaos in the present moment imagined by the text. An elaborate expansion in the targum reflects the linking of "In Gath, do not announce it" (1:10) with the same phrase—verbatim except for word order—within David's lament over the slain Saul and Jonathan (2 Sam 1:20), according to Kevin Cathcart and Robert Gordon (1989, 114n29). The expansion in Tg. Mic 1:11 opens with, "*Make lamentation bitterly for yourselves over the slaughtered of your warriors,*" and goes on to assign blame to the inhabitants for having seized "*houses . . . by violence joining one to the side of the other.*"

its place to take a stand. The meaning of *ʿemdâ*, a *hapax legomenon*, is conjectural (*HALOT* 2:842), and the referent for the 3ms pronominal suffix is unclear. David Kimḥi (1160-1235) envisions the one standing as the invader: "The enemy will demand payment for the time he spent standing in position while besieging the city" (Stavsky 2009, 10; similarly Naʾaman above). My translation coincides with that of Waltke (2007, 61). Other translational options: "his standing place" (Andersen and Freedman, who add,

Micah 1

"nobody knows what v. 11bC means," 2000, 224); "seine Unterstützung," Kessler (2000a, 98), who says the 3ms suffix must refer to Beth-ezel (106; similarly Allen 1976, 276); Marvin Sweeney (2000, 355), with the comment that the referent for the suffix is the enemy; Jeremias (2007, 141), elaborating that military support will be withdrawn; Johannes C. de Moor (2020, 100). Helmut Utzschneider prefers "sein fester Stand" but allows that "seine Unterstützung" is also possible (2005, 41). John Goldingay translates, "it will take up from you its stance" (2021, 419), with the explanation that Beth-ezel will "learn from the example of Zaanan" (427). Zapff offers, "he takes your position for his own" (2022, 50–51), saying the referent for the suffix could be Yhwh, a proposal I find implausible. Delbert Hillers says the consonantal text as written yields "nonsense"; he proposes to emend *mikkem* to *mimmāk* to tidy up the confusion of number in the pronoun, and more drastically, the term *ʿemdâ* becomes *ḥemdātēk*, "he takes away your treasures" (1984, 24, 26), which makes beautiful sense but is not what Micah^MT says.

1:12 though... surely. In the sequence *kî... kî*, I take the first as a concessive *kî*, "though" (*HALOT* 2:471), followed by an asseverative *kî* emphasizing a sure outcome contrary to that for which Maroth hopes. Micah^LXX 1:12 opens with a question: "Who began in good things? She dwells in pain," translated by Glenny (with italics expressing something he sees as implicit in the text) as, "Who began *to act* for good to her who dwells among pains?" (2015, 21).

Maroth. This place-name occurs nowhere else in the Hebrew Bible. Andersen and Freedman object to the identification of this locale with Maʿărat on the grounds that the *ayin* (ʿ) in the name constitutes a substantial lexical difference and the location is "too far south" to work in this topography (209). In one of the more subtle signals in Micah's deftly mapped soundscape, "Maroth" sounds like the root of a word, *mar*, that signifies bitterness, yielding a whisper of ominous homophony: "the inhabitant of bitterness waited [fruitlessly] for good." In Tg. Mic 1:12, the denizens of Maroth are accused of having "*refuse[d] to return to the law*," and the targum adds acidly, "What will you do?"

calamity has come down from Yhwh to the gate of Jerusalem. This is a stunning moment in the poetry. By means of the place-names in this section, the implied audience had been guided to think of calamity marching relentlessly across the landscape of Judah toward the gate of Jerusalem, in the form of an invading enemy army. Here Micah redeploys the verb *yrd*, last heard in 1:3 with Yhwh "coming down" from the heavens in judgment. The audience realizes that the inexorable doom filling them with dread is

Commentary

coming not (only) across the terrain of Judah laterally, but from above. The sense of inevitable destruction is heightened: there can be no escape. Jeremias (2007, 128) has noted that all of Mic 1–3 presses toward the culminating point articulated vividly in 3:12: the destruction of Jerusalem. Thus even at this early point, just twelve verses into the book of Micah, the audience is poised on the brink of disaster.

By the mid- to late eighth century BCE, Jerusalem was surrounded by massive walls, such that "the entire Judahite metropolis was heavily fortified" (Ussishkin 2003, 107). Though the city did not fall in the last third of the eighth century, the threats posed by the Syro-Ephraimite War in 734–732 and the assault of Sennacherib on Judah in 701 were serious indeed, and the denizens of Jerusalem at that time would not have had the benefit of hindsight about Jerusalem's endurance in those crises. For a noncombatant to see an enemy at their city gate arrayed in siege formation, intent on slaughtering the inhabitants, plundering their goods, and enslaving survivors, would have been one of the most terrifying experiences of life in antiquity.

1:13 Lachish. Ancient Lachish is identified with Tell ed-Duweir, southwest of Jerusalem. Marvin Chaney describes Lachish, "the large provincial 'capital' of the Shephelah," as having "dominated the surrounding towns and villages and their burgeoning agricultural production in Iron II" and having been characterized, as best can be determined from archaeological evidence, by "stark social stratification" (2017, 146). Its "double wall and gate system" (Hardin 2014, 749) did not save Lachish from being destroyed by Sennacherib in 701, an event portrayed in carved wall reliefs from the Assyrian king's throne room at Nineveh (Hays with Machinist 2016, 79; Sharon 2014, 60). Those wall reliefs served at least two political purposes: aggrandizing the Assyrian ruler, as all such monuments to military victory over enemies do, and intimidating vassal states whose leaders might consider rebelling. Christopher Hays and Peter Machinist observe of Sennacherib's reliefs that some "portray the awful fates of those who opposed the Assyrian Empire: exile, death, and torture. These were prominently placed . . . at the entry to Sennacherib's throne room to send a message to the emissaries of foreign cultures who visited his court" (2016, 79). Josette Elayi speculates on the absence of Lachish from Sennacherib's written inscriptions, "Lachish was not an exceptional city, and the victory against it was not considered by Sennacherib to be the high point of his western campaign"; in the wall relief, Lachish may have been "chosen among several others to illustrate the efficiency of Assyrian tactics against a strong fortress," and its "destruction

Micah 1

Fig. 9. The fall of Lachish: King Sennacherib reviews Judean prisoners. Detail from wall relief in the throne room of Sennacherib's Southwest Palace at Nineveh.

was not his objective, because he intended to leave loyal allies and vassals behind him" (2018, 75).

Years after Assyria's defeat by the Neo-Babylonian Empire, Babylonian troops advanced on Jerusalem to press what would be an eighteen-month siege from January 588 to July 587. Though "the Shephelah and northern Negev never fully recovered from the devastation wrought by Sennacherib" (Hardin 2014, 750), in the intervening years, Lachish had been refortified. As the end of Judean political autonomy drew near during the Babylonian onslaught, according to Jer 34:7, "when the army of the king of Babylon was fighting against Jerusalem and against all the cities of Judah that were left, Lachish and Azekah . . . were the only fortified cities of Judah that remained." In Micah's geography of destruction in Mic 1:10–16, those in Lachish will be harnessing the *rekeš*—warhorses for chariots—to battle invaders whom they cannot possibly defeat.

the beginning of sin for Daughter Zion. Clearly and dramatically, the prophet forges the link between the sins of (various) covenant constituencies and the brutal fate of Jerusalem. The noun *rē'šît* could mean not only first in historical time but preeminence (as, e.g., in Num 24:20, predicated of Amalek among the nations), and the LXX translates in the latter way as

170

"leader" or "originator" (the latter suggested by Glenny [21] for *archēgos*). Both meanings may be at play; as Cyril of Alexandria (ca. 375-444) suggests, Lachish "was perhaps the first of the cities subject to Judah and Benjamin that Sennacherib captured," but could also be understood "as the principal base of apostasy" due to its idolatry (*Comm.*^{CA}, 195).

1:14 Moresheth-gath. This town, likely the same Moresheth from which Micah is said to hail (1:1), was associated with the Philistine city of Gath as a "daughter-village" or "satellite village" (Nogalski 2011, 528-29), as its name, "possession of Gath," implies. Most scholars associate it with Tell ej-Judeideh, a site some six miles southeast of Tell eṣ-Ṣafi/Gath in the Shephelah, the hilly lowland region to the west of Jerusalem between the Judean mountains and the coastal plain (so, e.g., Schniedewind 2003, 385n33; Chaney 2017, 146). The identification of Moresheth-gath with Tell ej-Judeideh, per Andersen and Freedman, "is supported by early Christian tradition about the tomb of Micah" (210). Yigal Levin's alternative proposal of Tel Ḥarasim, a site about three miles northwest of Gath (2002), has not found significant support.

parting gifts. The meaning of *šillûḥîm* here is obscure. The interpretation of Andersen and Freedman that "Jerusalem has given away her endowment by ceding territory to Israel in settlement at the end of a losing war" (233) seems rather more elaborate than the context allows. But a similar reading had occurred to Kimḥi, albeit adducing a different historical background, on the logic that Moresheth-gath had earlier been the Philistine city of Gath: "It is as if Micah [were] saying . . . 'The city of Gath had been captured by King David and was our inheritance; but due to your sins it has now become a Philistine legacy. You must now humiliate yourselves and try to bribe the Philistines to offer you protection" (Stavsky 2009, 11).

Achzib. This town may be identified with Tell al-Bayḍā (or el-Beida) at Lavnin, some three miles south-southwest of Adullam (Avi-Yonah 2007, 356; Andersen and Freedman 2000, 211; Kessler 2000a, 103). A city called Achzib was also a major Phoenician port city. Many scholars, among them Henry McKeating, surmise that "Micah evidently has in mind some smaller place in his own locality" (1971, 161). Yet the semantic play in this line with the better-known Achzib may be important for Micah's point, especially if the thrust of the irony has to do with international trade. Otherwise, it would be difficult to imagine how "the houses of" an insignificant town in the Shephelah could have become "deception" for the rulers of Israel. Moshe Prausnitz describes the better-known Achzib as "an important city that was settled from the Middle Bronze Age until the Crusader period," located on the Via Maris, the coastal trade route running through the Fertile Crescent from Egypt to Syria; Achzib was "well protected by the Mediterranean Sea on the west and a natural bay on the south" (1993, 32).

Relevant to the time of Micah, "Assyrian sources relate that Sennacherib conquered the city . . . during his third campaign to Phoenicia and Palestine in the year 701" (32). Archaeologists have uncovered Iron Age storerooms with "rows of storage jars . . . along the walls of the buildings," and, from the end of the Iron Age and thus later than the time of Micah, "pottery figurines of women holding musical instruments" (32). There are ruins of four cemeteries on the site. The cemetery centrally located on the mound had "tombs dating to the Middle Bronze Age, the Iron Age, and the Roman-Byzantine period," while the three others had strata datable to the Hellenistic period and the Persian period as well as the Iron Age and the Roman period. Artifacts interred in the tombs on the mound included "flasks and juglets" and "an ivory bowl, cylinder seals, bronze bowls, . . . a double axehead, [and] a spear" (32). Many interred human bones and an impressive array of funerary artifacts demonstrate the importance of burial practices at Achzib over several centuries. Some tombs in the northern cemetery had "kraters filled with charred bones" that had been "passed through fire," and some had small tombstones, some of which "bore stylized engravings and inscriptions in Aramaic"; for Prausnitz, the evidence of charred bones points to the "continuity of Phoenician funerary rites in the three hundred years from the eighth to the fifth centuries BCE" (32, 34). In the southern cemetery "near the seashore, rock-cut and built tombs were found" that contained "the bones of two to three hundred bodies," which "apparently belonged to several generations of one family" (34–35). In the eastern cemetery and dating from "the eighth to the sixth centuries"—thus in use beginning during Micah's time—were shaft tombs holding burial chambers with "benches along three of their walls": "the deceased were laid on the benches along with burial offerings, such as pottery and personal belongings" (34). In that eastern cemetery, per Eilat Mazar, archaeologists have found seventeen graves, all "oriented from east to west," in which "the most common funerary gifts . . . were glass vessels, invariably laid at the deceased's feet," most often "candlestick bottles, bottles, plates, and bowls" (1993, 36). In the northern cemetery, excavations have yielded dozens of stelae; "a small number bear simple engraved symbols" likely representing a god and goddess, probably "the main Phoenician deity Ba'al" and "the main Phoenician goddess, Astarte" (Mazar 2008, 1562). Also found were burial gifts dating from the tenth to the sixth centuries, including "2 clay figurines—a donkey, and a monkey seated upon a chair . . . a clay mask depicting a woman's face; high quality silver and gold jewelry with inlays of a variety of polished precious stones; and two pairs of delicate bronze scales," as well as "a complete iron sword, a dagger, an axe, and many arrowheads" (1562-63).

deception for the kings of Israel. In Tg. Mic 1:14, this last clause is expanded along the trajectory of idolatry bringing divine retribution: "The houses of Achzib *shall be delivered to the nations because of the sins that* the kings of Israel *committed by worshipping idols in them.*"

1:15 *Mareshah.* Verse 15 in Micah[MT] is best read as Yhwh bringing a dispossessor (conqueror, invader) against the inhabitants of Mareshah, wordplay with the place-name being perceptible in the use of *yōrēš* earlier in the verse. The clause is translated in Micah[LXX] with a positive sense as Yhwh leading "the heirs," presumably of Lachish, homeward after exile (NETS). The Greek verb is read as 3pl by Glenny on the basis of several manuscripts, with an unspecified "they" doing the leading, but the sense remains positive (2015, 20, 60). Initially connected with Caleb, the heroic leader in the book of Joshua, through town lists in Judah (Josh 15:42), Mareshah is linked genealogically with the descendants of Caleb (1 Chr 2:42) and Shelah (1 Chr 4:21). The city was said to have been fortified by Rehoboam during his reign in the late tenth century BCE (2 Chr 11:8), and the Chronicler imagines a battle between the military force of Asa of Judah (r. 907-867) and an Ethiopian army at Mareshah in which, per the norms of holy-war ideology, Yhwh fights for Judah and defeats a million Ethiopian troops; the Judean soldiers carry away vast spoil from that conflict and their subsequent plundering of "all the cities of Gerar" (2 Chr 14:9-15). Thus, far from being an insignificant village, Mareshah would have been linked in ancient Israel's scribal memory with the mighty Caleb and with a miraculous military triumph before the time of Micah.

Identified by most scholars with contemporary Tell Ṣandaḥanna, Mareshah is located about a mile southeast of Beit Guvrin. Per Amos Kloner, "Ancient Mareshah comprised a high mound, a lower city with ancillary cave complexes, and a necropolis that encompassed the entire site" (2011). Mareshah continued to thrive centuries after the time of Micah, underlining its strategic importance to the region. Michael Avi-Yonah (2007) observes that in Hellenistic times, Mareshah was fortified and its streets were laid out in a Hippodamic grid—that is, arranged in right angles, a design attributed to Hippodamus of Miletus (498-408 BCE). Kloner writes, "Among the numerous Hellenistic finds were 328 Rhodian amphora handles

Micah 1

and three inscriptions. Sixteen small lead figurines and fifty-one limestone execration tablets attest magic practices at Hellenistic Mareshah" (2011). Further, connected by a "subterranean labyrinth . . . of extensive winding corridors" (Kloner 1997) are "hundreds of caves hewn into the soft chalky limestone of the hillsides," these used "for the manufacture of olive oil and for pigeon breeding," as well as for stables, cisterns, bathhouses, and storage rooms (Kloner 2011). Gerald Finkielsztejn notes the importance of Mareshah in trade: artifacts discovered by archaeologists included "local and imported wares, among which the amphoras are evidence for the relation of the Levant with the main production centers of wine, oil, and probably fish products of all the Mediterranean," as well as a "hidden hoard of silver coins" from the late second century (Avi-Yonah and Finkielsztejn 2007, 520). Mareshah was destroyed in 40 BCE.

Adullam. This locale, identified as Khirbet esh-Sheikh Madkur (Andersen and Freedman 2000, 211), is located "on the northeastern edge of the Shephelah hills" (Radashkovsky and Lazir 2017). Excavations in September 2015 uncovered "pottery sherds ranging in date from the Chalcolithic period to the Ottoman period" and "a hiding refuge from the time of Bar Kokhba"; among artifacts predating the time of Micah were "bifacial flint tools characteristic of the Pre-Pottery Neolithic" era and "a drill from the Chalcolithic period" (Radashkovsky and Lazir 2017).

As the hearer or reader reaches the end of the list of town names, retrospective understanding may dawn. According to Goldingay, this whole list may be structured with oblique allusions to King David at the beginning and the end. David flees from Saul and arrives at Gath (1 Sam 21), but still fearful, flees further to hide ignominiously in a cave at Adullam (1 Sam 22). Goldingay writes concerning the chiastic gesture via mentions of Gath and Adullam, "The glorious 'splendor' of the Davidic household . . . ends up in somewhere best known as the place where David the bandit had to take refuge" (2021, 428).

the Glory of Israel. This epithet would seem to be a title for YHWH in the horrifying guise of an enemy invader deployed as divine retribution—ironic scare quotes would not be out of place for this appellation. YHWH is bringing the Assyrians against YHWH's own people, as 1:12 makes abundantly clear. Comparable moves are made in Isaiah and Jeremiah, where Assyria is wielded as YHWH's war-club (Isa 10:5-6) and Nebuchadrezzar is thrice identified as YHWH's servant (Jer 25:9; 27:6; 43:10). Micah[LXX] adds "daughter" (Greek *thygatros* = Hebrew *bat*) to yield "the glory of Daughter Israel," which Gelston considers might have been "a vertical dittograph" triggered by the last two Hebrew letters of *yôšebet* earlier in the line (*BHQ*, 97). Andersen and Freedman give up: despite the clarity of the words and syntax here, they say, "we don't know what Micah is talking about" (236).

1:16 treasured children. A number of commentators over the centuries have interpreted this as pejorative. In Micah[LXX], the modifier *tryphera* is read by some as negative: "pampered," "self-indulgent" or "delicate" in the sense of frail, unable to endure pain, or effeminate, the latter construed negatively in misogynistic discursive frameworks (BDAG, 1018; CGL 2:1399–1400; so, e.g., Cyril of Alexandria, *Comm.*[CA], 197). But the positive valence of "delight" is possible for both the Hebrew *taʿănûg* and the Greek noun associated with this adjective. In my view, no negative valence should be heard here or at 2:9. Micah is describing elements of life in community that delight the covenant people but that will be stripped away due to the sins of elite oppressors among them.

baldness . . . as that of the vulture. In the Hebrew Bible, ritual acts of mourning include keening, tearing one's garments, donning sackcloth, prostrating oneself or sitting on the ground, throwing dust on the head, and fasting (Gen 37:34; Josh 7:6; 1 Sam 31:13; 2 Sam 1:11–12; 3:31; Esth 4:1; Ps 35:13; Isa 58:5; Jer 6:26; Lam 2:10). Relevant to the mention of baldness in Mic 1:16: Job shaves his head when his ten children are killed (Job 1:20; cf. Isa 22:12; Ezek 27:30–31). Maimonides (Moses ben Maimon, 1138–1204) and other medieval Jewish sources note the prohibition in Deut 14:1 on "the making of bald patches . . . as an expression of grief over death," but argue that "when done for any other reason, it is permitted" (Stavsky 2009, 13).

they have gone into exile. Forcible deportation creates extraordinary hardship and trauma for prisoners of war and noncombatants alike. In antiquity, many would not have survived the journey. For those who did survive, traumatized and saturated by grief, daily life in regions controlled by their enemy would have been precarious. The remembrance of deportations under Neo-Assyrian and Neo-Babylonian imperial forces unquestionably haunted Israelite and Judean scribes. Marks left by the trauma of exile are visible here and in many texts across the Hebrew Bible.

BIBLIOGRAPHY

Avi-Yonah, M. 2007. "Achzib." *EncJud* 1:356–57.
Avi-Yonah, M., and G. Finkielsztejn. 2007. "Mareshah." *EncJud* 13:519–21.

Baruchi-Unna, A. 2008. "Do Not Weep in Bethel: An Emendation Suggested for Micah i 10." *VT* 58:628-32. doi:10.1163/156853308X348240.

Boltvinik, J., and S. A. Mann. 2016. "Introduction." Pages 1-42 in *Peasant Poverty and Persistence in the 21st Century: Theories, Debates, Realities and Policies*. CROP International Studies in Poverty Research. London: Zed Books.

Day, P. L. 2008. "Metaphor and Social Reality: Isaiah 23.17-18, Ezekiel 16.35-37 and Hosea 2.4-5." Pages 63-71 in *Inspired Speech: Prophecy in the Ancient Near East; Essays in Honor of Herbert B. Huffmon*. Edited by J. Kaltner and L. Stulman. JSOTSup 378. London: T&T Clark.

DeGrado, J. 2018. "The qdesha in Hosea 4:14: Putting the (Myth of the) Sacred Prostitute to Bed." *VT* 68:8-40. doi:10.1163/15685330-12341300.

Ehrlich, C. S. 2016. "Philistia and the Philistines." Pages 353-77 in *The World around the Old Testament: The People and Places of the Ancient Near East*. Edited by B. T. Arnold and B. A. Strawn. Grand Rapids: Baker Academic.

Hardin, J. W. 2014. "Judah during the Iron Age II Period." *OHAL*, 743-56. doi:10.1093/oxfordhb/9780199212972.013.049.

Hoffman, Y. 2008. "The Wandering Lament: Micah 1:10-16." Pages 86-98 in *Treasures on Camels' Humps: Historical and Literary Studies from the Ancient Near East Presented to Israel Eph'al*. Edited by M. Cogan and D. Kahn. Jerusalem: Magnes.

Kloner, A. 1997. "Underground Metropolis: The Subterranean World of Maresha." *BAR* 23.2:24-25, 27, 29-30, 32-35, 67.

———. 2011. "Mareshah." *OEANE* online.

Kristeva, J. 1984. *Powers of Horror: An Essay of Abjection*. New York: Columbia University Press.

Levin, Y. 2002. "The Search for Moresheth-Gath: A New Proposal." *PEQ* 134:28-36. doi:10.1179/peq.2002.134.1.28.

Lloyd, K. 2021. *Abundance: Nature in Recovery*. London: Bloomsbury Wildlife.

Maeir, A. M., ed. 2012. *Tell es-Safi/Gath I: The 1996-2005 Seasons; Part I: Text*. ÄAT 69. Wiesbaden: Harrassowitz.

Mazar, E. 1993. "Achzib: Recent Excavations." *NEAEHL* 1:35-36.

———. 2008. "Achzib." *NEAEHL* 5:1562-63.

Na'aman, N. 1995. "'The House-of-No-Shade Shall Take Away Its Tax from You' (Micah I 11)." *VT* 45:516-27. doi:10.1163/1568533952662324.

Pachomius. 1980. *The Life of Saint Pachomius and His Disciples*. Translated by A. Veilleux. Pachomian Koinonia 1. CS 45. Kalamazoo: Cistercian.

Panitz-Cohen, N. 2014. "The Southern Levant (Cisjordan) during the Late Bronze Age." *OHAL*, 541-60. doi:10.1093/oxfordhb/9780199212972.013.036.

Prausnitz, M. W. 1993. "Achzib." *NEAEHL* 1:32-35.

Radashkovsky, I., and E. Liraz. 2017. "Khirbat esh-Sheikh Madkur (West): Final Report." *Hadashot Arkheologiyot: Excavations and Surveys in Israel* 129. https://www.jstor.org/stable/26693689.

Römer, T. 2010. Introduction and annotations to 2 Kings. Pages 485–529 in *The New Oxford Annotated Bible*. 4th ed. Oxford: Oxford University Press.

Schniedewind, W. M. 2003. "Jerusalem, the Late Judaean Monarchy, and the Composition of Biblical Texts." Pages 275–94 in *Jerusalem in Bible and Archaeology: The First Temple Period*. Edited by A. G. Vaughn and A. E. Killebrew. SymS 18. Atlanta: Society of Biblical Literature.

Shaw, C. S. 1987. "Micah 1:10–16 Reconsidered." *JBL* 106:223–29. doi:10.2307/3260634.

Suriano, M. J. 2010. "A Place in the Dust: Text, Topography, and a Toponymic Note on Micah 1:10–12a." *VT* 60:433–46. doi:10.1163/156853310X511696.

MICAH 2

Woe to Those Who Practice Injustice

2:1–5

> ¹Woe to those who devise wickedness
>   and those who work out evil on their beds!
> By the light of morning they perform it,
>   for their hand has dominion.
> ²So they covet fields and seize them,
>   houses, and take them away.
> They oppress a householder and [those in] his house,
>   a man and his estate.

³Therefore thus has Yhwh spoken: ^{Mark this:} I myself am devising against this family a calamity from which you {*mp*} will not be able to remove your necks! You will no longer go about with head held high, for it will be a calamitous time.

> ⁴On that day, they will take up a taunt about you,
>   and lament with bitter wailing:
> '"We have been utterly ruined!
>   He exchanges the portion of my people.
> How he removes what belongs to me!
>   To an apostate he apportions our fields!"'

⁵Therefore you {*ms*} will have no one to cast the boundary line by lot in the assembly of Yhwh.

Micah 2

The Insolence of Oppressors
2:6–11

⁶"Do not preach {*mp*}," they preach.
"They must not preach such things!
  Disgrace will not overtake [us]."
⁷ Should this be said, O house of Jacob?

"Has Yʜᴡʜ's forbearance been cut short?
  Are these [Yʜᴡʜ's] deeds?"
Are not my words beneficial
  when one behaves righteously?

⁸But of late, my people has risen as an enemy:
  from the front, robe [and] cloak you strip {*mp*}
from trusting passers-by,
  those who recoil from war.
⁹The women of my people you drive out,
  each from her treasured house;
from her young children
  you take away my splendor forever.

¹⁰Arise and go!
  For this cannot be the resting place.
Because it {*fs*} has become unclean, it causes ruin,
  and [the] destruction is horrific.

¹¹If someone were to go about "inspired," deceiving with
    falsehood—
"I will preach to you {*ms*} of wine and liquor"—
  such a one would be the preacher for this people!

Exile as Divinely Ordained Punishment
2:12–13

¹²I will assuredly gather Jacob—all of you!
  I will assuredly assemble the remnant of Israel!

> I will put them together like sheep in Bozrah,
>> like a flock in its pen,
>>> cacophonous with people.
> ¹³The one who breaks through will go up before them.
>> They will break through and pass on. A gate: they will go
>>> out by it.
> And their king will pass on before them,
>> Yhwh at their head.

INTERPRETATION

Micah 2 turns our gaze to the poisonous scheming and ethical breaches of oppressors within the Judean community. They are represented as responding with fierce objections to the prophet's indictment and his articulation of impending doom as a consequence for their actions. But the prophet persists in speaking the truth, in oracles textured by razor-sharp ironies. Micah calls his community to take stock, to tell the truth about the idolatries and ethical wrongs that have caused such harm in the social and political life of Judah. It must have been difficult for ancient Judeans to hear Micah's words of rebuke. But those committed to covenantal obedience, in the eighth century BCE and in later generations, might also have been heartened by the prophetic call to be resolute and fearless in taking spiritual inventory of self and community.

Woe to Those Who Practice Injustice (2:1-5)

A fiery oracle of woe opens Mic 2. At the end of Mic 1, the audience had watched as Yhwh commanded a devastated Daughter Zion to engage in a ritual action signifying mourning ("Cut off your hair because of your treasured children . . . for they have gone into exile from you," 1:16). In the opening verses of Mic 2, the audience is given to see the malefactors whose sins have occasioned this calamity (2:3). The extensive second-person address in Mic 1—feminine singular "you" for each threatened city, masculine plural and singular for its denizens, feminine singular for Zion—shifts, now, to the construction of a brutally oppressive group, "they," from whom the implied audience is invited in subtle ways to distance themselves. These malfeasant ones are powerful community leaders with authority and resources they deploy for their own gain. These scheming Judean elites, the prophet fulminates, use their privileged positions to seize agricultural lands and built structures belonging to families with less political and economic power, "inheritances" doubtless vital for subsistence that may have been held by these families for many generations. This elite group of oppressors, whom Micah sarcastically dubs a "family" unto itself (2:3)—kin by virtue of planning evil together—will soon confront a devastating force that will leave them ruined. For Yhwh too is scheming: an ironic reversal is limned clearly in 2:1 and 3. The deity will send retributive punishment against the "family" of Judah for the misdeeds of privileged malefactors in the form of enemies who will despoil and appropriate the lands of Judeans. They have been devising evil schemes; now Yhwh is devising retribution, in the form of a calamity from which they will not recover.

The tragedy is that those Judeans already living in poverty, too, will be swept up in the violence enacted militarily and economically against Judah by the Neo-Assyrian Empire. The harm done by systemic economic oppression and expropriation of land holdings continues to this day, in local regions and also enacted on a broader scale due to capitalist globalization of corporate interests and production processes. Kwadwo Appiagyei-Atua notes that "untold hardships on farmers in developing countries" have resulted from "environmental degradation, food insecurity, [and] land-grabbing," explaining further that food insecurity in many regions is caused by, among other things, monocropping designed to produce higher yields for export, an agricultural practice that results in "outbreaks of pests and disease, the depletion of soil fertility," and "loss of crop genetic diversity" that normally would have built resilience to adverse conditions (2015, 42–43). The harms that Micah decries have injured the well-being and future sustenance of families in countless localized settings—in Judah and more broadly across the ancient Near East—and continue to the present day, both in local development efforts that disenfranchise those living at subsistence or working-poor levels, and in the broader reach of profit-hungry globalized agribusinesses and other corporations. Appiagyei-Atua argues, "The monopolization of agricultural trade by transnational agribusiness . . . places farmers in developing countries at an enormous competitive disadvantage, and threatens to perpetuate poverty and hunger" (44). A lawyer, he advocates for a human-rights-based approach that empowers those living in poverty to be fully involved in policy-making, which requires moving away from a system geared toward "the financial enrichment of a few" (60). Micah will press Yhwh's "lawsuit," the disputation laid out brilliantly in Mic 6, to urge Judeans to practice justice (6:8), which assuredly requires ceasing the callous exploitation of those with less power.

The Insolence of Oppressors (2:6–11)

This passage is fascinating for the prophet's quoting of his adversaries, as well as for the interpretive ambiguity that suffuses several lines: it is not always immediately clear which utterances belong to Micah and which are being mouthed by his foes. The first ambiguous moment comes after the prophet has revealed the abuses of power that Judean officials have plotted in secret and are perpetrating against their own community (2:1–2), such that Yhwh has been engaged in divine machinations to stop them (2:3). The question in 2:4 is: Who is taking up a taunt about whom? Who will be wailing? And who is removing what belongs to the aggrieved party? "This family" is the target of Yhwh's retribution, but

Fig. 10. The prophet Micah, ca. 1099–1100, carved by Wiligelmo de Modena (fl. ca. 1099–1120). Detail from a frieze at the west portal of the cathedral in Modena, Italy.

Micah 2

it cannot be the whole family of Judah, for the oppressed peasants certainly have not been going about "with head held high." No, this oracle envisions the comeuppance of the "family" of the elites who conspire to enrich themselves at the expense of the powerless. In that light, their lament about "the portion of my people" being torn away and "our fields" being reallocated should be heard as savagely ironic ventriloquism on the part of the prophet. They had greedily exploited the portion of their people and callously expropriated the fields of others; now "you" (in a brutal masculine-singular address to a leader or representative of the elite as collective) will have no means to apportion further property to themselves (2:5).

Hostility had been signaled by the prophet's pronouncing "Woe!" at the beginning of the first oracle in Mic 2. Now Micah's adversaries bellow their antagonistic response: "Do not preach!" (2:6). Micah ventriloquizes their resistance here, and goes so far as to mimic what they'd like to hear instead, in his acidly sarcastic comment in 2:11, "I will preach to you of wine and liquor." The theology of 1:2-7 had depicted Yhwh as a cosmic ruler who descends in overwhelming power to crush the urban centers of power that have permitted idolatry, Samaria and Jerusalem. Here, the audience glimpses a God whose words are salutary to the righteous but—in a contrast that remains unexpressed but is thunderously audible—are harmful to those who do wrong (2:7c). The opening clause of 2:7 is brilliantly positioned to serve a Janus function. "Should this be said, O house of Jacob?" responds to what had just preceded: the opponents' false confidence that disgrace will not come to Jerusalem. But the prophet's rejoinder also looks forward, preparing the audience to reject the next misguided platitudes to come out of the elites' mouths: "Has Yhwh's forbearance been cut short?" Are these [Yhwh's] deeds?" Here, they continue to rely on the notion that Yhwh will not allow disaster to ravage Judah—and they are wrong. This is a second ambiguous moment in the reported dialogue crafted so artfully by Micah. It is orthodox Judean theology that Yhwh's patience and mercy are endless, and some interpreters have heard these rhetorical questions as uttered in the voice of Micah. Indeed, on the far side of disaster, after this community has been held accountable for the sins of its leaders, this theological claim will be articulated earnestly as the stirring and empowering claim that closes the scroll of Micah traditions (7:18-20). But here, such a claim is premature, facile, and self-serving, mouthed by those who do not wish to amend their ways. The unspoken answer to the second question is a rebuttal of the false premise underlying the question. The coming catastrophe is indeed the work of Yhwh.

Exile as Divinely Ordained Punishment (2:12-13)

This much-discussed passage signals with subtle irony the grim fate that awaits those who do not heed the word of Yhwh and amend their ways. Many interpreters have mistakenly read this as an oracle of hope added by a later redactor that sits uncomfortably in its current literary context. In fact, this is an oracle that lays out impending doom in brilliantly ambiguous terminology. The malfeasant Judean elites have barked at Micah not to preach of impending catastrophe (2:6), and the prophet has responded with scorn, mocking their desire for platitudes and deception (2:11). Now he provides an oracle that could be misheard as promise. Yhwh will "gather" this people, to be sure, but not in the way they are hoping—the deity will gather them for forcible deportation and lead them to slaughter. As I have articulated elsewhere (Sharp 2009, 169-76), the polysemy of this passage is effective in causing the implied audience to engage in the work of constructing meaning that—as becomes frighteningly clear—points to their own doom. Micah provides an artful mimetic performance of "false" prophecy, per the directive of the oppressive elites in 2:6. The images of sheep penned in Bozrah and moved toward a destination are ambiguous at best, and "the more Israel understands its own tradition history, the more chilling these ambiguities become" (172). Micah's relentless concern for ethical treatment of the vulnerable in his community has caused him to craft a razor-sharp oracle in which he mouths ostensible words of hope that actually eviscerate the malfeasant elites who are so eager for good news. This is a rhetoric of entrapment not unlike that on offer in Amos 1-2, wherein a sequence of oracles against enemy nations progresses inexorably toward the indictment of none other than Judah and Israel. "Just as the leaders should have been gently shepherding the people but in fact have been slaughtering and eating them" (Mic 3:2-3), "so too, with brilliant poetic justice, Micah purports to offer hope, but in fact, his prophetic word will ravage them" (174).

History of Consequences

For illustrative comments on Mic 2 in rabbinic midrash, see the introduction under §4.1.1 Midrashic Interpretations.

David Flusser (2007, 31) argues that in Matt 11:7-15, the casting of John the Baptist as Elijah redivivus reflects a rabbinic understanding of "the one who breaks through" in Mic 2:13 as Elijah, a position for

Micah 2

which he cites David Kimḥi (1160–1235). Flusser goes so far as to claim that Matt 11:12 and Luke 16:16 "reflect an ancient Jewish homily on Micah 2:13" (2007, 80).

Origen of Alexandria, the brilliant and controversial spiritualizing exegete, deploys the image of leaders being cast out, per Micah[LXX] 2:9, to illustrate a point he makes often in his reading of the Hebrew Scriptures: "Babylon" symbolizes the spiritual captivity of the sinful believer entangled in vices. "What is inwardly outside of salvation and foreign to blessedness," Origen says, "is *cast out*" by divine punishment that corrects, so the believer "is improved" (*Hom. Jer.* 28.4-5).

Hippolytus of Rome (d. 236) interprets 2:8-9 by means of the vision in Rev 19:11-16 of one coming down from heaven, riding a white horse and clad in a garment dipped in blood, "whose name is The Word of God" and whose name is inscribed as "King of kings and Lord of lords." Arguing that the garment sprinkled with blood symbolizes the flesh Christ put on in the incarnation, Hippolytus offers a conflation of Micah's language in 2:8 and 9, "they have risen up in enmity against His countenance of peace, and they have stripped off His glory," claiming that "this refers to Christ's suffering in the flesh" (*Noet.* 15, ANF 5:229).

Jerome practices his characteristically expansive hermeneutic when explicating the ruination lamented in 2:4: Micah foresees "the first captivity by the Assyrians and the captivity by the Babylonians, and the second by the Romans, because they [viz., the Jews] crucified the Lord, and the third one, the spiritual, by which each of us fell from paradise along with Adam . . . into the captivity of this world" (*Comm. Mich.*, 54). On the image of casting a boundary line (2:5), Jerome acknowledges the pragmatic reading of Judean fields being appropriated by the Assyrians and the Neo-Babylonian Empire, but first offers this: "Who does not lament when [seeing] human souls becoming so many pieces of furniture for demons . . . ? One demon casts a cord of fornication, another of avarice, another of murder; this one holds the strings of perjury. The portion of the people of God has been divided by a cord, and the fields of former holiness and paradise . . . have been handed over" (54). He interprets 2:12-13 as promise, reflecting John 10:7, 9 and Isa 40:3-5 per its reception in the Gospels (Matt 3:1-3; Mark 1:2-3; Luke 3:3-5; John 1:23): the one leading the people out is Christ the Good Shepherd, "he who has leveled all the steep ground . . . for he himself is the guide of their journey, the door of paradise, and he says, 'I am the gate'" (*Comm. Mich.*, 60). The believer who follows Christ out of the sheepfold of this world "will find pasture above the heavens, and [such a one] will feed on the words of God" (63).

Theodore of Mopsuestia (ca. 350-428) rightly recognizes 2:12-13 as an oracle of doom. He applies it to Israelites and Judeans deported in the eighth and sixth centuries: "You were all associated in the present punishment ... both those taken previously by the Assyrians and those later," when the Babylonian troops "took off everyone including the king into captivity through the gate" (*Comm.*^{TM}, 215). Theodore cites the biblical divine warrior tradition to explain Yhwh leading the captives (2:13): "the Lord acts as general amongst the enemy in fighting against you" (216). Cyril of Alexandria concurs, portraying the havoc of Israelites routed by the Babylonians: "many people aghast, others in flight, leaping walls and ditches, the very columns of the enemy breaking through gates," and God at the head of the enemy troops. In another layer of meaning, "this happened also to those who wreaked their frenzy on Emmanuel himself; their cities and towns were plundered by Vespasian and Titus, who ... discharged the divine anger on them" (*Comm.*^{CA}, 210-11).

The Franciscan theologian Bonaventure (Giovanni di Fidanza, 1221-1274) draws on the image in 2:13 of a king leading captives through a gate as he reflects on Christ's ascension in his *The Tree of Life*. This work, which per an editor "cannot be dated with any precision" (1978, xiv), is a lyrical meditation on Christ's incarnation and life, suffering and death, resurrection, ascension, and eternal reign. Mystical teachings for believers are presented in poetic strophes structured as twelve fruits from twelve branches of the Tree of Life (Gen 3:22). The tenth fruit portrays Jesus as "Leader of His Army" and, perhaps referencing Ps 68:18 [LXX 67:19] but more likely alluding to Mic 2:13, offers this: "with the gates of heaven now open, he made a way for his followers and led the exiles into the kingdom" (162).

Calvin's sermon on 25 November 1550 reads 2:6 as Micah's attempt to show all the people—not just professional seers—acting as false prophets: "The reprobate among them wanted the loudest voice and wanted to engage in a contest with God. Thus, when God speaks through [God's] prophets, the people shout back and pretend to be prophets themselves. Thus Micah wants to expose the diabolical among them" (88-89). Calvin urges the spiritually wise believer to listen to God's word quietly, rather than argue: "Let this passage serve as a mirror for us. ... When

God speaks to us, let us keep silent. Let us, in complete humility, open our ears to hear and receive everything that God might say" (91). Calvin continues, "Whenever we kick against God's Word, we are not simply engaging in a war with human beings . . . but we are confronting God [Godself], restricting [God's] Spirit, and provoking [God] against us. Is there any audacity more diabolical than that? Even the Devil trembles before the majesty of God" (100).

Congregationalist theologian and minister Edwards (1703-1758) says in his "Blank Bible" comments on 2:7, "Do not my words do good to [the one] that walketh uprightly?" that the righteous "are refreshed" by words of divine judgment, perceiving it not as "their rebuke and wound" but as "a precious ointment that heals, and revives, and invigorates them" (*WJE* 24:801).

Here is Jesuit peace activist Berrigan on elites' interdiction on truth-telling (2:6): the powerful write "their version of history. Lackeys are summoned, artists, architects, pseudo-prophets. Whether in word or work, the resultant fiction tells of virtue, glory and valor, of just causes and conquests, of the splendor and intelligence of rulers, the huzzahs and adulation of subject peoples. Micah is hardly impressed. Let us (we all but hear him) open a crack in this adamantine wall of—nonsense. Let us hear rather, and speak on behalf of . . . the slaves who built the mammoth tombs, the captives, the tortured and disappeared. Let us make our own history, and tell our story—from below" (1995, 213).

On 9 February 2020, Protestant minister and public theologian William J. Barber II preached a sermon on Mic 2 at the Greenleaf Christian Church Disciples of Christ in Goldsboro, North Carolina. Excoriating powerbrokers in Washington, DC, for greed and narcissistic hypocrisy, Barber says that while "all have sinned and fall short of the glory of God" (Rom 3:23), the purposeful and sustained "raising up of evil, constantly pushing evil" (Mic 2:1) by "lying politicians" and "lying preachers" (2:11) is a notorious sin that will incur divine wrath. Linking the economic predations in 2:2 with fourteen "marks of fascism" identified by Laurence Britt (2003), Barber deplores the United States' longstanding reluctance to provide universal healthcare and a living wage. Anticipating a march on Washington for moral revival in June 2020 to be led by the Poor People's Campaign, an economic justice advocacy group with roots in the civil rights movement, Barber thunders, "God is going to use poor people to straighten this nation out!"

RETROSPECT

The brutal economic exploitation perpetrated by elites against householders and their kinship groups has left few traces in the cultural artifacts of ancient Judah, but the oracles of Micah and other prophets (notably Amos) may be accounted as witness. Those whose houses and fields were expropriated in ancient Judah were likely to have been illiterate and without significant access to the means to inscribe and archive their experiences. But their voices can be heard through the lamenting and fiery polemics of one who stood in solidarity with them: Micah of Moresheth. Boer observes,

> As with most expressions of class consciousness, the exhibits left to us come from the ruling class (texts, artwork, monuments, and so forth). If we wish to locate some traces of the voices of those who have otherwise been obliterated by the economic structures of the time, then we need to be sensitive to the characterization of class opponents in these ruling-class documents. (2015, 123)

This requires critical interrogation of textual representations of those living in poverty as unintelligent, lazy, or sinful and valorization of those who work industriously to support ruling-class privilege as loyal and admirable. Boer's examples of such discursive moves in the Hebrew Bible are drawn from Gen 1–3 and the Joseph cycle, Ruth, and Proverbs; many other texts could be added. In the book of Micah, though a product of elite prophetic scribal memory, the indignation voiced by the prophet and by Daughter Zion can be taken seriously as amplifying other voices: the convictions and laments of those living in poverty whose voices were suppressed or simply ignored in ancient Judah, audible now only as whispers in the background of the dialogues Micah creates.

Micah's ventriloquizing of his opponents renders as dialogue the challenging nature of conflict between those who stand in solidarity with the vulnerable and those who uphold the exploitative status quo in an unjust social system. Ahmed underlines the pressure that can be placed on the feminist KILLJOY to stop naming what is amiss: "just stop noticing exclusions," others advise the KILLJOY, "and your burden will be eased" (Ahmed 2017, 235). But acquiescing and lapsing into silence cannot solve the problem. Micah 2 dramatizes a truth that Ahmed, too, observes: "you might have to become willful to hold on when you are asked to let go" (235). In every era, adversaries have advised prophetic truthtellers not to preach (2:6). Their

Micah 2

attempted censorship is one vector of "the violence reproduced by organizations that identify speaking about violence as disloyalty" (257). Ahmed's wry comment about feminist activists is something that can be predicated of Micah and other biblical prophets as well: "A committed killjoy has a lifetime of experience of being the cause of unhappiness" in their community (258). But the KILLJOY must not choose silence or, worse, the "willed oblivion" of denial of oppression: "We must refuse this oblivion," understanding that the truth spoken aloud should be welcomed by those who see what is at stake and who respond with integrity (cf. 2:7).

"Arise and go! For this cannot be the resting place. Because it has become unclean, it causes ruin, and [the] destruction is horrific." Micah 2:10 offers a powerful image of Judah as ruined terrain, as a landscape defiled and rendered unlivable because of the violence of Judean elites toward their own people (2:8–9). Bey argues that racism and gender policing make unlivable the modes through which Black trans persons have been taught to understand their identity, their place of origin writ metaphorically. Whenever "normative tentacles try to corral gendered unruliness back into the violence of the binary" (146), the gender-nonconforming FUGITIVE may choose to flee such impending ruin and destruction. Bey insists that with regard to gender normativity, "these given ontological skins we have come to love so dearly" cannot sustain authentic life; "they cannot be the home in which we dwell for the duration of our lives; we demand something more capacious and of our own coalitional choosing" (2022, 163). Through the notion of FUGITIVITY, Bey imagines flight as life-giving, claiming the chaotic, unsettled living of the Black trans FUGITIVE as far preferable to acquiescing to, or becoming assimilated into, hegemonies of white supremacist and gendered violence. Black trans feminism is prophetic resistance in solidarity with those who have been wounded, "a commitment to alleviate violences in all their forms, chief among which are the violences done by whiteness's racial taxonomy and gender's unbreachable binary" (163).

As articulated in the introduction, here is the spectrum of possibilities I have limned for contemporary responses to Micah's prophetic witness: → resilience → resistance → reformation → rejoicing. Micah 2 builds *resilience* through the prophet's assurance that the words of Yhwh are salutary and sustaining for all who comport themselves in their communal relationships with righteousness (2:7) and compassion (something implicit but crystal clear in 2:8–9). Micah 2 catalyzes *resistance* to the arrogance of elite malefactors who go about their invidious business with smug complacency (2:1–3). Micah 2 calls for *reformation* of predatory state-sponsored practices that allow the wealthy to seize householders' homes and farmers' lands, callously displacing women and children within the community (2:2, 9). Finally, Mic 2 holds space for *rejoicing* for those subsisting in the lower economic strata of the community: though they might perceive themselves to be powerless, Yhwh, their advocate and ally, is designing the comeuppance of elite oppressors (2:3–4).

MICAH 2 AND ECOLOGICAL JUSTICE

Micah 2 makes visible the displacement and forcible losses suffered by families due to economic exploitation and war. Micah voices the despair of the dispossessed: "We are utterly ruined! . . . How he removes what belongs to me!" (2:4). Throughout history, communities across the globe have relied on agriculture to secure and sustain their flourishing. Kinship groups and small villages rely on the produce of their own fields for their subsistence, and larger social entities support bigger towns, cities, and entire regions by means of trade in agricultural tools and crop yields. When an unscrupulous individual, elite group, or occupying army seizes farmland and built structures, as described in 2:2, 4, and 9, families are left vulnerable and, in some cases, can be catapulted into poverty (Braaten 2022, 150). Expropriation perpetrated by political elites or wartime enemies deprives kinship groups of places to live in which they have invested time, expertise, and labor for years or decades. The dispossessed are robbed of economic resources that could have sustained their children and future generations in the family lineage. In kinship groups surviving on the edge of economic precarity, expropriation of herds of livestock and fields could potentially lead to a cascade effect of deleterious consequences for generations to come. In our own day, insufficiently regulated agribusiness, oil drilling, strip mining, fracking, and other mechanisms designed to exploit natural resources have created enormous conflict and stress for indigenous communities and other families resistant to surrendering the land they tend. Extractive technologies have also enacted egregious harm on watersheds, on many biomes from forests to meadows to marshes, and on biodiversity in every ecosystem. The IPCC confirms, "Widespread deterioration of ecosystem structure and function, resilience and natural adaptive capacity, [and] shifts in seasonal timing have occurred due to climate change," with "hundreds of local losses of species . . . driven by increases in the magnitude of heat extremes . . . as well as mass mortality events on land and in the ocean" (IPCC 2022 §B.1.2).

Micah 2

Ayana Elizabeth Johnson and Katharine Wilkinson make a feminist argument for "gender-responsive strategies for climate resilience and adaptation" in addressing the ecological crisis, acknowledging, with numerous other experts, that women and children in many communities globally are disproportionately affected by ecological harms. Micah imagines women driven from their houses by oppressive economic practices (2:9). In our reception of the Micah traditions, we may amplify this prophetic indictment in a world in which countless villages are ruined, or their livability drastically reduced, through ecologically damaging policies underwritten by corporate greed, corrupt leadership, and willful ignorance about the climate emergency. The IPCC notes, "Climate and weather extremes are increasingly driving displacement in all regions. . . . Flood and drought-related acute food insecurity and malnutrition have increased in Africa . . . and Central and South America"; it is indisputable that "through displacement and involuntary migration from extreme weather and climate events, climate change has generated and perpetuated vulnerability" in countless families and communities, and "the number of people at risk from climate change and associated loss of biodiversity will progressively increase" (IPCC 2022 §§B.1.7; B.3.1). Johnson and Wilkinson articulate a feminist hope in the activism of the oppressed: "We see women and girls bringing their whole selves to this movement—fear, grief, fiery courage, wracking uncertainty, all of it—and doing the inner work that often precedes effective change" (2021, xix-xx). The challenges and costs of prophetic activism are perhaps best known from the laments of Jeremiah, but the emotional dynamics can be glimpsed also in the oracles of Micah, which move in turbulent and nonlinear ways from anger to lament to righteous indignation, from radiant hope to fear to resolve, the collection of oracles ending with a fragile claim on resilience through trust in Yhwh. Similarly, Johnson and Wilkinson note for contemporary prophets of ecological reformation "the immense emotional complexity of knowing and holding what has been done to the world, while bolstering our resolve never to give up on one another or our collective future" (xxii).

Ashlee Cunsolo speaks of the "abyssal sorrow" experienced by those who have lost loved ones, homes, or significant natural spaces to the effects of climate change (2017, xiii). Intense sorrow has saturated the lives of countless persons who have endured cultural dislocation and land loss over the centuries, from Micah's experience of the Neo-Assyrian military onslaught against Judah to contemporary communities experiencing increasingly powerful storms and inundation of coastal habitations, with growing numbers of living creatures coming under threat of endangerment or extinction. Andrew Solomon offers, "to be creatures who love, we must be creatures who despair at what we lose" (2001, 15; quoted in Cunsolo 2017, xvii). Ecological activists and theologians who work for the healing of creation recognize the need to "lament with bitter wailing" (2:4). Such performances of grief, expressed in writing, the arts, filmmaking, preaching and other public speaking, and political action, can harness the power of prophetic lament toward the goal of catalyzing solidarity with the suffering community of Earth.

COMMENTARY

Micah 2 lays bare the malevolent scheming and exploitation perpetrated by the powerful: subtle kinds of violence that fracture the covenantal obedience expected of Yhwh's people and make Judah vulnerable to terrible retribution at the hands of enemy nations. On that latter point, see Isa 10:5-6 for Yhwh wielding Assyria as a weapon of divine punishment; see also Jer 25:9; 27:6; 43:10; and Ezek 29:19-20 for Yhwh deploying Babylonia's ruler Nebuchadrezzar II as a death-dealing instrument of the divine will. Heschel notes, "The condemnation of violence (*ḥamas, shod, 'oshek*) is a major theme in the prophets' speeches," but the prophets also resisted imperial domination: "The denunciation of violence committed by private individuals applied a millionfold to the brutal wars of aggression waged by insatiable and arrogant empires. Although Assyria . . . was used as a tool" by Yhwh, "the prophets insisted that the guilt was the aggressor's" (2001, 206).

2:1 Woe! The taunting interjection *hôy* can be translated variously as "Ah!" or "Alas!" or "Ha!" or "Woe!" It occurs only here in Micah, but often in other books of the Latter Prophets, especially in Isa 1-55 and in a notable density in Hab 2.

For their hand has dominion. Hebrew *yeš-lǝʾēl yādām* may be translated idiomatically as "they have the power" or "it is in their power"; compare other instances of the idiom with *yād* at Gen 31:29; Deut 28:32; Neh 5:5; Prov 3:27. The Hebrew circumlocution indicates that which is appropriate to ʾEl, the chief god of the West Semitic pantheon: it is within their control to bring to fruition the evil they have devised. Because the vast majority of uses of *lǝʾēl* are referring to God earnestly, because the idiom is not common enough to seem prosaic in Biblical Hebrew, and because the way in which

Micah 2

malefactors in Micah's community are critiqued by the prophet as showing disregard for Yhwh, I prefer a translation with "dominion"—with its dominical valence—to render the undertone of irony in Micah's use of this phrase. Gelston observes that Micah^LXX, which renders *ouk ēran pros ton theon tas cheiras autōn*, "they did not lift their hands to God," seems to be interpreting *yeš* as a verb from *nś'* and "[inserting] a negative to improve" the sense (BHQ, 97).

2:2 *They covet fields and . . . houses.* The powerful elites exploit and defraud property owners under their jurisdiction, tearing fields and houses away from their rightful owners. Coveting (*ḥmd*) is expressly forbidden in the Ten Commandments (Exod 20:17; Deut 5:21). It is possible that the two nouns here, "fields" and "houses," are functioning metonymically: the elite are not restricting their predations only to agricultural plots and built residential structures, but are seizing all that their targets have. Chaney cites the work of William Moran (1967) on occurrences of the fixed word-pair "house and field" in property-transfer texts from Ugarit as being sometimes followed, as is the case in Exod 20:17 and Deut 5:21, by a phrase about everything belonging to the person (Chaney 2017, 72). The verb *gzl*, here rendered "seize," occurs also in Mic 3:2 as a metaphor for the rapacious greed of Israelite leaders who "tear the skin off" their people. As Chaney observes, the verbs "covet," "seize," and "take away" signal dimensions of a single "process of coveting, extortion, and appropriation" (73). The verb translated "oppress" in 2:3 can communicate the more precise valence of economic oppression, such as robbery, extortion, fraud, and withholding wages (cf. Deut 24:14; 28:33; Ps 62:11; Prov 22:16; Eccl 7:7; Jer 21:12; Ezek 18:18; 22:7, 12, 29; Hos 12:8 [Eng. 7]; Mal 3:5). As Harry Nasuti observes, such economic exploitation is forbidden in Lev 5:21-24 (Eng. 6:2-5); 19:13 (2004, 145). Practices codified in the Torah are designed to protect those living at the edge of poverty from life-threatening food insecurity and economic precarity generally (Lev 19:9-10; 23:22; Deut 15:7-11), from being cheated in dishonest trade (Lev 19:13, 35-36; Deut 25:13-16), from being subjected to protracted debt-slavery or unremitting debt (Exod 21:2-3; Lev 25:39-42, of Israelites only; Deut 15:1-2, 12-14), and from permanent loss of their ancestral lands (Lev 25:13-17, 25-28). Stephen Cook observes, "Micah upholds the right of permanent tenure of Israel's inherited land within the lineage categories of tribe, clan and family," and he indicts "the ruling stratum of Jerusalem . . . for ignoring rights to permanent land tenure and for subjugating Judean country farmers" (1999, 225).

Continuing with the interpretive trajectory that links Samaria and Jerusalem closely (Mic 1:5-7), Mic 2 can be illuminated by insights from Sergi and Gadot on the archaeology of ancient Samaria and Jezreel. Monumental buildings in those locations "were built on what were previously agricultural estates" and "reflect the power and wealth of a new, emerging elite in the Samarian highlands" who exploited the laboring class: "The substantial amount of work needed in order to erect these new centers of power required recruiting labor from the surrounding regions," thus "the palaces were . . . not only symbols of power but also a means to impose that power on local inhabitants" (2017, 109). Assuredly relevant to Micah's indictment of elite oppressors for their scheming to seize others' fields is this observation from Sergi and Gadot: "It was agricultural wealth that initially differentiated the emerging elite, and subsequently was translated into political hegemony" (109). Andersen and Freedman find undecidable the question of "whether the seizure of a person's house was to be taken literally, reporting the oppression of the poor by rich business interests, or whether this was a figure for the violent annexation of territory of one state by another, an act of military power" (2000, 389). Subsequent verses in Mic 2 gesture toward both possibilities. The first, that of internecine exploitation, is clearly supported by 2:8-9, where "my people has risen as an enemy." But the second possibility, that of forced displacement due to military defeat, comes into sharp focus in 2:10 and 2:12-13, when the latter bicolon is best interpreted as an oracle of doom that ironically mimics what the people would like to have heard from their (false) prophets.

they oppress a householder. Chaney sees Mic 2:1-2 and the tenth commandment as forbidding exploitation of "the agrarian population" by means of "practices of land consolidation so aggressive and coercive that they deprived a family of fellow Israelites of their ancestral plot of arable land and the subsistence and social inclusion that it supported" (2017, 74-75 [emphasis removed]).

2:3 Thus has Yhwh spoken. Only twice in Micah does this divine speech formula (sometimes called the "messenger formula") appear: here and at 3:5. Here, the formula introduces material in longer prose lines that signal semantic and syntactical difference from the surrounding shorter poetic bicola. While the distinction between prose and poetry in Biblical Hebrew texts is fluid and not to be taken as rigidly definable, here the speaker, Yhwh, pursues a thought with articulation of the speaker's own agency and a predicate that is substantially more complex than we discern in vivid, elliptical poetic phrases structured in bicola.

Micah 2

I myself am devising. Against scheming oppressors who have been "devising wickedness" (*ḥōšəbê-'āwen*), Yhwh has no choice but to "devise" calamitous punishment (*ḥōšēb . . . rā'â*) as retribution for their sin. The two sorts of planning are linked by use of the verb *ḥšb* (so many interpreters, including Dempsey 1999, 121), but the strategizing of Yhwh, of course, is understood as far more powerful. In the intensifying sequence of the semantic parallelism across 2:1-3, the divine plan overshadows and renders risible the erstwhile plotting of malfeasant Judean elites.

this family. The noun *mišpāḥâ* occurs only here in Micah and only a handful of other times in the Book of the Twelve, predominantly in prose material in Deutero-Zechariah (Amos 3:1, 2; Nah 3:4; Zech 12:12, 13, 14; 14:17, 18). By contrast, it is extremely common in the first four books of the Pentateuch and in Joshua, as well as in the genealogies of 1 Chronicles. This verse, Mic 2:3, fits reasonably well in its literary context, but the lines are far longer than is common in Micah's oracles otherwise. The syntax of the verse is anomalous in its prosaic character, marked by a notably lesser degree of poetic parallelism than is usual in Micah's oracular bicola and tricola. Thus Mic 2:3 has the character of a prose interpolation from a scribe anxious to render more clearly the judgment that looms in the penumbral transition from 2:1-2 to 2:4. Henri Cazelles and David Sperling suggest the opening verses of Mic 2 may point to territorial conflict between Israel and Judah:

> It is a clan (*mishpahah*, 2:3) [that] has angered the Lord and it is a stranger who reaps the benefit of the vengeful spoliation, without right of repurchase. The key phrase is in verse 7: the Lord does not abandon Israel. The sense of the passage becomes clearer if the prophet is assumed to be warning the ministers of Judah, who wish to expand at the expense of Israel. (2007, 162)

Many readers, including myself, will not be persuaded that conflict between Israel and Judah is the best framework for understanding the historical context here, given that an "apostate" will be receiving control of the disputed fields (2:4). This material is better understood as depicting forced expropriation of holdings by a militarily dominant foreign nation—conceivably Assyria, but equally or more likely given the character of 2:3 as a later prose interpolation, the Neo-Babylonian Empire.

Ben Zvi notes the lack of congruence between the identity of the malefactors in 2:1-2 (elite oppressors) and the identity of those who will experience punishment in 2:3-5, which seems to be the entire covenant people. He

Commentary

cites this as evidence that this oracular material was never intended to be read in a historicist way with hyperspecific referents enacting mimesis of historically performed prophecy: "neither the actual words of the historical Micah nor the precise historical situation in which they were uttered were among the main concerns of the community of writers and (re)readers" who created this material (1999b, 93). Instead, their literary strategies allow for reference to the monarchical period signaled in 1:1, but also "leave room for additional—not alternative—connoted meanings," something that "facilitates the continuous rereading" of Micah as a prophetic work relevant to future generations (98).

a calamity. The noun *rāʿâ* should be translated in ways that unfold the nuances of contextual usage within the relevant lexical field. Using "evil" in English would be inappropriate for many deployments of the word and, with its heavily moralistic and spiritually negative overtones in English, would constitute poor translation practice, though one may acknowledge the benefit for readers who do not know Biblical Hebrew in repeating the same translation to make evident the prevalence of the Hebrew root. Micah uses the noun *rāʿâ*, the verbal root *rʿʿ*, and the adjectival form *rāʿ* a total of nine times, making this a lexical motif of signal importance in the book. The instances are translated in this commentary as follows: 1:12, "calamity"; 2:1, "evil"; twice in 2:3, "calamity" and "calamitous"; 3:2, "evil"; 3:4, "evil"; 3:11, "calamity"; 4:6, "harmed"; 7:3, "evil." It is possible that aural resonances with instances drawn from a homographic verb, *rāʿâ*, "to pasture, to shepherd," which occurs in 5:3, 4, 5 and twice in 7:14, might have been audible to the prophet's original audience. Such sound-play would artfully highlight the contrast between the evil doings of Judean malefactors and the calamity looming as Yhwh's punishment of the same, on the one hand, and the tending and protection to be offered by the coming messianic ruler and by Yhwh as shepherd, on the other.

from which you will not be able to remove your necks. In this metaphor, the prophet draws on the image of an oppressive yoke, something dramatized in the vivid narrative in Jer 27. The book of Jeremiah, set narratively in the time of multiple assaults on Judah by Babylonia in the early sixth century, displays numerous prose interpolations that frame, disambiguate, and interpret the oracles of Jeremiah in light of the terrifying rise of the Neo-Babylonian Empire and that nation's conquest of Judah and Jerusalem in 587 BCE. The implicit image of an enemy's oppressive yoke links this material closely to the prose art—and perhaps, then, the narrative setting—of the Deutero-Jeremianic prose in the latter half of the book of Jeremiah.

Micah 2

with head held high. Some take *rômâ*, which occurs only here in the Hebrew Bible, as signifying that the addressees will no longer be able to walk erect (so NJPS; *HALOT* 3:1206); Andersen and Freedman elaborate that the term "refers to the bent attitude of bearing a yoke" and "thus reverses the liberation described in Lev 26:13," where the relevant adverb is taken not from *rwm* but from *qwm* (2000, 278). Others, including myself, see the term as signaling an attitude of insolence on the part of the scheming malefactors excoriated in the preceding two verses. My translation, "you will no longer go about with head held high," allows for both semantic possibilities.

for it will be a calamitous time. This precise phrase, *kî ʿēt rāʿâ hîʾ*, occurs elsewhere only at Amos 5:13. There, the clause serves as the culmination of a passage that laments Israel's population having been decimated (Amos 5:1-2), warns that Yhwh will punish Israel for having failed to perform the justice and righteousness expected of the covenant people (5:6-7), identifies Yhwh as the agent who brings destruction, and deplores malfeasant Israelites' unjust treatment of righteous adjudicators and those who are in need. Here in Mic 2 as well, Yhwh initiates devastating punishment for social and economic injustice.

2:4 ***On that day.*** This phrase and similar expressions, used widely in the corpus of the Latter Prophets, are construed by scholars as signaling a distant time or even an eschatological inbreaking of divine action into human history. The Hebrew phrase *bayyôm hahûʾ* occurs three times in Micah (2:4; 4:6; 5:9), in a pattern that traces catastrophe for Judah, restoration for Judah, and catastrophe for Judah's enemies. The phrase occurs no fewer than forty-five times in Isaiah, ten times in Jeremiah, thirteen times in Ezekiel, and thirty-seven times throughout the Book of the Twelve apart from Micah, most densely in Zechariah.

a taunt. This marvelous poetic line brims with alliterative and assonant sounds that manage to evoke both mourners and those who mock them. Repeated fricative sounds with the consonant *heh* sound like sobbing gasps, and repeated sibilant sounds with *shin* and (once) *sin* evoke the vocalizations of imagined mockers. Here Micah has created an artful sonic landscape that performs that to which it refers. Gelston remarks the difficulty ancient versions had with *nihyâ*, noting that some take it as a noun understood as cognate with *nhy*, as the present translation does (cf. *IBHS* §10.2.1g on cognate internal accusative nouns), while other translations "may simply represent guesses at an unknown word" (*BHQ*, 98).

A *māšāl* can be a proverb or maxim, an instructive riddle or poem, or a didactic parable or tale. In biblical traditions, the *māšāl* is represented as being orally performed by a speaker or speakers, whether depicted as known characters in narratives or, as is the case here, imagined as "hypothetical speakers" (Vayntrub 2019, 81). Andersen and Freedman insist that divergent utterances and contexts are in view here, an observation that one will "raise against you a proverb" and, then, the content of the lamentation wailed by the dispossessed: that is, "the two verbs, *yiśśāʾ* and *ʾāmar*, apply to two distinct speakers and imply two different kinds of speech" (2000, 257, 287). Kimḥi argues that the speaker is "a false prophet whose advice and predictions had not materialized and he therefore laments and recites dirges" (Stavsky 2009, 15). Nasuti reviews more recent proposals regarding the vexed question of speaker(s) in this passage (2004, 146–48). Are these the Judean oppressors lamenting, or is this the earnest protest of the compatriots whom they have dispossessed? These difficulties can be resolved when we perceive the onlookers to be ventriloquizing the lamenting oppressors with heavy sarcasm. I argue that in a powerful image of reversal, Micah is prophesying that unspecified onlookers (a 3ms generic subject) will use a taunt song or mockery concerning those who had formerly wielded their power to oppress; in this mockery, the onlookers are mimicking the lamenting of the now-dispossessed elites. The formerly elite malefactors will be economically ruined, dispossessed of their holdings by an enemy invader who distributes them to one of his subordinates, perhaps one tasked with ongoing administrative oversight of the decimated region. For a potentially analogous role in a later time period, the reader might consider the authority of Nebuzaradan over Jeremiah and other captive Judeans after the fall of Jerusalem, according to Jer 39:9–40:12. Less persuasive, to my mind, but not impossible, is Nasuti's suggestion that the lamenting speakers' land has been given to an "apostate" in the person of "a fellow Israelite who is perceived as violating the demands of the covenant" or may pertain to "a postexilic redivision of the land under the Persians" (2004, 148–50, on the latter position citing Kessler 2000a). The 3ms generic subject is deftly deployed in three 3ms *qal* verbs (*yiśśāʾ*, *nāhâ*, and *ʾāmar*): onlookers will relish this didactic taunt about the ruin of the elite oppressors, gleefully relaying the oppressors' wails as the Judean malefactors are being stripped of their ill-gotten gains and their corrosive influence.

lament with bitter wailing. This condensed phrase uses three forms of *nhh* with no other words in the clause, an artful poetic move that, with its heavy reliance on the voiceless fricative sound of *heh*, may be intended to mimic the gasping breaths of one who is wailing or sobbing uncontrollably.

He exchanges the portion of my people. The NJPS translation, "My people's portion changes hands," conveys the sense of the action well, but at a slight cost, obscuring the deft move effected by Micah via continued use of the 3ms subject. Here, the unexpressed agent cannot be a generic subject. Another shift has taken place in the referent for the 3ms verb, and this shift is nothing short of chilling: the agent of destruction has come fully into view, and it is Yhwh. There can be no question of this, as the verse continues: the God of Israel and Judah is giving the inheritance of the covenant people—the territory Israel had battled so hard to occupy in ancient days—to "an apostate," a godless enemy ruler. The term ʿammî, "my people," occurs three times in this chapter (2:4, 8, 9), in a broader sequence of nine instances throughout the book of Micah. This poignant formulation works rhetorically to underline the fear and grief experienced by the beleaguered community, or the prophet's sadness or righteous indignation on their behalf, or even, in Mic 6, the heightened emotions of Yhwh (see 1:9; 3:3, 5; 6:3, 5, 16).

"How he removes what belongs to me! To an apostate he apportions our fields!" Here, imagined mockers are cruelly quoting those whom they see being dispossessed. Thus the "bitter wailing" these onlookers will be performing "on that day" should be understood as heavily ironic. If it were being imagined as earnest mourning, Micah could easily have said (or written), "On that day you will lament with bitter wailing," but here, distance is created by the prophet's choice to stage this as a taunt coming from others. In *yāmîš*, the astute audience will hear an ironic echo of *tāmîšû* in 2:3. Judean oppressors will not be able to "remove" their necks from the yoke of enemy captivity, and the invaders will "remove" the patrimonial holdings of those elites from their possession. Intensifying the sense of ironic reversal is the wordplay discernible within 2:4 with *ḥēleq* and *yəhallēq*: the allotted territory "portion" of the covenant people will be "apportioned" to an apostate enemy. Andersen and Freedman suggest that the final three verbs, all nonperfective forms following the perfective *nəšaddūnû*, could be translated as present perfect, rather than by "a bland present tense" (2000, 284). But the present tense within this nested discourse need not be conceived as bland. One can interpret these quoted nonperfective forms—especially given the exclamatory ʾêk—as lending immediacy and urgency to the imagined utterances "in a present-time frame with reference to the act of speaking" (*IBHS* §31.3.b). The taunters witnessing Judah's despoliation are staring, or making as if to stare, in horror at these traumatizing events as they unfold: Micah is representing the bystanders as cruelly imitating the victims' shock in those chaotic moments.

The identity of the apostate conqueror is left elliptical in this suspenseful poetry. But the terror of the unnamed enemy's approach is already palpable in the final clause of 1:9. One has the sense that the identity of the adversary may be too terrifying to name in a direct and unvarnished way. Further, the aporia at the heart of referentiality here leaves open the shattering possibility that the enemy is none other than Yhwh. See above on *kî ʿēt rāʿâ hîʾ*, an expression found only in Amos 5:13 and Mic 2:4. Where Amos uses three devastating doxologies (4:13; 5:8-9; 9:5-6) to identify Yhwh with increasing intensity and semantic excessiveness as the source of destruction for those who oppose the divine purpose, Micah uses obliqueness, passive verbs focusing on the consequences of despoliation, and thunderous silence. A prophetic scribe will write the dreaded name fully into the witness of Micah only at 5:4b (Eng. 5b): only after a lyrical and powerful vision of a coming ruler who will shepherd God's people and secure peace for them. The feared conqueror is Assyria. The name is spoken aloud, as it were, only after strong promises of future deliverance have shored up the fortifications around the implied audience.

2:5 Cast the boundary line by lot in the assembly of Yhwh. The practice of determining the extent of tribal territories by lot-casting is established by divine command (Num 26:52-56; 33:50-54) and dramatized in Num 34 and Josh 14-19, 21. Andersen and Freedman speculate that having no one to cast lots on one's behalf would mean that an "individual, or more likely tribe, [would be] expelled and [would become] landless" (2000, 290). The cord or rope used in lot-casting (*ḥebel*) is echoed twice in 2:10 with use of the root *ḥbl* in another semantic arena connoting corruption, ruin, or destruction (*ḥbl* III, *HALOT* 1:285-86). As with 2:3, this verse has the character of a prose interpolation. It is not structured according to poetic parallelism and seems to serve an explicatory function, detailing a further harmful consequence of the sin of the scheming elites.

2:6 "Do not preach." The verb *nṭp* may suggest dripping or, meant pejoratively, speaking in a spirit-possessed frenzy with spittle flying. Sigmund Mowinckel (1884-1965) offers the definition, "to speak ecstatic words so that one froths at the mouth" (2002, 87). One notes a similar prohibition ventriloquized in an oracle of an older contemporary of Micah, Amos: Yhwh fulminates against the Israelites for having undermined those dedicated to holy work, "You made the nazirites drink wine, and commanded the prophets, saying, 'Do not prophesy'" (Amos 2:12). Here in Mic 2, the translation

Micah 2

"do not prophesy (ecstatically)" would be possible. But "preach" in English is fruitful for its diverse valences of thunderous remonstrance, revelation of divine purposes, and moralistic carping—that last sense assuredly in the foreground when Micah's critics are characterized by the second instance of the word. Further, to some readers, a translation of *nṭp* with the sense "to prophesy" might suggest foretelling, something that does not work to describe what Micah's opponents are doing in their critique. In Isa 30:9-11 is an elaborate parallel to this interdiction on intermediation in the quoted discourse of opponents. The "rebellious children" of Yhwh are ventriloquized as saying "to the seers, 'Do not see'; and to the prophets, 'Do not prophesy to us what is right; speak to us smooth things, prophesy illusions, leave the way, turn aside from the path, let us hear no more about the Holy One of Israel.'"

Isaac Abarbanel (1437-1508) reads the speakers of this prohibition as "the poor and the oppressed, whose causes the prophets champion," but who "are advising the prophets to refrain from speaking the word of God, for the nation will show no embarrassment or shame at the prophetic rebuke" (Stavsky 2009, 16). Andersen and Freedman are confident that this passage "documents Micah's confrontation with rival prophets" (296), but this is not, in my view, the best explanation of the antagonism dramatized here. The attempted silencing of Micah is coming from the community leaders described in the preceding verses as using their social and political capital for corrupt purposes. The utterances of Hosea, Amos, Jeremiah, and Ezekiel were remembered as having generated fierce political opposition; the rebuke of Micah here should be seen in that tradition. Hosea is mocked by his compatriots (Hos 9:7-9). Amos is warned by Amaziah, the priest of Bethel, not to preach (Amos 7:10-17, with *nṭp* in 7:16). Jeremiah is threatened by the violent antagonism of denizens of Anathoth, Pashhur son of Immer, and unnamed others toward him (Jer 11:18-23; 15:10, 15-21; 18:18-23; 20:1-12; and passim). Ezekiel addresses characterizations of the word of Yhwh as unfair and the way of Yhwh as unjust (Ezek 18:25-29; 33:17-20), and his prophetic authority is trivialized (33:30-33). The social authority of at least some of Israel's and Judah's prophets was portrayed as impressive by the scribes who preserved their traditions, for example, in the cases of prophets such as Isaiah and Jeremiah, who are described as consultants to monarchs. Yet it is equally clear that in their communities, the prophets' voices were, as Brueggemann says, "odd, abrasive, mostly unwelcome voices" (1997, 627).

"Disgrace will not overtake [us]." Those in positions of power are confident that disgrace—public shaming, political disempowerment, and cul-

Commentary

tural degradation in the wake of a devastating military defeat—will not overwhelm Judah. Many translations read *yissag* here as equivalent to a *qal* form from *nśg* with an unexpressed 1cpl object suffix (so McKane 1998, 86). Scholars of an earlier generation paid significant attention to the issue of the relation of textual charges of false prophecy to the historical realia that might have lain behind poetic passages such as Mic 2:6 and prose narratives such as Jer 28. For some interpreters, the falsity of prophecy may have been a matter of the content of the message being inappropriate or not relevant as regards the contextual application to the moment in which prophet and people found themselves. That is, it would not be prudent to assume that the "false" prophets had necessarily been malicious or intentionally deceitful—perhaps they trusted in Yhwh, as many passages in Deuteronomy, Joshua, Isaiah, and the Psalms adjure believers to do when under threat, and were unwilling to surrender that hope in the face of other prophets' jeremiads about Israel's or Judah's sin bringing inevitable calamity down on the community. James Crenshaw, drawing on the work of Hans-Joachim Kraus (1964, 112) and A. S. van der Woude (1969), offers that the false prophets in Micah may have been "profoundly moved by the ancient election faith and covenant promises" on offer in other authoritative traditions of Israel's heritage (Crenshaw 2007, 21). Citing the "theologies surrounding the themes of David, Sinai, the exodus, wilderness wandering and conquest, Zion, patriarchs, and the divine dwelling place (ark and temple)," Crenshaw avers that "every one of these tradition complexes contributed something worthwhile to Yahwism" and deserved respect; accordingly, some prophets might have reasonably assumed that "the God who made these promises contained in the traditions of election" would remain faithful in times of crisis (71).

2:7 Should this be said? Having quoted oppressors in 2:6 who would rather hear a (false) message of *šālôm* (see 3:5), Micah vigorously contests his opponents' assertion that Yhwh could not be behind the enemy invasion that has swept through Judah to the very gates of Jerusalem. McKane hears this clause as belonging to the quoted speech of the oppressors: "The opponents of Micah are questioning the premisses of the doom prophecy" (1998, 81). But it is better taken as Micah's indignant response to being told (with others prophesying doom) not to speak out. He quotes his adversaries further on how what is unfolding could not possibly be the actions of Yhwh, then asserts that indeed it is salutary to prophesy judgment. The structure, as I see it, proceeds through an overarching injunction by the powerful adversaries seeking to silence authentic prophecy, then two units, beautifully

Micah 2

Fig. 11. Jonah, Micah, and Isaiah. Stained glass, thirteenth century. In the Basilika St. Kunibert in Cologne, Germany. Photo by G. Freihalter.

parallel in that two lines are quoted from these adversaries, followed by Micah's retort.

"*Do not preach!*"
"*They must not preach such things! Disgrace will not overtake [us].*"
Micah: Should this be said, O house of Jacob?

"*Has Yhwh's forbearance been cut short? Are these [Yhwh's] deeds?*"
Micah: Are not my words beneficial when one behaves righteously?

"***Has Yhwh's forbearance been cut short?***" For *rûaḥ yhwh*, rendered in most contemporary translations as "Yhwh's patience," the targum supplies, "the Memra from the Lord," suggesting the word of Yhwh instead of a quality understood as essential to the being of the deity. Cathcart and Gordon note the targum avoids the imputation of "the human attribute of patience" to Yhwh "and—worse—the possibility of it coming to an end" (1989, 116n16). Micah quotes his opponents' disbelieving rhetorical question in order to refute it. With *qṣr*, a valence of limitation is implied (see, e.g., Num 11:23; Isa 50:2; 59:1), but precisely in what sense depends on the fuller predicate and cues from the larger literary context. In some instances, as here, elliptical expression may allow for interpretive options ranging from weakness to impatience to volatility. Many commentators translate *rûaḥ*, literally "spirit," here as patience, with *qṣr* yielding "impatient" (McKane 1998, 86; Sweeney 2000, 2:362; Waltke 2007, 115; O'Brien 2015, 20; cf. Job 21:4; *qṣr* + *nepeš* in Num 21:4). Kessler interprets the sense as being closer to divine irritation ("unmutig," 2000a, 126, 131; cf. *qṣr* + *nepeš* in Judg 16:16). Andersen and Freedman note that it is crucial to decide who is speaking in 2:7. Deciding that Micah is speaking (a position I consider mistaken), they argue that the phrase does not concern Yhwh's temperament but the apparent divine inability to stop evildoers from causing harm; thus the rhetorical question "probably means, 'Is Yahweh impotent?'" (2000, 309-11).

2:8 *of late . . . as an enemy.* Some translations ignore the adverbial expression of time *'etmûl*, but it is essential for the rationale Micah proffers regarding how the deity could turn punitive and send calamity upon the covenant people. Yhwh had indeed been gracious and forbearing in the past, and the prophet's words of remonstrance—those of Micah and perhaps, by implication, all authentic prophets—were salutary, because the people heeded and turned from disobedience. The people had behaved righteously,

Micah 2

the possibility articulated in the last clause of 2:7. But in recent times (*'et-mûl*), malfeasant oppressors among the people have become unregenerate and relentless in their predatory exploitation of others (2:8-9). Because these have risen up, as it were, in the role of enemy, Yhwh has been compelled to turn against them, leaving the land in a state of horrific destruction. The verb *qûm* is significant in Micah, occurring no fewer than seven times. Oppressors have risen up, making the land (morally) unclean, so now they—or the people as a whole—must rise up and depart (2:8, 10). Daughter Zion will arise to thresh her enemies (4:13), and Judah will raise up "shepherds" to tend to enemy Assyria (5:4 [Eng. 5]). A juridical advocate—elliptically expressed, but likely the prophet—is to rise and present Yhwh's case against the people. The corruption of Judah has become so pervasive that family members rise up against one another (7:6), but in this dark time when Zion has fallen, she will assuredly rise (7:8).

Many Hebrew Bible traditions utilize a trope known throughout the ancient Near East: figuring the deity as divine warrior, one who does battle on behalf of the deity's chosen people, but who is capable of turning against that same people when they are disobedient or fail to trust sufficiently in their divine sovereign. In Tg. Mic 2:8, the people of Judah are delivered to the enemy, rather than (MT) rising as an enemy themselves; they are dispossessed by their foes and "return *among them as those broken by war*."

from the front, robe [and] cloak you strip. Rapacious oppressors bent on stripping the very garments from the innocent make so bold as to approach their victims publicly, "from the front" rather than in stealth. The adverbial phrase sits somewhat awkwardly in the syntax, but emendation is ill-advised. The word is important for sound-play with the repeated *mem* that knifes through the first three clauses of this verse in *'etmûl*, *yəqômēm*, *mimmûl*, and *śalmâ*. Micah[LXX] has malefactors stripping off "his skin" instead. Glenny notes that the entire pericope of 2:6-11 in the Greek is "very rough and difficult to interpret. . . . The sentences are choppy and the connections between thoughts are difficult to understand" (2015, 67). As regards 2:8, Glenny speculates that the Greek translator may not have known the Hebrew word *'eder* (72). I would argue that the translator knew of the vivid flaying image coming soon in 3:2 and likely chose to interpret the "mantle" or "cloak" signified by *'eder* as a metaphor for the skin covering the bodies of those being assaulted.

2:9 *the women of my people.* It is rare for an authoritative figure from the Latter Prophets to mention the women of the covenant community with empathy, as Micah does here; one might commend one other text, Mal 2:14-15, for its sympathy articulated on behalf of women whose husbands have been faithless and cruel. Micah's precise and beautiful formulation, *nəšê ʿammî*, comes up nowhere else in the Hebrew Bible. The discursive practice in Isaiah, Jeremiah, Ezekiel, and the Book of the Twelve is normatively, and overwhelmingly, to ignore the lived reality of women within the community entirely, mentioning women and girls not at all or deploying female-gendered caricatures of pride (e.g., Isa 3:16-4:1) and unbridled sexual desire (Jer 3:1-5; Ezek 16 and 23; many other passages) as figures for covenantal infidelity or geopolitical alliance-making. The other option for nonmetaphorical mention of women exercised regularly by Israelite and Judean prophets is to level a blistering indictment against women as individuals or as a constituency within society: among other examples, see Amos 4:1-3 and Jer 44. By contrast, Mic 1:16 and 2:9 make visible the harms done to the least powerful within the community. These are "figures who can evoke pathos," as O'Brien notes (2015, 23), but this is not merely a prophetic exercise in manipulating the audience's emotions, *pace* O'Brien. Where she says that "the real-life plight of landless women in patriarchal systems is not named in Micah" (26), I would argue that in Mic 1-2, the prophet in fact does precisely that, showing the pathos and tragedy of women and children driven from their homes into exile. Micah[LXX] has it that "leaders of my people" (*hēgoumenoi laou mou*) are being driven out, presumably an exegetical decision in congruence with Micah's polemic against leaders elsewhere in this chapter and throughout the book.

treasured house. The noun *taʿănûg*, used at 1:16 with 2fs suffix and here with 3fs suffix, modifies something in which someone delights. It occurs in the Hebrew Bible otherwise only three times: in Prov 19:10 and Eccl 2:10 in semantic contexts suggesting its meaning has to do with luxurious pleasures, and in Song 7:7 as an intensifier portraying the romantic allure of the beloved. Here Mic 1:16 and 2:9, the prophet's sympathy is wholly with the women and children who are being forced into exile due to the corruption of those with political and economic power.

Micah[LXX] 2:9 has the "leaders of my people" being driven out (passive voice), rather than "the women," and adds a clause explaining the reason: *dia ta ponēra epitēdeumata autōn*, "on account of their evil practices." The Greek text trains the divinely ordained consequences of malfeasance on the oppressors whose evil deeds were described in 2:1-2. Where Micah[MT] continues the imagery of harms wreaked on families in the second half of 2:9, elaborating in wrenching detail the devastation of the whole com-

Micah 2

munity due to the greed of those in power, Micah[LXX] begins a new motif, syntactically unproblematic but not fully intelligible in terms of meaning, with the imperative line, "Approach everlasting mountains" (*engisate oresin aiōniois*), clearly linking this to "Arise and go" in 2:10. Gelston remarks, "G misread the noun and probably added the verb in an attempt to make sense of it" (*BHQ*, 99).

from her young children you take away my splendor forever. This enigmatic line may reflect an ancient Israelite understanding that the glory of YHWH, as seen in the pillar of cloud by day and pillar of fire by night during the exodus wandering, had a protective function. Midrashic commentary suggested that these children had been produced by sexual violence or adultery, and per Deut 23:3 (Eng. 2), such children were not allowed in the worshipping assembly (*Num. Rab.* 9.7 to Num 5:12; 246). But Micah is assuredly standing in solidarity with the young children to whom he refers here. Kimḥi considers internecine conflict that undermines the family to have profound implications for Israel's testimony to God, according to Yitzchok Stavsky: "A conjugal relationship that results in the fulfillment of God's command to be fruitful and bear children glorifies God's Name. By causing the wives to be driven away from their homes, they have hindered [YHWH's] glory and honor from being publicized" (2009, 18).

Invasion of Israel and Judah by the Neo-Assyrian and Neo-Babylonian Empires, destruction of homes and food production infrastructures, the forced deportation of captives in the immediate aftermath of battle, and long-term militarized colonization wreaked horrific trauma on kinship groups in Israel and Judah. Blessing Boloje underlines the importance of the family in ancient Israel and Judah: given that "for ancient Israel, the very existence, identity, security and happiness [that] found expression . . . in . . . intimate relationships within the community" were essential for community well-being, any "crisis that affects a family is undeniably a socio-culturally defining moment" (2020a, 2). For children to have been separated from their parents, deprived of their material inheritance as regards buildings and land, and alienated from the traditional means of learning religious and other meaningful values within their community would have constituted trauma.

2:10 *Arise and go! For this cannot be the resting place.* With most interpreters, Rashi (1040–1105) and Kimḥi identify the resting place as the land of Israel, as per Deut 12:9 (Stavsky 2009, 18). The plural imperative here urges the exploitative elites (2:8–9) to leave the place that has been destroyed due

Commentary

to their malfeasance. Reflecting on Micah^LXX, Cyril of Alexandria presents the prophet's words as conveying scathing sarcasm: "Leaders of the peoples, perhaps the comforts of home, life in your homeland, living in peace, and enjoying an existence befitting free people strike you as tedious and burdensome. Make your way to the enemy instead, since this seems to appeal to you" (*Comm.*^CA, 206–7). In Tg. Mic 2:10 is an explanation about who cannot rest: "this *land* is no place of rest *for the wicked.*"

because it has become unclean. Taking the 3fs *qal* form *tamə'â* ("it/she has become unclean") as it stands: the fs antecedent is *mənûḥâ*, the locale where the people are now—Judah or Jerusalem—that cannot remain a place of rest and security. Less likely but not impossible, the 3fs antecedent is unexpressed and could be taken implicitly to be Daughter Zion or the land more generally (*'ereṣ*) from which the people are about to be exiled. Hebrew *'ereṣ* in its meanings of "earth" or "land" occurs no fewer than fifteen times in Micah (1:2, 3; 4:13; 5:3, 4, 5 [thrice], 10; 6:2, 4; 7:2, 13, 15, 17). In 2:10 the sense is clear: what had been a resting-place has been defiled by the sinful corruption of the powerful elites.

2:11 *if someone were to go about "inspired."* The opening hypothetical particle *lû* introduces "subordinate clauses of unreal and concessive force" (*IBHS* §11.2.10i), in this case inviting the implied audience to imagine a risible turn of events: a "prophet" preaching about intoxication or the means to achieve the same. Andersen and Freedman complain that "the text is incoherent to the point of unintelligibility," even though "all the individual words are familiar and their meanings are plain" (297). In my view, the text is not so incoherent as all that, and their purposefully wooden rendering, "let man walking spirit and-deception he-lied," intended to demonstrate the syntactical difficulty, is a bit overdone. In many instances of translation of Hebrew Bible passages, undue literalism causes interpreters to obscure the point unwittingly. Here, the translator need only eschew overly rigid translation of the verbal aspect of *kizzēb* and signal that *rûaḥ* is being used ironically, something effected in the present translation by means of ironic scare quotes. Repointing *kizzēb* as a *qal* participle, *kōzēb* (as in Ps 116:11), would smooth the syntax but is not strictly necessary: Waltke and O'Connor cite Amos 8:14 and Hab 2:12 to demonstrate that "a relative participle may be continued by . . . a suffix form" (*IBHS* §37.7.2).

The targets of this irony are imagined hearers who would prefer such a message to the difficult truths offered by an authentic prophet, such as Micah himself. Micah's point is congruent with the broader Deutero-

Micah 2

Jeremianic view that the prophesying of ethical judgment and oracles of doom have been characteristic of authentic Israelite and Judean prophetic traditions since ancient times (Jer 28:8-9). Micah[LXX] renders here a "widely divergent translation" (*BHQ*, 100) that cannot easily be derived from the MT. In Tg. Mic 2:11 is a more elaborate description of the malfeasant people and the consequences of their sin: "*as they are accustomed to go astray after false prophets, so the people of this generation shall be exiled to a land of falsehoods.*"

wine and liquor. Compare Isa 28:7-18, a passage cited by Andersen and Freedman as an example of prophetic poetry intended to be unintelligible for mimetic purposes, a possibility they cite for Mic 2:6-11: "Like Isaiah's cruel, disgusting mockery of the gabble of the drunken prophets," this Micah passage might be intended as "deliberate gibberish" that scathingly reperforms the "meaningless jabber" of Micah's opponents (297). This is an interpretive option they finally decline, as I do. Deft sound-play links "falsehood," *šeqer*, with "liquor," *šēkār*.

2:12 *I will assuredly gather Jacob.* YHWH will gather the people, but toward what end? With some earlier interpreters, Waltke understands the gathering site as a place of sanctuary for those who would have "sought refuge in Jerusalem during Sennacherib's siege in 701" (2007, 134). But this pericope is best read as tonally congruent with 2:6-11 and 3:1-12: the "pen" for these sheep is no sanctuary, for divine punishment looms in the form of forced deportation. Those associated with Jacob will be confined in—as becomes chillingly clear—a transit site controlled by the enemy for the management of prisoners of war before they are removed to diaspora. A clear example of this practice can be seen in the narrative of Jer 40: after Jerusalem has fallen to the Babylonians, Judean captives are forcibly detained at Ramah (Jer 40:1).

Numerous scholars dismiss or fail to perceive the brilliant connection of these two verses with 2:6-11, misreading this as an oracle of promise (so, e.g., Smith 1974, 66-69; Barker and Baily 1998, 69-71; Dempsey 1999, 123; Andersen and Freedman 2000, 130; Jeremias 2007, 154-56; Nogalski 2011, 512, 540-41; Fretheim 2013, 201; Corzilius 2016, 191-200; Dempster 2017, 99-103; Hoyt 2019, 659-66; Boloje 2020b; Zapff 2022, 93-98). This misreading is generated by a failure to perceive Micah's subtle use of irony and ellipsis in the verbs and the overall perspective of these two verses. If this were a word of promise, it would be oddly situated among savage oracles of judgment, as virtually every interpreter concedes. Andersen and Freedman rightly cau-

Commentary

tion that we should not expect seamless congruence in prophet books—"the prophets were not systematic theologians"—and that the mixture of blistering polemic and lyrical words of hope here demonstrates "the complexity of the paradoxical, ambivalent, dialectical relationship" between Yhwh and Judah "in the ongoing covenant," which they term "at once conditional and unconditional" (343). Certainly ambiguity and paradox are at play here, but straightforward readings of these lines as promise miss the unspoken point of this fascinating material, especially when read in light of 2:6 and 10. Van der Woude (1969), Utzschneider (1999, 129-33), and a few others have suggested this is an oracle of promise being offered by false prophets, an intriguing possibility that has the merit of taking seriously the linkage with the preceding verses as establishing the sort of word Judean miscreants desire to hear. A stalwart minority of commentators have seen, correctly, that this is a devastating oracle of doom, including Gershon Brin (1989; see Sweeney 2004; Metzner 1998, 119-20, 125-29). On communal laments within the metaphor field of Yhwh harming the deity's own sheep, Brin cites Pss 44:10-15 and 74:1. Among earlier interpreters who read 2:12-13 as an oracle of judgment is Calvin. He first gestures toward the reading of this as promise: "Some interpret this passage as if the prophet meant to console the faithful, that they might trust in God's unfailing goodness" (2003, 125). But he goes on to argue for a different interpretive trajectory:

> After admonishing the Jews for their iniquities, calling them before the bar of God's judgment, and demonstrating how detestable and grave their sins are before God, [Micah's] method is to follow that with the theme we now find in this passage. . . . Our Lord frequently "assembles" people in order to execute his vengeance against all who would attempt to hide from him. . . . God finds it quite easy to execute his vengeance against all who deserve it, for he "gathers" them up in a single heap. (126-27)

Calvin explains further, "Although God always preserves some hope for his good and faithful servants, that does not mean that they will escape punishment. They will suffer just as others do" (127).

Bozrah. This form could be read as the preposition *bet* affixed to *ṣîrâ*, conjectural for "pen" (*HALOT* 1:149; 3:1054) in parallelism with the following noun *dōber*, "pen" or "pasture" in the sense of fenced enclosure, the meaning of the second term in the pair being clear, as per all of the ancient versions (*BHQ*, 100). The first term is best read as the place-name Bozrah,

Micah 2

with the acknowledgement that ironic sound-play may be subtly emphasizing the nature of the place not only as a literal shearing center (Andersen and Freedman, 339) but, figuratively, as a trap for the unwary. This city in Edom was significant; see the attention given Bozrah in Jer 49:13, 22. It may have been the capital, per Ronny Reich, as well as the royal seat of the Edomite king Jobab mentioned in Gen 36:33 as reigning before the establishment of the Israelite monarchy (1993, 264). The site may have been associated with sheep-shearing and livestock slaughter, if the metaphorical vehicle of the term as used in Isa 34:6 and 63:1 may be taken as indicating an intelligible cultural memory. Identified with Buṣeirah in contemporary Jordan, the site is "situated on a hilly ridge . . . and is surrounded on three sides by deep valleys. It is therefore a natural stronghold, linked to the surrounding plateau only at its southern end" (265). On the mound, the ruins of two buildings have been excavated. The "lower building stood on deep foundations that were essentially a system of retaining walls that created a raised platform," and had "two large wings . . . each containing a series of rooms around an inner courtyard," with a "very spacious courtyard" and a "flight of stone steps" in the center of the building; "cracks and other clear signs of a violent conflagration were found" (265). Interesting for consideration of the Neo-Assyrian period in which Micah prophesied: one room was designed on a plan that "resembles that of an Assyrian temple," indicating "an Assyrian influence at the site, perhaps even an Assyrian presence"; the building was used in the eighth and seventh centuries BCE (265). The upper building should be dated to a period later than the time of Micah. Artifacts discovered at Buṣeirah include "a bathtub and a lavatory bowl" and a "finely engraved Tridacna shell" as well as an inscribed pottery sherd earlier than Micah's era (266).

cacophonous with people. The 3fp *təhîmenâ*, from *hmh* "to make a noise, be tumultuous; to roar; to make a sound; to be restless, turbulent; to moan" (*HALOT* 1:250), has as its antecedent *ṣōʾn*, "sheep" taken as a collective noun, which can be feminine or masculine. The "flock" is tumultuous with the sounds of throngs of people confined at this transit site, awaiting forcible deportation by their enemies. Either the noise level is high generally from so many people being kept in one place, or the poet is evoking the tumult of many captives groaning in distress, as in other exilic and postexilic biblical passages depicting anguish (Ezek 7:16; Ps 55:18); as I have said elsewhere, "God will gather God's people as sheep headed for the blade," and the pen or pasture will be "cacophonous from far away with the bleating of these sheep waiting for slaughter" (Sharp 2009, 173). Some have taken the verb as from *hwm*; for example, Sweeney translates the clause, "'they/you shall be discomfited/confused by people,' which indicates that the people are not at all content about what is taking place" (2004, 320). I find unpersuasive the argument of Wagenaar (2000) that *mēʾādām*, "because of people," should be revocalized to *mēʾədōm*, "from Edom," not least because the defective spelling is anomalous for that place-name. The passage does trade on associations with Bozrah as a place of slaughter, but in this sophisticated mimesis of false prophecy that in fact communicates doom, Micah does not have in mind the relocation of Judeans from Edom.

2:13 *The one who breaks through.* The semantic ambiguities of this verse are chilling. Is this one who breaks out of the confining pen, or a deliverer who breaks in so as to rescue the sheep, or an invader who breaks through the fence or wall? In line with those who read this positively is Joseph Kara (ca. 1065-ca. 1135), who comments here, "The Messiah will break through all the barriers that have been restraining Israel's return to the land" (Stavsky 2009, 20). In his *Metzudot* commentary, David Altschuler (1687-1769) offers another positive identification of the "one who breaks through" as "Elijah the Prophet who will arrive prior to the final redemption to usher in the new era. He will break through to the hearts of the people, persuade them to repent and encourage them to turn their hearts to God" (Stavsky 2009, 20). Perceiving this as a negative oracle looking to the future, Kimḥi offers that the one breaking through is Zedekiah, "who tried to escape from Jerusalem by breaching . . . the wall of the city when it was besieged by the Babylonians," and that the images in 2:12-13 should be taken as "foretelling the catastrophic events that the Jewish people will endure" in the Neo-Babylonian era (Stavsky 2009, 20-21). This reading has a venerable pedigree in Christian interpretation as well, being represented in the writings of Ephrem the Syrian (ca. 306-373), Cyril of Alexandria (ca. 375-444), Theodoret of Cyrrhus (ca. 393-ca. 466), Theodore of Mopsuestia, Calvin (see further below), and Hugo Grotius (1583-1645), among others (Roukema 2019, 88-89; Zapff 2022, 93n7).

Reading this as an ironic oracle of judgment designed to mimic a promise of deliverance, I muster Amos 4:1-3 and 6:1-7 as analogous and highly instructive. Because callous elites on Mount Samaria and Zion, "the notables of the first of the nations," have the temerity to feast and "sing idle songs" while their people endure ruination, they shall be taken away "with fishhooks . . . through breaches in the wall" (Amos 4:3) and shall be at the head of the line of deportees, "the first to go into exile" (6:7). Here in Mic 2:12-13,

Micah 2

Yhwh is breaking through to lead Judean oppressors into diaspora. Many have suggested linkages between Amos and Micah, while inexplicably overlooking this crucial intertext. Per the theology of Micah, "God is one who breaks through—through the walls of a fortified city, and through the hermeneutical smugness of those who do not understand their own accountability" (Sharp 2009, 173-74).

Their king . . . Yhwh at their head. Further on the reading of this as a faux oracle of salvation eviscerating the complacency of Judean elites, see Ps 125:5 on Yhwh leading away the miscreant: "Those who turn aside to their own crooked ways, the Lord will lead away with evildoers." An early example of the mistaken positive reading of 2:13 can be found in the targum, which offers fulsome supplementary clauses: the king leading the people *"shall destroy the enemy oppressing them and conquer the mighty citadels; they shall inherit the cities of the nations, and their kings shall lead at their head, and the Memra of the* Lord *will be their support."* Here, as later in the history of interpretation, I would argue that the devastating ironic ambiguity of the MT has been missed. Rather than pointing to Amos 4:3 and 6:7, as I do, Calvin looks ahead historically to the gruesome fate of Zedekiah in the time of Jeremiah:

> When Micah adds that *the king will pass on before them*, at first glance they thought this was a blessing, since whenever the king passed before his subjects, it signaled that all was well. But . . . he was only leading the way into captivity. For as we have seen in our sermons on Jeremiah, the king was hardly leading them in a parade. Rather, when he was forced to pass in review at Riblah, he witnessed seeing his own sons' throats cut, had both of his eyes put out, then was enchained like a wild beast, and suffered innumerable other indignities. (127-28)

I concur with Calvin that Micah is saying, "your king will be the first to pass into destruction" (128). Guided by the iron will of Yhwh, malfeasant officials and oppressive elites will be forced to follow their defeated ruler into diaspora.

BIBLIOGRAPHY

Ben Zvi, E. 1999b. "Wrongdoers, Wrongdoing and Righting Wrongs in Micah 2." *BibInt* 7:87-99. doi:10.1163/156851599X00254.

Bibliography

Boloje, B. O. 2020a. "Micah 2:9 and the Traumatic Effects of Depriving Children of Their Parents." *HvTSt* 76.1:a5960. doi:10.4102/hts.v76i1.5960.

———. 2020b. "Micah's Shepherd-King (Mi 2:12-13): An Ethical Model for Reversing Oppression in Leadership Praxis." *Verbum et Ecclesia* 41.1:a2088. doi:10.4102/ve.v41i1.2088.

Bonaventure. 1978. *The Soul's Journey into God—The Tree of Life—The Life of St. Francis*. Translated by E. Cousins. CWS. New York: Paulist.

Brin, G. 1989. "Micah 2:12-13: A Textual and Ideological Study." *ZAW* 101:118-24.

Britt, L. W. 2003. "Fascism Anyone?" *Free Inquiry* 23.2. https://secularhumanism.org/2003/03/fascism-anyone/.

Crenshaw, J. L. 2007. *Prophetic Conflict: Its Effect upon Israelite Religion*. Atlanta: Society of Biblical Literature.

Cunsolo, A. 2017. "Prologue: She Was Bereft." Pages xiii-xxii in *Mourning Nature: Hope at the Heart of Ecological Loss and Grief*. Edited by A. Cunsolo and K. Landman. Montreal: McGill-Queen's University Press. doi:10.2307/j.ctt1w6t9hg.

Flusser, D., with R. S. Notley. 2007. *The Sage from Galilee: Rediscovering Jesus' Genius*. Grand Rapids: Eerdmans.

Kraus, H.-J. 1964. *Prophetie in der Krisis: Studien zu Texten aus dem Buch Jeremia*. BibS(N) 43. Neukirchen-Vlyun: Neukirchener Verlag.

Moran, W. 1967. "The Conclusion of the Decalogue (Ex 20,17 = Dt 5,21)." *CBQ* 29:543-54.

Reich, R. 1993. "Bozrah." *NEAEHL* 1:264-66.

Solomon, A. 2001. *The Noonday Demon: An Atlas of Depression*. New York: Scribner.

Sweeney, M. A. 2004. "The Portrayal of YHWH's Deliverance in Micah 2:12-13 Reconsidered." Pages 315-26 in *God's Word for Our World*. Vol. 1, *Biblical Studies in Honor of Simon John de Vries*. Edited by J. H. Ellens, D. L. Ellens, R. P. Knierim, and I. Kalimi. JSOTSup 388. London: T&T Clark.

Wagenaar, J. A. 2000. "'From Edom He Went Up . . .': Some Remarks on the Text and Interpretation of Micah II 12-13." *VT* 50:531-39. doi:10.1163/156853300506549.

MICAH 3

Indictment of Judean Leaders

3:1–4

> ¹I said further:
> "Pay attention, O heads of Jacob
>   and rulers of the house of Israel!
> Is it not your {*mp*} responsibility
>   to know justice?—
> ²you who hate good and love evil,
>   who tear the skin off them
>   and the flesh off their bones,
> ³ones who have devoured the flesh of my people
>   and have flayed their skin off them
> and have broken their bones in pieces
>   and spread [them] out as in a pot,
>   like meat in a cauldron!"
>
> ⁴Then they will cry out to Yhwh,
>   but [Yhwh] will not answer them.
> [Yhwh] will hide [Yhwh's] face from them at that time,
>   because they have made their deeds evil.

False Prophets Shamed, but Micah Empowered

3:5–8

> ⁵Thus has Yhwh spoken concerning the prophets,
>   those who lead my people astray,

Micah 3

    who strike with their fangs
        and proclaim "Peace!,"
    but against one who does not give per their direction,
        they sanctify war:
⁶Therefore it will be night for you {*mp*}, without vision,
        and darkness for you, without divination.
The sun will set on the prophets,
        and the day will darken over them.
⁷The seers will be shamed
        and the diviners disgraced;
all of them will cover their upper lips,
        for there will be no answer from God.
⁸But as for me, I am filled with the power of the spirit of
    Yhwh,
    and with justice and might,
to declare to Jacob his transgression
    and to Israel his sin.

The Razing of Jerusalem Foreseen

3:9-12

⁹Pay attention to this, O heads of the house of Jacob
    and rulers of the house of Israel,
you who abhor justice
    and make crooked all that is straight,
¹⁰who {*ms*} build Zion by means of bloodshed
    and Jerusalem by means of injustice!
¹¹Its {*fs*} heads offer adjudication for a bribe,
and its priests offer rulings for a price,
and its prophets offer divination for silver,
    yet they rely on Yhwh, saying,
"Is not Yhwh in our midst?
    Calamity will not come upon us!"
¹²Therefore because of you {*mp*},
    Zion will be plowed as a field,
    and Jerusalem will become heaps of rubble,
    and the mountain of the House high places of the forest.

INTERPRETATION

Micah 3 brings into the foreground the powerful figure of Micah of Moresheth himself. This is a prophet who dares to oppose the vicious harms perpetrated by corrupt officials and who, empowered by the spirit of Yhwh, speaks bold words of truth about the calamity looming over Judah and Jerusalem. The fierce and uncompromising contrast Micah draws between his own authoritative right to speak (3:1, 8) and the horrifying malfeasance of Judean authorities spurs the implied audience to listen with keenly focused attention to this prophetic discourse.

In Mic 3, the prophet focuses his hearers' attention on Jerusalem. Within the arc of descent, elevation, and dispersal that structures the book of Micah, we see in 3:9-12 the conclusion of the first great movement of descent: the monumental buildings and walls of Jerusalem will be dismantled and left in rubble. In 587, after an eighteen-month siege of Judah's holiest city, Babylonian troops poured into the streets of Jerusalem, plundered the temple, burned the monumental buildings of the city, slaughtered Judean combatants and noncombatants, and forced thousands into exile in Babylonia (see Jer 52). In light of that monumental catastrophe, postexilic prophetic scribes shaped the literature they had inherited, including the book of Micah. Whether one reads 3:9-12 as foretelling the future of Jerusalem from the perspective of the eighth century BCE, or, as I and many interpreters see it, as a postexilic reflection on a national catastrophe, it is certain that Judean scribes would struggle for generations to make sense of the enormous suffering, trauma, and loss their people had endured in the fall of Jerusalem and the Babylonian exile.

Indictment of Judean Leaders (3:1-4)

Drawn in hyperbolic terms, the officials and administrators of Judah are depicted, via a series of dramatic participial forms, as those who perpetrate terrible injury on their community. These predators are "haters" of that which is good, "lovers" of that which is evil, and "tearers-off" of their people's skin. The visceral imagery of cannibalism in the poetry that follows paints the leaders not just as malfeasant, not simply as greedy for self-enrichment at the expense of others, but as monstrous. What Micah decries—the exploitation of the powerless by moneyed and politically powerful elites—has been documented in many cultures across the centuries to the present day. Max Sklar, a graduate of Yale Divinity School, has given me permission to share this about his indigenous Guatemalan friend, Maria, who joined a group in Lynn, Massachusetts, to protest the United States' policy of turning refugees away at the border with Mexico. Her protest sign expressed what Micah dramatizes about the vulnerable being devoured by their oppressors: "How can you tell me to 'go back home' when my home is the mouth of a shark?"

Andrew Martin Fischer observes that in countries in which drastic economic inequality continues to ravage the poor while billionaire elites continue to grow richer, "national liberation leaders and movements [have been] intensely aware of the need to redistribute highly concentrated wealth inherited from the colonial era in support of decolonisation" (2018, 37). Most such emancipatory movements have failed, Fischer says, and while the causes are due to "complex political economy conjunctures" particular to each case, one shared factor has been this: "In the context of high inequality, as was typical in Latin America, policies of rural surplus extraction would tend to drive the poor into even further crippling poverty, as evidenced, for instance, by the way that colonial strategies of rural surplus extraction caused widespread and intense famines in India" (38). Such is the situation Micah paints of economic oppression in Jerusalem and the surrounding region: the elites' callous amassing of wealth continues as the struggling poor find themselves "cannibalized," dispossessed and driven away from their homes (2:2, 9).

Skeptics might venture that in eighth-century BCE Judah, as in twentieth- and twenty-first-century countries marked by high levels of economic inequity, prophetic cries for economic reform could not succeed. Fischer notes that reform movements are inevitably "blocked by powerful wealthy constituencies of landowners and associated elite factions, which is precisely a political economy characteristic of high-inequality settings" (39). This may be true. Change is slow, and oppressive systems that are frontally attacked can be reconfigured by their beneficiaries into different but still insidious forms, as the United States has seen with the abolition of chattel slavery: horrific physical and economic violence against Black persons in this country both continued and took new forms in the Jim Crow era, during the civil rights movement, and on into the present (Sharpe 2016; Alexander 2020). Yet the empowerment of dissenters and those committed to justice at every level of a community over time can indeed bear fruit. The prophetic witness of Micah constitutes a powerful articulation of that hope.

False Prophets Shamed, but Micah Empowered (3:5–8)

On behalf of Yhwh, Micah delivers a powerful indictment of intermediaries who claim to represent the will of the deity but who are motivated by economic self-interest. Often in the Latter Prophets, false prophecy is characterized by a message that all is well or will swiftly improve when, in fact, the Israelite or Judean community is roiled by pervasive social harms, political corruption, and the venality of the elites, and a significant threat looms. This is usually the approach of enemy invaders, sometimes expressly understood as having been dispatched by Yhwh as retribution for Israel's or Judah's sins. We see this perspective in Isa 10:5, where Yhwh thunders, "Ah, Assyria, the rod of my anger—the club in their hands is my fury!," and in the Deutero-Jeremianic prose, where the brutal Neo-Babylonian enemy commander Nebuchadrezzar is—shockingly—identified as the "servant" of Yhwh (Jer 25:9; 27:6; 43:10). False prophecies ventriloquized in the Hebrew Bible by the (authentic) prophets who dispute them include: "When the overwhelming scourge passes through it will not come to us" (Isa 28:15); "It shall be well with you" and "no calamity will come upon you" (Jer 23:17); "'Peace, peace,' when there is no peace" (Jer 6:14; 8:11; Ezek 13:10); and the misguided claim that Judean captives and looted temple vessels will be returned to Judah swiftly (Jer 28). Lying intermediaries are characterized as uttering "the deceit of their own minds," "the deceit of their own heart" (Jer 14:14; 23:26), and "empty consolation" (Zech 10:2). The false prophets and those desperate to believe their deceitful messages cling to the notion that the protective presence of Yhwh will ward off military disaster: "'Is not Yhwh in our midst? Calamity will not come upon us!'" (Mic 3:11; see also Jer 7:4). But Micah speaks terrifying words of authentic doom in the first three chapters of the book that bears his name. In this, he stands in a long lineage of prophets whose words were difficult to hear but were shown to be true. The integrity of Yhwh's righteous "servants the prophets" will be acclaimed, generations later, in the Deutero-Jeremianic prose, those scribes affirming the mighty Micah of Moresheth by name (Jer 26:18). True prophets are courageous in telling the truth about oppression, corruption, and the dire straits in which their sinful community will find itself, as Jeremiah argues in his dispute with the false prophet Hananiah: "The prophets who preceded you and me from ancient times prophesied war, famine, and pestilence against many countries and great kingdoms. As for the prophet who prophesies peace"—here, Jeremiah is registering skepticism—"[only]

Micah 3

Fig. 12. *Mystic Wheel (The Vision of Ezekiel)*, 1451–1452, by Fra Angelico (Guido di Pietro, ca. 1395–1455). Tempera on wooden shutter of the Armadio degli Argenti, a cabinet for silver. In the Museo di San Marco in Florence, Italy.

when the word of that prophet comes true, then it will be known that the Lord has truly sent the prophet" (Jer 28:8–9).

Here in Mic 3:5, this authentic prophet uses a concentrated and memorable dichotomy to characterize two kinds of false messages as "peace" and "war." In the context of the venomous harm they themselves inflict on their community ("they strike with their fangs," 3:5), the false prophets have the audacity to proclaim that all is well, that the community will flourish, that catastrophe will not befall them. When they are not bribed as they require, the false prophets "sanctify war," either metaphorically consecrating the oppressive circumstances against which the community is battling, or in fact launching a violent reprisal against the one who resists their sway. In this pericope overall, a powerful contrast is limned between false intermediaries and Micah. That contrast will be evoked in 7:7 as well: the prophet looks upon the confusion of the "sentinels" of corrupt leaders, then claims his own integrity as messenger of Yhwh.

The Razing of Jerusalem Foreseen (3:9–12)

The city of Jerusalem was not destroyed in the late eighth century by militarized violence, though one might argue that the injustice and corruption eroding the stability of Judean life—another kind of destruction—did make a profound impression on the historical record as refracted through the oracles of Isaiah of Jerusalem and Micah of Moresheth. Jerusalem's fortified walls would not be breached until 587 BCE, in the siege launched by Nebuchadrezzar of the Neo-Babylonian Empire. Jerusalem remained intact in the time of Micah, and Hebrew Bible traditions represent the siege of Jerusalem led by Sennacherib during the reign of Hezekiah as having been thwarted by Yhwh's intervention (Isa 36–37 // 2 Kgs 18–19). It is certainly possible that Mic 3:9-12 was added by a prophetic scribe after the fall of Jerusalem in 587, but the imagery here does not rely on precise *ex eventu* knowledge and could have been offered by the eighth-century Micah in visionary terms as concerning a future that had not yet occurred.

Parallel triads in 3:11-12 send a strong signal about the accountability of Jerusalem's malfeasant elites for the destruction of Zion. After opening this oracle in 3:9-10 with a robust indictment of the "heads of the house of Jacob" and "rulers of the house of Israel" for abhorring justice and twisting all that had been straight, Micah turns his attention to those inhabiting three specific roles—Jerusalem's heads, priests, and prophets—and indicts them for three kinds of corruption: offering adjudication of disputes for a bribe, offering halakic rulings for a price, and offering divination oracles for silver (3:11). As a direct consequence of their sins, Jerusalem will fall to the enemy. Artfully mirroring the three types of greedy officials and the three modes of corruption in which they are engaged, Micah describes the impending doom in three different ways, using three different designations for the city: "Zion" will be "plowed as a field," "Jerusalem" will be left as "heaps of rubble," and "the mountain of the House" will become nothing more than "high places of the forest." The prophet has created a chiastic structure, three distinct nouns plus three distinct predicates for the sins of the leadership, and three distinct nouns plus three distinct predicates for the terrible consequences for Jerusalem. At the center of the chiasm is the tragically ironic, and infuriating, theological claim of those whose sin will destroy the city: "Is not Yhwh in our midst? Calamity will not come upon us!" It is precisely because Yhwh is indeed present and does see their sin that catastrophe marches inexorably toward the entire community. In light of that prophetic truth, those hearing this oracle just before or after the fall of Jerusalem in 587 would be repelled by the smug pronouns ventriloquized

Micah 3

here: "*our* midst" and "*us*" would seem nothing short of appalling in the mouths of those whose sin had destroyed so many lives.

This oracle of doom focalizes the audience's attention on the third and most unusual designation of the Jerusalem temple on Mount Zion: "the mountain of the House." This brings into view a fascinating way in which Micah and later prophetic scribes work with the noun "house" (*bayit*) throughout these oracles. "House" comes up in every chapter of Micah. Instances of the term variously represent the temple as locus of the divine power of Yhwh, the traditional center of Israelite or Judean political power, the domestic site of a family's malfeasance or devastation, and "house" as a component of the place-name Bethlehem (5:1 [Eng. 2]), the origin place of the One of Peace who is to shepherd the people. In Mic 1, the "house of Israel" in 1:5 is met by "the houses of Achzib" that become "deception for the kings of Israel" in 1:14. In 2:2, those in a house are oppressed, the "house of Jacob" is rebuked by Micah for unwillingness to see the truth of its sinful exploitation (2:7), and women are driven out, "each from her treasured house," in 2:9, a chiastic structure that has distorted ideology at the center and the harmful practices generated by the same in the opening and closing positions. In Micah 3, the corruption of the "house of Israel" (3:1), broadened to those in power in the "house of Jacob" and the "house of Israel" (3:9), leads to the razing of the "mountain of the House," Mount Zion standing metonymically for Jerusalem (3:12). In a beautifully crafted joining of two blocks of disparate material, this instance of "mountain of the House" (*har habbayit*), the ruined center of Judean life reduced to rubble, is expanded semantically in the next verse, 4:1, with the "mountain of the House of Yhwh" (*har bêt-yhwh*) envisioned now as elevated above every mountain peak, now the center of learning and peacemaking, known as the House of the God of Jacob (4:2), drawing thither all the nations of the world. The power of divinely appointed reversal continues in 5:1 (Eng. 2) with "house" as a component of the name Bethlehem, from whence a royal deliverer is to arise, his insignificant origins eclipsed by his power "in the strength of Yhwh" to keep Israel secure and by his renown "to the ends of the earth" (5:3 [Eng. 4]). The lyrical uses of "house" in Mic 4–5 yield in Mic 6 to new iterations of condemnation, creating a perceptible chiastic macrostructure across the chapters of Micah. Yhwh had redeemed Israel from the "house of slavery" (6:4), but Israel had failed to honor Yhwh and must now be bidden to remember their own covenantal history. In the "house of the wicked one" are ill-gotten gains (6:10), and he has followed the illicit practices of the "house of Ahab" (6:16), to the detriment of the entire community. The final occurrence of "house" comes in 7:6, where disrespect and antagonism are said to create enmity within the householder's own house.

Micah 3:12 is marked by the MT scribes as the precise middle of the Book of the Twelve. This verse and 4:1-4, taken together, serve as a hinge between Micah's alarming vision of a Jerusalem plowed into rubble and the prophetic vision of the same holy city as restored and radiant, a beacon of peace for all nations, drawing to the Temple Mount pilgrims from across the world eager to learn the ways of Yhwh and live peaceably with all.

History of Consequences

Micah's polemic against Jerusalem leaders' bloodshed and injustice (3:10) is amplified in the Babylonian Talmud with details of specific sins enacted within the temple: not just bloodshed, but idol worship and forbidden sexual relationships (b. Yoma 9b). Reflecting on 3:11, R. Jose b. Elisha underscores the hubris of Judean elites who, despite their wickedness, dare to "place their confidence in Him who decreed, and the world came into existence" (b. Šabb. 139a). For illustrative comments on Mic 3 in rabbinic midrash, see the introduction under §4.1.1 Midrashic Interpretations.

Cyril of Jerusalem (ca. 315-386), with many Christian interpreters, construes Micah's claim to have strength "in the spirit of the Lord" (*en pneumati kyriou*) in 3:8 as a reference to the Holy Spirit, not just a divine spirit generally but the Third Person of the Trinity (ACCS 14:157). Cyril also reflects on Isa 1:8 about Zion being left "like a shelter in a cucumber field" and Mic 3:12 on Jerusalem being plowed like a field, offering that "a thousand years ago," during the lifetime of Isaiah of Jerusalem, Zion was "beautiful with public squares and clothed in honor," but "now the place is full of cucumber patches," taking this as confirmation of both prophecies: "Do you see how the Holy Spirit enlightens the saints?" (*Cat*.16.18). Alberto Ferreiro comments, "Cyril was catechizing only a few hundred yards from Mount Zion, so he had observed these cucumber patches. This was about A.D. 350" (ACCS 14:158).

Jerome applies Micah's indictment of false prophets (3:5) not only to Judean mercenary seers but also to later heretics who locate themselves within Christian tradition, false teachers who "promise ... peace and the kingdom of heavens, and ... say there is no need for you to live continently and holily, give credence to what we teach and you will obtain all the things promised by the Lord" (*Comm. Mich.*, 66). The

Micah 3

leaders and people indicted for corruption in 3:9-11 are "the Jewish people" in Micah's time and, per the anti-Judaic canard that was common through centuries of Christian interpretation, in the time of Jesus "on account of their shedding the blood of the Lord," but Jerome does not hesitate to apply the judgment also to ecclesial leaders in his own day, "the bishops, priests and deacons who, if they have not preserved their own heart with all watchfulness, 'abhor the judgment and pervert all righteous things'" (67). On mercenary motives for prophetic divination (3:11), Jerome cites the story of Peter and Simon Magus in Acts 8:15-24, observing, "The Holy Spirit can neither be sold nor bought" (68). He proceeds to level trenchant criticism against Christians who ignore the desperation of the poor, averring that in the eschatological judgment, "when charity has grown cold, and faith will be rare" (cf. Matt 24:12), the "temple of Christ . . . will be ploughed as a field" (69).

Cyril of Alexandria sees the indictment in 3:1-3 as applicable to the "scribes and Pharisees" who "cruelly abused the masses who believed in Christ" and tore apart "the saints, differing in no way from wild beasts" (*Comm.*^{CA}, 213). His analogy here moves away from Micah's metaphor of domestic food preparation, oddly conflating Jewish opposition to Christianity with the execution of Christians through exposure to wild animals, such as lions, leopards, bears, or bulls, in amphitheaters under Roman imperial authority (Kinzig 2021, 35-36, 56, 71-72). Though official persecution of Christians had been interdicted before Cyril was born, he would have been familiar with Paul's claim to have fought wild beasts at Ephesus (1 Cor 15:32) and stories of Christians (and others) tortured or executed through *damnatio ad bestias*, including Ignatius of Antioch (died ca. 107 to 115), Vibia Perpetua and Felicity (d. 203), and Euphemia (d. 303). Such martyrologies were constructed with sophisticated allusions to biblical texts, Jewish traditions, and tropes found in ancient Greek and Roman literatures (Moss 2012, 23-48). In ch. 4 of Ignatius's *Letter to the Romans*, we find this powerful theologizing of the impending horror: "Suffer me to become food for the wild beasts. . . . I am the wheat of God, and am ground by the teeth of wild beasts, that I may be found the pure bread" of Christ (ANF 1:75).

Calvin applauds the cannibalism metaphor in 3:2-3 as a powerful prophetic strategy to shock the implied audience into repentance. In a sermon on 29 November 1550, Calvin offers that these revolting images are meant "to strip away our own blindfolds, that we might recognize our sins for what they are, and not in our accustomed way of weighing and balancing them. Accordingly, Micah's text here is worthy of our highest regard" (2003, 143). For Calvin, the ethical implications are clear: "Whenever we oppress our neighbors, steal and devour their goods, or wrong and harm them in any way, God considers that equivalent to skinning them" (144). False prophets—linked with all the people earlier, and in this sermon linked to the pope—receive no answer from God (3:7) because, Calvin warns, "Micah confronts us here with the greatest evil that could ever befall us, that is, that God rejects those who reject him" (145). Of the destruction of the temple (3:12), Calvin preaches on 10 December 1550, "It was no easy matter to denounce the Temple. . . . For it had been built on the express command of God. . . . Later, it became a symbol for our Lord Jesus Christ. Not only was it the place where God wanted to be worshipped, but God had promised that his goodness would also be manifested there, until such time as the redemption of the world should occur" (187). He explains further, "The real meaning of the Temple's grandeur and glory lies in its connection with the coming of our Lord Jesus Christ. For that is when God would be revealed to all the world, resulting in a common assent and a common accord of faith" (190).

Peace activist Berrigan muses on the gruesome crimes of the powerful portrayed as cannibalism in 3:1-3, "One imagines them concluding their calamitous feast and turning with blood on their hands—in prayer to [Yhwh]. And God turns away, sickened. . . . War is a wanton feast of carrion. . . . And the churches nodding 'yes' with supine gravity, as though they spoke for any god but Mars" (1995, 219).

Ethnomusicologist Zoe Sherinian has studied reception of Tamil folk songs composed by the Dalit Christian minister Theophilus Appavoo (1940–2005) as resources for political resistance to caste-based oppression in South India. Sherinian notes Appavoo's creative refraction of the cannibalism metaphor in 3:2-3 in a 1993 song, "Tayi tagappanare," in the lines, "You make us your flock of sheep, but they cut us up and make briyani, they fry us up like a side dish and recklessly eat us" (Sherinian 2016, 141–42). In the interviews she conducted on this, "most Dalit villagers interpreted themselves as the flock of Jesus that was being cut or butchered by upper-caste non-Christians" (141). Sherinian observes that for some "newly middle-class" Dalits who heard the song, the imagery was felt to be "too graphic and frank for the passive spiritual setting" they preferred in worship (142), a response that speaks to the disruptive power of prophetic polemic.

Micah 3

RETROSPECT

The relentless prophetic polemic of Mic 3 hammers and fractures the falsehoods purveyed by corrupt officials, and by the priests and prophets coopted to support them. Kathleen Norris writes, "A prophet's task is to reveal the fault lines hidden beneath the comfortable surface of the worlds we invent for ourselves, the national myths as well as the little lies and delusions of control and security that get us through the day" (1996, 34). Micah roars his rebuke of those who offer deceitful reassurances and anodyne promises. The true prophet will dare to offer admonitions about the sinful behavior and lies that have caused the Judean people to experience Yhwh's retribution. To inhabit an alternative posture—callous disregard or outraged denial or scheming deceit—would be to become complicit in the destruction of the people of God. When the truth of sin is named, that truth is life-giving, because it illumines the path toward repentance, reform, and renewal of the covenant relationship. Thus the prophets cause trouble for the sake of renewal. Echoing Heschel, Judith Plaskow remarks, "The prophets were meddlers, troublesome busybodies. They were horrified by things that are daily occurrences all over the world, by abuses that are taken for granted as normal, if regrettable, aspects of complex social relations. They were unwilling to mind their own business, to stay away from wrongs that did not involve them personally, or to refrain from championing others' rights" (1990, 215).

Ahmed observes of the feminist killjoy, "Life matters; we are killjoys because life matters; and life can be what killjoys are fighting for. . . . We need to be unsettled by what is unsettling" (2017, 243). In stark contrast to the bland pieties of the false prophets, Micah offers his own forceful testimony, announcing the bone-crushing reality of oppression wreaked by the elite in his community, bearing witness to the value of those who are being metaphorically broken and flayed. Ahmed says, "The killjoy is testimony. She comes to exist as a figure, a way of containing damage, because she speaks about damage," calling the community to "care about the things that break off, the broken things" (260, 266). Micah boldly speaks of the damage done to the vulnerable in Judah by those with political and economic power. Tragically, the "evil doings" of rulers and officials (3:1, 4) will have catastrophic consequences for all who live under the shadow of the corrupt Jerusalem hierarchy in Micah's time and all who struggle under corrupt leadership in every age.

Retrospect

Critically interrogating the distorted ideation that undergirds hierarchies of violent oppression, Bey observes, "What has been given to us as the totality of the world is not, in fact, the totality of the world" (2022, 115). Micah 3:9-11 articulates the false worldview enacted by elites who "make crooked all that is straight," constructing community life by means of brutality and injustice while insisting that Yhwh remains present as divine protector even as corruption and bloodshed continue. Micah insists that the world on offer in these practices of exploitation is not the only world that can exist. Micah's discourse shares a grounding conviction with what Bey asserts for Black trans feminism: that "all systems, all modes of structuring subjectivity and life, are perpetually open to invention, revision, and reimagination." Harmful "normativities"—for Bey, racialized and gendered coercions; for Micah, economic brutality and juridical corruption—can be dismantled through a prophetic stance of "refusal to foreclose the radical possibility of things being not this," a position that expresses nothing less than "onto-epistemic insurrection" (115). Bey sees such insurrectionary refusal as spurred by "a fugitive impetus . . . constitutive of love" (119). Micah excoriates the leaders of his people for their love of evil (3:2), a cruel and poisonous way of dealing that mocks the love of God and love of neighbor to which Israel and Judah have been called (Deut 6:5; Lev 19:18). Fugitivity, then, is the intentional escape from such harmful systems, an unauthorized pressing on toward radical love—"love for self, love for others, love for life, love *regardless*" (119 [emphasis original])—that adamantly refuses conditions of violence that enslave and destroy.

As elaborated in the introduction, here is the spectrum of possibilities I have traced for contemporary responses to Micah's prophetic witness: → resilience → resistance → reformation → rejoicing. Micah 3 builds *resilience* in its audiences by confirming that the suffering of the vulnerable is taken with utmost seriousness as systemic injustice; the perpetrators will be shunned (3:4, 6-7) by a deity who stands in solidarity with the oppressed. Micah 3 catalyzes *resistance*, not least by means of its gruesome visceral imagery (3:2-3), toward the predatory economic practices of heartless individuals and corrupt processes that ravage the communal body. Micah 3 calls for *reformation* of many kinds of leaders at national and local levels—heads, rulers, prophets, seers, and priests (3:1, 5-7, 9-11)—whose role is to promote justice, but who instead oversee, enact, or are complicit with trajectories of economic violence that do terrible harm. Finally, Mic 3 holds space for *rejoicing* in the power of the Spirit-filled Micah of Moresheth (3:8) and every prophetic activist who has stepped forward courageously to tell the truth on behalf of their community.

MICAH 3 AND ECOLOGICAL JUSTICE

Micah 3 depicts the unnatural predations of which social and political elites are capable as they exploit those who are weaker in human communities. Economic violence is portrayed in idioms that, to impressive effect, mix the horrifying tearing and bone-breaking of carnivorous wild animals with the casual flaying and arranging of body parts carried out by a cook preparing a meal of stewed meat. Carnivores do not prepare their meals in coolly considered stages at the cookfire, and chefs do not devour chunks of flesh from still-living creatures. The interweaving of idioms yields something more chilling than either metaphor could have achieved on its own.

Micah rebukes the "heads of Jacob and rulers of the house of Israel" (3:1) for abdicating their responsibility to practice justice and safeguard the well-being of the vulnerable. Johnson and Wilkinson similarly rebuke officials and powerbrokers in our own day whose malfeasant choices have exacerbated, rather than mitigated, the looming ecological catastrophe. They write, "The climate crisis is a leadership crisis. For far too long, far too many leaders have been focused on profit, power, and prestige.... The climate crisis is the result of social, political, and economic systems that are wildly skewed to benefit those who already have so much," and further, an entangling web of complicity entraps many in the harms resulting from "unfettered economic growth, extractive capitalism, and the concentration of wealth and power in the hands of a few" (2021, xxi). The IPBES observes that those in positions of political power too often "move slowly" to enact policies that protect bioregions and biodiversity, yielding demonstrably harmful effects on human communities: "Economic instruments that may be harmful to nature include subsidies... subsidized credit, tax abatements, and prices for commodities and industrial goods that hide environmental costs," given that these practices support "unsustainable production and, as a consequence, can promote deforestation, overfishing, urban sprawl, and wasteful uses of water" (IPBES 2019 §B19). The IPCC reports, "Weather and climate extremes are causing economic and societal impacts across national boundaries through supply-chains, markets, and natural resource flows, with increasing transboundary risks projected across the water, energy, and food sectors," and notes, with diplomatic subtlety, an impact on fisheries that the astute reader will perceive to resonate with Micah's indictment of those who appropriate what belongs to others: "Climate change causes the redistribution of marine fish stocks, increasing risk of transboundary management conflicts ... and negatively affecting equitable distribution of food provisioning services as fish stocks shift from lower to higher latitude regions" (IPCC 2022 §B.5.3).

Micah's poetry invites the implied audience to experience in a visceral way the barbarous mutilations of the social body perpetrated by unjust economic practices. From our position in the reception history of Micah, we may amplify his metaphor to expose the injuries done to human bodies through failure to mitigate climate change, which is regularly a failure related to economic greed and political self-absorption. The IPCC observes, "In all regions extreme heat events have resulted in human mortality and morbidity. . . . The occurrence of climate-related food-borne and water-borne diseases has increased ... higher temperatures, increased rain and flooding have increased the occurrence of diarrheal diseases, including cholera"; further, "some mental health challenges are associated with increasing temperatures," and "increased exposure to wildfire smoke, atmospheric dust, and aeroallergens [has] been associated with climate-sensitive cardiovascular and respiratory distress" (IPCC 2022 §B.1.4). Climate scientists warn that failure to regulate and reduce industries' voracious cannibalizing of natural resources is already yielding significant economic imbalances that threaten the viability of local communities. In the mid- to long-range future, ecosystem collapse and the resulting exacerbation of the global refugee crisis could mean catastrophe for human civilization.

Micah's cannibalism metaphor may encourage us to consider injuries to nonhuman creaturely bodies entangled with ours in the teeming web of life that animates the Earth community. Avians from tiny songbirds to huge raptors, countless fish and other marine creatures, and an extensive array of land mammals are injured by human encroachment on wild habitats, trophy hunting and poaching, the torturous commodification of animals in laboratories for nonessential research, clearcutting of forests for timber, and ill-considered waste disposal practices on land and at sea that show callous disregard for the safety of wild creatures and the importance of regional biodiversity. Critically endangered, or extinct in the wild and extant only in captivity, are such creatures as the Spix's macaw, the northern white rhinoceros and western black rhinoceros, the Sumatran elephant, the Bornean orangutan, the baiji or Yangtze River dolphin, the Pyrenean ibex, and the Amur leopard, along with numerous other animals. Populations

Micah 3

of many creatures not technically endangered are measurably declining as well. Anthony Barnosky, Nicholas Matzke, Susumu Tomiya, Guinevere Wogan, and their colleagues argue that the modes of extraction, exploitation, and pollution that humans have developed are now causing the sixth mass extinction event in the history of this planet (2011; so also Ceballos et al. 2015). Harmful to countless creatures are the ways in which humans are "co-opting resources, fragmenting habitats, introducing non-native species, spreading pathogens, killing species directly, and changing global climate" (Barnosky et al. 2011, 51). They warn that "recovery of biodiversity will not occur on any timeframe meaningful to people," given that "evolution of new species typically takes at least hundreds of thousands of years, and recovery from mass extinction episodes probably occurs on timescales encompassing millions of years" (51). The hyperbole of Micah's cannibalism metaphor in 3:2-3 is more than matched by the sober realism of conclusions—using conservative benchmarks—suggesting that "pollution, overfishing and overhunting, invasive species and pathogens . . . and expanding human biomass are all more extreme ecological stressors than most living species have previously experienced" in the history of the world and could generate extinction at a magnitude of the five mass extinctions "in as little as three centuries" (55-56). The urgency of Micah's warning about the day darkening (3:6) and sacred space becoming uninhabited rubble (3:12) is all the more audible in light of these globally dire circumstances.

COMMENTARY

Micah 3 brings forward the prophet in his own voice once again, and the effect is startling. Micah levels a fierce polemic at the corrupt leaders of his community. Heschel offers that it would have been "an act of high treason" for Amos and others to countermand the pronouncements and deeds of those who governed the hierarchies under which they lived. "Yet the great prophets persisted in condemning the leaders—the kings, princes, priests, and false prophets—even more vehemently than the common people," for "while the prophets did not go so far as to call for the abolition of the monarchy, they insisted that the human pretension to sovereignty was dangerous" (2001, 613-14). Yhwh, the true sovereign, will bring not succor but a terrible silence—absence of vision, lack of divine response—to those whose rapacious greed and lies have led the Judean people toward destruction (Mic 3:5-7).

3:1 *I said further.* The express flagging of first-person discourse from this prophet is surprising. It helps secure a sharp contrast between what the malfeasant elites are reported to be saying (2:6, 11) and what the authentic prophet, Micah himself, says. Whether or not one believes 2:12-13 was added later to Mic 2, this dynamic of contrast would have been perceptible to an ancient audience. That is, 3:1 would not need to follow immediately after 2:11 for this valence to be audible to hearers and (re)readers of this text. "And I said" is certainly also possible as a translation of the simple *waw*. In that case, the sense would be, "And I continued," Micah then unleashing an oracle of judgment that elaborates further on the subtle oracle of doom just offered in 2:12-13, which might have sounded like an oracle of hope to the undiscerning audience—we cannot know whether 2:12-13 was performed publicly, and if so, whether with a "straight" vocal tone or with heavy sarcasm. But that material is, in fact, a devastating prophecy of doom along the lines of Amos 6:7. "But I said" is more effective, though, as a signal of the discursive contrast that, in my view, the prophet is drawing here. What would be unfortunate is for a translator to take 2:12-13 as an earnest oracle of promise—a common and regrettable misunderstanding—and then translate the *waw* here as "and" to mark the transition to the fierce oracle of doom that unfolds in Mic 3. The logic of those two choices in tandem would be cogent in no interpretive framework. Andersen and Freedman claim, "There is nothing in chapter 3 to indicate that it was intended to contradict 2:12-13" (2000, 348), but they have failed to discern the complexity of 2:12-13 as a brilliantly sharp-edged performance of precisely the kind of false prophecy demanded by Micah's interlocutors. They do allow, "3:1 could follow from 2:11, if Micah is responding to an attempt to silence him" (349); this comes closer to honoring the integrity of 2:6-11, 12-13 as an artfully crafted utterance, even though they have not seen the irony at work in 2:12-13.

Micah[LXX] 3:1 opens with a 3ms future indicative verb, *kai erei*, "And he will say." This makes clear, given the nearest antecedent three words earlier in 2:13, that the LXX translator sees the speaking subject as the Lord (*ho kyrios*). This gives the uncanny impression that Yhwh is thundering the indictment that follows to the very flock Yhwh is leading from the pen, congruent with the present author's reading of 2:12-13 as an oracle of judgment. Here is the sequence: "the Lord shall lead them. And he will say, Do hear these things, heads of the house of Iakob and remnant of the house of Israel . . . you . . . who hate the good things and seek the evil things," and so on (Glenny 2015, 23). The alternative, reading from the end of Mic 2 to the opening of Mic 3, would be that Yhwh is being portrayed as chiding the brutally corrupt devourers of their own people even as Yhwh leads them to freedom, something that would make little sense conceptually or rhetorically. Glenny reads 2:12-13 positively—"The unity of all Israel under a king with the Lord leading them points to a revitalized Davidic rule"—but concedes about the next verse, 3:1, "The human leaders are a stark contrast to the leadership of the Lord in 2:12-13" (77). To all who see 2:12-13 in such terms, whether reading Micah^MT or Micah^LXX, the counterargument can be raised that even in the postexilic community, a real-life king would not have been imagined as leading Judean captives personally from the diaspora location (this was never envisioned of Jehoiachin, the strongest candidate for a ruler in diaspora with other compatriots; cf. Jer 52:31-34). The best reading of Micah^LXX 2:12-3:12, taking sufficient account of that 3ms verb at the joining of 2:13-3:1, is that every verse of this material connotes Yhwh's fierce judgment on sinful leaders and their community.

O heads of Jacob and rulers of the house of Israel. The term *qāṣîn* ("ruler, leader") occurs in some Hebrew Bible passages as the designation of one tactically appointed to serve as a military chieftain in exigent circumstances (Josh 10:24; Judg 11:6, 11; Isa 3:6, 7). In the blistering polemic of Isa 1:10, *qāṣîn* is used to designate the leaders of "Sodom" in parallel with the people of "Gomorrah," derogatory references used in direct address to shame the Jerusalemite and Judean addressees. It is clear that the two usages of this noun in Micah (3:1, 9) are embedded within negative material in the broader context; whether any disrespect would have been heard as attached to the noun *qāṣîn* as such cannot be known.

your responsibility to know justice. The noun *mišpāṭ* occurs in Micah only five times, at 3:1, 8, 9; 6:8; and 7:9. But pertinent to every oracle in the book of Micah is the concept of rendering justice on behalf of those in the covenant community, and especially those who are most vulnerable—widows, those living in poverty or debt slavery, fatherless children, landless migrants (Houston 2015). A fierce prophetic commitment to *mišpāṭ* runs like a golden thread through every chapter of Micah.

In the Hebrew Bible, the broad and rich range of meanings for *mišpāṭ* includes: decisions and adjudications rendered by Yhwh, judges, or judicial courts; legal claims, disputations, and processes related to the disposition of matters of case law; legal statutes or laws; and, more informally, customs or practices (*HALOT* 2:651-52). Walter Houston notes the role of the ruler in ancient Near Eastern cultures as guarantor of economic justice for the people, "through decrees remitting debts and taxation, and through judicial action" that, theoretically at least, was to protect "the poor and marginalized from oppressors" (Houston 2015). In the Hebrew Bible, the prophets were seen to have a vital role in proclaiming the parameters of divinely ordained *mišpāṭ*, recalling for the community its obligations as regards ethical behavior, righteousness, and other dimensions of *mišpāṭ*, standing in solidarity with those who were exploited in a class-stratified community, and warning of the negative consequences of flouting the *mišpāṭ* of Yhwh. On that last possibility, we may adduce Hos 6:5, where Yhwh rebukes Ephraim and Judah for insubstantial covenantal fidelity, roaring, "Therefore I have hewn them by the prophets: I have slaughtered them by the words of my mouth, and your *mišpāṭ*"—the 2ms suffix suggesting a divine sentence of judgment leveled against the addressee—"goes forth as light" (my translation).

3:2 *who hate good and love evil.* The conceptual merism of "good" and "evil" spans all human behavior and interior motivation along the axes of ethical to unethical, righteous to unrighteous, and just to unjust. Micah's upbraiding of unjust and corrupt elites has resonances with the polemic in Ps 52:3-5 (Eng. 1-3) against scheming evildoers who "love evil more than good." Andersen and Freedman (2000, 352) note as relevant the triple imperative to "hate evil, and love good, and establish justice [*mišpāṭ*] in the gate" in Amos 5:15 (cf. Ps 45:8 [Eng. 7]). Israel and Judah are bid to love Yhwh their God as a covenantal mandate of the highest order (Exod 20:6; Deut 5:10; 6:5; 10:12; 11:1, 13, 22; 13:4; 19:9; 30:6, 16, 20; Josh 22:5; 23:11; Ps 31:24 [Eng. 23]). Those who obey Yhwh are to love the neighbor and the migrant or the stranger as themselves (Lev 19:18, 34; Deut 10:19). Here again, this love is understood as righteous and ethical comportment in relationship. Loving God and loving neighbor are celebrated in the Synoptic Gospels as mandates that lie at the very heart of the torah and Israel's prophetic traditions (Matt 22:36-40; Mark 12:28-31; Luke 10:25-28).

who tear the skin off them. The verb *gzl* here echoes an earlier instance in 2:2, expressing the predatory way in which the powerful tear away householders' fields. Here in 3:2, this is the third participial form in construct that Micah deploys in rapid succession (*śōnəʾê*, *ʾōhăbê*, and *gōzəlê*), lending the impression of hammer blows of verbal indictment. The viscerally shocking imagery of the MT is made less graphic in Tg. Mic 3:2, which clarifies the economic nature of the oppression, characterizing the malefactors as those who "violently take my people's belongings from their hand and take their precious wealth from them."

3:3 *devoured the flesh of my people.* The object of Judean elites' abhorrent depredations is made explicit only here, after the cannibalism is under-

Micah 3

way, as it were, in the minds of the implied audience. "My people" (ʿammî) is poignant, even wrenching. The audience has had to look closely at the gruesome scene of cannibalism, but only now can the audience see who is suffering the ravages of these corrupt leaders' greed. The term ʿammî occurs nine times in Micah, always in discursive moments in which the prophet is communicating heightened fear, grief, or outrage on behalf of his community, whether in his own voice or ventriloquizing others (see 1:9; 2:4, 8, 9; 3:3, 5; 6:3, 5, 16). The poignancy of "my people" here makes all the more appalling the harms that have been perpetrated by the heads and rulers of this riven communal body. The leaders have been not only derelict in their duty to protect the people but savage in their exploitation. As Boloje observes, the cannibalism metaphor depicts "the slow, systematic, and complete destruction of innocent life for selfish purposes," and "the inexorable progression" of the images here dramatizes "how the leaders and judges who should have been watchdogs turn out to be ravenous lions or wolves" (2021a, 3).

Micah's insistence on justice for the powerless is given intensity not only by the horror of his cannibalism imagery, but by the claim of solidarity he stakes via the possessive pronoun "my" in "my people." This remains true whether the interpreter takes this as Micah speaking in his own voice or Micah speaking on behalf of Yhwh. In proposing this claim, the prophet stands as spokesperson for covenantal fidelity. Brueggemann says about ancient Israel, "*what is most characteristic and most distinctive in the life and vocation of this partner of [Yhwh] . . . is the remarkable equation of love of God with love of neighbor*, which is enacted through the exercise of distributive justice of social goods, social power, and social access to those without leverage" (1997, 424 [emphasis original]). Daniel Carroll R. observes that the hyperbolic vividness of the cannibalism imagery and Micah's concern generally with the shedding of blood (3:10; 7:2) are "more than stylistic techniques designed . . . to shock the listener/reader"—these features of Micah's oracles speak to the prophet's "indignant anger" and "moral outrage" on behalf of Judeans who are oppressed (2007, 107).

as in a pot. Isaiah and Ezekiel, too, use the image of a cauldron in which gruesome things simmer. Isaiah 65 gives us a God who has been pleading with the rebellious covenant people with hands outstretched "all day long," to no avail. In language crafted to evoke revulsion, the poet depicts the idolatrous and corrupt people making illicit sacrifices, sitting with the dead in tombs, eating "swine's flesh, with broth of abominable things in their vessels," such that Yhwh has no choice but to punish their iniquities (Isa 65:1–

Commentary

7). Ezekiel 24 portrays Jerusalem in 588 BCE under the Babylonian siege as the flesh being cooked in a simmering pot; Judeans, seemingly "good pieces" of meat and "choice bones," will find themselves in a rusty pot—a "bloody city"—under which the fire blazes so fiercely that the stew will boil off, the copper of the pot will glow, and the rust will be consumed, a metaphor for YHWH using the Babylonian onslaught to "cleanse" the people from their "filthy lewdness" (24:1–13). In Mic 3:3, the breaking of bones "in pieces" in the MT imagery is rendered in Tg. Mic 3:3 as the oppressors dividing their ill-gotten gains among themselves.

3:4 [YHWH] will not answer. Twice in Mic 3, the implied audience must contemplate the alarming prospect that the deity to whom the community lifts their supplications will not answer them. In 3:4, the predatory elites will see that their evil deeds have broken the covenant relationship with YHWH, and in 3:7, the false prophets and illegitimate intermediaries will see that their efforts are fruitless, for God will not respond. Within the perspective of the theology Micah articulates, the abject bleakness of such a godforsaken landscape cannot be underestimated. Other eighth-century prophets, too, explore the silence or withdrawal of YHWH as punishment for corruption. Hosea crafts a polemic against inadequate priests in which YHWH rages, "Since you have forgotten the law of your God, I also will forget your children" (Hos 4:6). Amos imagines a time of divine withdrawal when Israel will be starved "of hearing the words of the LORD"; the people "shall run to and fro, seeking the word of the LORD, but they shall not find it" (Amos 8:11–12).

hide [YHWH's] face. The idiom of YHWH hiding the divine countenance from believers is a powerful idiom for purposive divine absence or silence. Per Micah[LXX], YHWH will "turn" the divine face from them (*apostrepsei*); Gelston finds it "most unlikely" that the Greek and Peshitta traditions are reflecting a Hebrew *Vorlage* based on *swr*, and "much more likely that they reflected an interpretive tradition" (*BHQ*, 101). It is not unknown in biblical wisdom literature for a believer to wish that God would be less engaged. Job laments to God, "Will you not look away from me for a while, let me alone until I swallow my spittle?" (Job 7:19). But usually in the Hebrew Bible, the lack of God's presence is to be mourned, whether it occurs for reasons unknown or unspecified—as is the case in some instances in Job and the Psalms—or as a consequence leveled by the deity against those adjudged guilty of ethical malfeasance or religious infidelity. Samuel Balentine notes the significance of this reference in Mic 3:4 occurring "within an oracle of judgment rather than within the petition of a suppliant" (1983, 69). The

Micah 3

threatened absence of the deity would surely have the effect of intensifying the terror of petitioners who might beg for mercy. This verse uses ironic reversal to dramatize the urgency of attending to those who are vulnerable: oppressors and callous rulers will learn firsthand what it is like to beg for divine intervention to no avail. William Brown remarks, "To shield ourselves from those who suffer, prophets and apostles alike have said, is to shield ourselves from God" (1996, 42). In Tg. Mic 3:4, Yhwh hiding the divine face from suppliants (MT) becomes Yhwh removing from them "his Shekinah"—the divine presence dwelling in the midst of the covenant people.

they have made their deeds evil. The indictment of the evil deeds of corrupt Judean elites here is amplified in 7:13 by a more expansive view of wrongdoing, where *maʿalêlêhem* is used of the (mis)deeds of all the inhabitants of the earth, those who have harmed Yhwh's people and will be made to suffer divine retribution. This noun, "deeds" or "doings," occurs only once in Deuteronomy (28:20) but is used seventeen times in polemical Jeremiah passages to signal that divine retribution is calibrated as recompense for Judeans' sustained wickedness.

3:5 Thus has Yhwh spoken. This divine speech formula occurs only at 2:3 and 3:5 in the book of Micah. At Mic 2:3, the divine speech formula introduces material that is syntactically closer to prose lines and thus different in degree from the poetic bicola that precede and follow it. Many take this semantic difference as indicative of 3:5-8, too, having the status of a later editorial interpolation (e.g., Arena 2020, 163).

the prophets . . . who lead my people astray. A number of Hebrew Bible texts address the challenge of adjudicating whether a prophet speaking in the name of Yhwh has offered an authentic oracle or vision (e.g., Deut 18:15-22; 1 Kgs 22:1-35; Jer 28; see Sharp 2022a, 120-22). Here, Micah deplores that mercenary prophets are compensated—bribed—to offer public authorization in the name of Yhwh for the political status quo as "peace," despite overwhelming evidence that Judeans are living in poverty intensified by unjust trading practices, corrupt judicial rulings, and the exploitation of farmers by economic elites.

who strike with their fangs. In this metaphor, Micah brilliantly deploys *nšk*. The verbal meaning "to charge interest" and the nominal form *nešek*, "interest," occur in passages forbidding the exploitative extraction of interest from financially needy members of the covenant community (Exod 22:24; Lev 25:36-37; Deut 23:19-20 [Heb. 20-21]; Ps 15:5; Ezek 18:8, 13, 17; 22:12). The verb *nšk* also describes predatory biting—literal or figurative—with a specific predator in view: a venomous snake striking its prey (Gen 49:17; Num 21:6, 8–9; Prov 23:32; Eccl 10:8, 11; Jer 8:17; Amos 5:19; 9:3). Some translators assume the false prophets are mercenaries who offer a benign message of *šālôm* when they are fed—that is, paid so they can support themselves (e.g., Allen 1976, 310; Sweeney 2000, 370-71). But this misunderstands both the vehicle and the tenor of Micah's metaphor: they are not chewing food. As Andersen and Freedman note, "the associations of *nšk* ('bite') are altogether sinister," and "the verb is never used to describe ordinary mastication" (2000, 362). Rather, the prophets are being characterized as striking with fangs as a viper or cobra would—a dramatic image that connotes painful or fatal toxicity and the tearing of flesh, and that would evoke fear.

does not give per their direction. The negative idiom with ʿ*al-peh* is not about failing to give food for the false prophets' actual mouths, as literal translations would have it (NRSV: "those who put nothing into their mouths"), even if that be taken metonymically as meaning to supply economic support. Rather, the idiom is best framed in the metaphorical realm of discourse and expresses not doing as the false prophets dictate; for other examples, see Gen 41:40; Job 39:27. Utzschneider understands this and translates, "wer nicht nach ihrer Forderung gibt" (2005, 75; similarly Arena 2020, 160-61). In Tg. Mic 3:5, the metaphorical vehicle of feeding is elaborated in terms that evoke a lavish royal setting: "whoever gives them a banquet of meat" will receive a prophecy of peace.

they sanctify war. The term *sanctify*, a priestly technical term, is used ironically here: the false prophets authorize "holy war," as it were, whenever they are not bribed. There is ambiguity in the semantic sense. Does this mean that these mercenary false intermediaries authorize the ongoing exploitative injustices that are ravaging the lives of those in the community who have no economic power, or that they prepare for battle, metaphorically speaking, against those who oppose them, or even that they invariably offer a message of doom regarding geopolitical enemies unless they are plied with bribes to offer a calming message congruent with the holy-war tradition that Yhwh will fight for Israel? While the third option seems least likely, any of these senses would be possible theoretically, in light of how prophecy is understood to work in the Latter Prophets. The interplay of possibilities makes for a layered condemnation of the false prophets, suggesting not only the baseness of their antagonistic relationship to those who do not pander to them but their appalling manipulation of a cherished tradition, that of Yhwh as divine warrior who protects Israel against their enemies, and this in a time—the Neo-Assyrian period, whether actually the histor-

Micah 3

ical context for the composition of these lines or a later scribal memory of same—when the people's fear of the enemy would have been intense.

For *qdš* + *milḥāmâ*, see Jer 6:4 and Joel 4:9 (Eng. 3:9). The Jeremiah usage evokes the terror and chaos roiling Jerusalem when a siege alarm is raised (Jer 6:1–8); in a chilling move, the prophet ventriloquizes an enemy shouting to ready the troops for an attack on Jerusalem at noon. The Joel usage, too, has to do with battle preparations, this time on an eschatologically broad scale involving multitudes of hostile nations (Joel 4:14–15 [Eng. 3:14–15]). The locution about sanctifying or preparing for battle precedes the Joel imperative that famously reverses the "swords to plowshares" trajectory envisioned in Isa 2:4 // Mic 4:3. Kessler emphasizes holy war as the underpinning to Mic 3:5 with "dem erklären sie den heiligen Krieg" (2000a, 152); ZUR does the same, albeit with a slightly different valence, with "erklären sie den Krieg für heilig." Both translations assist the reader in appreciating the ironic force of Micah's condemnation of prophetic misconduct: they muster the name of Yhwh for purposes of hostility or deceit.

3:6 it will be night ... and darkness. The rabbi known as the Malbim (1809–1879) sees poetic justice in this sequence of divine retributive actions against false intermediaries: "Seers claimed to see their visions at night; but instead of the night ushering in a vision, the vision will usher in the night. Diviners usually practiced their divinations in a dark place; instead of the darkness bringing the divination, the divination will bring on the darkness. The false prophets prophesied by day. Their punishment will be that the sun will set for them and their day will become dark" (Stavsky 2009, 24).

3:7 the seers will be shamed and the diviners disgraced. Of "seers" and "diviners," Andersen and Freedman aver, "In eighth-century usage the terms ... are equivalent and interchangeable" (374). The verb pairing *bwš* + *ḥpr* occurs in the Book of the Twelve only here at Mic 3:7. Evoking a span of modes of intermediation, the word pair can be found also in Isa 1:29; 24:23; 54:4; Jer 15:9; 50:12. In Tg. Mic 3:6–7, references to divination and diviners have been omitted, the sages presumably not wishing to encourage the impression that divination was happening in Judah. The targum renders instead, "you shall be too ashamed to prophesy and ... too embarrassed to teach," and uses the noun "teachers" where the MT has "diviners."

cover their upper lips. For clarification, the targum adds, "like mourners." This gesture of mourning (see Ezek 24:17, 22) emphasizes the publicly shameful inefficacy of these false intermediaries. They will not be

Commentary

able to facilitate access to the deity, so they will be humiliated and perhaps alienated from the community; Kessler (2000a, 156) points to Lev 13:45 in this regard.

3:8 *But as for me.* Micah draws a dramatic contrast between those mercenary seers and false prophets who deceptively declare *šālôm*, on the one hand, and his own proclamation of Yʜwʜ's impending judgment. The syntax of *wəʾûlām ʾānōkî* has enormous semantic force, calling the audience's attention to Micah's truth-telling over against the lies of the false prophets and signaling an awareness of the weightiness of his mission overall, that is, for the entire scroll of Micah. The resonance of this rhetorical move will be echoed in 7:7, where Micah underlines his own authentic stance as a true prophet watching for Yʜwʜ. Kessler has argued that much of Mic 1–3 (viz., 1:10–16; 2:1–3, 6–11; 3:1–12) functions as a "memoir" designed to justify Micah as a trustworthy prophet and "to save Micah's message for the future written by his followers after the events of 701 BCE," when Sennacherib's troops had invaded the region but were unable to bring down Jerusalem (2021b, 142–47; his Micha-Denkschrift argument is laid out in detail in 2000a, 94–97).

filled with the power of the spirit of Yʜwʜ. The particle *ʾet-* here signals an accusative of specification, expressing more precisely the kind of power with which the prophet is filled. Andersen and Freedman suggest that the second and third nouns in the clause may "constitute a second object, or instrumental adverb," and while there is no denying the syntactical awkwardness of the line, the latter two nouns are best read as being "in delayed coordination with *kōaḥ*" (2000, 376–77). To omit the specifying relationship, as some translations do—"I am filled with strength by the spirit of Yʜwʜ" (NJPS); "ich bin erfüllt von Kraft, durch den Geist des Hᴇʀʀɴ" (ZUR)— leaves the erroneous impression that the last clause is adverbial, modifying the verb rather than specifying the nature of the power suffusing Micah's prophetic proclamation. Some interpreters argue that the term "the spirit of Yʜwʜ" (*ʾet-rûaḥ yhwh*) is a scribal interpolation, flagged as such by the anomalous accusative marker (so Mowinckel 2002, 84, 146n3). But this cannot be proved, and the putative original line would make far less sense, with Micah simply claiming to be strong in some unspecified way. A century and a half later, another prophet will declare that he is filled with the energy of a divinely appointed message that is rejected by his community: Jeremiah laments that he is filled with the wrath of Yʜwʜ (*ḥămat yhwh*), and though his compatriots scorn his message of warning, Jeremiah is exhausted with the effort to hold it in and cannot keep silent (Jer 6:11; cf. 20:9). The book of

Micah 3

Fig. 13. Micah (top row, center). Victorian-era stained glass designed by John Richard Clayton (1827-1913) and Alfred Bell (1832-1895). St. Edmundsbury Cathedral in Bury St. Edmunds, Suffolk, England. Photo by Del Anson.

Jeremiah, of course, is the only book in the Latter Prophets to quote Micah by name (Jer 26:18).

to declare ... transgression. Mowinckel, a tradition historian, has explored differences between figures depicted in the throes of spirit possession in the Former Prophets (e.g., Saul in 1 Sam 10:5-6, 10-13; 18:10-11; 19:9-10) and figures such as Micah, whom he terms the "pre-exilic reforming prophets." He observes:

> Micah is endowed by [Yhwh] with "power" and "heroic might." The old prophets believed that they had a similar endowment. But in their case the power was first and foremost the magic, wonder-working power ... while in Micah's case it is the power to wield the scourge of chastisement and bear the attacks that this action would inevitably produce.... Micah is also endowed with "judgment" (*mišpāṭ*): the faculty of judging, acting rightly.... The ability to keep the community faithful to the right social, moral, and religious customs, which in earlier days was ascribed to and expected of the chief or king, is here claimed by the prophet. (2002, 96)

Drawing on the work of James C. Scott (1990), Gale Yee emphasizes that the authority enjoyed by prophets in ancient Judah made it possible for Micah to advocate on behalf of the marginalized in his community. Yee observes (2007, 23), "Spokespersons for the oppressed are not compelling because they have ... charisma. Rather, their strength lies in their willingness and ability to articulate the hidden transcript" regarding elites' misuses of power and brutal subordination of those who are economically vulnerable. Further, "renegade members of the dominant elite who ignore or protest the public transcript," that is, who dissent from explicit and implicit communications of the ideology that oppressive structures and processes are normal and cannot be changed, "present a very great threat to the balance of power" as they voice "the complaints, fears, rages, and hopes of the hidden transcript publicly" (23).

O'Brien (2015, 32) hears an echo of Mic 3:8 in Isa 61:1, where the prophet avers, "The spirit of the Lord God is upon me, because the Lord has anointed me; [Yhwh] has sent me to bring good news to the oppressed." In Luke 4:14-21, the Isa 61 passage is quoted by Jesus in the synagogue at Nazareth: described as "filled with the power of the Spirit" (Luke 4:1), Jesus publicly claims the Isaiah oracle as being fulfilled in his ministry. While not every scholar cites Luke 4 as alluding to Mic 3, I agree with O'Brien in hearing Mic 3:8 as vitally important source material for Isa 61, and Luke 4:1 seems to me to be a direct allusion to Mic 3:8.

3:9 heads... and rulers... who abhor justice. The prophet here returns to the strong claim with which he had opened the oracles of Mic 3, a rhetorical question requiring the assent of the implied audience that had asked whether it was not the responsibility of the rulers of Israel to know justice. Heightening is in evidence here across the intervening lines: indeed it is their responsibility, and not only are they failing to safeguard justice, they are abhorring it (3:9).

make crooked all that is straight. For wisdom teaching about thoughts, speech, deeds, or lifeways being upright (straight, pure) or crooked (ʻqš), see Job 9:20; Pss 18:27; 101:4; Prov 2:15; 8:8; 10:9; 11:20; 17:20; 19:1; 22:5; 28:6, 18. In the Latter Prophets, the trope occurs in Isa 59:8, in an impassioned diatribe against Judeans whose ways are tainted by corruption and violence.

3:10 who build Zion by means of bloodshed and... injustice. The targum to this verse reads, "those who build houses in Zion." Cathcart and Gordon explain, "The *Shekinah* dwells in Zion (see next verse) so it is unacceptable to give the impression that Zion was built with blood" (1989, 119n21). The noun ʻawlâ ("injustice") occurs six times in the Minor Prophets. Here and in Hab 2:12, it occurs with a verb of building (*bnh*) and an adverbial complement "by means of bloodshed" (*bədāmîm*). Gelston suggests that the builder (ms) might be understood as the king, tacitly included "alongside the groups listed in v. 11" (*BHQ*, 101). Hebrew ʻawlâ is found otherwise in the Twelve in Hos 10:13; Zeph 3:5, 13; and Mal 2:6.

Mays subtly references the blood of a primordial murder in Israel's founding traditions—Cain's murder of his brother Abel (Gen 4:10)—in his reflection on this verse: "The city has been built with bloodshed that cries out to God for the justice its leaders abhor" (1976, 87). Andersen and Freedman (2000, 382) consider references in the Hebrew Bible to the ritual sacrifice of children during the setting of foundations for monumental building projects. The proleptic malediction uttered by Joshua against anyone who seeks to rebuild the ruins of Jericho ("at the cost of his firstborn he shall lay its foundation, and at the cost of his youngest he shall set up its gates," Josh 6:26) does not reflect such a practice in itself, though the sacrifice of two children by Hiel of Bethel is identified in 1 Kgs 16:34 as a fulfillment of Joshua's prophecy. As I have argued elsewhere, Josh 6:26 "seems to be mixing two different ways of understanding the 'cost,' since an intentional foundation sacrifice cannot easily be understood as a calamitous effect of a curse that unleashes undesirable and unforeseen harm on the target" (Sharp 2019b, 171); in my view, neither understanding seems to lie in the background here. The observation of Carroll R. is cogent: "the 'blood' of 3:10 might be an ironic reference to the blood of the sacrifices in the temple, even as it is an indictment of the cruelty of the leaders. Whereas Zion should be the center of proper sacrifices of animals, it has devolved into the sacrifice of the powerless" (2007, 108). From a position of virtue ethics, Carroll R. writes, "The very institution that should have been the beacon of virtue had become its graveyard" (109).

3:11 *offer adjudication . . . rulings . . . divination.* Officials adjudicated disputes and other cases; priests offered halakic rulings to guide the community's domestic observance of torah stipulations regarding ethical and ritual practices; prophets were consulted to divine the will of Yhwh and intercede on behalf of rulers or the people. Micah excoriates each of those Judean constituencies for seeking personal enrichment and abdicating their responsibility to discharge their duties with integrity. Wary of suggesting that divination was taking place in Judah at all, Tg. Mic 3:11 offers the verb "teach" in place of the MT "offer divination."

They rely on Yhwh . . . "Is not Yhwh in our midst?" A central claim articulated in varied refractions of Israelite covenantal theology is that Yhwh has dwelled with the people of Israel and Judah. This notion is presented in texts set, narratologically speaking, from the ancient time of Israel's wilderness wandering, when the divine presence was represented as a pillar of cloud by day and pillar of fire by night and the divine resolve to accompany the people was seen as unwavering (Exod 13:21–22; 33:14–15; Deut 2:7) through the Israelites' obliteration of Canaanite indigenous groups on the strength of the divine promise that Yhwh would never leave Joshua and those under his leadership (Josh 1:5; 23:3, 9–10). But that orthodox claim of abiding divine presence becomes distorted in ideologies, such as the one Micah ventriloquizes here (cf. Jer 5:12) promulgated by malfeasant officials and false prophets. These insist, wrongly, that corrupt behavior will have no ill consequences for the divine protection that the people enjoy. The targum directs its audience away from the impression that Yhwh might dwell in any direct anthropomorphic way among the people, rendering: "They rely on the *Memra of* the Lord"—that is, on Yhwh's powerful word—and, "Is not the *Shekinah of* the Lord in our midst?"

"Calamity will not come upon us!" Some Hebrew Bible traditions promulgate a set of theological convictions expressing the inviolability or

Micah 3

resilience of Zion. Most audible in Yhwh's promise to David in 2 Sam 7, Solomon's prayer in 1 Kgs 8:12-61, numerous passages in Isaiah, and Pss 46 and 132, these traditions articulate, in a rich variety of ways, the convictions that Yhwh was enthroned in the temple on Mount Zion and that the holy city could not fall so long as the divine presence protected it, or would be rebuilt when military aggression had overwhelmed its defenses; further, Yhwh had established the Davidic monarchy to reign from Jerusalem forever. Hugh Williamson and many, including the present author, find the mercenary prophets in Mic 3:11 to be depicted as mouthing "a central tenet of Zion theology" when they mislead the people with the false reassurance, "Calamity will not come upon us!" (Williamson 2016, 145). Some biblical texts are unquestionably involved in open polemic against the Zion theology. As Andersen and Freedman observe (2000, 384), Amos 9:10 has Yhwh quote miscreants styled "all the sinners of my people" as saying something similar to what Micah attributes to mercenary false prophets in Mic 3:11. Also transparent in this regard is Jer 7:1-15 (Sharp 2003, 44-54), which ventriloquizes proponents of what the Deutero-Jeremianic scribes clearly knew to be a misguided politics.

3:12 *Zion will be plowed as a field.* While Jerusalem was not destroyed during the reign of Hezekiah, the city was conquered by Babylonian invaders several generations later, in 587 BCE. Jerusalem's fortifications were breached by the Babylonians, who then destroyed the city's buildings by fire, according to the prophetic scribal memory articulated in Jer 39:8 and 52:13. The latter passage says of the destruction wreaked by Nebuzaradan and his troops, "He burned the house of Yhwh and the house of the king and all the houses of Jerusalem; every house belonging to the powerful he set ablaze" (my translation). Micah 3:12 assuredly has this traumatic event in view. The positioning of this verse at the exact center of the Book of the Twelve has drawn the attention of many interpreters, including Zapff, who argues that Micah constitutes "a kind of theological *center* of the Book of the Twelve" in which a shift can be observed from Yhwh's punishment of Zion toward Zion's future restoration, a trajectory that continues to develop in the Book of the Twelve (2012 [emphasis original]). Zapff says, "Within the Book of the Twelve, the Micah document constitutes both a preliminary ending to the drama of Yhwh's judgment over [Yhwh's] people and a turning point and new beginning for Yhwh's saving action that . . . is open to the world of the nations" (2022, 19). This insight may be applied also to the "hinge" of 3:12-4:1 within the book of Micah.

Commentary

In Jer 26:18, in a passage of Deutero-Jeremianic prose composed after the fall of Jerusalem in 587, Micah's oracle of doom is quoted, a reperformance of Micah's prophesying that, Terence Fretheim notes, is "the longest quotation of one prophet by another" in the Hebrew Bible (2013, 189). The only difference is that the "heap of ruins" in Mic 3:12 is ʿiyyîn, whereas in Jer 26:18 it is rendered as ʿiyyîm. In the argument presented by the elders in Jer 26, the oracle is deemed to have been true and authoritative. It had gone unfulfilled during the time of Hezekiah only due to that king's humble petitionary prayer, which was efficacious in turning the purpose of Yʜᴡʜ away from divinely wrought destruction of Jerusalem via the Assyrian army (Isa 36–37 // 2 Kgs 18:13–19:37; cf. Isa 10:5–11; Josephus, *Ant.* 10.6.2). In their discussion of false prophecy and "'unfulfilled prophecy' [that] is authentic," David Noel Freedman and Rebecca Frey note the irony: "Hezekiah and the people responded to Micah's prophecy by modifying their behavior"—according to the reasoning of Jer 26:18-19—"so that nothing happened. . . . If God commanded Micah to speak, then the city ought to have fallen as he predicted." Rather than styling Micah a false prophet, "they say that his prophecy was so effective it prevented its own fulfillment" (2008, 83). Conrad observes that in Jer 26, the elders' verbatim quotation of Mic 3:12 could serve as evidence of the authority of the book of Micah as literary source: Micah's oracle "is written down and available to the elders, those who can read. These exact words of Micah could be quoted with precision because they were in writing" (2003, 143). While caution in dating biblical texts is generally to be commended, Andersen and Freedman are perhaps too cautious when they offer, "there is no way of dating the oracles in chapter 3" (2000, 387). It is possible that Mic 3 was composed with the Neo-Babylonian crisis in view, to be sure. But there is nothing substantial in this material that disconfirms another possibility: that the eighth-century prophet was here using dramatic imagery of wholesale destruction in a more general, albeit rhetorically powerful, way.

the mountain of the House [will become] high places of the forest. The magnificent and holy Temple Mount will revert to forested wilderness. The plural form of "high places" is clear, suggesting multiple illicit shrines and strongly evoking the *bāmôt* featured in the judgment oracle in 1:3, 5. Gelston observes that all versions apart from the Vulgate render the noun in the singular (see, e.g., Micah[LXX] *alsos drymou*, "the grove of a forest"), "but the pl. is supported by 4QXII[g] . . . by the citation of the text in Jer 26:18, and by the parallel" ʿ*yyn* (*BHQ*, 102), though the last point is not probative, as Biblical Hebrew parallelism could certainly move from a singular form to a

Micah 3

plural as well. From the opening of the book of Micah, YHWH has descended in judgment, treading upon the "high places of the earth" (1:3) and pronouncing doom against the "high places of Judah," shockingly identified as Jerusalem itself (1:5). Now, the prophet declares, YHWH is about to raze the literal monumental structures of Jerusalem, leaving that glorious city nothing more than elevation(s) in a devastated and wild terrain. The vibrancy of Zion as a cultural and religious center of unparalleled importance, alive with throngs of residents and visitors conducting trade and coming to offer sacrifices to YHWH at the temple—all that will be over, the sacred mount reduced to rubble, with no sign of the presence of the Holy One who had shepherded Israel and Judah. As the divine chariot of YHWH visibly departs Jerusalem in the spatial iconography of the prophet Ezekiel, so here the audience is left with no assurance of the presence of YHWH. Micah 3 ends in thunderous silence and desolation.

BIBLIOGRAPHY

Balentine, S. E. 1983. *The Hidden God: The Hiding of the Face of God in the Old Testament*. Oxford Theological Monographs. Oxford: Oxford University Press.

Barnosky, A. D., N. Matzke, S. Tomiya, G. O. U. Wogan, B. Swartz, T. B. Quental, C. Marshall, J. L. McGuire, E. L. Lindsey, K. C. Maguire, B. Mersey, and E. A. Ferrer. 2011. "Has the Earth's Sixth Mass Extinction Already Arrived?" *Nature* 471:51–57. doi:10.1038/nature09678.

Boloje, B. O. 2021a. "Exploring Religious Power: A Re-reading of Micah's Metaphor of Food (Mi 3:5) in the Context of African Religious Space." *Verbum et Ecclesia* 42.1:a2328. doi:10.4102/ve.v42i1.2328.

Freedman, D. N., and R. Frey. 2008. "False Prophecy Is True." Pages 82–87 in *Inspired Speech: Prophecy in the Ancient Near East; Essays in Honor of Herbert B. Huffmon*. Edited by J. Kaltner and L. Stulman. JSOTSup 378. London: T&T Clark.

Kinzig, W. 2021. *Christian Persecution in Antiquity*. Translated by M. Bockmuehl. Waco, TX: Baylor University Press.

Moss, C. R. 2012. *Ancient Christian Martyrdom: Diverse Practices, Theologies, and Traditions*. ABRL. New Haven: Yale University Press.

Norris, K. 1996. *The Cloister Walk*. New York: Riverhead.

Scott, J. C. 1990. *Domination and the Arts of Resistance: Hidden Transcripts*. New Haven: Yale University Press.

Sherinian, Z. C. 2016. "Transforming Christian Music, Transforming Social Identity in South India." Pages 126-44 in *Resounding Transcendence: Transitions in Music, Religion, and Ritual*. Edited by J. Engelhardt and P. Bohlman. Oxford: Oxford University Press. doi:10.1093/acprof:oso/9780199737642.003.0008.

Williamson, H. G. M. 2016. "History and Memory in the Prophets." *OHP*, 132-48. doi:10.1093/oxfordhb/9780199859559.013.8.

Zapff, B. M. 2012. "The Book of Micah—the Theological Centre of the Book of the Twelve?" Pages 129-46 in *Perspectives on the Formation of the Book of the Twelve: Methodological Foundations—Redactional Processes—Historical Insights*. Edited by R. Albert, J. D. Nogalski, and J. Wöhrle. BZAW 433. Berlin: De Gruyter. doi:10.1515/9783110283761.129.

MICAH 4

Zion as Pinnacle of Godly Peace

4:1–4

¹But in the latter days,
  the mountain of the house of Yhwh
will be established as the peak of the mountains;
  it will be elevated above the hills,
and peoples will stream to it.
  ²Many nations will set out and say,
"Come, let us go up to the mountain of Yhwh,
  to the house of the God of Jacob,
so [Yhwh] may instruct us in [Yhwh's] ways
  and we may walk in [Yhwh's] paths!"
For from Zion will go forth torah,
  and the word of Yhwh from Jerusalem.
³[Yhwh] will judge among many peoples
  and arbitrate with respect to mighty nations to a vast
    distance.
They will beat their swords into plowshares
  and their spears into pruning hooks.
Nation will not lift up sword against nation,
  and they will no longer study war.

⁴Each one will sit underneath their own grapevine and under
    their own fig tree,
  and there will be no one to terrify them—
    for the mouth of Yhwh of Hosts has spoken.

Micah 4

Communal Identity

4:5

> ⁵For each of the peoples walks in the name of its own god;
>   as for us, we will walk in the name of Yhwh our God
>   forever and ever.

Zion's Restoration and Renewed Dominion

4:6–8

> ⁶In that day—saying of Yhwh—
> I will gather those {fs} impaired in mobility,
>   and those {fs} who had been driven away I will assemble—
>   and those whom I had harmed.
> ⁷I will make those {fs} impaired in mobility into a remnant,
>   and those {fs} who had been banished into a mighty nation;
> and Yhwh will reign over them on Mount Zion
>   now and forever.
>
> ⁸And as for you, O Tower of Eder,
>   Hill of Daughter Zion,
> as far as you it {fs} will come:
>   the former dominion will come,
>   the sovereignty belonging to Daughter Jerusalem.

Catastrophe, Then Rescue by Yhwh

4:9–13b

> ⁹Now: Why do you {fs} cry out?
>   Is the King not in you,
>   or has your Counselor perished,
> that writhing has seized you
>   like that of a woman in labor?
> ¹⁰Writhe and shriek,
>   Daughter Zion, like a woman in labor!
> For now you will go out of the city
>   and dwell in the open field.

> And you will go to Babylon.
>> There you will be rescued;
> there Yhwh will redeem you
>> from the hand of your enemies.
> ¹¹Now many nations may be gathered against you,
> those who say, "Let her be defiled,
>> and let our gaze rove over Zion,"
> ¹²but they do not know
>> the plans of Yhwh,
> and they do not discern [Yhwh's] scheme:
>> that [Yhwh] will gather them like scythed grain to the threshing floor.
> ¹³Arise and thresh, Daughter Zion,
>> for your horn I will make iron
>> and your hooves I will make bronze,
> and you will crush many peoples.

Zion Pledges the Spoils to Yhwh

4:13c

> "And I will devote to Yhwh their ill-gotten gains,
> their wealth to the Lord of all the earth."

Israel under Threat

4:14 (Eng. 5:1)

> ¹⁴Now you should muster your raiders, Daughter Raider!
>> He has laid siege against us.
> With the rod they strike on the cheek
>> the judge of Israel.

INTERPRETATION

Micah 4 offers a luminous vision of hope for Jerusalem, Judah, and the nations of the world. At the end of Mic 3, the audience of these oracles had felt themselves to be standing in the rubble of their holy city (3:12). The un-

Micah 4

spoken horror: many Judeans had been killed by enemy invaders or forced into diaspora (2:12-13). Those who had survived had found themselves abandoned by Yhwh in a bleak landscape marked by cultural desecration, trauma, and loss. Now an incandescent light dawns. In a distant yet imaginable future, Jerusalem will have been rebuilt (language for this is in Isa 58:12 and Isa 60-62, not in Micah), and Mount Zion will be established as the elevated height to which peoples and governments across the globe look for guidance, rejoicing in what Judah has known and lived for centuries, taking a position of awe and veneration toward Israel's God. This vision at the opening of Mic 4 is eschatological, per many interpreters, having to do with an idyllic time of restoration for the righteous that comes at, or near, the end of human history. That may be, but the concreteness of the beautiful images here—swords and spears being hammered into farming tools, persons sitting in quiet enjoyment under their own grapevines and fig trees—speaks to a time that will unfold within lived history.

The material in 4:1-4 appears, virtually verbatim, in Isa 2:2-4. As every interpreter observes, the material that follows this shared oracle is, then, unique in each case. Isaiah 2:5 urges the "house of Jacob" to "walk in the light of the Lord," and the verses that follow elaborate on the idolatrous nature of foreigners who have influenced Judah toward sins of idolatry, pride, and oppression of the vulnerable in their midst (Isa 2:6-4:1). Micah 4:5 uses the same verb as that in Isa 2:5, *hlk* ("to walk" as a metaphor for choosing lifeways), but the point is different: while other peoples of the world calibrate their lifeways to their own deities, Judah (alone) looks to Yhwh for formative guidance. Interpreters have debated whether a direction of literary influence can be determined from Isaiah to Micah or vice versa, or whether the two prophetic corpora have drawn independently on another source, now lost to us, for the shared material. One feature that might seem promising, the reporting of others' discourse—here, "Come, let us go up to the mountain of Yhwh" and so forth—is a rhetorical move that is performed regularly in Micah's poetry (Mic 2:4, 6-7, 11; 3:5, 11; 4:11; 6:6-7; 7:10), but it occurs frequently in Isaianic poetry as well, particularly in material many consider to belong to earlier strata in the book (e.g., Isa 3:6-7; 5:19; 9:10; 10:13-14; 14:8, 10, 13-14, 16-17; 19:11; 21:8-9, 11-12; 22:13; 23:16; 28:9-10, 13, 15; 29:11-12, 15). In both Isaiah and Micah, it is usually opponents who are ventriloquized; this reported discourse of joyous allies in Isaiah 2 // Micah 4 is anomalous for both prophetic books.

My position is constructed from consideration of three distinct points within the broader arguments. First, the direction of literary dependence cannot be determined with certainty; eloquent and erudite interpreters are well able to construe evidence as pointing in one direction or the opposite direction, no position has commanded the field for long within Isaiah scholarship, and even if a position did muster broad assent, that would not mean the case had been proved. Second, the tropes and ideas in the shared material appear more native to the theology of Isaiah than to Micah. The glorification of Zion as the restored holy place of Yhwh and as an exquisite sanctuary of peace comes to stunning expression in Isa 11:6-10; 35:1-10; 52:7-10; 54:11-14; 58:11-14; 60:1-20; 61:10-11 (Daughter Zion is speaking); 62:1-12; 65:17-25; 66:10-13. But that could mean that later prophetic scribes worked to amplify the Isaiah traditions, as clearly has happened in the compositional history of that richly complex book; it cannot be taken to prove that the shared material must have originated with Isaiah rather than Micah. Third, this material makes excellent sense redactionally in Micah as a powerful response to the vision of desolation in Mic 3:12; the same cannot as readily be said of the material's location in Isaiah, where it follows blistering polemic against Jerusalem (Isa 1:21-25) and Yhwh's annihilation of unrepentant "rebels and sinners" (1:26-31). I believe it is likely, though it cannot be proved, that the material was quarried from Micah; see the commentary below.

Zion as Pinnacle of Godly Peace (4:1-4)

The contrast between Mic 3:12 and 4:1-2 is nothing short of astonishing. For readers or hearers proceeding sequentially through the scroll of Micah in antiquity, experiencing the dramatic shift to oracles of hope in Mic 4 would have been stirring. Calamity had leveled the city walls, the temple, and other central structures that supported Judean life in Jerusalem. Now the elevation of Zion brings floods of people from many nations to a rebuilt and glorious temple. They are eager to learn from Yhwh the lifeways that will ensure peace and flourishing, not just in Judah but—the sense of 4:4 is undeniable, given the preceding verses—across the whole earth.

In Mic 1, the prophet had portrayed Yhwh descending from the heavens to the high places of the earth to attend to the sins of Samaria and Jerusalem. This cataclysmic theophany would cause mountains to melt beneath the divine tread; the built structures of Samaria would crumble into rubble at the bottom of the steep slope on which the palace and other monumental structures had been sited. Samaria had indeed fallen to the Neo-Assyrian Empire in 722. Judeans watching developments at the time, and scribes of later generations studying the history of the Northern Kingdom as well, would have been chilled by prophetic proclamations of Yhwh's wrath. The

Micah 4

Fig. 14. Tympanum of Micah beating a sword into a plowshare, ca. 1220-1270. Pedimental sculpture in portal of south transept of the Basilique Cathédrale Notre-Dame d'Amiens. Photo by Manuel Cohen/Art Resource, NY.

imagery that traces the inexorable downward motion of Yhwh's descent in Mic 1 is met in Mic 4 by imagery that lifts the eyes of the audience to the radiance of Zion, now elevated above all other mountains. According to Micah, sin had caused the destruction of Samaria and would cause the destruction of Jerusalem. The remedy for sin is now at hand: nations will stream to Zion, the holy city shining atop the highest hill imaginable, and many peoples will learn together how to honor and obey Yhwh. After endless centuries of violence, peace will finally reign. From Zion will go forth "torah": this nuanced word can connote dimensions of halakic instruction, moral discipline, and spiritual formation in covenantal relationship. These precious gifts of Yhwh to Israel and Judah will be eagerly sought by many nations and peoples, underscoring the preeminence of Zion and the God enthroned in Jerusalem.

Communal Identity (4:5)

The prophetic scribe here lifts up "the name of Yhwh our God" as that to which this covenant community looks for its identity and path of life. Other peoples organize their communal life according to the names of their own deities, but Judah belongs to Yhwh. This stops short of explicitly asserting that Yhwh has allotted the worship of various deities to other nations, the astonishing claim we find in Deut 4:19-20, but the sharp contrast in Mic 4:5 between the observed polytheism of other peoples and Israel's dedication to Yhwh alone is powerfully resonant with that passage: "When you look up to the heavens and see the sun, the moon, and the stars, all the host of heaven, do not be led astray and bow down to them and serve them, things that the Lord your God has allotted to all the peoples everywhere under heaven. But the Lord has taken you and brought you out of the iron-smelter, out of Egypt, to become a people of [Yhwh's] very own possession, as you are now." Immediately following the parallel Isa 2 passage are verses that discuss other peoples as well, but the strong negative cast of those verses is quite different from the (arguably) studiedly neutral tone of Mic 4:5. In Isa 2:6-8 is a searing polemic attacking the "house of Jacob" for its relationships with "diviners from the east," "soothsayers like the Philistines," and foreigners who "bow down to the work of their hands." The calm statement in Mic 4:5, irenic by contrast, seems more in keeping with the tone of the preceding material shared in Mic 4:1-4 and Isa 2:2-4.

Zion's Restoration and Renewed Dominion (4:6-8)

A luminous oracle of restoration unfolds: Yhwh will gather from diaspora all those who had been injured and driven away. The motif of strength is central here. Yhwh had had the power to bring retribution on Judah, something made transparently clear in the last clause of 4:6, "those whom I had harmed," those upon whom the deity had purposefully brought catastrophe. Yhwh now has the power to draw Judean survivors from disparate locations into a cohesive remnant, refashioning a small community that, on the far side of disaster, can grow into a mighty nation and flourish anew. Daughter Jerusalem is to anticipate being empowered once again, enjoying political sovereignty to the impressive degree that the city had known in former days. While no temporal framework is specified by the prophetic scribe, it is plausible that the geopolitical power of the united monarchy is in view here.

Catastrophe, Then Rescue by Yhwh (4:9-13b)

As Mic 4 continues to unfold, the implied audience is compelled to turn from the rapturous prophetic vision of universal peace (4:1-4), consoling

Micah 4

images of Yhwh caring tenderly for those who had been driven away (4:6-7), and the restoration of sovereignty to Zion (4:8) to the terrifying reality of international warfare (4:9-10), with the concomitant threat of Zion's sexual violation by victorious enemies (4:11). It is a chilling transmutation. The "many nations" imagined as streaming eagerly to Zion to learn the ways of Yhwh in the future shape-shift back into the "many nations" in the present: adversaries eager to encamp in hostile array around Jerusalem. The prophet's words of hope are interleaved with minatory oracles about the inescapable harm done to Zion—as if the Micah traditions refuse to forget what Judah has suffered. The volatile oracular shifts in Mic 4-7, interweaving trauma and triumph, give the implied audience a wounded Zion who is transformed into an iconic figure of healing, victory, and peace. Here, as in other radiant passages of hope such as Jer 30-31 and Isa 60-62, Zion's former woundedness and apparent abandonment lend power to the imagery of Zion's magnificent vindication and resplendent honor in the envisioned future under Yhwh's universal sovereignty.

Micah 4:9 is best read as the prophet's sarcastic mockery of the people for not trusting in Yhwh. Here Micah is playing ironically on the deceptive reassurances offered by corrupt leaders as ventriloquized in 3:11c, "Is not Yhwh in our midst? Calamity will not come upon us!" The prophet's razor-sharp rhetorical questions in 4:9 do not mean, "Is there no king in your midst?" as if their human king were present and the prophet were excoriating the people for not trusting that king. No, the point is that Yhwh is their King—to their shame when they have ignored what Yhwh requires (see 6:8), but also for their redemption once they have paid the price for their malfeasance and sinful ways. The point of 4:9-5:1 (Heb. 4:14) is that Israel should trust in Yhwh as divine sovereign always, whether Israel is experiencing trauma or restoration. Calamity is indeed looming over Jerusalem, precisely because Judean leaders had not taken seriously their covenant obligations to Yhwh and to the vulnerable in their community. The horror of the Babylonian exile cannot be avoided—4:10 makes that clear, doubtless from the scribal perspective of hindsight—but Judah's divine King is indeed with the people, and thus Daughter Zion will be able to "arise and thresh" her enemies (4:13).

Daughter Zion's terrified screaming and violation by the Neo-Babylonian Empire are laid out in vivid, shocking imagery. Zion writhes and shrieks. Forced from her home, she is dragged by her captors out into the open field, a place where she is at grave risk of rape (cf. Deut 22:25-27), something made abundantly clear in Mic 4:11, where numerous adversaries snarl their

Israel under Threat 4:14 (Eng. 5:1)

intention to violate Zion sexually: "Let her be defiled, and let our gaze rove over Zion." That imagined scene of Zion's disempowerment and looming trauma is reversed, powerfully, in 4:12: Yhwh has been making plans of Yhwh's own, and the enemies of Judah will be cut down like scythed grain. Zion is bidden to arise in power, participating in the relentless "threshing" of all those who have gathered against Yhwh's people.

Zion Pledges the Spoils to Yhwh (4:13c)

The perspective here draws on the ancient Israelite tradition of holy war. Faithful Daughter Zion, envisioning her future triumph in battle, promises to dedicate the spoils of war to Yhwh the divine warrior, whose might will have secured victory for the covenant people. Holy-war traditions expressed in narrative form in Pentateuchal texts and in Joshua focus on the Israelite militarized conquest of indigenous Canaanite groups. Yhwh commands Israel to annihilate combatants and noncombatants alike (e.g., Deut 20:16-17; Josh 10:28-40), loot the villages and towns Israel has conquered (Josh 8:1-29 and other passages), and seize Canaanite land holdings as Israel's "inheritance." Here, the motif goes in a different direction. The "ill-gotten gains" amassed by enemy nations—likely meant is the plunder that Assyrian, Babylonian, and other invaders had seized from Israel, Judah, and other peoples—will be claimed by the victorious Zion and offered to Yhwh.

Israel under Threat (4:14 [Eng. 5:1])

Micah 4:14 in the Hebrew is 5:1 in the NRSV, RVR, and other translations influenced by the LXX. This variation in versification continues through Mic 5. The imagery of Judah's restoration and restored sovereignty (4:6-13) would have served to bolster the resolve of those loyal to Israel and Judah. This verse now returns to stark danger in the present: Zion is urged to muster armed resisters under conditions of siege. The identity of the enemy is left unexpressed. "He has laid siege against us" could theoretically call to mind Sennacherib's failed siege of Jerusalem in 701. But "Babylon" had been named explicitly in 4:10, and, for a postexilic audience, this verse would bring to mind the horror of Babylonian troops besieging Jerusalem from January 588 to the fall of the city in July 587. This dramatic note of fear and

Micah 4

resistance will yield, in Mic 5, to assurances that this time of tribulation will end and a messianic ruler will secure Israel's flourishing once more.

History of Consequences

For illustrative comments on Mic 4 in rabbinic midrash, see the introduction under §4.1.1 Midrashic Interpretations.

The Christian philosopher Justin Martyr (ca. 100–ca. 165) understands Micah's oracle about nations streaming to Zion as prophetic confirmation that the gentiles would repent when they had heard the preaching of Christ from Jerusalem (*Dial*. 109, ANF 1:253). On the divine word going forth, Justin offers that this was fulfilled in the preaching of the twelve apostles: "It did so come to pass.... For from Jerusalem there went out into the world men, twelve in number, and these illiterate, of no ability in speaking," yet they "were sent by Christ to teach to all the word of God" (*1 Apol*. 39, ANF 1:175-76). Numerous other Christian interpreters have promulgated this reading. Among them are Melito of Sardis (d. 180), who is surely alluding to the Prologue to the Gospel of John and 2 Cor 5:17 when he writes, "the law became Word, the old became new, together going forth from Zion and Jerusalem," and Clement of Alexandria (150–ca. 215), who waxes lyrical about that which proceeds from Zion as "'the heavenly Word, the true champion, who is being crowned upon the stage of the whole world,'" namely Christ (Roukema 2019, 104-5).

In *Against Heresies*, Irenaeus of Lyons (ca. 130–ca. 203) dismisses the notion that the rebuilding of the temple in the Persian period could be accounted the fulfilment of Micah's vision in 4:1-4. It was only the word of God "preached by the apostles" that effected "such a change in the state of things" that peace reigned across the world. Per Irenaeus, we know that Christ is the one who "made the plough," interpreted as the creation of Adam, "and introduced the pruning-hook," signaling the righteous by means of Abel, thereby preparing for "the gathering in of the produce in the last times by the Word" (*Haer*. 39.4, ANF 1:512).

To Methodius of Olympus (d. 311), bishop of Lycia and Tyre, is attributed a dialogue, *The Banquet of the Ten Virgins* (ANF 4:309-55), in which speakers debate the glories of virginity framed in theological and moral terms, characterizing this "supreme and blessed pursuit" as a virtue of those who, "vaulting over the stream of pleasure, direct the chariot of the soul upwards ... [to] contemplate immortality itself as it springs forth from the undefiled bosom of the Almighty" (310, 334). In this piece, Methodius refers to the idyllic scene in Mic 4:4 of God's people sitting peacefully under their own fig trees, noting that vines in Scripture often refer to Christ and fig trees signify the Holy Spirit. Placing the Micah passage alongside the healing of Hezekiah (2 Kgs 20:7 // Isa 38:21) and styling the fruits of the Spirit enumerated in Gal 5:22-23 as figs, Methodius cites Mic 4:4 as prophetic confirmation "that those who have taken refuge and rested under the Spirit, and under the shadow of the Word, shall not be alarmed, nor frightened by him [viz., Satan] who troubles the hearts of [humanity]" (350).

Jerome reads the nations streaming to Zion in light of the Pentecost scene in Acts 2 and the alacrity with which disciples follow Jesus when he calls: "The people will hasten when they together have believed in him, 'Parthians and Medes, Elamites and the inhabitants of Mesopotamia,'" and so on. Jerome continues, "Do they not seem to have hastened to the mountain to whom it is said, 'Follow me and I shall make you fishers of [people]?'" (Matt 4:19, of Simon and Andrew), then citing James and John, Matthew the tax collector, and the large crowds that follow Jesus to hear his teaching and be cured (*Comm. Mich.*, 71). The end of warfare indicates in historical terms the peace inaugurated by Constantine's acceptance of Christianity, when "Rome was allotted to the empire of Christ," but a spiritual reading suggests itself to Jerome as well: when a Christian "breaks the javelins and spears of insults" and "desires to harvest spiritual fruits," then "under the fig tree [that believer] plucks off the sweet fruits of the Holy Spirit: love, joy, peace, and all the rest" (72-73; for the fruits of the Spirit, see Gal 5:22-23). The "former dominion" or "first power" in Mic 4:8 refers, per Jerome, to the one "who said, 'I am alpha and omega, the beginning and the end, the first and the last'" (Jesus; Rev 22:13), elaborating this image of Christ via the figure of Wisdom in Prov 8:22 and three of Jesus's "I Am" sayings in John 6:51; 8:12; 15:1 (76-77). The horror evoked by Zion writhing and shrieking (Mic 4:9) is read by Jerome not as punitive but productive, linked to Paul's metaphor of being in labor until Christ be formed in believers in the churches in Galatia (Gal 4:19). The spiritual tenor of Jerome's readings is further evident in his interpretation of *bat gədûd*, translated in this commentary as "Daughter Raider," taken by Jerome as "the devil, who is always armed for the purpose of plundering" (80). The judge being struck upon the cheek (Mic 4:14 [Eng. 5:1]) is a prophecy of Jesus being struck during his interrogation (Matt 26:67-68; cf. Mark 14:65; Luke 22:63-64; John 19:3).

Micah 4

Cyril of Alexandria understands the prophesied restoration of Zion as effected by Christ in the incarnation: when "sacrifices according to the Law were at an end, the priesthood of the bloodline of Levi deserted ... and Jerusalem left desolate, Christ instituted the church from the nations ... at the end of this age, when he became like us," elaborating, "By *mountain*, therefore, he refers to the church, which is the house of the living God" (*Comm.*^{CA}, 221). Those who teach the ways of the LORD, per Cyril, are "clearly the disciples of the Savior ... to whom Christ said, "Go, make disciples of all nations, baptizing them ... [and] teaching them to observe all I have commanded you" (222, quoting Matt 28:19-20). Cyril frames the divine judging of peoples mentioned in Mic 4:3 as "the Word of God" having come "down to us from heaven" and becoming "for us *law* and lawgiver" (224 [emphasis original], quoting John 12:31). Micah's reference to a mighty or numerous nation in 4:7 is, for Cyril, best interpreted as "the holy multitude of those justified in Christ" (227).

The Franciscan friar Bonaventure (1221-1274) draws 4:1 into a discussion of the character of the "perfect prelate" in a sermon on the transfiguration for the second Sunday in Lent. The sermon, composed in 1267 or 1268 in Paris, has as its focal text Matt 17:1 (2008, 25-31). Taking Peter as representing clerical leadership throughout the history of the church, Bonaventure muses on ways in which ascending a spiritual "mountain" can be understood as moving from "the exercise of good works" to the higher plane of contemplation and elevation of the mind and the affections (211-12). The mountain's elevation means believers who ascend through contemplative praxis are better positioned to receive "divine radiance," the mountain's immovability conveys spiritual "stability for the virtuous toleration of all kinds of tribulation," and its visibility enables effective communication of the word of God through preaching (212). Bonaventure points to the peak of the mountains in Mic 4:1, then, as a symbol of the elevated position of prelates, who should display "the eminent excellence of evangelical perfection" through their "preached word and example of honest conduct" (213-14).

Calvin reads the opening lines of Mic 4 as prophesying the parousia. He preaches on 11 December 1550 that "all the world will be brought to God at the coming of our Lord Jesus Christ," for "Jesus Christ has been designated the Lord, not simply of one corner of the world, but of all nations" (2003, 200, 206). Calvin assures believers eager to walk in God's ways (4:2) that "the Gospel actually has the power to put us on the path that leads to obedience. It is no longer a matter of not knowing what to do, but of understanding the heart of life" (201–2). On the image of beating swords into plowshares, Calvin is more focused on local conflict than on wars among nations, urging that believers cease all "malice, cruelty, hate, and rancor" and help their neighbors (210–11), and expounding the spiritual meaning that sinners "were engaged in a moral war, in which God was forced to display [divine] wrath and vengeance" until they came to know peace in Christ (212). He pursues this trajectory further on 12 December 1550: "Since our Lord Jesus Christ's kingdom is spiritual, we ought not settle for a worldly peace based on our own appetites.... We must remember who we are and that this present life is only a passage through which we run in our haste" (217). His vitriolic opposition to Roman Catholicism issues in polemic regarding wars with "the papists, ... who have spewed their venom against the Gospel with a furious rage, so much so that they have gone to great lengths to destroy it by fire, sword, and numerous forms of torture" (219). Calvin laments the fragility of the peace believers should know in Christ: "it takes only a suggestion here and a whisper there to separate us from God," and "the slightest temptation is sufficient to distract us from the vocation to which God has called us" (225).

The image of all reclining under their own grapevine and fig tree in peace (4:4) is skillfully used by George Washington near the beginning of his term as first president of the United States, from 1789 to 1797. In Washington's letter of 18 August 1790 to a synagogue in Newport, Rhode Island, he responds warmly to a letter penned the previous day by Jewish civic leader Moises Seixas, averring that the United States supports all who are good citizens, not by a patronizing "tolerance" of difference but by active disavowal of bigotry and persecution. Washington writes, "May the Children of the Stock of Abraham, who dwell in this land, continue to merit and enjoy the good will of the other Inhabitants; while every one shall sit in safety under his own vine and fig tree, and there shall be none to make him afraid" (1996). Washington's letter has been influential in discussions of religious liberty in the United States (Fuchs 2021, 367); it is exhibited regularly at the National Museum of Jewish History in Philadelphia.

Among tablets written by Ḥusayn-'Alí, known as Bahá'u'lláh (1817–1892), the founder of the Bahá'í faith, is the tablet Bisəhárát ("Glad-Tidings"). Language about nonviolence in the fifth teaching there draws on 4:1–3: "Perchance the fire of animosity which blazeth in the hearts of some of the peoples of the earth may, through the living

Micah 4

waters of divine wisdom . . . be quenched, and the light of unity and concord may . . . shed its radiance in the world. We cherish the hope that through the earnest endeavors of such as are the exponents of the power of God . . . the weapons of war throughout the world may be converted to instruments of reconstruction and that strife and conflict may be removed from the midst of [humanity]" (Bahá'u'lláh 1978).

For an 1857 sermon by Rabbi David Woolf Marks in West London that evokes 4:1-3, and a 1917 sermon by Rabbi J. Leonard Levy in Pittsburgh that reads 4:4 as an ideal not relevant for pragmatic responses in wartime, see the introduction under §4.1.2 Modern Jewish Interpretations.

Micah's vision of peace is featured in a homily by Baptist minister Sutton E. Griggs (1872-1933) entitled "A Hero Closes a War," recorded with preacher, two sopranos, two altos, one tenor, and piano on 18 September 1928 and released in January 1929 (BVE-47056; for a transcript, see Tracy 1986, 161-62). Sutton opens with Mic 4:3b on not learning war any longer, then tells the story of a crew of "white and Negro men" whose boat capsized in the Chesapeake Bay during World War I. At first, the white sailors allowed only white crew members onto the bottom of the upturned craft. "Seeing the racial conflict, one Negro swam away" to rescue two white sailors first, then a Black sailor. The unspoken point was taken that "the ultimate good" of all could be preserved, and per Sutton, "the race war was over." The preaching event ends with the choral group singing six times, "Ain't gonna study war no more."

For a 1937 interview in which the formerly enslaved Nan Stewart (b. 1850) describes what it meant to her to hear Black preachers expound Mic 4:4, see the introduction under §4.2.3 Early Modern to Contemporary Christian Interpretations.

Claiming the swords-to-plowshares vision (4:1-3) as foundational for peace movements, Berrigan observes that in this oracle, the nations "have ceased to be—themselves: incurably, addictively, perennially violent. . . . Against the brutal derangement of our humanity wrought by war upon war, they discover—the ways of peace." Berrigan wonders, "Are we teachable at all?," given "the wars, the preparations for war, the enduring irreformable ways of war—in Vietnam, and Panama, and Iraq." The seasoned peace activist concludes with more ambivalence than Micah shows: "A hard lesson this, and never entirely learned: that we learn to behave humanly in a world which is manifestly and virulently inhuman" (1995, 226).

RETROSPECT

Zion's shattering military defeat by the Neo-Babylonian Empire, horrific as that had been, is acknowledged as the ground from which her repair and renewal will grow. Of the feminist KILLJOY's mandate to speak prophetic truth so as to disrupt denial about experiences of violence, Ahmed says, "Killing joy is a world-making project. We make a world out of the shattered pieces even when we shatter the pieces or even when we are the shattered pieces" (2017, 261). A crucial dimension of the power of visions of healing and peace is that they can form, in those who have survived violence and those who have witnessed it, an ethical commitment never to participate in such harms in future. Maintaining such a stance, for those gathered around the book of Micah as sacred Scripture, requires ongoing theological and political work. Plaskow writes,

> When spirituality is understood from a feminist perspective—not in otherworldly terms, but as the fullness of our relationship to ourselves, others, and God—it cannot possibly be detached from the conditions of our existence. Those ideologies and institutions that alienate us from ourselves and link us with others in relationships of domination and subordination militate against our spirituality on every level. In a sexist, heterosexist, anti-Semitic, class-ridden, and racist world, politics becomes the necessary work we do to make the world safe for the full realization and embodiment of spirituality. (1990, 213)

Ahmed underlines the feminist KILLJOY's commitment to nonviolent social transformation, work that "requires an ongoing and willful refusal to identify our hopes with inclusion in organizations predicated on violence" (2017, 264). While oracles of vengeance are not absent from the book of Micah, the effulgent promise of 4:3 can be mustered as a robust countertext for those seeking a peace that does not require the diminishment or destruction of the Other.

Bey ponders the ways in which Black and trans persons have been violated by injustice—by the "painful extirpative history" experienced by "black and trans flesh in the Western world"—and observes that in throwing off the ideological chains of cruelty, hatred, and incomprehension, they can learn to embrace FUGITIVITY as a mode in which they may "existentially thrive through the habitus of doing uprootedness" (2022, 108). Those who choose FUGITIVITY can make their way in a new landscape—not a pristine

Micah 4

"discovered" land to be colonized afresh, but a "hostile landscape" that is being transformed by their encounters with it, by the work of FUGITIVE resistance (98). What Bey says of this imagined terrain of freedom may also be said of the terrain in which Micah glimpses every Judean at peace and unafraid under their own grapevine: "I'm not sure we know this world, or can know it now, anytime before it comes. But it is imperative that we hope for this world and, even if it comes to pass that such a world is not possible, love it and live it *regardless*" (108 [emphasis original]).

Micah's vision might seem prosaic in its particulars, but quiet enjoyment of a fruiting vine near one's doorstep is surely something for which incarcerated persons, prisoners of war, refugees, and other dispossessed persons yearn. Carceral violence works not only through the enforcement of crushing social alienation, monstrous acts of torture, and outright execution, but also through the suppression or distortion of countless minor moments that would normally constitute the choices and textures of daily life. Bey urges us to recognize that it is in the quotidian that freedom is known: "Abolition, the world-making of fugitive hope, occurs in the mundane places of our subjectivity, or the minutiae of our living" (211). Such abolitionary moments sustain the vision of a transformed world. Bey calls us to join their visionary community, using language reminiscent of the first-person plural invitation in Mic 4:2 to ascend the holy mountain and learn peace:

> Come, radically imagine with us, with black trans feminism. Radically imagine what a world and our relation to others could be if we did not predicate sociality on transactional exchanges or violent presuppositions or ontological foreclosures or skewed life chances. . . . Imagine what abolition will feel like, that world in which prisons and logics of captivity—all forms of captivity—are, by definition of the existence of such a world, impossible. Imagine the kinds of beings we might dream ourselves into becoming. (228)

As described in the introduction, here is the spectrum of possibilities I have limned for contemporary responses to Micah's prophetic witness: → resilience → resistance → reformation → rejoicing. Micah 4 builds *resilience* in those struggling with the disorientation and grief caused by forcible separation from their community and heritage, sustaining them with the promise that a gracious God has not forgotten them and will return them, restored and strengthened, to their cherished homeland (4:6–7). Micah 4 catalyzes *resistance* to the shame and powerlessness imputed to a community by its enemies (4:11) or internalized in individuals' or groups' self-understanding: Micah thunders that the community's time will come to "arise and thresh" (4:13) all the adversaries who had violated and despised this people beloved of God. Micah 4 calls for *reformation* of ideologies of hopelessness, inviting those whose spirits are broken to trust that their circumstances will be transformed by a God who is indeed in their midst (4:9) even in times of trauma and bitter distress. Finally, Mic 4 holds space for *rejoicing* at the prospect of honoring justice and righteousness within a global community, celebrating the luminous vision of throngs of people eager to learn the precepts of YHWH and live out their new understanding peaceably (4:1-4).

MICAH 4 AND ECOLOGICAL JUSTICE

Micah 4 offers a spectacular vision of Mount Zion as cosmic beacon of holiness and peaceful coexistence for all the nations of the earth. In an imagined future saturated with obedience to the torah, warfare has ceased and the cultivation of agricultural abundance has become the focus of human expertise and meaningful work. As Braaten puts it, "The elites' instruments of war and domestic control will be fashioned into tools for the farmers, who will once again enjoy the full harvest of their Land" (2022, 160). This vision is promulgated in Isa 2 as well, amplified further in that prophetic book by Isaiah's stunning vision of God's peaceable kingdom, a vision that portrays harmony having transformed predatory and venomous interspecies relations into relationships of care and companionship (Isa 11:6-9). Since the dawn of human culture, disastrous consequences have unfolded from war, whether enacted at the level of regional disputes marked by sporadic combat and local ecological despoliation, or in sustained international warfare conducted through massive troop deployments and weapons of enormous destructive range that decimate large swaths of terrain.

Families and larger kinship groups, whole communities, and even entire cultures are ravaged by war. The material and financial costs of the war industry are incalculable. Paul Hawken updates a famous 1953 speech by Dwight Eisenhower to make this plain. Quoting Eisenhower's words, "Every gun that is made, every warship launched, every rocket fired signifies . . . a theft from those who hunger and are not fed, those who are cold and are not clothed," Hawken offers these contemporary statistics: "The cost of one B-2 bomber totals a new middle school in seventy-five cities, seventy-two solar

Micah 4

power plants serving 4.15 million people, thirty-six fully equipped hospitals, and 281,000 electric vehicle charging stations. We pay for a single F-35 Lightning fighter jet with 22 million bushels of wheat" (Hawken 2021, 226). Vast numbers of living creatures, not just human beings, are terrorized, maimed, and killed in armed conflicts, or are left to wander landscapes rendered desolate for a season, for years, or even for generations. War destroys built infrastructure and blocks access to urgently needed resources, inflicting terrible harms on combatants and noncombatants alike. Climate change and armed conflict have mutually intensifying effects on populations caught in their nexus, as the IPCC points out: "Vulnerability is higher in locations with poverty, governance challenges and limited access to basic services and resources, violent conflict and high levels of climate-sensitive livelihoods (e.g., smallholder farmers, pastoralists, [and] fishing communities)," and it is certain that "future human vulnerability will continue to concentrate where the capacities of local, municipal and national governments, communities and the private sector are least able to provide infrastructures and basic services" (IPCC 2022 §B.2.4-5). Deleterious effects of armed conflict include not only bodily injury and blocked access to needed resources, but also paralyzing anxiety and fear, grief, temporary or intractable pain, moral injury, emotional trauma, posttraumatic stress, and spiritual harm. These harms will become only more widespread as the ecological crisis worsens, for "at higher global warming levels, impacts of weather and climate extremes, particularly drought, by increasing vulnerability will increasingly affect violent intrastate conflict" (IPCC 2022 §B.4.7).

Justice-minded readers of Micah await the fulfilment of the prophet's vision of global *shalom*: people relaxing and refreshed under their own fruiting grapevines and fig trees, and all of God's creatures thriving with "no one to terrify them" (Mic 4:4). In the interregnum, we can work locally to transform the cultural terrains and biospheres of Earth into an expanding network of safe places. Debra Rienstra speaks of refugia, conceived as "small, humble, hidden places" in which we can "concentrate on protecting and nurturing a few good things, let what is good and beautiful grow and connect and spread," allowing them to "operate as microcountercultures ... where we prepare for new ways of living and growing" (2022, 5). For ancient audiences and contemporary readers, Mic 4:1-4 fosters hope, an essential and catalytic element of every initiative that spurs ethical action or political transformation. The alternatives are difficult indeed: cynicism, inaction, despair, or, worst of all, complicity with the distorted evil ideologies and violence that ground systems of oppression of the vulnerable within the living community of Earth. Veronice Miles writes, "Evil imaginings [make] those of us who surrender to such impulses unwitting accomplices in dehumanization's deep entrenchment in our world today.... Hope, on the other hand, calls us to a life of vocation, invites us to say yes to God's yes for creation and for our lives by adopting God's vision of *shalom* as our own.... Hope-filled imaginings engender life" (2021, 220). With its breathtaking imagery and powerfully hopeful perspective, the opening vision of Mic 4 draws readers deeper into torah traditions to learn lifeways of obedience that celebrate the purposes of God in globally constituted communities. The process of working together is arduous—politically, socially, and spiritually. But the suffering community of Earth needs believers to commit themselves to "work in equitable, just and enabling ways to reconcile divergent interests, values and worldviews, toward equitable and just outcomes" (IPCC 2022 §D.2.1). Micah's vision of globally joyful obedience to the Holy will not be realized overnight. Judean scribes in antiquity knew that as well as we do. But every moment of such obedience, every refugium created—no matter how modest in scope—can help foster the conditions for global peace and the flourishing of the interconnected communities of Earth.

COMMENTARY

Micah 4 directs our attention to the entanglements of visionary hope for the future and dread in the conflictual present. The prophet's portrayal of Zion as center of torah learning and radiant beacon of hope to the world (4:1-4) yields to consolation of a wailing and terrified Daughter Zion who is facing the threat of forced migration and violation (4:9-11). What Heschel says of the oracle in Isa 2:2-4 is equally true of its Micah parallel: "Politics is based on the power of the sword," and "war spawns death," so the prophetic task was to teach believers that their "security lies in the covenant with God" rather than in geopolitical machinations (2001, 92). "What to us seems inconceivable," Heschel writes, to Isaiah and Micah "was a certainty: War will be abolished. They shall not learn war any more because they shall seek knowledge of the word of God. Passion for war will be subdued by a greater passion: the passion to discover God's ways" (235).

Micah 4:1-4 appears in nearly identical form in Isa 2:1-4. The literature on this is vast and cannot be summarized here. Arguments about literary dependence have been presented in several directions. Some argue that the Micah traditions were influenced by Isaiah. Others aver that the scribes

Micah 4

responsible for Isaiah drew on Micah, which is my own position (so also, among others, Müller 2011; Spans 2018, 443). Yet others argue that both may have drawn independently on a third source, or that it is not possible to know. Robert Wilson suggests that "both Isaiah and Micah were edited by the same group" (1980, 275). Sweeney offers, "it appears that the two passages were written to engage intertextually in dialogue with each other," while stopping short of taking a position on literary priority (2020, 162). For Sweeney, reading in the context of Isa 2-4 and the Cyrus material in Isa 44-45, "Isaiah envisions a restored Israel as part of a larger Persian empire . . . under the sovereignty of Yhwh"; in the Micah material, framed with reference to Mic 4-5, the "dichotomy between the nations and Israel is . . . fostered throughout the book" and the prophet "points to the emergence of an independent state, ruled by a Davidic monarch, that will bring Yhwh's punishment to the nations" (2001, 121-22).

The opening oracle in Isa 2 echoes the vision of global illumination. The passage here in Mic 4 is not characteristic of the rest of Micah theologically, whereas the Servant Songs and other material in Deutero-Isaiah do underline that the light of Yhwh's teaching is for all peoples (Isa 42:1-4; 45:20-25; 49:1-6; 51:4-5; 55:1-5). But this oracle makes excellent sense positioned at the crucial transition from Mic 1-3 to the rest of the scroll of Micah, whereas in my view, the material sits more awkwardly in its Isaiah context.

In support of the position that the shared material has a literarily organic and compelling priority in the book of Micah, I offer the following. Reported discourse is important in Micah. In my view, the quoting of the nations in Mic 4:2 plays a crucial role as a structural hinge between the two panels of the diptych of the book of Micah. Each panel offers three instances of reported negative discourse of antagonists. The first panel (Mic 1-3) shows the oppressive elites' distorted thinking about the catastrophe that looms over Jerusalem (2:4, 6; 3:11), while in the second panel (Mic 4-7), Micah ventriloquizes Judah's enemies and a worshipper who purports not to understand what the covenant with Yhwh requires (4:11; 6:6-7; 7:10). The "hinge" quotation in 4:2 of the nations streaming to Zion to learn the ways of Yhwh expresses the exemplary eagerness for torah learning and obedience that will mark the relationship with Yhwh in the idyllic future: a covenantal fidelity that is to be cherished by every constituency, including Judah. As I see it, the shared material in Isa 2:2-4 // Mic 4:1-3 is of enormous importance structurally in the book of Micah; it plays no such role in Isa 2 or the broader immediate context there, beyond serving as a luminous island of hope in a sea of judgment oracles. This point, that the shared passage functions in

Commentary

Micah in a structurally vital role, while an analogous role cannot be predicated of the passage in its Isaiah locus, does not prove that the material was expressed first in the Micah traditions (as opposed to in another source now lost to us), nor does it prove that the material was retrieved from Micah by the Isaiah tradents, though both may have been true. But I do stake a claim for the organic and important role of the material in Micah, however the passage may have come to the attention of the prophetic scribe.

4:1 *in the latter days.* Often translated "in days to come," *bəʾaḥărît hayyāmîm* gestures proleptically toward time in the distant future of history, in a cultural perspective presented, implicitly or explicitly, as informed by a discerning perspective trained on the former times. Those days of old had been characterized by the wondrous deeds and salvific acts of Yhwh in delivering Israel from enslavement in Egypt, establishing the torah at Sinai, and prospering Israel's invasion and settlement of Canaan. Those events in the distant past are grounding for Israelite and Judean identity in history, moving forward. Other occurrences of *bəʾaḥărît hayyāmîm* in the Latter Prophets include the line in the parallel passage in Isa 2:2; Jer 23:20; 30:24; 48:47; 49:39; Ezek 38:16; Dan 10:14; and Hos 3:5.

mountain of the House of Yhwh. Christl Maier explains that "Zion," topographically speaking, "refers to the southeastern ridge from which the settlement of Jerusalem emerged," and in the Hebrew Bible, the appellation is used also "for the entire eastern hill including the temple precinct until early Byzantine time, when the name erroneously became attached to the southwestern hill" (2021, 261). In the verse following this one, the nations streaming to Zion urge one another to approach "the mountain of Yhwh," and there, the allusion to Mount Sinai is undeniably strong. Here, while Sinai may (also) be in view, the idea of the Zion temple as mountaintop abode of the deity is more likely trading on the trope of cosmic mountain in ancient Near Eastern traditions (Morales 2012, 1-20; Irudayaraj 2021). This ideology is perceptible in the background or foreground of many Hebrew Bible texts, including these: Exod 15:17 ("you brought them in and planted them on the mountain of your own possession, the place, O Lord, that you made your abode"); descriptions in Exod 19; 20; and 24 of the theophany of Yhwh on Sinai; and poetic texts such as Pss 3:5 (Eng. 4); 43:3; 48:1-2; 68:15-17; 74:2; 78:54; and 87:1-2.

established as the peak of the mountains. Literally the "head" of all earthly mountains, expressing the tenet of cosmic-mountain ideology that this sacred place is "the central and highest place of the world (*axis mundi*)"

Micah 4

with "its paradisiacal summit reaching into the divine abode" (Morales 2012, 2-3). For *nākôn*, Micah[LXX] has *emphanes* ("manifest, visible") here and at the parallel in Isa 2:2, but uses another modifier here as well, *hetoimon* ("ready, prepared"), that is absent from the Isaiah passage. Gelston suggests that this constitutes a "double interpretation" of *nākôn* (BHQ, 102). The semantic valence of unassailable preparation via divine purpose may be being emphasized in the second modifier: *nākôn* is used in a number of Hebrew Bible passages to articulate the motif of the irrevocably fixed and efficacious plan of YHWH (e.g., Gen 41:32; 2 Sam 7:16, 26; 1 Kgs 2:45; 1 Chr 17:14, 24; Ps 93:2). Explicating the elevation of Zion above other mountains important in Israel's history, Rashi (1040-1105) comments on the parallel verse in Isa 2:2, "On Mt. Sinai the nation received the Torah ... on Mt. Carmel, the prophet Elijah proved God's omnipotence through the descent of a heavenly fire ... and on Mt. Tabor, the Jewish armies defeated the armies of Sisera.... The miracles that will occur on the Temple Mount in Messianic times will greatly surpass these miracles" (Stavsky 2009, 28).

elevated above the hills. Zion's ascendancy is imaged topographically in an extended metaphor that expresses the visibility of YHWH's favor for Jerusalem before all the world, underscoring the cosmic significance of this temple. L. Michael Morales avers that given "its many mythic attributions in ... the Psalms and in the prophetic literature, Zion is perhaps the mountain most obviously cosmic in the religion of Israel, the ... gateway of both heaven and the underworld" (2012, 17). Mays muses, "With the elevation of Zion, the life-giving power of YHWH's *tōrāh*, creating justice and bringing salvation, is revealed, and a hunger and thirst for the word of YHWH draws a swelling tide of people to its source" (1976, 97).

peoples will stream to it. The verb *nhr* means "flow [like a river]" in Mic 4:1 // Isa 2:2 and Jer 51:44, with the subject articulated as peoples or nations. But the verb conveys a closely related semantic sense in biblical texts with literal or figurative liturgical overtones: "to shine, to be radiant (with joy)" (HALOT 2:676) in the presence of God who provides from limitless divine beneficence and in whose sovereign protection the believing community takes refuge. The verb occurs in this sense in Ps 34:6; Jer 31:12; and Isa 60:5, and the covenantal implications are clear. YHWH acts as divine warrior on behalf of those who know the stipulations of torah and obey them—"the angel of the LORD encamps around those who fear [YHWH] and delivers them" (Ps 34:7), and "YHWH has delivered Jacob ... from the hand of one stronger than he is" (Jer 31:11)—causing the people to beam with joyous gratitude as they delight in the abundant grain, wine, oil, and herds that YHWH

Commentary

has provided for their flourishing (Jer 31:12). The resplendent glory of Yhwh will illumine the holy place, Zion, when the rest of the earth is shrouded in darkness; Zion will "see and be radiant" as nations approach Yhwh's temple to offer tribute (Isa 60:2–7). As regards the verb *nhr* in Mic 4:1, then, the ancient audience might hear the streaming of nations to Zion as subtly evoking the covenant people's liturgical joy and the dazzling glory of Yhwh as Sovereign over all the earth. Andersen and Freedman go a step further in ascribing "eschatological fervor" to the worshippers (2000, 403), something we might more aptly imagine as having animated the prophetic scribe who composed the passage.

In the image of the nations offering tribute, the implication of Yhwh's subjugation of the entire earth is transparently clear. This connection is dramatically articulated in Isa 66, where the wealth of subdued nations comes like an "overflowing stream" to Zion (66:12), and Yhwh's burning "indignation" against enemies ensures their annihilation (66:14–16), such that all will have heard of Yhwh's military renown and (terrifying) glory. The streaming of the nations to Zion here is described in vivid terms as involving the return of diaspora Judeans: "They shall bring all your kindred from all the nations as an offering to the Lord, on horses, and in chariots, and in litters, and on mules, and on dromedaries, to my holy mountain Jerusalem, says the Lord" (66:20), and the Israelite priesthood will be rebuilt, for Yhwh will "take some of them as priests and as Levites" (66:21). While the imagery in Mic 4:1–3 does not provide such details, in the final form of Mic 4 there can be no question that the peace envisioned by the prophet does involve the military subjugation of enemy nations, for Yhwh "will gather them liked scythed grain to the threshing floor" and Zion will trample them with her mighty hooves of bronze (4:11–13).

4:2 "*Come, let us go up to the mountain of Yhwh!*" The streaming of peoples and nations to Zion foregrounds the Jerusalem temple and the torah teaching of the priests in a lyrical vision of global eagerness for wisdom and peace. Brueggemann observes a contrast here with the trope of subjugated nations honoring Judah in ritual signals of abjection or coming to render mandated tribute to Yhwh as victorious sovereign, a tradition expressed in a number of texts in the Latter Prophets (e.g., Isa 45:14; 49:7, 23; 60:5–16; 66:12). Here, "The nations come gladly, willingly, and expectantly. They are not coerced or compelled by the political force of the Davidic house, but have come in recognition that this is the only place where the way to peace and justice is available"; thus, "the intention of [Yhwh], as embodied in

Micah 4

the Torah, is the clue and guidance to world peace" (1997, 501, 594). An echo of this captivating motif can be heard in the so-called Book of Consolation, poetic oracles of restoration within the Deutero-Jeremianic prose traditions that likely were introduced into the book of Jeremiah late in its complex history of development. In Jer 31:5-6, Daughter Zion is assured that she will plant vineyards again on the mountains of Samaria, for there will be a day when northern sentinels on "the mountain of Ephraim" will call, "Come, let us go up to Zion, to Yhwh our God!" (Sharp 2022a, 166). The verb *nāhărû*, taken from *nhr* I in Mic 4:1 (// Isa 2:2) and translated as the action of the people "streaming" to Zion, occurs also in Jer 31:12, where it is taken from *nhr* II (*HALOT* 2:676) and translated as the quality of returning Judeans "being radiant" over the goodness of Yhwh on Mount Zion (so also Ps 34:6). In all instances of this verb in the Hebrew Bible, whether derived from root I or root II, the context suggests being drawn (in)to the abundance and security guaranteed by a powerful sovereign, though the image is one of reversal in Jer 51:44 regarding Babylonia: peoples will no longer stream toward Babylon, Jeremiah prophesies, when the Neo-Babylonian Empire is defeated. In Tg. Mic 4:2, the nations will go to "the house of *the Shekinah of* the God of Jacob," the characteristic targumic insertion designed to avoid too direct a suggestion of anthropomorphism regarding the deity.

instruct us in [Yhwh's] ways. The idea that the nations will learn torah in Zion draws Sinai into the center of this poetic imagery of the cosmic mountain. About the Sinai traditions, Morales says, "the fiery Presence upon its summit (Exod 19.16-20; 20.18-21; 24.9-18), perhaps Israel's ultimate experience of theophany, establishes Sinai as a cosmic mountain" (2012, 17). The nations' eagerness may refract something of the joy that believers are said to experience in studying torah per Ps 119: they discover "wondrous things" in the treasured, revivifying, sweet, and luminous word of Yhwh (Ps 119:11, 18, 25, 103, 105). For the MT phrase "[Yhwh's] ways," the targum offers a fuller and more precisely defined predicate: "that we may walk in *the teaching of his law*." Cathcart and Gordon explain, "According to the thinking of the Targumist humans can learn acceptable modes of conduct from God, but they and God do not act in the same way" (1989, 119n4).

From Zion will go forth torah. The absence of the definite article suggests this is not necessarily "the Torah" in the sense of the entire law given to Moses on Sinai. Yet the word "instruction," standing alone as, for example, in the NRSV and NJPS, signals no necessary association with that specific gift of Yhwh on Sinai, an association essential to the meaning of the Hebrew. Kessler observes that *tôrâ* occurs in eight books of the Twelve (Hosea, Amos,

Micah, Habakkuk, Zephaniah, Haggai, Zechariah, and Malachi). While at Mic 4:2 the term signifies concrete instruction, in other occurrences of the word across the Book of the Twelve, an eschatological perspective emerges, and "we get the vision of universal peace" (2016, 218-19). Andersen and Freedman find significant the absence of any mention of priests instructing the people: "Micah's silence on this detail is not just due to hostility against the priests in Jerusalem, who were condemned in 3:11. It contrasts with the apologetic concern of the postexilic community to legitimate the greater role of priests as givers of Torah" (2000, 405). O'Brien, who understands the scroll of Micah to be the product of Persian-period scribes, reads this material in precisely the opposite direction: "In its privileging of Torah, the vision of Mic 4 clearly reflects the interests of the scribal class. Those who preserve, copy, read, and interpret Torah mediate its power.... As a member of this scribal class, the writer of Micah would have clearly benefitted from a future in which all people recognize the importance of the texts in which he is an expert" (2015, 43-44). I acknowledge the acuity of her point, but I would valence this in a different way, as I consider the scribe who wrote this oracle. As one who cherishes Israel's and Judah's sacred traditions, who has devoted his life to mediating their transformative lifeways to his community and who glimpses their extraordinary potential for adjudicating conflicts, this prophetic scribe can see luminous benefit for all—not just himself—in attending deeply to Yhwh's torah.

The verb "go forth" (*yṣʾ*) may imply streaming forth from the summit of Zion. Diana Edelman (2015, 317) underlines "the association of Torah with a flowing or running river" here and in Sir 24, where the "book of the covenant of the Most High God" is said to overflow with wisdom and understanding like the rivers Pishon, Tigris, Euphrates, and Jordan; the torah "pours forth instruction like the Nile, like the Gihon" (Sir 24:23-27).

4:3 [Yhwh] will judge among many peoples. The characterization of Yhwh as divine judge has a venerable history in Hebrew Bible traditions. The deity, understood across biblical literature as "the Judge of all the earth" (Gen 18:25; cf. 1 Chr 16:33), is portrayed as assessing the righteousness or malfeasance of individuals and communities (Exod 5:21; 1 Kgs 8:31-32 // 2 Chr 6:23; Job 21:22; 23:7; Ps 7:9 [Eng. 8], 12 [Eng. 11]; Ps 9 and numerous other psalms; Lam 3:59; Ezek 5:10, 15 and passim), adjudicating conflicts between individuals (Gen 16:5; 31:53; 1 Sam 24:13 [Eng. 12], 16 [Eng. 15]; Jer 11:20), and rendering judgments on behalf of Israel and Judah against enemy nations and their gods (Exod 6:6; 7:4; 12:12; Num 33:4; Judg 11:27;

Micah 4

Fig. 15. *Let Us Beat Swords into Ploughshares*, by Evgeniy Vuchetich (1908-1974). Bronze sculpture. Gift in December 1959 from the USSR to the United Nations. In the garden of the United Nations headquarters in New York.

2 Chr 20:12; Isa 33:22; 66:16; Jer 25:31; Joel 4:1-17 [Eng. 3:1-17]). God's appointed messianic ruler, too, is capable of enacting God's divine power as judge of all nations (Isa 11:2-4).

to a vast distance. Yhwh's power to arbitrate—to adjudicate disputes and resolve matters governing the life of the community—extends across the known world. The point is not that some of the relevant nations are far away, but that the judicial power of Yhwh extends far beyond Zion, beyond Judah, and beyond the Levant.

swords into plowshares . . . spears into pruning hooks. Implements of maiming and death will be hammered into agricultural tools to cultivate the soil and coax abundant produce from fields and vineyards, imagery that would foster an affective response of peace and gladness in the implied audience as they contemplate tranquility and satiation. This captivating rhetorical move is reversed in Joel 4:10-13 (Eng. 3:10-13), where the nations are apostrophized with a bellicose imperative to "beat your plowshares into swords, and your pruning hooks into spears" in preparation for a warrior-led "harvest" as bloodbath among the nations.

no longer study war. J. J. M. Roberts has argued cogently that the peace envisioned in the parallel passages in Isa 2 and Mic 4 is tantamount to the cessation of warfare under the sovereignty of a restored Davidic monarchy, with "an idealized Davidic king and his court, as well as priests and prophets, as the human agents of Yhwh's imperial rule over the nations," and "the conceptual world behind the texts" assuredly "still that of an imperial state centered in Jerusalem" (2007, 123). Yet this oracle goes further than the acclamation of Yhwh in Ps 46:10 (Eng. 9) as one who "makes wars cease to the end of the earth," who "breaks the bow, and shatters the spear," and "burns the shields with fire." Here in Mic 4, the prophetic scribe limns a dramatic contrast between learning the ways of Yhwh (4:2) and learning the strategies and weaponry of warfare (4:3). Geopolitical relations among peoples will be transformed for all time.

Fig. 16. Schwerter zu Pflugscharen patch. Cloth, ca. 1980. Textile badge affixed by East German peace activists to clothing and bags.

4:4 *Each one will sit underneath their own grapevine.* The quiet enjoyment of shelter and agricultural produce one has tended with one's own hands is cherished across cultures in every historical era. Micah 1–3 has rendered in vivid terms the economic inequities and military exploitation of Judean people and land by agents of violence, leaving those subsisting in or near

Micah 4

poverty unable to support themselves. Micah's vision of tranquility in 4:4 represents an iconic view of sustainable life in a landscape in which war and economic predation are no more. Illuminating here are the terms of a 2003 report produced by La Comisión de Verdad Histórica y Nuevo Trato, an official body that sought to secure and safeguard such quiet enjoyment for oppressed communities in Chile, including indigenous peoples exploited by colonial powers for generations. According to Patricio Aylwin and José Aylwin, the report "acknowledges a set of rights for the indigenous peoples over natural resources that are found in their lands and territories," including "rights of protection for the ecosystems, panoramic beauties, and other patrimonial resources needed for their economic and cultural development" (2014, 88–91). This is precisely what the prophetic scribe envisions as the plan of Yhwh for the covenant people, already inscribed in the torah that will go forth from Zion to the nations in an idyllic future time of peace.

the mouth of Yhwh of Hosts has spoken. This is the only time the epithet "Yhwh of Hosts" appears in Micah, though it is common in the Hebrew Bible, occurring 265 times (*HALOT* 3:996). Within the Book of the Twelve, the term occurs most densely in the postexilic books Haggai, Zechariah, and Malachi. Not found in the Pentateuch, the appellation occurs in 1–2 Samuel, 1–2 Kings, 1 Chronicles, the Psalms, and very often in Isaiah and Jeremiah; similar formulations appear in other biblical books as well. While the semantic force of this divine title may not always be martial in a strictly formal sense (Quine 2019, esp. 754–55), it is clear that the term speaks to divine power: Yhwh is invincible as the Divine Commander of rank upon rank of heavenly beings, and the orders Yhwh gives will unfailingly be executed. Andersen and Freedman observe of the divine appellation that it "suits the theme of cosmic warfare in the prophets. At this point in Micah it befits the belligerent tone of the following prophecies, for a recapitulation of the *pax Solomonica* must be preceded by the wars of David" (2000, 410). Regarding Mic 4–5, Andersen and Freedman repeatedly press the claim that the "golden age of David and Solomon" funds the vision of the prophetic scribe (413, 495). The argument is not fully persuasive, especially when based on as thin a connection as the mention of "horses" in 5:9 (Eng. 10), which they link to Solomon having "introduced horses and chariots" in Israelite military history (491; 1 Kgs 10:26, 28 describes Solomon as having imported horses from Egypt and Kue [Cilicia], amassing "fourteen hundred chariots and twelve thousand horses").

4:5 in the name of its own god. This clause about other peoples following their deities is rendered euphemistically in Micah[LXX] with "each [walks] in its own way" (*hekastos tēn hodon autou*), avoiding the undesirable implication that there are, in fact, gods other than Yhwh (*BHQ*, 102). The targum moves in the opposite direction, making quite clear that non-Israelite peoples are committing idolatry, rendering, "Though all the peoples *shall be guilty because they worshipped idols*," Judah will rely only on Yhwh. This MT verse, the diction and ideology of which are unlike anything else in Micah, has the character of a secondary comment on 4:1-4. That it is contesting the earlier material is not clear, *pace* McKeating, who dubs it "astonishing" and "an explicit denial of the prophecy in the preceding four verses" (1971, 173). The apparently neutral tone of the comment that other peoples worship other gods finds a degree of resonance in Hebrew Bible traditions that refract a notion well known in many cultures of the ancient Near East, including West Semitic cultures, that there exists a pantheon of deities, or, in a more subordinative hierarchy, a divine council, that is, an assembly of lesser celestial beings who answer to the chief god. In Deut 4:19-20 is a polemical portrayal of the peoples of surrounding cultures worshipping the luminaries in the heavens, this behavior being prohibited to Israel because it had been Yhwh who had brought them "out of the iron-smelter," out of enslavement in Egypt, to be "a people of [Yhwh's] very own possession." Some emend Deut 32:8 to say the Most High "apportioned the nations" and "fixed the boundaries of the peoples according to the number of the gods" (Tigay 1996, 303), Israel being the portion of Yhwh; one way of reading this verse is that other deities are tacitly being acknowledged to be real, but hearing an ironic tone in this Deuteronomic discourse is equally possible. Other Hebrew Bible texts that trade on the notion of a heavenly council include: Gen 6:1-4; 1 Kgs 22:19-23; Job 1:6-2:6; Pss 29; 58; 75; 82; and 89; Isa 14:12-15; 40:3-6a; and Ezek 28:2-10.

4:6 *In that day.* This temporal locution is recognized as an eschatological formula by scholars. In some instances in the Hebrew Bible, the formula clearly marks a moment beyond historical time when the inbreaking of God's power will transform structures of injustice, the suffering righteous will be ushered into a life of blessedness and flourishing, and those who had perpetrated evil will face divine punishment. But in other instances—as here—the formula calls the audience's attention to something envisioned as possible within the constraints of human history.

***saying of* Yhwh.** This formulaic marker of divine speech occurs in Micah only here and in 5:9 (Eng. 10). It is a reflex that underscores the authority of prophetic speech in the name of Yhwh: as Andersen and Freedman note,

"Of the 376 occurrences of *něʾūm*" in the Hebrew Bible, "356 are in the Latter Prophets" (2000, 433).
those impaired in mobility, and those who had been driven away. Israelites and Judeans who had been forced into diaspora are assuredly the focus of the imagery here. David Kimḥi offers that "at the end of days, God will gather in the Israelite nation, who, due to their torturous exile, is likened to one who is ill, lame, and suffering" (Stavsky 2009, 31). Kessler notes shared language between Mic 4:6-7 and Zeph 3:19, arguing that since the noun *ṣōlēʿâ* occurs only in these two passages in the Hebrew Bible, this "must be seen as a sign . . . of an intentional allusion" (2016, 217), something certainly possible but not provable in either literary direction.

The imagery of divine ingathering of those impaired, banished, and harmed by Yhwh is of signal importance for the prophetic scribe's envisioning of the restored community. Judeans who have suffered alienation will be brought into the center of the divine plan for Judah's strength and flourishing, notwithstanding the geographical distance of diaspora groups and the social and religious challenges of reintegrating those who had been forced to subsist far from the temple-centered ritual praxes that had constituted belonging in the Judean community. From a disability-studies perspective, 4:6-7 could be taken to underscore the restored community's future solidarity with all who had been considered marginalized or abandoned by Yhwh. It is vital to observe that Micah does not speak of remediating or healing the mobility impairment flagged in the first clause. Contemporary readers might glimpse here what Thomas Reynolds has called an "expansive relational imagination," a communal prophetic resolve that "dismantles barriers of representation, attitude, and architecture and instead cultivates a wide sense of access that is ongoing and cocreated by and for all in community" (2023, 52). It is important not to underestimate the boldness of what Micah does here. It has implications for how the restored community is to understand its purpose and the status of its members in the radiant future to be lived under the sovereignty of Yhwh (4:7). What Reynolds offers is of relevance for how we understand the radical nature of the inclusion of those living with impairment in the prophetic vision of Mic 4:

> The reality of disability punctures the false illusions of normalcy in a community, unsettling and disrupting the status quo by exposing how dividing lines are constructed according to assumptions about what kinds of bodies are deemed normative and expected. The first task, then, is to notice this and accept the challenge as a provocation. . . .

> A prophetic belonging is one that names, denounces, and resists what distorts belonging. More, it marks a community's openness to self-examination and critique, confession and repentance. (2023, 57)

It would be anachronistic to claim that 4:6-7 can be accounted an articulation of ancient disability activism. But the prophetic scribe assuredly envisions a community in which all are welcomed home and the community comes alongside the returnees' (continuing) impairment and memories of traumatic abandonment in a relationship of solidarity as Yhwh makes these restored members into "a mighty nation." The community is not openly repenting here for ideologically uncompromising blame or vicious invective against diaspora Judeans. In Micah we have nothing of the sort of polemic that seethes through Jer 24-44 on that score. But it is clear that the transformed postexilic community envisioned in Mic 4 is to welcome all in a posture of openness and generosity.

those whom I had harmed. It is indisputable that in the view(s) of the book of Micah, Yhwh afflicts (NRSV), treats harshly (NJPS), and brings doom upon (ZUR) the covenant people. This is a central conviction of most books of the Latter Prophets. Though divine retributive judgment is decisive and unavoidable, in some traditions, notably in Isaiah, the biblical writer articulates a purifying or refining nature to the punishment that will leave the covenant people chastened and prepared for deeper obedience to Yhwh. In some passages, healing and restoration are offered by Yhwh to the same people Yhwh had designated to be violated, traumatized, and left desolate by enemies. Relevant passages in the prophetic corpus concerning Yhwh's purposeful affliction of Israel and Judah are far too many to list. An illustrative selection would include: Isa 3:1-4:1; 10:5-11; Jer 2:1-37; 7:8-8:3; 24:8-10; 32:26-35; 44:1-14; swaths of material in Ezek 5-16; 20-24; 33; Hos 2:1-13; 5:1-15; Joel 2:1-14; and Amos 4:6-11; 8:1-9:10. Though no single passage of Jonah can be listed here as a clear object lesson on divine retribution, I have argued elsewhere that the book of Jonah is brilliantly, though subtly, designed to show that Yhwh is a ruthless deity who has not been merciful to Israel (Sharp 2009, 176-86). In Tg. Mic 4:6, the agency of Yhwh in harming the covenant people has been replaced by the passive voice and an added emphasis on the people's sins, suggesting tacitly that divine retribution against them would have been justified: "those *who were* treated harshly *on account of the sins of my people.*"

4:7 Yhwh will reign . . . on Mount Zion. The glorious enthronement of Israel's God on Zion is an iconic image and chief tenet of the Zion theology that suffuses this material. For features of the Zion theology as discerned across several corpora of the Hebrew Bible, see Tryggve Mettinger (2015) and the bibliography there.

4:8 Tower of Eder. This proper name (per many, including Andersen and Freedman 2000, 439; Gelston, *BHQ*, 102) is a poetic designation for Mount Zion. As is the case with many place-names in the Hebrew Bible, it could theoretically be parsed as a common noun phrase—"tower of the flock." This is what Micah[LXX] does. Glenny observes that this sharpens the sense of a contrast with the characterization of the (destroyed) Jerusalem as a "garden-watcher's hut" in 3:12 (2015, 100). If such a translation is preferred, it should be rendered as an appellation, that is, as a proper noun in parallel construction with "Hill of Daughter Zion." In Tg. Mic 4:8 we find a lengthy elaboration: "you, Tower of Eder" has become "you, anointed one of Israel, who have been hidden away because of the sins of the congregation of Zion." Cathcart and Gordon note references to a hidden messiah in targumic expansions at Zech 4:7 and 6:12 as well (1989, 120n21). Juan Cruz observes the several metaphorical identities in which Daughter Zion is clothed in the book of Micah: "In 1:13 she is associated with Lachish, a fortress city said to be the source of her sin; in 4:8, she will be elevated in grandeur like a tower as her kingdom is restored to her, but in 4:10, she will suffer like a woman in childbirth as she leaves the city of Babylon; finally, in 4:12–5:1, she is summoned to gather her troops to destroy many nations" (2016, 113). I would argue that the figure of Zion maps a doubled trajectory through the poetic discourse of Micah. First, an association with fortification (the walled city of Lachish) yields only vulnerability to threat, since Lachish is preparing to meet the overwhelming force of invaders (1:13) and, historically, will not succeed; later, an association with fortification ("Tower of Eder") signals Zion's inviolability and renewed dominion (4:8). In the second iteration or doubling of that trajectory, we see Zion writhing and shrieking like a woman in birthing agony (4:10); shortly thereafter, she is encouraged to "arise and thresh," crushing her adversaries (4:13).

to you it will come: the former dominion will come. For a fleeting but powerful moment, this mysterious phrase could excite alarm in the implied audience, as it is reminiscent of the threat advancing toward the gate of Jerusalem in 1:9. But the resolution of the referential enigma brings joy: what approaches is restoration of the level of "dominion" (*memšālâ*) Judah had formerly enjoyed. This is a strong, albeit elliptical, signal of the prophetic scribe's anticipation of restored Davidic rule. Andersen and Freedman comment, "the plan to bring back kingly rule to Jerusalem is also intended to include a Davidic figure. David himself is not named, but who else could it be? The associations of Bethlehem, especially the use of the old name Ephratha, along with other allusive language, could have no other intention" (2000, 431). Micah[LXX] hears this as consonant with that earlier threat rather than reversing it: the translator adds a clarifying phrase, "out of Babylon," to modify the "former kingdom" that is coming. The move makes explicit that the authority to be reestablished is that of expatriate Judean leaders returning from the Babylonian diaspora (Glenny 2015, 101).

4:9 *Why do you cry out?* The Hebrew uses a cognate noun, *rēʿa*, to intensify the verb of crying out or shouting (from *rwʿ*). Mistaking the first root consonant *resh* for *dalet*, or translating a *Vorlage* that inscribed that change, Micah[LXX] reads the verb as from *ydʿ*, "to know," then taking the noun as "evil" from *rʿʿ* (BHQ, 102): *ti egnōs kaka*, "Why did you know evil?" or, rendered more idiomatically, "Why had you experienced harm?"

This verse opens an oracle that brims with gendered imagery: female Zion crying out, writhing, and shrieking like a woman in labor (4:9-10), though her male-gendered deity as king and counselor is nevertheless present to her; Zion forcibly removed to diaspora by male-gendered enemies (4:10), threatened and shamed by the violating gaze of male-gendered nations (4:11), and rising to demolish her adversaries with the horn and hooves of an enraged heifer (4:13). Feminist interpreters have analyzed the many effects such gendered imagery promotes, explicitly or implicitly, in ancient audiences and in the history of reception; among important researches on this rich and troubling nexus of issues, see the work of O'Brien (2008, esp. 140-51), Maier (2008), and Juliana Claassens (2018, 2021). Ruth Poser's work on trauma literature and the reality of gendered violence in warfare should be noted by every scholar of the Latter Prophets. Poser writes of biblical and other ancient Near Eastern literatures, "The conquest and domination of a city in war is pictured as the violent conquest and domination of a woman. In siege warfare, real violence against a city as metaphorical woman merged into real violence against *real* women living in the city," and it is "more than likely that rape of women was systematically applied as a weapon in ancient siege warfare" (2021, 342, citing Isa 13:16 and Zech 14:2).

Is the King not in you, or has your Counselor perished? It may be that the possessive pronoun "your" in the second clause does double duty implicitly, in retrospect, for the first clause (Andersen and Freedman 2000, 445); the referent is assuredly Judah's sovereign, understood not as a human

Micah 4

king who has failed (*pace* Biddle 2012, 255-56) but as the deity. Underlying these sharp rhetorical questions is a foundational claim of the royal Zion theology: Yhwh is cosmically enthroned as ruler in Jerusalem and is able to protect the holy city and its divinely appointed monarchical lineage from enemies. Jeremias observes that along with Zech 12-14, Mic 4-5 offers "the most elaborate and complex Zion theology in the Book of the Twelve" (2019, 275). The references here to Judah's "King" and "Counselor" function to taunt an implied audience that has lost faith in Yhwh, a brilliant move by a prophetic scribe who knew the Neo-Babylonian Empire had devastated Jerusalem and urges his audience to move beyond those material facts. Antti Laato argues that the tradition of Zion's inviolability visible in Pss 46; 48; and 76, as well as other Hebrew Bible passages, was originally rooted in Israelite holy-war traditions that were blended with "West Semitic mythical concepts," notably traditions of Canaanite deities battling the forces of chaos (2018, 113-16, 168-72). Whether or not the historical genesis of the Zion ideology can be traced with precision to an early stage in the formation of Hebrew Bible traditions, clearly in Mic 3:11 and 4:9, the prophet is articulating what has become a known view.

pain ... like that of a woman in labor. The trope of Israel/Judah in difficult straits being depicted as a woman in labor is pervasive in the prophetic corpus. While there is no denying that labor pains can be agonizing, the experience of childbirth can be a beautifully layered thing. The laboring woman works hard to bring new life into the world, trusting her body as it moves through the various stages of labor and delivery, supported by family and friends, perhaps aided by an expert midwife and spurred on by the anticipation of welcoming the newborn. Childbirth metaphors throughout the Latter Prophets present childbirth as a horror, something that weakens, emasculates, and engenders terror. This nexus of metaphorical valences is a product of the male gaze, conceived and portrayed by prophetic scribal onlookers—literally or figuratively—who have experienced neither the gradual hormonal and biological changes that ready the pregnant body for the birthing experience, nor the deep satisfaction of pushing in end-stage labor, nor the joy and physical relief of the neonate's emergence into the world. With Claassens and others, Maier sees possibilities for beneficial uses of this trope in contemporary interpretation: "The idea that the implicit male subject is constructed as a woman giving birth offers a culturally disruptive gender reversal that may be exploited as a resource for queer readings or as a 'counterlanguage,' which in the face of imperial threat may be useful for resistant reading in service of justice and cultural transformation" (2016, 475).

4:10 *Writhe and shriek.* The imagery of a woman in labor continues. The fs imperative from *gyḥ* seems to imply a sudden bursting forth (cf. Job 38:8), thus "shriek" in this translation, which arguably points to an unanticipated burst of vocalized fear or pain, as versus screaming, which can be protracted and even anticipated as a purposeful vocal response to looming threat. ZUR captures the sense well with "brich in Geschrei aus." Gelston observes that "all the versions reflect difficulty in understanding" *gyḥ* (BHQ, 103).

dwell in the open field. This image may evoke the plight of noncombatants fleeing from a besieged or breached city. But more likely, the prophetic scribe is describing a sight that would have been all too common after armed conflicts in the ancient Near East: a long line of prisoners of war being forcibly deported by victorious invaders. Such captives, some injured and all traumatized and lamenting the atrocities they had witnessed or endured ("writhe and shriek"), would suffer exposure to the elements and vulnerability to continued assault as they encamped in the open field en route to the country of the enemy.

you will go to Babylon. This reference, the only explicit mention of Babylon or Babylonia in Micah, secures the claim that the final form of this prophetic book can be dated to the exilic or postexilic era. Unlike the late prose of Jer 26–52, which is saturated with specific names, dates, and political details related to the Neo-Babylonian invasion of Judah, the book of Micah does not focus on markers of realism to supply the historical context(s) in which the prophesying of Micah is remembered to have taken place. This is not necessarily because the oracles of Micah are earlier than the Neo-Babylonian period. If "Babylon" occurs only once, the reader should note well that "Assyria" is mentioned only four times—once in 5:4, twice in 5:5, and once in 7:12—and further, the reference in Mic 7 serves to mark the eastern side of expansive geographical terrain rather than articulating a specific political point about Assyria as a nation. Thus the history of Israel and Judah as Yhwh's covenant communities has been framed through a complex lens that allows for a sightline to the Neo-Assyrian period, a sightline to the Neo-Babylonian period, and a future horizon in which Daughter Zion will "thresh" her enemies (4:13).

The literary dynamics of Mic 4 can be seen to be complex, when read attentively in the sequence in which the prophetic scribe has arranged them for the implied audience. Yhwh's torah will be the focus of international esteem in an era of peace (4:1–4), and Yhwh will restore Judeans from every kind of harm they had suffered (4:6–7), but that idyllic landscape will become recognizable only once Daughter Zion has fulfilled Yhwh's purposes (4:12) by pulverizing her enemies (4:13).

Micah 4

4:11 Many nations. Coalitions of regional adversaries did, of course, undertake militarized aggression against targeted geopolitical areas regularly in the history of the ancient world. But the prophetic scribe's image of "many nations" gathered against Zion is stylized in nature rather than realistic, and suggests that this battle will be apocalyptic in scope. Preeminent among prophetic passages envisioning an eschatological battle between the nations of the world and Yhwh's people is Ezek 38-39.

"Let her be defiled, and let our gaze rove over Zion." Many narrative and poetic traditions in the Hebrew Bible focalize the rape of women. For millennia, sexual violation has been enacted across many cultures in warfare, as torture and as a military strategy intended to leave survivors and their families traumatized and to shame the male authorities who failed to protect them. As Susanne Scholz argues, one salient dimension of sexual violation within patriarchal ideology is that "men rape women to mark their territory over other men" (2007, 91).

4:12 *like scythed grain to the threshing floor.* The notion of divine judgment as a terrifying "harvest" is regularly deployed in apocalyptic traditions, Joel Marcus notes (2000, 329). Examples can be seen at Isa 17:4-6; 18:3-6; 63:1-6; Hos 6:11; Joel 4:13 (Eng. 3:13), and in the earliest Christian literature, in the minatory preaching of John the Baptist (Matt 3:12; Luke 3:17) and in Rev 14:14-20.

4:13 *Arise and thresh.* The metaphor of a powerful heifer occurs also in Hos 10:9-15. Israel is indicted for having sinned since premonarchical times ("since the days of Gibeah," referring to the appalling events narrated in Judg 19-21). Ephraim, "a trained heifer that loved to thresh," is exhorted to turn its strength toward harrowing the ground so as to "sow . . . righteousness" and "reap steadfast love" (Hos 10:12), because, having "plowed wickedness" and having "reaped injustice" (10:13), Ephraim has called down the wrath of Yhwh. In Tg. Mic 4:13, the bidding to Zion has become "Arise and *kill, O congregation of* Zion," and the MT phrase "you will crush many peoples" has become "you shall *kill* many peoples."

"And I will devote to Yhwh . . ." Daughter Zion, who has been adjured to arise and thresh, is emboldened and responds eagerly that she will devote the spoils of war to Yhwh. Andersen and Freedman (2000, 454) and others continue the direct address to Zion here, arguing that this is an archaic 2fs form (see GKC §44h on the 2fs *qal* perf. occasionally displaying a vestigial *yod* at the end, cited by Gelston, *BHQ* 121). But the Hebrew of Micah does not

otherwise teem with archaic forms; the semantic effect of a scribe's deployment of a purposefully archaic form here would be entirely obscure, and Mic 4 is considered by most contemporary scholars, including the present writer, to have been composed late in the formation of the book. This word can be read as an unproblematic first-person singular form (see another occurrence in Num 21:2), and the line can be framed as dialogue, well in keeping with the poetic artistry of Micah elsewhere. Rather than hearing a stern directive to Zion, that she will (must?) devote the plunder from her victories to Yhwh, it is better to understand Zion responding to the exhortation to "arise and thresh" with a pledge of future spoils to the God who is empowering her to emerge from subjugation and rule over her enemies.

4:14 (Eng. 5:1) *muster your raiders, Daughter Raider!* The language here is difficult. The imagery plays on semantic possibilities of the verbal form *gdd* in the *hithpolel* ("gash oneself") as linked with the nominal form *gədûd*. Here, the term likely means "wall" or a "band of raiders" (Hos 6:9; 7:1; cf. Job 19:8, 12), though Shmuel Vargon construes it as the toponym of "an important site on the Azekah-Mareshah-Lachish highway" (1992, 559). NRSV chooses, "Now you are walled around with a wall," and NJPS translates, "Now you gash yourself in grief" (ZUR similarly), while de Moor translates, "Now gash yourself, O daughter of the band of robbers who have laid siege against us!" (2015, 193). The option involving mustering raiders is endorsed by Rashi, Joseph Kara (ca. 1065–ca. 1135), and Kimḥi (Stavsky 2009, 36), and that is the sense I find most coherent. The "wall" valence may gesture toward entrapment in siege, while the "troops" sense points to raiders' stealthy tactical movement against a force perceived to be stronger (1 Sam 30:8, 15, 23 and often in Samuel and Kings). Micah's artfully ambiguous poetic choice may be intended as polyphonous and is amplified by the repetition of the noun in the sobriquet for Daughter Zion, "Daughter Raider" (see similar wordplay in Gen 49:19).

He has laid siege against us. In view is the enemy commander attacking Jerusalem. This could be relevant to Sennacherib's siege during the Neo-Assyrian period or Nebuchadrezzar's siege in the time of Babylonia's dominance. The fluidity of the unspecified reference not only serves multiple generations of readers within the implied audience; it is poetically effective in heightening anxiety about the unseen but deadly enemy at the gate. It is also possible, though a bland translational choice in this dramatic oracle, to take this as a 3ms impersonal verb, as do NRSV ("siege is laid against us"), NJPS ("they have laid siege against us"), and ZUR ("man hat eine Belagerung gegen uns verhängt").

Micah 4

with the rod they strike on the cheek the judge of Israel. Most interpreters hear "judge" as referring to the king; the noun phrase "judge of Israel" (*šōpēṭ yiśrā'ēl*) comes up nowhere else in the Hebrew Bible. De Moor reads this as an allusion to the regicidal strife within Israel at the time of the Syro-Ephraimite crisis, and specifically the assassination of Pekah son of Remaliah by Hoshea son of Elah (2015, 195; see 2 Kgs 15:27-30). Other interpreters have spied here an allusion to a Mesopotamian ritual enacted in the *akītu*, the Babylonian New Year festival, a twelve-day event occurring twice a year in spring and autumn, then later, annually after the spring equinox, from the third millennium BCE on in Babylon, Uruk, and other cities (Debourse 2022, 14; for her reconstruction of the rituals over the twelve days, 21-25). On the fifth day of the festival, the Babylonian king was stripped of his royal regalia and made to kneel in a posture of abjection before the high priest, who would slap the king in the face, publicly enacting a ritual accusation (Mirelman 2021, 43). The king would respond by declaring he has not harmed "Babylon, its inhabitants, its temples or its god Marduk"; then he would be reclothed in his royal garb and the high priest would slap him a second time, it being considered "a good omen if tears came to his eyes" (Debourse 2022, 24). In Micah's portrayal, the ruler is struck with a rod, something that could cause injury and is not equivalent to being slapped. If the Mesopotamian ritual is in view—this commentator remains unpersuaded, as are Andersen and Freedman (2000, 460)—there would be a razor-sharp irony at play across Mic 4-5 that is complex indeed. The point of the reference might be that Babylonian invaders (see 4:10, 11) may humiliate the defeated Judean king with a blow, but that blow evokes the Babylonians' annual ritual humiliation of their own leader, after which he rises from his position of subjugation and rules in the strength of Marduk. So too the Judean king, only ostensibly humiliated—this would have to be the sense of the allusion, if it is present—will later rise and rule in might (5:3 [Eng. 4]) and will be victorious over Assyria, destroying those who had humiliated him earlier (5:4b-14 [Eng. 5b-15]). It is easier, though, to read this as simple assault. Wolff offers, "the best commentary on this is given by the account concerning the fate of Zedekiah in 2 Kings 25:4-7" (1990, 137) and the parallel account in Jer 52:8-11.

Micah[LXX] in Vaticanus has it that the "gates" of Israel are to be struck on the cheek. Glenny concedes that this could have resulted from a copyist's error—the scribe reading *pulas*, "gates," for *phulas*, "tribes"—but nevertheless reads it as it stands, arguing that this "obscure figure" may have been intended to convey a siege attack on city gates imagined as "a vulnerable and susceptible spot" (2015, 109).

the judge of Israel. Some translations paraphrase this as "the ruler of Israel" to make the sense clear. The identity of this "judge" has been suggested variously to be Hezekiah, another ruler, or Yhwh. That last is possible (though highly implausible to the present writer) despite the physicality of the image of striking on the cheek because any attack on the covenant people would be taken as "an affront to Yhwh" (Ben Zvi 2000, 120). The clause remains elliptical, which allows readers to entertain multiple inferences in keeping with their own historical understandings and social contexts.

BIBLIOGRAPHY

Bahá'u'lláh. 1978. *Tablets of Bahá'u'lláh Revealed after the Kitáb-i-Aqdas*. Haifa: Bahá'í World Centre. https://www.bahai.org/library/authoritative-texts/bahaullah/tablets-bahaullah/.

Biddle, M. E. 2012. "Dominion Comes to Jerusalem: An Examination of Developments in the Kingship and Zion Traditions as Reflected in the Book of the Twelve with Particular Attention to Micah 4-5." Pages 253-67 in *Perspectives on the Formation of the Book of the Twelve: Methodological Foundations—Redactional Processes—Historical Insights*. Edited by R. Albertz, J. D. Nogalski, and J. Wöhrle. BZAW 433. Berlin: De Gruyter. doi:10.1515/9783110283761.253.

Bonaventure. 2008. *The Sunday Sermons of St. Bonaventure*. Edited by T. J. Johnson. BTTS 12. St. Bonaventure, NY: Franciscan Institute.

Debourse, C. 2022. *Of Priests and Kings: The Babylonian New Year Festival in the Last Age of Cuneiform Culture*. CHANE 127. Leiden: Brill.

Jeremias, J. 2019. "Micha 4-5 und die nachexilische Prophetie." Pages 274-99 in *Studien zum Dodekapropheton II: Gesammelte Aufsätze zu Joel, Obadja, Micha und Nahum*. Edited by J. Gärtner and F. Hartenstein. FAT 133. Tübingen: Mohr Siebeck.

Mirelman, S. 2021. "Lament and Ritual Weeping in the 'Negative Confession' of the Babylonian *Akītu* Festival." *JANER* 21:42-74. doi:10.1163/15692124-12341318.

Müller, R. 2011. "Doubled Prophecy: The Pilgrimage of the Nations in Mic 4:1-5 and Isa 2:1-5." Pages 177-91 in *Changes in Scripture: Rewriting and Interpreting Authoritative Traditions in the Second Temple Period*. Edited by H. von Weissenberg, J. Pakala, and M. Marttila. BZAW 419. Berlin: De Gruyter. doi:10.1515/9783110240498.177.

Quine, C. 2019. "The Host of Heaven and the Divine Army: A Reassessment." *JBL* 138:741-55. doi:10.15699/jbl.1384.2019.3.

Roberts, J. J. M. 2007. "The End of War in the Zion Tradition: The Imperialistic Background of an Old Testament Vision of World Wide Peace." Pages 119-28 in *Character Ethics and the Old Testament: Moral Dimensions of Scripture*. Edited by M. D. Carroll R. and J. E. Lapsley. Louisville: Westminster John Knox.

Scholz, S. 2007. "Rape, Enslavement, and Marriage: Sexual Violence in the Hebrew Bible." Pages 76-99 in *Introducing the Women's Hebrew Bible*. Introductions in Feminist Theology 13. London: T&T Clark.

Spans, A. 2018. "Völkerbilder, Stadtbilder, Raumbilder: Ein Vergleich von Jesaja 60 und Micha 4." Pages 441-53 in *The Books of the Twelve Prophets: Minor Prophets—Major Theologies*. Edited by H.-J. Fabry. BETL 295. Leuven: Peeters.

Sweeney, M. A. 2001. "Micah's Debate with Isaiah." *JSOT* 25.93:111-24. doi:10.1177/030908920102509308.

———. 2020. *Jewish Mysticism: From Ancient Times through Today*. Grand Rapids: Eerdmans.

Tigay, J. H. 1996. *Deuteronomy*. JPS Torah Commentary. Philadelphia: Jewish Publication Society.

Tracy, S. C. 1986. "Saving the Day: The Recordings of the Reverend Sutton E. Griggs." *Phylon* 47.2:159-66. doi:10.2307/274542.

Vargon, S. 1992. "Gedud: A Place-Name in the Shephelah of Judah." *VT* 42:557-64. doi:10.1163/15685330-042-04-10.

Washington, G. 1996. "From George Washington to the Hebrew Congregation in Newport, Rhode Island, 18 August 1790." Pages 284-86 in vol. 6 of *The Papers of George Washington, Presidential Series*. Edited by D. Twohig. 21 vols. Charlottesville: University Press of Virginia.

MICAH 5

Rise of a Godly Ruler

5:1-4a (Eng. 2-5a)

> ¹And as for you {ms}, O Bethlehem of Ephrathah,
>   who are insignificant among the contingents of Judah,
> from you will come forth for me
>   one who is to be a ruler in Israel,
> whose origin is from of old,
>   from ancient days.
> ²Therefore he will give them up
>   until the time when she who is in labor has given birth,
> and the rest of his kin
>   return to the people of Israel.
> ³He will stand and perform the role of shepherd in the strength
>   of Yhwh,
>   in the majesty of the name of Yhwh his God.
> And they will dwell [securely], for now he will be great to the
>   ends of the earth.
>   ⁴He will be the One of Peace.

Israel's Defeat of Assyria

5:4b-8 (Eng. 5b-9)

> Assyria: when he invades our land
>   and treads within our fortresses,
> then we will raise up against him seven shepherds
>   and eight princes of mortals.

Micah 5

⁵They will "shepherd" the land of Assyria with the sword,
  and the land of Nimrod with the drawn blade.
He will rescue [us] from Assyria
  when he invades our land
  and treads within our territory.

⁶Then the remnant of Jacob will be in the midst of many peoples
  like dew from Yhwh,
  like spring showers upon the grass,
which does not depend on humans
  or put its hope in mortals.
⁷Then the remnant of Jacob will be among the nations,
  in the midst of many peoples,
like a lion among the creatures of the forest,
  like a young lion among flocks of sheep:
when it passes by, it tramples and tears to pieces,
  with none to rescue.

Ritual Shout to Yhwh as Divine Warrior
5:8 (Eng. 9)

⁸Let your {ms} hand be raised over your foes,
  and let all your enemies be cut down!

War Song of Divine Vengeance
5:9-14 (Eng. 10-15)

⁹In that day
  —saying of Yhwh—
I will cut down your horses from your midst,
  and I will destroy your chariots.
¹⁰I will cut down the cities of your land,
  and I will tear down all your fortifications.
¹¹I will cut down sorceries from your hand,
  and you will have no more soothsayers.
¹²I will cut down your idolatrous images and your sacred pillars
    from your midst,
  and you will bow down no longer to the work of your hands.

Rise of a Godly Ruler 5:1-4a (Eng. 2-5a)

¹³I will uproot your sacred poles from your midst,
and I will devastate your cities.
¹⁴I will exact vengeance with anger and fury on the nations
that have not heeded.

INTERPRETATION

Micah 5 draws us into the dramatic play of unexpected contrasts. From a humble and unimportant place, Bethlehem of Ephrathah, will come a mighty ruler who will shepherd his people in the strength of Yhwh and whose power will be magnified to the ends of the earth. An aggressive empire, Assyria, written in the third-person singular ("when he invades"), will be overwhelmed by a plurality of Judean resisters ("seven shepherds and eight princes of mortals") who will not only rebuff the invasion but will strike into Assyrian territory. Images of the "remnant of Jacob" as dew and spring rain—gentle and revivifying—yield to the image of a ferocious lion rampaging and tearing enemies to pieces. Finally, a war song voiced by Yhwh shows, blow by blow, how the deity will destroy or dismantle every piece of infrastructure with which enemy nations had built their idolatrous lifeways. Warhorses and chariots, cities and fortifications, illicit means of divination and idolatry: all will fall before the fury of Yhwh.

Rise of a Godly Ruler (5:1-4a [Eng. 2-5a])

Micah 5:1-14 Hebrew is 5:2-15 in NRSV, RVR, and other translations influenced by the LXX. This opening prophecy of a long-awaited righteous ruler has proved to be one of the most richly generative oracles in the history of reception of the Book of the Twelve. Micah 4 had given the audience to imagine a Jerusalem gloriously rebuilt in days to come, elevated in honor, with all the peoples of the earth streaming to Zion to learn the ways of Yhwh, which assuredly would include caring for the resident alien, the widow, and the orphan (Exod 22:21-24; 23:9; Deut 10:19; 14:28-29; 24:17-21; 27:19) and opening one's hand to the poor and needy within the community (Deut 15:7-11). To get to this luminous future, believers must be among those who stream to Zion. They would have to renounce their idols, look unflinchingly at the oppression and marginalization going on in their communities, tell the truth about what they see, and learn to live in covenantal fidelity with their neighbor. This would create the peaceable community over which the anticipated

Micah 5

Fig. 17: Virgin Annunciate and the prophet Micah, 1432. Detail from the Ghent Altarpiece by Jan van Eyck (1390-1441) with Hubert van Eyck (1370-1426). Oil paint on oak panels. In the Cathedral of St. Bavo in Ghent, Belgium.

Messiah—the one from Bethlehem "whose origin is from of old"—will rule. He will shepherd his flock in safety, securing a dominion marked by peace, this One of Peace heralded also by Isaiah as the Prince of Peace (Isa 9:6).

Israel's Defeat of Assyria 5:4b-8 (Eng. 5b-9)

The positioning of the short clause of 5:4a, with its unusual and thus memorable syntax—"He will be the One of Peace"—closes this luminous oracle of hope with the figure of the divinely appointed One of Peace in the foreground. The poetic art of the passage achieves a brilliant illumination of this emerging deliverer: he moves, as it were, from an origin shrouded in mystery in ancient days into the foreground of the audience's imagination. The mighty deliverer now stands ready to defeat the Assyrian invaders marching inexorably toward the audience in the next verse. The motif of shepherding "in the strength of Yhwh" (5:3a) finds ironic amplification in the "seven shepherds" whom the covenant community will raise up to "shepherd" Assyria with the sword (5:4-5) and then ironic reversal in 5:7, where the remnant of Jacob will itself become a marauding predator against its enemies among the peoples: this time, there will be "none to rescue," that is, no shepherd to assist those enemies in fending off the "lion" that is Judah.

Israel's Defeat of Assyria and Ritual Shout to Yhwh as Divine Warrior (5:4b-8 [Eng. 5b-9])

The imagery in this oracle is astonishing for its bold claim that Israel will defeat the seemingly invincible Neo-Assyrian Empire. The language here is neither about finding refuge from harm nor about creating an alliance with another ancient Near Eastern army, such as Egypt or the fearsome military machine of the Neo-Babylonian Empire, so as to defeat Assyria. No, here Israel is envisioned as itself empowered to overcome its enemies.

In the preceding lines of Mic 5, the implied audience has been spurred to joyous anticipation of the coming of a powerful ruler from the Davidic lineage whose strength is in Yhwh and who will be invincible for the cause of peace. Now, "Assyria" in 5:4b startles, drawing the rapt audience's attention away from the prophetic vision of eschatological peace and refocusing their gaze on the looming threat of military invasion of Judah in the time of Neo-Assyrian geopolitical dominance. The Assyrians will come—there is no doubt whatsoever about that. But in this prophetic perspective, Israel has the military capacity to respond effectively and turn the tide of battle such that Assyria will find itself on the defensive in its own territory. Stirring words, notwithstanding that they are not grounded in the reality of the relative strengths of the two nations.

Assyria's defeat having been envisioned and relished, the next two verses bring into close parallelistic relationship the theological hope of the flourish-

Micah 5

ing of the "remnant of Jacob" and its successful deterrence, or obliteration, of any further military threat from other nations. Micah 5:6 and 7 (Eng. 5:7 and 8) effect a reimagining of the "remnant of Jacob" as forces of nature that cannot be controlled by human beings and their paltry weapons. God's people will be like dew and rain, replenishing and unstoppable, and they will be like lions, fearsome apex predators from whom the other "creatures of the forest" cower in hiding. This material finishes with a ritual shout to Yhwh in 5:8 (Eng. 9) that expresses covenantal loyalty to the Divine Warrior, proleptically celebrating the ways in which Yhwh will destroy all enemies and positioning Micah's people as those who honor the sovereignty of their God.

War Song of Divine Vengeance (5:9-14 [Eng. 10-15])

Dramatic images of divine retribution conclude this set of oracles. There is a powerful ambiguity here as to the target of Yhwh's punitive wrath, given this war song's positioning between material that celebrates Israel's impending defeat of Assyria (5:4b-8 [Eng. 5b-9]) and material in which Yhwh calls Israel to account (6:1-2) in terms strongly reminiscent of the opening judgment oracle against Samaria and its idols, with "Jacob," Judah, and Jerusalem inextricably caught up in that avalanche of divine wrath (1:2-7). Here at the end of Mic 5, armies will be destroyed and cities razed, idols and sacred pillars obliterated, and the alarm of the implied audience grows. While Yhwh's fury against other nations is stated explicitly (5:14 [Eng. 15]), whether or not Israel belongs among the "nations that have not heeded" remains, ominously, an open question—one that is answered decisively in the affirmative in the disputation speech that follows in 6:1-5. Israel has not, in fact, heeded the words or the saving deeds of Yhwh throughout its own history.

As Yhwh rails at Israel in Mic 6, the Janus position of the war song of divine vengeance comes into focus with terrifying clarity. The implied audience is forced to revisit the language of divine destruction in breathless fear as they realize Yhwh has been speaking about them too, at least potentially, the entire time. As is widely acknowledged, Amos 1-2 uses a deft rhetoric of entrapment in a series of oracles against other nations: a stylized and compelling formula of divine vengeance unfolds against a group of enemies, and at the end, the implied audience sees with horror that Judah and Israel, too, are in the group to be punished (Amos 2:4-8). There, as we see in Mic 6, Amos immediately moves to remembrance of Yhwh's saving deeds on behalf of Israel as the grounds for punishing a recalcitrant people that has failed to remember what Yhwh has done for them (Amos 2:9-12). Just as in Amos 1-2, a rhetorical move of entrapment is performed through the larger block of material here at the transition from Mic 5 to Mic 6. The arc of Mic 5:4b (Eng. 5b) to 6:5 entraps the implied Judean audience in a way that is nothing short of brilliant.

History of Consequences

For illustrative comments on Mic 5 in rabbinic midrash, see the introduction under §4.1.1 Midrashic Interpretations.

The Gospel of Matthew quotes Mic 5:1, 3 (Eng. 2, 4) in the dramatic narrative in which King Herod consults the chief priests and scribes to learn where the Messiah would be born: Bethlehem, where traveling magi following the guidance of a star have arrived to pay homage to neonate Jesus (Matt 2:5-6). The Gospel of John relates that on the final day of the Festival of Sukkoth in Jerusalem, Jesus publicly exhorts those who thirst to come to him, spurring a debate about his identity in which some cite Mic 5:1 (Eng. 2): "Has not the scripture said that the Messiah is descended from David and comes from Bethlehem?" (John 7:42). Since the writing of the Gospels, in the apologetic discourses of Justin Martyr, the Micah commentary of Jerome, and innumerable other Christian sources, the Mic 5 oracle has been read as a prophecy of the birth of Jesus of Nazareth, whose coming from of old is accounted in the prologue of the Fourth Gospel (ANF 1:174, 237; *Comm. Mich.*, 82).

Jerome links the laboring woman in Mic 5:2 (Eng. 3) to the vision in Deutero-Isaiah of the desolate woman rejoicing in many children (Isa 54:1), then reaches for Rom 11 to argue that the fulfillment of this prophecy comes when faithful gentiles have been brought into the covenant people and all Israel has been redeemed (Rom 11:25-26; *Comm. Mich.*, 83). Of the Assyrian invasion anticipated in Mic 5:4 (Eng. 5), Jerome offers that "Assyria" is the malevolent power that had Paul lashed, beaten, stoned, shipwrecked, and confronted by other grave perils (2 Cor 11:23-27; *Comm. Mich.*, 84-85a). In defense of "the Word of God" stand seven shepherds and eight princes, whom Jerome identifies as "all the patriarchs and prophets and . . . holy men" of the Hebrew Bible and "all the people of the New Testament" from the apostles to Jerome's

Micah 5

own time, respectively (85). The restored "remnant of Jacob" in Mic 5:6 (Eng. 7) Jerome identifies as "the apostles and the first converts from the Jews," who destroy their enemies not in the sense of slaughter but in expurgation of their sinfulness: "not that the enemies perish... but the respect in which they are enemies perishes.... This killing does not signify annihilation but the cessation of wicked life.... It will not reduce them to nothingness, but it will be visited among them as long as the impiety that is among them needs to be devoured" (88).

Augustine of Hippo (354-430) musters 5:1 (Eng. 2) when he preaches on the objection of denizens of Jerusalem (John 7:27) that Jesus cannot be the Messiah since they know his birthplace but "no one will know where [the Messiah] is from." Through several homilies on John 7, Augustine has argued that Jesus going up to the Festival of Tabernacles in secret is meant to signify that it is not yet time for the revealing of Christ's glory, which is not worldly but is of God (John 7:6, 18). Augustine explains that Micah "had predicted where he [the Messiah] was from according to his humanness; according to his divinity he was concealed from the ungodly and was seeking to win the devout" (*Tract. Ev. Jo.* 31.3 [31]).

Theodore of Mopsuestia, an Antiochene exegete committed to expounding the historical sense of Hebrew Scripture texts, holds two levels of signifying together when commenting on 5:1 (Eng. 2). Zerubbabel is the leader of whom Micah speaks, Theodore insists, yet "in reality," this material "foretells Christ the Lord in the flesh, who as a successor of David exercises the true and abiding rule over all" (*Comm.*™, 226). In the "seven plus eight" Hebrew idiom of 5:4 (Eng. 5), Theodore avers that seven connotes perfection and eight connotes excess. Reflecting on the routing of Sennacherib in the time of Hezekiah (Isa 36:1-37:38 // 2 Kgs 18:13-19:37), Theodore says "seven shepherds" indicates "the severity of the divine retribution, which God inflicted on them [viz., the Assyrians] as perfect and complete through the angel's attack," while "eight bites" (per the LXX) points to "the excess of the troubles befalling them after their flight from there," including the assassination of the royal scions back in Assyria (232). He correctly reads the song of retribution at the end of Mic 5 as directed against the Neo-Assyrian Empire (234).

Cyril of Alexandria (ca. 375-444) joins Theodore and other Christian exegetes in reading much in Mic 5 christologically. Micah's oracle about the ruler's origin suggests to Cyril "either the Word's existence before the ages—he is co-eternal with the Father, and is himself the Maker of the ages," or alternatively, that "though he became [human] at a late point in time ... the mystery concerning him was predetermined" (*Comm.*^{CA}, 235). Cyril interprets the one of peace as Christ via Eph 2:14-15 and the "sword" imagery as alluding to "the blade of the Spirit, which is the word of God," per Eph 6:17. "Assyria" later in Mic 5 refers not to the historical empire, "but rather the inventor of sin—namely, Satan ... the implacable and warlike mass of demons which oppose everything holy and fight against the holy city, the spiritual Zion" (237). The "remnant of Jacob" in 5:7 (Eng. 8) refers to "descendants of Jacob who have been saved through faith in Christ and have emerged as heralds and ministers of the evangelical oracles" (242).

Peter Lombard (ca. 1100-1160) explores dimensions of the doctrine of the Trinity in the first volume of his *Four Books of Sentences*. In a catena of biblical proofs for the divine unity, the plurality and distinctiveness of the Trinitarian Persons, and the eternal begetting of the Son, Lombard ranges across well-known prooftexts such as Ps 2; Prov 8:22-30; and Eccl 24:3, then quotes Mic 5:2 as demonstrating "both the eternal generation of the Word and the temporal one from Mary" (*Sent*. I, d. 2, c. 5).

Among homiletical writings in the *Kirchenpostille* of Martin Luther (1483-1546) is a 1527 model sermon on Matthew 2 for the Festival of the Epiphany. Luther expounds the Micah 5 metaphor of the woman in childbirth in this way: "The church of the apostles is in travail; she experienced the sufferings of Christ and was in the anguish of birth, to bring forth a new spiritual people for this lord of Israel, as he himself foretold in John 16[:21-22]" (2013, 189).

Calvin affirms the christological reading of the opening of Mic 5 in a sermon on 23 December 1550: the coming ruler is "our Lord Jesus Christ, who is truly human, born of Abraham's seed by the Virgin Mary, but who is also the eternal Word of God" (2003, 262). He elaborates, "Our Lord chose the city of Jerusalem that it might serve as a living symbol of his Church.... In fact, the kingdom, the priesthood, and everything else also prefigured Christ's reign" (263). In Micah's oracle, Bethlehem serves as "a living image of the nature of the entire Church of God," for as "Jesus Christ, the Savior of the world, revealed himself in Bethlehem, a town of ostensible insignificance, so also will our Lord rescue his Church whenever events become confused and chaotic and appear destined for ruin" (269). Believers who lived prior to Christ's incarna-

Micah 5

> tion had full access to the grace of God. Preaching on 24 December 1550, Calvin ventriloquizes Micah saying to his Judean contemporaries, "we are nonetheless participants in [Christ's] grace.... This is true though he has not yet lived on earth... or been resurrected from the dead that we might have life. He is already our Redeemer, and we can claim this the moment we put our hope in him" (276). In tribulations, believers should be heartened by the power of Christ: "This world is like a forest of robbers, like a sea whipped by wind and storm... like a pit that could engulf us at any moment.... We are surrounded by enemies who are equipped and able to devour us the way wolves devour sheep. Nonetheless, with God on our side, we need never fear. And why? Because Jesus Christ is our shepherd" (284).
>
> In a "Blank Bible" annotation, Congregationalist preacher Edwards says of the plural noun in 5:1 (Eng. 2) "goings forth," translated as "origin" here and by many, that the term is "very fitly used to signify the eternal generation of him who is the Word of God, that was 'in the beginning with God,'" per the prologue of the Gospel of John (*WJE* 24:802).
>
> Jesuit peace activist Berrigan muses on Micah's linking of military resources and "sorceries" in 5:9–14 (Eng. 10–15): "Weaponry and war are not merely... a human aberration. Something more is at stake: a mystery of unutterable evil... as though the advisors, diplomats, strategists, policy-makers, power brokers, generals, were working a kind of vile magic." He continues, "All who make war stand as surrogates and guardians of the empery of death. They keep a universe that is a house of death," and "in such places, the worship of death proceeds," but as Mic 5 illustrates, "the obscene proceedings are also frequently, courageously, brilliantly interrupted; and this is our hope" (1995, 231).

RETROSPECT

Micah 5 opens with an acknowledgment of geopolitical subjugation and cultural trauma ("she who is in labor") that will yield to the joy of new birth: Judeans' return from diaspora and their flourishing in the land in peace. Micah 5 also offers sustained images of violence, imagining the restored people of YHWH as a lion that "tramples and tears to pieces" and understanding divine fury as cutting down not only abstract targets and inanimate objects— sorceries, idolatrous images, sacred pillars—but also entire cities (5:10, 13

[Eng. 11, 14]). In the troubling war song of 5:9-14 (Eng. 10-15), some feminist readers might appreciate the prophetic scribe's rhetoric of destruction, affirming the robust negation of all that distorts the purposes of the Holy. But for many gender-justice activists, the feminist KILLJOY position requires declining to participate in violence of any kind, including rhetorics of violence that inflame death-dealing antagonism toward adversaries, whether they be geopolitical or internecine. Jewish feminist theologian Plaskow points to the foundational idolatry of patriarchal religion, speaking of her own tradition in words that apply to the central ideation of many other traditions as well: "While Jews are used to thinking of idols as pillars and stones, verbal idols can be every bit as powerful as sculpted ones. . . . What will dislodge male idols . . . is not hammers or fire but structural changes in the patriarchal system and concurrent creation of new metaphors that lead the imagination down untrod paths" (1990, 128). Of biblical images of God as a powerful and vengeful male who destroys individual malefactors and enemy nations alike, Plaskow observes,

> Images of God's dominance give rise to the terrible irony that the symbols Jews have used to talk about God as ultimate good have helped generate and justify the evils from which we hope God will save us. The image of God as dominating Other functions as a fundamental and authorizing symbol in a whole system of hierarchical dualisms that includes . . . the hierarchical relationship between Israel and other peoples. . . . As traditionally depicted, God incorporates the "higher" qualities in a host of cleavages that correspond to various forms of human domination: He is male rather than female, regal rather than simple and poor, Jewish rather than pagan, spirit rather than flesh. . . . Such symbols undergird a worldview in which it seems "practical, humane, and moral" for people who identify with the higher side of these dualisms to oppress those they associate with the lower. (132)

The valorization of violence—power over a person or another living creature, bending another to one's will, seeking to disable or annihilate those who resist—lies at the heart of oppression and exploitation, and for many feminist theorists, including the present writer, such valorization must be roundly rejected.

Ahmed speaks of the "snap," that moment when the feminist KILLJOY rises up against the pressure to yield to distortion, erasure, or subjugation. The snap is not the originary inception of violence, though it can be per-

Micah 5

ceived that way. It is a reaction to pressure that had been building invisibly throughout "a longer history" of systemic injustice (2017, 188–90). The snap comes when a person, a constituency, or a community over time has been rendered so fragile that the status quo can no longer be sustained (163–64). Ahmed's observation that the KILLJOY "emerges from a scene of breakage" (168) is deeply relevant to the violent rhetoric in Mic 5. "We can be shattered by the force of what we come up against," Ahmed avers, "when our bodies are little objects thrown against the hard walls of history" (172). Standing in the contemporary reception history of Micah traditions, a feminist KILLJOY could read this portrayal as showing that YHWH "snaps" because the bodies and spirits of the covenant people had been manipulated, subjugated, and shattered for too long. The ambiguity in the war song at the end of Mic 5 telegraphs that not only will the deity "snap" against enemy nations, YHWH will also wreak vengeance on anyone, including those within Judah, who bow down to the work of their hands (5:12 [Eng. 13]).

Bey muses on the emancipatory disruption of oppressive categories, imagining fresh possibilities that emerge within and through "nonnormative corporeality's fractures" of white supremacy and carceral norms about how gender should be understood and lived. Bey calls for escape from "cisnormative and gender binaristic templates routed through whiteness"—for leaving behind those distorted ways of thinking about human persons, embracing instead a purposeful FUGITIVITY from "epidermalization and anatomized gendering" (2022, 74). Bey consoles those who might be alarmed by the prospect of living a FUGITIVE life, assuring them that their resistance to being wounded counts as a visionary and redemptive practice. Bey writes, "Know that you are held by the beckoning into the world after this world, a world that is not far from where you stand. The opening of that world is holding you, in every moment you question the ethics of how you've been treated" (74). Though FUGITIVITY can indeed lacerate former ways of being, requiring the relinquishment of that to which we have clung, Bey emphasizes that "even the things that might cut deep are there to help us glimpse what could be if we did not have to defend the violences that have come to be so familiar and thus thought unable to be discarded" (75). Similarly, Mic 5 urges his oppressed and scattered people to think beyond the material constraints of their history and, perhaps, their present lived experience. The prophet calls Judeans who had been taken forcibly into diaspora to understand their fearful ordeal as the birth pangs of a new reality. The people of YHWH will have to be given up (5:2 [Eng. 3]) until the birthing of the messianic age is complete; then they will be shepherded by one "whose

Micah 5 and Ecological Justice

origin is from of old" (5:1 [Eng. 2]), who in latter days "will be great to the ends of the earth" and whose dominion will be marked not by violence but by peace (5:4a [Eng. 5a]). Thus these two voices—Micah (or a postexilic prophetic scribe writing in the tradition of Micah) and Bey—utter words that acknowledge the trauma of their beloved people's lived oppression while calling fragile and fearful survivors to dare to envision a world without such violence, a world in which they will live in peace and flourishing.

As delineated in the introduction, here is the spectrum of possibilities I have traced for contemporary responses to Micah's prophetic witness: → resilience → resistance → reformation → rejoicing. Micah 5 builds *resilience* through the fresh image of dew and spring showers for the rejuvenated strength of God's people (5:6 [Eng. 7]), inviting readers daunted by oppressive political systems or traumatized by militarized conflict to imagine the sustaining power of divine care as inexhaustible and renewed every morning. Micah 5 catalyzes *resistance* to the disempowering fear that imperial invasion of one's homeland will be inexorable and inescapable. Here, in a confident asseveration of agency, those who face the prospect of invasion promise that the rescue of any captives will be effected by the community itself, its leaders unleashing retribution deep in enemy territory (5:4b-5 [Eng. 5b-6]). Micah 5 calls for *reformation* of the community's misdirected reliance on military resources and illicit cultic practices (5:9-13 [Eng. 10-14]), inviting readers in every age to understand that no weapon, fortification, or sorcery can stand against the purposes and power of God. Finally, Mic 5 holds space for *rejoicing* in the rich theological heritage of Israel and Judah, which has long known of succor "whose origin is from of old, from ancient days" (5:1 [Eng. 2]). Readers can thrill to the expectation of an incomparably powerful redeemer, one who will be "great to the ends of the earth" and who will secure the community's flourishing through the strength of none other than God (5:3 [Eng. 4]).

MICAH 5 AND ECOLOGICAL JUSTICE

Micah 5 lifts up the luminous hope that in the messianic age, one "whose origin is from of old" will restore the devastated community of Judah, making it possible for exiled kin to return home (5:2 [Eng. 3]). The "shepherd" whose advent has been divinely ordained "from ancient days" may be conceived as one who tends and cares for all living beings that long to dwell in safety. Those who would stand in the homiletical lineage of Micah can call out humanity's transgressions (cf. 3:8) against creaturely kin. Homiletician Leah Schade contends that "an other-wise ecological homiletic would have us 'exit' androcentric anthropocentrism and enable us to be open to 'the absolute mystery of the other,' which elicits compassion, resistance, justice, and hope, not just for a new vision for all humanity, but for the entire Earth community" (2015, 65).

Since the dawn of the industrial age, humans' unstinting commodification of natural resources and relentless exploitation of living creatures have been the cause of cascading disasters harmful to arboreal, botanical, amphibian, avian, and mammalian life. In 5:6 (Eng. 7), Micah emphasizes that Yhwh alone can give the seasonal rains that foster new growth: the grass "does not depend on humans, nor put its hope in mortals" as the source of its flourishing. Yet human agricultural practices must be reformed if the grasses made by the Creator are to flourish. Grasslands are harmed by overgrazing, monocropping, and habitat loss; the threat of desertification looms wherever global warming might reduce rainfall to a significant degree in a grassland biome. The IPBES notes that large-scale, profit-driven agribusiness is a major driver of harms to local bioregions: "Harmful economic incentives and polities associated with unsustainable practices in fisheries, aquaculture, agriculture (including fertilizer and pesticide use), livestock management, forestry, mining and energy (including fossil fuels and biofuels) are often associated with . . . overexploitation of natural resources, as well as inefficient production and waste management" (IPBES 2019 §B5).

Community activists may find their imaginations stirred by Micah's image of one who "shepherds" living beings by a mighty power that extends "to the ends of the earth" (5:3 [Eng. 4]). What might shepherding look like in a time of global ecosystem collapse? Some effects of human industrialization and pillaging of natural resources are not remediable, but other trajectories of harm can be blunted or ameliorated. The IPBES underscores the possibility of developing sustainable "food systems that ensure adaptive capacity, minimize environmental impacts, eliminate hunger, and contribute to human health and animal welfare," utilizing existing technologies that include "integrated pest and nutrient management, organic agriculture, . . . soil and water conservation practices . . . agroforestry, silvopastoral systems, [and] irrigation management" (IPBES 2019 §D36). The IPCC lifts up the importance of early warning systems in flood zones, restoration of wetlands and riverine environments, soil moisture conservation, improvements in use of cultivars and agroforestry, urban greening and agriculture, and collaborative consultation of indigenous peoples and their lifeways (IPCC 2022

Commentary

§§C.2.2-3, 5). Hawken elucidates many dozens of micro- and larger-scale ecological initiatives, drawing a vibrant portrait of what the communal role of "shepherd" could look like in an age desperately in need of ecological restoration and intentional protection of humans and other creatures. Shepherds will protect habitats in aquatic, arboreal, grassland, desert, and tundra biomes; honor indigenous knowledges; curtail overfishing, monocropping, and unwise use of biocides; reduce dependence on livestock and improve technologies of animal husbandry; promote rewilding, silvopasture, composting, and upcycling of food surpluses; better manage aerial particulates, the pollution of waterways, and the proliferation of nondegradable garbage; engage in seaforestation to restore undersea kelp forests and seagrass meadows; protect mangrove forests, coral reefs, peatlands, and tidal marshes; enhance carbon sequestration through proforestation, afforestation, and regenerative soil management; guard wildlife corridors and pollinator pathways; and advocate for public policies that reduce dependence on fossil fuels and incentivize practices such as electrification, green architecture, and the use of geothermal, solar, and wind energy, so as to support progress toward net-zero emission of greenhouse gases in cities (2021).

Schade argues for a holistic understanding of beloved community in our ecological age: preachers and activists should find language that "calls us to a home where everyone is loved and no one is lost—and *that* may look like a home we can scarcely imagine" (2015, 71 [emphasis original]). Habitat loss may be considered a kind of exile, with displaced creatures forced into endangered life on the run or compelled to settle into diaspora existence in another region that is not well suited to their needs. Schade articulates an ecofeminist goal that we may find congruent with Micah's prophetic vision: justice-minded truth-tellers should expose "the patterns of environmental destruction, nonhuman animal exploitation and cruelty, and social injustice in order to erase the logic and illusion that such patterns are natural or divinely sanctioned" (2015, 65).

COMMENTARY

Micah 5 opens with stirring words about the advent of an invincible ruler who will shepherd Yhwh's people and establish a reign of peace. Israel's and Judah's traumatic history of military defeat and diaspora may be a reality—5:2 (Eng. 3) acknowledges that "kin" must "return to the people of

Micah 5

Israel"—but deliverance is on the horizon. In the images of relentless divine vengeance that close Mic 5, Heschel is attuned to an implicit threat to all who are complicit with wickedness, including those within Judah. Heschel writes, "To the soul of Micah, the taste of God's word is bitter. . . . Micah does not question the justice of the severe punishment" Yhwh wreaks in fury on all who do not obey, "yet, there is reluctance and sorrow in that anger. It is as if God were apologizing for [the divine] severity, for [God's] refusal to be complacent to iniquity. This is God's apology to Israel" (2001, 126). Violence pervades the book of Micah, enacted by Judah's enemies and Judah's God alike, and suffered by all; but Yhwh is one who "delights in steadfast love," Heschel insists, taking Mic 7:18 as a governing claim that can ameliorate or frame the more difficult material (126).

5:1 (Eng. 2) *And as for you, O Bethlehem of Ephrathah.* Here the *waw* should be read as conjunctive, "and," rather than as adversative, since this verse continues the sense of the entire poetic unit, beginning with 4:14 (Eng. 5:1) and concluding with 5:8 (Eng. 9): an exhortation to Daughter Zion and Judah to engage in battle with steadfast resolve. Judah will assuredly succeed, the prophet announces, and a key element in Judah's success will be this leader from Bethlehem. Micah[LXX] has "house of Ephrathah" (*oikos tou Ephratha*), which Gelston suggests "originated as a facilitation, interpreting Ephrathah as community rather than location" (*BHQ*, 103).

insignificant among the contingents of Judah. The military imagery continues here. In 4:14 (Eng. 5:1), Daughter Zion had been urged to muster troops to repel Assyrian invaders. In such a muster, Judean towns and villages would be required to send their battle-ready fighters to assist in Judah's defense. For another example, see the poetic description of a muster of Israel's tribes in Judg 5:8–23. In Mic 5:1, the town of Bethlehem, though insignificant in military strength among the troop contingents of Judah (*'alpê yəhûdâ*) mustered for war, will play a decisive role. The quotation of 5:1 in Matt 2:6 negates the idea that Bethlehem is insignificant ("by no means least," *oudamōs elachistē*), an interpretive change also observable in some Greek manuscripts, per Gelston (*BHQ*, 103). The adjectival phrase in Micah[LXX], "few in number among thousands in Judah" (*oligostos . . . en chiliasin Iouda*), underlines that those in Bethlehem comprise only a small percentage of the thousands in Judah, having in mind perhaps not the population generally but those who could be mustered for battle.

from you will come forth . . . a ruler in Israel. In the scribes' memory of a time more than two centuries before Micah of Moresheth, Bethlehem had been the home of an Ephrathite named Jesse and his family, which included eight sons (1 Sam 16–17). Jesse's youngest son, David, would become a protégé of Israel's first king, Saul. David would come to contest Saul's leadership, strengthen his own power base, and finally take the throne himself. However one construes the complex interpretive issues involved in the Succession Narrative in the books of Samuel and Kings, the biblical sources agree that David came from Bethlehem, and the opening oracle of Mic 5 reflects on that tradition, prophesying the advent of a future ruler in continuity with the Davidic monarchy. Whether the Succession Narrative is to be dated in its final form to the tenth century, to 825–722 BCE, to the seventh century, to the exilic or postexilic era, or to the Persian period, and whether one sees that complex—or discrete strands within it—as legitimizing or delegitimizing the monarchy (Knapp 2021, 221–27), Micah is clearly in conversation with the David traditions from a positive vantage point. The Davidic house is presented in this oracle as the originary source of magnificent blessing and future deliverance. The addition of "anointed one/messiah" (*mšyḥʾ*, *BHQ*, 103–4) in Tg. Mic 5:1 amplifies the Micah^MT designation *môšēl*, underlining the divine approbation of this ruler and potentially eschatological implications of his sovereignty.

whose origin is from of old. This adverbial complement, *miqqedem*, is used of Yhwh being "from of old" as one who works salvation or wonders (Pss 74:12; 77:12 [Eng. 11]), who alone has declared long ago what was to be (Isa 45:21), and who is possessed of invincible power over enemies (Hab 1:12). Some see here a veiled reference to the Davidic monarchy, but paired with the locution "from ancient days," the temporal frame is better understood as evoking Yhwh having performed wonders during the exodus, as with "from ancient days" in 7:14. In Tg. Mic, "whose origin was from of old" is shaped into a more euphemistic and theologically cautious formulation: "whose name was mentioned from of old."

5:2 (Eng. 3) *she who is in labor*. This enigmatic reference may be an allusion to Mother Jerusalem birthing her children who are to return from diaspora, a trope expressed in Ps 87 and especially clear in the Greek (LXX Ps 86), where the Septuagint translator has added "mother" as a title for Zion in verse 5 (see Sharp 2022b, 31–36). Many interpreters have associated this verse with the sign described in Isa 7:14, in which a young woman will give birth to a son, "Immanuel," who is to be a sign of impending judgment. The Gospel of Matthew quotes Isa 7:14 and Mic 5:2 as prophecies of the birth of Jesus of Nazareth (Matt 1:23; 2:5–6).

Micah 5

Fig. 18. Micah with laboring Jerusalem in Tree of Jesse, ca. 1331. Marble façade of the cathedral in Orvieto, Italy, designed by Lorenzo Maitani (ca. 1275-1330). Photo by Georges Jansoone.

5:3 (Eng. 4) *perform the role of shepherd.* The royal leader as "shepherd" is a trope significant in many ancient Near Eastern cultures. The failure

Commentary

of human monarchs to tend and protect their "flocks" may lie in the background in a number of Hebrew Bible texts that promote Yhwh as shepherd, such as Ps 23 and Ezek 34, where that volatile prophet makes two promises: Yhwh will serve as shepherd of the sheep (Ezek 34:15-16), and Yhwh will appoint a royal shepherd in the lineage of David (34:23-24) under whose leadership Judah will flourish in conditions of peace, agricultural abundance, and "showers of blessing" (34:25-31). As regards Mic 5, Daniel Smith-Christopher dissents from those who hear positive Davidic overtones. In his view, "Micah's hope is precisely the opposite: a summary rejection of the line of David and a sentiment to go 'back to the drawing board' (i.e., back to Bethlehem) on Judean kingship," explaining, "in Micah's day, the central Jerusalem authorities responded to perceived Assyrian threats with force rather than diplomacy. Micah and his people are exhausted and angry," and Micah envisions a ruler who "will not resort to violence so easily" (2018, 48 [emphasis removed]). I am not persuaded, given what I believe "Bethlehem" connotes; but it is interesting that the name "David" does not occur in Micah. The tradition within the Twelve is polyphonous: there are gestures toward a Davidic restoration in Hos 3:5 and Amos 9:11 (arguably redactional), but the critique of those "like David" in Amos 6:5 is strong.

Glenny notes that this verse in Micah^{LXX} in Vaticanus "begins with a threefold description of the actions of the Lord" with the Lord as "the subject of the sentence, while in the modern editions of Rahlfs and Ziegler Lord is a genitive modifying 'strength'" (2015, 116), leaving the impression that the one tending the flock will be a Davidide monarch. Glenny's own interpretation combines these possibilities. Using LXX verse numbers and citing Ezek 34:11-31 as a source for the notion of two rulers, Glenny writes, "the imagery of a shepherd calls to mind the dual rule of the Lord and David over Israel," such that "in the first sentence of 5:4 in B the Lord . . . is the one who shepherds the nation, but . . . the Davidite in 5:2 [who] is prophesied to come out of Bethlehem . . . should be understood to rule with the Lord" (117).

great to the ends of the earth. The sovereignty of this "shepherd" will extend across the whole earth, something predicated of Yhwh and the divinely appointed ruler in many biblical traditions (e.g., 1 Sam 2:10; Pss 2:8; 22:28 [Eng. 27]; 67:8 [Eng. 7]; 72:8; 98:3; Isa 45:22; 52:10; Zech 9:10), and said of Yhwh and the servant in Isaiah using the diction of "coastlands" and "the corners of the earth" to signal the imagined edges of distant places (Isa 24:15; 41:5; 42:4, 10, 12; 49:1; 51:5; 59:18-19; 60:9; 66:19). The verb *hyh*, "to be, become," plays a powerful semantic role in Mic 5. The unfolding of divine blessing is signaled throughout the material by *wəhāyâ*, which occurs

309

Micah 5

earlier in Micah at only 2:11 and 4:1, then in a rich density of usage here in 5:4, 6, 7, 9 (Eng. 5, 7, 8, 10).

5:4 (Eng. 5) *He will be the One of Peace.* This powerful Hebrew sentence uses a designation—syntactically the equivalent of a title—to characterize the might of the messianic ruler as securing the cessation of hostilities. Many commentators rightly see as syntactically relevant and ideationally congruent the similar constructions in Judg 5:5 and Ps 68:9 (Eng. 8), as well as "prince of peace" in Isa 9:5 (Eng. 6; see, e.g., *IBHS* §19.5d; Andersen and Freedman 2000, 475–76; Utzschneider 2005, 117; Waltke 2007, 286–87; Goldingay 2021, 459). De Moor captures the sense colloquially: "And he will be a peace-maker!" (2020, 254). The three-word clause in Mic 5:4a could conceivably be translated in a more abstract sense: "This [set of circumstances] will constitute peace" or "This will ensure peace" (so Kessler 2000a, 230; Smith-Christopher 2015, 171). A minor addition in Tg. Mic nudges the syntax in this direction: "then it shall be peace *for us*." NJPS has made a similar decision: "and that shall afford safety"; ZUR renders, "und mit ihm wird der Frieden kommen." But more plausible in terms of the poetics of the strophe, as well as syntactically and conceptually, is the trajectory of interpretation that focalizes the agency of the rising deliverer.

Assyria. The geopolitical term "Assyria" occurs in Micah only at 5:4–5 and 7:12, yet fear of that nation suffuses the book of Micah from start to finish. At its zenith, the Neo-Assyrian Empire was mighty indeed. Kirk Grayson characterizes the "greatest period of the Assyrian empire" as the era from the early eighth century BCE to the early seventh century, a span that encompasses the time of Micah of Moresheth. During this era, Assyria's relentless militarized expansion westward had secured "all of the Fertile Crescent, including Egypt, as well as central Anatolia and western Iran" (Grayson 2011). The prospect of having one's region invaded by Assyria was a fearsome one. "The Assyrians were experts both at open-field warfare and sieges," Grayson comments; once a town was subdued, "it was thoroughly pillaged, and the inhabitants either were taken prisoner or slaughtered in gruesome ways as an example to other towns in the region."

Assyrian troops were notorious for their cruel practices of domination over subjugated enemies on the battlefield and those taken captive as prisoners of war. To understand what surely would have been widespread Judean anxiety concerning Assyrian martial tactics, consider the grim picture painted by Charlie Trimm, a scholar of warfare in antiquity, in what follows. Chariots having higher ground clearance meant that chariot-borne archers

Commentary

Fig. 19. Assyrian palace wall relief from Kalhu (Nimrud) during the reign of Tiglath-Pileser III, ca. 730-727 BCE, showing an Assyrian attack on an enemy town. In the British Museum in London. Photo by Allan Gluck.

would have an advantageous position from which to shoot (2017, 222). It was possible to affix scythes to chariot wheels—apparently the troops of Cyrus of Persia did this—to "cause extra damage to the enemy" (225); armored cavalry in the time of Sennacherib could wield both spears and bows (234). Assyrian epistolary materials and inscriptions document many sieges laid against the fortified cities of regions invaded by Assyrian troops, who deployed archers and stone-slingers, spear- and sword-wielding infantry, ladders and dirt ramps, battering rams, and hand tools such as axes. "Earlier spears," Trimm advises, "were around five feet long, but beginning during the reign of Sargon II they extended to nine feet" (521); short swords were often made of iron (523). Maces may have been used in battle or in ritual ceremonies (524).When besieging a fortified city, the Assyrians used tactics such as sapping, that is, digging covered trenches for protection of the advancing soldiers and, once close enough, to undermine the defenders' walls; flooding the city by means of deep-cut channels that reached groundwater; attacking by night; blockading avenues of food supplies so as to starve the trapped inhabitants into submission or death; and intimidating enemy resisters by displaying the mutilated bodies or heads of their fallen compatriots (251-60, 286). Trimm writes, "The frequent depiction of military scribes counting the severed heads of those defeated in battle in the Assyrian reliefs indicates that this was most likely a common practice throughout the Assyrian Empire," citing a relief from the reign of Assurnasirpal II "in which the soldiers carry severed heads while musicians play as part of a victory celebration" (342).

Boer comments sardonically on Assyrian priests' ritual support of pillaging, "Assyrians apparently were religiously hardwired for plunder," and goes on to note that a policy of militarized extraction as a chief source of

Micah 5

revenue meant that resource-hungry empires had to launch invasions on a continual basis, and were always "[teetering] on the perpetual edge of collapse" (2015, 211). "The gains from plunder are largely immediate," Boer remarks; "the wine is drunk; the human beings are molested, mutilated, and killed; the herds are driven off or slaughtered; the accumulated treasures in temple and palace are carted away. The Neo-Assyrians in particular preferred to engage in scorched-earth policies, slashing, slaughtering, and burning on their way through" (154-55). Trimm adds, "The taking of foreign items (especially luxury items) enhanced the Assyrian Empire through the visual demonstration of Assyrian superiority" (2017, 334). A harshly punitive culture of violence was enacted not only on the battlefield but within Assyrian society as well, according to Grayson: "Punishments for criminal acts were severe, commonly requiring physical mutilation, torture, and execution" (2011). Frahm observes of Assyria's enslavement of prisoners of war, "To make it as difficult as possible for slaves to abscond, it was not unusual to burn the names of their owners, or a message about their status, into their skin, a treatment originally applied to cattle" (2023, 315).

The articulation of the name "Assyria" here, for the first time in the Micah oracles, conveys a powerful shock of recognition and dread. The fearsome enemy unnamed at the opening of this prophetic book has marched inexorably toward the viewer, so to speak, and now the audience can see clearly: it is Assyria. In 5:4b-5 (Eng. 5b-6), we cannot look away from the advance of Assyrian troops—the enemy troops keep marching toward the audience, the repetition of the two-syllable *yidrōk* ("tread") underlining the point sonically within two longer repeated lines. The invaders march not only upon Judah, but also, as it were, upon the position of the implied audience that had been delighting in oracles of salvation in Micah 4 and 5:1-4a (Eng. 2-5a). Assyria's advance, depicted in spare language as inexorable, could reflect the historical context of the invasion of the Levant by Tiglath-Pileser III in 734-732, or the assault of Sennacherib on Judah and Jerusalem in 701, or the skilled interweaving of valences of both of those times of terror in this prophetic poetry.

Elayi observes that "the Syrian coast . . . [had been] incorporated into the Assyrian Empire in 738" (2022, 110). In Mic 5, Tiglath-Pileser's military campaign during the Syro-Ephraimite war may well be in view. Elayi writes that during this time, Tiglath-pileser's army "confronted Phoenician and Philistine cities; the kingdoms of Israel, Judah, and Damascus, and the Arabs," military incursions that are recorded in Assyrian "long and short inscriptions, on a fragmentary stela from Assur, on a relief in the palace at

Nimrud, and in several letters" (129). Tiglath-pileser's plundering of Gaza in 734 would have struck terror into the hearts of Judeans who had heard the news: Assyrian forces "carried off gold, 800 talents of silver, and people," including family members of the ruler of Gaza, Hanunu, who had fled to Egypt but was reinstated after paying "tribute of gold, silver, multicolored garments, linen garments, and large horses" (136).

Other regional entities sought in vain to defend against Assyrian aggression, something dramatized in 2 Kgs 15–17 and Isa 7–10 in narrative accounts and vivid poetry. Rebelling were Menahem of Samaria, Rezin (Rahiânu) of Aram, and Pekah of Israel, among others; Elayi cites Neo-Assyrian documentation of former vassals "Hanunu of Gaza, Mitinti of Ashkelon, and Samsi queen of the Arabs" in this regard (139, 150). The Assyrian ruler boasted of having overwhelmed Menahem "[like a snowstorm] and he... fled like a bird, alone.... I returned him to his place [and imposed tribute upon him, to wit:] gold, silver, linen garments with multicolored trimmings," and as regards Israel, "all its inhabitants (and) their possessions I led to Assyria.... I received from them 10 talents of gold, 1,000(?) talents of silver as their [tri]bute and brought them to Assyria" (*ANEATP*, 265). Tiglath-pileser's assault on Damascus in 733–732 bore the hallmarks of notorious Assyrian cruelty regarding prisoners of war: "he impaled the foremost men alive while forcing the people of Damascus to watch" (147), the kind of spectacle designed to intimidate and to suppress resistance. The anti-Assyrian coalition was unsuccessful and its members were subjugated by Tiglath-pileser. Among cities represented as captured in Assyrian reliefs and inscriptions are "Astaratu" and "Gazru," which Elayi notes are usually identified as Ashtaroth in Gilead and Gezer (143). The ruler of Judah, Ahaz, remained a vassal of the Neo-Assyrian Empire. Tiglath-pileser's descendant, Sennacherib, besieged Jerusalem thirty years later, during the reign of Hezekiah; this too may be within the visual frame of the prophetic scribe of Mic 5. Because the poetry in Micah is elliptical, identifying any specific contextual referent is not possible.

Some read "Assyria" in this verse as meaning the actual Neo-Assyrian Empire, but many who take Mic 5 to have been composed in the Neo-Babylonian era or later argue that "Assyria" is being deployed as a "codename for whatever great power threatens from the north" (Mays 1976, 120). The cipher "Babylon" used for Rome in the biblical book of Revelation is regularly cited as analogous. Hays and Machinist observe that as Hebrew Bible traditions developed, "Assyria took on a literary and ideological role as the second nation, alongside Egypt, to represent the prototypical foreign

Micah 5

imperial power that is judged by God" (2016, 103). Readers should be alert to the polysemous shimmer of possibilities in Micah's layered poetry about this destroyer. The once seemingly invincible Assyrians are in view here as fodder for a counternarrative in which Judah—not a coalition of Israel's allies, not Babylonia, but Judah—will have the resources to defeat any invader who treads upon Judean territory. The play of ambiguity in Mic 5:4b-8 (Eng. 5b-9) is artful: the prophetic scribe suggests the imminence of an invasion that may already have been a century old in Judah's lived history, rewriting the historical memory of the terror inflicted by Assyria in terms that would be relevant to fresh challenges faced by a later generation.

treads within our fortresses. The verb *drk*, "to tread upon, tread underfoot," is slightly awkward when linked syntactically with "fortresses" (*'armənōtênû*) in 5:4b (Eng. 5b), but the image is clear enough: enemy troops will tramp through the fortified cities that had sought to resist them. Some translations, including NRSV, emend to "our soil" (*'ădāmōtênû*) on the logic that, given that the image of invaders treading on soil makes excellent sense and the term stands in parallelism with *bə'arṣēnû* ("our land") three words earlier (BHQ, 104), the consonantal sequence *'rm* was likely a misreading of an original sequence *'dm*. Certainly the scribal confusion of *resh* and *dalet* is a widely recognized phenomenon in textual transmission generally. But emendation is not recommended here. Within the poet's imagined context of military invasion, the interpreter should note that Judean leaders of important and therefore fortified cities ("seven shepherds and eight princes of mortals") are in view as resistance fighters, and should also observe the stronger parallelism of the repeated lines in 5:4b and 5b (Eng. 5b and 6b), *kî-yābô' bə'arṣēnû wəkî yidrōk*, "when he invades our land and treads within" with divergent direct objects concluding the lines. It is best to read the text as it stands: Judah's fortresses will be attacked, and indeed—flagged with parallelistic heightening—not only targeted cities but the entire territory of Judah is under threat.

seven shepherds and eight princes of mortals. This phrase exhibits Biblical Hebrew parallelism in the formal "seven plus eight" construction, which here signals comprehensiveness or sufficiency beyond what is needed. Micah[LXX] has "bites" or "stings" for the second noun (*dēgmata*): "eight stings of people" is likely a misreading of the Hebrew *nsyk* as *nšk* (Glenny 2015, 119-20), the latter verb occurring in 3:5. It is a bold claim, if the prophetic scribe is envisioning eight mighty leaders from within Judah alone. One could also hear this as signaling that a number of nations, standing in alliance with Judah, will band together to dispatch the Assyrian threat. Midrashic interpretation and, centuries later, the Malbim suggest former rulers of Israel and Judah will arise in the messianic era: the seven shepherds are Hezekiah, Manasseh, Amon, Jehoahaz, Jehoiakim, Jehoiachin, and Zedekiah, while the eight princes are "the last eight monarchs [excluding Shallum... who only reigned for one month] who ruled the Northern Kingdom prior to the Assyrian invasion": Jehoahaz, Joash, Jeroboam, Zechariah, Menahem, Pekahiah, Pekah, and Hoshea (Stavsky 2009, 39).

5:5 (Eng. 6) *they will "shepherd" the land of Assyria.* Here, the poet seems to imagine Judean armed resistance driving the battle deep into Assyrian territory, a prospect that would have been entirely unrealistic in terms of Judah's actual military capacities, but, as an idea, would be encouraging to the implied audience. Cathcart (1978) argues for resonances in 5:4b-5 with Phoenician and Aramaic incantation texts, citing the position of van der Woude (1969) on the quoting of false prophets here as "quite plausible" and offering that the speakers here are represented as "people supremely confident of their own ability to overcome the Assyrians" (48). Fully agreed that the scroll of Micah does not promote human action as effective against foes without the leadership of Yhwh; but it is not impossible that this pericope is intended to follow on from the preceding verses as a pragmatic illustration of the way in which the "One of Peace" will secure the flourishing of Yhwh's people. A similar trope—that Yhwh can effect damage in the heart of enemy territory—may be audible in the prose narrative in Isa 37:36-38 (// 2 Kgs 19:35-37) about the angel of Yhwh slaughtering 185,000 Assyrian troops encamped around Jerusalem and the subsequent assassination of Sennacherib back in Nineveh by his sons.

land of Nimrod. Scribal traditions about Assyrian kingship lie in the background of Gen 10:8-12, where Nimrod is identified as "a mighty warrior" and "a mighty hunter before the Lord," as well as the builder of many cities across Mesopotamian territory (for judicious analysis of the Neo-Assyrian historical and literary background of the Nimrod reference, see Jones 2022). Nimrud, a site identified with ancient Kalhu on the Tigris River in what is now Iraq, was chosen by the Assyrian ruler Assurnasirpal II (r. 883-859) for what archaeologists call his Northwest Palace. Magnificent carved reliefs adorn several entryways, these described by Hays and Machinist as "colossal sculptures of supernatural composite beings" that, "viewed from the front... appear to be standing still, [while] viewed from the side they appear to be striding" (2016, 78). Nimrud also boasts "the most impressive surviving ruin of an Assyrian ziggurat" (71). "A rich horde

Micah 5

of finely carved ivories" and "jewelry of superb craftsmanship" have been found at Nimrud, and the Neo-Assyrian Empire left behind "hundreds of thousands" of inscriptions in Akkadian, including "hymns, prayers, magical incantations, medical texts, divinatory texts," libraries of myths and epic poetry, and more, including palace archives and pragmatic trade documents (Grayson 2011).

with the drawn blade. The Assyrians were known for their domination on the battlefield and their relentless cruelty in how they treated prisoners of war. Marian Feldman notes that Assyrian imperial representations purposefully reinforced Assyrian monarchs' reputation for cruel domination and plundering as an element of the identity formation of Assyrian elites. For example, in Sennacherib's "self-styled Palace without Rival (the Southwest Palace in Nineveh)" are reliefs that depict "an Assyrian soldier felling a Lachishite with his dagger," while "beyond them are two . . . individuals stretched out as they are flayed. Following these we see groups of men carrying sacks and boxes . . . oxen [that] pull carts filled with more sacks," and women and a camel carry yet more sacks, all symbolizing the "Assyrian imperial acquisition of wealth" (Feldman 2011, 136–37). Here in 5:5 (Eng. 6), the Judean prophetic scribe imagines fierce recompense enacted against the rapacious and cruel Assyria by indomitable Judean military leaders.

The present translation reads *pətīḥâ*, "drawn sword/dagger" (HALOT 3:989–90; BHQ, 104; Cathcart 1978, 43), for Micah^MT *pətāḥêhā*, "its doorways/entrances," an emendation based on presumed metathesis of *khet* and *yod* through scribal error. Earlier interpreters who argue for "swords" here include David Kimḥi and Abraham ibn Ezra (ca. 1092–ca. 1167), per Stavsky (2009, 40). But it would not be impossible to leave the noun as it stands. This poetic line could be portraying an incursion that breaches the entrances of Assyrian cities (NJPS: "in its gates"; ZUR, "in dessen Toren") or, alternatively, an invasion so relentless that there would be fierce hand-to-hand combat even in the doorways of Assyrian domiciles. The rare term *pətîḥâ*, found elsewhere only in Ps 55:22 (Eng. 21), there in the plural, makes good sense here and completes an elegant heightening in parallelistic construction with *ḥereb*, moving from a two-syllable common weapon to a three-syllable rarer term for a weapon. Nevertheless, one could argue for dramatic heightening enacted through an elaborate chiastic structure beginning in the preceding verse: if an Assyrian (grammatically singular, though obviously collective in sense) were to invade Judean territory and attack Judean fortresses, Judah's military reprisal will muster not one, not seven, but eight leaders (marked multiply for a plurality of commanders or their armies) who will invade Assyrian territory and press the battle even to the gates of Assyrian strongholds or, alternatively, to the doorways of Assyrian houses. The emended reading (*pətîḥâ*) is alarming in the spare elegance of its expression, inviting the implied audience to see before them an inescapable glittering blade; the reading of the text as it stands in Micah[MT] (*pətāḥêhā*) is alarming for the scope of reprisal envisioned throughout Assyria.

He will rescue . . . when he invades. This deliverer is the ruler (*môšēl*) whose rise to leadership has been prophesied in 5:1 (Eng. 5:2). Whether his act of deliverance comprises destroying Assyrian military hegemony or extracting Judean prisoners of war from Assyrian territory cannot be known. The *kî . . . kî* sequence could be translated via the conditional sense in English: "if he invades our land and [if he] treads within our territory" (so NRSV, NJPS). But the prophetic scribe is offering a vision of Judah as having been given up (5:2 [Eng. 3]) — militarily defeated, its people taken into exile. This material is best read as encompassing the horizon of that inescapable defeat and the subsequent overwhelming response of a Judean coalition, under the leadership of Yhwh or Yhwh's appointed ruler, to crush the Assyrian aggressor. A decisive intervention in Tg. Mic 5:5 adds negation: "He shall save us from the Assyrian *so that* he shall *not* come into our land and shall *not* tread upon our territory."

5:6 (Eng. 7) *the remnant of Jacob.* This phrase, *šə'ērît ya'ăqōb*, comes up in Micah only in 5:6, 7 (Eng. 7, 8). "Remnant" (*šə'ērît*) standing alone occurs at Mic 4:7, and the noun linked with other *nomina recta* occurs in Mic 2:12 (referring to the remnant of Israel) and 7:18 (referring to the remnant of God's inheritance). Micah[LXX] adds *en tois ethnesin* ("among the nations") here, presumably under the influence of that same phrase in 5:7.

like dew from Yhwh, like spring showers upon the grass. This beautiful imagery suggests new growth after a long period of winter dormancy. The term *rəbîbîm* occurs only six times in the Hebrew Scriptures. In Deut 32:2, it is used in a gorgeous sequence that characterizes Moses's teaching about the greatness of Yhwh. A literal usage in Ps 65:11 (Eng. 10) celebrates the agricultural growth fostered by the Creator. In Ps 72:6, the term evokes the justice, righteousness, and peace that flourish under the reign of the divinely appointed king. Two occurrences in Jeremiah underline the withholding of spring showers as divine punishment for Judah's sin (Jer 3:3) and articulate Judah's repentance through acknowledgment of Yhwh as the only one who can bring life-giving rains (14:22). The subject of the 3ms verbs *yəqawweh*

Micah 5

and *yəyaḥēl* is the grass, which relies not on human beings but on YHWH to provide spring rains.

does not . . . put its hope in mortals. Several books of the Latter Prophets, most notably Isaiah, draw a polemical contrast between faith in YHWH and political pragmatism in military planning and alliance-building with allies in the ancient Near East (e.g., Hos 5:13-15; 7:11-13; Isa 30:1-5; 31:1-3). Micah^{LXX} envisions the "remnant of Jacob" not as spring showers but as a flock ("like lambs upon the grass," *hōs arnes epi agrōstin*) so numerous that none will be able to assemble it. Gelston surmises that the Greek verb *sunagō* there, rendering the Micah^{MT} verb "to hope," was likely derived from *qwh* II, "to assemble, gather" (*BHQ*, 105; *HALOT* 3:1082-83).

5:7 (Eng. 8) *like a lion.* Lion iconography and leonine metaphors were prevalent in ancient Israel and Judah, Assyria, and other ancient Near Eastern cultures, especially as representing divine and royal power (Strawn 2016), but also to evoke the might or confidence of warriors in battle, malevolent adversaries generally, or the righteous (Strawn 2005, 46-66). Hearing the roar of a leonine predator would have evoked a response of terror. Claiming the power of the lion for one's deity or community—as for "the remnant of Jacob" here—underscores the fearsome political and military might enjoyed by a people under divine patronage or under the protection of an effective monarch.

tramples and tears to pieces. A lion wrestles a prey animal to the ground and suffocates it, rather than stomping on it with its paws. Wilhelm Rudolph translates, "zu Boden schlägt" (1975, 101), which is deft in the target language but a bit too free in its understanding of *rms* for me to adopt the English analogue here. Given that lions do not literally tread on prey or trample them as might hooved quadrupeds (2 Kgs 9:33; Ezek 26:11; Dan 8:7) or throngs of people (2 Kgs 7:17, 20), the poet's use of *rms* here may be intended subtly to evoke the semantic valence of an unstoppable horde—the vast and powerful troops of Jacob—rather than keeping too slavishly to the semantic range of *rms* within the vehicle of the metaphor. In Micah^{LXX} the metaphorical lion does not trample and rend its prey but, rather, "separates out" (*diasteilas*) and then "seizes" (*harpasē*) the prey. Perhaps, as per Gelston, the translator envisions "the predator separating the intended victim from the rest of the flock" (*BHQ*, 105), which works well to describe the predatory strategy of actual lions (the vehicle of the metaphor), but yields an odd sense for the tenor of the metaphor.

5:8 (Eng. 9) *Let your hand be raised . . . and let all your enemies be cut down!* The apocopated verb in the first clause is jussive in form and expresses volitional force, though more subtly in this elevated poetic bicolon than if this were a pragmatic narrative (*IBHS* §34.3.d). The referent for the ms addressee in view here is unlikely to be the "remnant," šəʾērît being a feminine noun. The referent could be "Israel," or the ruler or army commander of the forces of Israel/Judah, or "Jacob." Going further back in Mic 5 for an explicit antecedent, Bethlehem of Ephrathah is addressed via the syntactically emphatic ms pronoun "you" in 5:1 (Eng. 2). Bethlehem is functioning metonymically there as representative of the authoritative Davidic lineage. The "hand" in 5:8 (Eng. 9) could conceivably function as synecdoche for the military power of Judean troops commanded by that same royal figure.

Most likely, though, this is directed not to the envisioned human deliverer but to Yhwh (so also Wolff 1990, 157). Andersen and Freedman offer a chilling note regarding the sense, citing Deut 32:40 on the military commander's raised hand: in the spectrum of violence enacted in warfare, "this is the very last scene—not of casualties in battle, but of the execution of captives after it is all over" (2000, 487). The broader context of Deut 32:39–43 gives us the unmistakable voice of Yhwh as divine warrior: "There is no god besides me. I kill and I make alive" (Deut 32:39). The deity is the one who takes vengeance. In Deut 32:42, a poetic sequence unfolds from the battlefield ("arrows") to the execution of prisoners of war: Yhwh thunders, "I will make my arrows drunk with blood, and my sword shall devour flesh—with the blood of the slain and the captives." Here in Mic 5:8, the prophetic scribe is performing a ritual shout to Yhwh as the divine warrior acclaimed in the worshipping assembly. Several psalms make this rhetorical move, offering poetically crafted shouts to Yhwh to arise and fight on behalf of the speaker in battles literal or metaphorical. Among the relevant psalms are Ps 68:2 (Eng. 1), "Let God rise up, let [God's] enemies be scattered!" and Ps 132:8, "Rise up, O Lord, and go to your resting place, you and the ark of your might"; see also Pss 3:8 (Eng. 7); 7:7 (Eng. 6); 9:20 (Eng. 19); 10:12; 17:13; 44:27; 82:8; 94:16. Here, Yhwh responds in the war song that closes Mic 5.

5:9 (Eng. 10) *In that day—saying of Yhwh*. This sequence occurs in 4:6, here with a slightly fuller Hebrew prepositional phrase. See commentary on 4:6 for more.

I will cut down. The verb *krt*, "to cut, to cut down," is taken up from the preceding verse, with its affirmation that Yhwh will cut down Israel's ene-

Micah 5

mies, and amplified in a war song directed to an unspecified masculine singular adversary. This masterful ancient lyric uses a concatenation of short, powerful clauses with a repeated first-person verb (*hikrattî*) to evoke the continual slashing of a warrior wielding a sword on the battlefield, cutting down enemies, their cities, and more. Cazelles and Sperling say the theme of 1:7 is revisited here as regards the "extermination of idols" (2007, 162). While that is not wrong, I would counter that the imagery of forcible "cutting down" of warriors and massive fortifications in 5:9-14 has little in common with the diction of pulverizing and burning in 1:7. I hear a more decisive similarity, especially audible as regards dense syntagmatic repetition, to the rhetorical design of the Song of the Sword in Jer 50:35-38 and the chilling onomatopoeic effects of the Song of the Sword in Ezek 21:9-17.

Who is the target of these actions of divine destruction? The poetry is artful in its opacity. The masculine singular pronoun "you" occurs in 4:8 and 5:1 (Eng. 2), addressing the Tower of Eder and Bethlehem, respectively; speech to a masculine singular addressee in 5:8 (Eng. 9) is directed to Yhwh. But the addressee in the closing verses of Micah 5 is the target of Yhwh's fury, something surely destabilizing to the implied audience; as Erin Runions observes, "One moment *you* are an active and aggressive subject affiliated with [Yhwh] . . . the next moment *you* are a quite different subject, one whose activities are harshly curtailed by [Yhwh]" (2001, 227). Some of the imagery gestures toward other cultures, as with "sorceries" and "soothsayers" in 5:11 (Eng. 12; though these illicit means of intermediation are also critiqued within Israel, as, e.g., in Isa 2:6). Other images are congruent with Deuteronomistic polemic against Israel and Judah for their idolatrous practices, or warn about the threat of other nations leading Israel into the same, as with "sacred pillars" and "sacred poles" (e.g., Exod 23:24; 34:13; Deut 7:5; 12:3; Hos 10:2) and "bowing down to the works of your hands" (e.g., Isa 2:8, 20; 44:9-20; 46:6; Jer 1:16).

Wolff suggests the original addressee was the prophet's own community, with the nations expected to learn from "Micah's proclamation of [Yhwh's] judgment upon Israel and Judah, that they might understand the true basis for the course of history" (1990, 157, 160). I would argue that the pedagogy works in the opposite direction. Through a brilliant strategy on the part of the prophetic scribe, these violent images initially seem to be directed against enemy nations, as 5:8 (Eng. 9) suggests, but increasingly audible resonances with Deuteronomistic polemic against Yhwh's own people press the Judean implied audience into siding with an avenging Yhwh; the ambiguity allows for horrifying divine retribution on those within Judah who

Commentary

do not obey. Some might wish to argue that the ambiguity is resolved in 5:14 (Eng. 15), "I will exact vengeance . . . on the nations that have not heeded," but readers of Mic 1-3 would certainly realize that Judah could still find itself numbered among those nations, if Judeans do not refrain from idolatry. In early Christian interpretation were advocates of both views: that the target of divine retribution will be the nations or a specific adversary such as Assyria, as per Theodore of Mopsuestia, or alternatively, that the target is Judah under the Babylonian onslaught, as Cyril of Alexandria holds (Roukema 2019, 153). O'Brien opts for the nations as the target (2015, 69), yet frames the matter with some nuance, arguing that this material "indicates the writer's animosity against foreigners—either those outside of his land or those occupying his land" (70).

The artistic ambiguity and tension generated by the Hebrew are decisively resolved in Tg. Mic 5:9-14 through the addition of clarifying modifiers that create fuller and more precise predicates, in some instances accompanied by changes of pronominal suffixes from 2ms "you" to 3pl "their." It is the horses, cities, fortresses, and idolatrous images "of the peoples" that are to be cut down, and in the final clause, the nations "have not heeded *the teaching of the law*," that which sets Israel and Judah apart in covenant with Yhwh. Cathcart and Gordon note, "MT vv. 9-13 are an indictment of Israel for their trust in secular and non-Yahwistic religious practices," and the targumic alteration of the text "removes the condemnation . . . from Israel and [places it on] the enemies of Israel" (1989, 123n20). Kimḥi offers the other view: that Israel is the addressee, suggesting that "the prophet's intent, however, is to assure Israel that peace will prevail forever and therefore that the objects" identified as targets of destruction by Yhwh "will never again be needed" (Stavsky 2009, 42). I would underscore that the ambiguity of the Biblical Hebrew poetry allows for either Judah or the nations to be imagined as the target of Yhwh's wrath, effectively encouraging—or frightening—the implied audience into choosing to obey.

5:10 (Eng. 11) *the cities of your land, and . . . all your fortifications.* "Cities" here and in 5:14 (Eng. 15) signals the enemy's walled population centers as bastions of political power and military strength. The first two verses of Yhwh's war song focus on militarized destruction of the adversary's means of resistance, from warhorses and chariots to cities and their defensive fortifications. The penultimate verse in this passage revisits the fate of the doomed cities, as if to ensure that the implied audience will imagine them in rubble. The valence there may also be slightly different; see below.

Micah 5

5:11 (Eng. 12) *sorceries . . . soothsayers*. These avenues of intermediation between supplicants and their deities—including Yhwh—are sternly forbidden in Hebrew Bible texts (Exod 22:17 [Eng. 18]; Deut 18:10; Mal 3:5) and are used as terms of opprobrium to impute shame (2 Kgs 9:22; 2 Chr 33:6; Isa 47:9, 12; Jer 27:9; Nah 3:4).

5:12 (Eng. 13) *sacred pillars*. Standing stones were set up individually and in larger grouped installments in many ancient cultures across the globe, going back to the Neolithic period. Ritual and other functions of these stones were assuredly varied and cannot be fully known. In some cases, stones seem to have been aligned for astronomical purposes having to do with solstices, equinoxes, or other solar or lunar phenomena. Standing stones may well have served as places for making offerings to deities, honoring the dead, solemnifying agreements, memorializing events, or marking territory, as can be glimpsed in some Hebrew Bible texts (Gen 28:18-22; 31:13, 43-54; 35:20; Exod 24:4; Josh 4:1-9, 20-24; Isa 19:19; Hos 3:4; 10:1-2). The practice of setting up pillars or poles to honor deities other than Yhwh comes in for blistering polemic in the Deuteronomistic History. Laato observes of Israelite religion, "That *maṣṣēbôt* were an integral part of the Israelite Yahweh cult becomes clear not only from archaeological evidence but also from biblical texts. While the present form of the Hebrew Bible represents an intolerant attitude toward standing stones (Lev. 26:1; Deut. 16:22), many references in historical books indicate that such pillars were regularly used" (2018, 222).

5:13 (Eng. 14) *I will devastate your cities*. The enemy's urban centers here may stand for centralized cult infrastructures and the political and economic power that supported those. Andersen and Freedman observe that the city in enemy territory constituted "the most conspicuous symbol of idolatry," explaining, "In Mesopotamian religion certain cities attained renown because of a popular female deity, such as the Ishtar of Arbela. . . . Something similar in Israel lies behind the Ashimat of Samaria, and the Asherahs of the Judean cities" (2000, 492; on the Canaanite deity Ashima, see Amos 8:14 and 2 Kgs 17:30). The reading of "cities" here in terms of idolatry makes excellent sense, given that the focus in the preceding three verses has been on ritual practices perceived as illicit by the prophetic scribe. Perceptible, then, is a chiastic structure anchored by "cities" in 5:10 and 13 (Eng. 11 and 14): the devastating fury of Yhwh moves from the battlefield into the fortified cities, then to divine destruction of the various practices

Commentary

and associated ritual objects that facilitated worship of other gods within these cities, the chiasm concluding with a note about the leveling of the cities as the centers of idolatry.

5:14 (Eng. 15) *I will exact vengeance . . . on the nations that have not heeded.* Would the prophetic scribe have thought other nations had the opportunity to heed the teachings of Yhwh regarding idolatry and illicit means of divination? If not, the terrifying prospect moves into view, only in this last verse of the war song, that the enemy whom Yhwh will be cutting down and destroying might include Judah. In the larger redactional landscape that stretches beyond the literary borders of the book of Micah, Rainer Albertz cites the war song of divine vengeance in Mic 5 in his argument that "the editor of the Book of the Four interpreted the entire exile as a judgment of purgation (Hos. 3.1-5; Amos 9.7-10; Mic. 5.9-13; Zeph. 1.4-6; 3.9-11)," meaning, of course, purgation of Israel and Judah (2010, 18). See the interpretation section above for my argument that the war song of divine vengeance inhabits a Janus position, looking backward, as it were, to Assyria as the target of Yhwh's fury, but also looking ahead to Mic 6 for Yhwh's indictment of the covenant people for failing to obey. That Assyria is to be defeated is crystal clear from verses earlier in Mic 5. But Judah, too, stands under indictment. Mendel Hirsch (1833-1900) holds a position that allows for both Israel and other nations to be encompassed in the gaze of this oracle: "Verses 9-14 are directed toward Israel who had lost its glorious power and had suffered in exile," but other nations, "upon seeing the collapse of . . . Israel, should have understood that they too were threatened and should have changed their evil ways, but they did not," thus showing that they had not been paying attention (Stavsky 2009, 43).

In the final form of Mic 4-6, the implied audience has been taught to anticipate that nations across the world will indeed hear the invitation of Yhwh to come to Zion and learn the ways of torah (4:2). The lyrical prophecies of 4:1-8 and 5:1-3 (Eng. 2-4) direct the audience's imagination toward an irenic future marked by the covenant community's healing, restoration, and flourishing in safety, albeit with interspersed notes that trumpet Zion's dominion and subjugation of other nations (4:13; 5:4b-8 [Eng. 5b-9]). As Mic 5 closes, the ambiguity of this war song is chilling. These verses are brilliantly designed to capture the attention of the implied audience, subtly but unmistakably suggesting that throughout its history, Israel has been capable of covenantal disobedience, while at least theoretically, other nations might yet heed Yhwh. Micah 6 will drive the point home: God's

Micah 5

people have failed to honor their divine redeemer, though the path of obedience is beautifully clear and the journey of walking with Yhwh is neither complicated nor arduous.

BIBLIOGRAPHY

Albertz, R. 2010. "How Radical Must the New Beginning Be? The Discussion between the Deutero-Isaiah and the Ezekiel School." Pages 7–21 in *The Centre and the Periphery: A European Tribute to Walter Brueggemann*. Edited by J. Middlemas, D. J. A. Clines, and E. K. Holt. HBM 27. Sheffield: Sheffield Phoenix.

Cathcart, K. J. 1978. "Micah 5:4–5 and Semitic Incantations." *Bib* 59:38–48.

Feldman, M. H. 2011. "Assyrian Representations of Booty and Tribute as a Self-Portrayal of Empire." Pages 135–50 in *Interpreting Exile: Displacement and Deportation in Biblical and Modern Contexts*. Edited by B. E. Kelle, F. R. Ames, and J. L. Wight. AIL 10. Atlanta: Society of Biblical Literature.

Grayson, A. K. 2011. "Assyrians." *OEANE* online.

Jones, C. W. 2022. "The Literary-Historical Memory of Sargon of Akkad in Assyria as the Background for Nimrod in Genesis 10:8–12." *JBL* 141:595–615. doi:10.15699/jbl.1414.2022.1.

Knapp, A. 2021. "The Succession Narrative in Twenty-First-Century Research." *CBR* 19:211–34. doi:10.1177/1476993X20954841.

Luther, M. 2013. *The Works of Martin Luther*. Vol. 52, *Sermons, Volume 2*. Edited by H. J. Hillerbrand. Charlottesville, VA: InteLex Corporation. Originally published Philadelphia: Fortress, 1974.

Smith-Christopher, D. 2018. "Micah 5:2–5a." Pages 47–49 in vol. 1 of *Connections: A Lectionary Commentary for Preaching and Worship Year C*. Edited by J. B. Green, T. G. Long, L. A. Powery, and C. L. Rigby. 3 vols. Louisville: Westminster John Knox.

MICAH 6

Juridical Defense of Yhwh's Fidelity

6:1–5

¹Pay attention {*mp*} to what Yhwh is saying!
Rise {*ms*}, present the disputation before the mountains,
   and let the hills hear your voice!
²Pay attention {*mp*}, O mountains, to the disputation of Yhwh,
   and [pay attention], O everlasting foundations of the earth!
For Yhwh has a disputation against [Yhwh's] people,
   and with Israel [Yhwh] will argue.
³"O my people, what did I ever do to you {*ms*}?
   How have I wearied you?
      Answer me!
⁴For I brought you up out of the land of Egypt,
   and from the house of slavery I redeemed you.
And I sent before you
   Moses, Aaron, and Miriam.
⁵O my people, remember! What had Balak king of Moab
   contrived?
   And how had Balaam son of Beor answered him?
[Remember everything] from Shittim to Gilgal,
   in order to understand the righteous acts of Yhwh!

Dialogue on Covenantal Obligations

6:6–8

⁶"With what should I come before Yhwh,
   bow down before God on High?

Micah 6

> Should I come before [Yhwh] with burnt offerings,
>> with year-old calves?
> ⁷Will Yhwh be pleased with thousands of rams,
>> with myriad torrents of oil?
> Should I give my firstborn for my transgression,
>> the fruit of my body for the sin of my spirit?"

> ⁸[Yhwh] has told you, O mortal!
>> What is good?
>> What does Yhwh require of you?
> Nothing other than to do justice, to cherish fidelity,
>> and to proceed humbly with your God.

Indictment of the Corrupt City

6:9–16

> ⁹The voice of Yhwh summons the city
>> (and it is prudence to have regard for your name;
>> pay attention {*mp*}, O tribe, for Who appointed it {*fs*}?):
> ¹⁰ "Are there still in the house of the wicked one
>> treasures of wickedness,
>>> while the shorted ephah is cursed?
> ¹¹Can I remain blameless given wicked scales
>> and a bag of deceitful weights,
> ¹²when its {*fs*} wealthy are full of violence,
>> and its inhabitants speak falsehood
>> with treacherous tongues in their mouths?
> ¹³Thus I myself have made you {*ms*} weak by beating you,
>> left you desolate because of your sins.

> ¹⁴As for you: you devour but are not satisfied,
>> and there is bloating within you.
> You draw aside but cannot deliver;
>> and those whom you do deliver, I give to the sword.
> ¹⁵ As for you: you sow but cannot reap.
> As for you: you tread olives but cannot anoint with oil,
>> and [tread] grapes, but cannot drink wine.

¹⁶"For he has kept the statutes of Omri
   and all the practices of the house of Ahab.
And you {mp} have followed their counsels,
   so that I must make you {ms} a desolation
   and its {fs} inhabitants an object of hissing!
So you {mp} must bear the reproach of my people."

INTERPRETATION

Micah 6 presses a fierce challenge to the Judeans constructed as listeners within this artful prophetic book and to the broader implied audience of the Micah traditions as well. Micah 1 had the audience witness the power of YHWH reducing Samaria to rubble (1:3-7), the prophet wailing as a military threat pressed on into Judah, throwing every population center, from obscure unwalled villages to fortified Gath and Lachish to Jerusalem itself (1:8-15), into panic and mourning as their denizens were carried into captivity (1:16). Micah 2 gave us scheming elites (2:1-2) whose oppressive machinations had brought ruin to the entire community (2:3-5, 9-10, 12-13), their denials and suppression of prophetic truth-telling (2:6, 11) ineffective against a wrathful YHWH. Micah 3 showed us the savagery and deception of Judean oppressors and the false prophets who pandered to them (3:1-3, 5, 9-11), then elaborated the dire consequences (3:6-7, 12), leaving the audience no choice other than to trust the spirit-filled Micah himself in a time of darkness (3:8). Micah 4 offered a luminous vision of a future in which peace, restoration, and flourishing were the hallmarks of a global community that eagerly followed torah ethics (4:1-7); then the fierce geopolitical antagonisms of the present had come back into focus, albeit framed in the sure confidence that YHWH had planned Zion's eventual dominion (4:8-14). Micah 5 had envisioned a "shepherd" ruling in the strength of YHWH (5:1-4a [Eng. 2-5a]), with the "remnant of Jacob" now invincible (5:4b-7 [Eng. 5b-8]) and every antagonist feeling the full force of YHWH's vengeance (5:8-14 [Eng. 9-15]).

Here in Mic 6, the prophet turns his gaze directly on the implied audience, his incendiary words calling the people to attention and bidding the Creator—the boldness of this is shocking—to present the divine disputation. Towering mountains and rolling hills, the "everlasting foundations of the earth," are exhorted to bear witness as the dispute proceeds. Those topographical features of the landscape, whether imagined in literal or fig-

Micah 6

urative terms, signal that the Creator of all that has ever come into being is now training the divine gaze on a malfeasant Israel. As with the imagery in Mic 1:1-4, so here the perspective is framed from the immensity of cosmic divine enthronement downward toward that which is majestic in the landscape—in Mic 1, it was "the high places of the earth," the mountains, and the valleys—and finally down to that which is small and threatened. The force of the downward-sweeping trajectory, the gaze from eternity trained upon the misdeeds of officials and elites who seem minuscule by comparison, brilliantly dismantles the power they have seemed to hold over the vulnerable within their community.

Yhwh thunders: "I liberated you from enslavement, and I gave you prophetic leadership and priestly guidance!" The deity continues, "Remember your own history, O Israel": their ancient Moabite enemy had tried mightily to curse them via the utterances of the mercenary seer Balaam. Yhwh had turned the words of malediction into blessing, while Israel encamped, oblivious, below the ridges across which Balaam scurried, building multiple altars and making sacrifices, and then spectacularly failing to pronounce the cursing of Israel that Moab had wanted (Num 23-24). Yhwh's point in Mic 6:3-5 is unmistakable: throughout its history, Israel has been bathed in blessing even when enemies had enslaved them and sought to have them obliterated (Sharp 2009, 134-51).

Yet the abundantly blessed Israel had arrived at Shittim and had immediately engaged in exogamous sexual mixing with Moabites and Midianites, ignoring the torah stipulation that the covenant people remain separate from idolatrous nations, and worshipping the Baal of Peor (Num 25). An outraged Yhwh had sent retribution in the form of a devastating plague: twenty-four thousand Israelites had fallen. Gilgal, too, had been known as a site of sin, possibly for illegitimate shrines and the place where Saul had failed to wait for Samuel and had made sacrifices precipitously; Yhwh had torn the monarchy from Saul as a result (1 Sam 13:1-14). This is the history Yhwh now requires the people to remember.

Micah opposes his culture's false narratives, the stories the elite tell about power that are not true, the norms that lead people away from authentic relationship with one another and worship of Yhwh. False narratives, in the ancient world and today, create logics that deceive and mislead the gullible, the vulnerable, and those who do not dare to dissent. In Mic 6, the prophetic scribe urges his audience to ground their lives in the sacred narratives of old, stories that tell of the emancipation they have known only in Yhwh's redemptive power and the divine retribution that looms when they forget their God.

Juridical Defense of Yhwh's Fidelity (6:1-5)

Many of the prophets envisioned a time when justice and peace would reign. In Jer 31, Yhwh declares that it will become impossible for the covenant people to sin any longer. Where sin had once been engraved with an iron pen on the tablet of their hearts (Jer 17:1), in days to come, Yhwh says, "I will put my law within them, and I will write it on their hearts; and I will be their God, and they shall be my people. No longer shall they teach one another, or say to each other, 'Know the Lord,' for they shall all know me, from the least of them to the greatest, says the Lord; for I will forgive their iniquity, and remember their sin no more" (Jer 31:33-34). In Amos 9:13-15 and a number of passages in Isaiah (e.g., Isa 11:1-9; 19:24-25; 25:6-10; 60:1-62:12), too, are luminous promises of peace and flourishing. But first, Yhwh's people must be held accountable for their sin.

Micah's audience had seen Yhwh's torah lifted up as being of cosmic significance for the flourishing of all nations (Mic 4:1-4). Here in Mic 6, the prophet's community stands before a righteous God whose torah mandates have always been clear: believers should strive to be holy as Yhwh is holy (Lev 19:2) and learn to show mercy as Yhwh shows mercy (cf. Pss 18:26; 25:8-10). Leviticus 19 brims with powerful imperatives calling those who worship Yhwh to compassionate care for the vulnerable and integrity in all their dealings. Believers should neither defraud their neighbors (19:13) nor mock those living with disabling conditions (19:14). Believers should not oppress those who have come from another country to live in the land—the resident alien, the migrant (*gēr*, 19:33-34). Instead, those shaped by torah ethics are to bear no grudge, but to love the neighbor, whether vested landowner or day laborer, as themselves. Believers are to be holy and just, honoring the sanctity of Yhwh's holy name and practicing integrity in all their dealings because, Yhwh thunders, "I am the Lord your God who brought you out of the land of Egypt" (Lev 11:45; cf. 19:36; 22:33; 25:38; 26:13). A righteous and holy Yhwh delivered Israel from enslavement; Israelite and Judean believers owe Yhwh their very selves.

In Mic 6:3-5, Yhwh calls Israel and Judah into adjudication, citing as irrefutable evidence of divine care having sent Moses, Aaron, and Miriam as leaders on Israel's emancipatory journey out of slavery in Egypt. In Moses, Yhwh had given Israel a prophet, lawgiver, and judge to help them navigate faithfully their ordered life in community even in the wilderness, where they had relied daily on manna for food and on divine provision of fresh water, with fearful memories of the trauma of slavery behind them and

Micah 6

the threat of the unknown before them. In Aaron, Yhwh had given Israel a priest to preside over the ritual and liturgical life of the community, keeping the people safe from the awe-inspiring and death-dealing power of Yhwh's holiness and teaching them the ways in which they should honor Yhwh at the center of their common life. In Miriam we see further amplification of prophecy. She is called "the prophet Miriam" in the Song of the Sea (cf. Exod 15:20), possibly one of the most ancient poems preserved in the Hebrew Bible. Miriam the prophet had led the liturgical thanksgiving after the Israelites had crossed the Red Sea to escape the Egyptian army. Yhwh had delivered this people "from Shittim to Gilgal," leading and protecting the Israelite camp against threat after threat throughout the wilderness wandering. Such have been the "righteous acts of Yhwh" throughout Israel's history, meriting thanksgiving and obedience from this people saved from annihilation over and over again by their God.

Dialogue on Covenantal Obligations (6:6-8)

The prophet ventriloquizes a worshipper whose increasingly sarcastic rhetorical questions suggest that the deity cannot be appeased or pleased by what mortals offer. Burnt offerings and the slaughter of year-old calves (6:6) were to be expected in Israelite and Judean ritual sacrifices. The escalation to thousands of rams, myriad torrents of oil, and the speaker's own firstborn child are meant to render the idea of pleasing Yhwh ludicrous. But Micah has a rejoinder: Yhwh has, in fact, made clear what is needful. Not extravagant sacrifices, not the unthinkable slaughter of one's own child: only justice, fidelity, and humility. A similar exhortation can be found in Deut 10, where Moses declares these words before the Israelite congregation:

> So now, O Israel, what does the Lord your God require of you? Only to fear the Lord your God, to walk in all [Yhwh's] ways, to love [Yhwh], to serve the Lord your God with all your heart and with all your soul, and to keep the commandments of the Lord your God.... [Yhwh] is your praise; [Yhwh] is your God, who has done these great and awesome things that your own eyes have seen. (Deut 10:12-13, 21)

But Judah has not heeded its own history. The juridical defense of Yhwh's fidelity to the covenant people (Mic 6:1-5) and the dialogical elaboration of the people's obligations to their divine sovereign (6:6-8) give way to a blistering polemic against sinners.

Indictment of the Corrupt City 6:9–16

Fig. 20. *Michäas*, by Karl Mayer (1810-1876). Fresco (paint on plaster). In the Altlerchenfelder Pfarrkirche in Vienna. Photo by Renáta Sedmáková.

Indictment of the Corrupt City (6:9–16)

The prophet, speaking on behalf of Yhwh, levels a public indictment against an unidentified city and its merchants, who cheat others in order to secure higher profits for themselves, styled the "treasures of wickedness" (6:10). While Jerusalem would assuredly be in view for postexilic audiences, the mention of Omri and his son Ahab in 6:16 retrospectively may broaden the scope of possible referents to include Tirzah, where Omri had reigned initially for six years, and Samaria, where the Omride dynasty had been established (1 Kgs 16:15–29).

Micah 6

Here in Mic 6, the prophetic scribe's decision not to name the city allows for an inchoate sense of alarm in the implied audience: perhaps YHWH is indicting every city involved in economic practices that defraud and rob. In every age, prophets and other truth-tellers have decried the greed and corruption that they see harming subsistence farmers and those living in poverty in rural and urban contexts. For readers of Micah in the twenty-first century, journalists stand in the ranks of those who make known in the public square the consequences of profit-driven economic practices that injure communities living in precarious conditions. Roger Thurow and Scott Kilman have publicized the conditions in which families in Ethiopia struggle through famine and the failures of international development efforts (2009). Contemporary readers aware of disparities generated by capitalist globalization may perceive resonances with Micah's images of deprivation, displacement, and despair (2:2, 9; 3:2-3; 4:10; 6:14-15; 7:1) in passages from Thurow and Kilman such as these:

> In Ethiopia, while agricultural production increased at the dawn of the twenty-first century, the grain market was stuck in the Dark Ages. A farmer sold his surplus crop to a trader who showed up at his mud-and-sticks house with a take-it-or-leave-it price. . . . There were no institutions to establish prices, swap information, grade the quality of product, or enforce legal contracts. . . . The shock of feast begetting famine convinced her [Eleni Gabre-Madhin, an Ethiopian economist] that Ethiopia could never hope to feed itself without modern markets, in particular a commodities exchange that could lift some of the risk from the farmers. . . . "The farmers have to bear all the risk. They won't advance new technology use and fertilizer use so long as they also bear the volatility of the market. . . . It's all on the farmer." (79)

> It was . . . one of the continent's greatest mysteries. No matter where one roamed in Africa, be it a sandy settlement in the Sahara or a village deep in the thick equatorial bush, someone would be selling Coke, Pepsi, Fanta Orange, Guinness stout, or the beer from the national brewer. But why were the latest seeds and fertilizers rarely to be found in these distant outposts? . . . Most producers of seed, fertilizer, and farm implements didn't bother to sell to [local farmers] at all. They believed there was no market in subsistence farmers tilling only a few acres. . . . The competitive hustle driving the soft drink and beer distributors to penetrate the deepest bush—Coca-Cola's slogan was "a Coke within arm's reach," and it had achieved the goal almost everywhere—was a foreign

notion in the agricultural sector. The farm supply companies, be they government monopolies or private enterprises, were largely content to drop their wares in the larger towns and cultivate business with the bigger, wealthier commercial farmers. (196)

"The children and the old people were dying," remembered Gelesom Chimpopi, a peanut and corn farmer in Malawi's Mchinji district west of Lilongwe on the road to Zambia. "I lost a grandparent."
"I lost two children," volunteered farmer Henry Kangwelema, who joined a conversation at a peanut-sorting warehouse. "They were four and ten."
"I lost my four-year-old child and my grandmother," added Gerald Abudu, a third farmer.
The farmers didn't have enough to feed their families, let alone a surplus to sell to pay off their debts. Amid the dying, the creditors—the seed and fertilizer suppliers and the government-owned credit agency—came around and started dismantling houses. "They took the iron sheets from my roof," said Chimpopi. "They even took my kitchen utensils, and my blanket!" (256-57)

In 6:16, the charge that the corrupt ruler of this unnamed city has "kept the statutes of Omri" (r. 882-871) comes as a shock. It brings the implied audience back to the avalanche of divine punishment that reduced the seat of the Omride dynasty, Samaria, to rubble (1:2-7). Though Samaria is mentioned by name only in Mic 1, and Omri is mentioned only in 6:16, the lesson being elaborated throughout the scroll of Micah could not be clearer. Yhwh had made good on the threat against Samaria, and the treacherous denizens of the unidentified city in 6:9-16 are now experiencing a similarly grim fate. In Mic 3, the prophet had depicted in florid terms the figurative cannibalism of corrupt elites who flay and devour their people. Here in 6:13-16, Yhwh has been punishing the oppressors for their sins, and the terrible consequences are described in terms of poetic justice. Every exploitative action designed by greedy elites to secure their own wealth and well-being is thwarted.

History of Consequences

The most influential line in Micah is the prophet's exhortation "to do justice, to cherish fidelity, and to proceed humbly with your God" (6:8).

Micah 6

At the heart of the torah is the divine command to live faithfully with regard to justice and holiness. It may be traced back, in the memory of the ancient scribes, to the patriarchal era before the birth of Isaac: after Abraham has hosted three divine messengers by the oaks of Mamre and they have turned toward Sodom to destroy it, YHWH reflects on having brought Abraham into covenant so "that he may charge his children and his household after him to keep the way of the LORD by doing righteousness and justice" (Gen 18:19). In mishnaic and talmudic tradition, R. Simlai teaches that the prophet Micah distilled observance of the 613 torah *mitzvot* into the three divine mandates of Mic 6:8 (b. Mak. 24a). For more on this, and for other reflections on Mic 6 in rabbinic midrash, see the introduction under §4.1.1 Midrashic Interpretations.

The first vision of the Shepherd of Hermas (second century CE) may allude obliquely to the rhetorical questions of the petitioner in Mic 6:6-7: Hermas agonizes, "How shall I atone to God for my past sins? In what words can I ask the Lord to be reconciled with me?" (Herm. Vis. 1.1; trans. Osiek 1999, 46). In his *Stromateis*, Clement of Alexandria uses 6:7 in a catena of references drawn from Jeremiah, Job, the Psalms, Ephesians, and other texts to refute the position that birth itself conveys irreparable sin; the rhetorical question in the Micah passage is heard as an earnest appeal and is taken to demonstrate that the penitent sinner can turn again to faith (*Strom*. 3.16.101; trans. Ferguson 1991, 319).

Jerome reads the "mountains" in 6:1 as "the angels to whom the guidance of human affairs has been entrusted," finding a prooftext for this line of thinking in Deut 32:8 (*Comm. Mich.*, 90). The "foundations of the earth," then, are "the apostles and the prophets and the whole choir of martyrs" (91; see Eph 2:20; Rev 18:20, 24; and the fourth- to fifth-century text of the *Te Deum*). Jerome uses the rhetorical question of Mic 6:6 as an opportunity to highlight the inefficacy of material sacrifices (cf. Ps 50:12-14; Amos 5:21-24): "There is nothing worthy that could be offered to God for sin, and no humility is able to wash away the stains of transgressions" (93). Instead, believers should do justice and love mercy, for the one who "believes in Christ should walk even as he walked" (95). Those facing God's punishment—though here as elsewhere, for correction rather than for annihilation—include adversaries in the early church who followed, as it were, the counsel of Omri and Ahab: "the leaders of heresies, as were Marcion and Basilides, and more recently Arius and Eunomius" (98).

Cyril of Alexandria hears Micah's address to the "mountains and hills" as referring to "the spiritual powers that take care of everything by God's will, repelling the oppression of the demons from people on earth" (*Comm.*^{CA}, 246). As is characteristic of Cyril's expansive hermeneutic, he allows for another sense, that the figures of prominent topography represent "people of importance who outranked the common herd, and who . . . proved to be a path and a snare for the people subject to them" (247). Cyril paraphrases Yhwh's words in 6:3-4 with a heavy sarcasm that demonstrates the deity's frustration: "What was insufferable and completely burdensome in my decrees? . . . I infringed the bounds of reason in liberating you from harsh servitude," or "perhaps it is your instructor—Moses, I mean—whom you fault along with me for . . . clearly presenting what is pleasing to God so that you may be able unswervingly to live an edifying life and reach the peak of satisfaction" (248). A christological reading follows: "It was ourselves, too, whom the Savior led out of spiritual Egypt, that is, out of darkness and oppression by demons, and rescued us from mud and bricks, that is, fleshly passions and impure hedonism" (248). "Miriam" represents the church, which "[offers] glory to the saving God" (249). On 6:8, Cyril highlights compassion as the needful sacrifice from believers, weaving a tapestry of proofs from Col 3:12, Luke 6:36, Eph 5:2, and Hos 6:6. Doing justice, loving mercy, and being prepared to walk with God are, for Cyril, "the ornaments of life in Christ" (251). Micah's polemic in 6:10-15 is to be understood as indicting not only those engaged in avaricious dealings and profiteering, but also "the inventors of unholy teachings" and "deceitful sophistry," those who, "though they dabble in the sacred writings . . . gain no satisfaction from the teachings of truth," and "though crushing the spiritual olive, the sacred Scripture . . . are in no way enriched with the grace of the Spirit" (253-54, 256).

Calvin preached on 6:1-8 on 26 and 27 December 1550 (1551 per the Genevan calendar). His view, here as elsewhere, is supersessionist: "we [viz., Christians] have replaced the people of whom Micah speaks here," he avers, elaborating via the grafting imagery in Rom 11 (2003, 319). In this covenant lawsuit, Christians "have God as our adversary," and God "acts as both judge and criminal prosecutor. Yet we sleep on! We think nothing of it!" (313). Christian believers are deserving of a harsh sentence, for, as Calvin interprets the rhetorical indictment, "have we not betrayed our Baptism, insofar as we have engaged in our own abominations and idolatries? . . . When one probes our life, one finds about as much conformity with evangelical doctrine as with fire and water" (316). Indeed, "Satan has a thousand means for turning us away from our salvation," for "we are carnal," besotted with "love of self" that keeps us in denial about our sinfulness (322, 328). His polemic against Roman Catholicism is blistering here: "They have the audacity to engage in every form of evil and imagine that they are acquitted before God, so long as they keep their diabolical and abominable mass," hewing to a "cult" that is "filled with insignificant drivel" (332, 335).

In a sermon in June 1735 entitled "Our Weakness, Christ's Strength," Jonathan Edwards takes up the hyperbole of 6:7—"thousands of rams" and "myriad torrents of oil"—and elaborates in that mode, dramatizing the plight of the sinner confronted by the "abiding" wrath of God: "If we should weep an ocean of tears, and should spend all our lives in mourning in secret, and should weep tears of blood, or give our bodies to be burned, it would not do away [with] the guilt of our sin" (*WJE* 19:381).

Peace activist Berrigan reads the rhetorical gesture toward sacrifice of the firstborn (6:7) in light of war: "We are hardly free of the stench of human sacrifice; it continues to mock the hope of God. War upon war. A perennial inhuman predawn, and the works of darkness. War: a contrary, twisted version—atrocious, implacable, choleric, sanguinary—of 'the good.'" We ask earnestly what God desires because "waging war, complicit in war, we are powerless to imagine, summon, conjure up, the truth of our own humanity" (1995, 237).

In contemporary Jewish praxis, the rhetorical questions expecting negative answers in 6:6–7 about whether the believer should offer in ritual sacrifice burnt offerings, thousands of rams, torrents of oil, and their firstborn are, per Stephen Lewis Fuchs, often highlighted in Jewish sermons on the morning of Rosh Hashanah, as "the prophet speaks for contemporary Jews in categorically rejecting all of these practices" (2021, 366).

Micah 6:8 provides the theme of "Faith without Faithfulness is Faithlessness," a sermon preached on 29 October 2016 by Episcopal priest Wilda Gafney. Dramatizing the courtroom rhetoric of the passage, Gafney focalizes vulnerable constituencies with whom God expects righteous believers to stand in advocacy. The exhortation to "do justice," offered thirty-three times at the apex of the sermon, lifts up the plight of women and children (cf. 2:9) under intersectional oppressions: hearers are to do justice for "cis and trans women and men" and "little girls and grandmothers in their homes slaughtered by police," for "women who continue to be underpaid," for "LGBTQI persons who

> can still be fired for no reason," for survivors of sexual assault, for "children in underfunded school districts," for "our Muslim sisters and brothers who are under siege," and more. The sermon ends with a clarion call to do justice on behalf of the living community of Earth.
>
> Many Baptist services of ordination feature 6:8 as a call to the gathered community and the ordinand to give themselves to ministries marked by justice, mercy, and humility.

RETROSPECT

Grounding the testimony of the prophetic scribe in 6:1–8 is the fidelity of Yhwh to the covenant people as they confronted formative challenges in the distant past. Divine faithfulness had been displayed through the marvelous works of redemption Yhwh had wrought and the leadership Yhwh had raised up: towering ancestral figures whose vocations to guide and sustain the life of the community remained important as the centuries passed.

The ancestors cited by Micah as authoritative for Israel's and Judah's halakic formation and understanding of Yhwh are Moses, Aaron, and Miriam. Miriam is mentioned outside the Pentateuch only here in the Hebrew Bible as one in an iconic triumvirate of leaders sent by Yhwh. These three, Moses, Aaron, and Miriam, constituted the vanguard that led Israel out of enslavement in Egypt, and continue, via Micah's allusion, to lead the people of Yhwh by their venerable example. Yet scribal memory does not elaborate on Miriam in the Hebrew Bible beyond narratives in Exodus and Numbers, a reference in Deut 24:9, and a genealogical notice in 1 Chr 5:29 (Eng. 6:3). Yhwh calls the people to remember—implicitly in Mic 6:4, and explicitly in the following verse. What should they remember about Miriam? Jewish feminist interpreter Plaskow says: "The courage she showed in saving her brother from Pharaoh's decree that all newborn Hebrew males must be killed, her ecstasy by the shores of the Sea, her eager presence at Sinai, the agony and injustice of her punishment with leprosy all have become subjects for feminist reflection" (1990, 54). Ahmed theorizes the importance of ancestors—biological forebears, cultural antecedents, likeminded forerunners—in the cause of emancipatory politics. She portrays the feminist KILLJOY as one who remembers everything: the violence and erasures of the past, those who have been lost, and the inspiring exemplars of leadership and resolve that have made a transformative difference in the movement toward justice. For every feminist KILLJOY, "willfulness can be reclaimed as a collective source of energy, a way of being sparked into life by others" (2017, 77). Reflecting on the willful womanist brought to a position of prominence in emancipatory politics by Alice Walker (2005), Ahmed highlights the quality of perseverance, something assuredly relevant for Israel and Judah as they consider their history. If the willful womanist "comes up because she is necessary for collective survival, then she is a record of that survival" (2017, 79), of persistence through the terrifying prospect of Judah's subjugation by the Neo-Assyrian Empire (Mic 1; 5:4b-8 [Eng. 5b-9]) and later by Babylonia (3:12; 4:10).

The prophetic counternarrative Yhwh and Micah adduce in 6:1-8 is both remedial and aspirational. It remedies the people's cultural erasure of the emancipation Yhwh had already enacted historically on behalf of Israel and Judah, and it beckons the community to aspire to become the kinds of subjects whose foundational story is that narrative of deliverance and covenantal trust. I find relevant here the work of French Jewish philosopher Emmanuel Lévinas on the moral obligation to be present in solidarity to the stranger. Lévinas sees in "the face of the other . . . a defenseless exposure to the mysterious forlornness of death" and hears, then, "a voice that commands . . . me not to remain indifferent to that death, not to let the other die alone," for "there arises, awakened before the face of the other, a responsibility for the other to whom I was committed *before* any committing, before being present to myself or coming back to self" (1999, 29-31 [emphasis original]). Lévinas goes on to characterize "ethical peace," for the individual and for the community, as being constituted by nonviolent proximity in "relation to the inassimilable other, the irreducible other," by refusing to abandon the one who is not like oneself; choosing to respond ethically to "the impossibility of leaving [them] alone before the mystery of death" illustrates "the gravity of the love of one's neighbour" (199, 138, 141). What Lévinas expresses beautifully illuminates the ethical solidarity that is constitutive of *ḥesed* in relationship:

> The face looks at me, calls out to me. It claims me. What does it ask for? Not to leave it alone. An answer: Here I am. My presence, of no avail perhaps, but a gratuitous movement of presence and responsibility for the other. To answer, Here I am. . . . It is no longer just a question of going toward the other when [they are] dying, but of answering with one's presence the mortality of the living. That is the whole of ethical conduct. (1999, 163-64)

Retrospect

The Judean audience of Mic 1–5 has been compelled to consider the formation of their past as in a crucible, with multiple narrations of traumatizing violence generated from within and beyond their community (1:2-16; 2:1-13; 3:1-12; 4:9-10; 5:4b [Eng. 5b] and, with chilling ambiguity as to the referent, 5:9-14 [Eng. 10-15]). Now they are given the opportunity to imagine themselves otherwise. Relevant here is the way in which Bey describes the "queer counternarrative" articulated by Black trans feminism, with its "polyvocal interruption of ontological tenets" and its insistence on the abolitionary joy of nonnormativity: it is "the way that politicality engenders what we subsequently might mean and how we might literally matter or show up in the world . . . an indexation of what else might be possible for us to become unbeholden to the violences that have purportedly forged all we can be" (2022, 39–40, 43). The FUGITIVE living that Bey envisions—a fluid and free "nonviolated existence"—is crafted by the ways in which Black trans feminists decline to participate in "regulatory captivity" and instead "cultivate what it means, politically, to live among others on more ethical grounds" (40-41). Such freedom requires the persistent dismantling of hegemonic narratives that perpetuate distorted understandings as if they were natural and immutable. The Black trans feminist "[rejects] discourses that posit the steadfastness of the current situation," knowing that "our hope rests in the different story we tell, and it is thus ethically imperative not to rehash the same story" that permits carceral logics and horrific violence to continue (136). According to Micah's prophetic truth-telling, greed, economic oppression, and other violences have too long been constitutive of Judean social relations. His alternative vision in 6:8 lays out a way—through doing justice, cherishing fidelity, and proceeding humbly with God—through which Judah can live differently. Bey puts it this way in their own prophetic call for Black trans queer liberation: in a life marked by mutuality and justice, "we might come to live together differently, wherein all of us can indeed finally *live* together, can do life on nonviolent (under) grounds and permit a way to exist that is not tied to death or violence or normative constraints" (205 [emphasis original]).

As adumbrated in the introduction, here is the spectrum of possibilities I have limned for contemporary responses to Micah's prophetic witness: → resilience → resistance → reformation → rejoicing. Micah 6 builds *resilience* through the dynamic dialogical expression of a conviction central to faith: that all God has done for the community throughout its history can be met by a simple response (6:8) on the part of believers: to do justice, to cherish fidelity in relationship, and to move forward in humility with their

Micah 6

glorious redeemer. Micah 6 catalyzes *resistance* to the greed and corruption the prophetic gaze exposes in the chambers of imperial power, in inequitable trade practices, and in the treacherous manipulation that characterizes the behavior of deceitful powerbrokers more generally (6:10–12). Micah 6 calls for *reformation* of the violent misuses of power that have been permitted as standard ways of doing business for generations (6:16), officials' venal and unscrupulous actions regularly fracturing the community. Finally, Mic 6 holds space for *rejoicing* in the dazzling history of wonders Yhwh has performed on behalf of this community since the days of their enslavement in Egypt (6:4-5): in every age, readers can give thanks that God's power to deliver has been mightier than imperial machinations and threats.

MICAH 6 AND ECOLOGICAL JUSTICE

Micah 6 calls the believing community to humble fidelity to the purposes for which it was brought into being by the Creator. Yhwh had sustained Israel throughout its history, from the calling of Abram (Gen 12:1-3) and, focalized in Mic 6:4, in the Israelites' redemption from enslavement in Egypt. Yhwh is a deity who performs and expects "righteous acts" (6:5) from a people marked, generation after generation, by Yhwh's saving might and mercy. The solidarity in mutuality to which 6:8 calls the covenantal community is relevant to believers' relationships not only with other human beings within and beyond their own religious, social, and cultural constituencies but with all the living creatures God has made.

The agricultural imagery Micah uses in 6:14-15 depicts a landscape marked by futility—divinely appointed desolation as the consequences of wickedness and treachery on the part of the powerful Judean elites (6:9-13). The sinful wealthy can no longer be satisfied by all that their violent and deceitful ways had customarily procured for them. Harvesting olives and grapes and refining them into olive oil and wine may still be taking place, but exploitative merchants and corrupt officials are left with a "gnawing emptiness" that cannot be sated. The poetic imagery here is fluid, moving among metaphorical domains in which stark contrasts point up the shocking difference between anticipated feasting and the horror of famine, expectation of military protection and the reality of slaughter, strategies designed to yield agricultural bounty and consequences that leave the people without access to what has been harvested. As Maricel Ibita observes, ethical "problems in human interaction affect the individual, the community, and all of creation," and "creation's optimum capacity" to sustain life "is hindered" by human sin (2018, 486). Micah had claimed his endowment with the spirit of Yhwh (3:8) to cry out for justice with uncompromising rigor. Those who honor Micah's exhortation to justice understand that this requires the exercise of compassion not only within one's own community but across geopolitical borders and social barriers. Wealthy nations with an extremely high standard of living, especially in the West and often in the northern hemisphere, reap the benefits of avaricious practices that harm bioregions and communities far from their own territory. These economic "treasures of wickedness" (6:10) come at a terrible cost for persons living in conditions of precarity across the globe, some of whom may not have any idea of the factors involved in the deprivation and diminished access to resources they are experiencing. The IPCC puts it plainly: "Unsustainable land use and . . . unsustainable use of natural resources, deforestation, loss of biodiversity, pollution, and their interactions adversely affect the capacities of ecosystems, societies, communities and individuals to adapt to climate change," and further, "loss of ecosystems and their services has cascading and long-term impacts on people globally, especially for Indigenous Peoples and local communities who are directly dependent on ecosystems to meet basic needs" (IPCC 2022 §B.2.1). As the ecological catastrophe continues to unfold, "food security risks . . . will be more severe, leading to malnutrition and micro-nutrient deficiencies, concentrated in Sub-Saharan Africa, South Asia, Central and South America, and Small Islands" (§B.4.3).

The extractive policies Micah decries are still operative in today's world, and they cause even more far-reaching deleterious consequences now, due to the long reach of political imperialisms, global corporate greed, and technological advances. Ecological activist Hawken laments, "We take, we dam, we enslave, we exploit, we frack, we drill, we poison, we burn, we cut, we kill. The economy exploits people and the environment," and the causes of global ecological degeneration are "inattention, apathy, greed, and ignorance" (2021, 9). Working for ecological justice will restore balance within communities as well as within Earth's biomes. What Hawken says about the benefits of ecologically just praxis reads like an exposition of Mic 6:8:

> Regeneration is not only about bringing the world back to life; it is about bringing each of us back to life. It has meaning and scope; it expresses faith and kindness; it involves imagination and creativity. It is inclusive, engaging, and generous. . . . It restores forests, lands, farms, and oceans. It transforms cities, builds green affordable hous-

ing, reverses soil erosion, rejuvenates degraded lands, and powers rural communities. Planetary regeneration creates livelihoods—occupations that bring life to people and people to life, work that links us to one another's well-being. It offers a path out of poverty that provides people with meaning, worthy involvement with their community, a living wage, and a future of dignity and respect. (2021, 9)

COMMENTARY

Micah 6 dramatizes Yhwh's fierce indignation and grief at the persistent wickedness, violence, and deceit perpetrated by Judean elites (6:10-12). Between Yhwh and the covenant people is a venerable and precious relationship that should be marked by fidelity and trust. That relationship has become woefully fractured, per Micah, Hosea, Amos, Isaiah, Jeremiah, Ezekiel, Haggai, and Malachi. Heschel offers that reading the Latter Prophets, one would glean the impression that only the prophet seems to be aware of the truth of the corruption and failures of the community: "Answer Me! calls the voice of God. But who hears the call? . . . The prophet is a lonely man. His standards are too high, his stature too great, and his concern too intense for [others] to share. Living on the highest peak, he has no company except God" (2001, 127). The prophet Micah sees with a terrible clarity the outcome of the divine disputation: the leader of Judah is to become "a desolation" and Judah's inhabitants "an object of hissing" (6:16). With O'Brien (2015, 74), I see Mic 6 as an artistic whole engaging the issue of Yhwh's dispute with Israel. Beginning in 6:9, we see a justification for the retributive punishment that has already been carried out by the deity and that will continue to unfold for this recalcitrant covenant people.

6:1 *Pay attention! . . . Rise!* These two imperatives are directed to different addressees: the first command, to a plural audience, is likely imagined as spoken to the mountains and the foundations of the earth (see 6:2, where that is explicit). The second imperative is directed to a masculine singular addressee who is to take on the role of prosecutor. The reference is elliptical, but it would be congruent with 3:8 for the imagined prosecutor to be the prophet Micah himself. While *qûm* regularly functions in Biblical Hebrew as an auxiliary verb, here the imperative is best translated as rising or standing in order to present a legal case formally before adjudicators. That to which the implied audience should attend is expressed in an un-

Commentary

usual way: ʾēt ʾăšer-yhwh ʾōmēr, translated here as "what Yhwh is saying," occurs nowhere else in the Hebrew Bible. Micah[LXX] translates this by means of a syntactically awkward formulation, "the word of the Lord [that] the Lord says" (*logon kyriou kyrios eipen*) that, per Gelston following Wilhelm Rudolph (1975, 107), may be a "combination of a free and a literal rendering" (*BHQ*, 105).

present the disputation. The Hebrew term *rîb* can mean a dispute, controversy, or a conflictual matter requiring adjudication, fluid in nature but certainly involving a charge "stating what the defendant ought to do or ... has failed to do, or both" (Hillers 1984, 77). If the prosecuting of a legal case is in view here, it is wholly metaphorical (Mayfield 2023). Wolff says of 6:1–8, "As a didactic piece, it clearly presupposes characteristics of Deuteronomistic paraenesis and of the extended discourses found in the Deuteronomistic history," especially Samuel's historical review of the redemptive deeds performed by Yhwh on behalf of Israel in 1 Sam 12:6–15 and Joshua's speech on the same theme in Josh 24:1–15 (1990, 170).

before the mountains. Yhwh is sovereign over all the earth. Thus Yhwh has the authority to bid mountains and hills pay attention to the dispute between the Creator and the covenant people Yhwh had chosen from among all the peoples of the earth (Amos 3:1–2) and delivered from enslavement (Mic 6:4). This poetic language is capacious and elliptical, inviting a polyphony of understandings regarding figurative references for the topographical elements. The interpretation of the Malbim foregrounds the failure of "the leaders of Jacob to act as judges of Israel" (3:1–3; 7:3–4), compelling the deity to "[choose] new judges: the mountains and the hills," while Rashi and David Kimḥi expand the rich tradition history articulated in 6:4–5, offering that "the mountains represent the Patriarchs Abraham, Isaac and Jacob; and the hills represent the Matriarchs: Sarah, Rebecca, Leah and Rachel" (Stavsky 2009, 44). Joseph Kara and Mendel Hirsch (1833–1900) extend the interpretation of 5:14 (Eng. 15) as meaning the nations should pay attention to the divine punishment suffered by Israel and Judah: "the mountains represent the kings of the nations of the world and the hills are their officers. They should take to heart God's warning to Israel and thereby ensure their own future" (Stavsky 2009, 44).

6:2 everlasting foundations. In adjectival and nominal forms, ʾêtān suggests continual or enduring action, longevity, or immovable permanence (*HALOT* 1:44–45). Relevant here are instances at Num 24:21; Job 33:19; Ps 74:15; Jer 5:15; and, famously, Amos 5:24. Andersen and Freedman note the rare syntax of an adjective preceding the noun it modifies; though they do translate as "everlasting foundations," they remark that Hillers's proposal, "streams (from) the foundations of the earth," is possible (2000, 517, citing Hillers 1984, 76). Irudayaraj finds this image to constitute a reversal of the image of mountains melting under the divine tread in Mic 1:4 (2021, 713).

6:3 O my people. Here in Mic 6 is the apex of a rhetorical sequence using the term ʿammî, "my people," which occurs nine times in Micah. Earlier, the term had underscored the intense emotions of anguish and rage experienced by the prophet in solidarity with his devastated community, or the lamentation raised by Judeans being dispossessed (see 1:9; 2:4, 8, 9; 3:3, 5). Here in 6:3, 5, 16, it is none other than Yhwh who communicates heightened emotion during a review of earlier divine work to redeem a recalcitrant and ungrateful people and the unavoidable retribution that must now be exacted against the unjust.

6:4 brought you up. Wordplay is audible in 6:3-4 with "wearied" and "brought you up," which sound quite similar: helʾētîkā and heʿĕlîtîkā respectively. This resonance is echoed in 6:13 with a third word, "made you sick," heḥĕlêtî. The aural linkage of these three verbs is underscored conceptually by their shared subject: Yhwh. The structuring of the sound-play in this divine discourse is chiastic:

A = a theoretically negative sense: "How have I wearied you?" (6:3)
   B = a strongly positive sense: "I brought you up" out of enslavement in Egypt (6:4)
A' = a heightened negative sense: "I have made you weak" (6:13)

The intensifying logic of this chiastic sound-play propels the implied audience toward the judgment articulated in 6:14-16. Far from Yhwh having given Israel grounds to find the deity adversarial or irrelevant, Yhwh has in fact performed miraculous deeds of redemption for this people, a grounding theological claim that will be emphasized in 7:15. Judean elites' continuing disregard of their God and intransigence in violence and treachery will result in Yhwh bringing futility curses upon them (see below).

the house of slavery. The conviction that Yhwh delivered Israel from bondage in Egypt is central to emancipatory traditions throughout the Hebrew Bible, especially in the Psalms and Isaiah. The gritty poetic locution "house of slavery" occurs in the Torah (Exod 13:3, 14; 20:2; Deut 5:6; 6:12;

7:8; 8:14; 13:6, 11) and the Former and Latter Prophets (Josh 24:17; Judg 6:8; Jer 34:13; and here in Mic 6:4).

Moses, Aaron, and Miriam. Aaron is mentioned only here in the Latter Prophets (Andersen and Freedman, 521). The nine references to Aaron in the Psalms include instances where his name is paired with that of Moses, while Miriam's name is not present (Pss 77:21; 99:6; 105:26; 106:16). Miriam is mentioned here in Mic 6 not simply as the sister of Moses and Aaron, but as a prophet sent by Yhwh: the verb *šlḥ* in this line is being used in its technical sense as a term for prophetic deployment (Fischer 2002, 89). Feminist interpreters may highlight the uniqueness of Micah's drawing on tradition for this, "the only non-genealogical reference to Miriam outside the Pentateuch" (Cazelles and Sperling 2007, 162; see the overview of reception history of Miriam in Jewish and Christian tradition in O'Brien 2015, 77–84). The designation "prophet" is applied to only a handful of women in the Hebrew Bible, including the military adviser Deborah and the monarchy-shaping Huldah (see Fischer 2002; Gafney 2008).

Andersen and Freedman remark that apart from this reference, "nowhere in the tradition are the three siblings presented in a shared leadership role," the only other mention of them together being in the scene of conflict narrated in Num 12 (2000, 519). They say of Micah's collocation of the three, "it is hard to see what point he is making" (522). In Tg. Mic 6:4 are expansions functioning as clarification: "I sent before you *my three prophets*, Moses *to teach the tradition of judgments*, Aaron *to atone for the people*, and Miriam *to instruct the women*." Scholars have suggested that, put succinctly, the three figures stand for torah-teaching, priestly mediation, and prophecy; so, for example, Kessler (2000a, 264; 2001), who cites Deborah, Huldah, and Noadiah in the lineage, as it were, of Miriam the prophet. But we may say more.

Micah frames the point via the narratives of Yhwh's deliverance of Israel from Egypt. Israel's struggles in the wilderness are assuredly within the frame, which may be taken to span from the first mention of Aaron in the exodus tradition (Exod 4:14) through the mention of Miriam's role at the Red Sea (Exod 15:20-21) to the Num 12 conflict among the three at Hazeroth (Num 12:1-15; Deut 24:9), thence through the drama with Balaam and Balak and illegitimate mixing at Shittim (Num 22–25), and presumably to Israel's crossing of the Jordan River and setting up memorial stones at Gilgal (Josh 3–4). Within this richly complex narrative frame, one imagines Moses in fuller detail as lawgiver, judge, and advocate for the people; Aaron as representative of the priestly sacrificial cultus and spokesperson for Moses in the latter's absence; and Miriam as a powerful leader of the community.

6:5 O my people, remember! In the preceding clause, the mention of Miriam—unique in the Latter Prophets and exceedingly rare in the Hebrew Bible—may be taken to hint that this prophet's remembrance of ancient Israelite history is more expansive on issues of gender and power than are other historical texts of the Hebrew Bible. Plaskow suggests amplifying authoritative traditions through the lens of gender justice, something that may be considered relevant for Micah's inclusion of Miriam just prior to his call to remember: "We see a larger Torah behind the Torah, a Torah in which women's experience is rendered visible, and the social and religious forms to which they adhered are depicted in their complexity and power.... Remembering women's history, writing new midrash, empowers us to create more inclusive communities and prods us to challenge all the institutions of the Jewish community to perpetuate and live out of a richer Jewish memory" (1990, 43, 238).

Balak... and... Balaam. As related in Num 22–24, Balak had hired the seer Balaam to curse the war encampment of Israel, which lay spread across the plains of Moab, an Israelite "horde" so vast that "Moab was in great dread of the people" (Num 22:3-4). A West Semitic inscription found at Deir ʿAlla in Jordan in 1967, written on a plaster wall and likely dating to the ninth to eighth centuries BCE, discusses an elaborate vision of one "Balaam, son of Beor"; many scholars have connected that figure, not necessarily as a historical person but in ancient Near Eastern tradition history, to the Balaam of Num 22–24. Jewish and Christian reception history of Balaam offers both positive and negative evaluations of the seer (Sharp 2009, 135-36), but he is critiqued in Hebrew Bible traditions (Num 31:8, 16; Deut 23:4-6; Josh 24:9-10; Neh 13:2). In Mic 6:5, the formulation about how Balaam "answered" Balak may refer to the seer's uttering of oracles, per Abraham Malamat, who speculates that Balaam may be being portrayed as a type of prophet known at Mari as an *āpilum*, an "answerer, responder" (1995, 59).

In Num 23–24, Yhwh puts a beneficial word into Balaam's mouth on each of three occasions, compelling him to bless Israel. Unable to resist Yhwh, Balaam fails to pronounce curses despite his eagerness to do so and his overscrupulous preparations—offering seven bulls and seven rams on seven altars thrice, in three different locations, to create conditions favorable for his prophesying. The Balaam material satirizes the powerlessness of Moab to harm Israel, to be sure. But in the larger narrative, the irony takes an unexpected and devastatingly sharp turn (see Sharp 2009, 140-51). Israel, having remained oblivious to the dramatic machinations of Balak and Balaam and the hyperbolic blessings lavished upon them by an enemy,

Commentary

immediately moves to commit grievous sin: exogamous sexual mixing with Moabite women, something expressly contravening torah stipulations (Deut 23:3-6, a prohibition narratologically dramatized in Ezra 9-10 and Neh 13:23-31). Thus Israel brings divine wrath down upon themselves (Num 25:1-9): twenty-four thousand Israelites are killed, not by Moab but by a plague sent by Yhwh.

[*Remember everything] from Shittim to Gilgal.* The force of the imperative to "remember" carries on into this clause. The reference to Shittim assuredly alludes to Num 25:1-9, a recounting of Israelite infidelity fiercely punished by Yhwh; the three other mentions of Shittim in the Hebrew Bible (Josh 2:1; 3:1; Joel 4:18 [Eng. 3:18]) are not relevant here. Micah[LXX] does not understand the reference and gives a "mistranslation," as Gelston observes, here and with the same place-name in Joel 4:18 (*BHQ*, 78, 105). The Septuagint translator uses a noun for where reeds or rushes grow (*apo tōn schoinōn*; *CGL* 2:1351), which, per the relevant Hebrew term (*qāneh*) in Isa 19:6, Ezek 29:6, and, more elliptically, Ps 68:31 (Eng. 30), points to Egypt as the starting place of the trajectory of deliverance being sketched in Micah[LXX] at this verse. Gilgal has a richly storied past in Hebrew Bible traditions. Some traditions relate to the remembrance of Yhwh's miraculous stopping of the waters of the Jordan (Josh 4:19-24) and the Israelites' circumcision of males of the new generation on the journey into Canaan (5:9-10). Gilgal is also noted as the originary location of an angel of Yhwh who travels to Bochim—this travel itinerary for a divine intermediary being so odd as to signal the importance of both place-names—to rebuke the Israelites for not having driven Canaanite indigenous groups from the land (Judg 1:19-2:5), something that would initiate a volatile cycle of Israelite apostasy, divine punishment via enemy "plunderers," and deliverance through judges (Judg 2:11-19). Other biblical traditions associated with Gilgal involve the anointing and acclamation of Saul as ruler and Saul's subsequent premature sacrifice, construed as justification for Yhwh stripping the kingship from him (1 Sam 10-11, 13, 15), as well as events during the reign of David. The reference to Gilgal in Mic 6:5 may be echoing some of these traditions.

Also influential for this Gilgal reference in Micah may have been indictments of Israel in Hosea and Amos. Elliptical yet stern words linking Gilgal, illicit sacrifice, and engagement with cultic sex workers animate Hos 4:15. Illicit ritual praxis seems to be at issue also in Hos 12:12 (Eng. 11); Amos 4:4; and 5:5. Hosea 9:15 seems to foreground political malfeasance that has spurred Yhwh to withdraw covenantal fidelity ("Every evil of theirs began at Gilgal. . . . I will love them no more; all their officials are rebels").

Micah 6

In Mic 6:5, the reference to Gilgal is a brilliant gesture. It manages to sketch an expansive history of Israel's benefit from Yhwh's acts of deliverance, with a focus on Yhwh's dominance over rulers—the Egyptian pharaoh, Balak of Moab—who did not bow before the might of Israel's God, while also highlighting ways in which Israel itself had chosen not to obey Yhwh. Underscoring Saul's flaws, Rodney Hutton writes, "The name 'Gilgal' came to conjure up Israel's deepest failures: failure to consolidate the conquest; failure of the monarchy; and more specifically the failure of the northern (or more generally the non-Jerusalemite) political program" (1999, 100).

to understand the righteous acts of Yhwh. The verb *ydʿ* can signal not just recognition of something as factual or true, but also deeper understanding or discernment based on experience and wise reflection. The "righteous acts" (*ṣidqôt*) of Yhwh can be understood as the mighty acts of succor Yhwh performs for the oppressed (so Ps 103:6). Hebrew *ṣədāqôt* can also connote the ethical deeds and general comportment Yhwh expects of the covenant people (see the term in Ps 11:7 and Isa 33:15). Most relevant to Mic 6:3-5, *ṣədāqôt* is the term used for acts of military deliverance performed by the deity on behalf of Israel—signs of the patronage of the divine warrior that implicitly underline Israel's debt of gratitude and obligation to covenant obedience in light of those experiences of divine rescue, or what Brueggemann calls "acts of transformation" (1997, 131). The word *ṣədāqôt* appears in that sense in Judg 5:11 and Isa 45:24, in passages that laud Yhwh's martial victories. Notably, the judge Samuel cites the *ṣidqôt* of Yhwh in his blistering rebuke of the Israelites' demand for a (human) king, a speech trading on resonances of a legal proceeding and fully congruent with the thrust of Mic 6:3-5. Samuel roars that he will "enter into judgment with you before the Lord, and ... declare to you all the saving deeds [*ṣidqôt*] ... [Yhwh] performed for you and for your ancestors," since the people have found insufficient the sovereignty of Yhwh and insolently demanded a human monarch. Samuel calls upon Yhwh to level juridical punishment against the people by destroying their wheat harvest with "thunder and rain," which the deity does (1 Sam 12:6-18). The overarching narratological goal is to show Samuel's rebuke and the divine punishment as effectively catalyzing repentance in the people and exhorting them to reorient themselves to "the good and right way" in which they should go (12:19-25). The same may be said of the divine dispute in Mic 6:1-5, the ventriloquized confusion of a worshipper in 6:6-7, and the prophet's response in 6:8: those addressed within the poetry, and hearers and readers of the text, are to repent of their ingratitude toward

Commentary

Yhwh and recommit themselves to the torah norms of justice, fidelity in covenant relationship, and humility before God.

On one level, Israel's covenant relationship with God is straightforward: "[Yhwh] has told you, O mortal," in exquisite detail what is required as regards halakic obedience and theological praxis. But in the living of that relationship, much becomes obscure to the people, as the narratives in the Pentateuch and the Deuteronomistic History dramatize over and over again. Using the language of Martin Buber, Brueggemann observes of the intimate relationship between Israel and God, "Israel's life as a theological enterprise consists in coming to terms with this particular Thou": Yhwh, both as regards "the nonnegotiable purposes and commands" of the deity, "but also coming to terms with the immense problematic that [Yhwh] turns out to be: often uttering promise and command, but sometimes silent; often present and visible, but sometimes . . . absent." Yet Israel continues to bear testimony to the divine, through its prophets and in many other ways, for "in this very utterance Israel knew its own life to be differently characterized in holiness, sometimes beneficent and sometimes savage" (1997, 131-33).

6:6 *With what?* Here commences a powerful sequence of four questions that give the initial impression of being information-seeking but, as rapidly becomes clear, are rhetorical in nature. Yhwh had posed two rhetorical questions in 6:3 to Israel: "What did I ever do to you? How have I wearied you?," and two more in 6:5: "What had Balak contrived? And how had Balaam answered?" Here in 6:6, an imagined worshipper offers a cascade of rhetorical questions in response. The poetic balance is exquisite: four questions posed by Yhwh are met by four questions posed by the worshipper (Andersen and Freedman, 506), a point-counterpoint dynamic that heightens the dramatic conflict of the dialogue. The worshipper's questions can be understood in several ways. The questions might be passionately earnest and frantic, in the words of Hillers, a "hysterical offer" (1984, 79). They might be being represented as beginning earnestly and shading into sarcastic hyperbole. They might be being ventriloquized ironically (by Micah) as desperately earnest on the part of the questioner—the heightening toward hyperbole underscoring not sarcasm but emotional intensity—yet, implicitly in the view of the prophetic scribe, as nevertheless missing the point of covenantal relationship. In either case—a sarcastic and scoffing imagined worshipper, or an earnest imagined worshipper desperate to mollify Yhwh—the suggestion is that it would be hopeless to strive to please Yhwh, the implication

Micah 6

being that the deity is impossibly demanding or that even the most extravagant covenantal sacrifices cannot satisfy the divine desire.

God on High. The divine appellation "Yhwh" is paired with a more elaborate title for the deity, "God on High." Epithets, adjectives, and adverbs emphasizing the deity's exaltation can be found in many Hebrew Bible texts, including Job 31:2; Pss 56:3 (Eng. 2); 92:9 (Eng. 8); Isa 33:5; 57:15.

6:7 *thousands of rams ... myriad torrents of oil.* The hyperbole here undermines the earnestness of the ventriloquized speaker. Andersen and Freedman offer the animated interjection, "cosmic rivers!" (525). Gelston suggests the translation in Micah^LXX, "swollen streams" (NETS), was "occasioned by the unfamiliar notion of sacrifices of oil" (*BHQ*, 105), and Glenny supplies a fuller predicate in the LXX to avoid the problem: "ten thousands of rows of fat *lambs*" (2015, 31).

Should I give my firstborn ... the fruit of my body? This line, the culmination of an escalating series of dramatically hyperbolic misunderstandings of the purposes of ritual in worship of Yhwh, is intended to be rejected out of hand. The allusion here shows only that the abhorrent practice of child sacrifice is recognized as something others might theoretically consider or perform, as in 2 Kgs 23:10; 2 Chr 28:3; 33:6; Jer 7:31; 32:35. *Pace* Andersen and Freedman (2000, 382), this ironic gesture cannot be taken as evidence "that human sacrifice was a serious option" within the Judean community at the time this was written. They are misunderstanding the force of the rhetoric when they argue, "the climactic offer of the firstborn son in Mic 6:7 should not be read as the end of a movement from possible offers (v 6) through impossible ones (v 7a) to the most impossible of all (v 7b), as argued by [Martin] Buber and [Roland] de Vaux," but as the "'most valuable bid in the series'" (2000, 538, quoting G. C. Heider's 1985 study of the ancient Canaanite cult of Molech).

sin of my spirit. Translations of *nepeš* in this clause span a range of possibilities, including "soul," "life," and "my personal sin" (Allen 1976, 362; similarly Hillers 1984, 75) or "my personal wrongdoing" (Goldingay 2021, 470). Assuredly not in view here is any kind of dualistic understanding of material body versus eternal soul. The term *nepeš* is used in Hebrew Bible texts for the selfhood or living being of a person, and for creaturely desire, will, or appetite (*HALOT* 2:711–13).

6:8 *[Yhwh] has told you, O mortal!* The use of "mortal," *'ādām*, in direct address at this crucial juncture is rhetorically effective as a thunderous assertion of the distinction between (mere) mortals and the deity. The subject of *higgîd* is left unspecified, leading scholars to dispute whether the speaker is Micah assuring his compatriots that Yhwh has made clear the divine expectations over the centuries or, alternatively, Yhwh is confirming that the prophet Micah has made clear the divine expectations in his prophesying. Nasuti and others have noticed the repetition of *ngd hiph.* in Micah's self-designation as one authorized by the spirit of Yhwh "to declare to Jacob his transgression and to Israel his sin" (3:8). Nasuti suggests that 6:8 underscores the importance of the persona of the prophet in the book of Micah in much the way that 3:8 had done (2004, 157-58). My position is that Yhwh is more likely to be the subject of a verbal form having to do with communication of covenant stipulations. Tyler Mayfield perceives here not the end of a putative covenant lawsuit but, rather, a form more akin to a temple entrance liturgy, such as that perhaps audible in Ps 15. "Entrance

Fig. 21. *Micah Exhorting the Israelites to Repentance*, 1866, by Gustave Doré (1832-1883). Wood engraving in *La Grande Bible de Tours*. Published by Alfred-Henri-Armand Mame in Tours and by Cassell & Company in London. Photo by HIP/Art Resource, NY.

liturgies typically deal with the characteristics of a righteous person that enable them to enter the Temple," Mayfield observes; he hears 6:8 as expressing what is required of the character of the worshipper who would come into the presence of YHWH (2023, 155).

What is good? What does YHWH require of you? Taking the interrogative particles seriously as marking (rhetorical) questions is important, because it heightens the dramatic tension that suffuses this dialogue. Carroll R. rightly notes that this verse is polemical. It articulates not gentle spiritual counsel, "not a wise word of priestly guidance," but a "stinging rebuke" that is fully congruent with the "denunciations and announcement of judgment" in the following verses (2007, 112).

to do justice. Justice involves seeking equity, ensuring that power is not misused, holding perpetrators of unjust action to account, and pursuing vindication and reparations for those who have been unfairly harmed. Cruz reviews ways in which the Hebrew Bible has codified the preservation of justice in its regulations of communal life: first, "the law of weights and measures" was designed to ensure that economic transactions reflected YHWH's insistence on equity; second, "the judicial court" was to secure just adjudication of disputes, given that judges "were neither to be partial to the poor [nor to] pervert justice by accepting bribes"; third, "the law of money-lending" forbade charging interest in advance and selling food for a profit; fourth, "the law of tithing" provided for triennial distribution of tithed produce to Levites, resident aliens, widows, and orphans; fifth, the law of jubilee "meant that land ownership was to be equalised every fifty years"; sixth, the law of sabbath rest for agricultural holdings ensured that "the poor and needy of the people could ... collect any food that grew from the unploughed land"; seventh, "the law of gleaning" left remnants of produce during the harvest for those who needed sustenance (2016, 140). Brueggemann offers these definitions: "to 'do justice' ... is to be sure that the neighbor is well provided for; to 'love kindness' ... is to practice a life of reliable solidarity," and "'walking humbly,' in contrast to strutting, is to pay attention to *the other*," to attend to "the need and inescapability of the others who walk with us on the path of life" (2010, 14, 16 [emphasis original]). Brown offers an eloquent contemporary interpretation of 6:6–8: "What the worshipper is required to bring is a transformed self ... committed to an unwavering life of justice based on mercy ('kindness') and humble devotion to God" (1996, 59).

to cherish fidelity. As Gordon Clark notes, the expansive meanings of ḥesed encompass goodness, patience, constancy, trustworthiness, and commitment; when Yhwh shows *ḥesed* to Israel and Judah, the benefits include assistance, blessing, deliverance, and forgiveness (1993, 259-68; see Kosman and Gregory 2015). Yhwh's "tenacious commitment to Israel" is rooted in the divine character (Clark 1993, 267), and the covenant people is expected to show themselves trustworthy and kind in their own dealings with the deity and with others in and beyond the community. The audience is exhorted to cherish fidelity toward others in relationship—to show them "faithful love" (Hyatt 1952). Andersen and Freedman remark that the idiom with *ḥesed* would normally involve a verb of doing (*ʿśh*). This expression with *ʾhb* ("to love, to cherish") occurs only here in the biblical corpus, but it is "attested in the Damascus Document (XIII.18) and five times in the Rule of the Community at Qumran (II.24; V.4, 25; VIII.2; X.26)," in two cases occurring also with the infinitive of *hlk*, as in Mic 6:8 (2000, 528). One of those instances casts light on what Micah may have understood as the (unexpressed) alternative, when a believer is not proceeding (lit. "walking") humbly with God. In a section labeled as "the Rule for the men of the Community who have freely pledged themselves to be converted from all evil and to cling to [Yhwh's] commandments," it reads,

> They shall practise truth and humility in common, and justice and uprightness and charity and modesty in all their ways. No man shall walk in the stubbornness of his heart so that he strays after his heart and eyes and evil inclination, but he shall circumcise in the Community the foreskin of evil inclination and of stiffness of neck that they may lay a foundation of truth for Israel, for the Community of the everlasting covenant. (1QS V in Vermes 2011, 103-4)

The other instance in the Community Rule that uses "to proceed [walk]" in conjunction with *ḥesed* illumines further what faithful comportment looks like, for the scribes of the Qumran group and perhaps—there is no way to know for certain—for Micah, centuries earlier, as well. The Qumran document specifies that its council members should be

> perfectly versed in all that is revealed of the Law, whose works shall be truth, righteousness, justice, loving-kindness and humility. They shall preserve the faith in the Land with steadfastness and meekness and shall atone for sin by the practice of justice and by suffering the sorrows of affliction. They shall walk with all [people] according to the standard of truth and the rule of the time. (1QS VIII in Vermes 2011, 108-9)

Micah 6

The formulation in many English translations, "to love mercy," expresses one important part of the idea here, applicable to those circumstances in which a more powerful agent (as God) is bestowing mercy from above, as it were, in a hierarchical structure, to those who hold less power or have diminished capacity to act. As Katharine Doob Sakenfeld puts it, ḥesed "involves active concern for the well-being of all the people of God, but particularly for the weak and underprivileged among them—the poor or any whose status offers no ready advocate in the society" (1985, 102). Through centuries of interpretation, because God is so often the acting subject of verbs in the Hebrew Bible having to do with showing ḥesed, interpreters have emphasized the "mercy" aspect of the life-giving relationality envisioned by Micah. But the translation "to love mercy" is not fully adequate to express the solidarity in lateral relationships to which the prophet enjoins his people. Sakenfeld again: "Loyalty implies also the free taking on of . . . obligation for the other, even though the responsibility could easily be shirked," an ethical habitus that "requires constant reflection and renewed commitment" (103).

to proceed humbly with your God. The verb *hlk*, rendered in many translations as "to walk," has a rich metaphorical range in Hebrew beyond the pragmatic sense of locomotion: it can connote characteristic behavior in daily life, a state of mind, or a state of being that is unrelated to perspective or ideation. Kathleen O'Connor notes that for all three verbal clauses in 6:8, of vital importance are the believer's "focus and direction of life" and the refusal of "limp acquiescence to cultural norms that maintain an unjust status quo" (2016, 36). Additions in the final clause of Tg. Mic 6:8 direct the implied audience away from the anthropomorphizing notion that Yhwh walks with the people: *"You shall be modest by walking in the fear of your God."* My translation of the MT here, "to proceed humbly," reflects two decisions: no longer to use "walk" in an idiomatic sense of daily comportment that has become archaic in contemporary spoken and written English, and no longer to privilege the metaphorical vehicle of ambulation in light of an objection raised by advocates in the disability community that the expression can be experienced as ableist and alienating. Fundamental to the expression in this semantic context is the idea of "going with" God (see *BigS, mitgehen mit*) in a manner that evinces humility in one's daily comportment and in spiritual or affective orientation as well. Both "to act humbly with" and "to behave humbly with" are not ideal in English, and "act" and "behave" have some ambiguities attendant upon the sense of the verb; "to move forward humbly with" is slightly awkward, given the two contiguous adverbs.

Commentary

The hiph. inf. abs. *haṣnēʿ*, functioning here as adverbial modifier of *hlk*, is a *hapax legomenon*; the root *ṣnʿ* comes up nowhere else in the Hebrew Bible. Gelston observes that "the variant renderings all betray uncertainty as to the meaning of this rare word" (*BHQ*, 106). Micah[LXX] adds the divine epithet *kyrios* to the predicate and translates the verbal locution as *hetoimon einai tou poreuesthai*, yielding, "be ready to walk with the Lord your God" (Glenny 2015, 31).

6:9 the voice of Yhwh summons the city. The verb *qrʾ* with the preposition *lamed* can mean to summon or gather a solemn convocation. Its use here may underscore the seriousness of these imagined proceedings, even if hearing this as a summons to a juridical trial might be overreading. Smith-Christopher observes, "To refer to the 'voice of Yhwh' suggests peril or a significant announcement of events about to transpire," citing the dramatic judgment oracle in Isa 66:6, which shares with our Micah verse a number of important terms and ideas: "Listen, an uproar from the city! A voice from the temple! The voice of the Lord, dealing retribution to [Yhwh's] enemies!" (2015, 199). In Mic 6:9a, the targum has *"the prophets of* the Lord" calling out to the city.

As early as Jerome, commentators have seen the first bicolon of 6:9 to begin a new section in Micah[MT] but to conclude the previous section in Micah[LXX] (*Comm. Mich.*, 95). There is a thunderous ellipsis at the heart of this oracle of indictment: the city name is not stated. Early Christian and rabbinic interpretive debates have focused on two obvious contenders for what has been left unsaid: the referent could be Jerusalem, as per Joseph Kara and David Altschuler (1687-1769), or it could be a more distant antecedent last mentioned in Mic 1: Samaria, as per Jerome, taking Samaria as a figure for heretics in his own day (Roukema 2019, 174, 178-79), and also Abraham ibn Ezra and Kimḥi (Stavsky 2009, 49). In my view, Jerusalem is the best choice as the referent here, but even so, it is poetically significant that the identity of the city remains veiled. A similar move is made several times in Isa 24-27, where the poetry gives the implied audience to imagine an unidentified "city of chaos" (*qiryat-tōhû*, Isa 24:10); an unidentified fortified city (*qiryâ bəṣûrâ*) and "citadel of aliens" (*ʾarmôn zārîm*) that Yhwh has caused to fall into ruin (25:2); an unidentified "strong city" in Judah (*ʿîr ʿoz*, 26:1); and an unidentified "fortified city" (*ʿîr bəṣûrâ*) standing in isolation (27:10). Here in Mic 6:9, the summons to an unidentified corrupt city combined with an mp impv. to "pay attention" would keep listeners on edge, alert for their own complicity or another trajectory of relevance as this oracle of judgment unfolds.

Micah 6

to have regard for your name. Some read this verb not as a 3ms impf. from *rʾh*, "to see," but as a *qal* inf. from *yrʾ*, "to fear," which requires only the revocalization of *yirʾeh* to *yirʾâ* (e.g., Jeremias 2007, 205). But other occurrences of that infinitive in the Hebrew Bible have a prefixed *lamed* (Deut 4:10; 5:29; 6:24; 10:12; 14:23; 17:19; 28:58; 31:13; 1 Kgs 8:43; Neh 1:11; Ps 86:11; Jer 32:39). The absence of the expected preposition here constitutes more of a syntactical anomaly than some interpreters acknowledge. Gelston objects, "There is no direct evidence to support the attractive emendation of Rudolph," arguing instead for reading the MT as it stands, with *yirʾeh* "in the sense 'regard, feel respect for' as in Deut 33:9; Isa 5:12; 26:10" (BHQ, 106), and that is the position taken here. The LXX changes the pronoun to 3ms ("his name," *to onoma autou*), presumably to ameliorate the awkwardness of a parenthetical aside addressed to the deity. In a more daring decision that many will find unpersuasive, the NJPS moves this clause to follow immediately after 6:8, translating, "then will your name achieve wisdom" and keeping the implied subject within quotation marks signaling the reported discourse of Yhwh to the believer: when one does justice, cherishes fidelity, and walks humbly with God, one will enjoy the reputation of being wise. I see here instead refraction of a theology of the divine Name, which may have been developed by tradents responsible for Deuteronomy and Deuteronomistic literature but which would surely have become known in the postexilic period by prophetic scribes more generally (that is to say: I am not speculating here about Deuteronomistic editing of Mic 6). Mettinger observes, "this Name theology fulfilled a vital function in the new situation of the Exile," making a strong claim for a "transcendent God who is invulnerable to any catastrophe which could conceivably strike [Yhwh's] temple" (2015, 98–99).

O tribe. Gelston notes that "all the vrss. interpret the noun as a vocative referring to the subj." addressed by the imperative *šimʿû*, but he nevertheless prefers the interpretation of Dominique Barthélemy, "Listen to the rod (which strikes) and (learn) who is the one who has appointed it" (CTAT 3:764; BHQ, 106; similarly Cruz 2016, 148–49). That elegant proposal has support in rabbinic interpretation: Rashi suggests that "the people are told to bend their ear and hearken to the words of the prophets who have been rebuking them" (Stavsky 2009, 49). One might muster ancillary support from Hos 6:5, which utilizes a metaphor of prophetic rebuke as a sword that has hewn recalcitrant sinners. But that translation relies on the notion of "listening" to an implement of retributive punishment, mixing metaphorical fields in a way that I am convinced is too awkward for the

Commentary

normal signifying practices of Biblical Hebrew. Further, while *mî* can be used in a noninterrogative sense to mean "whoever" or "the one who," in the corpus of the Latter Prophets, the usage of the lexeme is overwhelmingly interrogative, with just a small handful of noninterrogative uses (Isa 54:15; Jer 44:28; Hos 14:10; Zech 4:10), and in Micah, the three other usages of *mî* are interrogative (Mic 1:5 twice; 7:18).

Goldingay retains the vocative as addressing the implement directly ("Listen, mace," as NJPS similarly, "Hear, O scepter"), interpreting this as a metonym for royal authority: Yhwh is "addressing the one who wields the mace, who has responsibility for directing the city's life," alluding "to the king without calling him the king" (2021, 470, 476). In biblical prose and poetic traditions, a staff could be used as a marker of identity (Gen 38:18), and a staff or war club could certainly be adduced metonymically as a symbol of royal power (Isa 9:3 [Eng. 4]; 10:5, 24; 14:5; Jer 48:17; Ezek 19:11). But if the intention of the prophetic scribe in Mic 6:9 was to signal a specific ruler in an elliptical way, the history of interpretation would indicate that in many quarters, this was not understood. I am persuaded that the best reading interprets this as vocative address to the "tribe" of Judah, indicting Judean elites (6:10) and other inhabitants (6:12) for corruption and deceitful practices congruent with the negative example of the Northern Kingdom, figured in the references to Omri and Ahab (6:16). A similar line of reasoning is followed by many, including Kessler (2000a, 277) and Smith-Christopher (2015, 200).

Who appointed it? The consonantal text of the last clause of 6:9 is uncertain. The emendation proposed in BHS is followed by many interpreters: taking the first word of 6:10 as well, and changing *ûmî yəʿādāh ʿôd* to *ûmôʿēd hāʿîr* yields, "and assembly of the city," a noun for a summoned constituency that works well in parallelism with "tribe" in the preceding clause. These emendations are too substantial for the present writer to support them. The LXX of these clauses, translated by Glenny as, "Hear, O tribe, and who shall bring order to a city?" (2015, 31, 174-75), is little help: Andersen and Freedman comment drily, "To recover a better text from the LXX would require almost every word of MT to be changed" (2000, 544; see McKane 1998, 193-94). Barthélemy observes that *yəʿādāh* occurs in Jer 47:7, and the expressed referent in the preceding verse is the sword of Yhwh (*CTAT* 3:764). Rather than follow him in seeing the Mic 6:9 noun *maṭṭeh* in an analogous role, I suggest that here, "the sword" is initially left unexpressed in a rhetorical move that is initially disorienting—provoking the question, "Who appointed what, exactly?"—and becomes chilling for those who hear

Micah 6

or reread Mic 6 on subsequent occasions. Those who have become familiar with the text now recognize all too clearly the as-yet-unexpressed instrument of Yhwh's wrath, for the deity is about to thunder, "those whom you do deliver, I give to the sword" (6:14).

6:10 Are there still? Hebrew *haʾiš* is likely an interrogative, the equivalent of *hăyēš*. Another instance of this interrogative form with suppression of the medial *yod* can be seen in 2 Sam 14:19 with *ʾim-ʾiš* (*BHQ*, 106). Here in Micah^LXX, the translator has read it as the noun "fire" (*pur* = *ʾēš*), but the Greek verse is nearly unintelligible, as is evident from George Howard's game rendering, "Will a fire and a lawless person's house [treasuring up] lawless treasure and a measure of pride—injustice?" (NETS, 799), and Glenny's slightly different rendering of the final words of the clause, "ill-gotten treasures and injustice with insolence?" (2015, 31).

the house of the wicked one. The referent for this enigmatic characterization is not known.

the shorted ephah. Reference to the shorted ephah and manipulated scales in 6:10–11 is reminiscent of Amos 8:4, as Cazelles and Sperling observe (2007, 162). See further on the following verse for unjust trade practices.

6:11 Can I remain blameless? The speaker here is the deity, defending the divine choice to allow an unspecified enemy—either the Neo-Assyrian Empire or Babylonia—to thrash Judah and leave the region desolate (6:13). Yhwh implicitly acknowledges that the decision to level harsh retributive punishment leaves the deity seeming to be at fault for allowing such harm to come to the covenant people. Yhwh justifies the divine action as a sovereign response that could not be avoided because of the wickedness and corruption of the Judean elites. The simple opening verb of divine accountability, *haʾezkeh*, is followed by a torrent of powerful poetic images of evildoing and immorality—"wicked scales ... a bag of deceitful weights ... wealthy full of violence ... inhabitants speak falsehood ... treacherous tongues in their mouths"—that serves to underscore Yhwh's juridical point. Some translators vocalize the form as *hiph.* or *piel* (*BHQ*, 106), as, for example, NJPS with, "Shall he be acquitted," presumably intending a subject other than Yhwh, but this move should be avoided. ZUR has it right with, "Bleib ich rein trotz ungerechter Waage?"

wicked scales ... a bag of deceitful weights. Structural economic inequity, the elites' financial disenfranchisement of the vulnerable, is a central theme of Mic 2, 3, 6, and 7. Here, deception in trade practices is the focus.

Commentary

The use of intentionally unbalanced scales or nonstandard weights to secure unfair advantage in a mercantile transaction is forbidden in the Torah (Lev 19:35-37; Deut 25:13-16), deplored in prophetic literature (Hos 12:8 [Eng. 7]; Amos 8:4-6), and characterized in wisdom traditions as abhorrent to Yhwh (Prov 11:1; 20:10, 23).

6:12 *its wealthy are full of violence, and its inhabitants speak falsehood.* Two subtle shifts amplify the drama of this indictment. First, within the verse poetic heightening is evident in the progression from the first clause, which accuses the wealthy of violence in a simple three-word sequence, to the rest of the line, which is more complex syntactically: it portrays all the city's inhabitants—not just the rich—as deceitful, then depicts multiple tongues speaking falsehood in a cacophony of treachery. Second and more broadly, the wickedness and deceit noted in 6:9-11 are intensified by the claim in 6:12 that the city's elites are "full of violence," something that will trigger a violent response from the deity in 6:13 ("beating you") and 6:14 ("those whom you do deliver, I will give to the sword").

6:13 *I myself.* Emphatic pronouns in 6:13-15 emphasize the agency of Yhwh ("I myself," 6:13) and the oppressive elites of Israel ("As for you," three times in 6:14-15). One effect of this poetic foregrounding of pronominal agency is that the implied audience has the sense of witnessing a pitched confrontation.

have made you weak by beating you. Gelston observes that many versions revocalize *heḥĕlêtî* (hiph. from *ḥlh*, yielding "to make weak, sick," HALOT 1:317) as from hiph. of *ḥll*, "to begin" (HALOT 1:320), but he notes, "the more difficult reading of M may find a parallel in Isa 53:10" (BHQ, 107). Indeed relevant is the deployment there of a hiph. form of *ḥlh* for divinely ordained harm administered to the suffering servant: ZUR, "Dem Herrn aber gefiel es, ihn mit Krankheit zu schlagen," and NJPS, "But the Lord chose to crush him by disease," illustrate well the divine intention to injure expressed in that verse, and most translators do not propose emendations there. In other prophetic texts, too, we find imagery of Zion beaten and wounded by Yhwh (e.g., Jer 30:12-14).

6:14 *you devour but are not satisfied.* The image here is of ravenous hunger that cannot be sated. Many interpreters see in 6:14-15 a series of deprivation or futility curses the effects of which are to be suffered in the future. The *yiqṭol* verbal forms could gesture toward a future that has not yet un-

359

Micah 6

folded, but such forms can also signal durative action in the present (Joüon §113.d), what Waltke and O'Connor describe as "similar to the customary non-perfective," which involves verbal action that "is conceived of as extended over an indefinite period," but "in a present-time frame with reference to the act of speaking" (*IBHS* §§31.2b, 3b). Here, the futility curses should be interpreted with close attention to the larger literary context of 6:13–7:4. Yhwh has already weakened Judah, raining blows upon the covenant community, and Daughter Zion bewails the terrible deprivation not expected in the future but constitutive of the present moment in which she is lamenting.

Maledictions in the ancient Near East were in numerous instances ritualized—that is, publicly performed as ritual actions—but in many other cases, they were embedded in written texts. In either circumstance, they were designed to convey the impetus and authority of divine judgment (Kitz 2014, 64–68). Laura Quick has studied nineteen futility curses in Old Aramaic and Akkadian inscriptions dating to between the ninth and seventh centuries BCE (2018, 70). Examples explored by Quick that dramatize the trope of "maximum effort but minimal gain" include: someone sowing but not harvesting, parallel curses about one hundred ewes/cows/women suckling a lamb/calf/child but the nursling not being satisfied, and a city of one thousand houses being reduced to a single house (75–76, 101, 103). Within the Hebrew Bible, scholars have identified no fewer than forty-four futility curses, if one includes the motif of crying out to or seeking Yhwh and being unsuccessful in that endeavor. I myself might bracket tropes of the silence or hiddenness of God as being different in nature from imprecations that effect the frustration of concrete actions necessary for the material flourishing or survival of a person, a household, or community. Nevertheless, the general similarity of these cursing traditions has been established across several ancient Near Eastern cultures, including Israel and Judah. The most famous biblical futility curses are articulated in vivid detail in Deut 28:15–68. Scholars have argued for deprivation or futility maledictions also in Leviticus, Job, Psalms, Proverbs, Isaiah, Jeremiah, Hosea, Amos, Zephaniah, Haggai, Zechariah, and Malachi, as well as Micah (Quick 2018, 107).

This cultural background of futility curses—assuredly familiar to biblical prophetic scribes in the time of Micah and later—lends drama to Micah's utterances when heard as predictive of future harms. But, importantly, Micah's words also perform a continued polemic against elite malefactors who have not stopped offending against the good of the community. Micah details the consequences of their sinful actions in the present moment: the

Commentary

speaker, Yhwh, is describing ways in which divine punishment has already made desolate those who have been malfeasant within the community. Their violent and exploitative ways have left them with a gnawing hunger that cannot be satisfied. The harvest may come, but the benefits—oil and wine—are withheld from these corrupt leaders and captains of trade. These futility curses sound a chilling warning to all who might consider acting in concert with the callous officials whom Micah confronts.

there is bloating within you. The noun *yešaḥ* is otherwise unattested and difficult. Andersen and Freedman decline to guess at the meaning and leave it untranslated (2000, 540, 549). According to Rashi, bowel discomfort or disease was the sense (Stavsky 2009, 50-51; "dysentery" per Ehrman 1973). *HALOT* gives the meaning as "filth," on the basis of an Arabic cognate (2:446); others cited by McKane (1998, 197) concur or suggest related intestinal meanings, including constipation, which is the choice of ZUR ("dein Kot bleibt in dir"). My translation here, "bloating," relies on the semantic context of the parallelistic couplet, as every translation must, and can accommodate blockage, infection, or emptiness as the cause, since bloating can be a symptom of constipation, bowel disease, malnutrition, or—likely in mind here—starvation. Micah[LXX] has, "you will grow dark within yourself" (*skotasei en soi*), taking the Hebrew *yšḥk* as a verbal form from *ḥšk*, "to be or grow dark," presumably on the assumption that metathesis of the inner consonants had occurred during scribal transmission. McKane surveys readings in the semantic arena of bowel dysfunction (dysentery or intestinal blockage), marking the phrase as a secondary addition and choosing "you will suffer from constipation" for his own translation (1998, 196-98).

you draw aside but cannot deliver. Presumably taking *swg* as a biform of *śwg* or *śgg* (see *HALOT* 3:1306, 1311), NJPS opts for the semantic realm of conception and delivery of infants, translating, "You have been conceiving without bearing young." Andersen and Freedman suggest "come to labor, but . . . not survive," but they concede, "this is a guess" (2000, 549). McKane (1998, 198) notes Rashi's reading of this as concerning forced migration: "Your enemies will lead your sons and daughters captive and you will not save them." I interpret the imagery as a fully congruent and powerful complex of images having to do with siege of the corrupt city (Jerusalem) and its military defeat, these taken as blows administered by a wrathful Yhwh (6:13). First, gnawing hunger ravages those trapped in the besieged city as food supplies are cut off; bloating is a medically documented effect of starvation, something widely feared in the ancient Near East (Kipfer 2021). Second, the besieged Judeans may be able to hide some denizens,

Micah 6

or possibly even draw them out of a line of captives designated for forced march into exile, but they are ultimately unable to deliver them; even those who had successfully hidden or been preserved initially will be executed by the sword. Third, those taken into exile will be unable to utilize what they have planted and otherwise prepared (6:15), whether grain, olive oil, or wine; alternatively or simultaneously, survivors who continue to engage in agriculture will have to yield their produce to the conquerors.

those whom you do deliver, I give to the sword. Several prophetic texts use the chilling trope of survivors of one dire threat succumbing to another threat; examples include Amos 5:19 and Jer 15:1-3. Laura Quick reads this line as being about the inability to protect harvested produce, observing that this is "the only futility curse in the Hebrew Bible concerning the frustration of the provision of preserves and food stocks" (123). The expansive range of the relative pronoun *ʾăšer* allows for this reading, but the verb *plṭ* ("to escape, to deliver") is used overwhelmingly with the accusative of persons, not inanimate things.

6:15 you sow but cannot reap . . . tread olives but cannot anoint . . . [tread] grapes, but cannot drink wine. This series of vivid metaphors shows that life will be relentlessly grim for those in the covenant community because of the sins of their leaders. The exploitative elites' disobedience to Yhwh—not doing justice, not cherishing fidelity, and not proceeding humbly with God—has triggered an avalanche of horrendous consequences. Again, I argue that 6:14-15 are best read as presenting a progression of deprivation images associated with the suffering of a besieged community, the slaughter that takes place when a city wall has been breached, and the ways in which those forced into exile must abandon the fields they had tended and survivors must surrender the fruits of their labor to the colonizers.

Fierce prophetic rhetoric in the Latter Prophets generally and throughout the book of Micah is designed to bring before the implied audience the inescapable truth that evil scheming and unethical practices wreak havoc on the covenant community. Those who understand should be spurred to reform their behavior, as per Yhwh's urgent exhortation in Jer 7:3, 5: "Amend your ways and your doings, and let me dwell with you in this place. . . . For if you truly amend your ways and your doings, if you truly act justly with one another, if you do not oppress the alien, the orphan, and the widow, or shed innocent blood . . . then I will dwell with you in this place." Mason Lancaster emphasizes, "The rhetorical purpose of judgment oracles is to provoke Israel to mourn, repent, and pray for mercy" (2021b, 419). Ezekiel

Commentary

makes the point with crystalline clarity: "I have no pleasure in the death of anyone, says the Lord God. Turn, then, and live" (Ezek 18:32).

6:16 ***the statutes of Omri.*** The closing verse of Mic 6 articulates an unmistakable warning of inexorable doom for Judah. Though neither Judah nor Jerusalem is mentioned by name, the prophet's chilling analogy with the fall of the Northern Kingdom is clear. Omri, ruler of Israel (r. 884–873), is remembered in biblical tradition for having fortified the hill of Samaria as the political seat of his monarchy after having reigned initially for six years in Tirzah, according to 1 Kgs 16:23–24. Archaeological excavations have uncovered the remains of monumental buildings at Samaria; see commentary on Mic 1:6 for details. In the formulaic judgment of the Deuteronomist, "Omri did what was evil in the sight of the Lord; he did more evil than all who were before him" in the Israelite monarchy, following Jeroboam son of Nebat in idolatrous practices (1 Kgs 16:25). Sergi observes that while the Omride rulers brought Israel to a position of considerable power, having "established their rule over vast territories in the southern Levant, in both cis- and trans-Jordan," their political achievements are all but ignored in biblical traditions, which focus on "the image of the Omrides as symbols of the ultimate offensive cultic sins of late monarchic Judah . . . [in] the cultural memory of the Judean intellectual elite of the Persian period" (2016, 504, 506). Elayi notes that the Northern Kingdom of Israel, "known to the Assyrians as *Bit-Humri*, 'House of Omri,' lost its northern territories and coastal regions after the conquest of Damascus by Tiglath-Pileser III in 732 BCE" (2017, 45).

practices of the house of Ahab. Ahab, the son of Omri and a king of Israel (r. 873–853 or 852), was, according to Avigad, "a great builder" like his father; he is thought to have "erected strong fortifications at Hazor and Megiddo" (1993, 1303). The lavish appointments of the royal palace may have contributed to the image of Israel's elites as corrupt. Avigad describes ivory preciosities discovered by archaeologists at Samaria, characterizing the trove as "the most important collection of miniature art from the Iron Age discovered in Israel" (1304). Among the finds were "a great number of ivory plaques and hundreds of ivory fragments," some "sculpted in the round," some "carved in low relief," and some "decorated with insets of precious stones, colored glass, and gold foil" (1304–5). These beautiful carvings "were probably used as inlays in the palace furniture of the Israelite kings," as per 1 Kgs 22:39 and Amos 6:4 (1306).

Ahab is adjudged by the Deuteronomist negatively, as was his father: painted as evil "more than all who were before him" (1 Kgs 16:30), Ahab is critiqued not only for allowing the idolatrous practices of Jeroboam son of Nebat to continue, but for taking initiative in that trajectory, per the Deuteronomist: having married the Sidonian princess Jezebel, Ahab built a shrine to Baal, worshipped there, and made a sacred pole (presumably for the cult of Asherah). Ahab is remembered as being predatory with regard to land acquisition, a theme that receives sustained attention in Micah. Andersen and Freedman observe that Micah's charge about elite powerbrokers coveting fields and scheming to tear them from their rightful owners (Mic 2:1-2) is precisely what the corrupt Ahab had done in having Naboth the Jezreelite falsely condemned and appropriating his vineyard (1 Kgs 21:1-16; 2000, 560). McKeating remarks, "Omri, and Ahab his son, were by any objective criteria outstandingly strong rulers, but to the writers of the Old Testament they were outstanding only in wickedness" (1971, 187). Cazelles and Sperling offer that the citing of Omri and Ahab "make it probable that the passage alluded (at least originally) to Samaria" and that the "tribe" apostrophized in 6:9 may be Ephraim. They point to the heavy use of the name "Ephraim" in Hosea—it occurs thirty-two times in the oracles of that northern prophet—and the explicit connection of Ephraim and Samaria in Isa 9:8 (Eng. 9) for "the kingdom of the North dismembered by Tiglath-Pileser III" (2007, 162). That the fall of Samaria is being taken as an object lesson is not in doubt; it is evident from the accusation, "you have followed their counsels," in Mic 6:16. That the oracle here would have been directed historically to Samaria is far less certain.

an object of hissing. The pairing of "desolation" (*šammâ*) and "an object of hissing" (*šərēqâ*) comes up often in late traditions in the book of Jeremiah (Jer 18:16; 19:8; 25:9, 18; 29:18; 51:37); *šammâ* also occurs many additional times in Jeremiah paired with other nouns. The specific pairing seen here occurs otherwise only once in the Hebrew Bible, in another late text (2 Chr 29:8), suggesting that the word pair was valued by scribes writing and shaping biblical materials after—perhaps long after—the fall of Jerusalem. Micah 6 closes with the stark image of Judah left in a state of utter ruination, with onlookers and passersby hissing in alarm or malice.

BIBLIOGRAPHY

Brueggemann, W. 2010. "Walk Humbly with Your God: Micah 6:8." *Journal for Preachers* 33:14-19.
Ehrman, A. 1973. "Note on Micah 6:14." VT 23:103-5. doi:10.1163/156853373X00243.

Bibliography

Ferguson, J. 1991. *Clement of Alexandria: Stromateis, Books 1–3.* FC 85. Washington, DC: Catholic University of America Press.
Fischer, I. 2002. *Gotteskünderinnen: Zu einer geschlechterfairen Deutung des Phänomens der Prophetie und der Prophetinnen in der Hebräischen Bibel.* Stuttgart: Kohlhammer.
Gafney, W. C. 2008. *Daughters of Miriam: Women Prophets in Ancient Israel.* Minneapolis: Fortress.
———. 2016. Sermon, "Faith without Faithfulness Is Faithlessness." Womanists Wading in the Word. https://www.wilgafney.com/2016/10/29/faith-without-faithfulness-is-faithlessness/.
Heider, G. C. 1985. *The Cult of Molek: A Reassessment.* JSOTSup 43. Sheffield: Sheffield Academic.
Hutton, R. M. 1999. "What Happened from Shittim to Gilgal? Law and Gospel in Micah 6:5." *CurTM* 26:94–103.
Hyatt, J. P. 1952. "On the Meaning and Origin of Micah 6:8." *AThR* 34:232–39.
Ibita, M. M. S. 2018. "'Plead Your Case before the Mountains': An Ecological Reading of the Royal Metaphor in Micah 6." Pages 477–90 in *The Books of the Twelve Prophets: Minor Prophets—Major Theologies.* Edited by H.-J. Fabry. BETL 295. Leuven: Peeters.
Kipfer, S. 2021. "'You Eat, but You Never Have Enough . . .': Fear of Famine and Food Shortage in the Hebrew Bible and in the Ancient Near East." *WO* 51:58–83. doi:10.13109/wdor.2021.51.1.58.
Kitz, A. M. 2014. *Cursed Are You! The Phenomenology of Cursing in Cuneiform and Hebrew Texts.* Winona Lake, IN: Eisenbrauns.
Kosman, A., and B. C. Gregory. 2015. "Ḥesed." *EBR* 11:962–83. doi:10.1515/ebr.hesed.
Malamat, A. 1995. "Prophecy at Mari." Pages 50–73 in *The Place Is Too Small for Us: The Israelite Prophets in Recent Scholarship.* Edited by R. P. Gordon. Sources for Biblical and Theological Study 5. Winona Lake, IN: Eisenbrauns.
Mayfield, T. D. 2023. "Genre Multiplicity in Micah 6:1–8: A Non-legal *rîb* and an Entrance Liturgy." Pages 149–56 in *A Sage in New Haven: Essays on the Prophets, the Writings, and the Ancient World in Honor of Robert R. Wilson.* Edited by A. A. Gruseke and C. J. Sharp. ÄAT 117. Münster: Zaphon.
O'Connor, K. M. 2016. "Reflections on Kindness as Fierce Tenderness: Micah 6:1–8." *Journal for Preachers* 39:32–36.
Osiek, C. 1999. *The Shepherd of Hermas.* Hermeneia. Minneapolis: Fortress.
Quick, L. 2018. *Deuteronomy 28 and the Aramaic Curse Tradition.* Oxford Theology and Religion Monographs. Oxford: Oxford University Press.
Walker, A. 2005. *In Search of Our Mothers' Gardens: Womanist Prose.* Phoenix: New Edition.

MICAH 7

Daughter Zion Laments

7:1-4a

¹Woe is me!
For I have become like the remnants of summer fruit,
    like what is left behind at the harvest:
There is no cluster of grapes to eat,
    no ripe fig, which I crave.
²The pious one has perished from the land,
    and there is no righteous one among humans.
All of them lie in wait for blood;
    they hunt one another with nets.
³Their hands are good at doing evil.
    The official asks, as does the judge, for illicit compensation,
and the powerful dictates per his greed:
    thus they conspire.
⁴The best of them are like a briar;
    the "upright," worse than a thorny thicket.

A Gibe at False Prophets

7:4b

A day for your {*ms*} sentinels: your punishment has arrived.
    Now their confusion is at hand.

Micah 7

Micah as Faithful Sentinel

7:5-7

⁵Do not rely {*mp*} on a friend;
  put no trust in an intimate.
With her who reclines at your {*ms*} chest,
  be guarded about what leaves your mouth!
⁶For son disrespects father;
  a daughter rises up against her mother,
a daughter-in-law against her mother-in-law;
  the enemies of a man are those of his own household.

⁷But as for me, for Yhwh I will keep watch;
  I will wait for the God of my salvation;
  my God will hear me.

Daughter Zion Speaks

7:8-10

⁸Do not rejoice {*fs*} over me, O my enemy!
  Whenever I have fallen, I have risen.
Whenever I have sat in darkness,
  Yhwh has been my light.
⁹I must bear the raging of Yhwh—
  for I have sinned against [Yhwh]—
until [Yhwh] adjudicates my case
  and renders justice for me.
[Yhwh] will bring me out into the light;
  I will see by means of [Yhwh's] righteousness.
¹⁰Then my enemy will see,
  and shame will cover her
who had been saying to me,
  "Where is Yhwh your God?"
My eyes will gaze upon her [in derision]:
  now she will become something to be trampled,
  like mud in the streets.

Micah Consoles Daughter Zion

7:11–13

> [11]A day for the rebuilding of your {fs} walls!
>   That very day, the boundary will lie distant.
> [12]That day, he will come to you {ms}
>   from Assyria and the cities of Egypt,
> and from Egypt to the River,
>   from sea to sea and mountain to mountain.
> [13]And the earth will become a desolation
>   because of its {fs} inhabitants, due to the fruit of their deeds.

Micah Intercedes and Yhwh Responds

7:14–15

> [14]Shepherd {ms} your people with your staff—
>   the sheep of your inheritance,
> one dwelling in solitude,
>   a forest in the midst of fruitful land.
> Let them graze in Bashan and Gilead,
>   as in ancient days,
> [15]as in the days when you {ms} came out of the land of Egypt.
>
> "I will show him wondrous things."

Micah's Doxology of Hope

7:16–20

> [16]Nations will see and be shamed
>   beyond all their strength.
> They will put their hands over their mouths;
>   their ears will be deafened.
> [17]They will lick dust like the snake,
>   like things that crawl on the ground;
>   they will come quaking out of their fortifications.
> They will approach Yhwh our God with dread,
>   and they will fear you.

Micah 7

¹⁸Who is a God like you,
   one who pardons iniquity
   and passes over transgression
      for the remnant of their inheritance?

[Yhwh] has not held fast to [Yhwh's] anger forever,
   for [Yhwh] delights in fidelity.
¹⁹[Yhwh] will once again have compassion on us;
   [Yhwh] will subdue our iniquities.

And you will hurl into the depths of the sea
   all of their sins.
²⁰You will render faithfulness to Jacob,
   fidelity to Abraham,
as you swore to our ancestors
   from days of old.

INTERPRETATION

Micah 7 opens with a powerful cry, "Woe is me!" This poetic pathos has the effect of unsettling the audience, pulling readers with magnetic force into oracles crafted as a dialogue between Daughter Zion and Micah. The dialogue expands in two key moments to include others. First, in 7:4b immediately after Zion has lamented at the pervasive corruption of Judean leadership, one of the speakers—it could be Zion or Micah—turns to excoriate someone who had not understood that divine punishment was coming. Jerusalem and Judah are desolate (7:1–3); thus the false prophets have been proved wrong about disgrace not coming upon Judean society (cf. 2:6). The masculine singular addressee, whose identity cannot be discerned, could be the ruler of the time, "your sentinels" meaning false prophets who had been functioning to underwrite corruption or had been coopted by the Jerusalem elite to justify a politically misguided position of faux optimism. Or the addressee could be someone perceived as leader of the false prophets, "your sentinels" signifying others who had been mustered, officially or unofficially, to overlook or actively support the malfeasance and wickedness poisoning the highest levels of government.

In a second expansion of the dialogue between Daughter Zion and Micah, Yhwh speaks, offering a response to Micah's intercession on behalf of

Interpretation

the covenant people (7:14-15a). Yhwh makes the stunning promise, "I will show them marvelous things" (7:15b), a clear allusion to the exodus traditions of old and thus a promise that a new and equally momentous time of deliverance is at hand. This divine promise functions as the catalyst for the turn to a prophetic paean of divine praise that closes the book.

Micah 7 is unlike any other poetry in Micah. Likely composed later than much of the preceding material in the book, it draws threads from other oracles in Mic 1-6, weaving them together in reversals and rearticulations that create an artfully embroidered tapestry of hope for the implied audience.

In Mic 1, a cascade of divinely appointed destruction had left Samaria in ruins, a dreaded military threat advancing on Jerusalem, and the prophet lamenting and howling like a wild animal. In Mic 7, it is Daughter Zion who laments, wailing her lived experience of the harms that oppression and covenantal infidelity have wrought. Zion staggers through a bleak and dangerous landscape, alone and ravenous, as rapacious officials lurk, hunting their people. In Mic 1, the prophet had evoked the dust and chaos of Judean towns scattering in terror during the enemy's military march through the Shephelah; the closing image was of Judeans being carried off into exile. In Mic 7, Zion has fallen to the enemy and now waits quietly in the darkness of exile, enduring the enemy's mockery as she waits for Yhwh to shine the light of vindication on her battered righteousness. The prophetic scribe foresees the unfolding of divine retribution on those who had harmed her.

In Mic 2, oppressors had sought to silence Micah's truth-telling, sneering that disaster would not overwhelm Judah and that he should cease prophesying about impending disgrace. Micah had responded that their corruption had rendered Judah a defiled landscape, then performed an ironic prophecy of doom that sounded like deliverance, per the rubrics of his detractors, but in fact was a devastating oracle about the people penned as animals awaiting slaughter, Yhwh leading the community not to safety but into diaspora. In Mic 7, the day of recompense has arrived for the false "sentinels" (prophets) who had insisted Jerusalem was not at risk. Deliverance will come, but only after defeat has shattered and displaced the community. As in the days when Yhwh brought the people out of enslavement in Egypt, so Yhwh will perform new miracles on Judah's behalf in terms recognizable to the faithful from of old: this will be a divine compassion that honors covenantal fidelity to founding ancestors Abraham and Jacob.

In Mic 3, the prophet had used graphic images of cannibalism to paint Judean officials and elite oppressors as horrifying predatory beasts. Against the backdrop of mercenary false prophets and exploitative cultic function-

Micah 7

aries, Micah had laid claim to the spirit of Yhwh as authorization for his speaking the truth about their vicious practices of injustice, which would leave Jerusalem in rubble. In Mic 7, Yhwh's deliverance of Zion is imminent. Against the backdrop of seething internecine suspicions and antagonism, Micah is portrayed as patiently trusting in Yhwh. The prophetic scribe envisions the rebuilding of Zion's walls; Judeans who had been being devoured by their corrupt officials would now feed on verdant pasturage in a land restored and fruitful.

In Mic 4, the prophetic scribe had portrayed a magnificent Zion, the mountain of the House of Yhwh, sending forth torah instruction as nations eagerly stream to Jerusalem for knowledge of Yhwh and for peace; the discourse then shifts to a fearsome Zion who will thresh her enemies. In Mic 7, diaspora Judeans will stream back to Zion from the many mountains bounding the geopolitical territories of the known world; a vindicated Zion will gaze on her erstwhile enemies in derision as they crawl toward Yhwh in dread. The torah teaching they will have learned is that no deity is like Yhwh, a God who is invincibly faithful to those in a covenantal relationship established from days of old.

In Mic 5, the prophetic scribe had articulated a luminous vision of the coming rule of a Davidic shepherd; the cruel invader Assyria was to be thwarted, and the remnant of Yhwh's people would trample and tear adversarial nations, with Yhwh demolishing the fortifications of those who had ravaged Judah. Micah 7 elaborates on this powerful shepherd imagery. In a landscape made desolate by the execrable deeds of malfeasant leaders, none other than Yhwh will shepherd the sheep of the covenant: divine protection will allow them to graze in safety. Forgiven their transgressions, Yhwh's people will flourish once again.

In Mic 6, Yhwh claimed the history of salvation wrought on behalf of Israel: deliverance from the house of slavery in Egypt; guidance through Moses the law-giver, Aaron the priest, and Miriam the prophet; and rescue of Israel from the machinations and violence of enemies in the wilderness. The covenant stipulations had always been simple: to do justice, to cherish fidelity, and to proceed humbly with God. In Mic 7, the prophetic scribe gives depth and texture to the implicit claim of every covenant in the Hebrew Bible, from the Noahide covenant to Priestly and non-Priestly expressions of Yhwh's promises of land and progeny to Abraham, Isaac, and Jacob, from the Mosaic covenant on Sinai and Yhwh's covenant with the Levites to the Davidic covenant and Jeremiah's vision of a new covenant to be written on the heart. That central claim: there is no god like

Interpretation

Yhwh. Micah 7 then teaches the grounding claim of the covenant people: that Yhwh is a deity who shows compassion and fidelity to the covenant people in every age.

Thus Mic 7 clearly draws on earlier oracles in the Micah traditions, echoing and reversing imagery in richly textured ways. Echoes with other Hebrew Bible texts are discernible in Mic 7 as well. For example, in 7:8, the trope of Yhwh being the light of the believer's eyes is reminiscent of Job 29:3; Pss 18:29 (Eng. 28); 27:1; 36:9; and 119:105. And the image in Mic 7:17 of the subjugated nations licking dust like the snake evokes Yhwh Elohim's curse on the snake in the garden of Eden (Gen 3:14) and the rearticulation of that tradition in Isa 65:25.

An exquisitely subtle but perceptible chiastic structure in Mic 7 frames the experience of the speaker by means of the time of the primordial flood. According to Israelite Priestly and non-Priestly Pentateuchal traditions in Gen 6–9, human wickedness and violence had been so pervasive that the deity unleashed the waters of the fountains of the great deep and the heavens, obliterating creaturely life so as to begin afresh with Noah and his family. Consider these gestures in Mic 7 to the flood narratives:

The Lord saw that the wickedness of humankind was great in the earth, and that every inclination of the thoughts of their hearts was only evil continually. (Gen 6:5)

Now the earth was corrupt in God's sight, and the earth was filled with violence. And God saw that the earth was corrupt; for all flesh had corrupted its ways upon the earth. (Gen 6:11)

> The pious one has perished from the land,
> and there is no righteous one among humans.
> All of them lie in wait for blood;
> they hunt one another with nets. (Mic 7:2)

So the Lord said, "I will blot out from the earth the human beings I have created—people together with animals and creeping things and birds of the air, for I am sorry that I have made them." (Gen 6:7)

And God said to Noah, "I have determined to make an end of all flesh, for the earth is filled with violence because of them; now I am going to destroy them along with the earth." (Gen 6:13)

Micah 7

> And the earth will become a desolation
> because of its inhabitants, due to the fruit of their deeds.
> (Mic 7:13)

> And you [Yhwh] will hurl into the depths of the sea
> all of their sins. (Mic 7:19b)

Daughter Zion Laments (7:1-4a)

Many interpreters identify the lamenting speaker as the prophet Micah, including Jerome and other early Christian theologians. But Daughter Zion, that is, personified Jerusalem as the honored center of theopolitical organization of the people of Judah, is the figure that has been left desolate. She hungers for righteousness, wailing in her diminishment, the integrity of her community left in useless fragments and discarded leavings as corruption has pervaded the land of Judah. The prophet attends deeply to Daughter Zion's lament, responding with a prophetic indictment directed at the malfeasant in his community. His address to (masculine plural) listeners in 7:5 is typical of prophetic polemic generally and of Micah's oracles otherwise, while such direct address of vitriolic indictment to a plural group is not typical of Zion's own speech.

Daughter Zion laments (7:1-4) that there are no pious or righteous persons remaining in the land. Her assessment could well take in the whole earth, since *'ereṣ*, translated "land" here, can also mean "earth." Lamentation and polemics concerning the moral and spiritual corruption of the whole earth can be found in texts early and late in the Latter Prophets (e.g., Isa 24:1-13; Jer 25:15-38; Hos 4:1-3; Amos 8:9-12; Zeph 1:2-3, 14-18; 3:8). The term *'ereṣ* occurs fifteen times in Micah, and its deployments encompass both senses: Yhwh enacts divine retribution and redemption upon the entire earth, and the consequences of sin also affect particular lands as bounded geopolitical territories.

> earth (1:2)
> earth (1:3)
> earth (4:13)
> earth (5:3)
>
> land (of Judah, 5:4)

land (of Assyria, of Nimrod, and of Judah, 5:5)
land (unspecified nation, 5:10)

earth (6:2)

land (of Egypt, 6:4)

earth *and/or* land (7:2)
earth (7:13)

land (of Egypt, 7:15)

earth (7:17)

The instance in 7:2 evokes ambiguity as to the scope of the human sin that has caused such suffering for Daughter Zion. That there is no righteous person left "among humans" gestures expansively toward the whole earth as the terrain on which inequity has become dominant. Yet the citing of roles of various corrupt elites—the official, the judge, the powerful—suggests keen-eyed observation of malfeasance in one's own community, and the lens focuses, then, even more tightly on social dishonor and conflicts within kinship groups. The poetry in the opening of Mic 7 moves artfully from a sweeping indictment of all humans on the earth and (or) within the land of Judah to a laser focus on corruption found in the chambers and city gates of Jerusalem and, finally, to breaches and antagonisms within Judean households (7:5-6). But Micah positions himself in opposition to the malfeasance poisoning his community: he signals to his compatriots that prophetic vision requires waiting for Yhwh.

A Gibe at False Prophets (7:4b)

In Mic 7, four times a note is struck regarding an imminent day on which justice will be upheld by Yhwh. The first occurrence, in 7:4, signals the recompense looming for malfeasant leaders and other malefactors among the people. In 7:11-12, three additional references to that "day" make clear that it will be a day in which the flourishing of Zion and Judah will unfold and exiled Judeans will stream homeward. In the fierce interpolation in 7:4b, the prophetic scribe taunts a masculine addressee; a corrupt ruler, venal judicial

Micah 7

official, or extortionate priest would seem to be in view (3:11; 7:3), whether an actual authority known to the scribe or a figure standing metonymically for the exploitative bureaucracy writ large. Divine retribution has arrived. Those "sentinels"—mercenary false prophets—who had pandered to the addressee, assuring him that "disgrace will not overtake [us]" (2:6) and that with Yhwh in their midst, "calamity will not come upon us" (3:11), will be thrown into confusion, their words revealed to have been deception.

Micah as Faithful Sentinel (7:5-7)

An important motif in Mic 7 is that of keeping watch: true prophets serve as sentinels, straining to glimpse an impending threat or to see and articulate that for which the community is waiting in hope. This idea is articulated as early as Hosea—"the prophet is a sentinel for my God over Ephraim" (Hos 9:8)—and is audible in the book of Ezekiel, where Yhwh says to the prophet, "Mortal, I have made you a sentinel for the house of Israel; whenever you hear a word from my mouth, you shall give them warning from me" (Ezek 3:17). As the divinely appointed doom of corrupt leaders approaches, the "sentinels" who have guarded the malfeasant will be thrown into chaos. Micah, by contrast, stands firm as he looks for divine succor: "But as for me, for Yhwh I will keep watch." The reversal here subtly echoes the stronger contrast drawn in 3:8, where Micah had excoriated false prophets and mercenary seers, then proclaimed, "But as for me, I am filled with power, with the spirit of Yhwh, and with justice and might." The voicing in 7:7 sounds less like a prophet thundering his authority granted by Yhwh to persuade a hostile audience, as in Mic 3, and more like a psalmist offering liturgical words of hope to the worshipping community.

Daughter Zion Speaks (7:8-10)

These lyrical strophes continue in the mode of liturgical expressiveness, as has often been noticed. Resonances with the ideation, voicing, and diction of the Psalms are indisputably in evidence here. Zion's bitter lament (7:1-4) yields to the claim of faith that, despite all evidence to the contrary, "Yhwh has been my light" and the light of her community. As with the psalmist who insists, "The Lord is my light and my salvation" (Ps 27:1), so Zion acknowledges Yhwh even as she continues to gaze on that which is broken and despoiled in the present landscape of Judah and in the community's history. The earlier lament in 7:1-4 and the warning in 7:5-6 focus on violence, corruption, and betrayal within the Judean community, while the enemy imagined in 7:8, 10 with feminine singular verbs and feminine pronominal suffixes seems to be a personified geopolitical adversary, Daughter Assyria or Daughter Babylon. A fascinating ambiguity is opened up by the taunt, "Where is Yhwh your God?" in 7:10, positioned, as it is, between blocks of material that explore familial conflict (7:5-6) and geopolitical militarized threats (implicit but clear in 7:11-13, 16-17). The taunt appears in the Hebrew Bible in the mouths of (ventriloquized) opponents, shaped in a variety of forms ranging from the sarcastic rhetorical question, "Where is your God?," to the arrogant claim that as regards evildoers' malfeasance, "Yhwh does not see" (Pss 10:11; 94:7; Jer 12:4; Ezek 9:9). It is deployed to ventriloquize both intracommunal antagonists (Ps 42:4, 11 [Eng. 3, 10]; Mal 2:17) and geopolitical enemies (Pss 79:10; 115:2; Joel 2:17). Notably, it is used in Isaiah in the context of Neo-Assyrian aggression against Jerusalem: the Rabshakeh mocks Hezekiah and his people by saying that Yhwh has assisted the Assyrian onslaught and is powerless to halt it (Isa 36:7-20). Here in Mic 7, one effect of positioning the taunt between material about injurious behavior within the community and material about enemy threats is that the identity of the "enemy" shifts fluidly, first signifying corrupt and callous Judeans, then signifying an enemy nation. This presents a powerful moment of decision for each implied hearer or reader of the entire scroll of Micah: whether to continue in self-serving ways, with no regard for the luminous torah teachings from Zion to which all the peoples of the world will stream and in which lifeways of peace and flourishing will be enjoyed (4:1-4), or continue in the ways of exploitation, extortion, and conflict, thereby becoming one of the enemies of Judah whom Yhwh will shame (7:10), destroy (7:13), or subjugate (7:16-17). Creating this Janus function for "Where is Yhwh your God" in 7:10 is a brilliant move on the part of the prophetic scribe to secure the implied audience's renewed commitment to Yhwh.

Micah Consoles Daughter Zion (7:11-13)

While some interpreters from Jerome (*Comm. Mich.*, 107) to the present day hear Yhwh addressing Zion here, it is better to hear the prophet responding to Zion's words, especially in light of the minatory character of 7:13, which has the character of a prophetic warning about divine retribution on all the nations of the earth that had harmed God's people. In three oracles in Micah (1:15; 5:4-5; 7:12), the prophet says a masculine singular subject will come. In 1:15, a "dispossessor" ironically styled "the Glory of Israel" will come as far as

Micah 7

Adullam. That this is a punitive enemy invader dispatched by Yhwh is clear; exactly how this invader could represent the Glory of Israel must be worked out by the implied audience, which has no choice but to see the enemy as the weapon of Yhwh. In 5:4-5, invasion by Assyria is expressly in view: the grammatically singular subject may be taken metonymically as the commander of Assyrian troops or as the Assyrian Empire personified. Here in 7:12, the unexpressed subject of the verb may be enigmatic, but the force of reversal is clear. Rather than an enemy coming, in this case the covenant people will come (back) from the diverse places of exile to which they had been scattered during the era of Neo-Assyrian hegemony (2 Kgs 17:5-6, 23) and, tacitly in this postexilic material, during the terror of Neo-Babylonian exile as well. The 3ms subject of "will come" in Mic 7:12 may be understood as the "people" and "sheep" of Yhwh, the one dwelling—note the 3ms participle—in peaceful solitude on Carmel (7:14) after repatriation.

Micah Intercedes and Yhwh Responds (7:14-15)

Having listened to the voice of lamenting Zion and having responded with compassionate assurances of restoration, Micah now calls on Yhwh: "Shepherd your people with your staff, the sheep of your inheritance" (7:14.) This clarion call to Yhwh for intervention is a strong theological assertion of Israel's covenantal right to divine care. Reading the prophet's intercessory petition is spiritually formative for the implied audience, who learn that they too may claim covenantal protection from Yhwh. The bucolic images of enjoying undisturbed solitude and peaceful grazing are framed, via 7:15, as the signs of the abundance that Israel and Judah have long known under Yhwh's sovereignty, ever since Yhwh had delivered them from enslavement in Egypt. And the deity responds to Micah's plea with confirmation of ongoing care: Yhwh will indeed show Israel and Judah "wondrous things" once more, new marvels that demonstrate the divine power to guide this covenant people through every kind of wilderness into rich pastureland.

Micah's Doxology of Hope (7:16-20)

The magnificent closing verses of the scroll of Micah achieve exquisite theological depth and rhetorical power through vivid imagery, allusions to venerable biblical traditions, and direct address that moves fluidly between the hearers and Yhwh.

First, the trauma of invasion in Mic 1 is put to rest: enemy nations, defeated and subjugated, will render obeisance to Yhwh and—this is implicit—will never again terrorize Yhwh's people (7:16-17). The enemies "[licking] dust like the snake" evokes Isa 65:17-25 (cf. 65:25, "but the serpent—its food shall be dust!"), where the glorious peace and fruitfulness of the restored Jerusalem make for a peaceable kingdom and kin-dom on Yhwh's holy mountain (Isa 11:6-9) like that envisioned in Mic 7:14.

Second, the prophetic scribe turns to Yhwh, offering praise of the deity's incomparable mercy in pardoning the sins of the covenant people. The authority of signifying Yhwh's character in this way is extraordinary. The rhetorical question, "Who is a God like you?" (mî-ʾēl kāmôkā), establishes the power of Yhwh and, further, gestures toward reiteration of the prophet's own name (mîkâ) in a more elaborate form that slows down the utterance of the phrase, as if to make every syllable count for the authority of this prophet who has spoken on behalf of Yhwh in oracle after oracle.

Third, the prophetic scribe turns back to the gathered people, and to the implied audience through subsequent generations, to explain that this God whom they worship "delights in fidelity"—the same fidelity to which the covenant community has been called throughout its history (6:3-8). This compassionate deity will meet the people in that joyous place of fidelity.

Finally, the prophetic scribe looks again to Yhwh, acclaimed as mighty in compassion, to articulate his trust that Yhwh will show clemency and faithfulness to the people of Abraham's lineage once again, as the deity had promised long ago.

History of Consequences

For illustrative comments on Mic 7 in rabbinic midrash, see the introduction under §4.1.1 Midrashic Interpretations.

In the Gospels of Matthew and Luke, Jesus warns that he comes to bring not peace but conflict, quoting Mic 7:6 (Matt 10:34-36; Luke 12:51-53). This saying and a passage in all three Synoptic Gospels about kin betraying kin (Matt 10:21-22 // Mark 13:12-13 // Luke 21:16-17) may reflect Jewish apocalyptic traditions about "end-time mayhem," expected to involve significant disruption to social relationships and persecution of

Micah 7

the faithful prior to the appearance of the Messiah and God's unleashing of retributive judgment on malefactors (Marcus 2009, 887-88).

Origen of Alexandria, preaching on Luke 3:11, uses Mic 7:19 to amplify the counsel of John the Baptist that faithful believers should attend to those in need. In his characteristically spiritualizing exegesis, Origen offers that the one who lacks a tunic, in John's ethically formulated example, is the one "who utterly lacks God," and Christians should "divest themselves" of all their "vices and sins," casting them into the depths of the sea—as envisioned in Mic 7:19—as a way of throwing them back onto "him who was the cause of them for us," presumably Satan (*Hom. Lk.*, 23.4).

Cappadocian theologian Basil of Caesarea (ca. 329-379) deploys 7:19 in his Homily 13, focused on Ps 28 LXX (MT 29). Basil explores dimensions of the soul's training in virtue, reflecting on the psalm's imagery of waters as "spiritual teaching which refreshes the souls of the hearers" and through which "they receive water which springs up to eternal life" (*Hom. Ps.*, 201). The floods over which YHWH sits enthroned are, for Basil, a sign of the "grace of baptism" as "a flood" in which, per Mic 7:19, believers' sins are washed away (210-11).

Jerome observes that though he sees the prophet as the lamenting speaker as Mic 7 opens, "there are those who think this is said under the persona of the Savior, who is pleading that among such a great multitude of believers and in the whole world of humankind he finds hardly any work worthy of his blood" (*Comm. Mich.*, 100). Jerome acknowledges grounds for such a reading might be found in Jesus's saying about the harvest being plentiful but the laborers few (Matt 9:37; Luke 10:2). He amplifies the prophet's counsel not to rely on a friend (Mic 7:5) by citing Ahithophel having betrayed David (2 Sam 15:12; 17:1-3) and Judas Iscariot having betrayed Jesus (per all four Gospels; 101). Jerome offers an apparent quotation of proverbial wisdom, "a sugar-coated tongue conceals the venom of the soul" (cf. Prov 5:3-4), and adds, "many are the friends of the rich, but even those who seem to be friends depart from the poor" (Prov. 19:4; 102). Jerome urges that those who long for true friendship should "be a friend of God, as Moses was," and follow Jesus, who called his disciples friends (John 15:15; 103). The spiritual sense of Mic 7:8-13, according to Jerome, suggests the soul speaking in soliloquy (108). Jerome hears the imperative to "shepherd your people" (7:14) as dialogue within the Trinity: "God the Father is speaking this to the Son, that is, to our Lord Jesus Christ, because he is the good shepherd, and he lays his life down for his sheep" (John 10:11, 14; 110). Shepherding with the staff sounds to Jerome like punishment for those keeping their own counsel, and he is scrupulously careful to draw distinctions between types of solitude: "I am not saying that the prophetic and solitary life that Elijah and John [the Baptist] led must be condemned, but that if someone despises others and becomes arrogant and lives in a forest of vices, [that one] needs to be chastised with a rod" (111).

Cyril of Alexandria finds warrant for Zion's hope (7:9) in Jerusalem having seen the rightness of its punishment by Yhwh, for the repentance of sinners yields their restoration, showing that "the Lord of all is good, and without delay ... gladdens them very abundantly with the good things of his clemency" (*Comm.*^{CA}, 266). This prophetic truth applies to Judah historically, and also "no less to the spiritual Zion, that is, the church," and finally to the soul of each individual who repents, "accepting the grace of salvation through Christ," for Christ "renders all who make their approach to him cleansed of their former sins through holy baptism, seals them in holiness with the Spirit, and enrolls them among God's children" (268–69). Citing Jer 15:17, Cyril avers that those "dwelling in solitude" (Mic 7:14) are the righteous, who "live an honorable and praiseworthy life" and whose minds are "filled ... with a kind of richness" through "exercising abundantly ... practical and contemplative virtue" (273). As regards the luminous promise that closes the book of Micah, Christians belong among those descended from Abraham and receiving the benefit of God's promises to the ancestors (7:20), a point Cyril secures via Rom 9:6-8 and Gal 3:6-9 (278).

Calvin preached on 7:1-12 on 7 and 8 January 1551; there is no record of him preaching on 7:13-20. He hears the despair of the speaker in the opening strophe as Micah wailing: "There is no point in hoping that my message will lead [humanity] to salvation, for they have totally given themselves up to malice and perversity" (2003, 367). Calvin consoles those who doubt the efficacy of their preaching: "though the world hasten toward its own ruin and perdition, God is still glorified. For when God executes his judgment against the wicked and the reprobate, [God's] justice shines in their damnation as equally as [God] is glorified in saving [God's] elect"; preachers should remember that no matter what consequences unfold, "God approves of the preaching of [God's] Gospel" (369-70). Perhaps drawing on his own experiences of opposition in Geneva, Calvin paraphrases Micah as lamenting, "'After several sermons, I expected to see God honored, but the season is too far gone now.' For a servant of God, that is a disappointing and bitter thing to have to acknowledge" (372). But preachers should remain resolute, like the sentinels of 7:4b, striving continually "to cry out against all evil, and to proclaim to those who remain asleep in their sins that they are not to mock God" (383). Calvin figures the gloating enemy of 7:8 as ecclesial adversaries, especially the "diabolical seat of Rome" (397). Acknowledging the spiritual reality of sitting in darkness, Calvin preaches, "We face constant troubles, sorrows, and temptations ... thus we appear like castles shrouded in fog, behind moats. Therefore, what must we do? Let us welcome God's light. . . . Let us come to his Word. Let us arm ourselves with the promises of the Holy Scripture" (401).

Reflecting on 7:9, Berrigan urges that believers be patient "with themselves" and, further, with "the extortionists, the oppressors. With vile forms of power that obdurately hold on, resistant to compunction or conversion. Little can be done. Very well, let us do that little. Let us, at the very least, not accept that we are abandoned, not yield before the thin margin of an awful present, as though no breakthrough were promised" (1995, 242). In light of divine forgiveness (7:18-19), Berrigan poses a rhetorical question: "Is our life in the empire to be marred by a kind of creeping acculturation and passivity, cynicism, silent scorn, questioning, skepticism—or refusal, non-conformity, nonviolent resistance?" His answer: violence and oppression are "to be resisted, at whatever cost," for "mercy has accepted us" (245).

Micah 7 is important for the festival of Rosh Hashanah in many Jewish communities. Micah 7:18-20 or 19-20 is recited in the *Tashlich* ceremony at a source of running water into which believers cast bread crumbs or pebbles, symbolically casting off their sins for the new year (cf. Fuchs 2021, 367). Isaac Gottlieb observes that this and similar rituals "show that the Rabbis considered repentance and the LORD's response of loving kindness to be major themes in the prophets" (2016, 403). Micah 7:20 is recited in its entirety within the *Uva L'Tzion* prayer that closes many Jewish services on weekdays, on the sabbath, and on special holy days (Stavsky 2009, 60).

As the scroll of Micah closes with praise of YHWH's incomparable compassion (7:18-20), the reception-history dimension of this commentary will close with praise of divine mercy by a medieval theologian. In *Wisdom's Watch upon the Hours* by Henry Suso (ca. 1300-1366), the figure known as Eternal Wisdom—who is Christ—assures the

> disciple of unfailing divine compassion in these stirring words: "See, if the whole world were a globe of fire, with a handful of tow in the middle of it, the flax would not more quickly by its natural inclination catch fire than is the abyss of my mercies moved to wish that a penitent sinner be turned back to me" (2019, 1.4.12).

RETROSPECT

In Mic 7, Zion laments the ongoing violence, corruption, and division that are sabotaging every level of communal life. Millennia later, liberation theologian Jon Sobrino confirms the pervasiveness of oppression and greed in contemporary communities: "In our present day we are basically still involved in a civilization of capital, which generates extreme scarcities, dehumanizes persons, and destroys the human family: it produces impoverished and excluded people and divides the world into conquerors and conquered" (2008, 37). Sobrino does not give up. Citing Mic 6:8, he urges activists to walk with God "in justice, love, and tenderness," continuing to work for the radical transformation of inequities as "we make our way toward absolute mystery," toward the ineffable "beloved nearness" that is God (96–97).

Neither does Zion give up. She confirms her own tenacity in the face of hostile adversaries, boldly claiming her power to rise from a posture of subjugation (7:8). Drawing on her 2014 work with a Brothers Grimm story of a willful child, Ahmed theorizes the feminist KILLJOY as one who refuses to stay down, who dares to persist and lifts her arm as a "signifier of hope" (2017, 84; 2014, 1–2). The raised arm performs a public display of resistance. As Ahmed describes the systemic oppressions experienced by feminists of color, her terms have resonance also for our imagining of the experiences of injured, traumatized, and forcibly displaced Judean captives of the Neo-Assyrian and Neo-Babylonian Empires: they must survive "the violence of enslavement, of colonization, of empire," and the violence of "the requirement to give up kin, culture, memory, language, land" (2017, 80). But the feminist KILLJOYS, in whose ranks I glimpse the proto-KILLJOY Daughter Zion, decline to yield to hopelessness: "We reclaim willfulness in refusing to give up ... to persevere embodies that refusal" (80). Observing, "willfulness is persistence in the face of having been brought down," Ahmed goes on to explicate the implicit call to solidarity and mobilization of the community that is audible in the KILLJOY's refusal to stay buried by patriarchal oppres-

Micah 7

sion: the feminist arm of resistance "has to disturb the ground, to reach up, to reach out of the grave, that tomb, that burial" (84). Her clarion call to feminist, womanist, and queer activists is "to join arms, to show the arms as joined. We assemble a feminist army in response to this plea. A feminist army of arms would pulse with shared life and vitality" (84). So, too, Mic 7:8-10 portrays Zion's tenacity as a call to the (postexilic) Judean community to refuse to remain broken and subjugated—to dare to rise.

Daughter Zion's willful resolve offers a powerful model for readers of Micah today who search for ways to decline the brutal economic, political, and social harms enacted through systemic oppression. The book of Micah begins and ends in willfulness: willful prophetic resistance to forms of domination that ignore the covenant stipulations of Yhwh, resolute resistance to actions of malfeasance and violence that mock the prophetic adjuration to do justice, to cherish fidelity, and to proceed humbly with God (6:8). What Ahmed says of willful subjects illuminates the history of consequences beautifully with regard to Micah's importance for justice-minded Jewish and Christian readers: "Willfulness becomes a vital and shared inheritance: bodies can remember what has not been fully erased from themselves and from other bodies that have become parts of a social body. Willfulness can be a trace left behind, a reopening of what might have been closed down, a modification of what seems reachable, and a revitalization of the question of what it is to be for" (2014, 140).

The "willfulness archive" of Mic 1-7 calls us in brilliant and artful ways to work toward hope. Though divine refusal of our sinfulness is urgently necessary for reformation of our communities, and the world may seem to be fracturing and falling into heaps of rubble around us (1:4-6), nevertheless, in the words of Ahmed, "There can be joy in creating worlds out of the broken pieces of our dwelling spaces" (169).

In 7:14, Micah implores Yhwh to establish Judah in verdant pasture, shepherding the covenant people in a bucolic meadow of geopolitical safety where Judah may graze in peace. Bey wants the same for Black and trans persons, who in countless cultural contexts have been insulted, assaulted, and violated by the hegemonic brutalities of white supremacy and cishetero ideology. Bey imagines FUGITIVITY for their community as a radically emancipatory resistance, which "requires a profound letting go and leap into other ways to become a subject and live, unfettered and unbounded" (2022, 112). In the prophetic imaginations of Micah and Bey, malevolent encroachments will no longer be able to invade and enslave the bodies and spirits of the beloved community. But where Micah imagines an emancipation characterized by peaceful rest and languid grazing, Bey imagines an emancipation characterized by unconstrained and lively movement. Citing the writing of "black queer gender-fluid trans woman" Venus Di'Khadijah Selenite (2016, 2017), Bey offers this: "Black and trans are textured echoes of the fugitive," the one who runs for their life as "a visceral escape from those attempting to harm one on the grounds of antiblackness and transantagonism," but who also embraces "life *as* running—a constant escape as freedom" (178 [emphasis original]).

As explicated in the introduction, here is the spectrum of possibilities I have traced for contemporary responses to Micah's prophetic witness: → resilience → resistance → reformation → rejoicing. Micah 7 builds *resilience* in its audiences through the image of a beleaguered Zion anchored by her trust in Yhwh and supremely confident that her laments will receive gracious attention from her God (7:7-9). Micah 7 catalyzes *resistance* to the violence, predatory cruelty, and extortionate malfeasance that have characterized political leadership, judicial processes, and economic transactions within the community (7:2-4). Micah 7 calls for *reformation* of the disrespect, antagonistic dealing, and betrayal that have ruptured the community's life in the public square and within households (7:5-6). Finally, Mic 7 holds space for *rejoicing* in captivating and consoling images of God as light (7:8), as shepherd (7:14), as endlessly forgiving and compassionate (7:18-19), and as eternally faithful to this community since their originary ancestor, Abraham, was first called from Ur (7:20) and commissioned to become a blessing to all the families of the earth (Gen 12:1-3).

MICAH 7 AND ECOLOGICAL JUSTICE

Micah 7 lays bare the wickedness and violence that have corrupted life at every level: across the earth, in the land of Judah, in Jerusalem, and within Judean households. Daughter Zion likens her stature to what has been discarded and abandoned in a harvested field, portraying her unfulfilled yearning for righteousness to the barrenness of a vineyard after the grapes have been harvested (7:1). The community of Zion has experienced the razor-sharp cuts and entanglements of sin: she depicts the community's tangle of unjust relationships as a briar and a thorny thicket. Her deep connection to the earth and its produce is powerful: Zion understands her life—the life of the covenant community—in terms of harmonious faithful living that yields an abundance of fruit, literal and metaphorical, with grain, wine, and oil (see Hos 2:8) and other agricultural produce sustaining the body and replenishing the spirit. Conversely, human malfeasance and large-scale injustice in ecological practices have resulted in agricultural barrenness, food precarity, and profound suffering. The IPCC explains, "Increasing weather and climate extreme events have exposed millions of people to acute food insecurity and reduced water security.... Sudden losses of food production and access to food compounded by decreased diet diversity have increased malnutrition in many communities ... especially for Indigenous Peoples, small-scale food producers and low-income households ... with children, elderly people and pregnant women particularly impacted." The IPCC report offers the staggering statistic that "roughly half of the world's population currently experiences severe water scarcity for at least some part of the year due to climatic and non-climatic drivers" (IPCC 2022 §B.1.3).

Micah 7 alludes to dire conditions of inequity and violence reminiscent of the corruption that engendered the divine response of the flood, per Israel's ancient narratives. Contemporary readers can choose, from their position in the history of reception of Micah, to draw on the theopoetic flood narratives of antiquity as a lens for clear-eyed prophetic vision regarding the pragmatic harms of our own day. Rising sea levels pose a serious threat to many coastal communities. The climate science is unequivocal: "Future sea level rise combined with storm surge and heavy rainfall will increase compound flood risks.... Risks to health and food production will be made more severe from the interaction of sudden food production losses from heat and drought, exacerbated by heat-induced labour productivity losses," resulting in "risks of malnutrition and heat-related mortality with no or low levels of adaptation, especially in tropical regions" (IPCC 2022 §B.5.1). Unwise agribusiness practices harm the fertility of croplands; urban "food deserts" present a near-insuperable obstacle to the flourishing of persons living with mobility impairment or reduced access to transportation; and in cultural contexts across the globe, class bias and racism can intensify the injurious effects for persons and families who seek remediation of these harms and deprivations.

Ecological activist and homiletician Leah Schade argues that faith communities need to take seriously the urgent threats facing the Earth due to climate change, and she urges that we build an "eco-ethical ark" to preserve life. Schade writes,

> Our eco-ethical ark must be built with planks of the strongest ethical teachings of each religion, faith, and spiritual group. It must be sup-

ported with joists of justice and beams of righteousness. And the ark must be sealed by compassion that fills in the cracks and binds us together. The first ones on this ark must be the people and species who are most affected by climate change, especially indigenous peoples, people of color, islanders, fisherfolk hut dwellers, climate refugees, those living in poverty, and the plants and animals that are on the brink of extinction. (2019, 20)

Micah stands as sentinel on the ramparts, keeping watch for the response of his God to the suffering of his community (7:7); Daughter Zion, too, waits for Yhwh (7:9). But we cannot wait quietly. The catalytic force of prophetic discourse and imagery throughout the book of Micah calls the community urgently to take action: to repent and return to the covenantal fidelity that should mark the identity and lifeways of every believer. Such reform will require that we listen deeply to those crying out in anguish and despair, as Daughter Zion has cried out. As Schade observes, "we must learn from those who have lived through and are currently suffering from the realities of the system's collapse" and, equally vital for transformational change, we must "cede our privilege and power to those with greater wisdom as we salvage what is left" of our injured planet and its creatures (2019, 20-21).

As believers learn to cultivate the fruits of compassion for all human constituencies, other living beings, regional biomes, and ecosystems across the Earth, we may find refreshment for this urgent and arduous work in an evocative image that comes near the close of Micah's oracles. The prophet looks toward a future in which Israel is a blessed community dwelling in peace, unthreatened, as a verdant forest surrounded by fruitful meadows and fields (7:14). Israel as forest is an apt metaphor for what Micah is offering about the interconnected ways in which those who follow the teachings of Yhwh (4:2) should help one another to breathe and grow. In a discussion of innovative ecospiritual practices, Rachel Wheeler considers the therapeutic wisdom that forests can teach those working for ecojustice and flourishing for the living communities of Earth. In the Japanese practice of *shinrin-yoku*, a mindful, relaxed, slow walking through forested terrain, the practitioner may benefit from physiological changes related to increased blood oxygen and the calming of the nervous system. But more, the practitioner may "[begin] to experience the reintegration of their fundamental identity as one member of the Earth community amid many other members" as they learn how to be more fully "present regarding all [they] see and hear, smell and feel, as sacred, as holy land" (2022, 131). Such an orientation to the living

Micah 7

community of Earth is well in keeping with Micah's opening call to attention to "the earth and all that fills it" (1:2) and his prophetic exhortation for believers to do justice, to cherish fidelity, and to proceed humbly with the Creator of all that is (6:8).

COMMENTARY

Micah 7 portrays deep shadows of ethical malfeasance, disloyalty, threat, and shame yielding to the light of hope: the covenant community can look for restoration and rebuilding, for peace and security, for the compassion of Yhwh. Heschel observes that the interplay of these oppositional realities is itself significant: "In spite of the gloom of his predictions, Micah insists that his message is for the good of his people," for "together with the word of doom, Micah proclaims the vision of redemption. God will forgive" (2001, 128). The intertwining of calamity and redemption in Mic 7 may be considered a gift, according to Heschel: "Among the great insights Micah has bequeathed to us is how to accept and to bear the anger of God. The strength of acceptance comes from the awareness that we have sinned . . . and . . . that anger does not mean God's abandonment of [us] forever. [God's] anger passes, [God's] faithfulness goes on forever" (2001, 128–29).

7:1 *Woe is me!* The lamenting speaker is Daughter Zion, as a number of interpreters have recognized in the history of interpretation (e.g., Wood 2000, 659; O'Brien 2015, 103; see de Moor 2000; 2020, 324–25). Other interpreters have heard the voice of Micah here, as is clear from rabbinic tradition and exegesis in the early church, for example in the work of Jerome (*Comm. Mich.*, 99), Theodore of Mopsuestia (*Comm.*^{TM}, 239), Rashi, David Kimḥi, and David Altschuler (Stavsky 2009, 52); the targum to Mic 7 expressly adds as the opening words, "*The prophet said.*" But the yearning and bitter diminishment expressed here are not in keeping with the persona of the prophet portrayed elsewhere in the book, and 7:1–13 is best read as a dialogue between Zion and Micah, with each speaking twice (I am agnostic regarding the implied speaker of 7:4b). Mays offers an objection characteristic of historicist thinking, a logic implicit in redaction-critical models to the present: "The tone and attitude of the piece is not congruent with the stance of Micah during the reign of Hezekiah. Those who assign the lament to Micah must extend his career into the reign of Manasseh to find a more appropriate setting" (1976, 150). At the end of the verse, Micah[LXX] amplifies the opening interjection of woe: *oimmoi psychē*, "Woe is me, O soul." This doubling may also serve as a chiastic device, as is subtly suggested by Glenny's observation that "the grief of the prophet in 7:1 is enclosed by the repetition" of the cry of woe (2015, 187).

what is left behind. The image evoked by ʿōləlōt is that of fruit or produce left behind after the rigorous threshing or beating of harvest is concluded: as Isa 17:6 puts it, "Gleanings . . . as when an olive tree is beaten—two or three berries in the top of the highest bough, four or five on the branches of a fruit tree." It is an image of scarcity and desolation, as the usage of ʿōləlōt in Isa 24:13 makes clear. The last clause turns the focus away from the stricken landscape to the hunger of Daughter Zion, longing for a ripe fig that cannot be found, with the particle of negation, ʾên, serving implicitly in the last clause as well as in what precedes.

Actual hunger—food insecurity—may be in view here, as well as the symbolic valence of Zion hungering to find justice and righteousness in a Judah that has become corrupt. The greed of powerful elites had disastrous consequences for the well-being of farmers and their families, according to Chaney. Chaney has analyzed the deleterious effects of the transition in ancient Israel and Judah from subsistence agriculture pursued in networks of kinship groups and villages to the monarchy, with its control of consolidated fields, its systems of monocropping and centralized international trade, and its economic structures designed to funnel profits to ruling-class officials. Chaney writes,

> As many small, subsistence plots were foreclosed upon and joined together to form large estates, a change in the method of tillage also took place. Upland fields previously intercropped to provide a mixed subsistence for peasant families were combined into large vineyards and olive orchards producing a single crop for market. . . . Since wine and oil were worth more than grain per unit of weight or volume, they were easier to export in exchange for the luxury and strategic imports coveted by members of the ruling classes. But the *efficiency* of these cash crops came at a brutal cost to the *sufficiency* of the livelihood that they afforded the peasants who actually produced them. . . . In the marketplace, the meager and irregular wages of field hands brought even less sustenance than they should have, because the vulnerable peasants were cheated with adulterated grain and rigged scales. (2017, 77 [emphasis original])

Micah 7

no cluster of grapes . . . no ripe fig. The noun *bikkûrâ*, "early" or "first-ripe" fig, signifies a fruit that would be ready at the beginning of the harvest. Andersen and Freedman observe that "it represents something utterly delectable and desirable" and "evidently had enormous emotional and symbolic value as welcome proof that the tree would bear and . . . that it would be a good season" (2000, 566–567). In this simile, the harvest is past and the lamenting Zion is not satisfied, something that bodes ill for the future of Jerusalem and its people. Zion's appetite (*nepeš*) is for piety and righteousness, and for those fruits, no harvest is imminent in the bleak landscape of Judah.

7:2 *the pious one has perished from the land.* Because the corruption of officials and judges is foregrounded in this lament (see 7:3), and that constitutes a chief concern of Micah regarding the malfeasance of leaders within Judah, "land" rather than "earth" is the best translation of *hā'āreṣ* here. But the noun's semantic bivalence means that the contours of a broader landscape can always be glimpsed as well. Rabbinic commentators heard this as decrying impiety and wickedness throughout the entire earth; the Micah verse is quoted in midrash this way: "The heavens wept and said, 'The godly [one] is perished out of the earth'" (*Deut. Rab.* 11.10 to Deut 31:14; 187). It would be possible to trace the poetic movement of Mic 7:1–7 as follows: 7:1–4 opens with an alarming view of the violence and greed that pervade the whole earth, as in the days of the flood (Gen 6:5, 11–12). Zion's lament spurs Micah to wheel upon the ruler (the masculine singular referent in 7:4b) and offer a taunt about the false prophets' unreliable assurances of safety. Then the prophet continues with a piercing gaze that has narrowed its focus to the dishonorable behavior and conflict even in the domestic sphere (7:5–7), claiming his own authority as prophetic sentinel once more as grounded in the power of Yhwh, just as he had done in 3:8.

no righteous one. There are several articulations in the Hebrew Scriptures of the motif of a community so corrupted that not a single righteous person can be found. In Gen 18:16–19:28, though Abraham successfully persuades Yhwh to spare Sodom and Gomorrah if even ten righteous persons are found there, the cities are destroyed. Commentators (e.g., Andersen and Freedman 2000, 566) point to Jer 5:1–5, which elaborates the trope of searching the streets and public squares of Jerusalem for even a single person who does justice and seeks truth: the search is fruitless, for those who are marginalized and those who are wealthy alike have "broken the yoke" and "burst the bonds" of covenantal fidelity. Psalm 14 and its close parallel, Ps 53, open with the complaint that no righteous person can be found.

Commentary

A refraction of the motif may underlie the image in Zeph 1:12 of searching Jerusalem with lamps as a prelude to punishing elites who are unconcerned about Yhwh's retribution for their misdeeds.

lie in wait for blood. The imagery here is of a fearsome predator—the most terrifying being the lion—lurking until the moment when hapless prey comes within range. The prophetic scribe's combining of this with net-hunting imagery in the following clause should be understood not as an awkward mixed metaphor (Strawn 2005, 334n37), but as skilled poetic work to transfer the sheer terror associated with a lunging lion to the human predation perpetrated by Judean elites.

they hunt one another with nets. Micah^{LXX} renders the verb with *ekthlibousin*, "they afflict one another," per Gelston having read the verb as from *ṣ-w-r* rather than *ṣ-w-d* and having "guessed at the meaning of this word from the context" (*BHQ*, 107).

7:3 *their hands are good at doing evil.* Metonymic use of "hand" or "hands" in the Hebrew Bible can represent agency or power. Andersen and Freedman suggest that only two examples of malfeasant officials are in view here: "the adjective *haggādôl*, 'the great one,' does not necessarily list a third functionary. . . . This adjective goes with both the preceding titles. It is the chief prince and the head judge who are guilty of graft" (2000, 564). But the syntax of *haśśar . . . wəhaššōpēṭ . . . wəhaggādôl* is better read as a paratactic unfolding of the chain of malfeasance that links multiple sectors of the community, signaled by "all of them" in the preceding verse: political leaders, judges, and other influential elites are all complicit in corruption, entangled with one another as thorny branches in a thicket (7:4).

The official asks, as does the judge. A number of passages in the Latter Prophets, including this one, indict malfeasant leaders in various influential roles seriatim, subtly suggesting that these elite powerbrokers are not only corrupt individually but are in league with one another in their venality. Among many examples—the trope is especially densely represented in Jeremiah—we may consider the polemic against an "oppressing city" in Zeph 3:3: "The officials within it are roaring lions; its judges are evening wolves that leave nothing until the morning. Its prophets are reckless, faithless persons; its priests have profaned what is sacred, they have done violence to the law." The targum to Mic 7:3 inserts a ventriloquized quotation from these corrupt functionaries: "*Act for me, that I might reward you.*"

illicit compensation. The term *šillûm* could signify a bribe, a kickback negotiated for malfeasance performed over time, or a fee charged in cir-

Micah 7

cumstances where no fee should have been assessed. Andersen and Freedman observe that the "reform of the judiciary attributed to Jehoshaphat" in 2 Chr 19 underlines the integrity with which magistrates were expected to serve: Jehoshaphat instructs his appointees, "You judge not on behalf of human beings but on the LORD's behalf; [YHWH] is with you in giving judgment. Now, let the fear of the LORD be upon you; take care what you do, for there is no perversion of justice with the LORD our God, or partiality, or taking of bribes" (2 Chr 19:6-7). In Hos 9:7 and Isa 34:8, *šillûm* represents punitive requital—directed against sinful Israel and intractable enemy Edom, respectively, in those loci—with YHWH as agent. Micah[LXX] has the judge not asking for a bribe but speaking "peaceable words" (*eirēnikous logous*), the Septuagint translator apparently reading the unvocalized Hebrew consonants later pointed by the Masoretes as *baššillûm* as the word *bəšālôm*, "in peace" (BHQ, 108).

thus they conspire. The root ʿbt signals a semantic field having to do with binding, twisting, or weaving together, metaphorically (e.g., Isa 5:18; Hos 11:4) or with literal ropes or cords (e.g., Judg 15:13, 14; 16:11, 12; Ezek 3:25; 4:8). The independent pronoun *hûʾ*, standing in apposition to the suffixed 3ms pronoun of the preceding word, underlines the agency of the powerful person in directing the malfeasant scheming (see *IBHS* §16.3.4). Gelston remarks, "None of the vrss. seem to have known the meaning of this *hapax legomenon*" (BHQ, 108).

7:4 The best of them . . . the "upright." The comparative superlative effected by the pronominal suffix on *ṭôbām* could serve both clauses, yielding "the most upright among them" (*IBHS* §14.5). But the heightening suggested by the poetic parallelism may be more subtly expansive than two simple superlatives, in which case the sense would be that the best of these malefactors is no better than a briar, and anyone who counts as "upright" in their ranks is worse than a thorny thicket. The targum modifies the imagery toward the idea that the righteous are entrapped by others' corruption: the upright find it as difficult to escape from the power of the malfeasant as if they were struggling to extricate themselves from a thorny thicket.

briar . . . thorny thicket. The "briar" (*ḥēdeq*) occurs only elsewhere in Prov 15:19 in an aphorism about laziness; the "thorny thicket" (*məsûkâ*) is a *hapax legomenon*, though a biform with *sin* occurs at Isa 5:5. Micah[LXX] draws its imagery not from the arena of woody botanicals but from the insect order Lepidoptera: in the Greek translation, the corrupt Judean elite are "like a moth eating and crawling on a rod" (NETS) or "like a moth larva devouring and crawling upon a weaver's rod" (Glenny 2015, 33), which Gelston dubs a "very free rendering" (*BHQ*, 108). The "moth" (*sēs*) in other LXX passages is deployed to represent decay (Prov 14:30, for Heb. *rāqāb*), the gnawing of sorrow (Prov 25:20), and something easily crushed (Job 4:19; Isa 33:1).

A day for your sentinels. The speaker of Mic 7:4b is unclear. The lamenting Zion could be imagined as wheeling upon the corrupt Jerusalem officials with a blistering direct address as the powerful conclusion to 7:1-4a. Alternatively, if spoken by Micah, this half-verse could be the opening salvo in his barrage of accusations about treachery going to the core of Judean communal life: the household (7:5-6). Neither proposal fully persuades me. A ferocious Zion is audible in 4:13c as well, so these two half-verses could have been interpolated by prophetic scribes to show Zion as fearsome adversary to enemy nations (4:13c) and internecine malefactors (7:4b) alike. The frontal assault is more characteristic of Micah's discourse, though; yet 7:4b does not lead as smoothly into 7:5 as one might like. Whatever the case regarding the imagined speaker, this half-verse provides a crucial literary function within Mic 7: expressly setting up the metaphor of prophet as sentinel, drawing on resonances with military personnel stationed on the ramparts of Jerusalem or in nearby watchtowers to characterize prophetic vigilance. This trope will be essential for understanding 7:7 as describing Micah's ongoing role in his community. "Sentinels" here in 7:4b is ironic, referring to the false prophets who have been pandering to corrupt officials (see Hos 9:8; Jer 6:17; Ezek 3:17; 33:7). The ambiguity of "sentinels" is artful and significant: those who should have been serving as metaphorical guardians of the people have failed, and now the literal sentinels can see that "punishment," in the form of an enemy army, "has arrived." This gibe at false prophets underlines that the imminent "punishment"—divinely appointed consequences for sin—will leave mercenary seers in confusion, as the grim reality will not accord with what they had prophesied, "disgrace will not overtake [us]" (2:6). The possessive pronoun in "your sentinels" addresses a masculine singular referent who might be Judah's unnamed ruler, or another official such as a judge, a priest, or the head of a prophetic group. The NRSV renders the 2ms pronominal suffixes as if they were 3pl ("their"), which is ill-advised.

their confusion. YHWH as divine warrior throws the enemy into confusion, and here, as is often the case in Micah, the enemy lurks within the community. The mercenary prophets who had offered deceptive blandishments to the corrupt leader are now shown to have been untrustworthy guides. The "confusion" (*məbûkâ*) imagined here could involve the cognitive

Micah 7

dissonance of seeing their counsel revealed publicly as worthless and witnessing their advisory authority evaporate. But the semantic force likely involves more than that—perhaps the collapse of the structures and rhetorics that had long sustained the elites' corrupt behavior and heedlessness about consequences. The noun *məbûkâ* occurs in one other place in the Hebrew Bible, in an elliptical oracle of doom in Isa 22:5 that is likely focused on Jerusalem, though the city remains unnamed. There, "confusion" is rendered in contextual terms reminiscent of the chaotic terror of invasion vividly dramatized in Mic 1:10-16. Below, I supply the preceding verse in the Isaiah passage as well, since it conveys key information about the prophetic speaker's grief over the unnamed Jerusalem:

> I said:
> Look away from me,
>   let me weep bitter tears,
> do not try to comfort me
>   for the destruction of my beloved people.
> For the Lord GOD of Hosts has a day
>   of tumult and trampling and confusion
>   in the valley of vision,
> a battering down of walls,
>   and a cry for help to the mountains. (Isa 22:4-5)

Here in Mic 7, the corruption of Judean society has meant that Daughter Zion has been overrun by her enemies. The tumult and darkness around her are overwhelming.

7:5 *do not rely on a friend; put no trust in an intimate.* In a society in disarray, under siege by armed invaders and rotting from within due to internecine corruption, the stress on family relationships can be profound. Disrespect, antagonism, and betrayal in intimate relationships can be responses to broader cultural anxiety and feelings of intimidation or hopelessness.

be guarded about what leaves your mouth! The idiom here, literally "guard the doors of your mouth," evokes wisdom teachings about circumspection in speech. Compare Prov 13:3, "Those who guard their mouths preserve their lives; those who open wide their lips come to ruin," and 22:23, "He who guards his mouth and tongue guards himself from trouble" (NJPS). Here, Micah has turned to the larger community and warns of treachery lurking in every corner, including within the family (7:6).

Commentary

7:6 *enemies . . . of his own household.* The intrafamilial conflict narrated here provides further evidence of the moral chaos roiling Judean society, adding the offense of younger persons dishonoring their elders to the cascade of ethical breaches that Micah has just decried in his community. Boloje discerns a heightening of relational disruption as the verse progresses: "the son treats his father contemptuously as a fool," and worse, "the close relationship between mother and daughter in this network of family relationship and responsibility would make insubordination an even more appalling contrast" (2021b, 5-6). Andersen and Freedman (2000, 573-74) remark similar teachings about familial strife or estrangement in ancient Near Eastern literatures, including the second-millennium BCE Mesopotamian legend of Naram-Sin (lines 138-141) and Akkadian *Šurpu* incantations (tablet II, lines 20-28), as well as the Egyptian Instruction of Amenemhet and Admonitions of Ipuwer. More than simply evidence of the intractability of the younger generation, these antagonisms may also signal the pervasive social disruption and agonistic volatility expected to precede the coming of eschatological judgment.

7:7 *But as for me, for Yhwh I will keep watch.* Micah positions himself as the appropriate alternative to the false prophets favored by corrupt political leaders, religious authorities, and powerful elites. Micah alone is a true sentinel, the lone prophet who watches anxiously for Yhwh and cries out for deliverance. The opening *waʾănî* here recalls the emphatic and contrastive *wəʾûlām ʾānōkî* in 3:8, a textual site in which we see a similar move: Micah claims his prophetic authority and authenticity over against those who have failed to see clearly and guide the people according to covenantal norms. The targum establishes some distance between the trustful speaker and the deity by inserting the word of Yhwh as mediating: "But I will *rejoice in the Memra of* the Lord." Similar insertions of "Memra" can be found in Tg. Mic 7:10, 14, and 19, as well as in other Micah chapters of the targum.

my God will hear me. Micah's relationship with Yhwh shines through the gloom of a society that the prophet says is fatally compromised in its ethical breaches and covenantal infidelity. Micah is speaking as the only righteous person left; all others are entangled in the "thorny thicket" of Judean bloodshed, corruption, greed, false prophecy, and household strife (7:2-6). He models for Daughter Zion the appropriate posture of faithful humility before Yhwh, the only possible source of deliverance. In the following verse, Zion shows that she has understood the lesson and will bear the indignities of violence, injustice, and diminishment that characterize

Micah 7

Judean life—which she had lamented in the opening lines of Mic 7—until Yhwh renders justice on her behalf.

7:8 *Do not rejoice . . . O my enemy!* "Enemy" here and in 7:10 is a fs noun. The personified gendering of a geopolitical adversary as feminine singular occurs regularly in Biblical Hebrew poetry; see, for example, "Daughter Egypt" in Jer 46:11, 19, 24; "Daughter Babylon" in Isa 47:1, 5; Jer 50:42; 51:33; Zech 2:11; Ps 137:8; and "Daughter Edom" in Lam 4:21, 22. In this passionate discourse, Zion is defending herself against the taunts of Daughter Assyria, which may be understood as the actual enemy Assyria or—in this crucial literary location at the end of the book of Micah—may be argued to represent all the geopolitical adversaries who have taunted and injured Zion. The similarity of diction here with poems in the book of Lamentations (per many, including Andersen and Freedman 2000, 577) could be taken to strengthen the position that this is a reflection of broader scope that sweeps artfully to 7:16–17, where the prophetic scribe envisions many nations submitting in dread to Yhwh. In Tg. Mic 7:8, 10, additions identify the enemy explicitly as "Rome." Cathcart and Gordon observe, "The historical reality reflected in this verse is such that a post-A.D. 70 dating should be assumed" for the targumic text (1989, 127n24).

Yhwh *has been my light.* No matter how often Daughter Zion has been violated and shamed, she has found her resilience and hope in Yhwh. Louis Stulman muses,

> How does literature so laden with loss operate as an artistic expression of hope? In the first place, it translates lived chaos into language and so creates a bearable distance between traumatic events and their symbolic representations. It refuses to indulge in denials about the nation's monstrous losses, generating space for the work of grief, a prerequisite to the work of hope. This trauma corpus puts virtually every facet of community life under a microscope and calls for action, transforming victims of violence into active meaning-makers. It creates alternatives to the old world, alternatives that contour a future for a people seemingly without one. (2016, 324)

7:9 *until Yhwh adjudicates my case.* A juridical metaphor reappears, linking this material to Yhwh's disputation with Israel in 6:1–8 and the further elaboration of the indictment in 6:9–16 of those within Jerusalem who have

Commentary

perpetrated violence and practiced deception. Both passages cite the history of Yhwh's saving deeds (6:4-5; 7:8). Zion's confession—"I have sinned against [Yhwh]" (7:9)—subtly suggests that Israel, too, must confess its transgressions in order to enjoy the light of Yhwh's righteousness.

7:10 *my enemy*. The identity of the enemy has been veiled by the prophetic scribe. The feminine singular suggests that a capital city here is personified as Zion's interlocutor. Given the likely postexilic context in which Mic 7 was composed, the referents closest to hand in this dramatic enactment of conflict are Daughter Nineveh (or Assyria writ larger) and Daughter Babylon. Daughter Egypt remains a possibility as well: "Egypt" occurs three times in Micah (6:5; 7:12, 15). Nogalski has argued for Nineveh as the personified antagonist, not least because, by his reckoning, "almost every verse in Mic 7:8-20 contains elements that also appear in the anti-Assyrian polemic of Isa 9-12" (2017b, 66-68, 71-72).

"Where is Yhwh your God?" This taunt occurs several times in the Hebrew Scriptures (see Pss 42:4, 11 [Eng. 3, 10]; 79:10; 115:2; Joel 2:17), ventriloquizing a hostile interlocutor who mocks the pious speaking subject: they trust in Yhwh but nevertheless have been overcome by adversity—why has their vaunted deity not come to their aid? Andersen and Freedman offer that this can be "a charge of incompetence"—or lack of divine compassion, one might add—"rather than nonexistence" (2000, 584).

***to be trampled, like mud in the streets*.** Invective of shame and denigration directed at enemies is a powerful means by which prophetic discourse effects the bolstering of Israelite or Judean communal cohesion. Misogynistic imputations of physical weakness and thinly veiled taunts regarding sexual assault can play a role in prophetic invective when the enemy is portrayed in the trope of a female figure (see, e.g., Isa 47:1-3).

7:11 *A day*. In 7:11-12, the prophetic scribe looks toward the distant future when the restoration of Zion will take place. A noun clause functioning adverbially occurs three times, gradually intensifying the joyous anticipation of the implied audience about the resplendent future. The clause is crafted in three slightly different forms and arranged in a chiastic structure with the most syntactically complex at the center, one effect of which would be to hold the audience's attention. "A day!" (*yôm*, 7:11a), "That very day!" (*yôm hahû'*, 7:11b), and "That day!" (*yôm hû'*, 7:12) direct the audience's attention to the yearned-for restoration of beloved Zion as a repeated festal shout might do. The rhetorical force of the repeated deixis here is strong. Micah[LXX]

Micah 7

instead links its interpretation of the first three words with the preceding image of the trampling of Zion's enemy like mud: "she shall become an object to be trampled like clay in the streets during a day of daubing of brick" (NETS). The targum makes clear that it is *"the congregations of Israel"* that will be rebuilt, while *"the decrees of the nations shall be abolished."*

for the rebuilding of your walls. Most interpret this as an oracle of consolation. According to Stavsky (2009, 57), Joseph Kara finds here an allusion to the imagery in Amos 9:11, presumably raising up the monarchy (the "booth of David") and repairing figurative breaches in that dynasty or literal breaches in the walls of Jerusalem. A minority opinion, found, for example, in the commentaries of David Kimḥi and Isaac Abarbanel (1437–1508), has it that the prophet is addressing an enemy whose day for rebuilding lies so distant that it "will never come" (Stavsky 2009, 57). The verb *bnh* can be used to signify building, repairing or fortifying an existing structure, or rebuilding (*HALOT* 1:139). The imagined context in which Micah addresses Daughter Zion is after her humiliation by the Neo-Babylonian Empire—after Jerusalem has been captured and profaned by enemy troops in 587 BCE. The narrative setting that introduces the prophetic oracles of Micah situates his activity well over a century earlier (1:1), of course. But the portrayal of Zion's desolation, in 3:9–12 as well as here in 7:1–10, likely reflects the enemy's disruption of Judah's agricultural infrastructure during months of siege that resulted in terrible famine for the inhabitants of Jerusalem (see Jer 52:4–6); the breaching of the Jerusalem city wall by Babylonian invaders; and the Babylonians' destruction of the gates and much of the city wall, along with all significant buildings in the city (see Jer 39:1–8; 52:12–14). The anticipated *rebuilding*, then, would signify Jerusalem's vindication by Yhwh when the period of Neo-Babylonian hegemony had been brought to an end by Cyrus of Persia, exiled Judeans were permitted to return home, and the massive project of rebuilding the city wall would commence (Ezra 4:12; Neh 2–6).

the boundary will lie distant. The promise here: one sign of Judah's flourishing will be that its territory has expanded significantly, such that the boundary (marker) will lie far in the distance, from the perspective of the speaker. This is the only occurrence in Micah of the enigmatic term *ḥōq*. This richly multivalent word can signify a statute or decree, frequently of Yhwh in the context of covenantal ideology (e.g., Exod 12:24; Lev 10:11; Deut 4:1 and often in Deuteronomy; Ezek 20:18, 25; 36:27; regularly in the Psalms, esp. Ps 119), or as promulgated or enforced by another authority literally or metaphorically (e.g., Gen 47:26; Josh 24:25; 1 Sam 30:25; Isa 10:1; Jer 32:11). In Isa 24:5, the prophet indicts the earth's inhabitants for having violated *ḥōq*,

Commentary

here imagined as a set of divinely ordained moral regulations brought into parallelistic relation with Yhwh's "eternal covenant" (bərît ʿôlām). The term ḥōq can express a prescribed boundary or an appointed portion (Lev 6:11 and often in Leviticus and Numbers), term, or time. In Job and the Latter Prophets, ḥōq is also deployed in a poetic register to evoke the delimiting power of Yhwh as Creator (Jer 5:22; 31:36) or the measureless realm of Sheol, for example, in Isa 5:14, where the gaping maw of Sheol is portrayed as having no limit (liblî-ḥōq).

7:12 *he will come to you*. It is not impossible that *hû* is simply an impersonal 3ms referent (*BHQ*, 109), but the identity of this unspecified ms figure is more likely to be (implicitly) "Jacob," understood as an iconic signifier of all the Israelites and Judeans living in diaspora across the known world. Within the thought-world of postexilic Judean tradition and the Mic 7 literary context of a desolate Daughter Zion being consoled, it is possible—though not explicitly said—that the returnees streaming back to Judah are envisioned as Zion's children. Judeans in diaspora had never lost their identity as Yhwh's people (on this motif in Ps 87, see Sharp 2022b, 31–35). Here, the anticipated influx of formerly exiled Judeans will serve both as confirmation of and impetus for the postexilic restoration and rebuilding envisioned by the poet. "To you": a ms addressee receives this good news, suggesting that the fractured community ("Jacob") will be reunited.

from Assyria and the cities of Egypt . . . to the River. In this verse is the only mention of the geopolitical term "Assyria" in Micah apart from three references in 5:4–5. In Mic 5, the chilling threat of Assyrian invasion had loomed. Assyria, one of the sites to which Israelites and Judeans had been deported as captives of war, is here identified as a locale from which those captives will stream homeward to Zion as Yhwh rebuilds the walls of Jerusalem (7:11) and again shepherds the covenant people (7:14). W. de Bruin discerns here enemies "seeking asylum because of the devastation of the whole earth" (2020, 331). While I am not persuaded of that reading, the possibility of polyvalence cannot be foreclosed. Where Deutero-Isaiah portrays diaspora Judeans singing joyously on their way home from exile (Isa 35:10), the imagery in Mic 7:12–17 would gain added layers of complexity, for those in agreement with de Bruin: Israelite and Judean returnees would be joined on the road to Zion by subjugated former enemies coming in dread to pay tribute to Yhwh (7:16–17).

The use of *māṣôr* ("Egypt") twice rather than the expected *miṣrayim* (only in 6:4; 7:15) can be seen elsewhere in the Hebrew Bible (2 Kgs 19:24; Isa 19:6;

Micah 7

37:25). Here in Mic 7:12, it may be for poetic effect or to foster an evocative sense of archaism congruent with the emphasis on Yhwh's deliverance of Israel in the distant past (7:14–15, 20; see Andersen and Freedman 2000, 587). The powerful nation of Egypt, a source of rich religious and cultural influences on other nations in the ancient Near East, has been refracted through Hebrew Bible traditions not only as the remembered site of Israel's enslavement in the distant past (as in 6:4), but as a geopolitical threat through centuries of Israelite and Judean survival in the region. Joel LeMon observes,

> The fortunes of Israel were inextricably linked to the political dramas constantly unfolding along the course of the Nile. As Egypt moved back and forth along the political spectrum between unity and diversity of power, the entire Near East felt its effects. When Egyptian political power was centralized, its leaders were invariably drawn toward military adventurism in the Levant. When power was decentralized, the Levant was left to its own devices. (2016, 189)

Hays and Machinist note that in later "mythologized" passages that mention Assyria, such as Zech 10:10–11, "Assyria loses its historical specificity; it is merely a hypostasis of the cosmic chaos that opposed [Yhwh's] order" (2016, 103). Egypt, too, came to be depicted in biblical traditions "as an archetypal foe" (LeMon 2016, 195).

7:13 *the earth will become a desolation.* Wholesale devastation will be wrought by Yhwh across many nations and regions: *hā'āreṣ* is not to be translated in terms of geopolitical boundaries ("land"), *pace* many translations and Nogalski (2017b, 73), but assuredly as "earth," as in Isa 24:1–13. In the preceding verse, Yhwh is envisioned as acting to save the covenant people from their captivity in all the places to which they had been scattered. The territory of the enemy nations, then, will be left devastated because of the harms they have visited upon Yhwh's people (7:10, 16–17). Yhwh's vengeance will leave the hostile parts of the earth in ruins and the covenant people living in glorious solitude, with none to harass them (7:14).

the fruit of their deeds. The noun "deeds" (*maʿălālîm*) can be positive or negative in semantic valence. Here, taken as referring to the deeds of those nations that held Judeans captive, the deeds clearly are considered as evil.

7:14 *Shepherd your people with your staff.* Ben Zvi argues that the noun *šēbeṭ*, absent the accusative particle *'et*, "serves as a double-duty form"

Commentary

that conveys two meanings: the sense adopted in my translation here, and "Shepherd your people, your tribe" (2000, 176-77). I am not persuaded by the argument of Nogalski that this is judgment material against Judah in which the speaker expresses "implicit acceptance of Yhwh's punishment and a petition that this punishment not be one of total annihilation" (2017b, 76-78). If the *šēbeṭ* here is meant to evoke Isa 10:5, the prophetic scribe is not echoing that grim text but reversing it, in keeping with the messianic shepherd image of Mic 5:3.

dwelling in solitude. This image is not of alienation or abandonment but of peaceful flourishing in a place unvisited by enemies (so also Van Hecke 2003). The covenant people are imagined as sheep grazing in tranquility under the protection of the divine Shepherd.

a forest in the midst of fruitful land. The noun *karmel* can function as a toponym for Carmel, located in the north, as are Bashan and Gilead. Carmel is taken as a toponym here in the Vulgate. But in many occurrences in the Hebrew Bible, *karmel* is more poetic in its valences, evoking the abundant natural bounty of the land as seen in newly ripe grain (Lev 2:14; 23:14; 2 Kgs 4:42), orchards of fruit trees and fields of fruit-bearing vines (Isa 16:10; 29:17; 32:15-16;), or cultivated trees of other kinds (see 2 Kgs 19:23 // Isa 37:24). "Carmel" can represent tranquil arable land bursting with magnificent produce (e.g., Isa 35:2; Jer 2:7; 50:2) or lushly forested terrain (Isa 37:24) the despoliation of which in times of political crisis (Isa 33:9; Jer 4:26; 48:33 of Moab; Amos 1:2; Nah 1:4) is adduced by biblical writers as an appalling consequence of divine judgment or militarized conflict. Many contemporary translations understand *karmel* here to be an image of fruitful land, as I do ("Obstgarten," *BigS*; "farmland," NJPS; "garden land," NRSV; "campo fértil," RVR; "Fruchtland," ZUR). Cazelles and Sperling read "Carmel" as a toponym, suggesting a political valence: "Carmel, Bashan, and Gilead," all northern sites, "were alienated in 733 B.C.E.," presumably during the Syro-Ephraimite war, and this verse is "probably aimed at encompassing Israel and Judah in the same gathering" (2007, 163). While political imagery is not impossible here, given the depiction of royal power in Israelite traditions via the trope of "shepherd" and the allusion to emancipation from Egypt in the distant past (7:15), I am persuaded that the vivid language of peace and abundance are more broadly significant in this particular oracle than a subtle expression of the healing of internecine conflict between Israel and Judah.

Bashan and Gilead. The prophetic signifying about these northern regions east of the Jordan River understands them as iconic representations

Micah 7

of verdant forests and lush meadows, as Carmel is, and as providing abundant support for grazing herds (cf. Deut 32:14; Isa 33:9; Jer 50:19; Ezek 39:18; Nah 1:4; Zech 11:2). Andersen and Freedman suggest one possible political framing of this material: "Since hope is set on the recovery of Transjordan (v. 14), the situation could be as early as the eighth century" (2000, 563); Bashan and Gilead "represent disputed territory whose recapture was often symbolic of recovery of ancient rights" (592). Whether the Neo-Assyrian period is meant to be perceived as the (remembered) historical backdrop for this material is not transparently clear, but Ben Zvi offers, "Bashan and Gilead . . . were certainly not included in the actual territory of Persian (or, for the sake of argument, Neo-Babylonian) Judah" (2000, 177). The immediately preceding images of the rebuilding of Zion's walls (7:11) and the anticipated return of diaspora Israelites or Judeans (7:12) suggest a historical backdrop in which Jerusalem's fortifications had been breached and left in rubble, thus later Babylonian incursions would likely be in view as well. This bucolic poetry remains elliptical and resists any overt linkage to one specific geopolitical context; the visionary hope here is crafted in poetic terms that could apply to Israel and Judah at any point from the Neo-Assyrian period onward. On my reading, this is an artfully shaped, expansive memory of past national trauma and restoration that includes all that Israel and Judah have suffered, the poetic "from sea to sea and mountain to mountain" tracing an arc through not only geography but time as the prophetic scribe envisions divine retribution against all who have ever harmed Yhwh's people (7:13) since Yhwh first brought Israel out of enslavement in Egypt (7:15).

as . . . when you came out of the land of Egypt. Here the prophet gestures toward a trope that finds lyrical expression in the oracles of Deutero-Isaiah: the hope of a new exodus. Yhwh will bring Israel out of diaspora once again, just as the deity had done in the days of Moses.

7:15 *"I will show him wondrous things."* Some scholars emend the verb to yield a third-singular agent ("he will show"), but this is ill-advised. Yhwh is speaking; so also Waltke (2007, 432), who adds, "[says I am]" to clarify this for the reader. The deity responds to the plea of the prophet with a breathtaking promise: the marvels with which Yhwh had effected Israel's deliverance from Egypt long ago will be seen by Israel—or "Jacob"—once again. Micah[LXX] has a second-person plural addressee here: "you will see marvelous things."

7:16 *Nations will see and be shamed. . . . Their ears will be deafened.* The Hebrew *bwš* ("to be ashamed, shamed") is used in 3:7 of false prophets

Commentary

Fig. 22. *Prophetarum Laudabilis Numerus*, 1447, by Fra Angelico (ca. 1395–1455). Fresco (paint on plaster). In the Capella di San Brizio of the cathedral in Orvieto, Italy.

within Micah's own community. There, disgraced Judean seers will cover their upper lips in a public gesture that acknowledges their inefficacy as intermediaries to whom God will not respond. Here, adversarial nations are envisioned as being shocked into speechlessness and stunned into being unable to hear, so astonishing will Yhwh's restoration of Judah be. The metaphorical field here is military in nature, as is clear from "fortifications" in 7:17. With the image of enemies becoming deaf, Micah may be gesturing to a known effect of extreme stress amid the chaos and noise of the battlefield: the compromising of auditory processing (Tepe et al. 2020).

7:17 [Nations] will lick dust like the snake. Micah may have in view here the curse on the snake in the garden of Eden (Gen 3:14), a tradition also refracted in Isa 65:25. I take this as imagery of the political subjugation of

403

Micah 7

enemy nations, who must surrender to the mighty Judah and its warrior deity, Yhwh, and thus "come quaking out of their fortifications." Micah[LXX] has the shamed and defeated nations remaining "confounded in their enclosure" (*syngythēsontai en synkleismō*), an image not of surrender but of continuing incarceration.

like things that crawl on the ground. This image constitutes a heightening of the disparagement of the enemy nations, who are depicted in terms reminiscent not only of the snake but of other unclean things that crawl, scuttle, or slither and that evoke repulsion in human observers across many cultures: ants, arachnids, beetles, fleas, myriapods, worms, and more would come to mind for the implied audience. While political subjugation seems to be the most transparent sense of this metaphor, Abarbanel reads it otherwise, suggesting that the image depicts "the fall of the nations in battle: they will fall to the ground mortally wounded and writhe in pain and lick the dust as snakes and worms" (Stavsky 2009, 60).

come quaking out of their fortifications. The image here is of a fortified city having been besieged and defeated. Once invaders have succeeded in breaking through the city wall, the inhabitants might still continue the battle in hand-to-hand combat in the streets for hours or days. But eventually, the only choice remaining—especially for noncombatants—would be to surrender to the enemy, to "come quaking out of" the fortified city as prisoners of war. Psalm 18, which celebrates the triumph of David over his enemies, offers the same trope of defeated antagonists coming "trembling out of their strongholds" (18:46 [Eng. 45]). Such captives would face a high likelihood of sexual violation, extreme deprivation, beatings, torture, and other traumas, if they were not summarily executed. If the enemy were an imperial force from a distant country rather than a regional adversary, many captives would not survive the forced march back to the invaders' home, where enslavement would likely have awaited them.

7:18 Who is a God like you? The opening clause of this verse is of unparalleled significance for Micah, given that the prophet is named by means of an apocopated form of this very question. Throughout the scroll of Micah, Yhwh has been portrayed as invincible in power and steadfast in covenantal fidelity, especially in solidarity with the powerless within the community. Andersen and Freedman speak of this material as a "hymnic recital with a credal effect" (2000, 595). This is a salutary way of articulating the resonance that many scholars of an earlier history-of-religions bent have heard. Earlier generations of scholars had speculated that Mic 7 reflects what must have been an actual liturgical context in ancient Judah; Nogalski cites eight scholars writing from 1904 to 1976 in this vein (2017b, 63n3). But this is a claim for which evidence has not been mustered (so also Ben Zvi 2000, 180). In Tg. Mic 7:18, the rhetorical question of the MT has been transformed into a robust assertion that there is no deity other than Yhwh: "*There is none besides you.*"

who pardons iniquity and passes over transgression. Many interpreters have noted the importance in the Book of the Twelve of the refrain in Exod 34:6-7 about Yhwh being merciful, slow to anger, and gracious in forgiving iniquity and transgression (e.g., Kessler 2016, 214-16; DiFransico 2017). Joel 2:13; Jon 4:2; and Nah 1:3 characterize Yhwh in language similar to that of Mic 7:18, though attempts to argue for a redactional layer in the Book of the Twelve emphasizing the graciousness of Yhwh have not commanded wide assent (Barker 2018, 700-701). The two figurative uses of the verb *nśʾ* in this chapter (in 7:9, where Daughter Zion must "bear the raging of Yhwh," and in 7:18, where God "pardons iniquity") are unlike the lexical uses of the verb elsewhere in Micah (2:2, 4; 4:1, 3; 6:16). Kessler observes, "where the Exodus text says: '*forgiving* iniquity and transgression and sin,' Mic 7:18 uses '*passing over*' the transgression," this alteration toward the verb '*br* constituting a matter of "high significance" given the importance of "passing over" in Amos 7:8 and 8:2; Kessler believes "the author of Mic 7:18-20 deliberately links Micah with Amos" (2020, 181).

the remnant of their inheritance. Here, as in 7:14, Micah underlines the idea of the chosen people as the "inheritance" of Yhwh: a covenant people chosen and dedicated to obedience, thus belonging to the deity over the eons, in an enduring and unique relationship that is nontransferable. A "remnant" may be all that remains in the wake of Neo-Assyrian invasion and Neo-Babylonian militarized colonial expansionism, which had left Samaria destroyed (1:6-7), Jerusalem in ruins (3:12), and the people of Judah terrorized and forced into diaspora. But the covenant relationship endures.

[Yhwh] delights in fidelity. Here and in 7:20, fidelity (*ḥesed*) is shown to be a grounding characteristic of Yhwh's relationship with Israel and Judah over the centuries. Wolff emphasizes that in the view articulated here, the "gracious kindness" of Yhwh "endures as an unconditional trustworthy bond" that "provides the foundation for [Yhwh's] readiness to forgive; forgiveness, in contrast to wrath, possesses the quality of permanence" (1990, 230).

7:19 *compassion.* In this lyrical poetic verse, divine faithfulness is acclaimed as Yhwh's practice of compassion for Israel and Judah, a practice upon

Micah 7

which the covenant people can rely. Sweeney asserts that the closing verses of Micah 7 "express the rhetorical goal" of the entire book: to console the implied audience and persuade them "that the punishment the people currently suffer will turn to forgiveness and restoration in the future" (2000, 413).

[Yhwh] *will subdue our iniquities.* The verb *kbš* signifies subjugation or suppression of resistance (see, e.g., Gen 1:28; Num 32:22, 29; Josh 18:1; 2 Sam 8:11; 2 Chr 28:10). Here, it is surprising as a term for what Yhwh will do to the iniquities of the covenant people: sin will be trodden underfoot as an enemy. While there is no articulation of repentance on the part of the prophetic speaker and his community here, this verse openly acknowledges the people's sinfulness. In the chastened and transformed community envisioned in Mic 4:1-7, the Judeans who had been punished for sin, driven away from Zion, or found themselves diminished or weakened by injury or impairment will be restored through the loving fidelity of Yhwh. That perspective is echoed here.

hurl into the depths of the sea. The suggestion that Yhwh's drowning of the Egyptian army in the Red Sea may give force to this image is less persuasive than the comparativist observation that "hurling something undesirable or harmful into deep water is part of ancient magic rituals" seen in Hittite and other ancient Near Eastern cultures (Andersen and Freedman 2000, 598).

7:20 *faithfulness to Jacob, fidelity to Abraham.* In Tg. Mic 7:20, the attention of the implied audience is directed to a foundational Torah narrative, Gen 28:10-22, about Yhwh's faithfulness to Jacob: "to Jacob *[and] to his sons, as you swore to him in Bethel.*" In Gen 12:1-3, Yhwh's calling of Abram includes the vocation to become a blessing to all the families of the earth. In the prophetic witness of Isaiah, Israel as God's servant had been called to be a light to the nations (Isa 42:6; 49:6). The targum elaborates as follows in the case of Abraham with reference to Gen 15, adding a mention of Isaac per Gen 22:1-18 to complete the triad of references to the patriarchs: "to Abraham *[and] to his seed after him, as you swore to him between the pieces; you will remember for us the binding of Isaac who was bound upon the altar before you.*" Abarbanel offers an expansive reading of the fidelity to Abraham: "The Assyrians and Ishmaelites, both descendants of Abraham, will accept God's Torah at that time and will dwell in peace, subservient to Israel" (Stavsky 2009, 63). The absence of Isaac's name in this verse has occasioned perplexity. Two rabbinic commentators, Ibn Ezra and Abarbanel, suggest that

Commentary

Isaac's link to Edom via his son Esau was considered problematic by the prophetic scribe, since the Edomites remained intractable enemies of Israel, and "there will be no remnant of Esau's descendants at the time of Israel's redemption" (Stavsky 2009, 63).

days of old. The history of Yʜᴡʜ's wondrous covenantal fidelity to Israel is evoked powerfully in the last clause of this extraordinary scroll, standing as an iconic remembrance that will bolster the people's resilience in every future circumstance.

Micah has moved his community toward transformation by lamenting the threats, wounds, and harms that are fracturing their lives, and by practicing holy memory: recalling the glorious deeds of Yʜᴡʜ on behalf of the community in ages past and laying claim to that narrative. Throughout his prophesying, Micah has rejected the distorted ideation and self-serving lies of those who relentlessly exploit others and assume that Yʜᴡʜ does not see. The true narrative, from antiquity to today—to this present moment in the reception history of Micah—is this: believers and those who struggle to believe are alike made in the image of a God who loves justice, who abounds in compassion and mercy, and who graces them with an unwavering fidelity far beyond anything they could ask or imagine.

Fig. 23. *Micah, Elijah, Gideon*, 1497. Russian Orthodox icon by unknown artist. In the Kirillo-Belozersky Monastery, Kirillov, in northern Russia.

BIBLIOGRAPHY

Barker, J. 2018. "From Where Does My Hope Come? Theodicy and the Character of Yhwh in Allusions to Exodus 34:6-7 in the Book of the Twelve." *JETS* 61:697-715.

Boloje, B. O. 2021b. "'The Godly Person Has Perished from the Land' (Mi 7:1-6): Micah's Lamentation of Judah's Corruption and Its Ethical Imperatives for a Healthy Community Living." *HvTSt* 77.4:a6757. doi:10.4102/hts.v77i4.6757.

Bruin, W. de. 2020. "Reading the Book of Micah as Mediation between Two Perspectives on the Enemy." Pages 315-37 in *Violence in the Hebrew Bible: Between Text and Reception*. Edited by J. van Ruiten and K. van Bekkum. OtSt 79. Boston: Brill. doi:10.1163/9789004434684_017.

DiFransico, L. 2017. "'He Will Cast Their Sins into the Depths of the Sea . . .': Exodus Allusions and the Personification of Sin in Micah 7:7-20." *VT* 67:187-203. doi:10.1163/15685330-12341272.

Gottlieb, I. B. 2016. "Rabbinic Reception of the Prophets." *OHP*, 388-406. doi:10.1093/oxfordhb/9780199859559.013.22.

Moor, J. C. de. 2000. "Micah 7:1-13: The Lament of a Disillusioned Prophet." Pages 149-96 in *Delimitation Criticism: A New Tool in Biblical Scholarship*. Edited by M. C. A. Korpel and J. M. Oesch. Pericope 1. Assen: Van Gorcum. doi:10.1163/9789004494367_008.

Schade, L. D. 2019. "Building the Eco-ethical Ark in the Age of Climate Disruption." Pages 17-22 in *Rooted and Rising: Voices of Courage in a Time of Climate Crisis*. Edited by L. D. Schade and M. Bullitt-Jonas. Lanham, MD: Rowman & Littlefield.

Selenite, V. K. 2016. *trigger: poems*. Scotts Valley, CA: CreateSpace.

———. 2017. *The Fire Been Here: Essays and Prose*. Scotts Valley, CA: CreateSpace.

Suso, H. 2019. *Wisdom's Watch upon the Hours*. Translated by E. Colledge. FCMC 4. Washington, DC: Catholic University of America Press.

Tepe, V., M. Papesh, S. Russell, M. S. Lewis, N. Pryor, and L. Guillory. 2020. "Acquired Central Auditory Processing Disorder in Service Members and Veterans." *JSLHR* 63:834-67.

Van Hecke, P. J. P. 2003. "Living Alone in the Shrubs: Positive Pastoral Metaphors in Micah 7,14." *ZAW* 115:362-75. doi:10.1515/zatw.2003.022.

Wheeler, R. 2022. *Ecospirituality: An Introduction*. Minneapolis: Fortress.

General Bibliography

Ahmed, S. 2014. *Willful Subjects*. Durham, NC: Duke University Press.

———. 2017. *Living a Feminist Life*. Durham, NC: Duke University Press.

Alexander, M. 2020. *The New Jim Crow: Mass Incarceration in the Age of Colorblindness*. 10th anniv. ed. New York: New Press.

Allen, L. C. 1976. *The Books of Joel, Obadiah, Jonah, and Micah*. NICOT. Grand Rapids: Eerdmans.

Alter, R. 2011. *The Art of Biblical Poetry*. Revised and updated. New York: Basic Books.

Andersen, F. I., and D. N. Freedman. 2000. *Micah: A New Translation with Introduction and Commentary*. AB 24E. New York: Doubleday.

Appiagyei-Atua, K. 2015. "Impact of the World Trade Organization's Agreements on Agriculture and on Trade-Related Aspects of Intellectual Property Rights on the Health of Citizens in the Developing World: A Poverty-Production-Based Critique." Pages 40-64 in *Protecting the Health of the Poor: Social Movements in the South*. CROP International Studies in Poverty Research. London: Zed Books.

Arena, F. 2020. "Promises of Peace in the Book of Micah." Pages 153-75 in *Prophetic Conflicts in Jeremiah, Ezekiel, and Micah: How Post-Exilic Ideologies Created the False (and True) Prophets*. FAT 2/121. Tübingen: Mohr Siebeck.

Arnold, B. T., and B. A. Strawn, eds. 2016. *The World around the Old Testament: The People and Places of the Ancient Near East*. Grand Rapids: Baker Academic.

Avigad, N. 1993. "Samaria (City)." *NEAEHL* 4:1300-1310.

Aylwin, P. A., and J. O. Aylwin. 2014. "The Option for the Poor and the Indigenous Peoples of Chile." Pages 83-96 in *The Preferential Option for the Poor beyond Theology*. Edited by D. G. Groody and G. Gutiérrez. Notre Dame: University of Notre Dame Press. doi:10.2307/j.ctvpj7bz3.8.

Barker, K. L., and W. Bailey. 1998. *Micah, Nahum, Habakkuk, Zephaniah*. NAC 20. Nashville: Broadman & Holman.

General Bibliography

Barthélemy, D. 2012. *Studies in the Text of the Old Testament: An Introduction to the Hebrew Old Testament Text Project*. Textual Criticism and the Translator 3. Winona Lake, IN: Eisenbrauns.

Baumann, G. 2003. *Love and Violence: Marriage as Metaphor for the Relationship between Yhwh and Israel in the Prophetic Books*. Collegeville, MN: Liturgical Press.

Beal, T. K. 1994. "The System and the Speaking Subject in the Hebrew Bible." *BibInt* 2:171–89. doi:10.1163/156851594X00204.

———. 2011. "Reception History and Beyond: Toward the Cultural History of Scriptures." *BibInt* 19:357–72. doi:10.1163/156851511X595530.

Becking, B. 2013. "Micah in Neo-Assyrian Light." Pages 111–28 in *"Thus Speaks Ishtar of Arbela": Prophecy in Israel, Assyria, and Egypt in the Neo-Assyrian Period*. Edited by R. P. Gordon and H. M. Barstad. Winona Lake, IN: Eisenbrauns. doi:10.5325/j.ctv1bxgz90.10.

Ben Zvi, E. 1998. "Micah 1.2–16: Observations and Possible Implications." *JSOT* 23.77:103–20. doi:10.1177/030908929802307708.

———. 1999a. "A Deuteronomistic Redaction in/among 'The Twelve'? A Contribution from the Standpoint of the Books of Micah, Zephaniah, and Obadiah." Pages 232–61 in *Those Elusive Deuteronomists: The Phenomenon of Pan-Deuteronomism*. Edited by L. S. Schearing and S. L. McKenzie. JSOTSup 268. Sheffield: Sheffield Academic.

———. 1999b. "Wrongdoers, Wrongdoing and Righting Wrongs in Micah 2." *BibInt* 7:87–99. doi:10.1163/156851599X00254.

———. 2000. *Micah*. FOTL 21B. Grand Rapids: Eerdmans.

Ben Zvi, E., and J. D. Nogalski. 2009. *Two Sides of a Coin: Views on Interpreting the Book of the Twelve/the Twelve Prophetic Books*. Introduction by T. Römer. Analecta Gorgiana 201. Piscataway, NJ: Gorgias.

Berrigan, D. 1995. *Minor Prophets, Major Themes*. Marion, SD: Rose Hill Books. Repr., Eugene, OR: Wipf & Stock, 2009.

Bey, M. 2022. *Black Trans Feminism*. Black Outdoors: Innovations in the Poetics of Study. Durham, NC: Duke University Press.

Bietenhard, S. 2012. "Micah: Call for Justice—Hope for All." Pages 421–32 in *Feminist Biblical Interpretation: A Compendium of Critical Commentary on the Books of the Bible and Related Literature*. Edited by L. Schottroff and M.-T. Wacker. Grand Rapids: Eerdmans.

Blenkinsopp, J. 1995. *Sage, Priest, Prophet: Religious and Intellectual Leadership in Ancient Israel*. LAI. Louisville: Westminster John Knox.

Boda, M. J., M. H. Floyd, and C. M. Toffelmire, eds. 2015. *The Book of the Twelve and the New Form Criticism*. ANEM 10. Atlanta: SBL Press.

Boer, R. 2015. *The Sacred Economy of Ancient Israel*. LAI. Louisville: Westminster John Knox.

Braaten, L. J. 2022. "God's Good Land: The Agrarian Perspective of the Book of the Twelve." Pages 145-65 in *The Oxford Handbook of the Bible and Ecology*. Edited by H. Marlow and M. Harris. Oxford: Oxford University Press. doi:10.1093/oxfordhb/9780190606732.013.3.

Brown, W. P. 1996. *Obadiah through Malachi*. Westminster Bible Companion. Louisville: Westminster John Knox.

Brueggemann, W. 1997. *Theology of the Old Testament: Testimony, Dispute, Advocacy*. Minneapolis: Fortress.

———. 2018. *The Prophetic Imagination*. 40th anniv. ed. Minneapolis: Fortress.

———. 2020. "The Litigation of Scarcity." *Journal for Preachers* 44.1:34-46.

Buber, M. 2016. *The Prophetic Faith*. Translated by C. Witton-Davies. With a new introduction by J. D. Levenson. Princeton: Princeton University Press.

Calvin, J. 2003. *Sermons on the Book of Micah*. Translated and edited by B. W. Farley. Phillipsburg, NJ: P&R Publishing.

Carroll, R. P. 1992. "Night without Vision: Micah and the Prophets." Pages 74-84 in *The Scriptures and the Scrolls: Studies in Honour of A. S. van der Woude on the Occasion of His 65th Birthday*. Edited by F. García Martínez, A. Hilhorst, and C. J. Labuschagne. VTSup 49. Leiden: Brill. doi:10.1163/9789004275737_008.

Carroll R., M. D. 2007. "'He Has Told You What Is Good': Moral Formation in Micah." Pages 103-18 in *Character Ethics and the Old Testament: Moral Dimensions of Scripture*. Edited by M. D. Carroll R. and J. E. Lapsley. Louisville: Westminster John Knox.

Cataldo, J. 2022. "Did the Prophets Teach Us to Protest?" *Religions* 13:487. doi:10.3390/rel13060487.

Cathcart, K., and R. P. Gordon. 1989. *The Targum of the Minor Prophets*. ArBib 14. Wilmington, DE: Glazier.

Cazelles, H., and S. D. Sperling. 2007. "Micah." *EncJud* 14:162-64.

Ceballos, G., P. R. Ehrlich, A. D. Barnosky, A. García, R. M. Pringle, and T. M. Palmer. 2015. "Accelerated Modern Human-Induced Species Losses: Entering the Sixth Mass Extinction." *Science Advances* 1.5. doi:10.1126/sciadv.1400253.

Chaney, M. L. 2017. *Peasants, Prophets, and Political Economy: The Hebrew Bible and Social Analysis*. Eugene, OR: Cascade.

Claassens, L. J. M. 2018. "From Traumatic to Narrative Memories: The Rhetorical Function of Birth Metaphors in Micah 4-5." *AcT* 26:221-36. doi:10.18820/23099089/actat.Sup26.13.

General Bibliography

———. 2021. "Between Excruciating Pain and the Promise of New Life: Birth Imagery in the Prophets and Trauma Hermeneutics." Pages 315-31 in *Prophecy and Gender in the Hebrew Bible*. Edited by L. J. Claassens and I. Fischer, with the assistance of F. O. Olojede. Bible and Women 1.2. Atlanta: SBL Press. doi:10.2307/j.ctv1p2gr81.17.

Clark, G. R. 1993. *The Word "Hesed" in the Hebrew Bible*. JSOTSup 157. Sheffield: Sheffield Academic.

Cohen, S. J. D., R. Goldenberg, and H. Lapin. 2022. *The Oxford Annotated Mishnah: A New Translation of the Mishnah with Introductions and Notes*. 3 vols. Oxford: Oxford University Press.

Conrad, E. 2003. *Reading the Latter Prophets: Toward a New Canonical Criticism*. JSOTSup 376. London: T&T Clark International.

Cook, S. L. 1999. "Micah's Deuteronomistic Redaction and the Deuteronomists' Identity." Pages 216-31 in *Those Elusive Deuteronomists: The Phenomenon of Pan-Deuteronomism*. Edited by L. S. Schearing and S. L. McKenzie. JSOTSup 268. Sheffield: Sheffield Academic.

Coomber, M. J. M. 2011. "Caught in the Crossfire? Economic Injustice and Prophetic Motivation in Eighth-Century Judah." *BibInt* 19:396-432. doi:10.1163/156851511X595576.

Corzilius, B. 2016. *Michas Rätsel: Eine Untersuchung zur Kompositionsgeschichte des Michabuches*. BZAW 483. Berlin: De Gruyter.

Counted, V., and F. Watts. 2017. "Place Attachment in the Bible: The Role of Attachment to Sacred Places in Religious Life." *JPsTh* 45:218-32. doi:10.1177/009164711704500305.

Cruz, J. 2016. *"Who Is Like Yahweh?" A Study of Divine Metaphors in the Book of Micah*. FRLANT 263. Göttingen: Vandenhoeck & Ruprecht.

Cuddon, J. A. 2014. *The Penguin Dictionary of Literary Terms and Literary Theory*. Revised by M. A. Habib. 5th ed. New York: Penguin Books.

Cuffey, K. H. 2015. *The Literary Coherence of the Book of Micah: Remnant, Restoration, and Promise*. LHBOTS 611. New York: Bloomsbury T&T Clark.

Davis, E. F. 2019. *Opening Israel's Scriptures*. Oxford: Oxford University Press.

Decorzant, A. 2010. *Vom Gericht zu Erbarmen: Text und Theologie von Micha 6-7*. FB 123. Würzburg: Echter.

Dempsey, C. J. 1999. "Micah 2-3: Literary Artistry, Ethical Message, and Some Considerations about the Image of Yahweh and Micah." *JSOT* 85:117-28. doi:10.1177/030908929902408507.

———. 2014. "Micah 1:1-16 and 7:1-10: A Poet's Cry of the Heart in the Midst of Tragic Vision." Pages 36-48 in *Why? . . . How Long? Studies on Voice(s) of*

Lamentation Rooted in Biblical Hebrew Poetry. Edited by L. S. Flesher, M. J. Boda, and C. J. Dempsey. LHBOTS 552. London: Bloomsbury.

Dempster, S. G. 2017. *Micah*. THBC. Grand Rapids: Eerdmans.

Di Pede, E., and D. Scaiola, eds. 2016. *The Book of the Twelve—One Book or Many? Metz Conference Proceedings 5-7 November 2015*. FAT 2/91. Tübingen: Mohr Siebeck.

Dobbs-Allsopp, F. W. 2015. *On Biblical Poetry*. Oxford: Oxford University Press.

Duhm, B. 1911. "Anmerkungen zu den Zwölf Propheten." *ZAW* 31:81-110. doi:10.1515/zatw.1911.31.2.81.

Edelman, D. V. 2015. "The Metaphor of Torah as a Life-Giving Well in the Book of Deuteronomy." Pages 317-33 in *History, Memory, Hebrew Scriptures: A Festschrift for Ehud Ben Zvi*. Edited by I. D. Wilson and D. V. Edelman. Winona Lake, IN: Eisenbrauns.

Elayi, J. 2017. *Sargon II, King of Assyria*. ABS 22. Atlanta: SBL Press.

———. 2018. *Sennacherib, King of Assyria*. ABS 24. Atlanta: SBL Press.

———. 2022. *Tiglath-Pileser III, Founder of the Assyrian Empire*. ABS 31. Atlanta: SBL Press.

Fabry, H.-J., ed. 2018. *The Books of the Twelve Prophets: Minor Prophets—Major Theologies*. BETL 295. Leuven: Peeters.

Fant, C. E., Jr., and W. M. Pinson, eds. 1971. *20 Centuries of Great Preaching*. 13 vols. Waco, TX: Word.

Finkelstein, I. 2011. "Stages in the Territorial Expansion of the Northern Kingdom." *VT* 61:227-42. doi:10.1163/156853311X571437.

Fischer, A. M. 2018. *Poverty as Ideology: Rescuing Social Justice from Global Development Agendas*. CROP International Studies in Poverty Research. London: ZED Books.

Fischer, I., and J. Claassens, eds. 2019. *Prophetie*. Die Bibel und die Frauen 2. Stuttgart: Kohlhammer.

Frahm, E. 2017a. "Assyria in the Hebrew Bible." Pages 556-69 in *A Companion to Assyria*. Edited by E. Frahm. Blackwell Companions to the Ancient World. Hoboken, NJ: Wiley Blackwell.

———. 2017b. "The Neo-Assyrian Period (ca. 1000-609 BCE)." Pages 161-208 in *A Companion to Assyria*. Edited by E. Frahm. Blackwell Companions to the Ancient World. Hoboken, NJ: Wiley & Sons.

———. 2023. *Assyria: The Rise and Fall of the World's First Empire*. New York: Basic Books.

Fretheim, T. E. 2013. *Reading Hosea-Micah: A Literary and Theological Commentary*. Reading the Old Testament. Macon, GA: Smyth & Helwys.

General Bibliography

Fuchs, S. L. 2021. "The Minor Prophets in Jewish Life Today." *OHMP*, 359-71. doi:10.1093/oxfordhb/9780190673208.013.25.

Gleich, P. von. 2022. *The Black Border and Fugitive Narration in Black American Literature*. American Frictions 4. Berlin: De Gruyter.

Glenny, W. E. 2015. *Micah: A Commentary Based on Micah in Codex Vaticanus*. Septuagint Commentary Series. Leiden: Brill.

Goldingay, J. 2021. *Hosea-Micah*. BCOTPB. Grand Rapids: Baker Academic.

Gordon, R. P. 1995. "Where Have All the Prophets Gone? The 'Disappearing' Israelite Prophet against the Background of Ancient Near Eastern Prophecy." *BBR* 5:67-86. doi:10.2307/26422127.

Hawken, P. 2021. *Regeneration: Ending the Climate Crisis in One Generation*. New York: Penguin.

Hays, C. B., with P. Machinist. 2016. "Assyria and the Assyrians." Pages 31-105 in *The World around the Old Testament: The People and Places of the Ancient Near East*. Edited by B. T. Arnold and B. A. Strawn. Grand Rapids: Baker Academic.

Heffelfinger, K. 2021. "Persuasion, Poetry, and Biblical Prophets." *PIBA* 43-44:38-53.

Heschel, A. J. 2001. *The Prophets*. New York: HarperCollins.

Hillers, D. R. 1984. *Micah*. Hermeneia. Philadelphia: Fortress.

Horrell, D. 2022. "Ecological Hermeneutics: Origins, Approaches, and Prospects." In *The Oxford Handbook of the Bible and Ecology*. Edited by H. Marlow and M. Harris. Oxford: Oxford University Press. doi:10.1093/oxfordhb/9780190606732.013.13.

Houston, W. J. 2010. "Exit the Oppressed Peasant? Rethinking the Background of Social Criticism in the Prophets." Pages 101-16 in *Prophecy and the Prophets in Ancient Israel: Proceedings of the Oxford Old Testament Seminar*. Edited by J. Day. LHBOTS 531. New York: T&T Clark.

———. 2015. "Justice." In *The Oxford Encyclopedia of the Bible and Law*. Edited by B. A. Strawn. 2 vols. Oxford: Oxford University Press.

Hoyt, J. M. 2019. *Amos, Hosea, Micah*. Evangelical Exegetical Commentary. Bellingham, WA: Lexham.

Irudayaraj, D. S. 2021. "Mountains in Micah and Coherence: A 'SynDiaTopic' Suggestion." *JBL* 140:703-22. doi:10.15699/jbl.1404.2021.4.

Jacobs, M. R. 2001. *The Conceptual Coherence of the Book of Micah*. JSOTSup 322. Sheffield: Sheffield Academic.

———. 2006. "Bridging the Times: Trends in Micah Studies Since 1985." *CurBR* 4:293-329. doi:10.1177/1476993X06064627.

Jeppesen, K. 1999. "'Because of You!': An Essay about the Centre of the Book of

the Twelve." Pages 196-210 in *In Search of True Wisdom: Essays in Old Testament Interpretation in Honour of Ronald E. Clements*. Edited by E. Ball. JSOTSup 300. Sheffield: Sheffield Academic.
Jeremias, J. 2007. *Die Propheten Joel, Obadja, Jonah, Micha*. ATD 24.3. Göttingen: Vandenhoeck & Ruprecht.
Jinbachian, M. 2012. "A Comparison of Micah 1 in the MT, the LXX, and Key Ancient Versions in Light of the Discoveries in the Judean Desert." Pages 135-61 in *Celebrating the Dead Sea Scrolls: A Canadian Collection*. Edited by P. W. Flint, J. Duhaime, and K. S. Baek. EJL 30. Atlanta: Society of Biblical Literature.
Joerstad, M. 2019. *The Hebrew Bible and Environmental Ethics: Humans, Non-Humans, and the Living Landscape*. Cambridge: Cambridge University Press.
Johnson, A. E., and K. K. Wilkinson. 2021. *All We Can Save: Truth, Courage, and Solutions for the Climate Crisis*. New York: One World.
Jones, B. A. 2016. "The Seventh-Century Prophets in Twenty-first Century Research." *CurBR* 14:129-75. doi:10.1177/1476993X14552928.
Kalmanofsky, A. 2016. "Postmodern Engagements of the Prophets." *OHP*, 548-68. doi:10.1093/oxfordhb/9780199859559.013.31.
Keimer, K. H. 2019. "Jerusalem in the First Temple Period." Pages 15-24 in *Routledge Handbook on Jerusalem*. Edited by S. A. Mourad, N. Koltun-Fromm, and B. der Matossian. London: Routledge.
Kelle, B. E., F. R. Ames, and J. L. Wight, eds. 2011. *Interpreting Exile: Displacement and Deportation in Biblical and Modern Contexts*. AIL 10. Atlanta: Society of Biblical Literature.
Kessler, R. 2000a. *Micha*. 2nd ed. HThKAT. Freiburg im Breisgau: Herder.
———. 2000b. "Zwischen Tempel und Tora: Das Michabuch im Diskurs der Perserzeit." *BZ* 44:21-36.
———. 2001. "Miriam and the Prophecy of the Persian Period." Pages 77-86 in *Prophets and Daniel*. Edited by A. Brenner. FCB 2/8. Sheffield: Sheffield Academic.
———. 2016. "The Twelve: Structure, Themes, and Contested Issues." *OHP*, 207-23. doi:10.1093/oxfordhb/9780199859559.013.12.
———. 2020. "Micah in the Book of the Twelve." Pages 176-85 in *The Book of the Twelve: Composition, Reception, and Interpretation*. Edited by L.-S. Tiemeyer and J. Wöhrle. VTSup 184. Leiden: Brill. doi:10.1163/9789004424326_012.
———. 2021a. "Micah." *OHMP*, 461-71. doi:10.1093/oxfordhb/9780190673208.013.35.

General Bibliography

———. 2021b. "Theodicy in Micah." Pages 143-56 in *Theodicy and Hope in the Book of the Twelve*. Edited by G. Athas, B. M. Stovell, D. Timmer, and C. M. Toffelmire. LHBOT 705. London: T&T Clark.

———. 2022. "Micha in der bildenden Kunst: Heilsprophet, Gerichtsprophet, Mahner." *Die Bibel in der Kunst* 6.

King, P. J. 1988. *Amos, Hosea, Micah—An Archaeological Commentary*. Philadelphia: Westminster.

Kugel, J. L. 1998. *The Idea of Biblical Poetry: Parallelism and Its History*. Baltimore: Johns Hopkins University Press.

Laato, A. 2018. *The Origin of Israelite Zion Theology*. LHBOTS 661. London: T&T Clark.

Lancaster, M. D. 2021a. "Metaphor Research and the Hebrew Bible." *CurBR* 19:235-85. doi:10.1177/1476993X20987952.

———. 2021b. "Wounds and Healing, Dew and Lions: Hosea's Development of Divine Metaphors." *CBQ* 83:407-24. doi:10.1353/cbq.2021.0082.

Landy, F. 2019. "Ancestral Voices and Disavowal: Poetic Innovation and Intertextuality in the Eighth-century Prophets." Pages 73-90 in *Second Wave Intertextuality and the Hebrew Bible*. Edited by M. Grohmann and H. C. P. Kim. RBS 93. Atlanta: SBL Press. doi:10.2307/j.ctvhn0933.8.

LeMon, J. M. 2016. "Egypt and the Egyptians." Pages 169-96 in *The World around the Old Testament: The People and Places of the Ancient Near East*. Edited by B. T. Arnold and B. A. Strawn. Grand Rapids: Baker Academic.

Lescow, T. 1995. "Zur Komposition des Buches Micha." *SJOT* 9:200-222. doi:10.1080/09018329508585068.

Lévinas, E. 1999. *Alterity and Transcendence*. European Perspectives. New York: Columbia University Press.

Levine, A.-J. 2022. "Supersessionism: Admit and Address Rather than Debate or Deny." *Religions* 13.2:155. doi:10.3390/rel13020155.

Linafelt, T. 2021. "Why Is There Poetry in the Book of Job?" *JBL* 140:683-701. doi:10.15699/jbl.1404.2021.3.

Lipschits, O., and A. M. Maeir. 2017. *The Shephelah during the Iron Age: Recent Archaeological Studies*. Winona Lake, IN: Eisenbrauns.

Luz, U. 2007. *Matthew 1-7*. Translated by J. E. Crouch. Hermeneia. Minneapolis: Fortress.

Maier, C. M. 2008. *Daughter Zion, Mother Zion: Gender, Space, and the Sacred in Ancient Israel*. Minneapolis: Fortress.

———. 2016. "Feminist Interpretation of the Prophets." *OHP*, 467-82. doi:10.1093/oxfordhb/9780199859559.013.26.

———. 2021. "Daughter Zion and Babylon, the Whore: The Female Personification of Cities and Countries in the Prophets." Pages 255-75 in *Prophecy and Gender in the Hebrew Bible*. Edited by L. J. Claassens and I. Fischer, with the assistance of F. O. Olojede. Bible and Women 1.2. Atlanta: SBL Press. doi:10.2307/j.ctv1p2gr81.14.

Marcus, J. 2000. *Mark 1-8: A New Translation and Commentary*. AB 27. New Haven: Yale University Press.

———. 2009. *Mark 8-16: A New Translation and Commentary*. AB 27A. New Haven: Yale University Press.

Marrs, R. R. 1999. "Micah and a Theological Critique of Worship." Pages 184-203 in *Worship and the Hebrew Bible: Essays in Honour of John T. Willis*. Edited by M. P. Graham, R. R. Marrs, and S. L. McKenzie. JSOTSup 284. Sheffield: Sheffield Academic.

Mason, R. 2004. *Micah, Nahum and Obadiah*. T&T Clark Study Guides. London: T&T Clark.

Mays, J. L. 1976. *Micah: A Commentary*. OTL. Philadelphia: Westminster.

McKane, W. 1998. *The Book of Micah: Introduction and Commentary*. Edinburgh: T&T Clark.

McKeating, H. 1971. *Amos, Hosea, Micah*. CBC. Cambridge: Cambridge University Press.

Meeks, C. 2020. "Superseding Patristic Supersessionism: Hilary of Poitiers and Cyril of Alexandria on Hosea 1-3." *JTI* 14:87-101. doi:10.5325/jtheointe.14.1.0087.

Menken, M. J. J., and S. Moyise, eds. 2009. *The Minor Prophets in the New Testament*. LNTS 377. London: T&T Clark.

Mettinger, T. N. D. 2015. "The Name and the Glory: The Zion-Sabaoth Theology and Its Exilic Successors." Pages 92-113 in *Reports from a Scholar's Life: Select Papers on the Hebrew Bible*. Edited by A. Knapp. Winona Lake, IN: Eisenbrauns. doi:10.5325/j.ctv1w36pqw.10.

Metzner, G. 1998. *Kompositionsgeschichte des Michabuches*. Europäische Hochschulschriften 635. Frankfurt am Main: Lang.

Middlemas, J. 2016. "Prophecy and Diaspora." *OHP*, 37-54. doi:10.1093/oxfordhb/9780199859559.013.3.

Miles, V. 2021. *Embodied Hope: A Homiletical Theology Reflection*. Eugene, OR: Cascade.

Moor, J. C. de 2015. "Jerusalem: Nightmare and Daydream in Micah." Pages 191-213 in *Open-Mindedness in the Bible and Beyond: A Volume in Honour of Bob Becking*. Edited by M. C. A. Korpel and L. L. Grabbe. LHBOTS 616. London: Bloomsbury T&T Clark.

———. 2020. *Micah*. HCOT. Leuven: Peeters.

General Bibliography

Morales, L. M. 2012. *The Tabernacle Pre-figured: Cosmic Mountain Ideology in Genesis and Exodus*. BTS 15. Leuven: Peeters.

Mowinckel, S. 2002. *The Spirit and the Word: Prophecy and Tradition in Ancient Israel*. Edited by K. C. Hanson. Fortress Classics in Biblical Studies. Minneapolis: Fortress.

Moyise, S. 2022. "The Use and Reception of the Prophets in the New Testament." *Religions* 13:304. doi:10.3390/rel13040304.

Nasuti, H. P. 2004. "The Once and Future Lament: Micah 2.1-5 and the Prophetic Persona." Pages 144-60 in *Inspired Speech: Prophecy in the Ancient Near East; Essays in Honor of Herbert B. Huffmon*. Edited by J. Kaltner and L. Stulman. JSOTSup 378. London: T&T Clark.

Nissinen, M. 2013. "Prophecy as Construct, Ancient and Modern." Pages 11-36 in *"Thus Speaks Ishtar of Arbela": Prophecy in Israel, Assyria, and Egypt in the Neo-Assyrian Period*. Edited by R. P. Gordon and H. M. Barstad. Winona Lake, IN: Eisenbrauns. doi:10.5325/j.ctv1bxgz90.6.

Nogalski, J. D. 2011. *The Book of the Twelve: Micah-Malachi*. 2 vols. SHBC 18. Macon, GA: Smyth & Helwys.

———. 2017a. "Jerusalem, Samaria, and Bethel in the Book of the Twelve." Pages 195-214 in *The Book of the Twelve and Beyond: Collected Essays of James D. Nogalski*. AIL 29. Atlanta: SBL Press. doi:10.2307/j.ctt1rfzzfs.16.

———. 2017b. "Micah 7:8-20: A Reevaluation of the Identity of the Enemy." Pages 63-81 in *The Book of the Twelve and Beyond: Collected Essays of James D. Nogalski*. AIL 29. Atlanta: SBL Press. doi:10.2307/j.ctt1rfzzfs.9.

———. 2017c. "Recurring Themes in the Book of the Twelve: Creating Points of Contact for a Theological Reading." Pages 181-94 in *The Book of the Twelve and Beyond: Collected Essays of James D. Nogalski*. AIL 29. Atlanta: SBL Press. doi:10.2307/j.ctt1rfzzfs.15.

———. 2018. "The Beginnings of the Twelve." Pages 97-134 in *Introduction to the Hebrew Prophets*. Nashville: Abingdon.

Nogalski, J. D., and M. A. Sweeney, eds. 2000. *Reading and Hearing the Book of the Twelve*. SymS 15. Atlanta: Society of Biblical Literature.

Nyong'o, T. 2019. *Afro-Fabulations: The Queer Drama of Black Life*. Sexual Cultures. New York: New York University Press.

O'Brien, J. M. 2008. *Challenging Prophetic Metaphor: Theology and Ideology in the Prophets*. Louisville: Westminster John Knox.

———. 2015. *Micah*. Wisdom Commentary 37. Collegeville, MN: Liturgical Press.

———. 2016. "Metaphorization and Other Tropes in the Prophets." *OHP*, 241-57. doi:10.1093/oxfordhb/9780199859559.013.14.

General Bibliography

———. 2022. "Forthtellers Not Foretellers: The Origins of a Liberal Orthodoxy about the Prophets." *Religions* 13:298. doi:10.3390/rel13040298.

Otto, E. 1991. "Techniken der Rechtssatzredaktion israelitischer Rechtsbücher in der Redaktion des Prophetenbuches Micha." *SJOT* 5:119-50. doi:10.1080/09018329108584976.

Phillips, R. D. 2010. *Jonah and Micah*. Reformed Expository Commentary. Phillipsburg, NJ: P&R Publishing.

Pioske, D. 2022. "'And I Will Make Samaria a Ruin in the Open Country' (Mic 1:6): On Biblical Ruins, Then and Now." *RB* 129:161-82. doi:10.2143/RBI.129.2.3290640.

Plaskow, J. 1990. *Standing Again at Sinai: Judaism from a Feminist Perspective*. San Francisco: Harper & Row.

Portier-Young, A. E. 2024. *The Prophetic Body: Embodiment and Mediation in Biblical Prophetic Literature*. Oxford: Oxford University Press.

Poser, R. 2021. "Embodied Memories: Gender-Specific Acts of Prophecy as Trauma Literature." Pages 333-57 in *Prophecy and Gender in the Hebrew Bible*. Edited by L. J. Claassens and I. Fischer, with the assistance of F. O. Olojede. Bible and Women 1.2. Atlanta: SBL Press. doi:10.2307/j.ctv1p2gr81.18.

Rad, G. von. 2001. *The Theology of Israel's Prophetic Traditions*. Vol. 2 of *Old Testament Theology*. Translated by D. M. G. Stalker. Louisville: Westminster John Knox.

Radford, CL W. 2022. *Lived Experiences and Social Transformations: Poetics, Politics and Power Relations in Practical Theology*. Theology in Practice 11. Leiden: Brill.

Redditt, P. L., and A. Schart, eds. 2003. *Thematic Threads in the Book of the Twelve*. BZAW 325. Berlin: De Gruyter.

Rees, A. 2020. "On Patting Snakes and Sitting under Trees: Just Peace Theory and Prophetic Witness." *IJPT* 14:135-48. doi:10.1163/15697320-12341608.

Reimer, D. 2013. "The Prophet Micah and Political Society." Pages 203-24 in *"Thus Speaks Ishtar of Arbela": Prophecy in Israel, Assyria, and Egypt in the Neo-Assyrian Period*. Edited by R. P. Gordon and H. M. Barstad. Winona Lake, IN: Eisenbrauns. doi:10.5325/j.ctv1bxgz90.15.

Reynolds, T. E. 2023. "Prophetic Belonging: Disability, Hospitality, and Being Church Together." *Spiritus* 23:51-65. doi:10.1353/scs.2023.a899754.

Rienstra, D. 2022. *Refugia Faith: Seeking Hidden Shelters, Ordinary Wonders, and the Healing of the Earth*. Minneapolis: Fortress.

Roth, M. 2005. *Israel und die Völker im Zwölfprophetenbuch: Eine Untersuchung*

General Bibliography

    zu den Büchern Joel, Jona, Micha und Nahum. FRLANT 210. Göttingen: Vandenhoeck & Ruprecht.

Roukema, R. 2019. *Micah in Ancient Christianity: Reception and Interpretation*. SBR 15. Berlin: De Gruyter.

———. 2022. "The Reception of the Hebrew Prophets in Ancient Christianity." *Religions* 13:408. doi:10.3390/rel13050408.

Rudolph, W. 1975. *Micha, Nahum, Habakuk, Zephanja*. KAT 13.3. Gütersloh: Mohn.

Runions, E. 2001. *Changing Subjects: Gender, Nation and Future in Micah*. Playing the Texts 7. London: Sheffield Academic.

Sakenfeld, K. D. 1985. *Faithfulness in Action: Loyalty in Biblical Perspective*. OBT 16. Philadelphia: Fortress.

Sawyer, J. F. A. 1996. *The Fifth Gospel: Isaiah in the History of Christianity*. Cambridge: Cambridge University Press.

———. 2021. "The Twelve Minor Prophets in Art and Music." *OHMP*, 279–95. doi:10.1093/oxfordhb/9780190673208.013.40.

Schade, L. D. 2015. *Creation-Crisis Preaching: Ecology, Theology, and the Pulpit*. St. Louis: Chalice.

Schütte, W. 2014. "Die Michaschrift und Israels Exil in Juda." *ZAW* 126:243–60. doi:10.1515/zaw-2014-0017.

Schwemer, Anna Maria. 2020. *Studien zu den frühjüdischen Prophetenlegenden Vitae Prophetarum II: Die Viten der kleinen Propheten und der Propheten aus den Geschichtsbüchern; Übersetzung und Kommentar*. TSAJ 50. Tübingen: Mohr Siebeck.

Schwienhorst-Schönberger, L. 2018. "Marcion on the Elbe." *First Things* 288:21–26.

Sergi, O. 2016. "The Omride Dynasty and the Reshaping of the Judahite Historical Memory." *Bib* 97:503–26. doi:10.2143/BIB.97.4.3186053.

Sergi, O., and Y. Gadot. 2017. "Omride Palatial Architecture as Symbol in Action: Between State Formation, Obliteration, and Heritage." *JNES* 76:103–11. doi:10.1086/690651.

Sharon, I. 2014. "Levantine Chronology." *OHAL*, 44–65. doi:10.1093/oxfordhb/9780199212972.013.004.

Sharp, C. J. 2003. *Prophecy and Ideology in Jeremiah: Struggles for Authority in the Deutero-Jeremianic Prose*. OTS. London: T&T Clark.

———. 2009. *Irony and Meaning in the Hebrew Bible*. ISBL. Bloomington: Indiana University Press.

———. 2010. "Hewn by the Prophet: An Analysis of Violence and Sexual Transgression in Hosea with Reference to the Homiletical Aesthetic of Jeremiah Wright." Pages 50–71 in *Aesthetics of Violence in the Prophets*. Edited by C. Franke and J. M. O'Brien. LHBOTS 517. London: T&T Clark.

———. 2011. "Micah." Pages 78–85 in *The Oxford Encyclopedia of the Books of the Bible*. Edited by M. D. Coogan. 2 vols. Oxford: Oxford University Press.

———. 2019a. *The Prophetic Literature*. Core Biblical Studies. Nashville: Abingdon.

———. 2019b. *Joshua*. SHBC 5. Macon, GA: Smyth & Helwys.

———. 2021. "Jeremiah and Homiletics." Pages 610–34 in *The Oxford Handbook of Jeremiah*. Edited by L. Stulman and E. Silver. Oxford: Oxford University Press. doi:10.1093/oxfordhb/9780190693060.013.12.

———. 2022a. *Jeremiah 26–52*. IECOT. Stuttgart: Kohlhammer.

———. 2022b. "Of Springs and Living Stones: Psalm 87 and the Memory of Zion in Christian Preaching." *IJH* 5:20–41. doi:10.21827/ijh.5.1.20-41.

Sharpe, C. 2016. *In the Wake: On Blackness and Being*. Durham, NC: Duke University Press.

Shaw, C. S. 1993. *The Speeches of Micah: A Rhetorical-Historical Approach*. JSOTSup 145. Sheffield: Sheffield Academic.

Sherwood, Y. 2000. *A Biblical Text and Its Afterlives: The Survival of Jonah in Western Culture*. Cambridge: Cambridge University Press.

Simundson, D. J. 2005. *Hosea, Joel, Amos, Obadiah, Jonah, Micah*. AOTC. Nashville: Abingdon.

Smith, J. M. P. 1974. *A Critical and Exegetical Commentary on Micah*. ICC. Edinburgh: T&T Clark.

Smith-Christopher, D. L. 2015. *Micah*. OTL. Louisville: Westminster John Knox.

Sobrino, J. 2008. *No Salvation Outside the Poor: Prophetic-Utopian Essays*. Maryknoll, NY: Orbis.

Stavsky, Y. 2009. *Trei Asar: The Twelve Prophets*. Vol. 2. *Micah, Nahum, Habakkuk, Zephaniah, Haggai, Zechariah, Malachi*. ArtScroll Tanach. Brooklyn, NY: Mesorah Publications.

Strawn, B. A. 2005. *What Is Stronger Than a Lion? Leonine Image and Metaphor in the Hebrew Bible and the Ancient Near East*. OBO 212. Fribourg: Academic Press; Göttingen: Vandenhoeck & Ruprecht. doi:10.5167/uzh-150391.

———. 2016. "Material Culture, Iconography, and the Prophets." *OHP*, 87–116. doi:10.1093/oxfordhb/9780199859559.013.6.

Stulman, L. 2016. "Prophetic Words and Acts as Survival Literature." *OHP*, 319–33. doi:10.1093/oxfordhb/9780199859559.013.18.

Sweeney, M. A. 2000. *The Twelve Prophets*. Vol. 2. *Micah, Nahum, Habakkuk, Zephaniah, Haggai, Zechariah, Malachi*. Berit Olam. Collegeville, MN: Liturgical Press.

General Bibliography

———. 2012. "Synchronic and Diachronic Concerns in Reading the Book of the Twelve Prophets." Pages 21-33 in *Perspectives on the Formation of the Book of the Twelve: Methodological Foundations—Redactional Processes—Historical Insights*. Edited by R. Albertz, J. D. Nogalski, and J. Wöhrle. BZAW 433. Berlin: De Gruyter. doi:10.1515/9783110283761.21.

Thurow, R., and S. Kilman. 2009. *Enough: Why the World's Poorest Starve in an Age of Plenty*. New York: PublicAffairs.

Tiemeyer, L.-S., and Wöhrle, J., eds. 2020. *The Book of the Twelve: Composition, Reception, and Interpretation*. VTSup 184. Leiden: Brill.

Tisdale, L. T., and C. J. Sharp. 2016. "The Prophets and Homiletics." *OHP*, 627-51. doi:10.1093/oxfordhb/9780199859559.013.35.

Tov, E. 2022. *Textual Criticism of the Hebrew Bible*. 4th ed. Minneapolis: Fortress.

Trimm, C. 2017. *Fighting for the King and the Gods: A Survey of Warfare in the Ancient Near East*. RBS 88. Atlanta: SBL Press.

Ussishkin, D. 2003. "Solomon's Jerusalem: The Text and the Facts on the Ground." Pages 103-15 in *Jerusalem in Bible and Archaeology: The First Temple Period*. Edited by A. G. Vaughn and A. E. Killebrew. SymS 18. Atlanta: Society of Biblical Literature.

Utzschneider, H. 1999. *Michas Reise in die Zeit: Studien zum Drama als Genre der prophetischen Literatur des Alten Testaments*. SBS 180. Stuttgart: Katholisches Bibelwerk.

———. 2005. *Micha*. ZBK 24.1. Zürich: TVZ.

Valk, J. 2020. "Crime and Punishment: Deportation in the Levant in the Age of Assyrian Hegemony." *BASOR* 384:77-103. doi:10.1086/710485.

Vargon, S. 2009. "The Prayer for the Restoration of the Israelite Kingdom in the Book of Micah: Literary and Historical Background." Pages 597-618 in *Homeland and Exile: Biblical and Ancient Near Eastern Studies in Honour of Bustenay Oded*. Edited by G. Galil, M. Geller, and A. Millard. VTSup 130. Leiden: Brill. doi:10.1163/ej.9789004178892.i-648.161.

Vayntrub, J. 2019. *Beyond Orality: Biblical Poetry on Its Own Terms*. Ancient Word. London: Routledge.

———. 2021. "Hearing the Voice of Biblical Poetry." *SEÅ* 86:20-38.

Vermes, G. 2011. *The Complete Dead Sea Scrolls in English*. Rev. ed. London: Penguin Books.

Vermeulen, K. 2022. "Of Cities, Mothers, and Homes: A Cognitive-Stylistic Approach to Gendered Space in the Hebrew Bible." Pages 173-93 in *The Mummy under the Bed: Essays on Gender and Methodology in the Ancient Near East*. Edited by K. De Graef, A. Garcia-Ventura, A. Goddeeris, and B. Alpert Nakhai. wEdge 1. Münster: Zaphon.

Wagenaar, J. A. 2001. *Judgement and Salvation: The Composition and Redaction of Micah 2-5.* VTSup 85. Leiden: Brill.
Waltke, B. K. 2007. *A Commentary on Micah.* Grand Rapids: Eerdmans.
Weaver, D. J. 2017. *The Irony of Power: The Politics of God within Matthew's Narrative.* Studies in Peace and Scripture 14. Eugene, OR: Pickwick.
Weingart, K. 2019. "Wie Samaria so auch Jerusalem: Umfang und Pragmatik einer frühen Michakomposition." *VT* 69:460-80. doi:10.1163/15685330-12341369.
Weisman, Z. 1998. *Political Satire in the Bible.* SemeiaSt 32. Atlanta: Scholars Press.
Wenzel, H., ed. 2018. *The Book of the Twelve: An Anthology of Prophetic Books or the Result of Complex Redactional Processes?* OSJCB 4. Göttingen: V&R Unipress.
West, T. C. 2016. "The Prophets and Ethics." *OHP*, 589-609. doi:10.1093/oxfordhb/9780199859559.013.33.
Williams, T. T. 2020. *Erosion: Essays of Undoing.* New York: Picador.
Willis, J. T. 2014. *Instruction Shall Go Forth: Studies in Micah and Isaiah.* Edited by T. M. Willis and M. W. Hamilton. Eugene, OR: Pickwick.
Wilson, R. R. 1980. *Prophecy and Society in Ancient Israel.* Philadelphia: Fortress.
Wilson, W. T. 2022. *The Gospel of Matthew.* 2 vols. ECC. Grand Rapids: Eerdmans.
Wolff, H. W. 1978. *Micah the Prophet.* Translated by R. D. Gehrke. Philadelphia: Fortress.
———. 1986. "Prophets and Institutions in the Old Testament." *CurTM* 13:5-12.
———. 1990. *Micah.* Translated by G. Stansell. CC. Minneapolis: Augsburg.
Wood, J. R. 2000. "Speech and Action in Micah's Prophecy." *CBQ* 62:645-62.
Woude, A. S. van der. 1969. "Micah in Dispute with the Pseudo-Prophets." *VT* 19:244-60. doi:10.1163/156853369X00491.
Yee, G. A. 2007. "Recovering Marginalized Groups in Ancient Israel: Methodological Considerations." Pages 10-27 in *To Break Every Yoke: Essays in Honor of Marvin L. Chaney.* Edited by R. B. Coote and N. K. Gottwald. SWBA 3. Sheffield: Sheffield Phoenix.
Zapff, B. M. 2022. *Micah.* Translated by L. M. Maloney. IECOT. Stuttgart: Kohlhammer.
Ziegler, Joseph. *Duodecim Prophetae.* 4th ed. SVTG 13. Göttingen: Vandenhoeck & Ruprecht, 2016.

Subject Index

Aaron: cloud of the divine presence and, 72; golden diadem for, 66; as guide, 72; leadership of, 9, 329, 330, 337; overview of, 345; as priest, 372; as representative of the law, 95, 345

Abelard, Peter, 96

Abel-Shittim, 5

Abraham: call of, 385; covenant with, 334, 371; descendants of, 381; fidelity to, 406–7; God's fidelity to, 77; mountain metaphor and, 343; persuasion of, 390; promises to, 372; reward to, 66; sacrifice of Isaac and, 76; as shepherd, 70

Achzib, 36, 135, 150, 164, 171–73, 224

Adullam, 36, 64, 135, 150, 163, 164, 174, 378

Ahab, 70, 138, 156, 224, 327, 331, 334, 357, 363–64

Ahaz, 133, 135, 147–48, 163, 313

Ahaziah, 138

Aiath, 150

akītu (Mesopotamian festival), 288

al-Baydā, 171

Alexander, Cecil Frances, 119

alliteration, 35

allusion: intentional, 280; overview of, 35–36; in strike on the cheek of judge of Israel, 288; to Amos imagery, 398; to biblical texts, 226; to biblical traditions, 378–79; to child sacrifice, 350; to emancipation, 401; to exodus traditions, 371; to King David, 174; to Mother Jerusalem, 307; to Mount Sinai, 271; to redemption, 76; to Song of the Bow, 165; to supersessionist theologizing, 94; to topographical high and low places, 153

ambiguity: as artful, 314; on divine retribution, 320–21; example of, 151, 211, 214, 339; in the Hebrew, 321; on human sin, 375; interpretive, 183; perception of, 38; in semantic sense, 239; of sentinels, 393; on target of Yhwh's punitive wrath, 296; in taunt, 377; in war song, 302, 323

Ammon, the Ammonites, 56, 73, 139

Amon, 315

Amos: commissioning of, 69; identity of, 31; place-name usage by, 138–39; political opposition to, 202; as prince, 70; treason of, 232;

425

Subject Index

warning to, 202; willfulness of, 52; as witness, 189
Amurru, 8
Anathoth, 150, 202
Angelica, Fra, 222, 403
āpilum, 346
apostrophe, 36, 62, 140, 142
Asa, 173
ascension (of Christ), 97, 187
Ashdod, 8, 164
Ashkelon, 164, 313
Ashtaroth, 313
assembly, heavenly. *See* council, divine
assonance, 35, 36
Assumption (of Mary), 97
Assurnasirpal II, 311, 315
Assyria, Neo-Assyrian empire: assassinations in, 298; as conqueror, 201; defeat of, 288, 291–92, 293, 295–96, 323, 372; feminine references to, 377; focus on, 8; as geopolitical term, 399; holdings of, 196; invasion by, 378, 399; judgment against, 61; lion iconography and, 318; meaning of, 69; overview of, 310–14; Paul and, 297; prisoners to, 53, 148; sex workers in, 158; shepherds against, 206, 315; sin and, 299; as threat, 8, 26, 138, 396; as Yhwh's weapon, 174, 193; Yhwh's wrath against, 162, 221, 321, 323, 400
Athaliah, 138

Babylon, Babylonia, Neo-Babylonian empire: assaults on Judah by, 197, 285, 321, 338, 358; Assyrian defeat by, 8, 170; defeat of, 7, 69, 149, 274; destruction from, 136, 208; exile of, 7, 90, 219, 258, 378; expansionism of, 405; feminine reference to, 377, 396, 397; humiliation rituals of, 288; Judean captives and, 5, 8, 56, 69, 175, 186, 187, 283, 383; Micah's visions regarding, 90; New Year festival of, 288; period of, 5; plundering by, 259; rise of, 197; routing of the Israelites by, 187; siege of Jerusalem and, 5, 11, 170, 210, 213, 219, 223, 237, 246, 259–60, 284, 398, 402; symbolism of, 186, 258–59, 282, 313; temple destruction by, 71; threat of, 6, 26; as Yhwh's revenge, 161, 193, 237, 398; Zion and, 258–59, 265, 398. *See also* Nebuchadrezzar/Nebuchadnezzar
Bach, Johann Sebastian, 118
Bahá'í faith, 263
Balaam son of Beor, 9, 70, 72–73, 325, 328, 345, 346–47
Balak, 9, 73, 325, 345, 346–47
Bar Kokhba, 24, 174
Bashan, 95, 150, 369, 401–2
Bayly, Albert F., 119
Beit Guvrin, 173
Beth-aven, 139
Bethel, 21, 148, 157, 165–66
Beth-ezel, 36, 135, 150, 164, 167–68
Beth-leaphrah, 134, 137, 140, 150, 164, 165
Bethlehem: David as from, 307, 309; hymns regarding, 119; Jesus's birth in, 83–84, 86, 119, 224, 283, 293–94, 297; personified, 36, 319, 320; prophecy regarding, 92, 98, 283, 293–94, 297; significance of, 88,

299; travelers to, 90; wrath and, 88. *See also* Ephrathah
Bît-Humria, 5
Black identity, 54-55, 118, 143-44, 190, 220, 229, 265, 339, 384-85
Bonar, Horatius, 118
Bozrah, 181, 185, 211-12, 213
Briggs, George Wallace, 118-19
Brooks, Phillips, 119
Buṣeirah, 212

Caleb, 173
Caravaggio, 89
Christology, 85, 87, 91, 92, 298-99, 335. *See also* Jesus of Nazareth
Chronicler, the, 173
climate crisis. *See* ecological justice
concatenation, 36-37
council, divine, 279
covenant lawsuit (*rîb*), 71-72, 150, 335, 351

Dalit identity, 227
Damascus, 5, 139, 312, 313, 363
Daw, Carl P., 118
Dead Sea Scrolls. *See* Qumran
Deir ʿAlla inscription, 346
deixis, 397
diaspora. *See* exile
Doré, Gustave, 351

Ebal, Mount, 82
ecological justice, 57-60, 117, 145-46, 191-93, 230-32, 267-69, 303-5, 340-42, 385-88
economic justice: cannibal, 21, 38, 219-20, 227, 231-32, 235-36, 333, 371-72; economic injustice, 30, 116, 198, 220, 228, 230-31, 277-78, 304, 358-59; exploitation, 42, 43, 44-45, 53, 123, 138, 182, 189, 191, 194, 238; extractive regime, 44, 146, 220, 232, 311-12; judges in, 352; poverty, 48, 59, 60, 149, 194, 341; predation, 143, 188, 229, 278; ruler for, 234-35; sacrifice, 118; for women, 121, 192
Eder, Tower of, 252, 282, 320
Edom, the Edomites, 8, 56, 139, 163, 212, 213, 392, 407
Egypt: Abram in, 77; as ally, 8, 295; Assyria and, 310; defeat of, 406; destruction in, 157; feminine reference to, 396, 397; fugitivity and, 56, 313; horses from, 278; imprisonment and enslavement in, 75, 76, 279, 340, 371, 378, 402; Israel's exodus from, 9, 37, 66, 71, 76, 271, 279, 329-30, 337, 340, 345, 371, 372, 378, 402; plagues in, 70, 152; redemption from, 76, 257, 340, 345, 372; salvation from, 372; significance of, 313-14, 400; symbolism of, 335, 344-45, 347; trade in, 172
Ekron, 8, 164
ellipsis, 40, 41, 210, 355
Ephrathah, 83, 88, 283, 291, 293, 306, 319. *See also* Bethlehem
Euphrates River, 37, 275
Eustochium, 90
exile: Assyrian, 9, 90, 140, 169, 317; Babylonian, 7, 90, 219, 258, 378; description of, 136, 140, 362; habitat loss and, 305; imagery of, 7; Jewish, 81; present, 69; as punishment, 68, 180-81, 185, 210, 323; restoration following, 303, 375, 378, 398, 399; Samaria and, 140; significance of, 5; symbolism of, 67; trauma of, 175, 207, 280, 362; of Zion, 371

427

Subject Index

Eyck, Hubert, 294
Eyck, Jan, 294
famine, 21, 77, 136, 220, 332, 340, 398
farmer(s): hardships on, 182, 191, 238, 332-33, 389; under Israelite and Judean monarchies, 44; Israelites as, 114; as laborers, 43; Micah as, 116; prophecy regarding, 267
fugitive, fugitivity: Black trans, 190, 384-85; curse of, 76; defined, 229; embracing, 265-66, 302; living as, 339; Micah and, 53-57; resistance, 266; solidarity with, 144

Gallim, 150
gapping. See ellipsis
Gath, 36, 134, 139, 150, 163-65, 171, 174, 327. See also Moresheth-gath
Gaza, 157, 313
Gebim, 150
Gezer, 313
Gibeah, 139, 150, 286
Gilead, 5, 95, 313, 369, 401-2
Gilgal, 10, 139, 325, 328, 330, 345, 347-48

Hanunu, 313
heightening, intensification: agricultural, 44; defined, 32-33; of disparagement of enemy nations, 404; example of, 244, 314, 316, 349, 359, 392; overview of, 37-38; of relational disruption, 395
Heseltine, Philip Arnold, 119
Ḥever, Naḥal, 24
Hezekiah: boast of, 73; healing of, 261; as judge, 289; mocking of, 377; as prince, 70; reforms of, 157; reign of, 147-48; repentance of, 61, 247; as shepherd, 315; spiritual landscape during time of, 142, 247, 388; verse mention of, 8, 133
Hiel of Bethel, 244
Hippodamus of Miletus, 173
Hosea, 20, 21, 52, 148, 158, 202, 237
Hoshea son of Elah, 288, 315
hymn, 118, 119, 316

idolatry, idol: of cities, 322-23; demolishing of, 94; of Israel, 65, 141, 320, 363; of Jeroboam, 363-64; of Judah, 254, 320, 321; of Lachish, 171; Micah as standing against, 51, 52, 142, 181; of non-Israelites, 279; of patriarchal religion, 301; polemics against, 46; prohibitions on, 71; prostitution and, 158; punishment for, 68; references to, 20; reformation of, 144; retribution for, 173; of Samaria, 34, 40, 148, 296; in the temple, 225, 236; verses referencing, 79, 134, 292; Yhwh's rage at, 143, 184, 293, 323
incarnation (of Christ), 92, 93, 98, 119, 140, 141, 186, 187, 262
indeterminacy. See ambiguity
injustice: economic, 30, 116, 198, 220, 228, 230-31, 277-78, 304, 358-59; gender-based, 43, 46, 48, 49-50, 54-55, 116, 124, 190, 229, 302, 346; racialized, 46, 54, 116, 124, 144, 190, 229, 302
irony: in biblical texts, 92; elements of, 41; example of, 28, 185, 288, 346; God and, 301; international trade and, 171; in Micah's response, 34, 194, 210; overview of, 39; percep-

Subject Index

tion of, 38; of the present age, 146; response to, 247; targets of, 209
Isaiah: commissioning of, 69, 159; as consultant, 202; Hezekiah and, 61, 73; Micah as compared to, 78, 269-70; peaceable kingdom of, 118; as prophet, 20, 147; temperament of, 31; writing style of, 48
Israel/Israelites: adultery of, 65-66; Assyria and, 5, 6, 53, 208, 295-96, 314; blessing of, 70, 328; Canaan and, 66, 72, 108, 271, 347; characteristics of, 114; David as ruler of, 306-7; defeat of, 6; disobedience of, 21, 67, 68-69, 71, 73-74, 139, 141, 194, 201-2, 203, 323-24, 347-48, 396-97; ecology in, 59; economy in, 43-45; Edomites and, 407; embalming of, 140; enslavement of, 75; exhortation to, 112, 330; exile of, 68, 90, 136, 187, 208, 280, 399; exodus of, 9, 51, 66, 75-76, 81, 279, 329-30; footwear in, 160; geopolitics of, 5; glory of, 174-75, 377-78; holy war and, 259, 284; house of, 224-25, 234; imagery regarding, 161, 284; inheritance of, 200; Jesus as shepherding, 83-84, 97, 309; to Judah, 155; Judah and, 196, 401-2; judgment of, 69, 135, 150, 151, 185, 275, 288, 289, 320, 329; land of, 194, 195; as lion, 70, 318; manna and water for, 72; map of, 132; metaphorization of, 157-58; Moab and, 346-47; peace of, 321, 387, 406; plague on, 328; poverty in, 42; punishment of, 6-7, 65, 67, 71-72, 118, 141, 145, 161, 198, 221, 224, 237, 281, 284, 286, 328, 342, 343, 347, 396-97; purgation of, 323; as refugees, 6; remnant of, 319; as resting place, 208-9; restoration/deliverance of, 5, 9, 12, 37-38, 68, 69, 75, 76, 213, 224, 270, 273, 279, 297, 306, 338, 340, 343, 344-45, 348, 372, 378, 387, 400, 402; sacrifices of, 109; under threat, 259-67; war song of, 296-97; wilderness wandering of, 35-36, 66, 70, 75, 152, 245, 345; as wounded, 161; Yhwh and, 15, 29, 51, 66, 76-77, 92, 208, 235, 237, 239, 245, 248, 257, 258, 279, 319-20, 348-49, 353, 378, 405-6, 407; to Zion, 37; Zion and, 272. *See also specific leadership*

Jacob: blessing to, 70, 76, 87-88; covenantal fidelity to, 371; deliverance of, 272; economic growth of, 66; failure of, 343; faithfulness to, 406-7; "fear not" exhortation to, 112; gathering of, 210-11; heads of, 223, 230, 234; as holiness model, 87-88; house of, 223, 224, 254, 257, 274; impiety of, 141; inheritance of, 65, 68; linkage with Christ, 88, 108; as political term, 155; promises to, 372; remnant of, 70, 109, 292, 293, 295, 296, 298, 299, 317, 318, 327; as shepherd, 70; symbolism of, 343, 399; transgression of, 141, 154, 351; wrath to, 296
Jehoahaz, 315
Jehoiachin, 234, 315
Jehoiakim, 315
Jehoram, 62, 138
Jeremiah: Baruch and, 14; execution of, 60; laments of, 29, 192, 241; on new covenant, 372-73; as prophet

429

Subject Index

for Christ, 96; skepticism of, 221-22; threats to, 202; as understood as Christ, 86-87; willfulness and, 52
Jeroboam son of Nebat, 70, 315, 363, 364
Jerusalem: Assyria and, 315, 377; ceding territory by, 171; corruption in, 21, 361, 375, 393; Daughter, 257; desolation of, 262, 370; destruction of, 5, 7, 34, 61, 80, 138, 139-40, 144, 153, 159, 160, 162, 168-69, 170-71, 247, 248, 256, 284, 402, 405; dispute about Jesus in, 84; economic oppression in, 220; enemies of, 36, 56, 138, 164; gate of, 150, 163, 168-69; geographical location of, 139-40; God as enthroned in, 256, 284; grief regarding, 394; history of consequences and, 225-27; hope for, 253; idolatry in, 184; imagery regarding, 237, 282; judgment against, 15-16, 28, 61; lament of, 69; as Mother, 307; as peace, 117, 225; personification of, 27, 36, 149, 166, 374; punishment of, 381; razing of, as foreseen, 223-25; rebuilding of, 254, 293, 398, 399; restoration of, 379; Samaria and, 148-49, 157, 195; siege/fall of, 5, 7, 18, 56, 80, 136, 148, 170, 197, 199, 210, 213, 219, 240, 246, 259-60, 287, 313; significance of, 27, 138; sinfulness in, 30, 154, 255-56; threat to, 29, 35, 159, 258, 282, 309, 371; warning to, 6, 7; worship in, 107; YHWH's favor toward, 272, 299
Jesus of Nazareth: betrayal of, 380; birth of, 83-84, 299, 307; confirmation of, 83; death of, 86, 89; destruction of the temple and, 227; exhortation of, 297; Festival of Tabernacles and, 298; followers of, 261; growth of, 98; on the harvest, 380; kingdom of, 263; as Lord, 262; mediation of, 114; as Messiah, 87, 96; ministry of, 84, 85, 94-95; mission of, 379; parable of the talents of, 84; as peace, 7, 86, 87, 92, 118-19, 186, 201, 263, 291, 294-95, 299, 305-6, 309, 310-14, 315, 379; on persecution, 85, 94; preexistence of, 108; Samaritan woman and, 91; as shepherd, 300, 380-81; titles of, 110, 187, 261; wedding banquet parable of, 98. *See also* Christology
Jezreel, 5, 139, 195
Joash, 315
John the Baptist, 185, 286, 380
Joram. *See* Jehoram
Jordan River, 275, 345, 347, 401
Jotham, 133, 135, 147

Kalhu, 311, 315
Khorsabad, 6
killjoy (in feminist theory), 52-53, 79, 143, 189-90, 228, 301-2, 337-38, 383

Lachish, 36, 93, 135, 139, 150, 163, 164, 169-70, 171, 173, 282, 327
Laishah, 150
Lavnin, 171
lineation (poetic), 22, 34, 35, 39
Loop, Henry Augustus, 105

Madmenah, 150
Manasseh, 70, 315, 388
Marduk, 288
Mareshah, 36, 135, 150, 164, 173-74

Subject Index

Maroth, 36, 135, 139, 140, 150, 164, 168
Mayer, Karl, 331
Memra, 151, 205, 214, 245, 395
Menahem, 313, 315
metaphor: of adultery, 157; of ambulation, 354; of battle, 239; of being in labor, 261; in Book of the Four, 21; of cannibalism, 226-27, 231-32, 236; of childbirth, 284, 299; of domestic food preparation, 226; of early-ripening figs, 98; of enemies, 153, 404; of feeding, 239; of a heifer, 286; in Hosea, 46; of idolatries, 51, 53, 158; of Israel and Judah, 150, 157, 387; of Israel's sinfulness, 73-74; juridical, 396-97; of a legal case, 343; of a lion, 318; military, 403; of oppressive yokes, 197; overview of, 39-40; of prophet, 393; of prophetic rebuke, 356; of prostitution, 158; relationship of, 162; of seizing, 194; of sentinels, 393; series of, 362-63; of sheep, 211-12; of skin, 206; of striking with fangs, 238-39; of trampling, 318; of violence against women, 283; of walking, 254, 354; of Yhwh, 237; of Zion, 272, 282
metonym, 67, 357
Micaiah ben Imlah, 62
Michmash, 150
Migron, 150
Miriam: death of, 72; leadership of, 9, 51, 53, 72, 329, 337; lineage of, 113; overview of, 345; as prophet, 330, 372; as representative, 95, 335
Mitinti, 313
Mizpah, 139
Moab, 8, 56, 325, 328, 346-47, 348, 401

Modena, Wiligelmo de, 183
Molech, 157, 350
Montgomery, James, 119
Moresheth, 3, 29, 36, 48, 59
Moresheth-gath, 36, 59, 135, 150, 164, 171. *See also* Gath
Moses: as barred from Canaan, 74; commandments and divine words to, 62, 65, 71, 73, 76, 274; death of, 74, 75; Deborah as compared to, 113; exhortation to, 112, 330; as friend of God, 380; as intercessor, 74; leadership of, 9, 66, 72, 82, 94, 95, 101, 317, 329, 337, 372; overview of, 345; at Red Sea, 81; as shepherd, 70; Song of, 66, 71; Ten Commandments and, 68, 274
Mount Zion. *See* Zion/Mount Zion
Murabba'at Wadi, 24

Nebuchadrezzar/Nebuchadnezzar, 7, 157, 174, 193, 221, 223
Nimrod, 292, 315-16, 375
Nimrud, 311, 313, 315-16
Nob, 150
nonviolence, 55, 121, 263-64. *See also* peace

Oatman, Johnson, 119
Odo of Tournai, 96
Omri, 9, 138, 156, 327, 331, 333, 334, 357, 363, 364
onomatopoeia, 40
Ophrah, 165-66
Ordo Lectionum Missae, 120
Osterwald, Georg, 100

Paula of Rome, 90
peace: of Canaan, 86; characteristics of, 263, 273, 277, 302-3, 377;

431

Subject Index

coming, 106; in community, 110; of community, 388; in desert lands, 60; ethical, 338; of false prophets, 162, 222; fragility of, 263; from God, 115; God's plan for, 278, 285; gospel of, 142; initiatives of, 121; inner, 98; of Israel, 69, 321, 387, 406; Jerusalem as, 117, 225; Jesus as, 7, 86, 87, 92, 118–19, 186, 201, 263, 291, 294–95, 299, 305–6, 309, 310–14, 315, 379; of Judah, 384; movements of, 264; *Pax Romana* and, 92; proclamation of, 221; universal, 106, 107, 257, 275; visions of, 61–62, 119, 264, 265, 277, 295, 327, 329; war and, 81–82; Zion as, 251, 255–56, 258, 267, 273. *See also* nonviolence

Pekah son of Remaliah, 288, 313, 315
Pekahiah, 315
Philistia, the Philistines, 114, 139, 157, 163, 164, 171, 257
Powell, Rosephanye, 119
Procter, Adelaide A., 118
prophets, false: as adversary, 34, 36; characteristics of, 203, 370; condemnation of, 232, 239; deception of, 199, 211, 241, 327; fruitlessness of, 237; gibe at, 367, 375–76, 393; holy war and, 239; idiom regarding, 239; indictment of, 225; manipulation by, 34; Micah as accused to be, 247; Micah as alternative to, 395; peace and, 162; as proven wrong, 370; punishment to, 240; seers as, 187; sentinels as, 393; shaming of, 217–18, 221–22, 402–3

question, rhetorical: example of, 3, 73, 117, 166–67, 184, 205, 244, 258, 283–84, 334, 352, 377, 379; function of, 10, 32, 154; Micah's name as, 147; overview of, 41; response to, 58; of Yhwh, 34, 72, 94, 349
Qumran, 24, 353
quotation: adversarial, 28; of authority, 247; function of, 96; hinge, 270; in Matthew, 83–84, 119; of Micah, 99, 247, 306; warning in, 98

repetition, 17, 35, 36, 40–41, 287, 312, 320, 351, 389
resurrection, 62, 91, 96, 97, 112–13, 187
reversal, 27, 75, 83, 165, 182, 199, 200, 224, 238, 274, 284, 295, 344, 376, 378
Revised Common Lectionary, 120
Rezin (Rahiânu), 313
rhetorical question. *See* question, rhetorical
Rimmon, 150
Roman, Johan Helmich, 118

Sacks, Jonathan, 82
sacrifice (in cultic praxis), 236, 244–45, 328, 336, 347; child sacrifice, 244, 330, 336, 350
Samaria: archaeology in, 363; Daughter, 161; exploitation in, 195; idolatry in, 34, 40, 148, 158, 184, 296; Jacob and, 155; Jerusalem and, 5, 148–49, 154, 157, 184, 195; judgment of, 26; personification of, 149, 157, 161; punishment of, 34, 135; siege/fall of, 3, 5, 6, 7, 8, 18, 29, 34, 36, 37, 135, 136–37, 138, 140, 144, 145, 148–49, 153, 155–57, 159, 255–56, 327,

333, 364, 371; significance of, 155, 355, 364
Samsi (Šamsi), 313
Ṣandaḥanna, 173
Sargon II, 6, 136, 140, 148, 311
Scott, K. Lee, 119
Seerveld, Calvin, 119
Sennacherib, 8, 61, 136, 169, 170, 171, 172, 223, 298, 311, 312, 313, 315
Shalmaneser V, 6, 136, 140, 148
Shaphir, 36, 140, 150, 164, 166, 167
Shekinah, 66, 67, 73, 152, 238, 244, 245, 274
shinrin-yoku, 387
Shittim, 10, 139, 325, 328, 330, 345, 347–48
Sidon, 8
simile, 40, 68, 69, 75, 390
spirit: defined, 205; Holy Spirit, 94, 96, 111, 225, 226, 243, 261; sin of, 350; of Yhwh, 25, 29, 30, 94, 102, 104, 116, 219, 241–42, 243, 341, 351, 372, 376
synecdoche, 41, 319

Tashlich (ritual), 382
Tel Ḥarasim, 171
Tell al-Bayḍā (el-Beida), 171
Tell ed-Duweir, 169
Tell ej-Judeideh, 3, 171
Tell el-'Areini (Tel Erani), 165
Tell eṣ-Ṣafi, 164, 171
Tell Ṣandaḥanna, 173
temple in Jerusalem: argument regarding, 67–68; dedication of, 16; destruction of, 61, 65, 71, 153, 219, 227, 247; field imagery regarding, 68; foregrounding of, 273; as peace, 225; photo, 163; plundering of, 219, 312; rebuilding of, 12, 67–68, 255, 260; restoration of, 149; sacrifices in, 245, 248; Second, 84; Shekinah in, 73; significance of, 224, 227, 271, 272; sin in, 225; symbolism of, 151–52, 224; worship in, 352; Yhwh as enthroned in, 227, 246
Theodorus of Tabennese, 141
Tiglath-Pileser III, 4–5, 9, 156, 311, 312–13, 363, 364
Tigris River, 275, 315
Tirzah, 331, 363
Torah, torah: disobedience to, 70–71, 73; establishment of, 271, 272; esteem from, 285; on exiles, 67; God's offering of, 70; house of slavery in, 344–45; as in Jerusalem, 27; observance/obedience of, 61, 62, 76, 245, 267, 269, 272, 273–75, 323, 329; overview of, 82; practices in, 194; significance of, 329; spread of, 82; stipulations in, 328, 329, 334, 347, 359, 372; women's experience in, 346; from Zion, 87, 246, 269, 270, 274–75, 278, 377
Tower of Eder, 252, 282, 320
transness, trans identity, 54–55, 119, 143–44, 190, 229, 265–66, 339, 384–85
Trinity, the, 87, 97, 108, 225, 299, 380–81

Uva L'Tzion (prayer), 382

violence: anti-Black, 54; of Assyria, 146; of Babylon, 69; of the binary, 190; carceral, 266; causes of, 121; culture of, 51; dehumanizing, 55;

Subject Index

economic, 124, 220, 229, 230; example of, 117, 118; fugitivity and, 55, 56; gender, 55, 124, 283; harms from, 124; hierarchies of, 56; imperial, 56; of Indian insurgents, 80; interpersonal, 54; in Judah, 182; of Judah, 78, 190; opposition to, 124, 193, 382, 385; patriarchal, 52, 53; peace following, 256, 303; racial, 190; in Samaria, 148; sexual, 124, 167, 208; subtle, 193; survival following, 265, 383, 396; sustained, 49; systemic, 54; trauma from, 339; valorization of, 301; in warfare, 319; of wealthy, 358, 359; as in the whole earth, 385, 390. *See also* war, warfare

Vitae Prophetarum, 62

Vuchetich, Evgeniy, 276

war, warfare: cosmic, 278; costs of, 267-68; Crimean, 80; demolishing of, 94; description of, 80; devastation of, 80, 81, 145, 191, 264, 267-68, 336; Divine Warrior, 152, 174, 187, 188, 239-40, 259, 272, 292, 295-96, 319, 348, 393; ending of, 162, 261, 267, 269, 277; gendered violence in, 283; harms from, 58; holy-war tradition, 173, 239-40, 259, 284; international, 258; Iraq, 264; lessons from, 264; moral, 263; Panama, 264; peace and, 81, 222; plundering in, 286; prisoners of, 9, 40, 43-44, 136, 175, 210, 266, 285, 310, 312, 313, 316, 317, 319, 404; rape in, 167, 286; refugees, 116, 124, 266; sanctifying, 222, 239-40; siege, 61; song of, 36-37, 41, 102, 292-93, 296-97, 301, 302, 319-20, 321, 323; Syro-Ephraimite, 4, 148, 163, 169, 312, 401; Vietnam, 264; violence in, 319; weapons of, 264; World War I, 81, 264. *See also* violence

Watts, Isaac, 108, 119

William of Champeaux, 96

Zaanan, 36, 135, 139, 150, 164, 166-67, 168

Zechariah (ruler), 315

Zedekiah, 70, 71, 213, 214, 288, 315

Zion/Mount Zion: appetite of, 390; building of, 244-45; call to, 87; as Christ, 85, 118; confession of, 397; consoling of, 369, 377-78, 399; Daughter, 5, 7, 10, 18, 21, 27, 28, 34, 40, 48, 56, 67, 69, 108, 112, 161, 166, 170-71, 181, 189, 206, 209, 258-59, 269, 274, 282, 285, 287, 306, 360, 367, 368-69, 370-71, 374-75, 376-78, 384, 385, 387, 388-89, 394, 395, 396, 398, 405; defeat of, 265; defense of, 396; description of, 225; destruction of, 153, 223, 371; dominion of, 28, 108, 252, 254, 256, 272-73, 327, 372; fugitive, 56; glorification of, 255; God's enthronement in, 281-82; hope of, 383, 385, 396; ideology of, 284; imagery regarding, 34, 47, 161; Israel's return to, 37; Jerusalem as, 138; lament of, 367, 370, 371, 374-75, 376, 383, 388-89, 390, 393; law from, 87; Mother, 140, 307; nations to, 106, 256, 260, 261, 270, 271, 273, 293, 323, 399; as peace, 255-56, 258, 267, 273; peace as, 251-52; as pinnacle of godly

Subject Index

peace, 251-52, 255-56; pledge of, 253, 259; plowed as a field, 67-68, 138, 223, 246-47; preeminence of, 256; razing of, 68; resilience of, 246; resolve of, 384; restoration of, 26, 28, 124, 252, 257, 258, 262, 372, 397-98, 402; return to, 37; rise of, 29, 206; sexual violation and, 286; significance of, 248, 267, 269, 272; sin for, 170-71, 258, 397; speaking by, 368, 376-77; structure of, 139; suffering in, 21, 56, 67, 258-59, 261, 359, 389, 398; temple in, 224, 246, 271; threat to, 161; topography of, 271; torah from, 87, 246, 269, 270, 274-75, 278, 377; wailing of, 40; Y*hwh*'s reign in, 281-82

Author Index

Aaron, Charles L., Jr., 115
Abarbanel, Isaac, 202, 398, 406-7
Abelard, Peter, 96
Aharoni, Yoḥanan, 24
Ahmed, Sara, 51-53, 57, 143, 189-90, 228, 265, 301-2, 337-38, 383-84
Aitken, J. K., 24
Albert the Great, 97
Albertz, Rainer, 5, 20, 323
Alexander, M., 220
Alfaro, J., 19
Alfonsi, Peter, 96-97
Allen, John, 112
Allen, Leslie C., 168, 239, 350
Alter, Robert, 32, 33, 38-39
Altman, Shalom, 82
Altschuler, David, 213, 355, 388
Ambrose of Milan, 4, 87-88, 94, 95
Andersen, Francis I., 15, 17, 33, 36, 147, 151, 154, 155, 157-58, 163, 164, 165, 167-68, 171, 174, 175, 195, 198, 199, 200, 201, 202, 205, 209, 210-11, 212, 233, 235, 239, 240, 241, 244, 246, 273, 275, 278, 279-80, 282-84, 286, 288, 310, 319, 322, 345, 349, 350, 353, 357, 361, 364, 390, 391-92, 395, 396, 397, 400, 402, 404, 406
Anderson, Wallace E., 106

Appavoo, Theophilus, 227
Appiagyei-Atua, Kwadwo, 182
Aquinas, Thomas, 97-98
Arena, Francesco, 5, 147-48, 238, 239
Aristotle, 41
Athanasius of Alexandria, 87
Augustine of Hippo, 85, 298
Avigad, Nahman, 156, 363
Avi-Yonah, Michael, 171, 173-74
Aylwin, José O., 278
Aylwin, Patricio A., 278

Baháʾuʾlláh (Ḥusayn-ʿAlí), 263-64
Bailey, W., 210
Balentine, Samuel E., 237
Baltzer, Klaus, 10
Barber, William J., II, 116, 188
Barker, J., 405
Barker, K. L., 210
Barnovsky, Anthony D., 232
Barthélemy, Dominique, 23, 356, 357
Baruchi-Unna, Amitai, 165-66
Basil of Caesarea, 95, 380
Baskin, Judith R., 72
Baumann, Gerlinde, 157
Beal, Timothy K., 158-59
Becking, Bob, 18
Benjamin, A., 55

Author Index

Ben Zvi, Ehud, 10, 11-12, 13, 25, 148, 151, 153, 196-97, 289, 400-401, 402, 405
Berlin, Adele, 32, 33
Berrigan, Daniel, 142, 188, 227, 264, 300, 336, 382
Bey, Marquis, 51, 54-56, 57, 143-44, 190, 229, 265-66, 302-3, 339, 384-85
Biddle, M. E., 284
Blenkinsopp, Joseph, 31
Boda, M. J., 13
Boer, Roland, 43, 146, 189, 311-12
Boloje, Blessing O., 208, 210, 236, 395
Boltvinik, Julio, 143
Bonaventure, 187, 262
Braaten, Laurie J., 58, 191, 267
Brin, Gershon, 211
Britt, Laurence W., 188
Brown, William P., 238, 352
Brueggemann, Walter, 115, 150, 202, 236, 273, 348-49
Bruin, W. de, 399
Buber, Martin, 78, 349, 350

Calvin, John, 57-58, 100-103, 142, 187-88, 211, 213, 214, 226-27, 262-63, 299-300, 335-36, 381-82
Carroll R., Daniel, 236, 245, 352
Cathcart, Kevin J., 63, 159, 167, 205, 244, 274, 282, 315, 316, 321, 396
Cazelles, Henri, 3, 196, 320, 345, 358, 364, 401
Ceballos, G., 232
Chalmers, D. M., 113
Chaney, Marvin L., 44, 169, 171, 194, 195, 389
Channing, William Ellery, 80
Chrysostom, John, 94
Claassens, L. J. M., 283, 284

Clark, Gordon R., 352-53
Clement of Alexandria, 140, 260, 334
Collier-Thomas, B., 112, 113
Conrad, Edgar, 149, 247
Cook, Stephen L., 30, 194
Corzilius, B., 210
Crenshaw, James L., 203
Crispin, Gilbert, 96
Cruz, Juan, 40, 162, 282, 352, 356
Cuddon, J. A., 35-36
Cuffey, Kenneth H., 14, 18
Cunsolo, Ashlee, 192
Cyril of Alexandria, 91-93, 95, 102, 159, 171, 175, 187, 209, 213, 226, 262, 298-99, 321, 334-35, 381
Cyril of Jerusalem, 225

Damian, Peter, 95-96
Davis, Ellen F., 30, 116-17
Day, Peggy L., 167
Debourse, C., 288
DeGrado, Jessie, 158
Dempsey, Carol J., 32, 196, 210
Dempster, S. G., 40, 210
De Troyer, Kristin, 24
Didymus of Alexandria, 94, 95
Dietrich, Walter, 10
DiFransico, L., 405
Dines, Jennifer, 19
Di Pede, E., 13
Dobbs-Allsopp, F. W., 33-34

Edelman, Diana V., 275
Edwards, Jonathan, 103-11, 188, 300, 336
Ego, Beate, 24
Ehrlich, C. S., 165
Ehrman, A., 361
Elayi, Josette, 4-6, 8, 169-70, 312-13, 363

437

Author Index

Elliger, Karl, 22
Ephrem the Syrian, 213
Eusebius, 83, 87

Feldman, Marian H., 316
Ferguson, J., 334
Ferreiro, Alberto, 225
Finkelstein, Israel, 156
Finkielsztejn, Gerald, 174
Fischer, Andrew Martin, 220
Fischer, Irmtraud, 345
Floyd, M. H., 13
Flusser, David, 185-86
Foote, Julia A. J., 112
Fraade, S. D., 64
Frahm, Eckhart, 53, 312
Freedman, David Noel, 15, 17, 33, 36, 147, 151, 154, 155, 157-58, 163, 164, 165, 167-68, 171, 174, 175, 195, 198, 199, 200, 201, 202, 205, 209, 210-11, 212, 233, 235, 239, 240, 241, 244, 246, 247, 273, 275, 278, 279-80, 282-84, 286, 288, 310, 319, 322, 345, 349, 350, 353, 357, 361, 364, 390, 391-92, 395, 396, 397, 400, 402, 404, 406
Fretheim, Terence E., 210, 247
Frey, Rebecca, 247
Fuchs, Stephen Lewis, 263, 336, 382
Fuller, Russell, 24

Gadot, Yuval, 156, 195
Gafney, Wilda C., 64, 77, 336-37, 345
Garton, Roy E., 20
Gelston, Anthony, 22, 151, 160, 194, 208, 244, 247, 272, 282, 285, 286, 306, 318, 347, 350, 355, 356, 391, 392, 393
Gervais, M., 121
Gleich, Paula von, 54

Glenny, W. Edward, 23, 166, 168, 171, 173, 206, 234, 282, 283, 288, 309, 314, 350, 355, 357, 358, 389, 393
Goen, C. C., 103
Goldingay, John, 168, 174, 310, 350, 357
Gordon, Bruce, 101-3
Gordon, Robert P., 159, 167, 205, 244, 274, 282, 321, 396
Gottlieb, David N., 63-64
Gottlieb, Isaac B., 382
Grayson, A. Kirk, 310, 316
Gregory, B. C., 353
Gregory of Nazianzus, 93
Griggs, Sutton E., 264
Grotius, Hugo, 213
Grunhaus, Naomi, 78
Guillaume, Philippe, 22

Ham, Clay Alan, 63, 83-84
Hardin, J. W., 169, 170
Harshav, Benjamin, 40
Hawken, Paul, 267-68, 305, 341-42
Hays, Christopher B., 6, 169, 313-14, 315, 400
Heider, G. C., 350
Herzog, Todd, 82
Heschel, Abraham J., 38, 78-79, 147, 161, 193, 228, 232, 269, 306, 342, 388
Heseltine, Philip Arnold, 119
Hesychius of Jerusalem, 93-94, 95
Heyden, Katharina, 96-97
Hilary of Poitiers, 90
Hill, Robert, 91
Hillers, Delbert R., 16, 168, 343, 344, 349, 350
Hippolytus of Rome, 186
Hirsch, Mendel, 323, 343
Hoffman, Yair, 164

Author Index

Hoke, Jimmy, 48
Honig, Bonnie, 51
Hoogland, Mark-Robin, 97-98
Houston, W. J., 234-35
Howard, George E., 358
Hoyt, J. M., 210
Hutton, Rodney M., 348
Hyatt, J. P., 353

Ibita, M. Maricel S., 340-41
Ibn Ezra, Abraham, 78, 154, 316, 355, 406-7
Irenaeus of Lyons, 83, 260
Irudayaraj, Dominic S., 153, 271, 344

Jackman, Christene, 82
Jacober, Amy E., 123
Jacobs, Mignon R., 14, 17
Jacobsen, David Schnasa, 115
Jeremias, Jörg, 16, 160, 168, 169, 210, 284, 356
Jerome, 88-90, 95, 141-42, 186-87, 225-26, 261, 297-98, 334, 355, 377, 380-81, 388
Jinbachian, Manuel, 24, 148
Johnson, Ayana Elizabeth, 192, 230
Johnson, C. W., 113
Jones, Christopher W., 315
Josephus, 247
Justin Martyr, 83, 96, 260, 297

Kadari, Tamar, 64
Kalmanofsky, Amy, 161
Kara, Joseph ben Simeon, 78, 213, 287, 343, 355, 398
Kessler, Rainer, 147, 152, 158, 168, 171, 199, 205, 240, 241, 274-75, 280, 310, 345, 357, 405
Kilman, Scott, 332-33
Kimḥi, David, 78, 167, 171, 186, 199, 208, 213, 280, 287, 316, 321, 343, 355, 388, 398
King, P. J., 162
Kinzig, W., 226
Kipfer, S., 361
Kitz, A. M., 360
Kloner, Amos, 173-74
Knapp, A., 307
Koskinen, Heikki J., 96
Kosman, A., 353
Kraus, Hans-Joachim, 203
Kristeva, Julia, 158
Kugel, James L., 32-33

Laato, Antti, 284, 322
Lancaster, Mason D., 39, 362
Lange, Armin, 24
Lasker, Daniel J., 96
LeMon, Joel M., 400
Lescow, Theodor, 16
Lesser, M. X., 103
Levin, Yival, 171
Lévinas, Emmanuel, 338
Levine, A.-J., 85
Levy, J. Leonard, 81-82, 264
Lichtenberger, Hermann, 24
Linafelt, Tod, 35
Liraz, E., 174
Lloyd, K., 161
Lombard, Peter, 299
Longenbach, James, 39
Lowance, Mason I., Jr., 108
Luther, Martin, 299
Luz, Ulrich, 84

Macchi, J.-D., 78
Machinist, Peter, 6, 169, 313-14, 315, 400
Maeir, Aren M., 164-65

Author Index

Maier, Christl M., 5, 271, 283, 284
Maimonides (Moses ben Maimon), 175
Malamat, Abraham, 346
Malbim (Meir Leibush ben Yehiel Michel Wisser), 152, 240, 343
Mann, Susan Archer, 143
Marcus, Joel, 83, 84, 286
Marks, David Woolf, 79-81, 264
Mason, Rex, 13, 149
Matzke, Nicholas, 232
Mayfield, T. D., 343, 351-52
Mays, James Luther, 15, 154, 244, 272, 313, 388
Mazar, Eilat, 172-73
McGowan, Andrew B., 118
McKane, William, 15, 16, 147, 151, 155, 165, 166, 203, 205, 357, 361
McKeating, H., 158, 171, 279, 364
McKenzie, Alyce M., 115
Meeks, Charles, 85
Melito of Sardis, 260
Menken, Maarten J. J., 84
Methodius of Olympus, 260-61
Mettinger, Tryggve N. D., 282, 356
Metzner, G., 211
Middlemas, Jill, 20
Miles, Veronica, 269
Minkema, Kenneth P., 103, 106, 107, 111
Mirelman, S., 288
Moor, Johannes C. de, 7, 24, 168, 288, 310, 388
Morales, L. Michael, 271, 272, 274
Moran, William, 194
Moss, C. R., 226
Mowinckel, Sigmund, 31, 201, 241
Müller, R., 270

Na'aman, Nadav, 163, 165, 167
Nagen, Yakov, 82
Nasuti, Harry P., 194, 199, 351
Nogalski, James D., 11, 13, 17-18, 20, 147, 155, 171, 210, 397, 400, 401, 405
Norris, Kathleen, 228
Nyong'o, Tavia, 54, 55

O'Brien, Julia M., 12, 38, 50, 149, 159, 205, 207, 243-44, 275, 283, 321, 345, 388
O'Connor, Kathleen M., 354
O'Connor, Michael, 154, 209, 360
Odo of Tournai, 96
O'Lynn, Rob, 115-16
Origen of Alexandria, 86-87, 140-41, 186, 380
Osiek, Carolyn, 334
Ottenheijm, E., 70-71

Pachomius, 141
Palmén, Ritva, 96
Panitz-Cohen, N., 164
Parsons, Michael, 100
Peter the Venerable, 96
Phillips, Richard D., 30
Plaskow, Judith, 47, 77-78, 228, 265, 301, 337, 346
Portier-Young, Anathea E., 159
Poser, Ruth, 283
Prausnitz, Moshe W., 171-72
Proclus of Constantinople, 94-95

Quick, Laura, 360, 362
Quine, C., 278

Rad, Gerhard von, 31
Radak. *See* Kimḥi, David
Radashkovsky, I., 174
Radford, CL Wren, 43

Author Index

Rambam. *See* Maimonides (Moses ben Maimon)
Randolph, Florence Spearing, 112-13
Rashi (Shlomo Yitzhaqi), 78, 208, 272, 287, 343, 356, 361, 388
Redditt, P. L., 13
Reich, Ronny, 212
Reynolds, Thomas E., 280-81
Rienstra, Debra, 268
Roberts, J. J. M., 277
Römer, Thomas, 147
Rosenzweig, Franz, 78
Roukema, Riemer, 85, 86, 87, 88, 93-95, 119-20, 213, 260, 321, 355
Rudolph, Wilhelm, 22, 318, 343, 356
Runions, Erin, 47, 320

Sacks, Jonathan, 82
Sakenfeld, Katharine Doob, 354
Sandt, Huub van de, 85
Sangster, William E., 114-15
Saperstein, Marc, 79-80, 81-82
Sawyer, John F. A., 85
Scaiola, D., 13
Scales, A. T., 100
Schade, Leah D., 117, 304, 305, 386-87
Schart, Aaron, 13, 20
Scheck, Thomas P., 88
Schniedewind, W. M., 171
Scholz, Susanne, 286
Schwemer, Anna Maria, 62
Scott, James C., 243
Selenite, Venus Di'Khadijah, 385
Sergi, Omer, 156, 195, 363
Sharon, I., 5, 169
Sharp, Carolyn J., 10, 14, 21, 26, 27, 39, 50, 57, 80, 123, 139, 185, 212, 214, 244-45, 274, 281, 307, 328, 346, 399
Sharpe, C., 220

Shaw, C. S., 163
Shepherd of Hermas, 334
Sherinian, Zoe C., 227
Sherwood, Yvonne, 85
Silverman, Jason M., 45
Simkovich, M. Z., 24
Simon, Maurice, 65, 69, 73-74
Smith, John Merlin Powis, 61, 210
Smith-Christopher, Daniel L., 309, 310, 355, 357
Sobrino, Jon, 383
Solomon, Andrew, 193
Spans, A., 270
Sperling, S. David, 3, 196, 320, 345, 358, 364, 401
Spurgeon, Charles, 80
Stade, Bernhard, 16
Stavsky, Yitzchok, 154, 167, 171, 175, 199, 208, 213, 240, 272, 280, 287, 315, 316, 321, 323, 343, 355, 382, 388, 398, 404, 406-7
Stein, Stephen J., 103-4, 107
Stewart, Nan, 113-14, 264
Strawn, B. A., 318, 391
Stulman, Louis, 396
Sumani, W., 120
Suriano, Matthew J., 163, 165, 166
Suso, Henry, 98-99, 382-83
Sweeney, Douglas A., 103
Sweeney, Marvin A., 168, 205, 211, 213, 239, 270, 406

Tepe, V., 403
Tertullian, 83
Theodore of Mopsuestia, 90-91, 187, 213, 298, 388
Theodoret of Cyrrhus, 93, 95, 213
Thompson, M. M., 84
Thurow, Roger, 332-33

Author Index

Tigay, J. H., 279
Tisdale, L. T., 26
Toffelmire, C. M., 13
Tomiya, Susumu, 232
Tov, E., 24
Tracy, S. C., 264
Trimm, Charlie, 310-11, 312

Ueberschaer, F., 61-62
Ussishkin, David, 169
Utzschneider, Helmut, 10, 168, 211, 239, 310

Valk, Jonathan, 9
Van Hecke, P. J. P., 401
Vargon, Shmuel, 287
Vaux, Roland de, 350
Vayntrub, Jacqueline, 199
Vermes, G., 353
Viezel, Eran, 78

Wagenaar, Jan A., 12, 213
Walker, Alice, 338
Waltke, Bruce K., 154, 158, 167, 205, 209, 210, 310, 360, 402
Warlock, Peter. *See* Heseltine, Philip Arnold

Washington, George, 263
Weaver, Dorothy Jean, 84
Weinbach, Ora, 82
Weisman, Ze'ev, 160
Weiss, D., 69
Wenzel, H., 13
Werse, Nicholas R., 20
West, Traci C., 119
Wheeler, Rachel, 387
Wilkinson, Katharine K., 192, 230
William of Champeaux, 96
Williams, Terry Tempest, 60
Williamson, H. G. M., 246
Wilson, Robert R., 270
Wilson, Walter T., 83, 84, 85
Wogan, Guinevere O. U., 232
Wöhrle, Jacob, 20-21
Wolff, Hans Walter, 15-16, 30, 156-57, 288, 319, 320, 405
Wood, Joyce Rilett, 10, 388
Woude, A. S. van der, 203, 211, 315

Yee, Gale A., 44-45, 243

Zapff, Burkard M., 148, 168, 210, 213, 246
Ziegler, Joseph, 22

Scripture Index

OLD TESTAMENT

Genesis
1–3	189
1:16–18	75
1:28	406
3:14	373, 403
3:22	187
4:8	67, 68
4:9	73
4:10	244
4:14–16	76
6–9	373
6:1–4	279
6:5	64–65, 373, 390
6:7	64–65, 373
6:11	373
6:11–12	390
6:13	373
10:8–12	315
12:1–3	340, 385, 406
12:10	77
15	406
16:5	275
18:8	66
18:16–19:28	390
18:19	334
18:21	140
18:25	275
19:24	70
21:17	112
21:22	74
22:1	73
22:1–14	76
22:1–18	406
26:24	112
27:27	68, 87–88
27:28	70
27:28–29	76
28:10–22	406
28:18–22	322
30:22	77
30:43	66
31:13	322
31:29	193
31:43–54	322
31:53	275
32:3	70
35:8	166
35:20	322
36:33	212
37:5–6	71
37:34	175
38:1	64
38:18	357
38:24	158
38:29	67
39:20–41:14	75
41:32	272
41:40	239
46:3	112
47:26	398
47:29	66
49:10	76
49:17	239
49:19	287
50:2–3	140

Exodus
1:13–14	75
3:11	72
4:14	345
5:21	275
6:6	275
7–12	70
7:4	275
8:26	75
11:1	152
12:1	68, 71
12:2	71, 72, 76
12:12	275
12:24	398
12:29	152
13:3	344

443

Scripture Index

13:14	344	33:14–15	245	25:36–37	238
13:21	66	34:1	68	25:38	329
13:21–22	245	34:6–7	19, 405	25:39–42	194
14:13	112	34:13	320	26:1	322
15:1	66	39:30	66	26:13	198, 329
15:17	271				
15:20	330	**Leviticus**		**Numbers**	
15:20–21	345	1:1	77	1:1	72, 73
16:1–18	72	2:14	401	1:4–5	72
16:4	70, 77	5:21–24 [Eng. 6:2–5]		1:36	67
16:10	72		194	2:3	67, 75
17:1–7	76	6:11	399	5:2	68
17:8	76	8:1–4	69	5:12	66, 208
19	271	9:1	70	6:2	67, 72
19:3	71	10:11	398	6:26	71
19:4	77	11:45	329	7:45	72
19:16–20	152, 274	12:2	86	7:48	70
20	271	13:45	241	11:23	205
20:2	344	17:3	68	11:24–25	69
20:6	235	19:2	10, 72, 329	12	345
20:17	194	19:9–10	194	12:1–15	345
20:18–21	274	19:13	194, 329	14:4	67
21–23	76	19:14	329	20:1	72
21:2–3	194	19:18	229, 235	20:2	72
22:17 [Eng. 18]	322	19:29	151	20:28–21:1	72
22:21–24	293	19:33–34	329	21:2	287
22:24	238	19:34	235	21:4	205
23:9	293	19:35–36	194	21:6	239
23:10–11	68	19:35–37	359	21:8–9	239
23:20–21	76	19:36	329	21:17–18	72
23:21	76	21:9	158	21:34	112
23:24	320	22:27	72	22–24	346
24	271	22:33	329	22–25	345
24:4	322	23:14	401	22:2	73
24:7	65	23:22	194	22:3–4	346
24:9–18	274	24:10	67	22:5	72
25:3–7	66	25:2–12	68	23–24	328, 346–47
32:1–8	65	25:13–17	194	24:17	108
32:8	65	25:25–28	194	24:20	170

444

Scripture Index

24:21	343	11:22	235	30:16	235
25	328	12:3	46, 320	30:20	235
25:1–9	347	12:9	208	31:13	356
26:52–56	201	13:4	235	31:14	74, 75, 390
31:8	346	13:6	344–45	32:2	317
31:16	346	13:11	344–45	32:8	279, 334
32:22	406	14:23	356	32:14	402
32:29	406	14:28–29	293	32:39	319
33:4	275	15:1–2	194	32:39–43	319
33:50–54	201	15:7–11	194, 293	32:40	319
34	201	15:12–14	194	32:42	319
		16:22	322	33:9	356
Deuteronomy		17:19	356	33:16	151
1:28	153	18:10	322		
2:7	245	18:15–22	238	**Joshua**	
3:24	110	19:9	235	1:5	245
4:1	398	20:8	153	2:1	347
4:10	356	20:16–17	259	2:11	153
4:15–30	158	22:25–27	258	3–4	345
4:19–20	257, 279	23:3 [Eng. 2]	65, 67, 208	3:1	347
4:34	110	23:3–6	347	4:1–9	322
5:6	344	23:4	73	4:19–24	347
5:10	235	23:4–6	346	4:20–24	322
5:21	194	23:19–20 [Heb. 20–21]		5:1	153
5:29	356		238	5:9–10	347
6:5	229, 235	24:9	337, 345	6:26	244–45
6:7	72	24:14	194	7:5	153
6:12	344	24:17–21	293	7:6	175
6:24	356	25:13–16	194, 359	8:1–29	259
7:5	46, 320	27:8	82	10:11	70
7:8	344–45	27:19	293	10:24	234
7:25	46	28:12	70	10:28–40	259
8:14	344–45	28:15–68	360	12	75
10:12	235, 356	28:20	238	14–19	201
10:12–13	330	28:32	193	15:42	173
10:19	235, 293	28:33	194	18:1	406
10:21	330	28:58	356	21	201
11:1	235	30:6	235	22:5	235
11:13	235	30:11	76	23:3	245

445

Scripture Index

23:9–10	245	10:5–6	243	**1 Kings**	
23:11	235	10:10–13	243	2:45	272
24:1–15	343	12:6–15	343	6:13	110
24:9–10	346	12:6–18	348	8:12–61	246
24:17	345	12:19–25	348	8:31–32	275
24:25	398	12:22	110	8:43	356
		13	347	10:26	278
Judges		13:1–14	328	10:28	278
1:19–2:5	347	15	347	12:1–20	64–65
2:1	166	16 [Eng. 15]	275	12:25–30	148
2:11–19	347	16–17	307	12:28–30	141
5:4–5	152	18:10–11	243	16:15–29	331
5:5	310	19–24	75	16:23–24	363
5:8–23	306	19:9–10	243	16:25	363
5:11	348	21	174	16:30	363–64
5:20	70	22	174	16:34	244
6:2	153	24:13 [Eng. 12]	275	21:1–16	364
6:6	153	30:8	287	22	62
6:8	345	30:15	287	22:1–28	147
9:21	153	30:23	287	22:1–35	238
11:6	234	30:25	398	22:19–23	279
11:11	234	31:13	175	22:24	62
11:27	275			22:28b	62
15:13	392	**2 Samuel**		22:39	363
15:14	392	1:11–12	175		
16:11	392	1:20	165, 167	**2 Kings**	
16:12	392	3:31	175	2:24	153
16:16	205	5:2b	83	4:42	401
19–21	286	7	246	7:17	318
20:26	166	7:16	272	7:20	318
21:2	166	7:26	272	8:12	153
		8:11	406	9:22	322
Ruth		14:19	358	9:33	318
1:1	73	15:12	380	10	156
		15:30	160	12:17	164–65
1 Samuel		17:1–3	380	15–17	4, 313
2:8	71	17:10	153	15:16	153
2:10	309	23:16	153	15:27–30	288
10–11	347			15:29	148

446

Scripture Index

15:33	147	**2 Chronicles**		4:19	393
16:6	163	6:23	275	4:20	157
17	140, 149	11:8	173	7:19	237
17–18	20	14:9–15	173	9:20	244
17:1-20	6	19	392	12:17	160
17:1-24	65	19:6–7	392	12:19	160
17:5-6	378	20:12	276	19:8	287
17:19	155	21:17	153	19:12	287
17:19-20	6	25:12	153	21:4	205
17:23	378	28:3	350	21:22	275
17:30	322–23	28:10	406	23:7	275
17:41	46	28:17–18	163	29:3	373
18–19	136, 223	28:20	4	29:22	40
18:13–19:37	61, 247, 298	29:8	364	30:29	161
		32:1	153	31:2	350
19:23	401	32:1–23	136	33:19	343
19:24	399	33:6	322, 350	38:8	285
19:35-37	315			39:27	239
20:7	261	**Ezra**			
20:12-18	73	4:12	398	**Psalms**	
23	46, 157	9–10	347	2	299
23:4-20	158			2:8	309
23:10	350	**Nehemiah**		2:9	95
25:4	153	1:11	356	3:5 [Eng. 4]	271
25:4-7	288	2–6	398	3:8 [Eng. 7]	319
		5:5	193	3:9	80
1 Chronicles		13:2	346	7:7 [Eng. 6]	319
2:42	173	13:23–31	347	7:9 [Eng. 8]	275
4:17	53			8	97
4:21	173	**Esther**		9	275
5:6	4	1:2	65	9:20 [Eng. 19]	319
5:29 [Eng. 6:3]	337	1:3	69	10:11	377
6:3	53	4:1	75, 175	10:12	319
11:18	153	8:15	75	11:7	348
16:33	275	9:2	70	12 [Eng. 11]	275
17:11–12	97			14	390
17:14	272	**Job**		15	62, 351
17:24	272	1:6–2:6	279	15:5	238
		1:20	175	17:13	319

447

Scripture Index

18:8-16 [Eng. 7-15]	152	61:4	153	98:3	309
18:26	329	62:11	194	99:6	345
18:27	244	65:11 [Eng. 10]	317	101:4	244
18:29 [Eng. 28]	373	67:8 [Eng. 7]	309	103:6	348
18:46 [Eng. 45]	404	68:2 [Eng. 1]	319	104:4	104
22:28 [Eng. 27]	309	68:2 [Heb. 3]	153-54	105:26	345
23	309	68:7-8	152	106:16	345
25:8-10	329	68:9 [Eng. 8]	310	115:2	377, 397
27:1	373, 376	68:15-17	271	116:11	209
28 LXX [MT 29]	380	68:18 [LXX 67:19]	187	118:22-23	94
29	279	68:31 [Eng. 30]	347	119	398
31:24 [Eng. 23]	235	72:3	71	119:11	274
34:6	272, 274	72:6	317	119:18	274
34:7	272	72:8	309	119:25	274
35:13	175	74:1	211	119:103	274
36:9	373	74:2	271	119:105	274, 373
42:4 [Eng. 3]	377, 397	74:12	307	125:5	25, 214
42:11 [Eng. 10]	377, 397	74:15	343	132	246
43:3	72, 271	75	279	132:8	319
44	97	76	284	137:8	396
44:10-15	211	77:12 [Eng. 11]	307	138:8	110
44:20 [Eng. 19]	161	77:16-20	152		
44:27	319	77:21	345	**Proverbs**	
45:8 [Eng. 7]	235	78:24-25	70	2:15	244
46	246, 284	78:54	271	3:27	193
46:10 [Eng. 9]	277	79:10	377, 397	5:3	40
48	284	82	279	5:3-4	380
48:1-2	271	82:1	66	8	99
50:7-10	109	82:8	319	8:8	244
50:12	151	82:21 [Eng. 20]	98	8:22	261
50:12-14	334	86:11	356	8:22-30	299
52:3-5 [Eng. 1-3]	235	87	307, 399	10:9	244
53	390	87:1-2	271	11:1	359
55:18	212	89	279	11:20	244
55:22 [Eng. 21]	316	89:12	151	13:3	394
56:3 [Eng. 2]	350	92:9 [Eng. 8]	350	14:30	393
58	279	93:2	272	15:19	392
60:9-10 [Eng. 7-8]	69-70	94:7	377	17:20	244
		94:16	319	19:1	244

Scripture Index

19:4	380	**Isaiah**		5:19	254
19:10	207	1–55	193	6:1–3	152
20:10	359	1:2	149	7–10	4, 149, 313
20:23	359	1:5	67	7:14	307
22:5	244	1:8	225	8:6	153
22:16	194	1:10	234	9	97
22:23	394	1:12–17	109	9–12	397
23:32	239	1:12–18	109	9:3 [Eng. 4]	357
25:20	393	1:18	71	9:5 [Eng. 6]	310
28:6	244	1:21–25	255	9:6	294
28:18	244	1:26–31	255	9:8 [Eng. 9]	364
		1:29	240	9:10	254
Ecclesiastes		2	96, 267	10:1	398
1:8	64	2–4	270	10:5	221, 357
2:10	207	2:2	271, 272, 274	10:5–6	162, 174, 193
3:8	81	2:2–4	82, 254, 257,	10:5–11	247, 281
4:1	67		269–71	10:13–14	254
5:9	68	2:3	87	10:24	357
7:7	194	2:4	49, 82, 87, 106, 107,	10:27b–32	150
9:11	66		240	10:30	150
10:8	239	2:5	254	11	97
10:11	239	2:5–21	68	11:1–9	329
24:3	299	2:6	320	11:2–4	276
		2:6–8	257	11:6–9	106, 107, 118,
Song of Solomon		2:6–4:1	254		267, 379
1:2	65	2:8	320	11:6–10	255
1:4	65	2:20	320	13:7	153
2:8	71	3:1–4:1	281	13:16	283
2:10	75	3:6	234	13:22	161
2:15	74	3:6–7	254	14:5	357
4	66	3:7	234	14:8	254
4:11	40	3:8	154	14:10	254
4:13	66	3:12	154	14:12–15	279
5:16	72	3:16–4:1	207	14:13–14	254
6:10	75	5:1–10	73	14:16–17	254
6:12	75	5:5	392	16:10	401
7:7	207	5:12	356	17:4–6	286
8:9	70	5:14	399	17:6	389
8:14	69	5:18	392	17:9	153

449

Scripture Index

18:3-6	286	33:5	350	45:21	307
19:1	153	33:9	401, 402	45:22	309
19:6	347, 399	33:15	62, 348	45:24	348
19:11	254	33:22	276	46:6	320
19:19	322	34:1	151	47:1	396
19:24-25	329	34:6	212	47:1-3	397
20:1-4	160	34:8	392	47:5	396
21:8-9	254	34:13	161	47:9	322
21:11-12	254	35:1-10	255	47:12	322
22:4-5	394	35:2	401	49:1	309
22:5	394	35:7	161	49:1-6	270
22:12	68, 175	35:10	399	49:6	406
22:13	254	36-37	29, 61, 136, 223, 247	49:7	273
23:16	254			49:23	273
24-27	355	36:1-37:38	298	50:2	205
24:1-13	374, 400	36:7-20	377	51:4-5	270
24:5	398-99	36:19	149	51:5	309
24:10	355	37:24	401	51:8	107
24:13	389	37:25	399-400	52:7-10	255
24:15	309	37:36-38	315	52:10	309
24:23	240	38:21	261	53:10	359
25	97	39:1-7	73	54:1	297
25:2	355	40	97	54:4	240
25:6-10	329	40:3-5	186	54:11-14	255
26:1	355	40:3-6a	279	54:15	357
26:10	356	41	97	55:1-5	270
27:10	355	41:5	309	56:1	62
28:7-18	210	42:1-4	270	57:15	350
28:9-10	254	42:4	309	58:1-4	109
28:13	254	42:6	406	58:5	175
28:15	221, 254	42:10	309	58:5-7	109
29:11-12	254	42:12	309	58:11-14	255
29:15	254	42:13	152	58:12	254
29:17	401	43:4	76	59:1	205
30:1-5	318	43:20	161	59:8	244
30:9-11	202	44-45	270	59:18-19	309
31:1-3	318	44:9-20	320	60-62	254, 258
32:15-16	401	45:14	273	60:1-20	255
33:1	393	45:20-25	270	60:1-62:12	329

Reference	Page(s)
60:2-4	107
60:2-7	273
60:5	272
60:5-16	273
60:9	309
61:1	243-44
61:10-11	255
62:1-12	255
62:4	110
62:11	112
63:1	212
63:1-6	286
65:1-7	236-37
65:17-25	255, 379
65:25	373, 379, 403
66:6	355
66:10-13	255
66:12	273
66:14-16	273
66:16	276
66:19	309
66:20	273
66:21	273

Jeremiah

Reference	Page(s)
1:16	320
2:1-37	281
2:7	401
3:1-5	207
3:3	317
4:26	401
5:1-5	390
5:12	245
5:15	343
5:22	399
6:1-8	240
6:4	240
6:11	241
6:13	109
6:14	221
6:17	393
6:26	166, 175
7:1-15	246
7:2-3	109
7:3	362
7:4	221
7:5	362
7:8-8:3	281
7:31	350
7:32-8:2	91
8:11	221
8:17	239
8:21-9:10	160
8:22-9:3 [Heb. 9:2]	159
9:10 [Eng. 11]	161
10:22	161
11:18-23	202
11:20	275
12:4	377
13:1-11	160
14:14	221
14:22	317
15:1-3	362
15:9	240
15:10	86, 202
15:15-21	202
15:17	381
17:1	329
18	69
18:16	364
18:18-23	202
19:8	364
20:1-12	202
20:9	241
21:12	194
23:13	149
23:17	221
23:20	271
23:26	221
24-44	281
24:8-10	281
25:9	174, 193, 221, 364
25:15-38	374
25:18	364
25:31	276
25:34	166
26	60-61
26-52	57, 285
26:2-6	61
26:18	30, 221, 243, 247
26:18-19	14, 247
27	197
27:6	174, 193, 221
27:9	322
28	203, 221, 238
28:8-9	210, 222
29:18	364
30-31	258
30:12-14	359
30:12-15	161
30:24	271
31:5	149
31:5-6	274
31:11	272
31:12	272-73, 274
31:33-34	329
31:36	399
32:11	398
32:26-35	281
32:35	350
32:39	356
33:9	107
34:7	170
34:13	345
39:1-8	398
39:8	56, 246
39:9-40:12	199

Scripture Index

40:1	210	**Lamentations**		19:7	151
41:5	149	1:2	69	19:11	357
43:10	174, 193, 221	1:10	73	20–24	281
44	56, 207	1:13	69	20:18	398
44:1–14	281	1:22	67	21:9–17	320
44:28	357	2:3	153	21:12	153
46:5	157	2:9	162	22:7	194
46:11	396	2:10	175	22:12	194, 238
46:19	396	3:25	76	22:29	194
46:24	396	3:33	111	23	207
47:7	357	3:59	275	23:11	149
48:17	357	4:21	396	24:1–13	237
48:30–33	158	4:22	396	24:15–24	160
48:33	401	4:33	161	24:17	240
48:47	271	5:9	153	24:22	240
49:13	212			25:25	398
49:22	212	**Ezekiel**		26:10	153
49:33	161	1:10	221	26:11	318
49:39	271	3:17	376, 393	27:30	166
50:2	401	3:25	392	27:30–31	175
50:12	240	4:8	392	28:2–10	279
50:19	402	5–16	281	29:6	347
50:34	76	5:10	275	29:19–20	193
50:35–38	320	5:15	275	30:12	151
50:42	396	7:16	212	30:16	153
51:30	162	9:9	377	33	281
51:33	396	14:14	74	33:7	393
51:37	161, 364	14:20	74	33:17–20	202
51:44	272, 274	16	207	33:30–33	202
52	219	16:9–10	77	34:11–31	309
52:4–6	398	16:10–13	66	34:15–16	309
52:7	153	16:51	149	34:23–24	309
52:8–11	288	18:8	238	34:24–25	110
52:12–14	398	18:13	238	34:25–31	309
52:13	56, 246	18:17	238	36:27	398
52:15	8	18:18	194	37:1–2	91
52:27–30	56	18:23	111	38–39	91, 286
52:28–30	8	18:25–29	202	38:16	271
52:31–34	234	18:32	111, 363	39:18	402

39:28–29	110	9	20	4:14	20
40:1–47:12	152	9:7	143, 392	4:14–15 [Eng. 3:14–15]	
		9:7–9	202		240
Daniel		9:8	376, 393	4:18 [Eng. 3:18]	347
7:1–27	73	9:15	347		
8:7	318	10:1–2	322	**Amos**	
10:14	271	10:2	320	1–2	139, 185, 296–97
		10:5–6	148	1:2	401
Hosea		10:7	148	1:5	162
1–3	29	10:9–15	286	1:7	21
2	20	10:12	286	1:10	21
2:1–13	281	10:13	244, 286	1:12	21
2:3	21	11	20	1:13	153
2:8	386	11:2	46	1:14	21
2:12	21	11:4	392	2	20
3:1–5	323	12	20	2:2	21
3:4	322	12:3	71	2:4–8	296–97
3:5	271, 309	12:5	166	2:5	21
4:1	150	12:8 [Eng. 7]	194, 359	2:9–12	297
4:1–3	374	12:12 [Eng. 11]	347	2:12	201
4:1–5	150	13	20	3	20
4:1–10	58	13:8	153	3:1	150, 196
4:6	237	14:1 [Eng. 13:16]	148, 153	3:1–2	343
4:7–10	21	14:10	357	3:2	196
4:15	347			3:3	41
5:1	150	**Joel**		3:4	41
5:1–15	281	1:2	149, 150	3:5	41
5:5	155	1:15	20	3:6	41
5:7	21	2:1	20	3:8	41
5:13–15	318	2:1–14	281	3:9–12	148
6:5	235, 356	2:11	20	3:12	148
6:6	335	2:13	405	3:13	150
6:9	287	2:17	377, 397	4:1	148, 150
6:11	155, 286	3:4	20	4:1–3	207, 213
7:1	148, 287	4:1–17 [Eng. 3:1–17]	276	4:3	25, 213, 214
7:7	21	4:9 [Eng. 3:9]	240	4:4	347
7:11–13	318	4:10–13 [Eng. 3:10–13]		4:6	21
8:5–6	148		277	4:6–11	281
8:14	155	4:13 [Eng. 3:13]	286	4:7–8	21

Scripture Index

4:9	21	8:4	150, 358	1:1-9	23
4:13	152, 201	8:4-6	359	1:1-6:4	24
5	20	8:8	41	1:2	36, 62, 141, 142, 145,
5:1	150	8:9-12	374		149-52, 153, 209,
5:1-2	198	8:11-12	237		374, 388
5:4	62	8:14	148, 209, 322-23	1:2-4	145, 151
5:5	347	9	20	1:2-3:12	26
5:6	21	9:3	239	1:2-5:14	10
5:6-7	198	9:5-6	152, 201	1:2-5:15	15
5:8-9	152, 201	9:7	41	1:2-6	143
5:13	198, 201	9:7-10	323	1:2-7	133-34, 136-38,
5:15	235	9:10	246		143-44, 153, 156,
5:18	20	9:11	309, 398		157, 158, 164, 184,
5:19	239, 362	9:13-15	329		296, 333
5:20	20, 41	**Obadiah**		1:2-9	24
5:21-24	109, 334	1	151	1:2-16	25, 339
5:24	49, 343	15	20	1:3	92, 133, 140, 151,
5:25	41	19	148-49		152-53, 168, 209,
6:1	67, 148				247-48, 374
6:1-7	160, 213	**Jonah**		1:3-4	104, 153
6:2	41	1-4	29	1:3-7	56, 327
6:3	41	4:2	19, 405	1:3b	152
6:4	363			1:4	40, 92, 93, 141,
6:4-7	7	**Micah**			153-54, 344
6:5	309	1	18, 60, 338, 355, 371	1:4-6	384
6:7	25, 213, 214, 233	1-2	18, 207	1:4b	37
6:12	41	1-3	7, 16, 17, 18, 20, 25,	1:5	41, 135, 140-41,
6:13	41		26, 28, 91, 144,		148, 151, 152-53,
7-9	29		169, 241, 270,		154-55, 157, 224,
7:1-2	21		277-78, 321		247-48, 357
7:2	41	1-5	15, 17, 339	1:5-7	36, 51, 79, 153, 195
7:4	21	1-6	371	1:5-13	164
7:5	41	1-7	7, 26, 32, 38-39, 384	1:5b	5, 155
7:8	405	1:1	16, 21, 29, 30, 32, 53,	1:5b-7	21
7:10-17	202		133, 136, 147, 148,	1:6	15, 37, 136, 145, 148,
7:16	202		157, 171, 197, 398		153, 155-57, 363
8:1-9:10	281	1:1-4	328	1:6-7	138, 144, 155, 405
8:2	405	1:1-7	5, 117	1:6-16	156-57
8:3	91			1:7	23, 34, 40, 46, 52,

Scripture Index

	64, 141, 142, 143, 144, 157–58, 320	1:16	51, 89, 136, 146, 175, 181, 207, 327		183–84, 206, 210, 233, 241
1:7b–13a	15	2	116, 358, 371	2:7	41, 58, 155, 184, 188, 190, 203–5, 206, 224
1:8	25, 36, 40, 106, 116, 141, 143, 144, 146, 158–61, 162	2–3	32, 117		
		2–5	18		
		2:1	15, 33, 64–65, 89–90, 182, 188, 193–94, 197	2:7c	184
1:8–9	7, 29, 134, 138, 144, 158–59, 162			2:8	65, 162, 163, 186, 200, 205–6, 236, 344
1:8–15	327	2:1–2	44, 51, 56, 154, 183, 195, 196–97, 207, 327, 364		
1:9	21, 36, 56, 88, 138, 150, 161–63, 200, 201, 236, 282, 344			2:8–9	51, 56, 186, 190, 195, 206, 208
		2:1–3	190, 196, 241	2:8–10	28
		2:1–4	15	2:9	37, 51, 65, 92, 93, 163, 175, 186, 191, 192, 200, 206–8, 220, 224, 236, 332, 336, 344
1:9–16	160	2:1–5	120, 179, 181–83		
1:10	23, 88, 140, 163–66, 167	2:1–13	339		
		2:2	51, 188, 191, 194–95, 220, 224, 235, 332, 405		
1:10–11	144				
1:10–12	139, 163			2:9–10	144, 327
1:10–15	35, 136, 142, 160	2:3	22, 32, 56, 90, 133, 181–82, 183, 194, 195–98, 200, 201, 238	2:10	65, 93, 118, 190, 195, 206, 208–9
1:10–16	3, 35, 36, 56, 134–35, 138–40, 150, 162, 164, 165, 170, 241, 394			2:11	34, 143, 184, 185, 188, 209–10, 211, 233, 254, 310, 327
		2:3–4	24, 191		
		2:3–5	196–97, 327	2:12	40, 97, 155, 210–13, 317
1:10–3:4	23	2:4	28, 35, 37, 40, 65, 93, 163, 183, 186, 191, 193, 196, 198–201, 236, 254, 270, 344, 405		
1:11	140, 144, 166–68			2:12–13	16, 18, 25, 26, 28, 34, 117, 144, 180–81, 185–87, 195, 211, 213–14, 233–34, 254, 327
1:11bC	168				
1:12	36, 56, 139–40, 166, 168–69, 174, 197				
		2:5	32, 184, 186, 201		
1:12–15	23	2:6	28, 29, 34, 40, 65, 143, 184, 185, 187–88, 189, 201–3, 211, 233, 270, 327, 370, 376, 393	2:12–3:12	234
1:12b	21			2:13	66–67, 97, 185–86, 187, 213–14, 233
1:13	139, 157, 163, 166, 169–71, 282				
				2:13–3:1	234
1:13–15	163				
1:14	144, 160, 171–73, 224			3	17, 358, 371–72
		2:6–7	25, 254	3–5	18
1:14–16	15	2:6–8	89	3:1	29, 41, 149, 155, 219,
1:15	36, 64, 93, 166, 173–75, 377–78	2:6–11	3, 15, 180,		

455

Scripture Index

	224, 228, 229, 230, 233–35	3:9–10	223		267, 268–70, 279, 285, 329, 377
3:1–2	106	3:9–11	56, 226, 229, 327		
3:1–3	21, 226, 227, 327, 343	3:9–12	45, 218, 219, 223–25, 398	4:1–5	28, 115, 120
				4:1–7	119, 327, 406
3:1–4	56, 154, 217, 219–20	3:10	225, 236, 244–45	4:1–8	323
		3:10–11	51	4:1–5:15	23
3:1–12	15, 210, 241, 339	3:11	28, 34, 41, 53, 67, 106, 197, 221, 223, 225, 226, 245–46, 254, 270, 275, 284, 376	4:1–7:20	26
3:1–4:8	18			4:2	27, 28, 87, 91, 155, 224, 262–63, 266, 270, 273–75, 277, 323, 387
3:2	117, 194, 197, 206, 229, 235				
3:2–3	34, 37, 38, 51, 93–94, 115, 144, 185, 226, 227, 229, 232, 332	3:11–12	223	4:3	40, 49, 82, 87, 106, 118, 120, 122, 162, 240, 262, 265, 275–77, 405
		3:11c	258		
		3:12	7, 18, 24, 28, 34, 56, 61, 67–68, 80–81, 138, 152, 153, 155, 169, 224, 225, 227, 232, 246–48, 253, 255, 282, 327, 338, 405		
3:3	94, 163, 200, 235–37, 344			4:3–4	92
				4:3b	264
3:4	197, 228, 229, 237–38			4:4	61, 82, 86, 88, 107, 113–14, 121, 255, 261, 263, 264, 268, 277–78
3:4–7	56				
3:5	23, 162, 163, 195, 200, 203, 222, 225, 236, 238–40, 254, 314, 327, 344	3:12–4:1	246	4:5	32, 68, 252, 254, 256–57, 278–79
		4	17, 25, 293, 372		
		4–5	4, 15, 16, 17, 18, 224, 270, 278, 284, 288	4:6	34, 68–69, 197, 198, 257, 279–81, 319
3:5–7	52, 229, 232				
3:5–8	217–18, 221–22, 238	4–6	26, 323	4:6–7	18, 56, 120, 258, 266–67, 280–81, 285
		4–7	15, 25–26, 28, 91, 258, 270		
3:5–12	23, 120	4:1	18, 23, 82, 224, 262, 271–73, 274, 310, 405	4:6–8	252, 257
3:6	232, 240			4:6–13	120, 259
3:6–7	229, 327			4:7	262, 280, 281–82, 317
3:7	227, 237, 240–41, 402–3	4:1–2	24, 85, 255		
		4:1–3	81, 82, 96, 107, 263–64, 270–71, 273	4:8	258, 261, 282–83, 320
3:8	25, 29, 94, 155, 219, 225, 229, 234, 241–44, 304, 327, 341, 342, 351, 376, 390, 395			4:8–12	24
		4:1–3a	85	4:8–14 [Eng. 5:1]	36, 327
		4:1–4	56, 117, 118, 144, 225, 251, 254, 255–56, 257, 260,	4:9	41, 83, 258, 261, 267, 283–84
3:9	149, 155, 224, 234, 244			4:9–10	258, 283, 339

456

4:9-11	26, 56, 269	
4:9-13b	252-53, 257-59	
4:9-5:1 [Heb. 4:14]	258	
4:9-5:15	18	
4:10	5, 7, 258, 259, 282, 283, 285, 288, 332, 338	
4:11	28, 254, 258-59, 267, 270, 283, 286, 288	
4:11-13	108, 273	
4:12	259, 285, 286	
4:12-14 [Eng. 5:1]	26	
4:12-5:1	282	
4:13	29, 108, 112, 206, 209, 258, 267, 283, 285, 286-87, 323, 374	
4:13c	7, 253, 259, 393	
4:14 [Eng. 5:1]	35, 62, 69, 253, 259-60, 261, 287-89, 306	
5	25, 83-84, 102, 372	
5:1 [Eng. 2]	36, 83, 85, 88, 91, 92, 96-97, 98, 108, 119, 224, 297, 298, 300, 303, 306-7, 317, 319, 320	
5:1-3 [Eng. 2-4]	323	
5:1-4a [Eng. 2-5a]	7, 85, 118, 120, 291, 293-95, 311, 327	
5:1-5 [Eng. 2-8]	10	
5:1-6 [Eng. 2-7]	119	
5:1-14 [Eng. 2-15]	293	
5:2 [Eng. 3]	69, 99, 297, 299, 302, 303, 305-6, 307, 309, 317
5:2 [Heb. 1]	108
5:2-4	116, 120
5:2-5	120
5:2-5a	120
5:3 [Eng. 4]	56, 83, 197, 224, 288, 297, 303, 304, 308-10, 374, 401
5:3a	295
5:4 [Eng. 5]	69-70, 91, 197, 206, 209, 285, 297, 298, 309, 310-15, 374
5:4-5	295, 310, 377-78, 399
5:4a	295, 303, 310
5:4b [Eng. 5b]	41, 82, 201, 297, 314, 339
5:4b-5 [Eng. 5b-6]	40-41, 311, 315
5:4b-6 [Eng. 5b-6]	303
5:4b-7 [Eng. 5b-8]	327
5:4b-8 [Eng. 5b-9]	7, 291-92, 295-96, 314, 323, 338
5:4b-14 [Eng. 5b-15]	26, 288
5:5 [Eng. 6]	197, 209, 285, 315-17, 375
5:5b [Eng. 6b]	41, 295, 314
5:5b-6	8
5:6 [Eng. 7]	70, 155, 296, 298, 303, 304, 310, 317-18
5:6-7	18, 24
5:7 [Eng. 8]	70, 155, 295, 296, 299, 310, 317, 318
5:7-8	109
5:8 [Eng. 9]	292, 296, 306, 319, 320
5:8-14 [Eng. 9-15]	327
5:9 [Eng. 10]	198, 278, 279, 319-21
5:9-13 [Eng. 10-14]	21, 94, 303, 323
5:9-14 [Eng. 10-15]	26, 36-37, 41, 292-93, 296-97, 300, 301, 320, 323, 339
5:10 [Eng. 11]	209, 300-301, 321, 322-23, 375
5:11 [Eng. 12]	320, 322
5:11-13 [Eng. 12-14]	51, 79
5:12 [Eng. 13]	46, 52, 302, 322
5:13 [Eng. 14]	300-301, 322-23
5:14 [Eng. 15]	70-71, 296, 321, 323-24, 343
6	9-10, 20, 25, 117, 224, 358, 372
6-7	15, 17, 18
6:1	23, 71, 149, 334, 342-43
6:1-2	117, 296
6:1-4	120
6:1-5	296, 325, 329-30, 348
6:1-8	120, 144, 150, 335, 337-38, 343, 396-97

457

Scripture Index

6:1–9b	23, 119–20		122, 123, 182,	7:1	21, 40, 73–74, 84,
6:1–2:20	10, 15		234, 258, 333–34,		87, 98, 332, 385,
6:1–7:7	17		335, 336–37, 339,		388–90
6:2	36, 71, 91, 149, 209,		340, 341–42, 348,	7:1–2	86–87
	342, 343–44, 375		350–55, 356, 383,	7:1–3	95, 370
6:2–3	71–72		384, 388	7:1–4	10, 56, 374,
6:2–4a	21	6:8–10	24		376–77, 390
6:2–7:7	16	6:9	36, 41, 73, 111, 149,	7:1–4a	7, 367, 374–75,
6:3	34, 41, 72, 94, 163,		342, 355–58, 364		393
	200, 236, 344, 349	6:9–11	359	7:1–7	390
6:3–4	335, 344	6:9–13	340	7:1–10	398
6:3–4a	120	6:9–16	26, 326–27,	7:1–12	381
6:3–5	36, 328, 329, 348		331–33, 396–97	7:1–13	388
6:3–8	379	6:9a	21, 355	7:2	74, 98, 209, 236,
6:4	37–38, 51, 53, 72,	6:9b	23		373, 375, 390–91
	94–95, 113, 209,	6:9c–7:6	23	7:2–3	24, 51
	224, 337, 340, 343,	6:10	41, 224, 331, 341,	7:2–4	56, 385
	344–45, 375, 399,		357, 358	7:2–6	395
	400	6:10–11	358	7:3	44, 112, 197, 376,
6:4–5	10, 36, 340, 343,	6:10–12	340		390, 391–92
	397	6:10–15	21, 335	7:3–4	343
6:5	72–73, 163, 200, 236,	6:11	41, 73, 358–59	7:4	53, 391, 392–94
	297, 340, 344,	6:11–12	56	7:4b	26, 36, 367, 370,
	346–49, 397	6:12	357, 359		375–76, 382, 388,
6:6	73, 330, 334, 349–50	6:13	56, 344, 358, 359,		390, 393
6:6–7	28–29, 38, 254,		361	7:5	374, 380, 393, 394
	270, 334, 336, 348	6:13–16	333	7:5–6	375, 376–77, 385,
6:6–8	114, 120, 325–26,	6:13–7:4	360		393
	330, 352	6:14	21, 358, 359–62	7:5–7	10, 368, 376, 390
6:6b	38	6:14–15	332, 340, 359,	7:6	63, 74–75, 84–85,
6:7	41, 109, 334, 336,		362		98, 99, 206, 225,
	350	6:14–16	24, 344		379, 394, 395
6:7–8	109	6:15	84, 111, 362–63	7:7	23, 30, 34, 82,
6:7a	38, 350	6:16	156, 163, 200,		85, 95, 98, 222,
6:7b	38, 350		224, 236, 331, 333,		241, 376, 387, 393,
6:8	29, 36, 49, 56,		340, 342, 344, 357,		395–96
	58, 62–63, 73,		363–64, 405	7:7–9	120, 385
	83, 110–11, 115,	7	10, 20, 25, 26, 358,	7:7–20	23, 120
	116, 118, 119, 120,		371–74	7:8	75, 95, 206, 373,

458

	377, 382, 383, 385, 396, 397	7:16–17	26, 51, 377, 379, 396, 399, 400	1:4–6	323
				1:7	20, 21, 151
7:8–10	10, 48, 56, 368, 376–77, 384	7:16–20	369–70, 378–79	1:12	391
				1:14	20
7:8–13	7, 380	7:17	34, 98, 209, 373, 375, 403–4	1:14–18	374
7:8–20	16, 397			3:3	21, 391
7:9	26, 234, 381, 382, 387, 396–97, 405	7:18	3, 18, 41, 76, 82, 111, 120, 147, 306, 317, 357, 404–5	3:5	244
				3:8	374
7:10	26, 29, 41, 95, 254, 270, 377, 396, 397, 400			3:9–11	323
		7:18–19	118, 382, 385	3:13	244
		7:18–20	19, 36, 56, 115–16, 120, 184, 382, 405	3:19	280
7:11	397–99, 402			**Haggai**	
7:11–12	3, 41, 375, 397			1–2	29
7:11–13	10, 36, 369, 377–78	7:19	76, 95, 99, 119, 380, 405–6	2	20
7:11a	41, 397	7:19–20	382		
7:11b	41, 397	7:19b	374	**Zechariah**	
7:12	37, 41, 285, 310, 377–78, 397, 399–400, 402	7:20	24, 77, 120, 155, 381, 382, 385, 400, 405, 406–7	1–8	29
				2:11	396
				4:2	67
				4:7	282
7:12–17	399	**Nahum**		4:10	357
7:13	26, 51, 209, 238, 374, 375, 377, 400, 402	1:2–3	19	6:12	282
		1:3	405	7:2–10	109
		1:4	401, 402	8:4	61
7:13–20	381	2:11	153	8:20–22	107
7:14	95, 120, 197, 307, 378, 379, 380, 381, 384, 385, 387, 399, 400–402, 405	3:4	196, 322	9:9	112
		3:13	162	9:10	309
				10:2	221
		Habakkuk		10:10–11	400
7:14–15	56, 120, 369, 378, 400	1:2–4	17	11:2	402
		1:12	307	12	97
7:14–15a	30, 371	2	193	12–14	284
7:14–20	10, 29, 120	2:4	62	12:12	196
7:15	36, 76, 117, 209, 344, 375, 378, 397, 399, 401, 402	2:12	209, 244	12:13	196
		3:3–15	152	12:14	196
				14:2	283
7:15b	371	**Zephaniah**		14:17	196
7:16	76, 111, 120, 402–3	1:2–3	374	14:18	196

Scripture Index

Scripture Index

Malachi

1–3	20
1:1	20
1:3	161
1:5b–7	20
1:9	20
2:3	20
2:6	244
2:12–13	20
2:14–15	207
2:17	377
3	20
3:5	194, 322
3:23	20
4–5	20
6	20
6:9–16	20

NEW TESTAMENT

Matthew

1:23	307
2:1	83
2:1–6	119
2:4	83
2:5–6	297, 307
2:6	83, 98, 306
2:16	88
3:1–3	186
3:8–9	93
3:12	286
4:19	261
9:12	86
9:36	84
9:37	380
10:21–22	84, 379
10:22b	85
10:34–36	379
10:35–36	84
11:7–15	185–86
11:12	186
15:3–9	109
15:24	84
17:1	262
21:5	112
21:18–19	84
21:33–41	93
21:42–45	94
22:36–40	235
23:37–39	86
24:12	226
25:24	84
26:67–68	261
27:22–23	89
28:19–20	262

Mark

1:2–3	186
2:17	86
8:22–25	141
11:12–13	84
12:28–31	235
13:12–13	84, 379
13:13b	85
14:65	261
15:13	89
16:6	113

Luke

2:4–16	83
2:52	98
3:3–5	186
3:8	93
3:10–11	109
3:11	380
3:17	286
4:1	243–44
4:14–21	243–44
5:31	86
6:36	335
10:2	380
10:25–28	235
11:11–13	110
12:51–53	379
12:52	85
12:53	84
13:34–35	86
14	98
16:16	186
19:21	84
21:16–17	84, 379
21:19b	85
22:63–64	261
23:21	89

John

1:3	88
1:23	186
3:13	140
4:7–26	91
6:33	88
6:41	88
6:51	88, 98, 261
7:1	84
7:6	298
7:18	298
7:27	298
7:42	83, 84, 297
8:12	261
9:1–7	141
10:7	186
10:9	186
10:11	381
10:14	381
12:15	112
12:31	262
15:1	261

Scripture Index

15:15	380
16:21–22	299
19:3	261
19:6	89

Acts
2	261
8:15–24	226
9:4	94

Romans
3:23	188
6:1–11	112
9–11	93
9:6–8	381
11	89, 335
11:25–26	297
13:14	141

1 Corinthians
15:32	226

2 Corinthians
4:10	86
5:17	260
8:9	86
11:23–27	297

Galatians
3:6–9	381
3:27	141
3:28	113
4:19	261
5:22–23	261

Ephesians
2:14–15	299
2:19	93
2:20	334
4:10	97
4:22–24	141
5:2	335
6:12	86
6:15	142
6:17	112, 299

Philippians
2:6–8	86
2:7	140

Colossians
3:9–10	141
3:12	335

Hebrews
12:18–24	94

James
2:18	109

2 Peter
3:12	104

1 John
3:8	112
4:21	110

Revelation
14:14–20	286
18:20	334
18:24	334
19:11–16	186
22:13	261

Ancient Sources Index

Ancient Near Eastern Texts

Akkadian *Šurpu* incantations
Tablet II,
lines 20-28 — 395

Mesopotamian Legend of Naram-Sin
Lines 138-141 — 395

Deuterocanonical Books and Pseudepigrapha

Wisdom
8:2 — 99

Sirach
24 — 99
24:23-27 — 275
44:1-50:29 — 61
49:10 — 61

1 Maccabees
14:4 — 61-62
14:8-9 — 61-62
14:12 — 61-62

1 Enoch
56:7 — 63

Jubilees
23:16-19 — 63

Dead Sea Scrolls

1QS (Rule of the Community)
II.24 — 353
V — 353
V.4 — 353
V.25 — 353
VIII — 353
VIII.2 — 353
X.26 — 353

1Q14 (1QpMic) — 24

4Q76 (4QXII^a) — 23, 24

4Q77 (4QXII^b) — 24

4Q78 (4QXII^c) — 24

4Q80 (4QXII^e) — 24

4Q82 (4QXII^g) — 23, 24, 247

4Q168 (4QpMic) — 24

8Ḥev 1 (8ḤevXIIgr) — 24

CD (Damascus Document)
XIII.18 — 353

MurXII — 24

Ancient Jewish Writers

Josephus

Jewish Antiquities
10.6.2 — 247

Ancient Sources Index

Rabbinic Works

Babylonian Talmud (Bavli)

Baba Batra
14b-15a — 19

Makkot
23b-24a — 62
24a — 62, 334

Šabbat
139a — 225

Soṭah
32a — 82
36a — 82
49b — 63

Sukkah
49b — 62-63

Yoma
9b — 225

Midrash

Genesis Rabbah
22.7 — 68
28.5 — 65
48.10 — 66
54.1 — 74
55.5 — 73
65.23 — 68
69.5 — 66
73.2 — 77
73.11 — 66
75.8 — 70
84.10 — 71
85.1 — 64
85.14 — 67
96 — 66
99.8 — 76

Exodus Rabbah
15.4 — 71
15.7 — 71
15.11 — 76
15.14 — 72
15.15 — 68
15.26 — 71
23.5 — 66
25.1 — 70
25.6 — 77
26.2 — 76
28.2 — 71
32.4 — 76
42.7 — 65
46.4 — 68

Leviticus Rabbah
1.4 — 77
10.2 — 69
11.7 — 70
22.2 — 68
24.1 — 72
27.6 — 72
32.8 — 67

Numbers Rabbah
1.2 — 72
1.3 — 73
2.10 — 67, 75
7.10 — 68
9.7 — 66, 208
10.1 — 72
10.3 — 67
13.20 — 72
14.1 — 70
20.5 — 72
20.6 — 73

Deuteronomy Rabbah
8.1 — 76
11.10 — 74, 75, 390

Ruth Rabbah
1.2 — 73

Esther Rabbah
Proem 11 — 70
Proem 16 — 70
1.2 — 65
1.18 — 69
10.11 — 70
10.14 — 75

Ecclesiastes Rabbah
1.8.3 — 64
4.1 — 67
5.8f.3 — 68
9.11.1 — 66

Song of Songs Rabbah
1.2 — 65
1.4.3 — 65
2.13.4 — 75
2.15.2 — 74
4.12.2 — 66
6.10.1 — 75
6.12.1 — 75
8.9.3 — 70
8.14.1 — 69
10.1 — 72

Lamentations Rabbah
Proem 24 — 68
Proem 25 — 73
Proem 50-51 — 73
1.25 — 69
1.38 — 73
1.41 — 69
1.57 — 67

Ancient Sources Index

3.9	76
Tanḥuma-Yelammedenu	68, 69, 70

Targumim

Targum Micah

1:3	152
1:5	154
1:8	159
1:11	167
1:12	168
1:12–18	63
1:14	173
2:8	206
2:10	209
2:11	210
3:2	235
3:3	237
3:4	238
3:5	239
3:6–7	240
3:11	245
4:2	274
4:6	281
4:8	282
4:13	286
5:1	307
5:5	317
5:9–14	321
6:4	345
6:8	354
7:8	396
7:10	395, 396
7:14	395
7:18	405
7:19	395
7:20	406

EARLY CHRISTIAN AND GNOSTIC WRITINGS

Ambrose of Milan

Jacob and the Happy Life	88

Athanasius of Alexandria

Letter 6.11	87
Letter 59.2	87
On the Incarnation	87

Augustine of Hippo

City of God

Book 18, chapter 30	85

Tractates on the Gospel of John: 28–54

31.3	298

Basil of Caesarea

Homilies on Psalms

Homily 13	380

Bonaventure

Sermon on the Transfiguration	262
The Tree of Life	187

Clement of Alexandria

Stromateis

3.16.101	334
4.26	140

Cyril of Alexandria

Commentary on the Twelve Prophets

185	92
186	92
188	92
190	92, 159
195	171
197	175
202	93
206–7	92, 209
207	93
210–11	187
213	226
221	262
222	262
224	262
225–26	92
227	262
231	92
233	92–93
233–34	93
235	299
237	299
242	299
244	102
246	335
247	335
248	335
249	335
251	335
253–54	335

Ancient Sources Index

256	335
266	381
268–69	381
273	381
278	381

Cyril of Jerusalem

Catecheses 13–18
16.18	225

Gospel of Thomas
Logion 16	85

Hippolytus of Rome

Against the Heresy of One Noetus
15	186

Irenaeus of Lyons

Against Heresies
39.4	260

Jerome

Commentariorum in Michaeum libri II
xxiii	88
42–43	141
43	141
45	141
49	88
50	88
51	89
52	89
53	90
53–54	90
54	90, 186
55–56	89
59	89
60	187
63	187
66	225
67	226
68	226
69	226
71	261
72–73	261
74–75	90
75–76	90
76–77	261
80	261
82	297
83	297
84–85a	297
85	297–98
88	298
90	334
93	334
95	334, 355
98	334
99	388
100	380
101	380
107	377
108	380
110	381
111	381

John Chrysostom

Homilies on the Gospel of Saint Matthew
29	94
68	94

Justin Martyr

Dialogue with Trypho
109	260

First Apology
39	260

Martyrdom of Polycarp
6	85

Methodius of Olympus

The Banquet of the Ten Virgins   260–61

Origen of Alexandria

Homiliae in Genesim
108	140
213	141

Homiliae in Jeremiam
14.5–14.6	86–87
15.3	87
28.4–5	186

Homiliae in Joshua
5.2	86
15.7	86
16.4	86

Homiliae in Leviticum
8.4.3	86

Homiliae in Lucam
23.4	380

Pistis Sophia
Book 3.113	85

Ancient Sources Index

Shepherd of Hermas

Visions
1.1   334

Theodore of Mopsuestia

Commentary on the Twelve Prophets
206   90
209   90
214   91
215   187
216   187
219   91
219–22   90
220   91
226   298
226–28   91
229   90
230–31   91
232   90, 91, 298
234   298
235   91
239   388
242   91

MEDIEVAL WRITINGS

Albert the Great

On Resurrection   97

Peter Alfonsi

The Dialogue against the Jews   96–97

Peter Damian

Letter 1   95–96

Peter Lombard

Sentences, Book I
d. 2, c. 5   299

Henry Suso

Wisdom's Watch upon the Hours
1.4.12   338–39
1.1   98–99
1.3.1   99
1.3.20   99
1.4–11   99
1.5–11   99
1.5.1–2   99
1.5.6   99
1.6.6   99
1.14.1   99

Thomas Aquinas

Sermon 1   97–98
Sermon 8   98
Sermon 13   98
Sermon 16   98